ZAGAT
2014

New York City
Restaurants

With my Best Wishes
for a Happy New Year
Avida

Zagat Survey, LLC
76 Ninth Avenue
New York, NY 10011
E: feedback@zagat.com
www.zagat.com

ACKNOWLEDGMENTS

We thank Stefanie Tuder, as well as the following members of our staff: Danielle Borovoy (editor), Brian Albert, Sean Beachell, Maryanne Bertollo, Reni Chin, Nicole Diaz, Kelly Dobkin, Jeff Freier, Alison Gainor, Michelle Golden, Justin Hartung, Marc Henson, Anna Hyclak, Ryutaro Ishikane, Michele Laudig, Natalie Lebert, Mike Liao, Vivian Ma, Molly Moker, James Mulcahy, Polina Paley, Josh Siegel, Albry Smither, Amanda Spurlock, Chris Walsh, Jacqueline Wasilczyk, Art Yagci, Sharon Yates, Anna Zappia and Kyle Zolner.

We also sincerely thank the thousands of people who participated in this survey – this guide is really "theirs."

ABOUT ZAGAT

In 1979, we asked friends to rate and review restaurants purely for fun. The term "user-generated content" had yet to be coined. That hobby grew into Zagat Survey; 35 years later, we have loyal surveyors around the globe and our content now includes nightlife, shopping, tourist attractions, golf and more. Along the way, we evolved from being a print publisher to a digital content provider. We also produce marketing tools for a wide range of corporate clients, and you can find us on Google+ and just about any other social media network.

The reviews in this guide are based on public opinion surveys. The ratings reflect the average scores given by the survey participants who voted on each establishment, while the text is based on quotes from, or paraphrasings of, the surveyors' comments. Ratings and reviews have been updated throughout this edition based on our most recent survey results. Phone numbers, addresses and other factual data were correct to the best of our knowledge when published in this guide.

JOIN IN

To improve our guides, we solicit your comments – positive or negative; it's vital that we hear your opinions. Just contact us at **nina-tim@zagat.com.**

Contents

Ratings & Symbols

Name	Symbols		Cuisine		Zagat Ratings			
					FOOD	DECOR	SERVICE	COST

Area, Address & Contact

Tim & Nina's ◗ *Ozarks*   ▽ 23 | 9 | 13 | $15

Chelsea | 76 Ninth Ave. (bet. 15th & 16th Sts.) |
212-977-6000 | www.zagat.com

Review, surveyor comments in quotes

Lowlifes love this "down-and-out" dump under the High Line, a "former food truck" turned restaurant after its customers stole the wheels; ignoring repeated "C-grade" health inspections, fans praise Nina's "haute hot plate" Ozarks cuisine, but concede that the "reclaimed cardboard" decor and Tim's "offhand service" need work; it has just "a few seats", "charges bupkis" and "doesn't take rezzies", yet somehow there's "never a line."

Ratings

Food, Decor & **Service** are rated on a 30-point scale.

26 – 30   extraordinary to perfection

21 – 25   very good to excellent

16 – 20   good to very good

11 – 15   fair to good

0 – 10   poor to fair

▽   low response | less reliable

Cost

The price of dinner with a drink and tip; lunch is usually 25% to 30% less. For unrated **newcomers,** the price range is as follows:

I $25 and below   E $41 to $65

M $26 to $40   VE $66 or above

Symbols

◗   serves after 11 PM

Ⓢ   closed on Sunday

Ⓜ   closed on Monday

⊘   cash only

Maps

Index maps show restaurants with the highest Food ratings and other notable places in those areas.

New York City at a Glance

WINNERS:

- **Le Bernardin** (Food, Most Popular)
- **Asiate** (Decor)
- **Per Se** (Service)
- **Mighty Quinn's Barbecue** (No. 1 Newcomer)

SURVEY STATS:

- 2,084 restaurants covered
- 48,114 surveyors
- In our recent Dining Trends Survey, New York City respondents reported that they eat 4.9 meals out per week, spending an average of $48.56 per person for dinner, well above the national average of $40.53.
- When presented with a list of dining irritants, surveyors chose noise as the most annoying, with 72% saying they avoid restaurants that are too loud.
- Fifty-six percent of NYC participants typically make restaurant reservations online, and 43% will not wait more than 30 minutes at a place that doesn't take reservations.

SANDY AFTERMATH: The year's biggest restaurant story was certainly the devastation caused by Hurricane Sandy. Dumbo, Red Hook, the Rockaways and the Seaport were particularly hard hit, and iconic places like the **Bridge Cafe, Nathan's, Perry St.**, the **River Café** and the **Water Club** were among the many temporarily shuttered.

BIG-NAME OPENINGS: April Bloomfield (**Salvation Taco**), Saul Bolton (**Red Gravy**), Mario Carbone/Rich Torrisi (**Carbone, ZZ's Clam Bar**), Andrew Carmellini (**Lafayette**), Harold Dieterle (**The Marrow**), Hugue Dufour (**M. Wells Dinette**), Wylie Dufresne (**Alder**), Paul Liebrandt (**The Elm**), Laurent Tourondel (**Arlington Club**), Jean-Georges Vongerichten (**ABC Cocina**), Michael White (**The Butterfly, Costata**)

TRENDS: Epic tasting menus at epic prices: **Aska, Luksus, New York Sushi Ko**; fast-casual dining on the rise: **Clarke's Standard, Harlem Shake, Umami Burger**; long-shuttered landmarks poised to reopen: the **Rainbow Room, Tavern on the Green** and the **Oak Room** (under the aegis of the Plaza's new culinary director, Geoffrey Zakarian)

HOT NEIGHBORHOODS: East Village (**Alder, Jeepney, L'Apicio, Mighty Quinn's Barbecue**), NoHo (**Lafayette, Le Philosophe**), NoLita (**The Cleveland, Musket Room, Pearl & Ash, Uncle Boons**), West Village (**Chez Sardine, El Toro Blanco, The Marrow, Murray's Cheese Bar**), Williamsburg (**Antica Pesa, Aska, BrisketTown, The Elm, Xixa**)

MOST SEARCHED ON ZAGAT.COM: NoMad, Gramercy Tavern, Daniel, Nobu, Rosa Mexicano, Jean Georges, The Modern, Bouley, The Smith, Mas (Farmhouse)

New York, NY
October 1, 2013

Nina and Tim Zagat

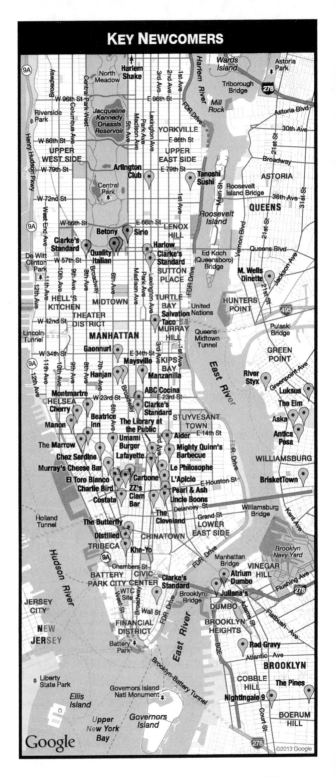

KEY NEWCOMERS

Key Newcomers

Our editors' picks among this year's arrivals. See full list at p. 303.

BIG NAMES/BIG TICKETS

ABC Cocina
Beatrice Inn
The Butterfly
Carbone
Costata
The Elm
Juliana's
Lafayette
M. Wells Dinette
Sirio
ZZ's Clam Bar

CULINARY CUTTING-EDGE

Alder
Aska
The Elm
Luksus
Manzanilla
Pearl & Ash

NEW OLD-SCHOOL

The Butterfly
Carbone
Le Philosophe
Quality Italian
Red Gravy

COCKTAIL FOCUS

Aska
Atrium Dumbo
Betony
The Butterfly
Costata
Distilled
Manon
Maysville
ZZ's Clam Bar

STRIKING SPACES

Antica Pesa
Cherry
Harlow
Lafayette
The Library at the Public
Manon
River Styx

ASIAN COOL

Chez Sardine
Gaonnuri
Hanjan
Khe-Yo
Nightingale 9
Tanoshi Sushi
Uncle Boons

QUICK BITES

Clarke's Standard
Harlem Shake
Salvation Taco
Umami Burger

MEAT-CENTRIC

Arlington Club
Brisket Town
Costata
The Marrow
Mighty Quinn's Barbecue

NEIGHBORHOOD STARS

Charlie Bird
The Cleveland
El Toro Blanco
L'Apicio
Montmartre
Murray's Cheese Bar
The Pines

PROJECTS ON TAP

American Cut: Marc Forgione brings his steakhouse concept to TriBeCa

Empire Diner: Amanda Freitag moves into Chelsea's iconic diner digs

Gato: TV toque Bobby Flay does Spanish-Mediterranean in the Village

La Cenita: The old Abe & Arthur's space goes Latin via Akhtar Nawab

Mission Cantina: LES Mexican by Mission Chinese's Danny Bowien

M. Wells Steakhouse: LIC meatery from the M. Wells Dinette dynamic duo

Saul: The Boerum Hill destination moves inside the Brooklyn Museum

Branches on the way: Oyster Bar (Park Slope), RedFarm (UWS), Bubby's (Meatpacking), Butter (Midtown), Tao (Chelsea), Telepan (TriBeCa)

Most Popular

This list is plotted on the map at the back of this book.

1. Le Bernardin | *French/Seafood*
2. Gramercy Tavern | *American*
3. Peter Luger | *Steak*
4. Daniel | *French*
5. Bouley | *French*
6. Eleven Madison | *French*
7. Gotham B&G | *American*
8. Union Square Cafe | *American*
9. Jean Georges | *French*
10. 21 Club | *American*
11. Atlantic Grill | *Seafood*
12. Babbo | *Italian*
13. Marea | *Italian/Seafood*
14. Per Se | *American/French*
15. Balthazar | *French*
16. Becco | *Italian*
17. Del Posto | *Italian*
18. La Grenouille* | *French*
19. ABC Kitchen | *American*
20. Café Boulud | *French*
21. Modern | *American/French*
22. Palm | *Steak*
23. Telepan | *American*
24. Rosa Mexicano | *Mexican*
25. Shake Shack | *Burgers*
26. Jean-Georges' Nougatine | *Fr.*
27. Katz's Deli | *Deli*
28. Capital Grille | *Steak*
29. 5 Napkin Burger | *Burgers*
30. Blue Water Grill | *Seafood*
31. Nobu | *Japanese*
32. 2nd Ave Deli | *Deli/Kosher*
33. Il Mulino* | *Italian*
34. Del Frisco's | *Steak*
35. Four Seasons | *American*
36. Aureole | *American*
37. A Voce | *Italian*
38. Aquagrill | *Seafood*
39. Boulud Sud | *Mediterranean*
40. Ai Fiori | *Italian*
41. Maialino | *Italian*
42. Bar Boulud | *French*
43. Milos* | *Greek/Seafood*
44. Carmine's | *Italian*
45. Eataly | *Italian*
46. db Bistro Moderne | *French*
47. Blue Smoke | *BBQ*
48. Keens | *Steak*
49. Carnegie Deli | *Deli*
50. SD26* | *Italian*

Many of the above restaurants are among NYC's most expensive, but if popularity were calibrated to price, a number of other places would surely join their ranks. To illustrate this, we offer a Best Buys section comprising 26 lists starting on page 22.

* Indicates a tie with restaurant above

Top Food

<table>
<tr><td>29</td><td>Le Bernardin | French/Seafood
Bouley | French</td></tr>
<tr><td>28</td><td>Per Se | American/French
Daniel | French
Eleven Madison | French
Jean Georges | French
Sasabune | Japanese
Sushi Yasuda | Japanese
La Grenouille | French
Gramercy Tavern | American
Sushi Seki | Japanese
Marea | Italian/Seafood
Degustation | French/Spanish</td></tr>
<tr><td>27</td><td>Gotham B&G | American
Mas (Farmhouse) | American
Peter Luger | Steak
Chef's Table/Brooklyn Fare | Fr.
Soto | Japanese
Annisa | American
Picholine | Fr./Med.</td></tr>
</table>

Kyo Ya | *Japanese*
Lucali | *Pizza*
Torrisi | *Italian*
L'Artusi | *Italian*
Scalini Fedeli | *Italian*
Milos | *Greek/Seafood*
Blue Hill | *American*
Sripraphai | *Thai*
Union Square Cafe | *American*
Momofuku Ko | *American*
Jean-Georges' Nougatine | *Fr.*
Nobu | *Japanese*
Gari | *Japanese*
Masa/Bar Masa | *Japanese*
NoMad | *American/European*
Al Di La | *Italian*
Babbo | *Italian*
Pylos | *Greek*
Four Seasons | *American*
Grocery | *American*

Top Decor

28	Asiate		Buddakan
	Per Se		Morimoto
	Daniel		One if by Land
	Eleven Madison		Jean Georges
	Four Seasons		Del Posto
	La Grenouille	26	Kittichai
	Le Bernardin		Riverpark
27	Bouley		Le Cirque
	River Café		Modern
	Tao		Spice Market

Top Service

29	Per Se		Mas (Farmhouse)
28	Le Bernardin		Del Posto
	Eleven Madison		Annisa
	Daniel		Tocqueville
	La Grenouille		Picholine
	Jean Georges		Marea
	Bouley		Blue Hill
27	Gramercy Tavern		Union Square Cafe
	Four Seasons		Villa Berulia
26	Gotham B&G		Scalini Fedeli

Excludes places with low votes, unless otherwise indicated

TOPS BY CUISINE

AMERICAN

28	Per Se
	Gramercy Tavern
27	Gotham B&G
	Mas (Farmhouse)
	Annisa
	Blue Hill
	Battersby
	Union Square Cafe
	Momofuku Ko
	NoMad
	St. Anselm
	Four Seasons

ASIAN

25	Asiate
	Buddakan
24	Wong
	Shi
	Tao
23	Spice Market
	China Grill
22	Fatty 'Cue

AUSTRIAN/GERMAN/ SWISS

26	Wallsé
25	Seäsonal
24	Zum Stammtisch
23	Mont Blanc
	Edi & The Wolf
22	Blaue Gans
	Café Sabarsky/Fledermaus
21	Zum Schneider

BARBECUE

26	Fette Sau
23	Dinosaur BBQ
	Hill Country
22	Smoke Joint
	Fatty 'Cue
	Blue Smoke
21	Daisy May's
20	Virgil's Real BBQ

BURGERS

24	Burger Joint
22	Bonnie's Grill
	Burger Bistro
	Corner Bistro
	BareBurger
	BLT Burger
21	Island Burgers
	Shake Shack*

CARIBBEAN

24	Sofrito
23	Cuba
	Sazon
	Negril
	Amor Cubano
	Café Habana/Outpost
22	La Taza de Oro
	Victor's Cafe

CHICKEN

24	Pies-N-Thighs
23	Pio Pio
21	BonChon
	Flor de Mayo
	Coco Roco
20	Kyochon
–	Blue Ribbon Fried Chicken
	Hybird

CHINESE

26	Prosperity Dumpling
25	RedFarm
24	Shanghai Café
	Spicy & Tasty
	Xi'an Famous Foods
	Shun Lee Palace
	Cafe China
	Wa Jeal

DELIS

(See also Sandwiches)

24	Barney Greengrass
	Katz's Deli
23	Mile End
	Ben's Best
	Liebman's Deli
22	Mill Basin Deli
	Carnegie Deli
	B & H Dairy

DESSERT

25	ChikaLicious
	Chocolate Room
24	L&B Spumoni
	La Bergamote
	Bouchon Bakery
23	Ferrara
22	Café Sabarsky/Fledermaus
	Lady Mendl's

DIM SUM

25	RedFarm
22	Oriental Garden
	Lychee House

Excellent Dumpling
21 Nom Wah Tea Parlor
Shun Lee Cafe
Dim Sum Go Go
Golden Unicorn

EASTERN EUROPEAN

22 Lomzynianka∇
21 Mari Vanna
20 Tatiana
Russian Tea Room
Russian Samovar
FireBird
Veselka
Little Poland

ECLECTIC

26 Traif
25 Good Fork
Graffiti
Carol's
WD-50
24 Stanton Social
23 Sojourn
Nook

FRENCH

29 Le Bernardin
Bouley
28 Daniel
Eleven Madison
Jean Georges
La Grenouille
27 Chef's Table/Brooklyn Fare
Café Boulud

FRENCH BISTRO

25 Raoul's
db Bistro Moderne
24 JoJo
Tournesol
La Sirène
La Silhouette
Bar Boulud
23 Bistro La Promenade

GREEK

27 Milos
Pylos
26 Taverna Kyclades
25 Eliá
Yefsi Estiatorio
Avra
24 Agnanti
Thalassa

INDIAN

26 Tamarind
25 Amma
24 Junoon
Tulsi
23 Dhaba
Banjara
Yuva
Vatan

ITALIAN

28 Marea
27 Torrisi
L'Artusi
Scalini Fedeli
Il Bambino
Al Di La
Babbo
26 Tratt. L'incontro
Pepolino
Del Posto
Ai Fiori
Bar Corvo

JAPANESE/SUSHI

28 Kurumazushi
Sasabune
Sugiyama
Sushi Yasuda
Ushiwakamaru
Sushi Seki
27 Soto
Kyo Ya
Nobu
Gari
Masa/Bar Masa
26 Takashi

KOREAN

26 Jungsik
25 Hangawi
Danji
23 Moim
Cho Dang Gol
22 Miss Korea BBQ
New WonJo
Kunjip

KOSHER

25 Solo
Azuri Cafe
24 Mike's Bistro
23 Prime KO
Ben's Best
Peacefood Café
Caravan of Dreams
Colbeh

LOBSTER ROLLS

26 Pearl Oyster Bar
25 Mary's Fish Camp
24 Red Hook Lobster Pound
 Ed's Lobster Bar
23 Luke's Lobster
22 Brooklyn Fish Camp
21 Mermaid
- Cull & Pistol

MEDITERRANEAN

27 Picholine
25 Il Buco
 Little Owl
 Alta
 Aldea
 Boulud Sud
 Convivium Osteria
23 Red Cat

MEXICAN

26 Tortilleria Nixtamal
24 Barrio Chino
 Mercadito
 Pampano
 Toloache
 El Paso
23 Tacombi/Fonda Nolita
 Fonda

MIDDLE EASTERN

26 Tanoreen
 Taïm
25 Azuri Cafe
24 Ilili
 Taboon
 Mimi's Hummus
23 Balaboosta
 Mamoun's

NOODLE SHOPS

26 Totto Ramen
25 Ippudo
 Donguri
24 Momofuku Noodle
 Soba Totto
 Xi'an Famous Foods
23 Soba-ya
 Great NY Noodle

PIZZA

27 Lucali
26 Luzzo's
 Paulie Gee's
 Di Fara Pizza
 Denino's
 Roberta's
25 Franny's
 Motorino

RAW BARS

26 Aquagrill
 Pearl Oyster Bar
25 Blue Ribbon
24 Esca
 Oceana
 John Dory Oyster
 David Burke Fishtail
 Ocean Grill

SANDWICHES

(see also Delis)
27 Il Bambino
26 Leo's Latticini/Corona
25 Num Pang
24 Porchetta
 Taboonette
 Press 195
 Meatball Shop
 Defonte's

SEAFOOD

29 Le Bernardin
28 Marea
27 Milos
26 Aquagrill
 Taverna Kyclades
 Pearl Oyster Bar
25 Avra
 Mary's Fish Camp

SMALL PLATES

28 Degustation (French/Spanish)
26 Traif (Eclectic)
 Salt & Fat (American/Asian)
 Zenkichi (Japanese)
25 Graffiti (Eclectic)
 Sakagura (Japanese)
 Alta (Mediterranean)
 Danji (Korean)

SOUTH AMERICAN

24 Caracas
 Buenos Aires
 Arepas
23 Churrascaria
 Chimichurri Grill
 Ipanema
 Pio Pio
22 Circus

SOUTHERN/SOUL

24 Pies-N-Thighs
Egg
23 Peaches
Seersucker
22 Redhead
Char No. 4
Miss Mamie's/Maude's
Amy Ruth's

SPANISH/TAPAS

25 Casa Mono
Tía Pol
El Quinto Pino
24 Tertulia
Txikito
Solera
23 Bar Jamón
Beso

STEAKHOUSES

27 Peter Luger
26 Quality Meats
Porter House NY
Keens
25 Wolfgang's
BLT Prime
Sparks
Strip House
Benjamin Steak
Christos
BLT Steak
Del Frisco's

THAI

27 Sripraphai
26 Ayada

25 Kuma Inn
Pure Thai Cookhouse
24 Kin Shop
Kittichai
Song
23 Am Thai

TURKISH

25 Taci's Beyti
22 Turkish Kitchen
Sahara
Beyoglu
21 Uskudar
Akdeniz
Bodrum
Hanci

VEGETARIAN

26 Taïm
25 Dirt Candy
Hangawi
Candle 79
24 Pure Food & Wine
Candle Cafe
23 Vatan
Gobo

VIETNAMESE

24 Omai
22 Nha Trang
Pho Bang
Baoguette
Bo-Ky
21 Le Colonial
An Choi
Indochine

TOPS BY SPECIAL FEATURE

BREAKFAST

27 Jean-Georges' Nougatine
25 Clinton St. Baking Co.
Locanda Verde
Norma's
24 Balthazar
Egg
23 Breslin
21 Rosemary's

BRUNCH DOWNTOWN

25 Prune
24 Hearth
Blue Ribbon Bakery
DBGB

22 Saxon & Parole
Paradou
Beaumarchais
21 Miss Lily's

BRUNCH MIDTOWN

26 Maialino
25 db Bistro Moderne
24 Petrossian
23 Bar Americain
Artisanal
22 Lambs Club
Americano
21 Eatery

BRUNCH UPTOWN

26 Telepan
24 Ouest
   Ocean Grill
23 Community Food
22 Atlantic Grill
   Lido
21 Calle Ocho
   Cascabel Taqueria

BUSINESS DINING
FINANCIAL DISTRICT

24 North End Grill
   MarkJoseph Steak
23 Bobby Van's
   Cipriani Club 55
22 2 West
   Harry's Cafe
21 Wall & Water
20 Les Halles

BUSINESS DINING
MIDTOWN

29 Le Bernardin
28 Eleven Madison
   Marea
27 Milos
   Union Square Cafe
   Nobu
   Four Seasons
23 Casa Lever

CHILD-FRIENDLY

24 L&B Spumoni
22 Rosa Mexicano
   Blue Smoke
21 Landmarc
20 Serendipity 3
19 Ninja
18 Ruby Foo's
17 Cowgirl

DINING AT THE BAR

27 Gotham B&G
   Union Square Cafe
26 Aquagrill
25 Colicchio & Sons
24 Hearth
23 Red Cat
22 Plaza Food Hall
   Oyster Bar

GROUP DINING

23 Má Pêche
   Hill Country
22 Beauty & Essex

Almayass▽
21 Carmine's
   Fig & Olive
   Hurricane
20 Almond

HISTORIC PLACES

27 Four Seasons
26 Keens
25 Old Homestead
24 Minetta Tavern
23 21 Club
22 Oyster Bar
21 Waverly Inn
20 Monkey Bar

HOTEL DINING

28 Jean Georges (Trump Int'l)
27 NoMad (NoMad)
   Café Boulud (Surrey)
26 Ai Fiori (Langham Pl.)
   Maialino (Gramercy Park)
25 Asiate (Mandarin Oriental)
   Locanda Verde (Greenwich)
   Benjamin Steak (Dylan)

HOT SERVERS

23 La Esquina
   Lure Fishbar
22 44 & X/44½
21 Miss Lily's
20 General▽
   Dos Caminos
17 Coffee Shop
- Manon

HUSH-HUSH

26 Zenkichi
25 Kuma Inn
   Sakagura
   Bohemian
24 Burger Joint
23 Hudson Clearwater
   Armani Ristorante
20 Pulqueria▽

LATE DINING

28 Sushi Seki
24 Spotted Pig
23 Wollensky's
   La Esquina
22 Beauty & Essex
   Kang Suh
21 Umberto's Clam House
20 Pulino's

LOCAVORE

27 Blue Hill
   Union Square Cafe
26 Telepan
   Roberta's
25 RedFarm
24 Diner
   Northern Spy
22 Back Forty

PATIOS/GARDENS

24 Pure Food & Wine
22 Salinas
   Barbetta
21 New Leaf
20 Battery Gardens
19 Brasserie Ruhlmann
   Bryant Park Grill/Cafe
18 Boathouse

PRIVATE ROOMS

29 Le Bernardin
27 NoMad
26 Del Posto
   Craft
   Ai Fiori
25 Il Buco
23 21 Club
19 Lafayette∇

QUICK BITES

26 Taïm
25 Azuri Cafe
24 Caracas
   Arepas
   Pommes Frites
23 Mamoun's
   Crif Dogs
22 Bark

ROMANCE

27 Mas (Farmhouse)
26 Zenkichi
25 Il Buco
24 Erminia
23 Place
22 Water's Edge
21 House
‒ Cherry

SINGLES SCENES

24 Perla
23 Hudson Clearwater
   Catch
22 Beauty & Essex

21 Rosemary's
   Miss Lily's
   Hurricane
20 General∇

SOCIETY WATCH

25 David Burke Townhouse
24 Elio's
   Arabelle
22 Sirio∇
21 Ze Café
   Sant Ambroeus
19 Harlow∇
17 Swifty's

24/7

23 Empanada Mama
   Coppelia
22 Miss Korea BBQ
   New WonJo
   Sanford's
   Kunjip
21 Cafeteria
20 Bubby's

VIEWS

26 River Café
25 Asiate
24 Lincoln
   Shi
23 Sea Grill
21 Gaonnuri∇
   Michael Jordan's
20 Robert

WINE BARS

26 Danny Brown
25 Il Buco Alimentari
   SD26
24 Aroma
   Peasant
   Bar Boulud
23 Otto
22 Corkbuzz

WINNING WINE LISTS

29 Le Bernardin
   Bouley
28 Per Se
   Daniel
   Eleven Madison
   Jean Georges
   Gramercy Tavern
25 Veritas

TOPS BY OCCASION

Some best bets in a range of prices and cuisines for these occasions.

ANNIVERSARY WORTHY

29	Bouley
28	La Grenouille
27	Mas (Farmhouse)
26	Del Posto
	Zenkichi
	Marc Forgione
22	Water's Edge
21	House

BRIDAL/ BABY SHOWERS

23	Bobo
22	Lady Mendl's
21	Ze Café
	Kings' Carriage House
	Mari Vanna
	Palm Court
20	Sarabeth's
	Alice's Tea Cup

DRINKS DOWNTOWN

24	North End Grill
	DBGB
23	Spice Market
	Dutch
	Catch
22	Acme
	Freemans
20	Macao Trading

DRINKS MIDTOWN

27	NoMad
26	Keens
22	Zengo

Lambs Club
La Fonda del Sol

21	Lavo
20	Monkey Bar
19	Harlow∇

DRINKS UPTOWN

24	Lincoln
	Ouest
	Bar Boulud
22	Mark
	Red Rooster
21	Cafe Luxembourg
	Crown
20	Penrose∇

JURY DUTY

25	Takahachi
23	Great NY Noodle
22	Nha Trang
	Amazing 66
	Excellent Dumpling
21	Pongsri Thai
20	Red Egg
19	Forlini's

THANKSGIVING

28	Gramercy Tavern
27	Blue Hill
26	Telepan
24	One if by Land
	DBGB
23	21 Club
	Cookshop
18	Fraunces Tavern

TOPS BY LOCATION

CHELSEA

27	NoMad
26	Del Posto
	Morimoto
	Scarpetta
25	Colicchio & Sons
	Da Umberto
	Tía Pol
	El Quinto Pino

CHINATOWN

24	Xi'an Famous Foods
23	Great NY Noodle
22	Oriental Garden
	Peking Duck

Nha Trang
Joe's Shanghai
Wo Hop
Amazing 66

EAST 40s

28	Kurumazushi
	Sushi Yasuda
26	Aburiya Kinnosuke
25	Sakagura
	Sparks
	Benjamin Steak
	Num Pang
	Avra

EAST 50s

28	La Grenouille
27	Four Seasons
26	Caviar Russe
	Felidia
25	SushiAnn
	Wolfgang's
	Le Cirque
	Aquavit

EAST 60s

28	Daniel
	Sushi Seki
26	Il Mulino
25	Tiella
	David Burke Townhouse
24	Rouge Tomate
	Scalinatella
	JoJo

EAST 70s

28	Sasabune
27	Gari
	Café Boulud
25	Candle 79
	Caravaggio
	Yefsi Estiatorio
24	Candle Cafe
	Sette Mezzo

EAST 80s

25	Sandro's
	Sistina
	Donguri
24	Elio's
	Spigolo
	Poke
	Erminia
	Wa Jeal

EAST 90s & 100s

25	San Matteo
24	Pinocchio
	El Paso
23	Nick's
	Sfoglia
	Paola's
	Amor Cubano
	Rizzo's Pizza

EAST VILLAGE

28	Degustation
27	Kyo Ya
	Momofuku Ko
	Pylos
26	Luzzo's
25	Dirt Candy
	Jewel Bako
	Graffiti

FINANCIAL DISTRICT

24	North End Grill
	MarkJoseph Steak
	Capital Grille
	Toloache
23	Adrienne's Pizza
	Luke's Lobster
23	Delmonico's
	Bobby Van's

FLATIRON/UNION SQ.

28	Eleven Madison
	Gramercy Tavern
27	Union Square Cafe
	Tocqueville
26	Craft
	15 East
	Tamarind
	ABC Kitchen

GARMENT DISTRICT

26	Ai Fiori
	Keens
23	Delmonico's Kitchen
	Cho Dang Gol
	Uncle Jack's
	Szechuan Gourmet
	Colbeh
22	Frankie & Johnnie's
	Miss Korea BBQ

GRAMERCY

26	Maialino
25	BLT Prime
	Casa Mono
	Novitá
24	Pure Food & Wine
	Posto
	Defonte's
23	Bar Jamón

GREENWICH VILLAGE

28	Ushiwakamaru
27	Gotham B&G
	Blue Hill
	Babbo
26	Il Mulino
	Tomoe Sushi
25	Strip House
	Alta

HARLEM

24	Melba's
23	Dinosaur BBQ

Covo

22 5 & Diamond

Lido

Red Rooster

Miss Mamie's/Maude's

Amy Ruth's

LITTLE ITALY

24 Pellegrino's

Shanghai Café

23 Nyonya

La Esquina

Angelo's/Mulberry

Ferrara

Il Cortile

22 Wild Ginger

LOWER EAST SIDE

26 Prosperity Dumpling

25 Kuma Inn

Clinton St. Baking Co.

Ápizz

WD-50

24 Barrio Chino

Katz's Deli

Stanton Social

MEATPACKING

25 Old Homestead

24 Valbella

23 Spice Market

STK

Catch

22 Sea

Paradou

Standard Grill

MURRAY HILL

25 Wolfgang's

Hangawi

Sushi Sen-nin

Marcony

SD26

24 Villa Berulia

Riverpark

Ben & Jack's

NOHO

26 Bianca

25 Il Buco

Bohemian

Bond St

24 Aroma Kitchen

23 Mile End Sandwich

Hecho en Dumbo

22 Forcella

NOLITA

27 Torrisi

26 Taïm

24 Lombardi's

Peasant

Ed's Lobster Bar

23 Parm

Rubirosa

Tacombi/Fonda Nolita

SOHO

26 Aquagrill

Blue Ribbon Sushi

25 Blue Ribbon

Raoul's

24 Osteria Morini

Kittichai

L'Ecole

Balthazar

TRIBECA

29 Bouley

27 Scalini Fedeli

Nobu

26 Pepolino

Jungsik

Brushstroke

Tamarind

Marc Forgione

WEST 40s

27 Gari

26 Sushi Zen

Aureole

25 Wolfgang's

Del Frisco's

db Bistro Moderne

24 Esca

Koi

WEST 50s

29 Le Bernardin

28 Sugiyama

Marea

27 Milos

Nobu 57

Gari

26 Modern

Totto Ramen

WEST 60s

28 Per Se

Jean Georges

27 Picholine

Masa/Bar Masa

26 Telepan

Porter House NY

| 25 | Asiate |
| | Boulud Sud |

WEST 70s

27	Gari
25	Dovetail
	Salumeria Rosi
24	Mike's Bistro
	Ocean Grill
23	'Cesca
	Saravanaa Bhavan
	FishTag

WEST 80s

24	Barney Greengrass
	Ouest
	Candle Cafe
23	Momoya
	Celeste
	Luke's Lobster
	Prime KO
	Peacefood Café

WEST 90s & UP

25	Pisticci
24	Gennaro
23	Thai Market
	Max SoHa/Caffe
	Community Food
	Vareli
	Pio Pio
22	Indus Valley

WEST VILLAGE

27	Mas (Farmhouse)
	Soto
	Annisa
	L'Artusi
26	Takashi
	Perilla
	Pearl Oyster Bar
	Perry St.

BROOKLYN

BAY RIDGE

26	Tanoreen
25	Eliá
	Tuscany Grill
24	Gino's
	Areo
	Chadwick's
23	Fushimi
	Pearl Room

BKLYN HTS/DUMBO

26	River Café
25	Colonie
	Henry's End
	Noodle Pudding
24	Queen
23	Grimaldi's
	Jack the Horse
20	ChipShop

BOERUM & COBBLE HILLS

25	Hibino
	Chocolate Room
	Ki Sushi
24	Rucola
23	Mile End
	Joya
	Boca Lupo
	South Brooklyn Pizza

CARROLL GARDENS

27	Lucali
	Battersby
	Grocery
25	Buttermilk Channel
24	Fragole
23	Prime Meats
	Frankies Spuntino
	Seersucker

FORT GREENE

23	Caffe e Vino
	Walter's
	Madiba
	Olea
	Habana Outpost
22	Smoke Joint
	No. 7
21	67 Burger

GREENPOINT

26	Paulie Gee's
	Five Leaves
24	Fornino
	Xi'an Famous Foods
22	No. 7 Sub
21	Calexico
-	Luksus
	River Styx

PARK SLOPE

27 Al Di La
25 Rose Water
    Franny's
    Blue Ribbon
    Talde
    Chocolate Room
    Applewood
    Convivium Osteria

PROSPECT HEIGHTS

26 Bar Corvo
24 James
23 Chuko▽
    606 R&D
    Amorina
21 Vanderbilt
    Tom's
20 Zaytoons

WILLIAMSBURG

27 Peter Luger
    St. Anselm
26 Traif
    Fette Sau
    Zenkichi
25 Rye
24 Caracas
    Marlow & Sons

OTHER AREAS

27 Chef's Table/Brooklyn Fare (Downtown)
26 Di Fara Pizza (Midwood)
    Locanda Vini/Olii (Clinton Hill)
    Roberta's (Bushwick)
25 Good Fork (Red Hook)
    Taci's Beyti (Midwood)
24 Totonno's (Coney Island)
    Vinegar Hill House (Vinegar Hill)

OTHER BOROUGHS

BRONX

26 Roberto
24 Patricia's
    Zero Otto Nove
    Jake's
23 Dominick's
    Enzo's
    Beccofino
    Tosca Café

QUEENS: ASTORIA

27 Il Bambino
26 Tratt. L'incontro
    Taverna Kyclades
    Vesta
25 Piccola Venezia
    Christos
    Basil Brick Oven
24 Agnanti

QUEENS: FLUSHING

24 Spicy & Tasty
    Xi'an Famous Foods
23 Szechuan Gourmet
22 Sik Gaek
    Pho Bang
    Joe's Shanghai
21 Kum Gang San
20 Kyochon Chicken

QUEENS: LONG ISLAND CITY

24 Tournesol
    Shi
23 Manetta's
    Manducatis
22 Corner Bistro
    Bella Via
    Water's Edge
21 Riverview

QUEENS: OTHER AREAS

27 Sripraphai (Woodside)
26 Tortilleria Nixtamal (Corona)
    Salt & Fat (Sunnyside)
    Ayada (Woodside)
    Leo's Latticini (Corona)
    Danny Brown (Forest Hills)
25 Don Peppe (Ozone Park)
    Park Side (Corona)

STATEN ISLAND

26 Denino's
25 Bocelli
    Carol's Cafe
    Trattoria Romana
23 Angelina's
    Joe & Pat's
    Fushimi
    Bayou

TOPS BY DESTINATION

A selection of the best bets in a range of prices and cuisines near these points of interest.

BARCLAYS CENTER

- 25 Convivium Osteria
- 24 Rucola
- 23 South Brooklyn Pizza
- Habana Outpost
- 22 Smoke Joint
- Bark
- 21 Vanderbilt
- Flatbush Farm

BROOKLYN BRIDGE PARK

- 27 Smorgasburg
- 25 Colonie
- 24 Pok Pok Ny▽
- 23 Luke's Lobster
- 22 No. 7 Sub
- 20 Teresa's
- Henry Public
- Red Gravy▽

HIGH LINE (GANSEVOORT ST. EXIT)

- 23 Spice Market
- 22 Sea
- Standard Grill
- Pastis
- 21 Fig & Olive
- 20 Dos Caminos
- 19 Bill's Bar & Burger
- 18 Serafina

HIGH LINE (23RD ST. EXIT)

- 25 Tía Pol
- 24 Txikito
- Co.
- 23 Red Cat
- Cookshop
- 22 Artichoke Basille's
- 21 La Lunchonette
- Bottino

INSIDE GRAND CENTRAL

- 22 Oyster Bar
- La Fonda del Sol
- Cipriani Dolci
- 21 Cafe Centro
- Michael Jordan's
- 19 Junior's
- Naples 45
- Two Boots

METROPOLITAN MUSEUM

- 27 Café Boulud
- 23 Giovanni Venticinque
- 22 Café Sabarsky/Fledermaus
- 21 Sant Ambroeus
- 20 E.A.T.
- 19 Caffe Grazie
- 18 Serafina
- Le Pain Quotidien

MoMA

- 26 Modern
- 23 China Grill
- 22 Soba Nippon
- Michael's
- 21 PizzArte
- Benoit
- 19 Menchanko-tei
- La Bonne Soupe

9/11 MEMORIAL

- 24 North End Grill
- 22 Blue Smoke
- 21 Shake Shack
- Zaitzeff▽
- 20 Les Halles
- 19 Bill's Bar & Burger
- Baluchi's
- 17 P.J. Clarke's

THEATER DISTRICT DELUXE

- 26 Aureole
- 25 Wolfgang's
- db Bistro Moderne
- 24 Esca
- Oceana
- 23 Triomphe
- Hakkasan
- 22 Lambs Club

THEATER DISTRICT OLD-SCHOOL

- 22 Frankie & Johnnie's
- Patsy's
- Chez Napoléon
- Barbetta
- 21 Le Rivage
- 19 Joe Allen
- 18 Sardi's
- Landmark Tavern

Best Buys

Top-rated restaurants $25 and under, unless otherwise indicated

1. Il Bambino | *Italian*
2. Di Fara Pizza | *Pizza*
3. Tortilleria Nixtamal | *Mexican*
4. Denino's | *Pizza*
5. Ayada | *Thai*
6. Leo's Latticini/Corona | *Deli/It.*
7. Totto Ramen | *Japanese/Noodles*
8. Prosperity Dumpling | *Chinese*
9. Taïm | *Israeli/Vegetarian*
10. Num Pang | *Cambodian/Sand.*
11. Pure Thai Cookhouse | *Thai*
12. Basil Brick Oven | *Pizza*
13. Azuri Cafe | *Israeli/Kosher*
14. Totonno Pizza | *Pizza*
15. Caracas | *Venezuelan*
16. L&B Spumoni | *Dessert/Pizza*
17. Lombardis | *Pizza*
18. Mighty Quinn's BBQ | *BBQ*
19. Porchetta | *Italian*
20. Katz's Deli | *Deli*

BEST BUYS BY NEIGHBORHOOD

CHELSEA

- 24 La Bergamote
- 22 La Taza de Oro
- Friedman's Lunch
- No. 7
- BareBurger

CHINATOWN

- 24 Xi'an Famous Foods
- 23 Great NY Noodle
- 22 Nha Trang
- Wo Hop
- Amazing 66

East 40s

- 25 Num Pang
- 21 99 Miles to Philly
- 19 Two Boots
- Menchanko-tei
- 17 'Wichcraft

EAST 50s/60s

- 22 John's Pizzeria
- Kati Roll Company
- Hide-Chan
- 21 BonChon
- Angelo's Pizzeria

EAST 70s

- 24 Meatball Shop
- 22 BareBurger
- 21 Dos Toros
- 20 Al Forno Pizzeria
- 19 Blue 9 Burger

EAST 80s

- 23 Luke's Lobster
- 22 Naruto Ramen
- Burger Bistro
- 21 Shake Shack
- Papaya King

EAST VILLAGE

- 24 Caracas
- Mighty Quinn's BBQ
- Porchetta
- Pommes Frites
- Xi'an Famous Foods

FLATIRON/UNION SQ.

- 23 Grimaldi's
- 22 City Bakery
- 21 Shake Shack
- Maoz
- 20 Hill Country Chicken

GREENWICH VILLAGE

- 25 Num Pang
- 22 BareBurger
- Kati Roll Company
- Creperie
- Artichoke Basille's

LOWER EAST SIDE

- 26 Prosperity Dumpling
- 24 Katz's Deli
- Meatball Shop
- 22 Creperie
- 21 Vanessa's Dumpling

MURRAY HILL

23 Vezzo
S'MAC
Saravanaa Bhavan
22 Tiffin Wallah
Shorty's

WEST 40s

22 John's Pizzeria
Shorty's
Pam Real Thai
21 Shake Shack
Maoz

WEST 50s/60s

26 Totto Ramen
25 Pure Thai Cookhouse
Azuri Cafe
24 Burger Joint
18 Le Pain Quotidien

WEST 70s

23 Saravanaa Bhavan
22 Hummus Place
21 Shake Shack
Maoz Vegetarian
20 Gray's Papaya

WEST 80s

23 Luke's Lobster
Peacefood Café
21 Island Burgers
Flor de Mayo
Hampton Chutney

WEST VILLAGE

26 Taïm
24 Meatball Shop
23 Joe's Pizza
22 John's Pizzeria
Hummus Place

BROOKLYN: PARK SLOPE

24 Song
23 South Brooklyn Pizza
22 Bonnie's Grill
Burger Bistro
BareBurger

BROOKLYN: WILLIAMSBURG

24 Caracas
Best Pizza
Pies-N-Thighs
Meatball Shop
Egg

BEST BUYS BY CATEGORY

ALL YOU CAN EAT

- [24] Mercadito ($23)
- [23] La Baraka ($14)
- Yuva ($14)
- [22] Nirvana ($13)
- Turkish Kitchen ($22)
- Indus Valley ($15)
- Yuka ($21)
- [21] Brick Lane Curry ($10)
- Sapphire Indian Cuisine ($16)
- Darbar ($13)

BYO

- [26] Di Fara Pizza
- [25] Azuri Cafe
- [22] Pho Bang
- [21] Oaxaca
- Wondee Siam
- Hampton Chutney
- [20] Zaytoons
- Little Poland

CHEAP DATES

- [25] Pure Thai Cookhouse
- [24] Mimi's Hummus
- Song
- [23] Nyonya
- Café Habana/Outpost
- [22] Cafe Orlin
- [21] Nom Wah Tea Parlor
- Pequena ▽
- Cubana Café
- [20] Zaytoons

EARLY-BIRD

- [25] Takahachi ($20)
- [22] La Gioconda ($20)
- Turkish Kitchen ($22)
- Ponty Bistro ($25)
- [21] Carmine's ($17)
- Good ($25)

- Osteria Laguna ($25)
- [20] Chez Oskar ($22)
- [18] Our Place ($23)
- Arté Café ($13)

PRE-THEATER

- [28] Sugiyama ($32)
- [27] Milos ($49)
- Tocqueville ($44)
- [25] db Bistro Moderne ($45)
- [24] Bar Boulud ($45)
- [23] 21 Club ($42)
- Circo ($38)
- Uncle Jack's ($40)
- China Grill ($38)
- [21] South Gate ($35)

PRIX FIXE LUNCH

- [28] Jean Georges ($38)
- Sushi Yasuda ($23)
- [27] Gotham B&G ($25)
- Milos ($25)
- [26] Morimoto ($25)
- Telepan ($28)
- Aureole ($36)
- Porter House NY ($25)
- [25] Colicchio & Sons ($25)
- [23] 21 Club ($37)

PRIX FIXE DINNER

- [28] Sushi Yasuda ($28)
- [26] Danny Brown ($28)
- [25] SushiAnn ($35)
- [24] Tournesol ($25)
- Yerba Buena ($38)
- Kittichai ($38)
- [23] Periyali ($37)
- [22] Remi ($38)
- Etcetera Etcetera ($38)
- Brasserie 8½ ($38)

RESTAURANT DIRECTORY

	FOOD	DECOR	SERVICE	COST

NEW Aamanns-
Copenhagen ⬤Ⓜ *Danish/Sandwiches* — ▽ 20 | 18 | 19 | $45

TriBeCa | Tribeca Film Bldg. | 13 Laight St. (bet. 6th Ave. & Varick St.) |
212-925-1313 | www.aamanns-copenhagen.com

A "chefly take on smørrebrød" – an open-faced sandwich on "delicious rye bread" – is the specialty of this midpriced offshoot of a Copenhagen favorite, deemed a "Danish gem" in TriBeCa; its "plain, modern" space exudes "Scandinavian" "cool", but its casual vibe has many suggesting "think lunch."

Abboccato *Italian* — 21 | 19 | 20 | $56

W 50s | Blakely Hotel | 136 W. 55th St. (bet. 6th & 7th Aves.) |
212-265-4000 | www.abboccato.com

It boasts "convenient" coordinates – near both "City Center and Carnegie Hall" – and this Midtown Italian "sleeper" follows through with "dependably good" eats, "prompt" service and "intimate" environs; the $38 dinner prix fixe is a "bargain" vis-à-vis the otherwise "higher-end" tabs.

NEW ABC Cocina *Pan-Latin* — - | - | - | E

Flatiron | ABC Carpet & Home | 38 E. 19th St. (bet. B'way & Park Ave. S.) |
212-677-2233 | www.abccocinanyc.com

The follow-up to Jean-Georges Vongerichten's runaway hit, ABC Kitchen, is also located in the Flatiron's ABC Carpet & Home, but here chef Dan Kluger's expansive (and expensive) menu of farm-fresh small plates skews Latin, with elaborate tacos, guacamole, wood-grilled meats and the like matched with margaritas; the moody, meticulously designed space is outfitted with fixtures you can buy in the store.

ABC Kitchen *American* — 26 | 24 | 23 | $59

Flatiron | ABC Carpet & Home | 35 E. 18th St. (bet. B'way & Park Ave. S.) |
212-475-5829 | www.abckitchennyc.com

An "eco-friendly delight" from Jean-Georges Vongerichten, this "refreshingly" "whimsical" American in the Flatiron's ABC Carpet & Home "continues to amaze" as chef Dan Kluger's "organic sourcing" and "farm-to-table approach" yield an "exquisite", "seasonal menu" presented by a "knowledgeable" staff; access to the "energized space" remains a "challenge", but "keep on trying" for a rez – it's "worth it."

Abigael's *Eclectic/Kosher* — 20 | 16 | 19 | $49

Garment District | 1407 Broadway (bet. 38th & 39th Sts.) |
212-575-1407 | www.abigaels.com

The menu spanning "short ribs to sushi" gives kosher cuisine an "upscale" gloss at this double-decker Garment District Eclectic overseen by "creative" chef Jeff Nathan; "bland" atmospherics and "spotty service" detract, but it remains a "staple" for observant folks.

Aburiya Kinnosuke ⬤ *Japanese* — 26 | 20 | 22 | $56

E 40s | 213 E. 45th St. (bet. 2nd & 3rd Aves.) | 212-867-5454 |
www.aburiyakinnosuke.com

"The real deal" in Midtown, this "classic izakaya" "transports you" to Japan with a "top-notch", sushiless lineup starring "grilled robata" bites and housemade tofu; since "course after course" can do some "damage to your wallet", bargain-hunters are "bummed that they no longer serve lunch."

| | FOOD | DECOR | SERVICE | COST |

ABV ◐ *American*
20 | 19 | 20 | $33

E 90s | 1504 Lexington Ave. (97th St.) | 212-722-8959 | www.abvny.com
"Something different" for Carnegie Hill, this "with-it" wine bar matches "interesting" American nibbles (who knew foie gras fluffernutter was the "ultimate snack"?) with an "eclectic" list of wines; the "communal" space exhibits "lots of energy" and even a touch of "downtown" "swagger."

Acappella ⊠ *Italian*
24 | 21 | 24 | $69

TriBeCa | 1 Hudson St. (Chambers St.) | 212-240-0163 |
www.acappella-restaurant.com
Dining is "an event" at this "old-world" TriBeCa Northern Italian renowned for "excellent" food, "over-the-top" service and *"Godfather* opulent" decor; "try not to faint when you get the check" or you'll miss out on the complimentary grappa.

A Casa Fox Ⓜ *Pan-Latin*
23 | 20 | 21 | $34

LES | 173 Orchard St. (Stanton St.) | 212-253-1900 | www.acasafox.com
What this "little" LES Pan-Latin joint lacks in legroom is made up for in "homey", "candlelit" ambiance and a "fab assortment" of tapas and clay pots; given the "friendly" hospitality, modest tabs and "cozy fireplace", it's sure to "warm your soul."

Acme *American*
22 | 18 | 19 | $54

NoHo | 9 Great Jones St. (Lafayette St.) | 212-203-2121 | www.acmenyc.com
A "hot" ticket in NoHo, this "former down-home roadhouse" is now "delighting diners" with "fabulous" New American fare featuring chef/"vegetable wizard" Mads Refslund's "Nordic" "twists"; it's a "buzzing scene" with "tight quarters" and "noise", but trendsetters who "welcome" the "hip vibe" will "definitely return" all the same.

Acqua *Italian/Pizza*
20 | 18 | 19 | $40

W 90s | 718 Amsterdam Ave. (95th St.) | 212-222-2752 |
www.acquanyc.com
This "casual" UWS Italian "staple" keeps it simple and "satisfying" with a "dependable" outlay of "really good" brick-oven pizzas and "hearty" trattoria standards; "reasonable" prices, "friendly" service and convenience to Symphony Space make the "uninspired" decor easy to overlook.

Adrienne's Pizzabar ◐ *Pizza*
23 | 16 | 17 | $25

Financial District | 87 Pearl St. (Hanover Sq.) | 212-248-3838
Brace yourself for "lunchtime madness" when "Wall Street suits" and "casual passersby" descend on this FiDi pizzeria for its "outstanding" thin-crust pies; "adequate" service and "nonexistent decor" are part of the package, making it best enjoyed at an alfresco seat on "picturesque Stone Street."

Afghan Kebab House *Afghan*
20 | 13 | 18 | $26

E 70s | 1345 Second Ave. (71st St.) | 212-517-2776
W 50s | 764 Ninth Ave. (bet. 51st & 52nd Sts.) | 212-307-1612
Jackson Heights | 74-16 37th Ave. (bet. 74th & 75th Sts.) | Queens |
718-565-0471
"Mouthwatering" kebabs get skewered at this "authentic" Afghan trio hailed for "flavorful", "substantial" grub for "bargain-basement"

dough; "no-frills" service and "dark", "nothing to write home about" settings are the downsides.

Agave *Southwestern*
20 | 19 | 19 | $36

W Village | 140 Seventh Ave. S. (Charles St.) | 212-989-2100 | www.agaveny.com

Sure, the chow is "decent" enough, but according to this Village Southwesterner's "young" fan base it's the "killer margaritas" that "keep the place buzzing"; though service skews "slow", time is on your side during the "all-you-can-drink" weekend brunch.

A.G. Kitchen *Nuevo Latino*
18 | 15 | 16 | $35

W 70s | 269 Columbus Ave. (73rd St.) | 212-873-9400 | www.agkitchen.com

This "bustling" UWSer from chef Alex Garcia (Calle Ocho, Copacabana) turns out Nuevo Latino "comfort food for the masses" as well as burgers with some "creative touches"; its "casual" style includes "irregular service", but "fun vibes" and "strong" drinks make for "a big draw."

Agnanti *Greek*
24 | 15 | 20 | $36

Astoria | 19-06 Ditmars Blvd. (19th St.) | Queens | 718-545-4554 | www.agnantimeze.com

A "notch above the typical Astorian", this "tried-and-true" Hellenic taverna rolls out "delicious", "reasonably priced" meals that conjure up the "Greek isles"; the decor is on the "forgettable" side, so regulars request seats on the "wonderful" patio facing Astoria Park and the East River.

Agora Taverna *Greek*
21 | 19 | 19 | $35

Forest Hills | 70-09 Austin St. (70th Ave.) | Queens | 718-793-7300 | www.agorataverna.com

"They know how to grill fish" at this Forest Hills taverna, whose "varied menu" ups the local ante for "traditional Greek dishes"; it can get "noisy", but it's "amiable" if you're "not in the mood to go to Astoria."

Ai Fiori *Italian*
26 | 25 | 25 | $91

Garment District | Langham Place Fifth Avenue Hotel | 400 Fifth Ave. (bet. 36th & 37th Sts.) | 212-613-8660 | www.aifiorinyc.com

"Michael White's empire" encompasses this "culinary treasure" in the Langham Place Fifth Avenue Hotel, where you "feel like a swell" relishing "lovely" Italian cuisine (notably "exquisite pastas"), "interesting" wines and "gracious service"; the "plush surroundings" befit a "class act" that's "splurgy" but "worth every century note" – "especially for an occasion."

Aji Sushi *Japanese*
20 | 16 | 19 | $30

Murray Hill | 519 Third Ave. (bet. 34th & 35th Sts.) | 212-686-2055

Maybe it's "just a standard sushi spot", but Murray Hill locals swear by this "reliable" Japanese "staple" for its "good variety" and "value" tabs; "swift delivery" seems the preferred way to go, given the "bland" atmosphere and just "adequate" service.

Akdeniz ☒ *Turkish*
21 | 14 | 19 | $32

W 40s | 19 W. 46th St. (bet. 5th & 6th Aves.) | 212-575-2307 | www.akdenizturkishusa.com

It's all about "value" at this Midtown Turk offering a "can't-be-beat" $25 dinner prix fixe that's a showstopper for theatergoers; the "tiny", "relaxed" room can feel a bit "claustrophobic" and "shabby", but the grub's "tasty" and the service "accommodating."

	FOOD	DECOR	SERVICE	COST

Aki *Japanese* | 24 | 16 | 23 | $43

W Village | 181 W. Fourth St. (Barrow St.) | 212-989-5440
"Not your regular sushi place", this "atypical" Villager plies a "creative" East-meets–West Indies "fusion" concept that "sounds crazy but actually works"; smooth service and "affordable" tabs mean most take the "smaller-than-a-studio-apartment" dimensions in stride.

NEW Alameda ◐Ⓜ *American* | - | - | - | I

Greenpoint | 195 Franklin St. (Green St.) | Brooklyn | 347-227-7296 | www.alamedabk.com
The team from Williamsburg's Brooklyn Star is behind this midpriced Greenpointer, where a gorgeously grungy staff serves creative cocktails and high-end (yet affordable) takes on American snack fare; a U-shaped bar dominates the stylish space, which is decked out in white tile and handsome wood.

A La Turka *Turkish* | 19 | 14 | 17 | $37

E 70s | 1417 Second Ave. (74th St.) | 212-744-2424 | www.alaturkarestaurant.com
"Surprisingly good" Turkish food is yours at this "reliable" Upper Eastsider where the prices are "affordable" and the noise level "manageable"; those who shrug "nothing exceptional" cite "drab" decor and "spotty" service.

Alberto *Italian* | 23 | 19 | 22 | $47

Forest Hills | 98-31 Metropolitan Ave. (bet. 69th & 70th Aves.) | Queens | 718-268-7860 | www.albertorestaurant.com
A "Forest Hills find", this "marvelously old-fashioned" "upscale" Italian remains a "steady" "neighborhood institution" (since '73) thanks to "well-prepared classics" and "staff and owners who greet you like family"; the "romantic" white-tablecloth vibe (abetted by a fireplace) and "high prices" suggest "special occasion."

Al Bustan *Lebanese* | 21 | 20 | 20 | $48

E 50s | 319 E. 53rd St. (bet. 1st & 2nd Aves.) | 212-759-5933 | www.albustanny.com
"Hidden" on an East Midtown side street, this upscale double-decker delivers "succulent" Lebanese classics in a "modern", chandeliered room; although the "big space" can feel "empty" at dinner, at least it's "comfortable" and you can "hear yourself speak."

Alcala *Spanish* | 21 | 18 | 21 | $49

E 40s | 246 E. 44th St. (bet. 2nd & 3rd Aves.) | 212-370-1866 | www.alcalarestaurant.com
"Basque country" comes to a residential block near the U.N. via this "muy bueno" Spaniard that's touted for its "excellent" tapas, "flavorful" large plates and "liquid-courage" sangria; "caring" service and an "attractive" setting embellish the "low-key" vibe, while a "romantic" back garden seals the deal.

NEW Alchemy, Texas *BBQ* | - | - | - | I

Jackson Heights | 71-04 35th Ave. (bet. Leverich & 72nd Sts.) | Queens | 718-899-9553
Tucked in the back of Jackson Heights' Legends Bar, this low-cost 'cue joint from John Brown Smokehouse owner Josh Bowen puts a fresh spin

on the genre, spicing up Texas-style ribs, brisket and esoterica (Spam, anyone?) with ingredients like saffron and foie gras; counter service and a no-frills, checkered-tablecloth setting complete the picture.

Aldea Ⓢ *Mediterranean* | 25 | 22 | 23 | $68

Flatiron | 31 W. 17th St. (bet. 5th & 6th Aves.) | 212-675-7223 | www.aldearestaurant.com

"Tantalize your taste buds" with George Mendes' "top-end" modern Med cuisine at this "refreshing" Flatiron "delight", where coastal Iberian specialties "well-served" by "total pros" justify the "high prices"; to really "treat yourself", sit at the chef's counter and enjoy "dinner and a show."

NEW Alder *American/Eclectic* | ▽ 20 | 16 | 22 | $60

E Village | 157 Second Ave. (bet. 9th & 10th Sts.) | 212-539-1900 | www.aldernyc.com

Wylie Dufresne follows up WD-50, his famed temple of molecular gastronomy, with this relatively "casual" East Villager offering "creative", "high-end" takes on American pub fare; the space, which features a metal bar in the front and a no-frills rectangular dining room in back, is decorated with touches of the namesake white birch.

Al Di La *Italian* | 27 | 19 | 22 | $49

Park Slope | 248 Fifth Ave. (Carroll St.) | Brooklyn | 718-783-4565 | www.aldilatrattoria.com

The trattoria "everyone wishes was in their neighborhood", this "all-time-favorite" Park Sloper "deserves its reputation" for "inspired" Venetian cooking that's a "bargain" to boot; no reservations means "obligatory" waits ("bummer!"), though "lunch is easier" and there's always its "wine bar around the corner."

Al Forno Pizzeria *Pizza* | 20 | 13 | 18 | $25

E 70s | 1484 Second Ave. (bet. 77th & 78th Sts.) | 212-249-5103 | www.alfornopizzeria77.com

This "neighborhood" Yorkville pizzeria churns out "quality" brick-oven pies on the "quick" for low dough; "typical" Italian pastas and salads are also on offer, but given "lots of kids" and little atmosphere, "home delivery" may be the way to go.

Ali Baba *Turkish* | 20 | 16 | 18 | $35

E 40s | 862 Second Ave. (46th St.) | 212-888-8622
Murray Hill | 212 E. 34th St. (bet. 2nd & 3rd Aves.) | 212-683-9206
www.alibabaturkishcuisine.com

Ottoman expats say these "convivial" Midtown Turks "taste like home", then up the ante with "generous portions" at real-"value" tabs; proponents praise Second Avenue's "lovely roof deck", though the "neon sign", "seedy" looks and "so-so service" are another story.

Alice's Tea Cup *Teahouse* | 20 | 22 | 19 | $26

E 60s | 156 E. 64th St. (Lexington Ave.) | 212-486-9200
E 80s | 220 E. 81st St. (bet. 2nd & 3rd Aves.) | 212-734-4832
W 70s | 102 W. 73rd St. (bet. Amsterdam & Columbus Aves.) | 212-799-3006
www.alicesteacup.com

"Go with the girls (little girls especially)" to these "frilly" American tearooms where the "storybook" surroundings make the "light" menu's "excellent scones" and array of "wonderful" brews "more en-joyable"; even with "amateurish service", tabs "on the pricey side" for the genre and "crazy" waits that'll have you feeling "like the Mad Hatter", they're a "super-cute" treat.

Alison Eighteen ● ⓢ *American*

FOOD	DECOR	SERVICE	COST
21	20	21	$68

Flatiron | 15 W. 18th St. (bet. 5th & 6th Aves.) | 212-366-1818 | www.alisoneighteen.com

A haven of "tasteful adult" dining, this "reintroduced old favorite" in the Flatiron furnishes "fine", French-inflected American cuisine deliv-ered by an "attentive" staff in "spacious, classy and quiet" environs; however, hedgers contend it's "pricey for what it is" and a recent chef change means "the jury's back out."

Ali's Roti ⌦ *Caribbean*

FOOD	DECOR	SERVICE	COST
∇ 25	18	21	$23

Bed-Stuy | 1267 Fulton St. (Arlington Pl.) | Brooklyn | 718-783-0316
Crown Heights | 337 Utica Ave. (Carroll St.) | Brooklyn | 718-778-7329
Prospect Heights | 589 Flatbush Ave. (bet. Midwood St. & Rutland Rd.) | Brooklyn | 718-462-1730

"Mouthwatering" rotis with "fresh dough" and meaty fillings ("ask for them spicy") bring the "Trini flavor to Brooklyn" at these low-cost Caribbeans; despite bare-bones setups and sparse seating, expect a "line of loyal customers" at prime times.

Alloro *Italian*

FOOD	DECOR	SERVICE	COST
23	17	23	$58

E 70s | 307 E. 77th St. (bet. 1st & 2nd Aves.) | 212-535-2866 | www.alloronyc.com

"Original" is the consensus on this "small" UES Italian "sleeper" where "imaginative", "ambitious" dishes from a "skilled" chef are conveyed by an "eager-to-please" crew; loyalists are so grateful it's "not just an-other red-sauce joint" that they overlook the "bland" setting.

Allswell ● *American*

FOOD	DECOR	SERVICE	COST
∇ 23	18	20	$40

Williamsburg | 124 Bedford Ave. (N. 10th St.) | Brooklyn | 347-799-2743

"Just like the name says", this Williamsburg pub fields a "fresh, inven-tive" American menu that showcases "local ingredients" and "changes daily"; a "small", old-timey "rustic" setting equipped with a communal table makes its "hipster" following feel at home, despite a few gripes about the pricing.

Alma *Mexican*

FOOD	DECOR	SERVICE	COST
20	21	18	$37

Carroll Gardens | 187 Columbia St., 2nd fl. (Degraw St.) | Brooklyn | 718-643-5400 | www.almarestaurant.com

"Mind-altering" Manhattan skyline views from a "year-round" rooftop are the bait at this Carroll Gardens Mexican where the chow is as "solid" as the margaritas are "strong"; an "off-the-beaten-path" ad-dress "not close to public transportation" makes "walking shoes" the footwear of choice.

Almayass ⓢ *Armenian/Lebanese*

FOOD	DECOR	SERVICE	COST
∇ 22	20	20	$48

Flatiron | 24 E. 21st St. (bet. B'way & Park Ave. S.) | 212-473-3100 | www.almayassnyc.com

For a "delicious" introduction to Lebanese-Armenian cooking, this "lovely", "welcoming" Flatiron branch of a Beirut-based chain offers a share-worthy menu headlining an "amazing range" of cold and hot meze; the "overall enjoyable" scene includes a room "spacious" enough to "go with a few people so you can try more", plus there's an adjacent bar/lounge for "grabbing a drink."

Almond *French* | 20 | 20 | 20 | $45 |

Flatiron | 12 E. 22nd St. (bet. B'way & Park Ave. S.) | 212-228-7557 | www.almondnyc.com

"Comforting" French fare meets "rustic charm" at this "buzzing" Flatiron bistro, a Bridgehampton spin-off where the tabs are "reasonable" and the crowd "young"; it's an "easy choice" for "big groups", so expect "noisy" decibels and a "happening" brunch.

Alta *Mediterranean* | 25 | 22 | 20 | $52 |

G Village | 64 W. 10th St. (bet. 5th & 6th Aves.) | 212-505-7777 | www.altarestaurant.com

An "inventive" array of "delectable" Med small plates ("two words: Brussels sprouts") chased with "wonderful sangria" keeps this duplex Village boîte "hopping" with "discerning" sorts who know "sharing is key"; be ready for "big prices", including a $490 option to "order the whole menu" (a "boatload of fun").

Amali *Mediterranean* | 21 | 19 | 20 | $57 |

E 60s | 115 E. 60th St. (Park Ave.) | 212-339-8363 | www.amalinyc.com

"Classic Mediterranean flavors" with "farm-to-table" sensibilities are a "tempting" mix at this Periyali sib "tucked" away near Bloomie's, which also "surprises" Midtowners with a "biodynamic wine list"; "pleasant" service and rustically "stylish" decor help justify the "high price" tag.

Amaranth *Mediterranean* | 21 | 18 | 19 | $62 |

E 60s | 21 E. 62nd St. (bet. 5th & Madison Aves.) | 212-980-6700 | www.amaranthrestaurant.com

Aka "air-kissing central", this "buzzy" Madison Avenue–area Med is the kind of place where the "better-than-average" food is incidental to the "social scene"; service is "diffident" if you've got a "European title", "inattentive" if you don't, but the "expensive" pricing applies to all.

Amarone ● *Italian* | 20 | 16 | 20 | $44 |

W 40s | 686 Ninth Ave. (bet. 47th & 48th Sts.) | 212-245-6060 | www.amaroneristorantenyc.com

"Unassuming" is the word on this "reliable" Hell's Kitchen trattoria that supplies "reasonably priced" Italian standards in a setting that's "pleasant" though "hardly exciting"; "convenience to the theater" is its trump card, and "timely" staffers "get you in and out" on time.

Amazing 66 *Chinese* | 22 | 13 | 16 | $24 |

Chinatown | 66 Mott St. (bet. Bayard & Canal Sts.) | 212-334-0099

"Cheap and filling" says it all about this "solid" C-town Cantonese plying an encyclopedic menu of "familiar" items in "old"-looking digs; the "pushy" service comes with language-barrier issues, but no one notices when its "kick-ass lunch specials" are on offer.

Amber *Asian* | 19 | 18 | 18 | $36 |

E 80s | 1406 Third Ave. (80th St.) | 212-249-5020 ●
Murray Hill | 381 Third Ave. (bet. 27th & 28th Sts.) | 212-686-6388 | www.ambergramercy.com ●
W 70s | 221 Columbus Ave. (70th St.) | 212-799-8100 | www.amberwestside.com ●

(continued)

Amber

W Village | 135 Christopher St. (bet. Greenwich & Hudson Sts.) |
212-477-5880

This "up-tempo" Pan-Asian mini-chain provides "right-on-the-money"
sushi and "consistent" cooking in "dark", "trying-to-be-trendy" settings (with "Buddha watching over you"); "noisy" decibels and "party"
atmospherics are part of the "nice young vibe."

The Americano *French*

FOOD	DECOR	SERVICE	COST
22	23	22	$46

Chelsea | Americano Hotel | 518 W. 27th St. (bet. 10th & 11th Aves.) |
212-525-0000 | www.hotel-americano.com

Located in Chelsea's High Line–adjacent Americano Hotel, this "vibrant"
contender offers midpriced French fare with "Latin flair" in a "cooler-
than-cool" setting with lots of marble, black leather and polished con-
crete; its "trendy" following says the most "fun" is on its roomy patio.

Amma *Indian*

25	17	22	$46

E 50s | 246 E. 51st St. (bet. 2nd & 3rd Aves.) | 212-644-8330 |
www.ammanyc.com

"Breaking away from the clichés", this Midtown "contender" provides a
"tantalizing array" of "refined" Northern Indian fare served by a "kind,
calm" crew in a setting that falls somewhere between "intimate" and
"cramped"; tabs skew a bit "high", except for the $12 lunch deal.

Ammos ● *Greek/Seafood*

21	20	20	$55

E 40s | 52 Vanderbilt Ave. (bet. 44th & 45th Sts.) | 212-922-9999 |
www.ammosnewyork.com

The "only thing missing is the plate-breaking" at this "authentic"
Grand Central–area Greek that offers a "hustle-bustle" lunch for
"expense account"–wielding "suits" as well as a more "quiet" dinner
hour; tabs are a bit on the "high" side, but expect serious "sticker
shock" if you order whole fish, priced by the pound.

Amor Cubano *Cuban*

23	17	20	$32

Harlem | 2018 Third Ave. (111th St.) | 212-996-1220 |
www.amorcubanorestaurant.com

Giving "Miami" a run for its money, this "hopping" East Harlem Cuban
doles out "tasty, traditional" chow right out of "pre-Castro Havana",
paired with "amazing" mojitos; "live music" via a "loud band" adds
"authenticity" and distracts from the just "ok" ambiance.

Amorina *Italian/Pizza*

23	16	20	$27

Prospect Heights | 624 Vanderbilt Ave. (Prospect Pl.) | Brooklyn |
718-230-3030 | www.amorinapizza.com

When in the mood for "delicious" Roman-style pizzas and pastas, all
at "low, low prices", locals turn to this Prospect Heights Italian; the
"small", red-checkered-tablecloth setting exudes a "homey" vibe and
is overseen by a "hard-working" staff.

🆕 Amsterdam Burger Company *Burgers/Kosher*

▽ 25	16	19	$26

W 90s | 654 Amsterdam Ave. (92nd St.) | 212-362-0700

The burgers are "excellent" and "they're kosher" too exalt the observant of the "enormous, juicy, perfectly seasoned" patties at this UWS

arrival; kvetchers say it's a bit "expensive" for the genre, with service and "rustic, laid-back" digs that are nothing to write home about, but still to most it's a "welcome" addition to the area.

Am Thai Bistro *Thai* | 23 | 16 | 22 | $24 |

Ditmas Park | 1003 Church Ave. (bet. 10th & 11th Sts.) | Brooklyn | 718-287-8888 | www.amthaibistro.com

Am-Thai Kitchen ⇗ *Thai*

Kensington | 359 McDonald Ave. (Albemarle Rd.) | Brooklyn | 718-871-9115 | www.amthaikitchen.com

With "generous" portions of "wonderful" Thai "staples", these "local" Brooklyn standouts appease Siamese "cravings" at "reasonable" rates; the Ditmas Park branch offsets a "tiny venue" with "welcoming service" while the seatless, cash-only Kensington outlet dispenses "absolutely great takeout."

Amy Ruth's *Soul Food* | 22 | 14 | 19 | $26 |

Harlem | 113 W. 116th St. (bet. Lenox & 7th Aves.) | 212-280-8779 | www.amyrutshsarlem.com

Those jonesing for a taste of "classic Harlem" head to this low-budget soul food "stalwart" for "hearty" cooking highlighted by "amazing" chicken and waffles; regulars "ignore the decor" and "lackadaisical" service, and get there early "before the tourist buses arrive."

NEW Anassa Taverna ◐ *Greek* | - | - | - | M |

E 60s | 200 E. 60th St. (3rd Ave.) | 212-371-5200 | www.anassataverna.com
The Avra team is behind this upscale Greek arrival to East Midtown, serving up grilled seafood and other traditional faves; the rustic-chic bi-level space fills up quickly after work, with many crowding around the lively bar for wine and cocktails.

An Choi Ⓜ *Vietnamese* | 21 | 17 | 20 | $27 |

LES | 85 Orchard St. (bet. Broome & Grand Sts.) | 212-226-3700 | www.anchoinyc.com

There's an "authentic" feel pervading this "funky" LES Vietnamese touted for its "original", "delicious", "addicting" takes on pho and banh mi; low prices and a "hole-in-the-wall" space with a Saigon "back-alley" feel add extra legitimacy.

NEW Andanada 141 *Spanish* | ▽ 21 | 22 | 20 | $57 |

W 60s | 141 W. 69th St. (bet. B'way & Columbus Ave.) | 646-692-8762 | www.andanada141.com

Inhabiting the former Gastroarte space, this "lovely" UWS arrival follows in its predecessor's footsteps with tapas and other Spanish classics "done with modern flair" offered within sleek, graffiti-mural-adorned digs; the vibe is "lively but allows for conversation", and "high prices" notwithstanding, it's tailor-made for the "pre–Lincoln Center" set.

Andre's Café *Bakery/Hungarian* | 19 | 12 | 18 | $27 |

E 80s | 1631 Second Ave. (bet. 84th & 85th Sts.) | 212-327-1105 | www.andrescafeny.com

The "main event is pastry and coffee" at this "little" UES bakery/cafe, though its "basic" Hungarian menu is "hearty" and "authentic" enough; it's "one of the last bastions" of the genre in Yorkville with "easy-to-digest" tabs and "hole-in-the-wall" decor that makes "take-out a viable option."

	FOOD	DECOR	SERVICE	COST

Añejo Tequileria ●Ⓜ *Mexican* — 22 | 20 | 21 | $43

W 40s | 668 10th Ave. (47th St.) | 212-920-4770 |
www.anejonyc.com

"Such a find", this Hell's Kitchen haute Mexican showcases chef
Angelo Sosa's "expertly prepared" small plates and "excellent" cocktails crafted from a "fine tequila selection"; "courteous" staffers man
a "pseudo-rustic" space that's occasionally "cramped and noisy" but
"totally worth it."

Angelica Kitchen Ⓟ *Vegan/Vegetarian* — 22 | 17 | 19 | $25

E Village | 300 E. 12th St. (2nd Ave.) | 212-228-2909 |
www.angelicakitchen.com

A longtime East Village vegan "standard-bearer", this "go-with-
the-flow" BYO is a "wholesome" destination for "your-body-as-a-
temple" dining at a "reasonable" (if cash-only) cost; though the
decor is "spartan" and the service "loose", there's "always a line
for a table."

Angelina's Ⓜ *Italian* — 23 | 23 | 21 | $57

Tottenville | 399 Ellis St. (Arthur Kill Rd.) | Staten Island | 718-227-2900 |
www.angelinasristorante.com

"Fine dining" comes to Tottenville at this "highly recommended" Italian
offering "fabulous" food and "professional" service in a "stunning" tri-
level mansion; sure, it's "expensive" for SI and the crowd can be a bit
"Jersey Shore", but to most it's a bona fide "special-occasion" hub.

Angelo's of Mulberry Street Ⓜ *Italian* — 23 | 17 | 19 | $46

Little Italy | 146 Mulberry St. (bet. Grand & Hester Sts.) | 212-966-1277 |
www.angelomulberry.com

It doesn't get more "old-school" than this circa-1902 Little Italy "favorite" that stays popular thanks to "good, old-fashioned" Italian
cooking and "top-notch" service; maybe the "stereotypical" decor
could use "a little touching up", but otherwise fans "feel the love" –
"maybe the tourists know something" after all.

Angelo's Pizzeria *Pizza* — 21 | 14 | 17 | $25

E 50s | 1043 Second Ave. (55th St.) | 212-521-3600 |
www.angelospizzany.com
W 50s | 117 W. 57th St. (bet. 6th & 7th Aves.) | 212-333-4333 |
www.angelospizzany.com
W 50s | 1697 Broadway (bet. 53rd & 54th Sts.) | 212-245-8811 |
www.angelosnyc.com

These "family-friendly" Midtown pizzerias turn out "worthy"
brick-oven pies with "generous" toppings for "economical" dough; ok,
"ambiance is not their strong point", ditto the "hit-or-miss" service,
but regulars say a "glass of wine always helps."

NEW Angolo SoHo ● *Italian* — ∇ 24 | 18 | 18 | $60

SoHo | 331 W. Broadway (Grand St.) | 212-203-1722 |
www.angolosoho.com

Chef Michael Berardino (The Cannibal) presents midpriced, market-
driven Italian fare – notably "excellent" housemade pastas and salumi –
at this "bright, cheerful" SoHo arrival; the casual-chic interior has a
1970s feel abetted by vintage black banquettes, orange racer chairs
and exposed-brick walls.

	FOOD	DECOR	SERVICE	COST

Ann & Tony's ☒ *Italian* — 21 | 16 | 20 | $36

Fordham | 2407 Arthur Ave. (bet. 187th & 188th Sts.) | Bronx |
718-933-1469 | www.annandtonysonline.com
Talk about "classic" – this circa-1927 "Arthur Avenue mainstay" remains a steady "favorite" thanks to its "healthy portions" of "old-fashioned" Italiana served by a "treat-you-like-family" crew; "great prices" mean most don't notice the "decor from the '70s."

Annisa *American* — 27 | 24 | 26 | $87

W Village | 13 Barrow St. (bet. 7th Ave. S. & W. 4th St.) | 212-741-6699 |
www.annisarestaurant.com
"Anita Lo's care and craft" continue to "pay off" at this "high-end" West Village "gem", a "civilized respite" renowned for its "brilliant, Asian-inspired" New American fare, "superb service" and "understated elegance"; a "smart", "soothing" space where you "can actually have a conversation" rounds out this "rare treat."

Anthony's *Italian/Pizza* — 21 | 17 | 21 | $29

Park Slope | 426 Seventh Ave. (bet. 14th & 15th Sts.) | Brooklyn |
718-369-8315 | www.anthonysbrooklyn.com
"Disguised as a pizza joint", this "comfortable" Park Slope Italian goes beyond "fantastic" brick-oven pies with "classic" red-sauce dishes that are "tasty" and "priced right"; too bad about the "meh" decor, but the "can't-do-enough-to-please-you" staff adds warmth.

NEW Antica Pesa ● *Italian* — ∇ 23 | 23 | 23 | $68

Williamsburg | 115 Berry St. (bet. N. 7th & 8th Sts.) | Brooklyn |
347-763-2635 | www.anticapesa.us
"One of the posher" options in Williamsburg, this American branch of a Rome stalwart puts forth "cooked-to-perfection pastas" and other Italian classics delivered by a "welcoming" staff; the space breaks from the nabe's shabby-chic norm, offering instead an "elegant" fine-dining vibe and a salonlike, fireplace-equipped lounge.

Antique Garage *Mediterranean* — 20 | 24 | 19 | $46

SoHo | 41 Mercer St. (bet. Broome & Grand Sts.) | 212-219-1019 |
www.antiquegaragesoho.com
It's all about the "delightful" decor at this "repurposed" SoHo auto-body shop that's been turned into a Med eatery where the "cool" antique furnishings are for sale; maybe the "friendly" service "needs work" and the menu's somewhat "limited", but the "funky" ambiance is fine as is.

Antonio's Trattoria *Italian* — ∇ 23 | 18 | 22 | $61

Fordham | 2370 Belmont Ave. (Crescent Ave.) | Bronx | 718-733-6630 |
www.antoniostrattoria.com
This "welcoming" resident of the Bronx's Little Italy proffers "tasty" Italian "standbys" ("nothing you haven't seen before") at "nice prices"; its "hoot" of a "singing bartender" is one more reason it's a "popular option for out-of-towners."

Antonucci Cafe *Italian* — 23 | 18 | 20 | $58

E 80s | 170 E. 81st St. (bet. Lexington & 3rd Aves.) | 212-570-5100 |
www.antonuccicafe.com
In a "neighborhood filled with Italian restaurants", this "nice and easy" UES trattoria holds its own with "authentic" fare highlighted by espe-

cially "excellent pastas"; seating is "tight" and tabs "pricey for every-day", but "warm" vibes and "unhurried" service help compensate.

A.O.C. Bistro *French*
20 | 18 | 18 | $41

Park Slope | 259 Fifth Ave. (Garfield Pl.) | Brooklyn | 718-788-1515 | www.aocbistro.com

A.O.C. L'aile ou la Cuisse ● *French*

W Village | 314 Bleecker St. (Grove St.) | 212-675-9463 | www.aocnyc.com

"Genuinely French", these "straightforward" West Village–Park Slope bistros roll out "better-than-expected" Gallic menus for A-ok tabs; service may skew "indifferent" and the decor "pleasant" but "nothing special", though all is forgiven in Bleecker Street's "lovely" back garden "escape."

Apiary *American*
23 | 19 | 21 | $55

E Village | 60 Third Ave. (bet. 10th & 11th Sts.) | 212-254-0888 | www.apiarynyc.com

Buzzy folks "make a beeline" to Scott Bryan's "bustling" East Village New American, a "gem in a kebab neighborhood" boasting "exceptional" cooking, "polished service" and "modern", "stylish" looks; however, this "terrific" little "hive has a loud hum", so conversationalists "go early."

Ápizz Ⓜ *Italian*
25 | 22 | 22 | $49

LES | 217 Eldridge St. (bet. Rivington & Stanton Sts.) | 212-253-9199 | www.apizz.com

One of the "coziest" joints in town, this "sexy" LES Italian purveys "excellent" pizza and other "melt-in-your-mouth" dishes straight from a "wood-burning oven"; despite "quality" service, "accessible" rates and "intimate" "rustic" digs, it remains something of a "hidden gem" – maybe because of the "tucked-away" location.

Applewood Ⓜ *American*
25 | 21 | 22 | $47

Park Slope | 501 11th St. (bet. 7th & 8th Aves.) | Brooklyn | 718-788-1810 | www.applewoodny.com

"Inventively prepared farm-fresh ingredients" lure "locals and food-ies" to this "charming" New American that's "like going to the country without leaving Park Slope"; sure, it's "a tad pricey", but "welcoming" service, "cozy" atmospherics and a "fabulous brunch" mean to most it's "worth it."

Aquagrill *Seafood*
26 | 19 | 23 | $62

SoHo | 210 Spring St. (6th Ave.) | 212-274-0505 | www.aquagrill.com

"Definitely a winner", this "classic" SoHo seafooder continues to de-liver with a "top-notch" team serving up "well-executed fish" ("any fresher and it would still be on the boat") and "oysters galore" from a "superior raw bar"; even given "high" prices, it stays "crowded and loud."

Aquavit Ⓩ *Scandinavian*
25 | 24 | 25 | $78

E 50s | 65 E. 55th St. (bet. Madison & Park Aves.) | 212-307-7311 | www.aquavit.org

Midtown's "exemplar of Scandinavian dining" remains an "impres-sive" destination for "exquisitely executed" cuisine with "stellar ser-vice to match" (not to mention "every aquavit known to man"); the "formal" space's "modern Nordic design" provides further grounds for "expense-account" pricing.

Arabelle *American/French*   24 | 26 | 25 | $71

E 60s | Plaza Athénée Hotel | 37 E. 64th St. (bet. Madison & Park Aves.) | 212-606-4647 | www.arabellerestaurant.com

"Civility" is alive and well at this "sumptuous" Franco-American "secluded" in the Plaza Athénée Hotel and favored by "ladies of a certain age"; while the "refined" menu exhibits "no culinary pyrotechnics", the "elegant" environs and "sky-high" tabs make an impression.

Areo ⓜ *Italian*   24 | 20 | 21 | $52

Bay Ridge | 8424 Third Ave. (bet. 84th & 85th Sts.) | Brooklyn | 718-238-0079

"Fuhgeddaboudit" – this "busy" Bay Ridge "staple" continues to "stand the test of time" as a supplier of "wonderful" Italiana and "old-world" service; assuming "you can handle the noise", its "lively scene" and "local color" are an all-around "hoot."

Arepas Café *Venezuelan*   24 | 16 | 20 | $18

Astoria | 33-07 36th Ave. (bet. 33rd & 34th Sts.) | Queens | 718-937-3835

NEW Arepas Grill *Venezuelan*

Astoria | 21-19 Broadway (21st St.) | Queens | 718-355-9686 www.arepascafe.com

"Flavors straight out of Caracas" are stuffed into "fluffy", affordable arepas at these "something-different" Astoria Venezuelans; the bite-size Café original sports a "diner atmosphere" that suggests "take-out", but its new Grill offshoot is roomier, with a broader menu that spans Caribbean and Med dishes.

Aretsky's Patroon ⓢ *American*   22 | 22 | 23 | $73

E 40s | 160 E. 46th St. (bet. Lexington & 3rd Aves.) | 212-883-7373 | www.patroonrestaurant.com

Ken Aretsky's "polished" East Side "business" "oasis" remains a place to "impress clients" with "solid" American fare and "first-class service" in "men's club" digs done up with "classic photos"; "especially nice" are the private rooms and roof bar, but just "watch out for those prices."

Arirang Hibachi Steakhouse *Japanese*   21 | 19 | 21 | $39

Bay Ridge | 8814 Fourth Ave. (bet. 88th & 89th Sts.) | Brooklyn | 718-238-9880

Great Kills | 23 Nelson Ave. (Locust Pl.) | Staten Island | 718-966-9600

www.partyonthegrill.com

"Interactive" is the philosophy of these cross-borough "Benihana wannabes", where the Japanese steaks and sides arrive "projectile-style" from "amusing" hibachi chefs "swinging their implements around"; "kids can't get enough of it", but adults sigh "hokey" even though the pricing's pretty "reasonable for dinner and a show."

Arirang Korean ❶ *Korean/Noodle Shop*   ▽ 22 | 13 | 18 | $28

Garment District | 32 W. 32nd St. (bet. B'way & 5th Ave.) | 212-967-5088 | www.koreanrestaurantnyc.org

"Delicious" Korean soups that showcase "handmade noodles" and are ladled out in "generous", "vat-of-goodness" portions deliver "comfort-food" satisfaction at this third-floor K-town slurp house; quite "decent" prices, "no-fuss" service and "minimal" decor (save for some "colorful" murals) complete the picture.

NEW Arlington Club *Steak*   21 | 22 | 19 | $87

E 70s | 1032 Lexington Ave. (bet. 73rd & 74th Sts.) | 212-249-5700 | www.arlingtonclubny.com

Already "wildly popular", Laurent Tourondel's "much-needed" addition to the UES "redefines the steakhouse" for a "more adult" clientele, serving "delicious" meats (plus sushi) in split-level digs themed as a "steampunk" "train station" with a "hopping bar scene" made for "Tom Wolfe wannabes"; "expensive" tabs and "incredibly noisy" acoustics can't quell the "buzz."

Armani Ristorante *Italian*   23 | 25 | 22 | $70

E 50s | Armani/5th Avenue Bldg. | 717 Fifth Ave., 3rd fl. (56th St.) | 212-207-1902 | www.armanilifestyle.com

"Serious shoppers" in Giorgio Armani's Fifth Avenue flagship unwind at this "hidden" third-floor Italian whose "chic", "beautiful" space "floating above Fifth Avenue" is populated with equally "pretty people"; it's a "favorite for lunch", but the food's "delectable" at dinner too (the pricing less so).

Arno ⓈItalian   20 | 16 | 21 | $51

Garment District | 141 W. 38th St. (B'way) | 212-944-7420 | www.arnoristorante.com

A "go-to place" in the Garment District "culinary desert", this "old-fashioned" Northern Italian is targeted to the "garmento" business-lunch trade; the "down-to-earth" cooking is "fine" though "not exotic", but the decor seems a bit "tired" given the tabs.

Aroma Kitchen & Winebar ❶ *Italian*   24 | 18 | 22 | $46

NoHo | 36 E. Fourth St. (bet. Bowery & Lafayette St.) | 212-375-0100 | www.aromanyc.com

For a "big surprise" in a "tight" but "delightful" space, sniff out this NoHo "hideaway" where "wonderful" Italian flavors are matched with "nicely picked" wines and delivered by "friendly" staffers; it fills the bill "if you're going to the Public Theater", and its private party rooms are perfect "for an intimate get-together."

Arté Café *Italian*   18 | 17 | 17 | $36

W 70s | 106 W. 73rd St. (bet. Amsterdam & Columbus Aves.) | 212-501-7014 | www.artecafenyc.com

It's all about "bang for the buck" at this Upper West Side Italian, renowned for its $13 "blue-hair special" early-bird and "amazing" bottomless-booze brunch; since the chow is just "passable", the service "slow" and decor "nothing to brag about", "don't expect inspiration", just "excellent value."

Arthur on Smith Ⓜ *American*   ▽ 21 | 18 | 19 | $60

Boerum Hill | 276 Smith St. (bet. Degraw & Sackett Sts.) | Brooklyn | 718-360-2340 | www.arthuronsmith.com

Farm-to-fork dining is the thing at this Smith Street American offering an "excellent" Italian-accented seasonal menu paired with craft beers and a local wine list; some say the exposed-brick, reclaimed-wood setting "needs a little atmosphere", but it's "lively" all the same.

	FOOD	DECOR	SERVICE	COST

Artichoke Basille's Pizza ◐ *Pizza* — 22 | 10 | 14 | $15

Chelsea | 114 10th Ave. (17th St.) | 212-792-9200
E Village | 328 E. 14th St. (bet. 1st & 2nd Aves.) |
212-228-2004 ⌷
G Village | 111 MacDougal St. (bet. Bleecker & 3rd Sts.) |
646-278-6100
www.artichokepizza.com

"Gooey ooey pizza" spread with "rich" artichoke dip is the "amaze-balls" "trademark" that puts this "flourishing" chainlet in a "class by it-self" for a "substantial" "late-night munch"; if it's "overpriced" for the "typical" format, try telling that to everyone "stumbling out of the bars" and "getting in line."

Artie's *Seafood/Steak* — 22 | 17 | 22 | $37

City Island | 394 City Island Ave. (Ditmars St.) | Bronx | 718-885-9885 |
www.artiesofcityisland.com

"Actual City Island residents" eat at this "been-there-forever" surf 'n' turfer offering a "retro" Italian-accented menu; true, it's "not on the water" and the decor is "generic seafooder", yet "unhurried" service and fair pricing keep locals "happy as clams."

Artisanal *French* — 23 | 20 | 20 | $55

Murray Hill | 2 Park Ave. (bet. 32nd & 33rd Sts.) | 212-725-8585 |
www.artisanalbistro.com

An "all-time fave" among fromage fanciers, Terrance Brennan's Murray Hill brasserie boasts a "dreamily" "deep" cheese selection bolstered by "flavorful" French staples ("fondue is a must"); the "cheery open space" "channels Paris" complete with "a lot of hubbub", "loud acous-tics" and "perfunctory service", but still it "never gets old."

Arturo's Pizzeria ◐ *Pizza* — 23 | 15 | 18 | $26

G Village | 106 W. Houston St. (Thompson St.) | 212-677-3820

"Old Greenwich Village" endures at this 1957-vintage pizzeria where a "slice of the past" comes via "delicious, no-nonsense" pies "straight out of the coal oven"; a live "jazz combo" and an "unpre-tentious" mood compensate for decor that's somewhere between "faded" and "dingy."

A Salt & Battery *British* — 22 | 13 | 18 | $20

W Village | 112 Greenwich Ave. (bet. 12th & 13th Sts.) | 212-691-2713 |
www.asaltandbattery.com

Fish 'n' chips fanciers say this "clevely named" Village "hole-in-the-wall" does a "jolly good" rendition of the British staple for an "afford-able" sum; "anti–health food" treats like "deep-fried candy bars" fill out the "greasy" bill, but since there's "no decor" and seating's just a "few stools", most get the goods to go.

Asellina *Italian* — 20 | 23 | 18 | $55

Murray Hill | Gansevoort Park Avenue Hotel | 420 Park Ave. S. (29th St.) |
212-317-2908 | www.togrp.com

Designed with "the Kardashians" in mind, this "big", "dimly lit" Murray Hill Italian is "more about atmosphere than food", leading some to de-clare the "bar scene's the thing" here; fans praise the "stylish" setting, but the "spotty service", "noisy" acoustics and "pricey-for-the-quality" tabs are another matter.

	FOOD	DECOR	SERVICE	COST

Asiate *American/Asian* | 25 | 28 | 26 | $117 |

W 60s | Mandarin Oriental Hotel | 80 Columbus Circle, 35th fl. (B'way) | 212-805-8881 | www.mandarinoriental.com

"High in the sky" over Central Park, this "sophisticated" Asian–New American in the Mandarin Oriental matches "breathtaking views" with a "gorgeous setting" – once again voted NYC's No. 1 for Decor – and "equally stunning" prix fixe spreads; "exceptional service" ensures all are "treated like royalty", and lest "ridiculously expensive" outlays bring things back down to earth, there's a "reasonable" $34 prix fixe lunch.

NEW Aska *Scandinavian* | ∇ 23 | 19 | 25 | $86 |

Williamsburg | Kinfolk Studios | 90 Wythe Ave. (N. 11th St.) | Brooklyn | 347-799-2946 | www.askanyc.com

One of the "brilliant chefs" behind Williamsburg's pop-up Frej is back in Kinfolk Studios serving "innovative, delicious and beautifully plated" Scandinavian fare – think "Nordic avant-garde" in a tasting menu format – matched with botanically focused cocktails; the casual-but-polished space features lots of natural wood, plus there's a "hopping front bar" with its own à la carte menu.

Astor Room Ⓜ *American/Continental* | 20 | 22 | 21 | $42 |

Astoria | Kaufman Astoria Studios | 34-12 36th St. (bet. 35th & 36th Aves.) | Queens | 718-255-1947 | www.astorroom.com

It "feels like the 1920s" at this American-Continental, once the Paramount Pictures commissary during the silent film era and now a supper club in Kaufman Astoria Studios; "retro" eats (e.g. shrimp cocktail, beef Wellington), "speakeasy" looks and "vintage" drinks embellish the "old-school" vibe.

Atera Ⓢ Ⓜ *American* | ∇ 25 | 23 | 25 | $254 |

TriBeCa | 77 Worth St. (bet. Church St. & W. B'way) | 212-226-1444 | www.ateranyc.com

Expect the "unexpected" from "genius at work" Matthew Lightner at this 18-seat "open-kitchen concept" in TriBeCa, where "foraged elements" "become high art" on an "intriguing" American tasting menu likened to a multicourse flow of "marvelous" "culinary surprises"; the $195 prix fixe-only "theatrical experience" ain't cheap, but diners with deep pockets and an "adventurous palate" will be "rewarded."

Atlantic Grill *Seafood* | 22 | 20 | 21 | $56 |

E 70s | 1341 Third Ave. (bet. 76th & 77th Sts.) | 212-988-9200
W 60s | 49 W. 64th St. (bet. B'way & CPW) | 212-787-4663
www.atlanticgrill.com

"Another Steve Hanson success story", these "sprawling" "sea-tastic" crosstown "mainstays" are "still going strong" with "delish" fish, land-lubbing "basics" and an "excellent brunch" delivered by a "capable staff"; though "a bit pricey", they're "packed" with "energetic", "high-decibel" fans who say you "can't go wrong."

NEW Atrium Dumbo ● *French* | – | – | – | M |

Dumbo | 15 Main St. (bet. Plymouth & Water Sts.) | Brooklyn | 718-858-1095

Alums of db Bistro Moderne have taken over the Dumbo space that formerly housed Hurricane Sandy victim Governor, supplying contemporary, Provençal-inspired French fare; the airy bi-level setup looks largely unchanged from its former incarnation, down to the verdant plant wall and compact front bar mixing au courant cocktails.

August *European* 22 | 21 | 19 | $49

W Village | 359 Bleecker St. (bet. Charles & W. 10th Sts.) | 212-929-8727 | www.augustny.com

"Really romantic", this "lovely" West Village European seduces diners with "candlelight", "charming" service and "quality", wood-fired-oven cooking that's "adventuresome without being bizarre"; insiders tout the "delightful" all-seasons back garden for "intimate dining."

Aureole *American* 26 | 24 | 25 | $88

W 40s | Bank of America Tower | 135 W. 42nd St. (bet. B'way & 6th Ave.) | 212-319-1660 | www.charliepalmer.com

A rare "civilized" "oasis" near Times Square, Charlie Palmer's "first-class" New American "does not disappoint" those anticipating "inspired" cuisine, a "fabulous wine list", "pampering" service and an overall "polished" milieu; the "formal" main dining room's prix fixe-only pricing is an "indulgence" for "expense-accounters", but going à la carte in the "vibrant" front bar is "lighter on the wallet."

Aurora *Italian* 23 | 20 | 21 | $47

SoHo | 510 Broome St. (bet. Thompson St. & W. B'way) | 212-334-9020
Williamsburg | 70 Grand St. (Wythe Ave.) | Brooklyn | 718-388-5100
www.auroraristorante.com

At these "quaint" Williamsburg and SoHo Italians, the "delectable" rustic cooking is a match for the "Tuscan countryside" settings, complete with a "lovely garden" at the Brooklyn original; "hip" crowds, midrange prices and "helpful" service ensure "enjoyable" repasts.

A Voce *Italian* 24 | 23 | 23 | $67

Flatiron | New York Merchandise Mart Plaza | 41 Madison Ave. (26th St.) | 212-545-8555 🅢
W 60s | Time Warner Ctr. | 10 Columbus Circle (60th St. at B'way) | 212-823-2523
www.avocerestaurant.com

Known for "grown-up" dining that "delivers", these "tasteful", "upscale Italians" furnish "serious" cuisine (especially the "fabulous pastas") via an "informed" staff; the Columbus Circle site carries over the Flatiron original's "sleek, modern" style to quarters "overlooking Central Park"; P.S. chef Missy Robbins' departure may put the Food rating into question.

Avra ◑ *Greek/Seafood* 25 | 21 | 21 | $63

E 40s | 141 E. 48th St. (bet. Lexington & 3rd Aves.) | 212-759-8550 | www.avrany.com

"Fabulously grilled" fish so "super-fresh" "you can practically smell the ocean" lures Midtown's "expense-account" set to this "lively" Greek seafooder despite "costly" per-pound pricing; service is "peppy", and "alfresco" seating skirts the "close" quarters and "enthusiastic" noise levels.

Awash *Ethiopian* 22 | 14 | 18 | $26

E Village | 338 E. Sixth St. (bet. 1st & 2nd Aves.) | 212-982-9589
W 100s | 947 Amsterdam Ave. (bet. 106th & 107th Sts.) | 212-961-1416

(continued)

Awash

Cobble Hill | 242 Court St. (bet. Baltic & Kane Sts.) | Brooklyn | 718-243-2151
www.awashny.com

"Different experience" seekers tout this "unsung", utensil-free Ethiopian trio where "delectable" stews are scooped up with "just-right" injera flatbread; "decidedly relaxed" service and settings that "need sprucing up" come with the territory, but at least you'll walk out awash with cash.

Ayada *Thai*

26 | 14 | 20 | $24

Woodside | 77-08 Woodside Ave. (bet. 77th & 78th Sts.) | Queens | 718-424-0844

"Behind a nondescript storefront", this "authentic" Woodside Thai supplies "exceptional" takes on "all the favorites" ("don't order 'spicy' unless you mean it") "without breaking the bank"; service is "efficient", but "crowds" form in the "smallish" space now that "the secret is out."

Ayza Wine & Chocolate Bar ⏺ *French/Mediterranean*

20 | 19 | 19 | $35

Garment District | 11 W. 31st St. (bet. B'way & 5th Ave.) | 212-714-2992
W Village | 1 Seventh Ave. S. (Carmine St.) | 212-365-2992
www.ayzanyc.com

Made for a "night out with the girls", these "novel" French-Med wine bars in the Garment District and West Village put out the "perfect trifecta" of "wine, cheese and chocolate" in "tiny" settings augmented with "pleasant outdoor" seating; "decadent" cocktails and "nice energy" ensure they're "always hopping."

Azuri Cafe *Israeli/Kosher*

25 | 9 | 14 | $17

W 50s | 465 W. 51st St. (bet. 9th & 10th Aves.) | 212-262-2920 |
www.azuricafe.com

Falafel "from heaven" and other "cheap", "delicious" Israeli eats offset the "dumpy" decor at this Hell's Kitchen "hole-in-the-wall"; just "don't expect a warm welcome" – the "short-tempered" owner is the neighborhood's "favorite curmudgeon."

Babbo ⏺ *Italian*

27 | 23 | 24 | $82

G Village | 110 Waverly Pl. (bet. MacDougal St. & 6th Ave.) |
212-777-0303 | www.babbonyc.com

"Year after year", the Batali-Bastianich team's Village "standard-bearer" for "elevated Italian" cooking "lives up to its rep" with a "daring and fulfilling" menu that highlights "unrivaled pasta" in "warm" carriage-house surrounds filled with "energized" "music and hubbub"; it's still "worth the Byzantine reservations policy" and "big bucks" for a "dynamic" outing that's "not to be missed."

Bacchus *French*

20 | 17 | 19 | $40

Boerum Hill | 409 Atlantic Ave. (bet. Bond & Nevins Sts.) | Brooklyn | 718-852-1572 | www.bacchusbistro.com

Francophiles tout the "classic French bistro" fare at this "charming little" Boerum Hill wine bar/eatery; "reasonable" rates, "no pretension" and a "beautiful" back garden lend "lazy-day" appeal, even if a few Francophobes feel it has "no particular distinction."

	FOOD	DECOR	SERVICE	COST

Back Forty *American*
E Village | 190 Ave. B (12th St.) | 212-388-1990   22 | 18 | 20 | $39
Back Forty West *American*
SoHo | 70 Prince St. (Crosby St.) | 212-219-8570
www.backfortynyc.com

Early "proponent of farm-to-table" Peter Hoffman turns to the "local markets" to craft these "easygoing" eateries' "comforting", "everyday" New Americana, notably "terrific burgers" and "outstanding" brunch; the East Village original boasts a "bucolic" back patio, while the SoHo follow-up has all-day hours.

Bagatelle ◗ *French*   ▽ 20 | 22 | 18 | $76
Meatpacking | 1 Little W. 12th St. (9th Ave.) | 212-488-2110 |
www.bistrotbagatelle.com

"Hot and cool at the same time", this Meatpacking jet-setter central bolsters its splurgy but "better-than-average" French fare with exuberant "funday mentality"; the "party brunch" featuring "expensive champagne", "throbbing Euro-house" sounds and "dancing on the tables" is most definitely "not for the faint of heart" (or wallet).

Bahari Estiatorio ◗ *Greek*   24 | 18 | 21 | $34
Astoria | 31-14 Broadway (32nd St.) | Queens | 718-204-8968 |
www.bahariestiatorio.com

Astoria is "lucky to have" this hopping Greek "haunt" cooking up "awesome" "homestyle dishes" that "taste like mom use to make"; the "brightly lit" digs offer little more than the "bare essentials", but still, "sweet staffers" and nice prices "make you want to return."

Balaboosta *Mediterranean/Mideastern*   23 | 18 | 20 | $50
NoLita | 214 Mulberry St. (Spring St.) | 212-966-7366 |
www.balaboostanyc.com

Med-Mideastern "comfort food" gets an "imaginative" and "delicious" boost at this "homey" NoLita "favorite" from the Taïm team; the "understated" space may seem "cramped", but the "welcoming" staff and relatively "affordable prices" help ensure it's a "player."

Balthazar ◗ *French*   24 | 23 | 21 | $57
SoHo | 80 Spring St. (Crosby St.) | 212-965-1414 | www.balthazarny.com
There's "never a dull moment" at Keith McNally's "high-profile" SoHo brasserie, where the "belle epoque" decor, "heady Parisian atmosphere" and "memorable" French fare ("can't-be-beat" breakfasts included) are a "magnet" for a "SoHo microcosm" of "locals", "moneyed tourists" and stray "celebrities"; the "controlled chaos" comes with "rushed" service and "daunting" decibels, but it's a certified "classique."

Baluchi's *Indian*   19 | 16 | 17 | $30
E 80s | 1724 Second Ave. (bet. 89th & 90th Sts.) | 212-996-2600
Murray Hill | 329 Third Ave. (25th St.) | 212-679-3434
TriBeCa | 275 Greenwich St. (bet. Murray & Warren Sts.) | 212-571-5343
Park Slope | 310 Fifth Ave. (2nd St.) | Brooklyn | 718-832-5555
Forest Hills | 113-30 Queens Blvd. (76th Ave.) | Queens |
718-520-8600
www.baluchis.com

This "Americanized" Indian chain is popular for its "serviceable" food and "economical" tabs (lunch is a particular "bargain"); but critics citing "conventional" cooking, "mundane" settings and "dull-witted" service say "don't expect nirvana."

Bamonte's Italian
22 | 17 | 22 | $45

Williamsburg | 32 Withers St. (bet. Lorimer St. & Union Ave.) | Brooklyn | 718-384-8831

"Auld Brooklyn" lives on at this circa-1900 Williamsburg Italian, a "throwback" for "real" "red-sauce" fare and "lots of it" (the "only things locally sourced are the waiters"); ok, it may be "short on decor", but the tabs are "reasonable" and the ambiance "right out of *The Godfather.*"

B&B Winepub ◖ American
22 | 19 | 19 | $35

SoHo | 25 W. Houston St. (bet. Greene & Mercer Sts.) | 212-334-7320 | www.burgerandbarrel.com

"Trendy" burgers, "barrel beers" and "wine on tap" collide in a "high-energy" setting at this "happy" SoHo gastropub from the Lure Fishbar folks; sure, it's "loud", with "lighting so low you can barely see your food", but its "cool", cost-conscious crowd considers it fine as is.

B & H Dairy Deli/Vegetarian
22 | 11 | 19 | $15

E Village | 127 Second Ave. (bet. 7th St. & St. Marks Pl.) | 212-505-8065

This "hole-in-the-wall" East Village "patch of history" has been filling bellies with "veggie" borscht-and-blintz fare (aka "Jewish soul food") since the 1940s; talk about kickin' it "old school" – the "diner" ambiance "hasn't changed since your grandpa ate there" way back when.

Banjara ◖ Indian
23 | 16 | 20 | $34

E Village | 97 First Ave. (6th St.) | 212-477-5956 | www.banjaranyc.com

"A cut above" its Sixth Street neighbors, this "upscale" subcontinental "doesn't bow to American tastes", purveying "authentic" Northern Indian fare that "stands out from the rest"; "worn" decor and "so-so" service" are trumped by "low prices."

Bann Korean
21 | 21 | 20 | $46

W 50s | Worldwide Plaza | 350 W. 50th St. (bet. 8th & 9th Aves.) | 212-582-4446 | www.bannrestaurant.com

"Classy" Korean barbecue is no oxymoron at this Theater District "change of pace" where the smokeless tabletop grills impress do-it-yourselfers and the "modern" setting thrills aesthetes; maybe the tabs skew "upscale", but the food's "exciting", the service "caring" and the overall experience "satisfying."

Bann Thai Thai
20 | 18 | 20 | $29

Forest Hills | 69-12 Austin St. (bet. 69th Rd. & Yellowstone Blvd.) | Queens | 718-544-9999 | www.bannthairestaurant.com

Admittedly "off the beaten path", this "reliable" Forest Hills Siamese is worth seeking out for "zesty" vittles that are "as fresh as the decor is colorful" – and "reasonably priced" to boot; purists find the cooking a bit "Americanized", but ultimately "not bad for the neighborhood."

Baoguette Vietnamese
22 | 6 | 13 | $12

Murray Hill | 61 Lexington Ave. (bet. 25th & 26th Sts.) | 212-532-1133 🗷
W Village | 120 Christopher St. (Bedford St.) | 212-929-0877
www.baoguette.com

"They guette how to make the perfect sandwich" at these "no-frills" Vietnamese standbys, where "nontraditional" banh mi are assembled from "ultrafresh bread" and "fiery fillings"; "cheap" tabs make "rude" service and "hole-in-the-wall" looks easier to swallow.

BaoHaus ❶ *Chinese*

23 | 11 | 17 | $14

E Village | 238 E. 14th St. (bet. 2nd & 3rd Aves.) | 646-669-8889 | www.baohausnyc.com

"Un-bao-lievable" rave fans of the "seriously delicious" Taiwanese steamed buns at Eddie Huang's East Villager, whose "fast-food vibe" gets a boost from "blaring hip-hop music"; despite "teenage" service and "no decor to speak of", "cheap" checks keep its "college" crowd content.

Bar Americain *American*

23 | 23 | 23 | $63

W 50s | 152 W. 52nd St. (bet. 6th & 7th Aves.) | 212-265-9700 | www.baramericain.com

Ever "full of energy", this Midtown brasserie shows off "Bobby Flay's special flair" via "spot-on" New American plates served "without skip-ping a beat"; the "cavernous", "clubby" space and "vibrant bar" host a "loud" "scene", but it's considered a "cut above" for "business or pre-theater" (even more so "when someone else pays").

Baraonda ❶ *Italian*

19 | 18 | 18 | $51

E 70s | 1439 Second Ave. (75th St.) | 212-288-8555 | www.baraondany.com

"Euro types" gravitate to this longtime UES Italian where the "good but not sensational" chow plays second fiddle to late-night "rowdy" revel-ing involving "loud music" and "dancing on tables"; critics say it's "past its prime", unless "plastic surgery and pasta" is your thing.

Barbès ❶ *French/Moroccan*

20 | 16 | 21 | $41

Murray Hill | 21 E. 36th St. (bet. 5th & Madison Aves.) | 212-684-0215 | www.barbesrestaurantnyc.com

An "exotic escape from *la vie ordinaire*", this Murray Hill "sure thing" purveys "toothsome" French-Moroccan vittles in a setting akin to an "Algerian bistro in Marseilles"; it may be "cramped" and "noisy", but "pleasant" service and "value" pricing help to distract.

Barbetta ❶Ⓜ *Italian*

22 | 23 | 22 | $66

W 40s | 321 W. 46th St. (bet. 8th & 9th Aves.) | 212-246-9171 | www.barbettarestaurant.com

For "upscale Theater District dining", there's this "gracious", 1906-vintage Northern Italian offering an "old-world" blend of "tasty" food, "elegant" decor, "refined" service and an "escape-from-Manhattan" garden; sure, it's "pricey", but you're paying for a "NY classic."

Barbone *Italian*

23 | 17 | 22 | $47

E Village | 186 Ave. B (bet. 11th & 12th Sts.) | 212-254-6047 | www.barbonenyc.com

"Hidden away in the East Village", this "no-tourists" Italian sleeper earns raves for "well-prepared" classic dishes ferried by "friendly" folks overseen by a "charismatic" chef-owner; "good overall value" and a "great backyard patio" keep the locals coming.

Bar Boulud *French*

24 | 20 | 22 | $63

W 60s | 1900 Broadway (bet. 63rd & 64th Sts.) | 212-595-0303 | www.barboulud.com

Daniel Boulud's trademark "quality shines through" in a "less formal setting" at this "handy" French bistro–wine bar mash-up opposite

| | FOOD | DECOR | SERVICE | COST |

Lincoln Center, where a "memorable" menu starring "celebrated" charcuterie "delights" at a relatively "accessible price point"; the "tunnel-like" digs can be "tight", but "bonus" sidewalk seating is a "welcome detour" "pre- or post-performance."

Barbounia *Mediterranean*

21 | 22 | 19 | $50

Flatiron | 250 Park Ave. S. (20th St.) | 212-995-0242 | www.barbounia.com
"Stylish" and "upbeat", this "cacophonous" Flatiron Med lures "see-and-be-seen" "Gen-X" types with a "tasty", "something-for-everyone" menu (and one "crazy brunch"); still, it's the "beautiful", "airy" setting – replete with vaulted ceilings – that's the star of the show.

Barbuto *Italian*

24 | 19 | 21 | $55

W Village | 775 Washington St. (bet. Jane & W. 12th Sts.) | 212-924-9700 | www.barbutonyc.com
Parked in a "chic converted garage", this "unpretentious" West Village Italian showcases Jonathan Waxman's "simple but classy" cooking highlighted by a "life-changing" roasted chicken; the atmosphere's "upbeat" – ok, "noisy" – but it's somewhat "quieter in summer" when they roll up the doors and it becomes "semi-alfresco."

Bar Corvo *Italian*

26 | 21 | 23 | $40

Prospect Heights | 791 Washington Ave. (bet. Lincoln & St. Johns Pls.) | Brooklyn | 718-230-0940 | www.barcorvo.com
Hailed as a "boon to the area", this Prospect Heights "Al Di La off-spring" fields a "well-curated menu" of "superior" Italian cooking in "cozy" quarters run by an "attentive" team; "real-steal" prices ensure it "does fill up", though a patio helps stretch the space.

BareBurger *Burgers*

22 | 16 | 19 | $22

Chelsea | 153 Eighth Ave. (bet. 17th & 18th Sts.) | 212-414-2273
E 70s | 1370 First Ave. (73rd St.) | 212-510-8559
E Village | 85 Second Ave. (5th St.) | 212-510-8610
G Village | 535 Laguardia Pl. (bet. 3rd St. & Washington Square Vill.) | 212-477-8125
Murray Hill | 514 Third Ave. (bet. 34th & 35th Sts.) | 212-679-2273
Park Slope | 170 Seventh Ave. (bet. 1st St. & Garfield Pl.) | Brooklyn | 718-768-2273
Astoria | 23-01 31st St. (23rd Ave.) | Queens | 718-204-7167
Astoria | 33-21 31st Ave. (34th St.) | Queens | 718-777-7011
Bayside | 42-38 Bell Blvd. (bet. 42nd & 43rd Aves.) | Queens | 718-279-2273
Forest Hills | 71-49 Austin St. (bet. 71st Rd. & 72nd Ave.) | Queens | 718-275-2273
www.bareburger.com
Additional locations throughout the NY area
The "health-conscious" approach "plays well" at this "fast-rising" fran-chise, where "organic" beef and " exotic meats" (wild boar, bison, etc.) yield "flavorful burgers" with "tons" of "inventive toppings"; patty pun-dits find it "a little spendy" but "worth it" for "something different."

Bar Italia ● *Italian*

19 | 18 | 18 | $55

E 60s | 768 Madison Ave. (66th St.) | 212-249-5300 | www.baritalianyc.com
"Wanna-be-seen" Euros flock to this "fashion-forward" Madison Avenue Italian where the "better-than-expected" cooking takes a backseat to the "sleek" white setting and *Real Housewives* people-watching; ex-pect serious tabs and "lots of attitude."

| | FOOD | DECOR | SERVICE | COST |

Bar Jamón ● *Spanish* — 23 | 19 | 20 | $44

Gramercy | 125 E. 17th St. (Irving Pl.) | 212-253-2773 |
www.casamononyc.com

Mario Batali's "convivial" Gramercy tapas bar–cum–"holding pen" for his
'round-the-corner Casa Mono puts out "top-of-the-line" Spanish small
plates paired with an "extensive" wine list; it's a "tight squeeze" and the
tabs are "not cheap", but most don't mind given the "sexy-time" mood.

Bark *Hot Dogs* — 22 | 16 | 18 | $16

Park Slope | 474 Bergen St. (bet. 5th & Flatbush Aves.) | Brooklyn |
718-789-1939 | www.barkhotdogs.com

The "dogs are hot and the crowd cool" at this Park Sloper where the
"artisanal dawgs with "great snap" are made from "locally sourced",
"pedigreed ingredients" and paired with "oustanding" sides and
Brooklyn craft beers; "hip-minimalist" digs where "everything's recy-
cled" help justify prices kinda "high-end" for wieners.

Barney Greengrass Ⓜ⇄ *Deli* — 24 | 9 | 16 | $30

W 80s | 541 Amsterdam Ave. (bet. 86th & 87th Sts.) | 212-724-4707 |
www.barneygreengrass.com

Still "as good as when grandpa ate here", this UWS institution has
been slinging "old-style Jewish deli food" and "gold-standard" smoked
fish since 1908; "fading" decor, "no credit cards" and "borderline rude
service" are all "part of the charm", as the "lines out the door" attest.

Barosa *Italian* — 22 | 19 | 22 | $41

Rego Park | 62-29 Woodhaven Blvd. (62nd Rd.) | Queens | 718-424-1455 |
www.barosas.com

"Tasty" red-sauce fare "like mom used to make" is available for a
"good price" at this "neighborhood favorite" Rego Park Italian; its "upscale" ambitions are apparent in the "polite" service, while "fantastic
specials" seal the deal.

Bar Pitti ●⇄ *Italian* — 23 | 16 | 18 | $44

G Village | 268 Sixth Ave. (bet. Bleecker & Houston Sts.) | 212-982-3300
Home to "many a celeb sighting", this "jet-set" Village Italian is
best known for its "excellent people-watching", even if the "easygoing" fare is pretty "delicious" as well; no reservations, no plastic,
"no discernible decor" and "far-from-friendly" service don't faze its
"paparazzi"-ready patrons.

NEW Barraca ● *Spanish* — ∇ 15 | 16 | 12 | $58

W Village | 81 Greenwich Ave. (Bank St.) | 212-462-0080 |
www.barracanyc.com

Classic paellas for two or more are the specialty at this "casual", midpriced West Village Spaniard, which also turns out "flavorful" tapas
and other favorites; the space is modeled after the traveling theaters
in Spain, plus sidewalk seating is perfect for watching the "parade of
fun people" passing by.

Barrio Chino ● *Mexican* — 24 | 18 | 20 | $31

LES | 253 Broome St. (bet. Ludlow & Orchard Sts.) | 212-228-6710 |
www.barriochinonyc.com

Its Spanish name translates as 'Chinese neighborhood', and sure
enough this "rustic", "microscopic" LES cantina specializes in "un-

usual" Mexican-Sino fusion fare; it's still "something of a scene" after more than a decade, maybe because of its "highly affordable" price point and "lay-you-out-flat" tequila list.

Basil Brick Oven Pizza *Pizza*
25 | **19** | **21** | **$23**

Astoria | 28-17 Astoria Blvd. (bet. 27th & 29th Sts.) | Queens | 718-204-1205 | www.basilbrickoven.com

Some of the "best pizza in Astoria" emerges from the "wood-burning oven" of this "tiny" Italian that also vends "delicious" pastas and panini; a "good location", "reliably fast delivery" and affordable tabs have fans wondering why it's so "little known."

Basso56 *Italian*
23 | **18** | **23** | **$51**

W 50s | 234 W. 56th St. (bet. B'way & 8th Ave.) | 212-265-2610 | www.basso56.com

An "excellent Carnegie Hall resource", this Midtown Italian features a "nicely put-together menu" with "modern flair" ferried by an "accommodating" team; some sniff at the "narrow", "nothing-fancy" setting, but admit the prices are "reasonable for the quality."

Basta Pasta *Italian*
23 | **17** | **20** | **$44**

Flatiron | 37 W. 17th St. (bet. 5th & 6th Aves.) | 212-366-0888 | www.bastapastanyc.com

"Japanese-style Italian food" begs the question "where else but NY?" – and this "unusual" Flatiron "change of pace" comes through with "interesting" vittles led by a signature "pasta tossed in a Parmesan wheel"; if the decor's getting "dated", the "hospitable" service and "reasonable" rates are fine as is.

Battersby *American*
27 | **17** | **23** | **$59**

Carroll Gardens | 255 Smith St. (bet. Degraw & Douglass Sts.) | Brooklyn | 718-852-8321 | www.battersbybrooklyn.com

A "red-hot phenom" on Smith Street, this "quintessential Brooklyn" "foodie destination" supplies "sophisticated, creative" New American cuisine via an "earnest" crew "without the fuss and stiffness" – or quite the "hefty cost" – of its "high-end" counterparts; however, its "teeny", basic digs can't keep pace with "extreme popularity", so plan to "go early" or "do the tasting menu" (for which it takes rezzies) – "these guys won't let you down."

Battery Gardens *American/Continental*
20 | **24** | **20** | **$49**

Financial District | SW corner of Battery Park (State St.) | 212-809-5508 | www.batterygardens.com

The "harbor is at your feet" at this "shoreline" Battery Park bastion where the "peerless" views of the harbor and Lady Liberty are matched with "better-than-expected" American-Continental fare; for the most "priceless" experience, go for "outdoor cocktails at sunset."

Bayou *Cajun*
23 | **23** | **21** | **$41**

Rosebank | 1072 Bay St. (bet. Chestnut & St. Marys Aves.) | Staten Island | 718-273-4383 | www.bayounyc.com

"Ragin' Cajun" cooking and "real Southern hospitality" comes to Staten Island via this Rosebank "favorite" where the "tasty" cooking is as "true" to N'Awlins as the "Big Easy" decor; "affordable" tabs and "designated-driver-recommended" drinks ratchet up the "festive" vibrations.

| | FOOD | DECOR | SERVICE | COST |

B. Café *Belgian*

21 | 16 | 19 | $39

E 70s | 240 E. 75th St. (bet. 2nd & 3rd Aves.) | 212-249-3300
W 80s | 566 Amsterdam Ave. (bet. 87th & 88th Sts.) | 212-873-0003
www.bcafe.com

"Belgian pub grub" is yours at these "satisfying" crosstown "reliables" offering "consistently fine" mussels and frites washed down with "high-test" brews; ok, the "railroad" settings are a bit "drab" and "squashed", but the staff "tries its best" and you do get "lots for your money."

NEW Beatrice Inn *American*

▽ 17 | 22 | 21 | $68

W Village | 285 W. 12th St. (bet. 8th Ave. & W. 4th St.) | 917-556-7400 | www.thebeatriceinn.com

This longtime West Village basement recently enjoyed a short life as a too-hip-for-words nightspot and is now back as a "standard" American chophouse courtesy of editor/restaurateur Graydon Carter (Monkey Bar, Waverly Inn); look for dual dining rooms exuding downtown "townhouse" charm, uptown pricing and a relatively democratic door policy, despite the "celebrities" in attendance.

Beaumarchais ●Ⓜ *French*

22 | 22 | 19 | $65

Meatpacking | 409 W. 13th St. (bet. 9th Ave. & Washington St.) | 212-675-2400 | www.brasseriebeaumarchais.com

"French food" meets "French kissing" at this Meatpacking District "Eurotrash" magnet better known for its "blaring music", "party vibe" and "hot brunch" than the "surprisingly good" grub; all the "grinding", "champagne spraying" and "dancing on tables" distracts from the sticker shock.

Beauty & Essex ● *American*

22 | 26 | 20 | $61

LES | 146 Essex St. (bet. Rivington & Stanton Sts.) | 212-614-0146 | www.beautyandessex.com

A "scene-and-a-half" hidden behind a "functioning pawn shop", this Lower East Side phenom seduces "beautiful" folks with its "sexy", eclectic New American edibles offered up in an "over-the-top", AvroKO-designed duplex space; it may come at a "high price", but "free bubbly in the ladies' room" compensates.

Becco ● *Italian*

22 | 18 | 21 | $47

W 40s | 355 W. 46th St. (bet. 8th & 9th Aves.) | 212-397-7597 | www.becco-nyc.com

For a "legitimate Italian" "fill-up", this Bastianich Restaurant Row "standby" supplies an "ever-popular" $23 bottomless pasta "binge" and a $25 wine list that "clinches the deal" for "tourists as well as in-the-know" locals; its "down-to-a-science" service is tailored to the "multitudes" who indulge "pre-show."

Beccofino *Italian*

23 | 17 | 20 | $36

Riverdale | 5704 Mosholu Ave. (bet. Fieldston Rd. & Spencer Ave.) | Bronx | 718-432-2604

Pretty "happening" for Riverdale, this "traditional" Italian offers "Manhattan-quality" red-sauce cooking at Bronx prices; its "neighborly atmosphere" draws huzzahs, but "no reservations" and "small" dimensions mean you must "come early or be prepared to wait."

	FOOD	DECOR	SERVICE	COST

Beco ◗⊄ *Brazilian* ▽ 23 | 19 | 20 | $39

Williamsburg | 45 Richardson St. (Lorimer St.) | Brooklyn | 718-599-1645 |
www.becobar.com

A "well-kept Williamsburg secret", this "cozy", cash-only Brazilian
styled after the *botecos* (neighborhood hangouts) of São Paolo is "like
a little vacation" offering "yummy" dishes like "grandma used to
make" plus native cocktails; weekends bring on a feijoada brunch and
"live music" till you think "you're in Rio."

Beecher's Cellar *American* 23 | 19 | 20 | $30

Flatiron | 900 Broadway (20th St.) | 212-466-3340 |
www.beechershandmadecheese.com

Upstairs, this Flatiron cheese factory vends artisanal varieties "made
right in front of your eyes", while downstairs a "secret" lounge/eatery
features a "limited" but "tasty" American menu highlighted by a
"magical mac 'n' cheese"; "personable" service and a "candlelit" setting with "cozy armchairs" enhance the "low-key" vibe.

Bella Blu *Italian* 21 | 18 | 19 | $55

E 70s | 967 Lexington Ave. (bet. 70th & 71st Sts.) | 212-988-4624

"Well-to-do" Upper Eastsiders "get happy" at this "popular" Italian
serving a "high-quality" menu led by "fantastic" pizzas; granted, it's
"pricey", the seating's "cheek-by-jowl" and service depends on "how
familiar you look", but "superior people-watching" saves the day.

Bella Via *Italian* 22 | 18 | 20 | $32

LIC | 47-46 Vernon Blvd. (48th Ave.) | Queens | 718-361-7510 |
www.bellaviarestaurant.com

"Funky Long Island City" is home to this "reliable" Italian known for its
"fresh" pastas and coal-fired pizzas at prices that "won't break the
bank"; set in a big-windowed storefront, it features "simple" decor
that contributes to its "pleasant", "friendly" mien.

Bell Book & Candle ◗ *American* 20 | 19 | 19 | $49

W Village | 141 W. 10th St., downstairs (bet. Greenwich Ave. &
Waverly Pl.) | 212-414-2355 | www.bbandcnyc.com

Best known for an aeroponic "roof garden" that supplies most of its
produce, this "cozy-chic" West Villager is appreciated for its "delicious" "seasonal" Americana; the "dark" basement setting has
"great date" potential, but it's also "worth checking out" for its "ridiculously awesome happy-hour" deals.

Ben & Jack's Steak House *Steak* 24 | 20 | 23 | $69

Murray Hill | 255 Fifth Ave. (bet. 28th & 29th Sts.) | 212-532-7600 |
www.benandjackssteakhouse.com

Among the "best of the Luger's imitators", this "solid" Murray Hill
carnivorium features "humongous", "cooked-to-perfection" steaks
matched with "man-size" sides; "boys'-club" looks and "attentive"
staffers offset the predictably "expensive" tabs.

Benchmark *American/Steak* 22 | 21 | 21 | $48

Park Slope | 339 Second St. (bet. 4th & 5th Aves.) | Brooklyn |
718-965-7040 | www.benchmarkrestaurant.com

Nestled in an "intimate" carriage house, this "somewhat overlooked"
Park Slope steakhouse offers "terrific" chops as well as "quite good"

American accompaniments; fans admire its "calm" mood and midrange tabs, while a "lovely patio" allows it to "double in size" in good weather.

Benjamin Steak House *Steak*

| 25 | 22 | 24 | $75 |

E 40s | The Dylan Hotel | 52 E. 41st St. (bet. Madison & Park Aves.) | 212-297-9177 | www.benjaminsteakhouse.com

"Tucked away" in Midtown's Dylan Hotel is this "well-run" steakhouse where the "top-end" chops are priced for "corporate credit cards"; further assets include "engaging" service, a "high-ceilinged", fireplace-equipped setting and convenience to Grand Central, just a block away.

Benoit Bistro *French*

| 21 | 21 | 20 | $64 |

W 50s | 60 W. 55th St. (bet. 5th & 6th Aves.) | 646-943-7373 | www.benoitny.com

Long having "hit its stride", Alain Ducasse's Midtown French bistro puts forth "classic", "true-to-its-roots" dishes (including a "roast chicken of the gods") in a "well-lit" room that feels "like Paris"; though on the "pricey" side, most agree it's "worth a try."

Ben's Best *Deli/Kosher*

| 23 | 10 | 17 | $24 |

Rego Park | 96-40 Queens Blvd. (bet. 63rd Dr. & 64th Rd.) | Queens | 718-897-1700 | www.bensbest.com

For an "authentic artery-clogging experience", look no further than this circa-1945 Rego Park Jewish deli known for "old-time" kosher fare ("don't miss the pastrami") "and lots of it"; the "oy!" decor is "just what you'd expect", but "Queens prices" and "ok service" compensate.

Ben's Kosher Deli *Deli/Kosher*

| 19 | 13 | 16 | $26 |

Garment District | 209 W. 38th St. (bet. 7th & 8th Aves.) | 212-398-2367
Bayside | Bay Terr. | 211-37 26th Ave. (Bell Blvd.) | Queens | 718-229-2367
www.bensdeli.net

"Sandwiches built for two" and other fresser's delights turn up at these "decent" kosher delis in Bayside and the Garment District; "dated" "luncheonette" looks and "uneven" service lead critics to pronounce the overall going "routine", but the tourists don't seem to care.

Beso *Spanish*

| 23 | 22 | 22 | $42 |

St. George | 11 Schuyler St. (Richmond Terr.) | Staten Island | 718-816-8162 | www.besonyc.com

A "short walk from the ferry", this St. George Spaniard rolls out "outstanding" tapas and sangria in a "relaxed" setting that "feels very far away from Staten Island"; admirers "wish it were bigger", though the staff that "never misses a beat" and "reasonable" rates are fine as is.

Best Pizza ● *Pizza*

| 24 | 15 | 19 | $15 |

Williamsburg | 33 Havemeyer St. (bet. N. 7th & 8th Sts.) | Brooklyn | 718-599-2210 | www.best.piz.za.com

"They picked a ballsy name", but this pizza "joint" in Williamsburg (a Roberta's sib) "does itself proud" with a succinct lineup of "excellent" brick-oven pies, slices and sandwiches; paper plate–adorned digs that "leave a lot to be desired" encourage takeout or delivery.

	FOOD	DECOR	SERVICE	COST

Betel *SE Asian* | 21 | 20 | 20 | $52
W Village | 51 Grove St. (bet. Bleecker St. & 7th Ave. S.) | 212-352-0460 | www.betelnyc.com

"Unique spins" on Southeast Asian street food are slung at this "cool" West Villager; its "stiletto"-clad fan base likes the "dark, dimly lit" setting and "jumping scene", the "tight tables" and "pricey" tabs not so much.

NEW Betony 🗷 *American* | - | - | - | E
W 50s | 41 W. 57th St. (bet. 5th & 6th Aves.) | 212-465-2400 | www.betony-nyc.com

Helmed by Eleven Madison Park alums, this upscale arrival in Midtown's former Brasserie Pushkin space puts forth playful, artfully plated New American dishes matched with a creative cocktail list; the quiet upstairs dining room is suited to intimate dinners, while a bar area with vaulted ceilings is prime for a pre-curtain tipple before heading to nearby Carnegie Hall.

Bettola ● *Italian* | 19 | 15 | 18 | $37
W 70s | 412 Amsterdam Ave. (bet. 79th & 80th Sts.) | 212-787-1660 | www.bettolanyc.com

"Comfortable" is the word on this "popular" UWS trattoria, offering "simple but tasty" Italiana highlighted by thin-crust pizzas; given the "reasonable" tabs, its "neighborhood" following ignores the "inconsistent" service and so-so decor.

Beyoglu *Turkish* | 22 | 16 | 18 | $37
E 80s | 1431 Third Ave. (81st St.) | 212-650-0850

"Craveable" meze is the calling card of this "perennially popular" Turk on the UES; those who want to "hear their tablemates" opt for the upstairs dining room, but wherever you sit, the tabs are "affordable", the mood "upbeat" and the service "variable."

Bianca 🍽 *Italian* | 26 | 18 | 21 | $33
NoHo | 5 Bleecker St. (Bowery) | 212-260-4666 | www.biancanyc.com

The "hearty" Emilia-Romagna dishes are "clearly made with love" and a "fabulous bargain" to boot, making this cash-only NoHo Italian "gem" well worth the "tight squeeze"; no reservations means there's "definitely a wait", which those in the know spend "next door at the wine bar."

Biang! 🍽 *Chinese/Noodle Shop* | ▽ 24 | 15 | 15 | $23
Flushing | 41-10 Main St. (bet. 41st Ave. & 41st Rd.) | Queens | 718-888-7713 | www.biang-nyc.com

"Tease your taste buds" with "spicy goodness" at this Flushing "table-service" site spun off from the Western Chinese staple Xi'an Famous Foods, a biang-up source of "amazing" hand-ripped noodles and "excellent skewers" at "extremely reasonable" (cash-only) rates; seekers of the "authentic" say it's "worth the schlep."

Bice ● *Italian* | 21 | 20 | 20 | $65
E 50s | 7 E. 54th St. (bet. 5th & Madison Aves.) | 212-688-1999 | www.bicenewyork.com

For "entertaining" people-watching, there's always this "elite" Midtown Italian where the "lively" crowd ranges from blasé "Euros" to wide-eyed "tourists" and "power"-lunchers; the food's "solid" enough, but servicewise it helps to "look like a big spender", and consider having a couple of Bellinis to "ease the pain of the bill."

Big Wong ⏞ Chinese

FOOD	DECOR	SERVICE	COST
22	6	12	$15

Chinatown | 67 Mott St. (bet. Bayard & Canal Sts.) | 212-964-0540
"Genuine, moan-provoking" Cantonese fare ("amazing congee", "out-standing roast meats") explains the "mob scene" at this cash-only C-towner; given the "insanely inexpensive" checks, it's easy to over-look the "nonexistent" decor, "rushed" service and unfortunate name.

Bill's Bar & Burger Burgers

FOOD	DECOR	SERVICE	COST
19	15	18	$26

NEW Financial District | Marriott NY Financial Ctr. | 85 West St. (Washington St.) | 212-894-3800 ☽
Meatpacking | 22 Ninth Ave. (13th St.) | 212-414-3003 ☽
W 50s | 16 W. 51st St. (bet. 5th & 6th Aves.) | 212-705-8510
www.billsbarandburger.com
"Good ol' fashioned burgers" and "craft beer on tap" are the highlights at Steve Hanson's "hopping" hamburger hamlets, where "authentic" disco fries and "creative" alcoholic shakes add zest; expect "efficient" service" and "fair pricing" at all locations, but look out for "tourist hordes" at Rock Center.

Bill's Food & Drink ☽⊠ American/Steak

FOOD	DECOR	SERVICE	COST
▽ 18	23	19	$66

E 50s | 57 E. 54th St. (bet. Madison & Park Aves.) | 212-518-2727 | www.bills54.com
Prohibition-era speakeasy Bill's Gay Nineties reboots as this Midtown American grill, where chef John DeLucie (Crown, The Lion) focuses on "juicy" steaks; a townhouse setting replete with vintage artwork and taxidermy recalls '20s Gotham and "the Wild West", though some wonder if retro chic is "too cool" for this turf.

Biricchino ⊠ Italian

FOOD	DECOR	SERVICE	COST
21	15	21	$39

Chelsea | 260 W. 29th St. (bet. 7th & 8th Aves.) | 212-695-6690 | www.biricchino.com
Set in a "neighborhood with few choices", this MSG-convenient Chelsea vet rolls out "real-deal" Northern Italiana, particularly its "incredible" housemade sausages; true, the decor may leave "much to be desired", but service is "attentive" and the pricing as "low-key" as the mood.

Birreria Italian

FOOD	DECOR	SERVICE	COST
20	21	18	$44

Flatiron | Eataly | 200 Fifth Ave. (bet. 23rd & 24th Sts.) | 212-937-8910 | www.eataly.com
"Hard to beat on a nice summer" day and ideal for "out-of-towners", this "beer-lover's garden" atop Eataly is an all-seasons, retractable-roofed "experience" dispensing an "excellent" selection of cask ales soaked up with "light" Italian bites (mostly cheeses and salumi); the place is "hopping" from lunch till late, so "to actually gain access, go early."

Bistango Italian

FOOD	DECOR	SERVICE	COST
21	17	23	$40

Murray Hill | 415 Third Ave. (29th St.) | 212-725-8484 | www.bistangonyc.com
While the Italian offerings at this "old-school" Murray Hill perennial are certainly "tasty", it's the "wonderful gluten-free" options – "even beer" – that earn the most praise; "reasonable" pricing and "accom-modating" service led by an "engaging host" seal the deal.

	FOOD	DECOR	SERVICE	COST

Bistro Cassis *French*   20 | 18 | 18 | $48

W 70s | 225 Columbus Ave. (bet. 70th & 71st Sts.) | 212-579-3966 |
www.bistrocassis.com

For a serving of "old Paris on the UWS", this French bistro can be
counted on for "traditional", "satisfying" dishes at a relatively "reasonable price"; the "no-reservations" policy is a turnoff, but the "intimate" interior and "expeditious" service make it "good pre–Lincoln
Center", an "easy walk" away.

Bistro Chat Noir *French*   20 | 19 | 21 | $56

E 60s | 22 E. 66th St. (bet. 5th & Madison Aves.) | 212-794-2428 |
www.bistrochatnoir.com

A "low-key fave" in a "chic" address off Madison Avenue, this
Gallic Eastsider caters to "fashionable" folk with "Parisian inti-
macy" and "quite good" French bistro fare dispensed in a "snug"
setting; tabs are "expensive", but a "fantastic" owner and "convivial
staff" keep customers satisfied.

Bistro Citron *French*   20 | 18 | 20 | $46

W 80s | 473 Columbus Ave. (bet. 82nd & 83rd Sts.) | 212-400-9401 |
www.bistrocitronnyc.com

UWSers fancying a "taste of Paree" head to this "relaxed", "old-style"
bistro purveying "reliably good" French country cooking in a "happy" milieu; it "won't drain your bank account" and is just the "place to take your
mom or girlfriend du jour", hence it's a "neighborhood favorite."

Bistro La Promenade *French/Italian*   23 | 22 | 21 | $59

Chelsea | 461 W. 23rd St. (bet. 9th & 10th Aves.) | 212-255-7400 |
www.lapromenadenyc.com

"Cute and hip", chef Alain Allegretti's "inviting" Chelsea bistro channels the Côte d'Azur with a breezily "comfortable" setting, "warm service" and traditional French fare centered on "fabulous seafood";
however, in keeping with the Riviera style, prices run *un peu* steep.

Bistro Les Amis ❶ *French*   22 | 19 | 22 | $45

SoHo | 180 Spring St. (Thompson St.) | 212-226-8645 |
www.bistrolesamis.com

Bringing a soupçon of the "Left Bank" to SoHo, this seasoned French
bistro lures fans with its "comforting" cooking vs. cost ratio; ok, there's
"no scene" going on, but sidewalk seats provide prime people-watching
and the "*charmant*" staff lives up to the promise of its name.

Bistro Le Steak *French*   18 | 15 | 18 | $48

E 70s | 1309 Third Ave. (75th St.) | 212-517-3800 | www.bistrolesteak.com
A "neighborhood anchor" for the "10021 set", this "not trendy" UES
bistro dispenses "simple", "understated" French food "without sky-
high prices" or attitude; although certainly "nothing fancy" (and perhaps "in need of renovation"), it's a perennial where you just "might
run into" Mayor Bloomberg.

Bistro Milano *Italian*   21 | 19 | 21 | $51

W 50s | 1350 Sixth Ave. (bet. 54th & 55th Sts.) | 212-757-2600 |
www.bistromilanonyc.com

"Fresh pastas", "excellent pizzas" and a "spacious" outdoor terrace
combine to make this "midpriced" Northern Italian from the Bice folks

a "reliable" drop-in; given its "convenience to City Center" and "Fifth Avenue shopping", it's a natural for theatergoers and "tourists" alike.

Bistro 61 *French*
19 | 15 | 20 | $43

E 60s | 1113 First Ave. (61st St.) | 212-223-6220 | www.bistro61.com
Upper East Side locals tout this "everyday" French bistro near the Queensborough Bridge for its "flavorful", Moroccan-accented cooking "served with a smile" by an "earnest" crew; "decent" pricing and a "relaxing" (if "nothing-fancy"), brick-walled setting add to the overall "charming" effect.

Bistro S K ⊠ *French*
∇ 26 | 23 | 27 | $57

City Island | 273 City Island Ave. (bet. Carroll & Hawkins Sts.) | Bronx | 718-885-1670 | www.bistrosk.com
This Gallic bistro brings a welcome "touch of France" to City Island's dining scene, which is generally in full-on "seafood overload"; its "very good" midpriced standards arrive via "attentive" "pro" staffers in an ambiance that Romeos rate conducive to "romantic" repasts.

Bistro Ten 18 *American*
19 | 17 | 19 | $39

W 100s | 1018 Amsterdam Ave. (110th St.) | 212-662-7600 | www.bistroten18.com
It's "slim pickings" for decent dining in Morningside Heights, and this "shabby-chic" American is "one of the better options" given its "solid" menu and "relaxed" service; while tabs are "budget-friendly", the view of St. John the Divine from its sidewalk seats is "priceless."

Bistro Vendôme *French*
22 | 20 | 20 | $54

E 50s | 405 E. 58th St. (1st Ave.) | 212-935-9100 | www.bistrovendomenyc.com
"Sutton seniors" gather at this "upscale bistro" for French fare dispatched by "Gallic-accented staffers" who are as "charming" as the tri-level townhouse setting; the less-impressed shrug "nothing special", but those who love the "particularly pretty" terrace call this a "neighborhood jewel."

Black Duck *American/Seafood*
22 | 19 | 21 | $49

Murray Hill | Park South Hotel | 122 E. 28th St. (Lexington Ave.) | 212-448-0888 | www.blackduckny.com
"Dark" and "cozy", this "sleeper" hotel tavern on kind of a "nothing" Murray Hill block provides "upmarket" New Americana with a seafood slant for a "fair price"; service is "spot-on", while a "mood-setting fireplace", "wonderful weekend jazz" and "clubby but not stuffy" vibe add allure.

Black Iron Burger ❶ *Burgers*
21 | 14 | 17 | $20

E Village | 540 E. Fifth St. (Ave. B) | 212-677-6067 | www.blackironburger.com
"Pretty damn good" "no-frills" burgers paired with draft pints "go down easy" at this East Village "hole-in-the-wall"; though the "earthy" setting's on the "small" side, the staff is "fun", the tabs "reasonable" and the late-night hours a bonus.

Black Whale *American*
22 | 20 | 21 | $30

City Island | 279 City Island Ave. (Hawkins St.) | Bronx | 718-885-3657
The "offbeat" nautical decor conjures up "Cape Cod in the Bronx" at this "cute" City Island vet where the "inexpensive" New American

menu includes some notably "decadent desserts"; fans find the "terrific" Sunday brunch and "lovely" back patio equally "memorable."

Blanca ⌧Ⓜ️ American ▽ 29 | 21 | 27 | $254

Bushwick | 261 Moore St. (Bogart St.) | Brooklyn | 347-799-2807 | www.blancanyc.com

The "spectacular" fine-dining adjunct of Bushwick darling Roberta's, this "must-try" (if you can get in) New American in spare, "cool" loft digs delivers an "amazing experience" with its lavish tasting menu, offered at a single seating nightly to "only 12 lucky diners"; chef Carlo Mirarchi's "exquisite" "morsels" arrive artfully plated on high-end china, appropriate to the $195 prix fixe-only price tag – the few who've tried it say this is "as good as it gets."

Blaue Gans Austrian/German 22 | 18 | 20 | $48

TriBeCa | 139 Duane St. (W. B'way) | 212-571-8880 | www.kg-ny.com

"First-rate" Wiener schnitzel heads the list of "hearty" Austro-German dishes at Kurt Gutenbrunner's "down-to-earth" "neighborhood" TriBeCan, abetted by "wonderful" Teutonic brews; the "artsy poster-clad" room is "simple" but "cool", while "fair prices" and "pleasant" staffers add to the "gemütlich" mood.

Blossom Vegan/Vegetarian 23 | 18 | 21 | $35

Chelsea | 187 Ninth Ave. (bet. 21st & 22nd Sts.) | 212-627-1144 | www.blossomnyc.com

Blossom du Jour Vegan/Vegetarian

W 40s | 617 Ninth Ave. (bet. 43rd & 44th Sts.) | 646-998-3535
W 60s | 165 Amsterdam Ave. (bet. 67th & 68th Sts.) | 212-799-9010
www.blossomdujour.com

Cafe Blossom Vegan/Vegetarian

W 80s | 466 Columbus Ave. (bet. 82nd & 83rd Sts.) | 212-875-2600
W Village | 41-43 Carmine St. (bet. Bedford & Bleecker Sts.) | 646-438-9939
www.blossomnyc.com

"Plant-based food" gets a "delicious" spin at these "guilt-free" vegans known for dishes so "inventive" they could "convert meat eaters"; "friendly" staffers and "peaceful" digs come along with the "affordable" tabs, while the du Jour take-out venues vend "healthy meals on the run."

BLT Bar & Grill ⓓ American 22 | 20 | 20 | $50

Financial District | W Hotel Downtown | 123 Washington St. (bet. Albany & Carlisle Sts.) | 646-826-8666 | www.bltrestaurants.com

A "classier" option in the "barren Financial District", this American tavern in the W Downtown serves "upscale" standards to "expense-account" wielders and "9/11 Memorial" visitors; the ceilings in this duplex are as "high" as the bills, but the after-work scene is "lively."

BLT Burger Burgers 22 | 16 | 19 | $29

G Village | 470 Sixth Ave. (bet. 11th & 12th Sts.) | 212-243-8226 | www.bltburger.com

"High-end burgers" are flipped in a "low-key" setting at this "diner"-esque Villager where "decadence" comes in the form of "big, juicy" patties, "top-notch" sides and "thick shakes" (some of them "boozy"); service lies somewhere between "prompt" and "rushed", while critics call it "overpriced" for what it is.

	FOOD	DECOR	SERVICE	COST

BLT Fish ☒ *Seafood*   23 | 21 | 21 | $63

Flatiron | 21 W. 17th St. (bet. 5th & 6th Aves.) | 212-691-8888 |
www.bltfish.com
"Straight-out-of-the-water" fish is the bait at this Flatiron seafooder
famed for its "expertly prepared" catch, "exceptional" service and
"stylish" setting beneath a "giant skylight"; brace for "a whopper of a
tab" in the "more genteel" upstairs room, or set your anchor in the
more "funky" ground-floor Fish Shack where it's "cheaper" and "louder."

BLT Prime *Steak*   25 | 22 | 23 | $76

Gramercy | 111 E. 22nd St. (bet. Lexington Ave. & Park Ave. S.) |
212-995-8500 | www.bltprime.com
"They know their way around a cow" at this "chic" Gramercy steakhouse touted for "perfectly cooked" chops and "light-as-a-feather"
popovers; "stellar" wines, "solicitous" service and "sleek" decor add
to the overall "special experience" and help explain tabs that may
"leave your credit card smoking."

BLT Steak *Steak*   25 | 22 | 23 | $78

E 50s | 106 E. 57th St. (bet. Lexington & Park Aves.) | 212-752-7470 |
www.bltsteak.com
Frequented by "suits", "big spenders and pretty ladies", this Midtown
chop shop sizzles with "outstanding" steaks accompanied by "first-
rate" sides and popovers "on steroids"; "super service" and a "swanky"
setting amplify the "power-scene" vibe, but just "bring lots of money" –
the pricing's "sky high."

Blue Fin ◑ *Seafood*   23 | 22 | 20 | $57

W 40s | W Hotel Times Sq. | 1567 Broadway (47th St.) | 212-918-1400 |
www.bluefinnyc.com
"Dependable results" ensure this "energetic" Steve Hanson seafooder
remains a "popular" "oasis" amid the "tumult of Times Square", with
"delicious" catch served by "pros" in a "spacious" setting with a "cacophonous" lower level and "quieter" mezzanine; though "pricey", it's
a "civilized" curtain-raiser that's "convenient to most Broadway shows."

Blue Ginger *Asian*   21 | 17 | 19 | $33

Chelsea | 106 Eighth Ave. (bet. 15th & 16th Sts.) | 212-352-0911
Handy for a "quick bite before a show" at the nearby Joyce Theater,
this "fun" Chelsea Pan-Asian slices sushi that's "pleasing to the eye"
and also offers "mouthwatering" cooked items, all "well priced";
"friendly" staffers take your mind off the "typical" decor.

Blue Hill *American*   27 | 23 | 26 | $89

G Village | 75 Washington Pl. (bet. MacDougal St. & 6th Ave.) |
212-539-1776 | www.bluehillfarm.com
Dan Barber's "farm-to-table" "temple", this "top-tier" Village American
"consistently wows" with "heavenly" "locavore" cuisine that "brings
together the best ingredients and makes them shine"; a "serene", "sophisticated" venue where the staff "couldn't be more engaged", it's
"well worth" the rez drama and "high-end" cost ("what's good enough
for Mr. President . . .").

Blue 9 Burger ◑ *Burgers*   19 | 7 | 13 | $13

E 70s | 1415 Second Ave. (bet. 73rd & 74th Sts.) | 212-988-8171

(continued)

Blue 9 Burger

E Village | 92 Third Ave. (bet. 12th & 13th Sts.) | 212-979-0053

Though the mood's "fast food" and there's "no ambiance to speak of", the burgers are "quite delectable" at these "quick, cheap" patty places; the East Village original is an "after-hours" magnet for the "student" set, though snobs turn to it only for "delivery" given the "indifferent service" and "unexciting" digs.

Blue Ribbon ● *American*   25 | 20 | 23 | $54

SoHo | 97 Sullivan St. (bet. Prince & Spring Sts.) | 212-274-0404

Blue Ribbon Brooklyn ● *American*

Park Slope | 280 Fifth Ave. (bet. 1st St. & Garfield Pl.) | Brooklyn | 718-840-0404

www.blueribbonrestaurants.com

The Bromberg brothers "deserve a blue ribbon" for this "nifty" SoHo New American (with a Park Slope counterpart), rolling out a "sublime" menu that runs the gamut "from foie gras to matzo ball soup"; "personable service", an "unpretentious" setting and "night-owl" hours balance out "loud" acoustics, "pricey" tabs and "long waits" due to the "no-rezzie challenge."

Blue Ribbon Bakery ● *American*   24 | 18 | 21 | $43

W Village | 35 Downing St. (Bedford St.) | 212-337-0404 | www.blueribbonrestaurants.com

The "wonderful smell" of bread perfumes the air at the Bromberg brothers' "crusty" West Village American, a bistro-bakery combo supplying the "epitome of comfort food", "enthusiastic" service and a particularly "standout" brunch; both its "shoebox"-size ground floor and bigger "wine-cellar"-esque basement are "long on charm."

🆕 Blue Ribbon Fried Chicken   *Chicken*   - | - | - | I

E Village | 28 E. First St. (2nd Ave.) | 212-228-0404 | www.blueribbonrestaurants.com

The Bromberg brothers do Southern-style fried chicken – long a popular menu item at their other eateries – at this casual East Villager dishing up by-the-piece bird, chicken burgers and a few salads and sides; the airy counter-service setup features lots of white subway tile, plenty of tables and windows looking out on Second Avenue.

Blue Ribbon Sushi ● *Japanese*   26 | 19 | 22 | $64

SoHo | 119 Sullivan St. (bet. Prince & Spring Sts.) | 212-343-0404 | www.blueribbonrestaurants.com

Long a "standard-bearer of cool" in SoHo, this Bromberg brothers Japanese slices "top-flight", "work-of-art" sushi along with a "wonderful array" of cooked items; "proactive service" and "cozy", "denlike" digs offset "pretty-penny" price tags and that "frustrating" no-rez thing.

Blue Ribbon Sushi Bar & Grill ● *Japanese*   25 | 20 | 22 | $63

W 50s | 6 Columbus Hotel | 308 W. 58th St. (bet. 8th & 9th Aves.) | 212-397-0404 | www.blueribbonrestaurants.com

Somewhat "swankier" than its "bohemian kin", this "inviting" Japanese "tucked away" in a Columbus Circle hotel is touted for its "fresh-off-the-boat" sushi and "impeccable" grilled fare; it shares the "mellow" vibe, late-night hours and "steep tabs" of its Downtown siblings.

	FOOD	DECOR	SERVICE	COST

Blue Ribbon Sushi Izakaya ● *Japanese* ▽ 21 | 19 | 19 | $66

LES | Thompson LES Hotel | 187 Orchard St. (bet. Houston & Stanton Sts.) |
212-466-0404 | www.blueribbonrestaurants.com

The Bromberg brothers' take on the traditional izakaya, this Thompson
LES Hotel Japanese offers an extensive menu that "ain't cheap" but includes a "terrific" signature fried chicken plus "delish sushi"; still,
many "go more for the location" and the "cool" feel of its loungey,
dimly lit digs.

Blue Smoke *BBQ* 22 | 18 | 20 | $42

Financial District | 255 Vesey St. (bet. North End Ave. & West St.) |
212-889-2005
Murray Hill | 116 E. 27th St. (bet. Lexington Ave. & Park Ave. S.) |
212-447-7733
Flushing | Citi Field | 126th St. & Roosevelt Ave. (behind the scoreboard) |
Queens
www.bluesmoke.com

"Join the exuberant crowds" relishing "succulent ribs" at Danny
Meyer's "real-deal BBQ" outlets, which "definitely satisfy a meat craving" even if you need "a shower afterward"; the bourbon list and
"super-friendly staff" distract from settings that suggest "child-
friendly" "suburbia" (and Murray Hill's original offers refuge in the
Jazz Standard club downstairs).

Blue Water Grill *Seafood* 24 | 23 | 22 | $58

Union Sq | 31 Union Sq. W. (16th St.) | 212-675-9500 |
www.bluewatergrillnyc.com

"Still a top draw", Steve Hanson's "vibrant" Union Square "institution"
is "tried and true" for "prime seafood" and "personable" service in a
"swanky" repurposed bank building sporting "vaulted ceilings",
"beautiful marble" and "high-energy crowds"; embellished with an
"outdoor terrace" and a "cool" downstairs jazz venue, it's "not inexpensive", but "worth the cost."

Boathouse *American* 18 | 26 | 19 | $54

E 70s | Central Park | Central Park Lake, enter on E. 72nd St. (Park Dr. N.) |
212-517-2233 | www.thecentralparkboathouse.com

It's all about the "unbeatable location" at this lakeside American,
where "the decor is Central Park" and watching the rowboats drift by
"feels like being on vacation"; the menu's "not overly exciting" and the
service just "so-so", but for tourists and natives alike, this "must-have"
NYC experience "sells itself."

Bobby Van's Grill *Steak* 23 | 20 | 22 | $66

W 40s | 120 W. 45th St. (bet. 6th & 7th Aves.) | 212-575-5623
W 50s | 135 W. 50th St. (bet. 6th & 7th Aves.) | 212-957-5050

Bobby Van's Steakhouse *Steak*

E 40s | 230 Park Ave. (46th St.) | 212-867-5490 ⓢ
E 50s | 131 E. 54th St. (bet. Lexington & Park Aves.) | 212-207-8050
Financial District | 25 Broad St. (Exchange Pl.) | 212-344-8463 ⓢ
New York John F. Kennedy Airport | Terminal 8, across from Gate 14 |
JFK Access Rd. | Queens | 718-553-2100
www.bobbyvans.com

This "steady" chainlet "does the trick" for "business" types who "hobnob" at lunch over "solid" steaks from "old-time waiters" amid the

"requisite muscular decor" (including a "subterranean vault" in the FiDi); just "use your expense account" since the "enormous portions" come "with prices to match."

Bobo *French* | 23 | 23 | 21 | $57 |

W Village | 181 W. 10th St. (7th Ave. S.) | 212-488-2626 | www.bobonyc.com

The "ambiance is the selling point" at this "low-lit" West Village townhouse serving "well-prepared" French fare to a "Euro"-heavy following either in an "ornate dining room", outdoor terrace or "more youthful" downstairs bar; it may be a tad "expensive", but service is "friendly" and the vibe "charming."

Bocca *Italian* | 22 | 18 | 21 | $47 |

Flatiron | 39 E. 19th St. (bet. B'way & Park Ave. S.) | 212-387-1200 | www.boccanyc.com

It "feels like Rome" at this "enjoyable" Cacio e Pepe sibling in the Flatiron known for its "expert" Italian cooking, "appealing" modern look and "reasonable" rates; regulars say "pasta is the thing to eat" here, notably its "cool" signature dish tossed tableside in a wheel of pecorino.

Bocca di Bacco *Italian* | 21 | 20 | 19 | $44 |

NEW Chelsea | 169 Ninth Ave. (20th St.) | 714-404-6491 ●
W 40s | 635 Ninth Ave. (bet. 44th & 45th Sts.) | 212-262-2525 ●
W 50s | 828 Ninth Ave. (bet. 54th & 55th Sts.) | 212-265-8828
www.boccadibacconyc.com

Bocca East ● *Italian*

E 70s | 1496 Second Ave. (78th St.) | 212-249-1010 | www.boccadibaccoeast.com

"Old-world Italy" comes to Manhattan via these Italians vending "jazzed-up" standards bolstered by "sure-hit" wines by the glass and "rustic", brick-walled settings; "up-and-down" service strikes off-notes, but given the "decent prices" and "positive energy", most "go home happy."

Bocca Lupo ● *Italian* | 23 | 20 | 21 | $36 |

Cobble Hill | 391 Henry St. (Warren St.) | Brooklyn | 718-243-2522

Cobble Hill denizens tout this "terrific local" enoteca for "seductive" Italian small plates paired with a "great wine list", also via The Boot; the "cozy quarters" are "super kid-friendly" during the first wave but transition to a "busy late-night" scene for singletons.

Bocelli *Italian/Seafood* | 25 | 23 | 24 | $50 |

Grasmere | 1250 Hylan Blvd. (Parkinson Ave.) | Staten Island | 718-420-6150 | www.bocellirest.com

With "delicious" seafood specialties that "aren't lacking in pizzazz", "professional" service and "pretty elegant" "Tuscan" decor, this Grasmere Italian "definitely stands out" among its Staten Island peers; despite city-style pricing, "reservations are a must" on weekends.

Bodrum *Mediterranean/Turkish* | 21 | 14 | 19 | $37 |

W 80s | 584 Amsterdam Ave. (bet. 88th & 89th Sts.) | 212-799-2806 | www.bodrumnyc.com

"Small and cozy", this UWS "neighborhood" Med is the "real deal" for "inexpensive" dining on "stellar" Turkish meze and "tasty thin-crust pizza"; though service is "speedy", it's often "crowded and cramped", so insiders flee to the "outside tables."

	FOOD	DECOR	SERVICE	COST

Bogota Latin Bistro *Pan-Latin*   24 | 20 | 23 | $30

Park Slope | 141 Fifth Ave. (St. Johns Pl.) | Brooklyn | 718-230-3805 | www.bogotabistro.com

"It's always a party" at this "hyper-popular" Park Slope Pan-Latin, where the "awesome", "Colombian-style" eats and "exotic drinks" whisk you "to Bogota"; "decent prices" and an "incredible staff" help keep the "good times" and "noise level" going strong.

Bohemian ●🅼 *Japanese*   25 | 25 | 25 | $73

NoHo | 57 Great Jones St. (bet. Bowery & Lafayette St.)

"You'll need a reservation" and a referral (there's "no listed phone number") to access this "exclusive" NoHo Japanese hidden "behind a butcher shop", where the "exceptional" food and cocktails are presented by "truly wonderful people"; an "intimate", denlike room furnished with "low couches" conduces conversation, and while prices run "steep", it'll leave a "lasting memory."

Bo-Ky 🅿 *Noodle Shop*   22 | 7 | 13 | $15

Chinatown | 80 Bayard St. (bet. Mott & Mulberry Sts.) | 212-406-2292
Little Italy | 216 Grand St. (Elizabeth St.) | 212-219-9228

One of the few "good things about jury duty" is the chance to lunch at these Chinatown–Little Italy noodle shops churning out "authentic" Chinese and Vietnamese soups for ultra-"cheap" coin; "dreary" decor, "busy" atmospherics and "poor" (albeit "quick") service come with the territory.

Bombay Palace ● *Indian*   20 | 18 | 19 | $42

W 50s | 30 W. 52nd St. (bet. 5th & 6th Aves.) | 212-541-7777 | www.bombay-palace.com

On the Midtown scene since 1979, this "spacious" Indian remains a "solid standby" for all the "standards"; maybe the once-"sumptuous" surroundings are getting "a little tired", but no one's weary of its "good-value" $17 lunch buffet.

Bombay Talkie *Indian*   20 | 17 | 17 | $39

Chelsea | 189 Ninth Ave. (bet. 21st & 22nd Sts.) | 212-242-1900 | www.bombaytalkie.com

"Change-of-pace" seekers tout this "not-typical" Chelsea Indian for its "clever" takes on "less commonly seen" street food items; a "fun vibe" and semi-"stylish" digs decorated with "Bollywood" murals compensate for the slightly "upscale" pricing.

BonChon *Chicken*   21 | 13 | 15 | $22

E 50s | 957 Second Ave. (bet. 50th & 51st Sts.) | 212-308-8810
Garment District | 207 W. 38th St. (bet. 7th & 8th Aves.) | 212-221-3339
Murray Hill | 325 Fifth Ave. (bet. 32nd & 33rd Sts.) | 212-686-8282 ●
Bayside | 45-37 Bell Blvd. (bet. 45th Dr. & 45th Rd.) | Queens | 718-225-1010 ●
www.bonchon.com

"Habit-forming" is the verdict on the "out-of-sight" Korean fried chicken with "crispy, parchmentlike skin" vended at this international chain; since the birds are cooked to order, expect "forever" waits, not to mention "slipshod" service, "no decor" and just-"decent" prices.

	FOOD	DECOR	SERVICE	COST

Bond 45 ◐ *Italian/Steak* — 19 | 18 | 19 | $52

W 40s | 154 W. 45th St. (bet. 6th & 7th Aves.) | 212-869-4545 |
www.bond45.com

Shelly Fireman's "cavernous", "vibrant" trattoria in Times Square's
old Bond clothing store presents a "straight-up", "something-for-
everybody" Italian steakhouse menu in a "well-decorated barn" of a
setting; "service with alacrity" suits theatergoers, though "loud"
acoustics and kinda "high" prices are less well received.

Bond St ◐ *Japanese* — 25 | 23 | 22 | $69

NoHo | 6 Bond St. (bet. B'way & Lafayette St.) | 212-777-2500 |
www.bondstrestaurant.com

"They've still got it" at this NoHo Japanese "knockout", where the "work-
of-art" sushi and "swanky" space with a "cool" downstairs lounge deliver
both "style and substance"; "beautiful" people out "to see and be seen"
readily bond with the "trendy vibe", less so with the "expensive" tabs.

Bonnie's Grill *Burgers* — 22 | 14 | 19 | $22

Park Slope | 278 Fifth Ave. (bet. 1st St. & Garfield Pl.) | Brooklyn |
718-369-9527 | www.bonniesgrill.com

Park Slopers refuel at this "short-order joint" slinging "damn good
burgers" and other basics in "classic diner" digs; it's "fun sitting at the
counter" and the grub's "well priced", but since the dimensions are
"slim", "good luck getting a seat on the weekend."

Boqueria *Spanish* — 23 | 19 | 20 | $47

Flatiron | 53 W. 19th St. (bet. 5th & 6th Aves.) | 212-255-4160
SoHo | 171 Spring St. (bet. Thompson St. & W. B'way) | 212-343-4255
www.boquerianyc.com

"Graze your way" through "top-class tapas" at these "happening"
Spaniards bringing a "transported-to-Barcelona" feel to the Flatiron
and SoHo; a "competent" crew navigates the "no-room-to-spare" settings and "well-priced" wines offset tabs that "add up pretty quickly",
but the no-rez rule results in "discouraging" waits.

Bottega *Italian* — ▽ 21 | 19 | 22 | $59

E 70s | 1331 Second Ave. (bet. 70th & 71st Sts.) | 212-288-5282

Not unlike "so many Italian places in the neighborhood", this UES trattoria turns out "accessible" staples from The Boot in "pleasant" confines;
still, its "large, comfortable" digs with a "busy bar" and "terrific outdoor"
seating, not to mention the "friendliest staff", help set it apart.

Bottega Del Vino *Italian* — 22 | 20 | 21 | $63

E 50s | 7 E. 59th St. (bet. 5th & Madison Aves.) | 212-223-2724 |
www.bottegadelvinonyc.com

"Situated near everything" – or at least Bergdorf's, the Plaza and the
Apple Store – this "relaxed" Midtown "replica of the Venice original"
dispenses "tasty" Italiana backed by an "immense" wine list; buoyant
staffers maintain the "happy mood", at least until the bill arrives.

Bottino *Italian* — 21 | 20 | 19 | $47

Chelsea | 246 10th Ave. (bet. 24th & 25th Sts.) | 212-206-6766 |
www.bottinonyc.com

Convenient to West Chelsea's "gallery district" and the High Line, this
"all-around pleasant" Tuscan "pioneer" delivers "solid" meals at

"moderate-to-a-bit-expensive" prices; the "unhurried" pace suits its "arty" constituents, though the "charming", "spacious" garden is bound to please everyone.

Bouchon Bakery *American/French* | 24 | 17 | 19 | $27 |

W 40s | 1 Rockefeller Plaza (48th St., bet. 5th & 6th Aves.) | 212-782-3890
W 60s | Time Warner Ctr. | 10 Columbus Circle, 3rd fl. (60th St. at B'way) | 212-823-9366
www.bouchonbakery.com

"Thomas Keller bestows" a "degree of quality that's a real treat" at these "casual" crosstown cafes/patisseries supplying "phenomenal" pastries, sandwiches and other "fast bites"; Rock Center's site "across from the *Today Show*" is favored for takeout, though on Columbus Circle "shoppers" can snare tables with "views of Central Park."

Boukiés ● *Greek* | ▽ 23 | 20 | 21 | $50 |

E Village | 29 E. Second St. (2nd Ave.) | 212-777-2502 | www.boukiesrestaurant.com

Younger "sister to Pylos", this "low-key" East Villager is making its name with "delightful" Greek meze from "servers who are good guides" for neophytes; add an "appealing" "open space" and "affordable" tabs, and it's "a find in the neighborhood"; P.S. the "prix fixe dinner is a steal."

Bouley Ⓩ *French* | 29 | 27 | 28 | $116 |

TriBeCa | 163 Duane St. (bet. Hudson St. & W. B'way) | 212-964-2525 | www.davidbouley.com

"Engaging all the senses", David Bouley's TriBeCa "masterpiece" presents "superb", "French-decadence-at-its-best" cuisine, "consistently superior" service and a "beautiful", "formal" (jackets required) setting that add up to a "wonderful overall experience"; it's "among NYC's true elite", with prices to match, but when you seek an "unforgettable" repast, it's "hard to beat"; P.S. the $55 lunch prix fixe is a "bargain."

Boulud Sud *Mediterranean* | 25 | 23 | 24 | $75 |

W 60s | One Lincoln Plaza | 20 W. 64th St. (bet. B'way & CPW) | 212-595-1313 | www.danielnyc.com

Whether or not you're "hitting Lincoln Center", Daniel Boulud's "civilized" "masterpiece" adjacent to Bar Boulud is "prized" for "sumptuous" "twists on Mediterranean cuisine" and "deft" service in "a bright, sophisticated" room; for its "well-heeled" habitués, the "pristine" performance is "completely worth the significant tab."

Bowery Diner ● *Diner* | 18 | 17 | 17 | $29 |

LES | 241 Bowery (Prince St.) | 212-388-0052 | www.bowerydiner.com
Parked next to the New Museum, this all-day Lower Eastsider conjures up "nostalgia" with "diner standards" dispensed in faux vintage digs equipped with an old-fashioned soda fountain counter; critics contend the chow is "just ok" and the prices "far from retro."

Braai ●Ⓜ *S African* | 20 | 19 | 20 | $40 |

W 50s | 329 W. 51st St. (bet. 8th & 9th Aves.) | 212-315-3315 | www.braainyc.com

Diners with a "taste for adventure" mingle with "homesick expats" at this "different" Hell's Kitchen outpost specializing in South African barbecue; the "flavorful", "unique" eats (think ostrich and venison) arrive in a "hut"-like, "thatched-roof" setting that adds to the "novelty."

Brasserie *French* — 22 | 21 | 21 | $53

E 50s | Seagram Bldg. | 100 E. 53rd St. (bet. Lexington & Park Aves.) | 212-751-4840 | www.patinagroup.com
Descending its "sleek catwalk" entrance makes fans feel "cosmopolitan" at this "ultracool" brasserie in the Seagram Building, a "longtime favorite" for "top-notch", all-day French dining; "high" prices and a "cacophonous" racket are counterbalanced by "pro" service and "streamlined", "spaceship" decor.

Brasserie Cognac ● *French* — 19 | 19 | 18 | $48

W 50s | 1740 Broadway (55th St.) | 212-757-3600 | www.cognacrestaurant.com
NEW Brasserie Cognac East *French*
E 70s | 963 Lexington Ave. (70th St.) | 212-249-5100 | www.cognaceast.com
"Homesick Parisians" feel at home at this "proper" Midtown brasserie and its new East 70s offshoot, where "simple, tasty" standards come at relatively "gentle" prices; the West 50s original is "convenient to Carnegie Hall" and City Center, but both locations are deemed "attractive" enough for a "romantic" tête-à-tête.

Brasserie 8½ *French* — 22 | 23 | 22 | $61

W 50s | 9 W. 57th St. (bet. 5th & 6th Aves.) | 212-829-0812 | www.patinagroup.com
"Glamorous" is the word for this Midtown brasserie accessed via a "Gloria Swanson"-style "grand stairway", where the equally "spiffy" French fare is served in a room lined with artwork by "Matisse and Leger"; it's "sedate" enough for "conversation without shouting", though very "active at the bar" after work.

Brasserie Ruhlmann *French* — 19 | 20 | 19 | $57

W 50s | 45 Rockefeller Plaza (bet. 50th & 51st Sts.) | 212-974-2020 | www.brasserieruhlmann.com
"Hobnob with the NBC crowd" and others "happily expensing their meals" at Laurent Tourondel's "heart-of-Rock-Center" brasserie providing a "sumptuous art deco" setting for "good" (if "not spectacular") French cooking; the "fascinating people-watching" from its patio may be the most "fun" here.

Bread ● *Sandwiches* — 21 | 18 | 18 | $31

NoLita | 20 Spring St. (bet. Elizabeth & Mott Sts.) | 212-334-1015
There's "much more than bread" on offer at this "low-key" NoLita nook dishing up "affordable" Italiana highlighted by "satisfying" panini and "wonderful tomato soup"; service and "elbow room" may be in short supply, but its "cool hipster" fan base doesn't seem to mind.

Breeze *French/Thai* — 21 | 15 | 18 | $28

W 40s | 661 Ninth Ave. (bet. 45th & 46th Sts.) | 212-262-7777 | www.breezenyc.com
"Bright-orange decor" draws attention to this "unique" Hell's Kitchen venue that plies "serious" Thai-French fusion vittles backed by "fruity drinks" in "long, narrow" digs; "rapid" service and "too-good-to-be-true" pricing make it a "great first act" pre-theater.

	FOOD	DECOR	SERVICE	COST

Brennan & Carr ●⇗ *Sandwiches*
22 | **11** | **17** | **$18**

Sheepshead Bay | 3432 Nostrand Ave. (Ave. U) | Brooklyn | 718-646-9559

More than 75 years old, this cash-only Sheepshead Bay "tradition" still "rocks" thanks to "outrageous" double-dipped roast beef sandwiches "drowned in au jus"; it's something of a "dive" with "table-mat menus", but enthusiasts of "old-fashioned goodness" keep returning "with the new generation in tow."

The Breslin ● *British*
23 | **21** | **18** | **$48**

Chelsea | Ace Hotel | 16 W. 29th St. (bet. B'way & 5th Ave.) | 212-679-1939 | www.thebreslin.com

A "carnivore's heaven", April Bloomfield and Ken Friedman's Ace Hotel "hipster'" magnet features "bold" British fare (don't miss the "to-die-for" lamb burger) dispensed in a dark, "noisy" pub setting; "fashionable" cachet means it's usually "pack to the gills", and no reservations means it's "nigh impossible to get a table" without a wait.

Brgr *Burgers*
19 | **14** | **15** | **$17**

Chelsea | 287 Seventh Ave. (bet. 26th & 27th Sts.) | 212-488-7500
E 60s | 1026 Third Ave. (bet. 60th & 61st Sts.) | 212-588-0080
www.brgr.com

"Brgr lvrs" plug these "highbrow fast-food" places for their "solid" "grass-fed beef" patties "made to order" with "neat toppings" and augmented with "excellent" shakes; however, critics find "only average" goods that "can be pricey" for their "abbreviated" size.

Bricco *Italian*
21 | **18** | **21** | **$45**

W 50s | 304 W. 56th St. (bet. 8th & 9th Aves.) | 212-245-7160 | www.bricconyc.com

This Hell's Kitchen Italian hideaway is a "steady" source of "well-prepared" pasta and wood-oven pizza delivered by the "nicest staff"; "reasonable rates" and "warm" atmospherics (check out the lipsticked kisses on the ceiling) buttress its "reliable" rep.

Brick Cafe *French/Italian*
21 | **20** | **21** | **$34**

Astoria | 30-95 33rd St. (31st Ave.) | Queens | 718-267-2735 | www.brickcafe.com

Astorians assemble at this "neighborhood standby" for "tasty" French-Italian eats served in rustic digs so atmospheric it's "hard to believe you're in Queens"; "reasonable" rates, weekly live music and "can't-be-beat" alfresco tables are further reasons why it's "always packed."

Brick Lane Curry House *Indian*
21 | **15** | **19** | **$29**

E 50s | 235 E. 53rd St. (bet. 2nd & 3rd Aves.) | 212-339-8353 | www.bricklanetoo.com
E 90s | 1664 Third Ave. (bet. 93rd & 94th Sts.) | 646-998-4440 | www.bricklanecurryhouse.com
E Village | 306-308 E. Sixth St. (bet. 1st & 2nd Aves.) | 212-979-2900 | www.bricklanecurryhouse.com

There's "no need to go to London – let alone India" – thanks to this curry-savvy East Side mini-chain purveying "real-deal" dishes with heat levels ranging from "mild to crazy hot" (the "fiery phaal" requires "extra napkins to wipe away the sweat and tears"); like the decor, the tabs are distinctly "low budget."

	FOOD	DECOR	SERVICE	COST

Brio *Italian* | 20 | 17 | 18 | $45

E 60s | 137 E. 61st St. (Lexington Ave.) | 212-980-2300
Flatiron | 920 Broadway (21st St.) | 212-673-2121
www.brionyc.com

These "bustling" Italians in the Flatiron and near Bloomie's are "handy" options for "basic" refueling on "relatively inexpensive" pastas and pizzas; "efficient" service compensates for "dark", "lacking" settings, but then again the dining is "grown-up" and "civilized."

NEW BrisketTown *BBQ* | ▽ 25 | 16 | 20 | $26

Williamsburg | 359 Bedford Ave. (bet. S. 4th & 5th Sts.) | Brooklyn | 718-701-8909 | www.delaneybbq.com

Young pitmaster Daniel Delaney has a hit on his hands with this new Williamsburg joint smoking "melt-in-your-mouth" BBQ – notably "unequaled" brisket – plus "good breakfast tacos"; a "friendly" counter crew and casual hipster-roadhouse digs are part of the package – just know it "can be crazy" at prime times, and when they run out of meat, it's closing time.

Brooklyn Farmacy *Ice Cream* | ▽ 23 | 24 | 21 | $16

Carroll Gardens | 513 Henry St. (Sackett St.) | Brooklyn | 718-522-6260 | www.brooklynfarmacy.blogspot.com

"Nostalgia" and seasonal, locally sourced ice cream add up to "a lot of fun" at this Carroll Gardens homage to "old-school soda shops", where the sundaes, egg creams and such – plus "simple, satisfying" diner staples – are "expertly" dispensed by "friendly" staffers and "hit the spot" for "adults and kids" alike; housed in a "beautiful" restored pharmacy, it's "retro" to the core.

Brooklyn Fish Camp ⊠ *Seafood* | 22 | 16 | 19 | $42

Park Slope | 162 Fifth Ave. (Degraw St.) | Brooklyn | 718-783-3264 | www.brooklynfishcamp.com

"Peerless freshness" makes for happy campers at this "laid-back" Park Slope sequel to Mary's Fish Camp that "hits the mark" with "robust" seafood and "spot-on" lobster rolls; the tabs may be "pricey" considering its "clam-shack", "wine-in-a-juice-glass" approach, but that backyard garden sure is "fantastic."

Brother Jimmy's BBQ *BBQ* | 17 | 13 | 16 | $28

E 70s | 1485 Second Ave. (bet. 77th & 78th Sts.) | 212-288-0999 ☽
Garment District | 416 Eighth Ave. (31st St.) | 212-967-7603
Gramercy | 116 E. 16th St. (bet. Irving Pl. & Union Sq. E.) | 212-673-6465 ☽
Murray Hill | 181 Lexington Ave. (31st St.) | 212-779-7427 ☽
W 80s | 428 Amsterdam Ave. (bet. 80th & 81st Sts.) | 212-501-7515 ☽
NEW Brother Jimmy's BBQ To Go *BBQ*
Meatpacking | 521 West St. (bet. Gansevoort & Horatio Sts.) | www.brotherjimmys.com

"Totally fratty" throngs pile into this "trashy" BBQ chainlet for "filling" snoutfuls of "edible" grub served in "redneck Riviera" settings; the "weak service", "franchise feel" and "stale beer smell" can detract, but at least the pricing's "decent" for a hoot and a howl; P.S. the West Village satellite is for takeout or delivery only.

	FOOD	DECOR	SERVICE	COST

Brushstroke ●⊠ *Japanese* | 26 | 25 | 26 | $133 |

TriBeCa | 30 Hudson St. (Duane St.) | 212-791-3771

Ichimura at Brushstroke ⊠ *Japanese*

TriBeCa | Brushstroke | 30 Hudson St. (Duane St.) | 212-513-7141
www.davidbouley.com

A "joint venture" between David Bouley and Osaka's Tsuji Culinary Institute deemed a "dream come true", this "transporting" TriBeCa Japanese presents "ethereal" kaiseki menus and "extraordinary" sushi enhanced by the "elegant service" and "beautiful, austere" setting (and matched with a "high-rolling" price tag); at the side-pocket Ichimura, the namesake "master" chef delivers "traditional omakase at its best" (menus start at $160).

Bryant Park Grill/Cafe *American* | 19 | 22 | 19 | $49 |

W 40s | 25 W. 40th St. (bet. 5th & 6th Aves.) | 212-840-6500 | www.arkrestaurants.com

"Primo" Bryant Park scenery is the main "selling point" of this American pair, where "location, location, location" trumps the "pricey" tabs and rather "average" food and service; the Grill's the more "handsome" of the pair with both indoor and outdoor seats, while the alfresco-only Cafe is more of a "tourist magnet."

B. Smith's *Southern* | 19 | 19 | 20 | $48 |

W 40s | 320 W. 46th St. (bet. 8th & 9th Aves.) | 212-315-1100 | www.bsmith.com

For a "change of pace" on Restaurant Row, check out this "slick" Southern comfort-food practitioner from TV personality Barbara Smith; maybe it's "not what it used to be" and "pricier than it should be", but a "great location" for showgoers and a "decent" overall performance keep it humming.

Bubby's ● *American* | 20 | 16 | 17 | $33 |

TriBeCa | 120 Hudson St. (N. Moore St.) | 212-219-0666 | www.bubbys.com

"Wholesome" breakfast fare served 24/7 in "glorified diner" digs sums up the scene at this "unfussy" TriBeCa bastion of American "home cooking", best known for its "weekend brunch crunch", replete with "crazy lines", "slow service" and "ill-behaved" kids; P.S. a Meatpacking offshoot is in the works.

Buddakan ● *Asian* | 25 | 27 | 22 | $67 |

Chelsea | 75 Ninth Ave. (bet. 15th & 16th Sts.) | 212-989-6699 | www.buddakannyc.com

"Get ready for sensory overload" at Stephen Starr's "dynamic" Chelsea "bacchanal", which matches a "knockout" backdrop with "memorable" Asian dishes served in "style" to "trendy" types "hell-bent on" creating a "scene" that's "deafening" "but so vibrant you won't care"; while "on the expensive side", it's "a gas."

Buddha Bodai *Chinese/Kosher* | ▽ 23 | 12 | 19 | $23 |

Chinatown | 5 Mott St. (Worth St.) | 212-566-8388 | www.chinatownvegetarian.com

"It may be fake meat", but the "sheer variety" and "excellent quality" of the "inventive" kosher vegetarian options "blow your mind" at this Chinatown dim sum dojo; an "eclectic" following also feels blessed that it's so "reasonably priced."

	FOOD	DECOR	SERVICE	COST

Buenos Aires ❶ *Argentinean/Steak* | 24 | 15 | 21 | $45 |

E Village | 513 E. Sixth St. (bet. Aves. A & B) | 212-228-2775 |
www.buenosairesnyc.com

Beef eaters convene at this East Village Argentine steakhouse for
"mouthwatering", chimichurri-slathered chops that you can "cut with
a fork" and wash down with a "great selection of Malbecs"; forget the
"don't-judge-a-book-by-its-cover" decor: "super" service and "gentle"
tabs make this often-crowded spot a "keeper."

Bukhara Grill *Indian* | 21 | 15 | 19 | $40 |

E 40s | 217 E. 49th St. (bet. 2nd & 3rd Aves.) | 212-888-2839 |
www.bukharany.com

They "spice it up" at this "authentic" North Indian near the U.N.,
where the cooking's "tasty" and the service "courteous"; if it seems a
bit "pricey" given the "dowdy" digs, at least the $17 lunch buffet is
a "terrific bargain."

Bull & Bear ❶ *Steak* | 22 | 23 | 22 | $81 |

E 40s | Waldorf-Astoria | 540 Lexington Ave. (bet. 49th & 50th Sts.) |
212-872-1275 | www.bullandbearsteakhouse.com

"Time travel" to *Mad Men* days at this circa-1960 Waldorf-Astoria
steakhouse where "professional" servers ply *Wall Street Journal* sub-
scribers with "superb" cuts ("strong" cocktails gratify those on a "liq-
uid diet"); it's a NYC "tradition", assuming one can "bear what they
charge" for those bulls.

NEW Bunker Vietnamese Ⓜ *Vietnamese* | - | - | - | I |
(aka Bún-Ker)

Ridgewood | 46-63 Metropolitan Ave. (Woodward Ave.) | Queens |
718-386-4282 | bunkervietnamese.com

Ridgewood's industrial fringe is the unexpected home of this Vietnamese
arrival from an Eleven Madison Park alum; it puts forth a seasonal
lineup of street-food favorites made from top-quality ingredients, but
the prices are more in line with the nothing-fancy, thatch-lined room;
P.S. it's BYO until the beer and wine license comes through.

Burger Bistro *Burgers* | 22 | 17 | 20 | $21 |

NEW E 80s | 1663 First Ave. (bet. 86th & 87th Sts.) | 646-368-1134
Bay Ridge | 7217 Third Ave. (bet. 72nd & 73rd Sts.) | Brooklyn |
718-833-5833
Park Slope | 177 Fifth Ave. (bet. Berkeley & Lincoln Pls.) | Brooklyn |
718-398-9800
www.theburgerbistro.com

"So many options to choose from" is the hallmark of this born-in-
Brooklyn "build-your-own-burger" chainlet offering "perfectly cooked"
patties accessorized with "every topping imaginable"; "friendly" service and "cute", casual quarters help keep the trade brisk.

Burger Joint *Burgers* | 24 | 13 | 14 | $17 |

NEW G Village | 33 W. Eighth St. (MacDougal St.) | 212-432-1400
W 50s | Le Parker Meridien | 119 W. 56th St. (bet. 6th & 7th Aves.) |
212-708-7414 ❶⇄
www.burgerjointny.com

Probably NYC's "worst-kept secret", this burger "speakeasy" hidden
behind a "giant curtain" in the Parker Meridien draws "crazy lines" for

its "damn fine" patties – voted "tops" in NYC – offered in "tacky" digs with "lacking service" quite at odds with its "luxurious" hotel setting; for those seeking elbow room there's now a roomier Village outpost, which also pours liquor.

Butcher Bar *BBQ*

▽ 24 | 22 | 22 | $25

Astoria | 37-08 30th Ave. (bet. 37th & 38th Sts.) | Queens | 718-606-8140 | www.butcherbar.com

"When you just crave some smoky meat", this Astoria BBQ outlet (and organic butcher shop) ups the ante with "high-quality", "grass-fed" beef that yields "damn good dry rub" coupled with down-home sides; an "amazing backyard" boosts both the limited space and the folksy feel.

NEW Butcher's Daughter *Vegetarian*

- | - | - | M

NoLita | 19 Kenmare St. (Elizabeth St.) | 212-219-3434

NoLita is home to this all-day vegetarian cafe/juice bar from a Pulqueria alum that's drawing crowds with a fancy mix of pricey soups, sandwiches and salads; the bleached-wood, white-tiled space exudes sunny vibes, and it's in the process of expanding into an adjacent storefront.

Butter ☒ *American*

23 | 24 | 21 | $62

E Village | 415 Lafayette St. (bet. Astor Pl. & 4th St.) | 212-253-2828 | www.butterrestaurant.com

A "beautiful" setting, "creative" cookery and "slinky" staffers lend "sophistication" to this "upscale" New American duplex near the Public Theater, overseen by chef Alex Guarnaschelli; the "dramatic", birch-forest decor on the ground floor gives way to a "dark", "sceney" cellar that's a magnet for "*Gossip Girl*" types; P.S. an Uptown outpost is in the works at 70 West 45th Street.

NEW The Butterfly ❷ *American*

- | - | - | M

TriBeCa | 225 W. Broadway (bet. Franklin & White Sts.) | 646-692-4943 | www.thebutterflynyc.com

At this TriBeCa ode to the '50s, chef Michael White eschews pasta in favor of nostalgic American comfort fare – think shrimp cocktail, relish plates, patty melts – washed down with the real stars of the show, re-jiggered retro cocktails via mixologist Eben Freeman; the functional midcentury-modern design is a match for the sensibly modest tabs.

Buttermilk Channel *American*

25 | 21 | 22 | $41

Carroll Gardens | 524 Court St. (Huntington St.) | Brooklyn | 718-852-8490 | www.buttermilkchannelnyc.com

"Welcoming" "neighborhood vibes" and "terrific" "comfort food with a twist" make this "quaint" Carroll Gardens New American an "absolute fave", especially for brunch; since reservations aren't accepted, the peak-time waits can be "excruciating" – but "well worth it" to most.

Buvette ❷ *French*

24 | 22 | 21 | $46

W Village | 42 Grove St. (bet. Bedford & Bleecker Sts.) | 212-255-3590 | www.ilovebuvette.com

"Ooh-la-la!", this West Village "godsend" "oozes charm" thanks to chef-owner Jody Williams' "glorious" French 'gastrotheque' small-plate fare served in "cute", "pint-size" quarters by an "easygoing" crew; the "upbeat" vibe includes "chairs bumping" at peak hours, but in warm weather there's always the "lovely" (but equally "tiny") back garden.

	FOOD	DECOR	SERVICE	COST

BXL Café ◕ *Belgian* | 19 | 13 | 18 | $34 |
W 40s | 125 W. 43rd St. (bet. 6th & 7th Aves.) | 212-768-0200
BXL East ◕ *Belgian*
E 50s | 210 E. 51st St. (bet. 2nd & 3rd Aves.) | 212-888-7782
BXL Zoute ◕ *Belgian*
NEW Flatiron | 50 W. 22nd St. (bet. 5th & 6th Aves.) | 646-692-9282
www.bxlcafe.com

"Moules frites done right" chased with "awesome beers" explain the "crush" at these "friendly" Belgian pubs in Midtown; they're "nothing fancy" and can be "way too noisy" at prime times, but the "price is right", particularly the "endless mussel" special on Sunday and Monday nights.

Byblos *Lebanese* | ▽ 19 | 16 | 20 | $43 |
Murray Hill | 80 Madison Ave. (bet. 28th & 29th Sts.) | 212-687-0808 | www.byblosny.com

After a two-year hiatus, this "endearing" longtime family-owned Murray Hill Lebanese is back in "warm" new Madison Avenue digs where "old-world values reign"; happily, the same "fresh, authentic", "reasonably priced" charcoal-grilled meats and "fabulous" weekend music and belly dancing are on offer.

Cabana *Nuevo Latino* | 22 | 19 | 19 | $37 |
E 60s | 1022 Third Ave. (bet. 60th & 61st Sts.) | 212-980-5678 ◕
Seaport | Pier 17 | 89 South St. (bet. Beekman & John Sts.) | 212-406-1155
Forest Hills | 107-10 70th Rd. (bet. Austin St. & Queens Blvd.) | Queens | 718-263-3600 ◕
www.cabanarestaurant.com

It "always feels like a party" at these "casual", "colorful" Nuevo Latinos where "nicely spiced" chow and "rocket-fuel" mojitos make for a "happening" vibe; the "noise factor" and "erratic" service may be sore points, but tabs are "reasonable" and the Seaport outlet sports "gorgeous" water views.

Cacio e Pepe *Italian* | 20 | 15 | 18 | $42 |
E Village | 182 Second Ave. (bet. 11th & 12th Sts.) | 212-505-5931 | www.cacioepepe.com

The "titular" signature pasta served in a "massive round" of pecorino is the star of the "traditional Roman" menu at this "sweet" East Village Italian; "pleasant" service and "fair prices" keep things "bustling", so regulars take "respite" in the "pretty" back garden.

Cafe Asean ⊄ *SE Asian* | 22 | 14 | 19 | $29 |
W Village | 117 W. 10th St. (bet. Greenwich & 6th Aves.) | 212-633-0348 | www.cafeasean.com

"Modest" (but "cute") looks belie the "well-crafted" Southeast Asian lineup purveyed at this "tiny" West Villager where the "inexpensive", cash-only menu "takes you further East with every bite"; an "easy vibe", "accommodating" service and a "serene" garden round out this "offbeat find."

Café Boulud *French* | 27 | 24 | 26 | $82 |
E 70s | Surrey Hotel | 20 E. 76th St. (bet. 5th & Madison Aves.) | 212-772-2600 | www.danielnyc.com

Daniel Boulud's "mastery shows through" at this Upper East Side "oasis" of "refinement", where "perfectionist chef" Gavin Kaysen wows a "smartly dressed", "blue-blood" crowd with "exquisite French cuisine" set down by "discreet" servers who "make you feel special"; the "soothing" atmosphere is "perfect for conversation" so long as "you can afford the tab" – for tighter budgets, the "prix fixe lunch is a terrific bargain."

Cafe Centro 🖼 *French/Mediterranean*   21 | 19 | 20 | $50
E 40s | MetLife Bldg. | 200 Park Ave. (45th St.) | 212-818-1222 | www.patinagroup.com
There's always a "big hubbub" at lunchtime at this "steady" Grand Central–area magnet for "networking" suits who dig the "satisfying" French-Med cooking, "prompt" service and "modern", patio-equipped setting; it's "quieter" at dinner, despite a weeknight $35 prix fixe "deal."

Cafe China *Chinese*   24 | 18 | 18 | $35
Murray Hill | 13 E. 37th St. (bet. 5th & Madison Aves.) | 212-213-2810 | www.cafechinanyc.com
"You don't need to eat under fluorescent lights" to enjoy "authentically spicy Sichuan" fare thanks to this "inviting" Murray Hill Chinese, which offers "outstanding" specialties in the guise of a "circa-1930 Shanghai teahouse"; "moderate" prices make some amends for "spotty service."

Cafe Cluny ❶ *American/French*   22 | 21 | 20 | $46
W Village | 284 W. 12th St. (W. 4th St.) | 212-255-6900 | www.cafecluny.com
A "wonderful vibe" has evolved at this "cute" West Village bistro, a once-"trendy" joint that's now a bona fide "neighborhood favorite" thanks to "terrific" Franco-American cooking served in a "charming", "sun-filled" space; since the weekend brunch can be a "free-for-all", regulars say "arrive early."

Cafe Dada *French/Hungarian*   ▽ 22 | 18 | 22 | $25
Park Slope | 57 Seventh Ave. (Lincoln Pl.) | Brooklyn | 718-622-2800 | www.cafedadany.com
This "warm, inviting" French-Hungarian arrival to Park Slope's former Ozzie's space (still sporting those "old-timey drugstore cabinets") has been embraced as a "comfortable neighborhood stop" that's one part bistro, one part coffeehouse; the affordable offerings include "wonderful sandwiches, salads and pastries" served by an "attentive" team.

Café d'Alsace *French*   21 | 18 | 18 | $46
E 80s | 1695 Second Ave. (88th St.) | 212-722-5133 | www.cafedalsace.com
Particularly "great on a cold winter day", this "Euro-authentic" Yorkville brasserie rolls out "hearty" Alsatian eats backed by an "endless" beer list curated by a suds sommelier; given the "on-top-of-each-other" tables and "intense" prime-time "clamor", the sidewalk seats are "a plus."

Cafe Du Soleil *French/Mediterranean*   19 | 16 | 17 | $38
W 100s | 2723 Broadway (104th St.) | 212-316-5000 | www.cafedusoleilny.com
"Simple but tasty" French-Med staples priced for "value" make this "upbeat" Columbia-area entry a "popular neighborhood" fallback, though service skews "spotty"; when the "bistro-ish" interior gets too "cramped and loud", insiders flee to the "wonderful" sidewalk terrace.

	FOOD	DECOR	SERVICE	COST

Cafe Espanol ● *Spanish*   `20` `16` `20` `$38`
G Village | 172 Bleecker St. (Sullivan St.) | 212-505-0657 |
www.cafeespanol.com
W Village | 78 Carmine St. (7th Ave. S.) | 212-675-3312 |
www.cafeespanolny.com
When you "don't want to spend much" on "traditional" Spanish fare,
these separately owned, "been-there-forever" Villagers provide "satisfying" basics doled out in "generous", "paella-for-days" portions; sure, the
space is "tight" and "hokey", but the sangria "always calls you back."

Cafe Fiorello ● *Italian*   `20` `18` `19` `$52`
W 60s | 1900 Broadway (63rd St.) | 212-595-5330 | www.cafefiorello.com
Lincoln Center ticket-holders like this "long-standing" Italian "work-
horse" for "dependable" classics including "scrumptious" pizza and a
"surefire" antipasti bar; insiders "go after curtain time" and request
"outside tables" to sidestep the "cheek-by-jowl seating", "rushed service" and overall "hullabaloo."

Café Frida   *Mexican*   `21` `18` `19` `$37`
W 70s | 368 Columbus Ave. (bet. 77th & 78th Sts.) | 212-712-2929
W 90s | 768 Amsterdam Ave. (bet. 97th & 98th Sts.) | 212-749-2929
www.cafefrida.com
"Young" folks consider these "uncomplicated" UWS Mexicans "well
worth the money" for "flavorful", "hearty" dining lubricated with
"killer margaritas" (the *mañana* service is another story); the
Amsterdam Avenue site adds a rear garden "oasis" to the incentives.

Café Gitane ● *French/Moroccan*   `21` `19` `17` `$31`
NoLita | 242 Mott St. (Prince St.) | 212-334-9552 ⊟
W Village | Jane Hotel | 113 Jane St. (bet. Washington & West Sts.) |
212-255-4113
www.cafegitanenyc.com
The food's a match for the "trendy vibe" at these "fashionable" French-
Moroccan lairs where "affordable" bites like "fabulous" couscous are
dispensed by a "gorgeous" staff; the NoLita original is on the "tight"
side, but the more spread-out Jane Hotel spin-off is just as "energetic."

Café Habana ● *Cuban/Mexican*   `23` `17` `17` `$21`
NoLita | 17 Prince St. (Elizabeth St.) | 212-625-2001 | www.cafehabana.com
Habana Outpost ●⊟ *Cuban/Mexican*
Fort Greene | 757 Fulton St. (Portland Ave.) | Brooklyn | 718-858-9500 |
www.habanaoutpost.com
Don't miss the "killer grilled corn" and other "delicious" Mexican-
Cuban bites at these "lovable" "hipster paradises"; "happening"
hordes endure "long waits" for a table at the "funky" NoLita original
and its "environmentally friendly" Fort Greene sibling, while "eco-
nomic" tabs and "amazing" libations keep this duo *"muy caliente."*

Café Henri ● *French*   `20` `16` `18` `$27`
W Village | 27 Bedford St. (bet. Downing & Houston Sts.) | 212-243-2846
LIC | 10-10 50th Ave. (Vernon Blvd.) | Queens | 718-383-9315
"Quaint" and "always inviting", these "Parisian-style cafes" in the
West Village and LIC supply "pretty good" crêpes and other "simple"
French bites at an agreeable "quality-to-price ratio"; they're "relaxed"
jour et nuit "if you need a place to chat."

		FOOD	DECOR	SERVICE	COST

Cafe Lalo ● *Coffeehouse/Dessert*

20 | 22 | 16 | $23

W 80s | 201 W. 83rd St. (Amsterdam Ave.) | 212-496-6031 |
www.cafelalo.com

Famously "featured in *You've Got Mail*", this veteran UWS "sweetery"
is ever a "tempting" rendezvous for "decadent desserts"; despite
"wall-to-wall" tourists and "can't-be-bothered" service, it still makes
fans "fall in love with NYC all over again."

Cafe Loup ● *French*

19 | 18 | 21 | $47

W Village | 105 W. 13th St. (6th Ave.) | 212-255-4746 |
www.cafeloupnyc.com

Long a Village "neighborhood standby", this "timeless" bistro is a
"grown-up" nexus for "fairly priced" French fare "like *grand-mère* used
to make" dispatched by a "personable" crew; the room may need
"updating", but loyalists attest it's "worth repeating", especially for
"Sunday jazz brunch."

Cafe Luluc ●⇗ *French*

21 | 15 | 18 | $31

Cobble Hill | 214 Smith St. (bet. Baltic & Butler Sts.) | Brooklyn |
718-625-3815

An "easy way to feel Parisian", this "cash-only" Cobble Hill French bistro offers "satisfying" food served "sans attitude" at "Brooklyn prices";
just "be ready to wait" on weekends – it's a renowned "brunch destination", flipping some of the "world's best pancakes."

Cafe Luxembourg *French*

21 | 19 | 20 | $54

W 70s | 200 W. 70th St. (bet. Amsterdam & West End Aves.) |
212-873-7411 | www.cafeluxembourg.com

"Still a real draw", this long-standing "bastion of UWS hip" is catnip
for a crowd of "good-lookers" and "A-listers" who show up for its "terrific" French bistro cooking, "legitimate Paris" mien and cool "insider
vibe"; "intelligentsia" celeb sightings compensate for the "loud",
"shoulder-to-shoulder" conditions at prime times.

Cafe Mogador ● *Moroccan*

23 | 17 | 19 | $30

E Village | 101 St. Marks Pl. (bet. Ave. A & 1st Ave.) | 212-677-2226
Williamsburg | 133 Wythe Ave. (bet. N. 7th & 8th Sts.) | Brooklyn |
718-486-9222
www.cafemogador.com

Popular with the "tattooed, leathered" set, this "go-to" East Village
Moroccan and its newer garden-equipped Williamsburg sibling "have
it down to a science", providing "memorable" tagines for "super-
affordable" dough; to avoid "long waits" for the "delicious" brunch, go
for "early dinner."

Cafe Noir ● *Moroccan*

20 | 19 | 19 | $36

SoHo | 32 Grand St. (Thompson St.) | 212-431-7910 | www.cafenoirny.com

A "fun Eurotrash" crowd frequents this "cool", "sultry" SoHo Moroccan
where "tasty tapas" and sangria are served in "small" but atmospheric
digs; it's an "all-around good deal" that grows more "flirty" after dark.

Cafe Orlin ● *American*

22 | 17 | 18 | $22

E Village | 41 St. Marks Pl. (2nd Ave.) | 212-777-1447 | www.cafeorlin.com

A "neighborhood institution", this East Villager vends "very good"
American basics with some Mideastern accents in a "mellow" ambiance

(servers "let you be"); it's a weekend brunch fave, so "get there early" to avoid the "line" – and even earlier to snag a "coveted" outdoor seat.

Cafe Ronda   *Mediterranean/S American*   20 | 16 | 17 | $36
W 70s | 249-251 Columbus Ave. (bet. 71st & 72nd Sts.) | 212-579-9929 | www.caferonda.com

"Very UWS", this Med–South American "port in a storm" is a local magnet for "delicious" tapas and "refreshing" sangria that "won't break the bank"; since the quarters are "cramped" and it's "always busy" ("especially for brunch"), claustrophobes "sit outside" and watch the Columbus Avenue parade go by.

Café Sabarsky   *Austrian*   22 | 24 | 20 | $45
E 80s | Neue Galerie | 1048 Fifth Ave. (86th St.) | 212-288-0665
Café Fledermaus   Ⓜ *Austrian*
E 80s | Neue Galerie | 1048 Fifth Ave., downstairs (86th St.) | 212-288-0665
www.kg-ny.com

Kurt Gutenbrunner's "civilized" Neue Galerie cafes transport you to "fin de siècle Vienna", with "exquisite pastries" and "vonderful" Austrian savories dispensed in "glorious", "old-worldy" settings; Sabarsky is the "prettier" of the pair while Fledermaus is "easier to get into", but both are "pretty expensive."

Cafe Steinhof   *Austrian*   18 | 17 | 19 | $28
Park Slope | 422 Seventh Ave. (14th St.) | Brooklyn | 718-369-7776 | www.cafesteinhof.com

Park Slopers "raise a stein" to this Austrian "change of pace" purveying "stick-to-your-ribs" grub for comfortingly "low" dough (Monday's $7 goulash night may be the "best deal in the 'hood"); "fantastic" brews and a "spirited" "bar culture" shore up the appealingly "informal" mood.

Cafeteria   ◗ *American*   21 | 19 | 18 | $34
Chelsea | 119 Seventh Ave. (17th St.) | 212-414-1717 | www.cafeteriagroup.com

With a 24/7 open-door policy, this longtime Chelsea "after-the-clubs" spot serves "dressed-up" American comfort classics with "unwarranted attitude" to a crowd that "clearly expects to be watched"; though it's lost the "allure of years past", it's reassuring to know that it's there when you feel like "meatloaf and a Cosmopolitan at 3 AM."

Caffe e Vino   *Italian*   23 | 17 | 22 | $41
Fort Greene | 112 DeKalb Ave. (bet. Ashland Pl. & St. Felix St.) | Brooklyn | 718-855-6222 | www.caffeevino.com

"Delightful", "rustic" Italian food is the thing at this "tiny but terrific" Fort Greene trattoria near BAM; the "unpretentious" setting (complete with "requisite brick wall") can be "cramped", but the "attentive" servers will "get you out well-fed" before curtain time.

Caffe Grazie   *Italian*   19 | 16 | 20 | $50
E 80s | 26 E. 84th St. (bet. 5th & Madison Aves.) | 212-717-4407 | www.caffegrazie.com

With its "dignified" townhouse setting and "quite creditable" Italian cooking, this veteran UES duplex off Museum Mile is a "restful" respite "before, after or instead of the Met"; maybe it's "a bit pricey", but the $16 set-price lunch is a "bargain considering the neighborhood."

	FOOD	DECOR	SERVICE	COST

Caffe Storico Ⓜ *Italian* — 20 | 22 | 20 | $47

W 70s | NY Historical Society | 170 Central Park W. (77th St.) |
212-485-9211

From restaurateur Stephen Starr, this Upper Westsider "hits all the
right marks" with an "innovative", Venetian-influenced Italian menu
featuring "delicious" cicchetti (small plates); set in the New-York
Historical Society, the "airy", "grand", "white-and-bright" room is
lined with "antique dishes from the museum's collection."

Calexico *Mexican* — 21 | 13 | 17 | $21

NEW LES | 153 Rivington St. (bet. Clinton & Suffolk Sts.) | 646-590-4172 |
www.calexico.net ●

Carroll Gardens | 122 Union St. (bet. Columbia & Hicks Sts.) | Brooklyn |
718-488-8226 | www.calexicocart.com ⊟

Greenpoint | 645 Manhattan Ave. (Bedford Ave.) | Brooklyn |
347-763-2129 | www.calexicocart.com ●

Mexican mavens "all abuzz" over these "rough-and-ready" street-cart
spin-offs call out their "outstanding", "Cali-inspired" tacos, tortas and
burritos; "fabulous prices" and "fast service" offset the "simple"
"hole-in-the-wall" settings; P.S. "make sure to get the 'crack' sauce on
anything you order."

Calle Ocho *Nuevo Latino* — 21 | 21 | 20 | $43

W 80s | Excelsior Hotel | 45 W. 81st St. (bet. Columbus Ave. & CPW) |
212-873-5025 | www.calleochonyc.com

The "gourmet aspirations" are still "interesting" and the "fabulous
mojitos" still flowing at this Upper West Side Nuevo Latino vet, now
firmly settled in its "attractive" Excelsior Hotel digs; weekends the
"party" picks up during the "unlimited sangria brunch" (just "bring
a designated driver").

Calliope *French* — 22 | 15 | 21 | $55

E Village | 84 E. Fourth St. (2nd Ave.) | 212-260-8484

Hailed as a "neighborhood find", this "unpretentious" East Village bistro delivers a "limited" but "distinctive" lineup of "down-home French"
dishes via a "welcoming staff"; the communal table–equipped space
has a suitably "Left Bank feel", down to the "cramped" and "noisy"
conditions "when packed."

Camaje ● *American/French* — 20 | 14 | 20 | $39

G Village | 85 MacDougal St. (bet. Bleecker & Houston Sts.) |
212-673-8184 | www.camaje.com

A "sweet place in the heart of the Village", Abigail Hitchcock's
"small, funky" bistro matches "homey yet sophisticated" Franco-
American meals with "mellow" vibes; it also hosts "cooking lessons" and 'dark dining' events ("you're blindfolded before you enter")
that are "a blast."

Campagnola ● *Italian* — 23 | 19 | 21 | $71

E 70s | 1382 First Ave. (74th St.) | 212-861-1102

All eyes are on the "floor show" at this "old-school" UES veteran where
the stellar people-watching is on par with the "excellent", "garlicky"
Italian cooking and "all-business" service; for best results, "go with
somebody they know" – it's much "better if you're a regular" – and better yet if you bring "someone else's expense account."

	FOOD	DECOR	SERVICE	COST

Canaletto *Italian* | 21 | 16 | 21 | $57 |

E 60s | 208 E. 60th St. (bet. 2nd & 3rd Aves.) | 212-317-9192
Something of a "hidden gem", this "genuine" Northern Italian near Bloomie's purveys "dependable", "traditional" dishes to an "older crowd"; a "well-seasoned staff" and "comfortable" environs that are "not unduly loud" mute "pricey" tariffs.

Candle Cafe *Vegan/Vegetarian* | 24 | 17 | 21 | $34 |

E 70s | 1307 Third Ave. (bet. 74th & 75th Sts.) | 212-472-0970
Candle Cafe West *Vegan/Vegetarian*
W 80s | 2427 Broadway (bet. 89th & 90th Sts.) | 212-769-8900
www.candlecafe.com
Candle 79's "cheaper", "more utilitarian" cousins, these crosstown joints feature "intriguing" vegan eats "prepared with love" in "cramped", "unpretentious" environs; though they're "often crowded" with "Gwyneth Paltrow wannabes", the "right-on" cooking is "worth the wait."

Candle 79 *Vegan/Vegetarian* | 25 | 22 | 24 | $47 |

E 70s | 154 E. 79th St. (bet. Lexington & 3rd Aves.) | 212-537-7179 | www.candle79.com
"Tasting is believing" at this UES vegan "fine-dining" "phenom" that "sets the standard" with "quality-sourced", "distinctive" organic dishes and wines delivered by "enthusiastic" servers in "intimate", "classic" digs; a "pleasant departure from meaty fare", it's "so worth" the "premium price."

The Cannibal ● *Belgian*   ∇ | 24 | 19 | 23 | $43 |

Murray Hill | 113 E. 29th St. (bet. Lexington Ave. & Park Ave. S.) | 212-686-5480 | www.thecannibalnyc.com
A spin-off of Murray Hill's Resto, this next-door butcher shop–cum–Belgian gastropub plies a "meat-heavy" menu of "superlative" small plates backed up by an "amazing" selection of brews; maybe the snug, communal table–equipped setting is "not comfortable", but few "headhunters" mind given the "swoon"-inducing chow.

NEW **Cantine Parisienne** *French* | - | - | - | M |

Financial District | Nolitan Hotel | 40 Kenmare St. (Elizabeth St.) | 212-966-2740 | www.cantineparisienne.com
A wall of art and fashion magazines invites diners to linger at this airy, chic-yet-casual French cantine on the ground level of the Nolitan Hotel; the midpriced menu includes original cocktails and American-inflected bistro fare, from ricotta pancakes to beef tartare.

The Capital Grille *Steak* | 24 | 22 | 23 | $71 |

E 40s | Chrysler Ctr. | 155 E. 42nd St. (bet. Lexington & 3rd Aves.) | 212-953-2000
Financial District | 120 Broadway (Pine St.) | 212-374-1811 ⍓
W 50s | Time-Life Building | 120 W. 51st St. (bet. 6th & 7th Aves.) | 212-246-0154
www.thecapitalgrille.com
Whether for "corporate" or "celebratory" dining, this "higher-end" steakhouse threesome does it right with "superbly prepared cuts" and "dedicated" service that make it "easy to forget it's a chain"; the Chrysler Center locale stands out for "stunning decor" with "swooping

glass overhead", but all are "reliably good" – especially when "someone else is paying."

Caracas Arepa Bar *Venezuelan*

| | 24 | 15 | 18 | $21 |

E Village | 93½ E. Seventh St. (bet. Ave. A & 1st Ave.) | 212-529-2314

Caracas Brooklyn *Venezuelan*
Williamsburg | 291 Grand St. (bet. Havemeyer & Roebling Sts.) | Brooklyn | 718-218-6050

Caracas to Go *Venezuelan*
E Village | 91 E. Seventh St. (1st Ave.) | 212-228-5062

Caracas Rockaway ⊐̶ *Venezuelan*
Rockaway Beach | 106-01 Shore Front Pkwy. (Beach 106th St.) | Queens
www.caracasarepabar.com

An "amazingly delicious" "change of pace", these "authentic" Venezuelans churn out "crisp arepas" loaded with "flavorful" fillings "on the cheap"; to bypass "insane" waits at the "chaotic" East Village "hole-in-the-wall", try the "funky" Williamsburg branch (complete "with a cute backyard") or hang "at the beach" in Rockaway.

Cara Mia *Italian*

| | 20 | 16 | 20 | $40 |

W 40s | 654 Ninth Ave. (bet. 45th & 46th Sts.) | 212-262-6767 | www.nycrg.com

"Not fancy but plenty comfortable", this Hell's Kitchen "red-sauce" Italian is a Theater District "standby" for "homemade pasta" and "spot-on" service; granted, it's "space-challenged" and "crazy busy" pre-curtain, but at least you can mangia "without paying an arm and a leg."

Caravaggio *Italian*

| | 25 | 24 | 25 | $86 |

E 70s | 23 E. 74th St. (bet. 5th & Madison Aves.) | 212-288-1004 | www.caravaggioristorante.com

More than "just dining out", this "refined" UES Italian is a "special-occasion" nexus owing to its "sophisticated" cooking, "flawless" service and "exquisite" modern setting; "money is no object" for most of its "mature" fan base, though frugal folks find the $28 prix fixe lunch quite "enticing."

Caravan of Dreams *Kosher/Vegan*

| | 23 | 16 | 20 | $29 |

E Village | 405 E. Sixth St. (1st Ave.) | 212-254-1613 | www.caravanofdreams.net

A dream come true for "healthy food" fanatics, this East Village vet offers "transformative" kosher vegan fare in "mellow", "bohemian" quarters; fair prices and occasional "live music" enhance its "aura of peace and satisfaction", making followers "feel good inside and out."

NEW Carbone ● *Italian*

| | ∇ 21 | 21 | 21 | $93 |

G Village | 181 Thompson St. (bet. Bleecker & Houston Sts.) | 212-254-3000 | www.carbonenewyork.com

Among NYC's "hottest" tickets, the Torrisi boys' "upscale" ode to Italo-American nostalgia in the Village's erstwhile Rocco's space delivers "fine" red-sauce classics theatrically presented by "jovial" tuxedoed waiters; it's an "upbeat", "celeb"-sprinkled "scene" with a '60s soundtrack, and while some find its "stagey" touches a bit much – ditto the "lotta moolah" prices – "when you see Jake Gyllenhaal and Jerry Seinfeld, you know the place has got to be good."

	FOOD	DECOR	SERVICE	COST

Carlyle Restaurant *French* | 23 | 26 | 25 | $90 |

E 70s | Carlyle Hotel | 35 E. 76th St. (Madison Ave.) | 212-570-7192 |
www.thecarlyle.com

"Synonymous with class", this "old-world" room in the Carlyle Hotel
holds "fond memories" for a "blue-blood" fan base in thrall to its "refined"
New French fare, "royal-treatment" service and "Dorothy
Draper"–esque digs; plan to wear your "finest baubles" (jackets required
for dinner) and be prepared for "super-premium prices."

Carmine's *Italian* | 21 | 17 | 19 | $43 |

W 40s | 200 W. 44th St. (bet. 7th & 8th Aves.) | 212-221-3800 ◑
W 90s | 2450 Broadway (bet. 90th & 91st Sts.) | 212-362-2200
www.carminesnyc.com

"Sharing is a must" at these "convivial" Italian "crowd-pleasers",
where "red sauce reigns" as "mobs" "mangia" on "hearty", "garlicky"
staples served in "monstrous" family-style portions; "tourists flock" to
the "hectic-paced" Theater District "feed hall", while the UWS original
is "a little quieter" but still "very social."

Carnegie Deli ◑☞ *Deli* | 22 | 11 | 15 | $30 |

W 50s | 854 Seventh Ave. (55th St.) | 212-757-2245 |
www.carnegiedeli.com

"Unhinge your jaw" for "a whole lot of a good thing" at this Midtown
"landmark" of "deli debauchery", home since 1937 to "legendary",
"knock-your-socks-off" sandwiches stacked "taller than the Empire
State Building"; prices are "steep" for the genre ("bring cash"), service
"growly" and the "bare-bones" setting "overrun" by a "crush of tourists",
but you "definitely get the big-city experience."

Carol's Cafe ☒Ⓜ *Eclectic* | 25 | 21 | 21 | $50 |

Dongan Hills | 1571 Richmond Rd. (bet. 4 Corners Rd. & Garretson Ave.) |
Staten Island | 718-979-5600 | www.carolscafe.com

"Thoughtful", "Manhattan-quality" cooking via chef Carol Frazzetta is
yours at this "pretty" Eclectic standby in Staten Island's Dongan Hills;
maybe the tabs run "a little high" for these parts, but "perfect-ending"
desserts and weekly "cooking lessons" sweeten the pot.

Casa Enrique ◑ *Mexican* | ∇ 24 | 15 | 23 | $29 |

LIC | 5-48 49th Ave. (bet. 5th St. & Vernon Blvd.) | Queens |
347-448-6040

The Cafe Henri crew goes south of the border at this "cozy, comfortable"
LIC Mexican where "enticing", "expertly prepared", "aesthetically
presented" fare inspired by the cuisine of the Chiapas region
comes in "comfortable", "no-pretenses" environs; "fantastic" service
and moderate tabs are two more reasons locals declare they've "died
and gone to heaven."

Casa Lever ☒ *Italian* | 23 | 24 | 23 | $77 |

E 50s | Lever House | 390 Park Ave. (53rd St.) | 212-888-2700 |
www.casalever.com

Luring Park Avenue "power" players, this Midtown Milanese from the
Sant Ambroeus team offers "delicious" chow delivered by an "attentive"
crew; set in the "historic" Lever House, the "modernist" room
lined with "wall-to-wall Warhols" is so "fashionable" that many say
you're "paying for the style" here.

	FOOD	DECOR	SERVICE	COST

Casa Mono ◐ *Spanish* — 25 | 18 | 20 | $62

Gramercy | 52 Irving Pl. (17th St.) | 212-253-2773 | www.casamononyc.com
"Inspired" tapas and an "encyclopedic" selection of Spanish vintages
pack the house nightly at this "standout" Gramercy tapas bar from the
Batali fam; sure, it's "like eating in a phone booth", and tabs "can mount
up", but "who cares when the grub's this good?"

Casa Nonna *Italian* — 21 | 21 | 21 | $49

Garment District | 310 W. 38th St. (bet. 8th & 9th Aves.) | 212-736-3000 |
www.casanonna.com
A "big surprise" in the Garment District, this Italian has its "act together" offering "perfectly fine" Roman-Tuscan standards served with
"quick" "professionalism"; it's a "relaxing" option in a "lacking" dining
zone, with well-spaced tables allowing for "private conversations."

NEW Casa Pomona *Spanish* — - | - | - | M

W 80s | 507 Columbus Ave. (bet. 84th & 85th Sts.) | 212-362-3200 |
www.casapomonanyc.com
This spacious UWS Spaniard puts forth a traditional, midpriced tapas
lineup served in two distinct areas: a front bar with pub-height tables
(and soccer on the TVs) and a more formal back dining room anchored
by a colorful mural; sherry-spiked cocktails and affordable Iberian
wines highlight the small libations list.

Cascabel Taqueria ◐ *Mexican* — 21 | 14 | 16 | $28

E 80s | 1538 Second Ave. (80th St.) | 212-717-8226
W 100s | 2799 Broadway (108th St.) | 212-665-1500
www.nyctacos.com
"*Ay caramba*", these "popular" taquerias are about as "legitimate" as
you'll find in these parts, slinging "league-of-their-own" tacos in "funky"
quarters; "bargain" tabs and "downtown" vibes keep them "overwhelm-
ingly busy", so expect service that's "cheerful" but "not very polished."

NEW Cata ◐🅱 *Spanish* — - | - | - | M

LES | 245 Bowery (bet. Rivington & Stanton Sts.) | 212-505-2282
A catalogic menu of midpriced Spanish tapas and tipples – the bar offers 27 types of gin and tonics alone – befits the château-meets-
industrial warehouse vibe at this Bowery Spaniard from the Alta folks;
ceramic tile, copper tables and a case displaying seafood on ice add to
the authentic experience.

Catch *Seafood* — 23 | 23 | 19 | $75

Meatpacking | 21 Ninth Ave. (bet. Little W. 12th & 13th Sts.) |
212-392-5978 | www.emmgrp.com
"Beautiful people" and random "Kardashians" populate this "trendy"
Meatpacking "scene" where "outstanding" seafood via *Top Chef* winner Hung Huynh is dispensed by "Abercrombie model"–like staffers in
a sprawling, "pumping" duplex; reservations can be hard to catch despite the "expensive" tabs.

Ça Va *French* — 21 | 20 | 21 | $58

W 40s | InterContinental NY Times Sq. | 310 W. 44th St. (bet. 8th &
9th Aves.) | 212-803-4545 | www.cavatoddenglish.com
Todd English assumes a "straightforward French" accent at this pleasing Theater District brasserie; though the "nondescript", "hotel-

	FOOD	DECOR	SERVICE	COST

"lobby" decor may be at odds with the "high-end" prices, "thoughtful" service and a "convenient" address make it a natural "pre-theater."

Caviar Russe *American*   26 | 23 | 25 | $95

E 50s | 538 Madison Ave., 2nd fl. (bet. 54th & 55th Sts.) | 212-980-5908 | www.caviarrusse.com

The "decadent experience" at this East Side New American "conjures up tsars" as patrons are "pampered" with "exquisite caviar" and crudo from an "attentive, knowledgeable staff" in "deluxe" digs suitable for an "illicit affair"; prices are predictably "astronomical", but big spenders urge "indulge in this when you can."

Cávo ●Ⓜ *Greek*   21 | 24 | 19 | $45

Astoria | 42-18 31st Ave. (bet. 42nd & 43rd Sts.) | Queens | 718-721-1001 | www.cavoastoria.com

A "cool-looking", "spacious" setting is the lure at this "upscale" Astoria Greek offering "solid" Hellenic fare that's upstaged by its "spectacular", waterfall-equipped garden; just be aware it "can get pricey" and "loud" – as the evening progresses, it becomes "more of a nightclub."

Cebu ● *Continental*   20 | 19 | 19 | $39

Bay Ridge | 8801 Third Ave. (88th St.) | Brooklyn | 718-492-5095 | www.cebubrooklyn.com

"Large" and "busy", this "reasonably priced" Continental brings a bit of "Manhattan chic" to Bay Ridge via an "enjoyable" menu, "on-the-ball" service and night-owl noshing "till 3 AM"; "younger" folks with "fake tans" keep the bar scene "buzzing."

Celeste ⊅ *Italian*   23 | 12 | 17 | $34

W 80s | 502 Amsterdam Ave. (bet. 84th & 85th Sts.) | 212-874-4559

"Celestial" Neapolitan cooking, "wonderful" cheese plates and "tough-to-beat" tabs make for "crammed" conditions at this UWS "winner" whose engaging owner is "part of the experience"; despite "no rezzies", "no credit cards" and "little ambiance", "long lines" are the norm here.

Cellini *Italian*   22 | 18 | 22 | $57

E 50s | 65 E. 54th St. (bet. Madison & Park Aves.) | 212-751-1555 | www.cellinirestaurant.com

A "staple" for "entertaining clients", this "expense-account" Midtowner draws a "chatty lunch crowd" with "authentic", "sure-bet" Italian standards served in a "not-so-fancy" setting; it's more subdued come suppertime, but you can expect "comfortable, grown-up" dining at any hour.

Cercle Rouge ● *French*   19 | 20 | 18 | $48

TriBeCa | 241 W. Broadway (N. Moore St.) | 212-226-6252 | www.cerclerougeresto.com

There's "no need to go to Paris" thanks to this "under-the-radar" TriBeCa bistro purveying "classic" Gallic grub that conjures up a "certain je ne sais quoi"; it's a "comfy" fallback for local boulevardiers who sit outside and "pretend" they're on the Champs-Elysées.

'Cesca *Italian*   23 | 22 | 22 | $63

W 70s | 164 W. 75th St. (Amsterdam Ave.) | 212-787-6300 | www.cescanyc.com

"Fine-dining" fanciers frequent this Upper West Side "standout" for its "delectable" Italian fare, "stellar" wine list and "warm", "no-rush" service; although it's "as expensive as it is sophisticated", payoffs include a "relaxing" rustic setting, acoustics perfect for "normal conversation" and an open kitchen that's catnip for "armchair chefs."

Chadwick's American
24 | 20 | 23 | $44

Bay Ridge | 8822 Third Ave. (89th St.) | Brooklyn | 718-833-9855 | www.chadwicksny.com

On the Bay Ridge scene since '87, this American "stroll down memory lane" bats out a "solid" menu dispatched by "old-time waiters" who "treat you right"; the decor may "need a little uplift", but the "value" is intact, notably its "early-bird specials" Monday–Thursday.

Chai Home Kitchen Thai
22 | 18 | 19 | $25

W 50s | 930 Eighth Ave. (55th St.) | 212-707-8778
Williamsburg | 124 N. Sixth St. (Berry St.) | Brooklyn | 718-599-5889 ●
www.chai-restaurants.com

"Incredibly reasonable prices" keep the trade brisk at these Siamese twins in Williamsburg and Hell's Kitchen vending "spot-on" Thai food ferried by a "prompt" crew; the seating's strictly "sardine"-style in Manhattan, with more room at the Brooklyn original.

NEW Charlie Bird M American
- | - | - | M

SoHo | 5 King St. (6th Ave.) | 212-235-7133 | www.charliebirdnyc.com

Something hip comes to SoHo via this newcomer whose Italian-accented American cuisine is backed by a wine list from a former Cru sommelier; the bi-level, banquette-lined space, decorated with random microphones and boombox artwork, exudes effortless cool and is already a hit with happening locals.

Char No. 4 ● Southern
22 | 21 | 21 | $40

Cobble Hill | 196 Smith St. (bet. Baltic & Warren Sts.) | Brooklyn | 718-643-2106 | www.charno4.com

"Brooklyn edge" is everything at this Cobble Hill "pork-and-bourbon paradise" that matches "memorable" Southern eats with a "world-class selection" of brown liquids; "knowledgeable", professional service and "one heck of a weekend brunch" draw flocks of "young, trendy" folk.

Château Cherbuliez ● French
- | - | - | M

Flatiron | Limelight Mktpl. | 47 W. 20th St. (bet. 5th & 6th Aves.) | 212-203-7088 | www.chateaunyc.com

Anchoring the troubled Limelight Marketplace, this good-looking, St. Tropez–inspired arrival from Todd English serves French fare in a ground-floor wine bar or more exclusive upstairs dining room; still, it's the sprawling outdoor garden that's the real place to be.

Chef Ho's Peking Duck Grill Chinese
22 | 15 | 19 | $34

E 80s | 1720 Second Ave. (bet. 89th & 90th Sts.) | 212-348-9444 | www.chefho.com

De-ho-tees say you "won't find better Peking duck" than at this "old-school" Yorkville Chinese, a "neighborhood favorite" also lauded for its "above-average" cooking, "below-average" tabs and "efficient" service; fans say it's so good that there's "no need to go to Chinatown."

	FOOD	DECOR	SERVICE	COST

Chef's Table at Brooklyn Fare ⑧ *French* — 27 | 20 | 25 | $332

Downtown Bklyn | 200 Schermerhorn St. (bet. Bond & Hoyt Sts.) | Brooklyn | 718-243-0050 | www.brooklynfare.com

Affirming "Brooklyn's continued place" on the "NYC cuisine scene", this 18-seat prep kitchen in a Schermerhorn Street grocery presents Japanese-influenced French cooking from "extraordinary chef" Cesar Ramirez, favoring the "privileged" few who score "elusive" reservations with 20-plus "magical" small plates and "close-to-flawless" service; it may "take a second mortgage" to settle the $255 prix fixe-only tab, but "save up the dough" and "keep redialing" – "you won't regret it."

Chef Yu *Chinese* — 21 | 19 | 17 | $23

Garment District | 520 Eighth Ave. (bet. 36th & 37th Sts.) | 212-736-6150 | www.chefyu-nyc.com

An "easy" option near Penn Station, this "well-located" Garment District Chinese offers "tasty" traditional dishes in "airy", "modern" double-decker digs; the pricing's "reasonable" with lunch specials the "best value", but opinion splits on the service: "friendly" vs. "eat, pay, leave."

NEW Cherry ● *Asian* — - | - | - | E

Chelsea | Dream Downtown Hotel | 355 W. 16th St. (bet. 8th & 9th Aves.) | 212-929-5800 | www.cherrynyc.com

In the Dream Hotel, this swanky downstairs den supplies Asian-fusion fare (including sushi) and a nightlife-friendly vibe courtesy of the folks behind Bond Street; appointed with lush red-velvet banquettes and offering plenty of quiet nooks for dates, it draws a crowd set to head out to one of the area's many clubs post-meal.

Chez Jacqueline *French* — 19 | 18 | 19 | $51

G Village | 72 MacDougal St. (bet. Bleecker & Houston Sts.) | 212-505-0727 | www.chezjacquelinerestaurant.com

"Unassuming", "been-there-forever" Village bistro that has a "winning way" thanks to "satisfying" traditional French fare served by a "charming" staff that "keeps the *vin rouge* flowing"; critics site "ordinary" decor and feel the "flair is missing" sans Jacqueline.

Chez Josephine ●Ⓜ *French* — 20 | 22 | 21 | $54

W 40s | 414 W. 42nd St. (bet. Dyer & 9th Aves.) | 212-594-1925 | www.chezjosephine.com

"Josephine Baker lives on" at this "campy" Theater District "tribute" via her "flamboyant", "silk-pajama'd" son Jean-Claude; the "dark", "midnight-in-Paris" setting works well with the "throwback" French food and "energetic" live piano – no wonder it's been "popular" since 1986.

Chez Lucienne *French* — 21 | 18 | 21 | $37

Harlem | 308 Lenox Ave. (bet. 125th & 126th Sts.) | 212-289-5555 | www.chezlucienne.com

"Parisian soul" is the thing at this French bistro on a happening stretch of Harlem's Lenox Avenue, where the midpriced Gallic grub is as "genuine" as the "accommodating" service; it's a "great alternative" to Red Rooster next door, and sidewalk seats supply people-watching galore.

	FOOD	DECOR	SERVICE	COST

Chez Napoléon ⑤ *French*

22 | 15 | 22 | $49

W 50s | 365 W. 50th St. (bet. 8th & 9th Aves.) | 212-265-6980 |
www.cheznapoleon.com

"*Vérité*" could be the motto of this circa-1960 Theater District "relic"
where an "old-school" crew dispatches "time-stood-still" French bistro classics à la escargot, frogs' legs and calf's brains; the "tiny" setting exudes "faded elegance", but prices are "moderate" and you're
"there to eat, not sight-see."

Chez Oskar ● *French*

20 | 19 | 19 | $33

Fort Greene | 211 DeKalb Ave. (Adelphi St.) | Brooklyn | 718-852-6250 |
www.chezoskar.com

"Very Brooklyn", this veteran Fort Greene bistro continues to show
its "staying power" with "enjoyable" French plates purveyed in
"laid-back" surrounds enhanced by frequent "live music"; its hipster fan base appreciates its "lack of pretension", not to mention the
rather "reasonable" prices.

NEW Chez Sardine *Japanese*

∇ 20 | 19 | 21 | $64

W Village | 183 W. 10th St. (4th St.) | 646-360-3705 |
www.chezsardine.com

"Tiny and always crowded", this "immediate-hit" addition to Gabe
Stulman's West Village empire gratifies nose-to-tail piscivores
and foie gras connoisseurs alike, thanks to a "wonderful" menu
emphasizing Japanese seafood (just know "those little plates can
add up"); slatted wooden ceilings and low tables lend the "cute"
quarters a streamlined feel.

ChikaLicious *Dessert*

25 | 16 | 21 | $22

E Village | 203 E. 10th St. (bet. 1st & 2nd Aves.) | 212-475-0929 |
www.chikalicious.com Ⓜ
E Village | 204 E. 10th St. (bet. 1st & 2nd Aves.) | 212-475-0929 |
www.dessertclubnyc.com ●

"Sophisticated sweet tooths" applaud this "blink-and-you-missed-
it" East Village "dessert nirvana" for its "scrumptious", three-
course prix fixes paired with "perfect" wines; those sour on the
"postage stamp"–size digs get takeout from the counter-service satellite across the street.

Chimichurri Grill ● *Argentinean/Steak*

23 | 17 | 21 | $52

W 40s | 609 Ninth Ave. (bet. 43rd & 44th Sts.) | 212-586-8655 |
www.chimichurrigrill.com

"Well-cooked" Argentine steaks topped with the namesake sauce
thrill carnivores at this "tiny" Hell's Kitchen hideout; "efficient" staffers and "reasonable" pricing make it a natural for the "pre-theater"
crowd, who only "wish it had more tables."

China Grill *Asian*

23 | 21 | 21 | $57

W 50s | 60 W. 53rd St. (bet. 5th & 6th Aves.) | 212-333-7788 |
www.chinagrillmgt.com

Long a bastion of "upmarket chic", this Midtown "powerhouse" offers "fancy takes" on Asian cuisine served in "dark", airy digs with
an "'80s James Bond" atmosphere; it's "deafeningly loud" and
"definitely not a bargain", but "business" types still belly up for its
"fun bar scene."

| | FOOD | DECOR | SERVICE | COST |

Chin Chin ❶ *Chinese*   23 | 18 | 22 | $54

E 40s | 216 E. 49th St. (bet. 2nd & 3rd Aves.) | 212-888-4555 |
www.chinchinny.com

On the scene since 1987, this "fancy" Midtowner is a nexus for
"impressive" haute Chinese cuisine (don't miss the "off-the-menu"
Grand Marnier shrimp) served by a "crisp" crew led by owner
Jimmy "Energizer-bunny" Chin; despite rather "expensive" tabs, the
"crowds keep coming."

ChipShop *British*   20 | 16 | 20 | $22

Brooklyn Heights | 129 Atlantic Ave. (bet. Clinton & Henry Sts.) |
Brooklyn | 718-855-7775
Park Slope | 383 Fifth Ave. (6th St.) | Brooklyn | 718-832-7701 🍽
www.chipshopnyc.com

The "British invasion" comes to Brooklyn via these kinda "divey"
pub-food places decorated with "'80s punk memorabilia" and specializing in "cardiologist-disapproved" items like "killer fish 'n'
chips" and "seriously deep-fried" candy bars; "homesick Brits" dub
it "bloody wonderful."

Chocolate Room *Dessert*   25 | 19 | 20 | $18

Cobble Hill | 269 Court St. (bet. Butler & Douglass Sts.) | Brooklyn |
718-246-2600
Park Slope | 86 Fifth Ave. (bet. St. Marks Pl. & Warren St.) | Brooklyn |
718-783-2900
www.thechocolateroombrooklyn.com

Dedicated to "all things chocolate", these "brilliant" Brooklyn dessert
specialists vend "sinful" homemade desserts best paired with a glass
of vino to cut the "sugar rush"; the Cobble Hill satellite is roomier, but
the staffers are as "sweet" as the goods at both locations.

Cho Dang Gol *Korean*   23 | 14 | 18 | $31

Garment District | 55 W. 35th St. (bet. 5th & 6th Aves.) | 212-695-8222 |
www.chodanggolny.com

"Real-deal" Korean cooking is offered at this "step-above" Garment
District joint that's famous for its "luscious" homemade tofu; "low
prices", "utilitarian" decor and "typical" service are all part of the
package, along with a "full house" at prime times.

Chola *Indian*   23 | 16 | 19 | $39

E 50s | 232 E. 58th St. (bet. 2nd & 3rd Aves.) | 212-688-4619 |
www.cholany.com

"Spices abound" at this "delectable" Indian on East 58th Street's subcontinental strip, supplying a "wide-ranging" roster of "complex"
dishes; tariffs are generally "moderate", but for "quality and selection"
the $14 buffet lunch provides true "value for the money."

Chop-Shop *Asian*   ▽ 22 | 14 | 21 | $49

Chelsea | 254 10th Ave. (bet. 24th & 25th Sts.) | 212-820-0333 |
www.chop-shop.co

"Why this place isn't packed is a mystery" marvel mavens of this
"pleasant" Chelsea Pan-Asian presenting "delish" dishes via a
competent crew; an ideal "pit stop if you're gallery-hopping or
strolling the High Line", it boasts a sleek white-on-white interior and
a verdant patio.

	FOOD	DECOR	SERVICE	COST

Christos Steak House *Steak*
25 | 20 | 24 | $62

Astoria | 41-08 23rd Ave. (41st St.) | Queens | 718-777-8400 |
www.christossteakhouse.com

"Fabulous" cuts of meat plus apps and sides with a "Greek twist" are
"cheerfully served" at this Astoria "neighborhood steakhouse"; it's
"not cheap" for these parts and the space could "be fixed up", but hey,
the valet parking's a "real winner."

Chuko *Japanese/Noodle Shop*
▽ 23 | 17 | 21 | $26

Prospect Heights | 552 Vanderbilt Ave. (Dean St.) | Brooklyn |
718-576-6701 | www.barchuko.com

Supplying a "solid ramen experience", this popular, cash-only Prospect
Heights Japanese presents "toothsome" noodles, "amazing broth"
and some "nontraditional accoutrements", along with a slim list of
"delicious" appetizers; "polite service" helps slurpaholics justify the
"wait time" to access its small, sleek digs.

Churrascaria Plataforma *Brazilian/Steak*
23 | 20 | 22 | $82

W 40s | 316 W. 49th St. (bet. 8th & 9th Aves.) | 212-245-0505 |
www.churrascariaplataforma.com

Churrascaria TriBeCa *Brazilian/Steak*

TriBeCa | 221 W. Broadway (bet. Franklin & White Sts.) |
212-925-6969 | www.churrascariatribeca.com

Brace yourself for a "food coma" after dining at these Brazilian rodizio
all-you-can-eat "extravaganzas", where "skewer-bearing" waiters
bring on a "nonstop" barrage of "cooked-to-perfection" meats;
since they're "kinda expensive", gluttons "try not to fill up" at the
"bountiful" salad bar.

Cibo *American/Italian*
20 | 19 | 21 | $47

E 40s | 767 Second Ave. (41st St.) | 212-681-1616 |
www.cibonyc.com

A "grown-up" favorite in the land of "limited" options around Tudor
City, this "comfortable" Tuscan–New American plies "fresh seasonal"
fare in a "spacious", "white-tablecloth" milieu; "excellent value" (e.g. the
$39 dinner prix fixe) makes it "worth coming back to."

Cilantro *Southwestern*
19 | 16 | 18 | $32

E 70s | 1321 First Ave. (71st St.) | 212-537-4040 ◑
E 80s | 1712 Second Ave. (89th St.) | 212-722-4242 ◑
W 80s | 485 Columbus Ave. (bet. 83rd & 84th Sts.) | 212-712-9090
www.cilantronyc.com

"Ample portions" and "low prices" keep these "serviceable"
Southwesterns enduringly "popular" with twentysomethings on a
budget; "gigantic" margaritas help blot out the "excessive noise",
"predictable" grub and "fake adobe" decor.

Cipriani Club 55 *Italian*
23 | 24 | 23 | $71

Financial District | 55 Wall St., 2nd fl. (William St.) | 212-699-4099 |
www.cipriani.com

"One-percenters" who relish the "high life" "feed their egos" at this
FiDi branch of the Cipriani empire, where "excellent" Italiana is dispensed in "posh" environs that include a jaw-dropping columned terrace; "prestige"-wise, it's a "solid" investment "when you have
money to burn."

	FOOD	DECOR	SERVICE	COST

Cipriani Dolci *Italian*
22 | 21 | 20 | $61

E 40s | Grand Central | 89 E. 42nd St. (Vanderbilt Ave.) | 212-973-0999 | www.cipriani.com

It's all about the view from the balcony at this Grand Central Venetian overlooking the "mass of humanity" thronging the Concourse and the Apple store; the "quality" food and signature Bellinis "warm the heart" and "empty the wallet", but it's still "a treat if you're waiting for a train."

Cipriani Downtown ◑ *Italian*
23 | 22 | 21 | $73

SoHo | 376 W. Broadway (bet. Broome & Spring Sts.) | 212-343-0999 | www.cipriani.com

The only thing missing is "Fellini" at this SoHo slice of "la dolce vita", a "ritzy" nexus where "international" types "park their Lamborghinis" out front, then tuck into *molto bene* Italian food and "delicious" Bellinis; "astronomical" price tags and "attitude" galore come with the territory.

Circo ◑ *Italian*
23 | 24 | 23 | $66

W 50s | 120 W. 55th St. (bet. 6th & 7th Aves.) | 212-265-3636 | www.osteriadelcirco.com

Exhibiting its "Le Cirque DNA", this "big-top" Midtowner from the Maccioni family purveys "wonderful Tuscan fare" in a "playful" room festooned with "circus-themed decor"; given the "high-end" price tags, the "prix fixe deals" draw bargain-hunters, especially "pre- or post–City Center."

Circus ☒ *Brazilian/Steak*
22 | 21 | 21 | $53

E 60s | 132 E. 61st St. (bet. Lexington & Park Aves.) | 212-223-2965 | www.circusrestaurante.com

There's "no clowning around" in the kitchen at this Brazilian "sleeper" near Bloomie's where a "marvelous", meat-centric menu is served by a "jolly staff" that keeps the "knockout" caipirinhas flowing; "intimate" digs with a "circus motif" add to the "pleasant" vibe.

Citrus Bar & Grill *Asian/Nuevo Latino*
20 | 19 | 18 | $41

W 70s | 320 Amsterdam Ave. (75th St.) | 212-595-0500 | www.citrusnyc.com

"Festive" is putting it mildly at this UWS Latin-Asian fusion specialist where the "interesting" chow takes a backseat to the "awesome" specialty tipples shaken at the "lively bar"; bargain-hunters drawn by "decent-value" pricing "go early" to avoid the "loud" decibels later on.

City Bakery *Bakery*
22 | 14 | 15 | $20

Flatiron | 3 W. 18th St. (bet. 5th & 6th Aves.) | 212-366-1414 | www.thecitybakery.com

It's beloved for its "ever-so-rich" hot chocolate, "one-of-a-kind" pretzel croissants and "scrumptious" sweets, but this Flatiron bakery also wins favor with its "wholesome" salad and juice bars; maybe prices are "out of whack" given the "mess-hall" decor and "unhelpful service", but that doesn't faze the "crazed" lunch crowds.

City Crab & Seafood *Seafood*
19 | 16 | 18 | $47

Flatiron | 235 Park Ave. S. (19th St.) | 212-529-3800 | www.citycrabnyc.com

"Casual" and "commercial", this "straightforward" Flatiron fixture offers "no surprises", just a "wide assortment" of "simple", "fresh" seafood dispatched in a "big, boisterous" duplex; "decent" tabs compensate for "spotty" service and "not much character."

	FOOD	DECOR	SERVICE	COST

City Hall ⊠ *Seafood/Steak* | 22 | 22 | 21 | $59 |

TriBeCa | 131 Duane St. (bet. Church St. & W. B'way) | 212-227-7777 | www.cityhallnyc.com

"Politicos" and "power" players rub elbows at Henry Meer's TriBeCa "mainstay" where "attentive" staffers ferry "superb" surf 'n' turf in a "lofty", "sophisticated" setting that feels like "old NY"; bonuses include "space between tables" and "lovely private rooms" downstairs.

City Island Lobster House ● *Seafood* | 22 | 18 | 20 | $46 |

City Island | 691 Bridge St. (City Island Ave.) | Bronx | 718-885-1459 | www.cilobsterhouse.com

Crustacean cravers commend this "basic" City Island "throwback" as a "fine and dandy" option for "abundant", satisfying seafood; aesthetes note it offers "not much decor", but "budget" pricing and alfresco dining "overlooking Long Island Sound" give it "staycation" status.

City Lobster & Steak *Seafood* | 20 | 18 | 20 | $52 |

W 40s | 121 W. 49th St. (6th Ave.) | 212-354-1717 | www.citylobster.com

For "standard" surf 'n' turf with "no surprises", this "convenient" harbor is a "good all-around" performer in the "touristy" turf around Rock Center; foes crab about shelling out for "nothing special", but then again the pre-theater prix fixes are a "best buy."

NEW Clarke's Standard *American* | ▽ 20 | 13 | 16 | $18 |

E 50s | 636 Lexington Ave. (54th St.) | 212-838-6000
Financial District | 101 Maiden Ln. (Pearl St.) | 212-797-1700
Flatiron | 870 Broadway (bet. 17th & 18th Sts.) | 212-529-9100
W 50s | 977 Eighth Ave. (bet. 57th & 58th Sts.) | 212-245-2200
www.clarkes-standard.com

These counter-service offshoots of P.J. Clarke's have a retro look inspired by old NYC delis and soda shops, and their "reasonably priced", nostalgia-driven American lineup stars "delicious, juicy burgers"; sit at one of the communal tables while listening to jukebox classics.

NEW Clarkson ● *American* | ▽ 20 | 16 | 21 | $54 |

W Village | 225 Varick St. (Houston St.) | 212-675-2474 | www.clarksonrestaurant.com

From the owner of Cercle Rouge comes this "large, publike" New American in the "out-of-the-way" West Village space that has previously been home to Steak Frites, Lucy Browne's, Charolais and others; a Thistle Hill Tavern vet mans the burners.

NEW The Cleveland ● *American* | - | - | - | M |

NoLita | 25 Cleveland Pl. (bet. Kenmare & Spring Sts.) | 212-274-0900 | www.theclevelandnyc.com

Lodged in a compact, whitewashed space that expands into a verdant back garden, this new NoLitan provides a rustic refuge for locals; the American market menu with Med inflections touches all the bases, and is paired with regional beers and eclectic wines.

Clinton St. Baking Company *American* | 25 | 14 | 18 | $26 |

LES | 4 Clinton St. (bet. Houston & Stanton Sts.) | 646-602-6263 | www.clintonstreetbaking.com

"Bring *War and Peace*" to pass the time in the "brunch line" at this "tiny" LES bakery/cafe where the "ridiculous" waits pay off when

	FOOD	DECOR	SERVICE	COST

homespun Americana "made with love" (especially those "divine pancakes") arrives; insiders hint "dinner is just as good" – and "you can get in."

Club A Steak House ☒ *Steak*

| 24 | 23 | 24 | $68 |

E 50s | 240 E. 58th St. (bet. 2nd & 3rd Aves.) | 212-688-4190 | www.clubasteak.com

Set in the "lesser known" area near the Queensboro Bridge, this bi-level steakhouse draws "older" locals with "A-1" chops, "top-notch" service and a "sexy", "bordello"-hued, fireplace-equipped setting; sure, it's on the "pricey" side, but "live music" and a "relaxed" mood compensate.

Co. *Pizza*

| 24 | 16 | 18 | $34 |

Chelsea | 230 Ninth Ave. (24th St.) | 212-243-1105 | www.co-pane.com

It's all about the "love of dough" at this Chelsea pizzeria where "bread guru" Jim Lahey serves "gourmet" pies flaunting "innovative toppings" and crust that "hits the magic spot between crispy and pillowy"; just don't expect much "elbow room" – this baby is "always busy."

NEW Cocina Economica Mexico *Mexican*

| ▽ 22 | 15 | 17 | $33 |

W 80s | 452 Amsterdam Ave. (82nd St.) | 212-501-7755 | www.cocinaeconomicamexico.com

"Fresh, fresh, fresh" is the word on the Mexican fare at this "terrific" UWS arrival from the chef at Land Thai next door; the "reasonably priced" menu includes classics as well as less-typical offerings (e.g. salmon in banana leaf), all made from "good ingredients", while the kitschy, religious decor is a knickknack collector's dream.

Coco Roco *Peruvian*

| 21 | 15 | 18 | $28 |

Cobble Hill | 139 Smith St. (bet. Bergen & Dean Sts.) | Brooklyn | 718-254-9933
Park Slope | 392 Fifth Ave. (bet. 6th & 7th Sts.) | Brooklyn | 718-965-3376
www.cocorocorestaurant.com

"Juicy-crisp" rotisserie chicken is the signature of these Park Slope-Cobble Hill Peruvians known for their "substantial portions" of "hearty", well-marinated grub that "won't empty your wallet"; "no atmosphere" leads aesthetes to fly the coop via takeout or delivery.

NEW Cocotte ◑ *French/Spanish*

| – | – | – | M |

SoHo | 110 Thompson St. (bet. Prince & Spring Sts.) | 212-965-9100 | www.cocotte-ny.com

Dark, moody and cellarlike, this wine-focused SoHo boîte offers up a menu of small plates and cocottes (little casseroles) with French and Spanish Basque accents, all spelled out on the chalkboard walls; communal tables and a little bar to the back boost the convivial mood.

Coffee Shop ◑ *American*

| 17 | 14 | 14 | $31 |

Union Sq | 29 Union Sq. W. (16th St.) | 212-243-7969 | www.thecoffeeshopnyc.com

One of NY's "quintessential" late-night scenes, this longtime Brazilian-American rolls out a "diner-esque menu" delivered by a "leggy" staff that's "more attractive than you" – and "less hardworking" too; since the chow's just "so-so" and the decor "tired", regulars take sidewalk seats to "watch Union Square pass by."

	FOOD	DECOR	SERVICE	COST

Colbeh *Kosher/Persian* — 23 | 19 | 20 | $41

Garment District | 32 W. 39th St. (bet. 5th & 6th Aves.) | 212-354-8181 | www.colbeh.com

"Authentic Persian" cooking augmented with sushi is the "pleasant" scenario at this kosher Garment District sleeper where the portions are as "generous" as the flavors are "intense"; however, the "glitzy" decor divides voters – it's "stylish" or "tacky Miami" depending on whom you ask – but you "won't leave hungry."

NEW Cole's Greenwich — ▽ 21 | 22 | 20 | $62

Village *American*

W Village | 118 Greenwich Ave. (13th St.) | 212-242-5966 | www.colesgreenwichvillage.com

The operators of the popular penthouse bar Jimmy have taken over the West Village wedge space that formerly housed Lyon, and their well-heeled followers are flocking to sample its high-end American fare; a bar area dubbed the Bottle Room is lit by a pink neon sign, while the dining space is split into a casual cafe and more formal room with decorative flourishes that evoke the 1950s.

Colicchio & Sons *American* — 25 | 25 | 25 | $75

Chelsea | 85 10th Ave. (bet. 15th & 16th Sts.) | 212-400-6699 | www.craftrestaurantsinc.com

"As you would expect from" *Top Chef*'s Tom Colicchio, this Chelsea "standout" is "top-notch all the way" from the "stellar" American "smart plates" and "first-class service" to the "striking", "spacious" surrounds; "stratospheric" tabs are the only catch, but the Tap Room delivers similar "excellence" for a "lower price."

Colonie ◑ *American* — 25 | 24 | 23 | $51

Brooklyn Heights | 127 Atlantic Ave. (bet. Clinton & Henry Sts.) | Brooklyn | 718-855-7500 | www.colonienyc.com

"Vibrant atmosphere meets inspired menu" at this Brooklyn Heights New American, where a seasonal lineup of "exceptional locavore" dishes pairs with "top-notch" service in a space sporting a "lush garden" wall; it's an acknowledged "keeper", though the "lively" "crowds" and no-reservations rule can make it "hard to snag a table."

Commerce *American* — 23 | 20 | 19 | $60

W Village | 50 Commerce St. (Barrow St.) | 212-524-2301 | www.commercerestaurant.com

The "good surprises" include a "delicious bread basket" preceding the "fabulous" New American plates at this "hidden" West Villager, which draws an "attractive crowd" into "charming", retro-chic digs with a "scene at the bar"; just be ready for "noisy" acoustics and that "funky" "credit-cards-only" policy.

Community Food & Juice *American* — 23 | 17 | 18 | $32

W 100s | 2893 Broadway (bet. 112th & 113th Sts.) | 212-665-2800 | www.communityrestaurant.com

"Beloved by its own community", this "buzzy" Morningside Heights New American is a "healthy" haven in "Columbialand" for "nourishing" eats with "locavore-ish" leanings; exuding "good vibes" for three meals a day, it's "wildly popular" for brunch, thus there's "always a line."

	FOOD	DECOR	SERVICE	COST

Congee Bowery ◐ *Chinese* — 20 | 12 | 13 | $24
LES | 207 Bowery (bet. Rivington & Spring Sts.) | 212-766-2828
Congee Village ◐ *Chinese*
LES | 100 Allen St. (bet. Broome & Delancey Sts.) | 212-941-1818
www.congeevillagerestaurants.com

The namesake porridge is "fantastic" at these kinda "tacky" Lower
Eastsiders, which also ply a laundry list of "pleasing" Cantonese
plates; "major miscommunication" with staffers isn't uncommon, but
the "congeenial" (read: "oh-so-cheap") pricing keeps 'em packed with
bargain-hunters "devouring" their meals.

Convivium Osteria *Mediterranean* — 25 | 23 | 22 | $54
Park Slope | 68 Fifth Ave. (bet. Bergen St. & St. Marks Ave.) | Brooklyn |
718-857-1833 | www.convivium-osteria.com

"Park Slope's Restaurant Row" is home to this "dreamy" Mediterranean
"experience" that melds "sumptuous cuisine" with a "serious" vino list
and "polite" service; done up in "warm", "rustic" style with "polished
wood", "mood lighting" and a "wonderful" garden, it boasts an especially "romantic" downstairs wine cellar.

Cookshop ◐ *American* — 23 | 19 | 21 | $50
Chelsea | 156 10th Ave. (20th St.) | 212-924-4440 |
www.cookshopny.com

"Always bustling", this ever "trendy" Chelsea American right off the
High Line fields a "fab" "farm-to-table" menu that's "sensibly priced
for the quality"; "prompt" servers oversee a wide "open" room that's
"lively" and "loud", particularly when the "pretty people" come out in
droves for brunch.

Coppelia ◐ *Diner/Pan-Latin* — 23 | 18 | 20 | $29
Chelsea | 207 W. 14th St. (bet. 7th & 8th Aves.) | 212-858-5001 |
www.coppelianyc.com

An "interesting" spin on a Cuban diner, this "friendly" Chelsea luncheonette slings "accomplished" Pan-Latin comfort chow in "casual",
"colorful" confines; the "low tabs", "no-rush atmosphere" and 24/7
open-door policy make it a hit with early-risers and "all-nighters" alike.

Coppola's *Italian* — 21 | 17 | 20 | $42
Murray Hill | 378 Third Ave. (bet. 27th & 28th Sts.) | 212-679-0070 ◐
W 70s | 206 W. 79th St. (bet. Amsterdam Ave. & B'way) | 212-877-3840
www.coppolas-nyc.com

"Like an old friend", these longtime Upper West Side–Murray Hill
Southern Italians are "relaxing", "reliable" fallbacks for "comfort"
chow heavy on the "red sauce"; maybe the "homey" settings are be-
coming "outdated", but "plentiful" portions, "courteous" service and
"moderate" prices compensate.

Corkbuzz ◐ *Eclectic* — 22 | 22 | 23 | $53
G Village | 13 E. 13th St. (bet. 5th Ave. & University Pl.) | 646-873-6071 |
www.corkbuzz.com

Its Eclectic share plates are "tasty", but it's wine that stars at this
Village bôite where "lovely" pairings are culled from a "vast" list of vintages, including an "extensive" by-the-glass selection; "expertise
flows freely" in the "modern", narrow space with communal tables in
the rear deemed a "must-try."

	FOOD	DECOR	SERVICE	COST

Cornelia Street Cafe ❶ *American/French* — 19 | 16 | 19 | $37

W Village | 29 Cornelia St. (bet. Bleecker & W. 4th Sts.) | 212-989-9319 |
www.corneliastreetcafe.com

"Old-school West Village" dining thrives at this circa-1977 "charmer"
with a "yoga vibe", offering "perfectly acceptable" Franco-American fare
and a "cheap and cheerful" brunch; although "starting to show its age",
it gets "bonus" points for the "cool" performance space downstairs.

Corner Bistro ❶ *Burgers* — 22 | 12 | 14 | $20

W Village | 331 W. Fourth St. (Jane St.) | 212-242-9502 ⊟
LIC | 47-18 Vernon Blvd. (47th Rd.) | Queens | 718-606-6500
www.cornerbistrony.com

"Memorable", "messy" burgers dished out on paper plates in "sticky
booths" make for classic "slumming" at this "dingy" Village perennial
(with a slightly "nicer" LIC spin-off); "cheap beer", "long waits" and
"student crowds" are all part of the timelessly "cool" experience.

Corner Social ❶ *American* — ∇ 17 | 19 | 17 | $38

Harlem | 321 Lenox Ave. (126th St.) | 212-510-8552 |
www.cornersocialnyc.com

True to its name, this Harlem American hosts a "meet-up" scene "of
the moment" fueled by familiar "quick bites" and "a little sip of something"; some label it a "bar with higher intentions", but regardless it's
a welcome "addition to the neighborhood."

Corsino ❶ *Italian* — 21 | 17 | 20 | $45

W Village | 637 Hudson St. (Horatio St.) | 212-242-3093 |
www.corsinocantina.com

They "get simplicity right" at this "stylish" West Village Italian where
"delectable" small plates are paired with a "vast, affordable" wine list;
patronized by "beautiful, thin" types and patrolled by a "thoughtful"
team, it's a "vibrant" – verging on "boisterous" – scene.

NEW Corvo Bianco *Italian* — - | - | - | M

W 80s | 446 Columbus Ave. (81st St.) | 212-595-2624 |
www.corvobianco.com

TV chef Elizabeth Faulkner makes her Manhattan debut with this midpriced arrival bringing coastal Italian cooking to the UWS; it inhabits
the old Calle Ocho space, with an airy front bar and a roomy rear dining room topped by a dramatic skylight.

NEW Costata *Italian/Steak* — - | - | - | VE

SoHo | 206 Spring St. (bet. 6th Ave. & Sullivan St.) | 212-334-3320 |
www.costatanyc.com

In SoHo's former Fiamma space, this new high-end steakhouse from
Michael White serves up the expected dry-aged beef plus ample seafood and pastas, matched with a smart cocktail list; the three-story,
lushly appointed space features plenty of elbow room between tables,
cushy leather chairs and large, colorful artwork.

Cotta *Italian* — 22 | 21 | 20 | $36

W 80s | 513 Columbus Ave. (bet. 84th & 85th Sts.) | 212-873-8500 |
www.cottanyc.com

"Busy and lively", this "rustic" UWS "neighborhood" Italian puts forth
"delicious" pizza and "tapas-type" plates in a ground-floor wine bar or

"cozy upstairs" (watch out for those "candles on the stairs"); it's "perfect for a casual date", with equally casual tabs to match.

The Counter *Burgers*
20 | 13 | 17 | $20

W 40s | 1451 Broadway (41st St.) | 212-997-6801 | www.thecounterburger.com

"Near-infinite" burger options are the lure at this Times Square link of the "build-it-yourself" national chain, where diners customize their orders "from bun to patty to toppings"; some shrug "nothing stellar", but most agree it's an "easy, cheap pre-theater bite."

Courgette ●⊘ *Mediteranean*
▽ 26 | 24 | 23 | $52

W 50s | 204 W. 55th St. (bet. B'way & 7th Ave.) | 212-333-7799 | www.courgette.us

From the MPD folks, this "stylish" Med bistro in the Dream Hotel makes a "friendly" choice "near City Center"; that the "surprisingly good" fare comes via "outstanding" staffers helps justify kinda "high" prices.

Covo ● *Italian*
23 | 19 | 21 | $36

Harlem | 701 W. 135th St. (12th Ave.) | 212-234-9573 | www.covony.com

"Solid" is the word on this "tucked-away" Harlem Italian supplying "tasty" pizza and pastas for "bang-for-the-buck" tabs in a "spread-out", brick-walled setting; "caring" servers distract from the "ear-ringing" noise, but night owls tout the "upstairs lounge."

Cowgirl *Southwestern*
17 | 18 | 18 | $30

W Village | 519 Hudson St. (W. 10th St.) | 212-633-1133 | www.cowgirlnyc.com

Cowgirl Sea-Horse *Southwestern*

Seaport | 259 Front St. (Dover St.) | 212-608-7873 | www.cowgirlseahorse.com

"Down-to-earth" says it all about this West Village Southwesterner slinging "decent" chow in a "kitschy", "retro rodeo" setting that's "kid-friendly" by day and a "high-octane" margaritaville after dark; the Seaport satellite gets a "fishy spin" with a seafood focus.

Crab Shanty ● *Seafood*
23 | 18 | 21 | $36

City Island | 361 City Island Ave. (Tier St.) | Bronx | 718-885-1810 | www.originalcrabshanty.com

They "pile it on" at this "informal" City Island vet where the "king-size" Italian seafood servings are both "tasty" and "affordable"; the fare's "fresh", but the nautical decor may have been out of the water too long.

Craft *American*
26 | 24 | 25 | $78

Flatiron | 43 E. 19th St. (bet. B'way & Park Ave. S.) | 212-780-0880 | www.craftrestaurantsinc.com

A "longtime favorite" "still going strong", *Top Chef* star Tom Colicchio's Flatiron American earns "high marks" for "pure", "ingredient-centric" cooking that makes for "delectable" results; "impeccable" service and "chic", "beautiful" digs boost the "delightful" but "pricey" experience.

Craftbar *American*
23 | 20 | 22 | $55

Flatiron | 900 Broadway (20th St.) | 212-461-4300 | www.craftrestaurantsinc.com

Craft's Flatiron "baby brother" is a "more casual" option for "Colicchio fans" seeking the chef's "inventive, seasonal" New Americana at a "lower" price point; "super" staffers oversee the "understated" "loft-like space" that's typically "hopping" with a "noisy" clientele.

Crave Fishbar *Seafood*
▽ | 25 | 19 | 20 | $53

E 50s | 945 Second Ave. (bet. 50th & 51st Sts.) | 646-895-9585 |
www.cravefishbar.com
Adding some "much needed" "cool" to Midtown East, this "fun", "friendly" little seafooder delivers "delicious", "foodie"-approved ocean fare amid "casual" coastal-rustic digs; relatively "reasonable" rates and "$1 oysters during happy hour" are further lures.

Crema *Mexican*
23 | 17 | 20 | $45

Chelsea | 111 W. 17th St. (bet. 6th & 7th Aves.) | 212-691-4477 |
www.cremarestaurante.com
"French techniques" give an "innovative" lift to the modern Mexican cooking at chef Julieta Ballesteros' "tucked-away" Chelsea "sleeper"; it's a "relaxed" enclave for "elevated" eating and "energetic" service, and "affordable" enough for *fanáticos* to "go back again and again."

Creperie ●⊄ *French*
22 | 13 | 18 | $15

G Village | 112 MacDougal St. (bet. Bleecker & Houston Sts.) | 212-253-6705
LES | 135 Ludlow St. (bet. Rivington & Stanton Sts.) | 212-979-5521
www.creperienyc.com
"Savory or sweet", the "comprehensive" roster of "custom-made" crêpes "hits the spot" at these counter-service standbys that are a no-brainer for folks "on a budget"; it's one of the "only games in town" for "late-night" noshing, though "tiny", "hole-in-the-wall" settings encourage ordering "to go."

Crif Dogs ● *Hot Dogs*
23 | 13 | 17 | $12

E Village | 113 St. Marks Pl. (bet. Ave. A & 1st Ave.) | 212-614-2728
Williamsburg | 555 Driggs Ave. (N. 7th St.) | Brooklyn | 718-302-3200
www.crifdogs.com
"Spunky", "deep-fried" hot dogs are a "guilty pleasure" at these "gritty" tubesteak twins famed for their "fun toppings" (like bacon, avocado and cream cheese); they're a natural for "cheap", "late-night munchies", and the East Village original features a secret "speakeasy" bar accessed through a "phone booth."

Crispo ● *Italian*
23 | 19 | 20 | $51

W Village | 240 W. 14th St. (bet. 7th & 8th Aves.) | 212-229-1818 |
www.crisporestaurant.com
Pastaphiles are "blown away" by this "favorite" West Village trattoria purveying "gratifying" Northern Italiana led by a signature spaghetti carbonara that "has no rivals"; its "increasing popularity" results in "loud, cramped" conditions, so insiders head for the "all-seasons garden."

Crown *American*
21 | 25 | 22 | $87

E 80s | 24 E. 81st St. (bet. 5th & Madison Aves.) | 646-559-4880 |
www.crown81.com
"Luxurious" is the mind-set at this destination from chef John DeLucie (Bill's, The Lion), luring "UES billionaires" and "plastic-surgery" practitioners with its "gorgeous" townhouse setting, "upper-class-club" mood and "glass-walled" garden room; "excellent" American fare and "courteous" service round out this "royal treat", best savored when "someone else is paying."

	FOOD	DECOR	SERVICE	COST

Cuba *Cuban*
| | 23 | 19 | 21 | $42 |

G Village | 222 Thompson St. (bet. Bleecker & 3rd Sts.) | 212-420-7878 | www.cubanyc.com

Everyone's "Havana great time" at this "high-energy" Village supplier of "authentic" Cuban standards and "heavenly" mojitos "charmingly" served in "funky" Latin digs; "live bands", "relatively affordable" tabs and a "cigar-rolling man" lend a "vacation" vibe to the proceedings.

Cubana Café ⊄ *Cuban*
| | 21 | 17 | 19 | $23 |

Park Slope | 80 Sixth Ave. (St. Marks Ave.) | Brooklyn | 718-398-9818 | www.cubanacafenyc.com

An "enjoyable little spot", this "bright, cheery" Cuban on the Park Slope-Prospect Heights border offers up "solid" standards and "really good mojitos" at "even better prices"; just be aware there's "not much elbow room", service is "casual" and the payment's cash only.

NEW Cull & Pistol *Seafood*
| | - | - | - | M |

Chelsea | Chelsea Mkt. | 75 Ninth Ave. (bet. 15th & 16th Sts.) | 646-568-1223 | www.cullandpistol.com

A real sit-down eatery from Chelsea Market's Lobster Place, this next-door, subway tile-lined seafooder offers up lobster rolls and other midpriced shore faves, plus raw-bar items, matched with a respectable drinks list; it takes its name from crustacean talk: a 'cull' is a lobster who's lost a claw and a 'pistol' is one who's lost both.

Da Andrea *Italian*
| | 23 | 17 | 22 | $39 |

G Village | 35 W. 13th St. (bet. 5th & 6th Aves.) | 212-367-1979 | www.daandreanyc.com

"Delicious" housemade pastas and other Emilia-Romagna standards are a "steal" at this "cozy", "unpretentious" Villager; with "warm", "friendly" staffers keeping the vibe copacetic, it's no wonder "neighborhood" denizens come back "time after time."

Da Ciro *Italian/Pizza*
| | 22 | 16 | 20 | $48 |

Murray Hill | 229 Lexington Ave. (bet. 33rd & 34th Sts.) | 212-532-1636

"Mouthwatering" focaccia Robiola is "reason enough" to frequent this Murray Hill duplex that's also a "reliable" source for wood-fired pizza and other "delicious" Italiana; upstairs is quieter than down, but no matter where you wind up, tabs tilt "a bit high."

Dafni Greek Taverna *Greek*
| | 19 | 14 | 19 | $36 |

W 40s | 325 W. 42nd St. (bet. 8th & 9th Aves.) | 212-315-1010 | www.dafnitaverna.com

Set on a "no-man's-land" block opposite Port Authority, this "genuine" Greek comes across with "decent" renditions of "typical" Hellenica; "convenience to the theater", a short trip to Jersey and "affordability" are its trump cards, though the "nothing-special" decor needs work.

Daisy May's BBQ USA *BBQ*
| | 21 | 8 | 13 | $26 |

W 40s | 623 11th Ave. (46th St.) | 212-977-1500 | www.daisymaysbbq.com

"Fall-off-the-bone" ribs and other "darn-good" BBQ allow patrons to "get in touch with the caveman within" at Adam Perry Lang's Clinton 'cue hut; despite "cafeteria-style" service, decor "best left undescribed" and a "nearly-in-the-Hudson River" address, fans feel "lucky to have it."

	FOOD	DECOR	SERVICE	COST

Da Nico *Italian*
21 | 17 | 20 | $42

Little Italy | 164 Mulberry St. (bet. Broome & Grand Sts.) | 212-343-1212 |
www.danicoristorante.com

A "Mulberry Street staple" for more than 20 years, this "traditional"
Italian rolls out "gargantuan" portions of "tasty" vittles that are "a cut
above the local" norm; "attentive" service, "nominal" prices and a
large back garden complete the overall "comfortable" picture.

Daniel ⑤ *French*
28 | 28 | 28 | $146

E 60s | 60 E. 65th St. (bet. Madison & Park Aves.) | 212-288-0033 |
www.danielnyc.com

Still the "hautest of haute" after two decades, Daniel Boulud's "magnificent" Eastsider offers a "religious experience" via "otherworldly"
prix fixe-only New French cuisine, an "exquisite", jackets-required
setting and near-"flawless" service; sure, you'll need a "Brinks truck"
to settle the bill, but "it's worth the gold" to "dine in heaven"; P.S. the
comparatively casual lounge offers à la carte dining.

Danji ❶⑤ *Korean*
25 | 18 | 20 | $50

W 50s | 346 W. 52nd St. (bet. 8th & 9th Aves.) | 212-586-2880 |
www.danjinyc.com

"Fantastic, elegant" cooking and a "lively, energetic" vibe means this
"upscale" Hell's Kitchen "Korean tapas" specialist remains a "tough
table to get" (brace for an "interminable wait"); a pleasant "pared-
down" setting and capable – if slightly "indifferent" – service help ensure it's a "fun place to be."

Danny Brown Wine Bar & Kitchen Ⓜ *European*
26 | 22 | 25 | $53

Forest Hills | 104-02 Metropolitan Ave. (71st Dr.) | Queens |
718-261-2144 | www.dannybrownwinekitchen.com

Delivering "Manhattan-style" fine dining at Queens prices, this Forest
Hills "culinary heaven" serves up "inventive", "lovingly prepared"
European fare matched with "wonderful" vintages; a "charming", "sophisticated" setting and "knowledgeable", "attentive" service complete
the "first-class" experience.

Da Noi *Italian*
23 | 19 | 22 | $49

Shore Acres | 138 Fingerboard Rd. (Tompkins Ave.) | Staten Island |
718-720-1650
Travis | 4358 Victory Blvd. (Crabbs Ln.) | Staten Island | 718-982-5040
www.danoirestaurant.com

"Old-world" "red-sauce" cooking "like nonna's" draws fans to these
"congenial" Staten Island Italians where "generous portions" turn
"pricey" tabs into "money well spent"; the crowd's right out of a "scene
from *The Godfather*", while the sound level's a bit on "da noisy" side.

Darbar *Indian*
21 | 16 | 19 | $36

E 40s | 152 E. 46th St. (bet. Lexington & 3rd Aves.) | 212-681-4500 |
www.darbarny.com

Darbar Grill *Indian*

E 50s | 157 E. 55th St. (bet. Lexington & 3rd Aves.) | 212-751-4600 |
www.darbargrill.com

Aficionados of "high-quality Indian" cuisine patronize these Midtowners
for a "standard repertoire" of "solid", "well-prepared" dishes served

by a "gracious" team in "comfortable" confines; even better, there's "no sticker shock", particularly at the "can't-be-beat" $13 lunch buffet.

Da Silvano ❶ *Italian*   22 | 17 | 20 | $65

G Village | 260 Sixth Ave. (bet. Bleecker & Houston Sts.) | 212-982-2343 | www.dasilvano.com

The "glitterati" draw the "paparazzi" to this ever-"trendy" Villager where "celeb-spotting" is the "main course", though the Tuscan eats are almost as "delicious"; it costs "wads of cash" and the staff can be "snooty" to outsiders, so for best results, bring "George Clooney" – and get him to pick up the check.

Da Tommaso ❶ *Italian*   20 | 16 | 20 | $49

W 50s | 903 Eighth Ave. (bet. 53rd & 54th Sts.) | 212-265-1890 | www.datommasony.com

The "quality never falters" at this veteran Hell's Kitchen Italian purveying "lovely old-school" cooking with "waiters to match"; maybe da "dated" room "could use a face-lift", but "reasonable" rates and a "near-the–Theater District" address keep it "crowded" before a show.

Da Umberto 🗷 *Italian*   25 | 19 | 23 | $68

Chelsea | 107 W. 17th St. (bet. 6th & 7th Aves.) | 212-989-0303 | www.daumbertonyc.com

"Still a classic", this 25-plus-year-old Chelsea "favorite" rolls out "serious" Northern Italian cuisine with "vibrant" flavors in a "simple" space where the white-tablecloth "elegance" is matched by "impeccable" service; "costly" tabs aside, it fits the bill for a "romantic" or otherwise "special" occasion.

David Burke at   19 | 14 | 16 | $38
Bloomingdale's *American*

E 50s | Bloomingdale's | 150 E. 59th St. (bet. Lexington & 3rd Aves.) | 212-705-3800 | www.burkeinthebox.com

Assuage a "shopping hangover" with "high-fashion" New American "quick bites" à la David Burke at this "fast-paced" cafe in Bloomie's (and its grab 'n' go counterpart); despite "uninspiring" surroundings and "sloppy service", it's "convenient" and thus "continuously crowded."

David Burke Fishtail *Seafood*   24 | 23 | 23 | $68

E 60s | 135 E. 62nd St. (bet. Lexington & Park Aves.) | 212-754-1300 | www.fishtaildb.com

"Fabulous" seafood dished up in "lovely townhouse" digs by a "chipper" crew is the lure at David Burke's UES piscatorium, where "cheerful", "modern" decor distinguishes the downstairs bar ("hopping" at happy hour), upstairs dining room and terrace; it's "pricey" – even factoring in the "complimentary peanut brittle" – but the $24 lunch prix fixe is a "bargain."

David Burke Kitchen *American*   24 | 21 | 22 | $60

SoHo | James Hotel | 23 Grand St., downstairs (6th Ave.) | 212-201-9119 | www.davidburkekitchen.com

"Creative" but "casual", this far-from-cheap "farm-to-fork" option from David Burke matches "delightful" New Americana with "on-point" service and a "semi-subterranean" setting in SoHo's James Hotel; the Treehouse Bar upstairs adds an extra dimension to the "inviting" package.

	FOOD	DECOR	SERVICE	COST

David Burke Townhouse *American*   25 | 24 | 24 | $71

E 60s | 133 E. 61st St. (bet. Lexington & Park Aves.) | 212-813-2121 |
www.davidburketownhouse.com

It's "David Burke at his best" at this UES townhouse where the "exquisitely complex" New American cuisine and "beautiful" (if "tightly packed") setting are only "outclassed by the people-watching" its Social Register clientele provides; you'll "empty your pockets", but "hospitable" service takes out the sting – and there's always the $25 lunch prix fixe "steal."

Dawat *Indian*   23 | 19 | 21 | $49

E 50s | 210 E. 58th St. (bet. 2nd & 3rd Aves.) | 212-355-7555
Midtown's Indian "pioneer" (since 1986) "still pleases", thanks to actress/chef Madhur Jaffrey's "sophisticated" cooking, "graciously served" in a "quiet", "contemporary" room that's "conducive to conversation"; it may look "a little worn", but loyalists avow the tabs are "worth the extra cost."

db Bistro Moderne *French*   25 | 22 | 23 | $68

W 40s | City Club Hotel | 55 W. 44th St. (6th Ave.) | 212-391-2400 |
www.danielnyc.com

"Less formal than the mother ship", Daniel Boulud's Theater District French is nonetheless a "sleek", "upscale" option applying "artful", "Daniel-like" preparation to modern bistro fare – including a "ridiculous", "delicious" foie gras–stuffed $32 burger; things can get a bit "noisy and crammed" pre-curtain, but "accommodating" service and that "bargain" $45 prix fixe compensate.

DBGB ● *French*   24 | 22 | 21 | $52

E Village | 299 Bowery (bet. 1st & Houston Sts.) | 212-933-5300 |
www.danielnyc.com

"Uptown chic" meets "downtown casual" at Daniel Boulud's "boisterous" Bowery French destination, a "carnivore heaven" where "out-of-this-world" sausages and "epic" burgers meet "killer cocktails" and "premium" suds; sure, it's "noisy" and "packed", but to most the "scene's a scream", with relatively "reasonable" rates as the crowning touch.

Dee's Ⓜ *Mediterranean/Pizza*   22 | 18 | 21 | $31

Forest Hills | 107-23 Metropolitan Ave. (74th Ave.) | Queens |
718-793-7553 | www.deesnyc.com

Dee-votees depend on this "homey" Forest Hills outlet for "wonderful" brick-oven pizzas, Mediterranean "comfort" classics and burgers and other grill items; "fair prices", a "huge" space and "ample seating" bolster the "amicable", "family-friendly" mood.

Defonte's *Sandwiches*   24 | 9 | 17 | $16

Gramercy | 261 Third Ave. (21st St.) | 212-614-1500 |
www.defontesofbrooklyn.com
Red Hook | 379 Columbia St. (Luquer St.) | Brooklyn | 718-625-8052 |
www.defontesinbrooklyn.com Ⓢ ⊟

"Don't eat for a week" before attacking the "two-handed" "Dagwood" sandwiches at these "lip-smacking" Italian sub shops; the '20s-era Red Hook original "used to feed the longshoremen" and still exudes a whiff of "old-fashioned Brooklyn", while its "Manhattan outpost" continues the tradition in a no-frills Gramercy storefront.

	FOOD	DECOR	SERVICE	COST

DeGrezia ⑤ _Italian_ | 24 | 22 | 24 | $66 |

E 50s | 231 E. 50th St. (bet. 2nd & 3rd Aves.) | 212-750-5353 |
www.degreziaristorante.com

A "real sleeper" hidden below street level, this Eastsider is a model of
"old-world elegance", offering "first-rate" Italian food, "expert" service and a "civilized" milieu where "one can actually talk"; though "expensive", it's "worth it for special occasions" and "business lunches."

Degustation ● _French/Spanish_ | 28 | 20 | 24 | $84 |

E Village | 239 E. Fifth St. (bet. 2nd & 3rd Aves.) | 212-979-1012 |
www.degustation-nyc.com

"Intimate" and "extraordinary" in equal measure, Grace and Jack
Lamb's "tiny" Franco-Spanish East Villager serves up "exquisite",
"smack-in-the-taste-buds" small plates via "friendly" chefs who work
their "magic" in an open, behind-the-bar kitchen; be warned though,
the "dollar-to-calorie ratio" isn't always favorable.

Del Frisco's ● _Steak_ | 25 | 23 | 23 | $77 |

W 40s | 1221 Sixth Ave. (bet. 48th & 49th Sts.) | 212-575-5129 |
www.delfriscos.com

Del Frisco's Grille _Steak_

W 50s | Rockefeller Ctr. | 50 Rockefeller Plaza (51st St.) | 212-767-0371 |
www.delfriscosgrille.com

"High-energy" "power scenes" are the deal at this "cavernous" Midtown
chop shop and its smaller Rock Center sibling, where "brontosaurus-size
steaks" are delivered to carnivorous "corporate" types via a "personable" crew; it's best when "someone else is paying", but for the "expense
account"-challenged there's a "must-try" $50 prix fixe.

Delicatessen ● _American_ | 19 | 19 | 18 | $35 |

NoLita | 54 Prince St. (Lafayette St.) | 212-226-0211 |
www.delicatessennyc.com

NoLita is home to this wannabe "trendy" spot slinging "filling"
Americana (e.g. "fantastic" mac 'n' cheese) in "minimalist" digs outfitted with retractable walls; cynics feel it "tries too hard", but concede that the staff is "pretty" and the downstairs bar "lively."

Dell'anima ● _Italian_ | 25 | 19 | 22 | $59 |

W Village | 38 Eighth Ave. (Jane St.) | 212-366-6633 | www.dellanima.com
Ever "jam-packed" thanks to its "wonderful" rustic Italian fare (including "the best housemade pastas"), this "cozy", "warm" West Villager
showcases a chef's counter where you can watch the "magic" happen;
"reservations are a must", or plan to while out the "long wait" in its adjacent wine bar, Anfora.

Delmonico's ⑤ _Steak_ | 23 | 23 | 23 | $72 |

Financial District | 56 Beaver St. (William St.) | 212-509-1144 |
www.delmonicosny.com

NEW Delmonico's Kitchen _Steak_

Garment District | 207 W. 36th St. (bet. 7th & 8th Aves.) | 212-695-5220 |
www.delmonicosrestaurantgroup.com

A "piece of NY history", this "revived" FiDi meatery trades in "days-of-
yore" "charm" but also "choice cuts" that "melt in your mouth" and arrive
via "courteous", "pro" staffers; the new Garment District offshoot cred-
ibly upholds the tradition, including "Wall Street tycoon"-worthy pricing.

| | FOOD | DECOR | SERVICE | COST |

Del Posto *Italian*

26 | 27 | 26 | $111

Chelsea | 85 10th Ave. (bet. 15th & 16th Sts.) | 212-497-8090 | www.delposto.com

Another "incredible dining experience" delivered by Mario, Joe and Lidia, this Chelsea "stunner" serves up "masterful" "upscale Italian" cuisine and "unrivaled" wines in "opulent" balconied environs overseen by a "first-class" crew; yes, the prices can seem "punitive" – "have a grappa ready when the check arrives" – but hey, it's "cheaper than flying to Italy."

Delta Grill ● *Cajun/Creole*

20 | 16 | 18 | $33

W 40s | 700 Ninth Ave. (48th St.) | 212-956-0934 | www.thedeltagrill.com

"N'Awlins comes to Ninth Avenue" at this "funky" Hell's Kitchen roadhouse that channels the "Big Easy" with "reliable" Cajun-Creole grub that "somehow tastes better when a band is playing"; "cheery" vibes and "reasonable" tabs keep the "patrons marching in."

Denino's Pizzeria ⊅ *Pizza*

26 | 13 | 20 | $21

Port Richmond | 524 Port Richmond Ave. (bet. Hooker Pl. & Walker St.) | Staten Island | 718-442-9401 | www.deninos.com

"In Staten Island, this is the place for pizza" declare devotees of the "fantastic" "thin-crust" pies this "low-price" Port Richmond parlor has been producing since 1937; "don't worry about the decor", the noise from the adjoining tavern or the "no-plastic" policy – there's a reason it's "rarely empty."

Dervish ● *Mediterranean*

19 | 15 | 19 | $39

W 40s | 146 W. 47th St. (bet. 6th & 7th Aves.) | 212-997-0070 | www.dervishrestaurant.com

"Well established" as a "dependable" curtain-raiser, this Theater District Med specializes in "satisfying" "homestyle" cooking ferried by "expeditious" servers who "whirl you in and out"; "modest prices" – i.e. that $28 early-bird prix fixe – make the "tired" decor easy to swallow.

Destino *Italian*

19 | 19 | 20 | $59

E 50s | 891 First Ave. (50th St.) | 212-751-0700 | www.destinony.com

Sutton Place "locals" like this "classy" joint for its "well-prepared" Southern Italian cooking via a Rao's alum who knows his way around a meatball; "understated" atmospherics, luxe furnishings and an "occasional piano player" make the "high prices" more palatable.

Deux Amis *French*

20 | 18 | 22 | $48

E 50s | 356 E. 51st St. (bet. 1st & 2nd Aves.) | 212-230-1117 | www.deuxamisnyc.com

The "warm" owner and "agreeable staff" lend a "feel-at-home" air to this East Midtown bistro, an approximation of "side-street-Paris" dining featuring "solid" French country cuisine; the interior's "*plaisant*" if "a bit close", so some find it's "best sitting outside."

Dévi *Indian*

23 | 21 | 21 | $54

Flatiron | 8 E. 18th St. (bet. B'way & 5th Ave.) | 212-691-1300 | www.devinyc.com

Among the first of NYC's "high-end Indians", this Flatironer still delivers with "delicious" subcontinental cooking (including "veggies a carnivore could die for") served up in "exotic" environs; to some "it's not

	FOOD	DECOR	SERVICE	COST

the same" since Suvir Saran exited the kitchen, but the majority calls it an overall "wonderful experience."

Dhaba ● *Indian*

| 23 | 15 | 17 | $31 |

Murray Hill | 108 Lexington Ave. (bet. 27th & 28th Sts.) | 212-679-1284 | www.dhabanyc.com

"Delicious and different", this "simple" Curry Hill Indian turns out "impressive", "pungently spiced" specialties – even "'regular' is hot, hot, hot" – at "terrific-value" tabs; there's "always a line" at the "sliver" of a space for the "bargain" $11 lunch buffet.

Di Fara Ⓜ✉ *Pizza*

| 26 | 6 | 11 | $18 |

Midwood | 1424 Ave. J (15th St.) | Brooklyn | 718-258-1367 | www.difara.com

Taste the "magical" pies "lovingly prepared" by octogenarian "pizza alchemist" Dom DeMarco at this '60s-era Midwood "temple" and "all is good in the world"; "unnerving" waits, decidedly "nothing-fancy" digs and smile-free service are just part of the "total experience" – acolytes insist it's more than "worth the trouble" for a "slice of heaven."

Dim Sum Go Go *Chinese*

| 21 | 12 | 16 | $24 |

Chinatown | 5 E. Broadway (bet. Catherine St. & Chatham Sq.) | 212-732-0797 | www.dimsumgogo.com

"Cheap", "no-frills" dim sum ordered off a menu rather than snagged from a trolley makes this "utilitarian" Chinese "less chaotic" than the typical C-town outfits; however, traditionalists "miss the ladies schlepping the carts" and report "perfunctory service" and "run-of-the-mill" decor.

Diner ● *American*

| 24 | 17 | 21 | $40 |

Williamsburg | 85 Broadway (Berry St.) | Brooklyn | 718-486-3077 | www.dinernyc.com

The "memorable", "daily changing", locally sourced New Americana – "far from diner fare" – is as "tops as the crowd" at this "cool, laid-back" Williamsburg pioneer; its "blast-from-the-past" 1927 dining car digs are a "snug fit", but the helpful staff ("don't be afraid to ask for direction") and "good wine/cocktail list" help keep the mood copacetic.

Dinosaur Bar-B-Que *BBQ*

| 23 | 18 | 18 | $32 |

Harlem | 700 W. 125th St. (12th Ave.) | 212-694-1777
NEW Gowanus | 604 Union St. (4th Ave.) | Brooklyn | 347-429-7030
www.dinosaurbarbque.com

This "biker-approved" West Harlem BBQ barn (and its long-awaited Gowanus offshoot) slings "heaping plates" of "glorious", "five-napkin" 'cue backed by an "amazing beer selection" in a "Deep South roadhouse" setting; "working-man's" prices and a "free-for-all" atmosphere suggest it "won't go extinct" anytime soon.

Dirt Candy Ⓢ Ⓜ *Vegetarian*

| 25 | 17 | 24 | $50 |

E Village | 430 E. Ninth St. (bet. Ave. A & 1st Ave.) | 212-228-7732 | www.dirtcandynyc.com

"Clever", "complex" vegetarian dishes that "look mouthwatering" and "taste even better" are the calling card of this "fun" East Villager where chef-owner Amanda Cohen's "brilliant invention" "wins over" even "devout carnivores"; the "unassuming" digs are seriously "tiny", though, so "snag a reservation."

	FOOD	DECOR	SERVICE	COST

NEW Distilled ◐ *American*

| - | - | - | M |

TriBeCa | 211 W. Broadway (bet. Franklin & White Sts.) | 212-601-9514 | www.distilledny.com

A Momofuku Noodle Bar vet mans the burners at this self-styled TriBeCa 'public house' where the upscale takes on American comfort faves are matched with creative cocktails as well as NY-made meads; set in a landmark building, it boasts floor-to-ceiling windows and an open kitchen with a chef's counter where you can take in the action.

Divino *Italian*

| 19 | 16 | 20 | $46 |

E 80s | 1556 Second Ave. (bet. 80th & 81st Sts.) | 212-861-1096 | www.divinonewyork.com

Yorkville denizens "always feel welcome" at this "neighborhood" vet thanks to "gracious" staffers serving "dependable Italian staples" in calm, "comfortable" environs; weekend "live music" lends this "oldie but goodie" a "fun atmosphere."

Docks Oyster Bar *Seafood*

| 20 | 18 | 20 | $55 |

E 40s | 633 Third Ave. (40th St.) | 212-986-8080 | www.docksoysterbar.com

"Reliable" fish and bivalves galore reel in the masses at this "cavernous" seafood standby near Grand Central; "briskly professional" servers tend to schools of "biz lunchers" and "after-work" revelers who dive in for its "active" happy hour and high-octane "social" scene.

Do Hwa *Korean*

| 22 | 18 | 18 | $39 |

W Village | 55 Carmine St. (bet. Bedford St. & 7th Ave.) | 212-414-1224 | www.dohwanyc.com

"Authentic" eats packing "lots of spice" chased with "creative" cocktails fuel the "cool vibe" at this "hip" West Village Korean, a slightly "upscale" take on the "traditional" with grill-equipped tables on hand for hands-on types; sure, it may cost "a little more than K-town", but it's a much "sexier" experience.

Dominick's ♯ *Italian*

| 23 | 12 | 19 | $40 |

Fordham | 2335 Arthur Ave. (bet. 184th & 187th Sts.) | Bronx | 718-733-2807

Patrons have been filling the communal tables of this "iconic" Arthur Avenue Italian since 1966, despite no decor, "no menus" ("you eat what they're cooking"), "no checks" ("trust the waiter") and no reservations or credit cards; "off-the-charts" food and "cost performance" make the "daunting waits" bearable, but to save time, go early.

Don Antonio *Pizza*

| 24 | 16 | 18 | $31 |

W 50s | 309 W. 50th St. (bet. 8th & 9th Aves.) | 646-719-1043 | www.donantoniopizza.com

Pizzaphiles ascend to "pie heaven" via the dozens of varieties built on "light, flaky" crusts at this "excellent" Hell's Kitchen Italian (linked to a famous Naples pizzeria), though its flash-fried rendition is considered especially "scrumptious"; the digs are "cramped" and "hectic" yet "civilized" nonetheless – and those "mmm" wood-fired pies "overcome all."

Donatella *Italian*

| 20 | 18 | 18 | $44 |

Chelsea | 184 Eighth Ave. (bet. 19th & 20th Sts.) | 212-493-5150 | www.donatellanyc.com

"Glitz" meets garlic at Donatella Arpaia's "cheerful" Chelsea pizzeria, a "jumping" joint turning out "rich, flavorful" Neapolitan pies along

| | FOOD | DECOR | SERVICE | COST |

with "appetizing" Italian standards; "gracious" staffers patrol the "trattoria"-like setting, dominated by a gold-tiled oven that hints at the "pricey"-for-the-neighborhood tariffs.

Don Giovanni ● *Italian/Pizza* `20` `14` `18` `$32`

Chelsea | 214 10th Ave. (23rd St.) | 212-242-9054
W 40s | 358 W. 44th St. (bet. 8th & 9th Aves.) | 212-581-4939
www.dongiovanni-ny.com

The thin-crust pizza's "a cut above" at these Chelsea–Times Square Italians, home of coal-fired pies that are "heavy on the cheese but light on the price"; regulars straying from the slices "stick to the basics" on the "pretty good" Italian menu and opt for "outdoor seating" – there's "not much ambiance" inside.

Donguri Ⓜ *Japanese* `25` `15` `23` `$70`

E 80s | 309 E. 83rd St. (bet. 1st & 2nd Aves.) | 212-737-5656 |
www.dongurinyc.com

"Tiny but lovely", this "side-street" Yorkville Japanese specializes in dishes from the Kansai region – think "brilliantly prepared" soba, udon and sashimi (there's no sushi, however); "hospitable" servers who "don't rush you" make for "relaxing" dining, that is until the "expensive" check arrives.

Donovan's *American* `20` `18` `19` `$29`

Bayside | 214-16 41st Ave. (Bell Blvd.) | Queens | 718-423-5178 |
www.donovansofbayside.com
Woodside | 57-24 Roosevelt Ave. (58th St.) | Queens | 718-429-9339 |
www.donovansny.com ●⇴

"Something-for-everyone" menus lure the "family" trade to these separately owned Queens vets lauded for "perfect" hamburgers along with "solid", "Irish-tinged" pub grub; the Bayside outlet has been "redecorated" and Woodside is "cash only", but both enjoy "bargain" tabs and "pleasant" service.

Don Peppe Ⓜ⇴ *Italian* `25` `12` `19` `$47`

Ozone Park | 135-58 Lefferts Blvd. (149th Ave.) | Queens | 718-845-7587
An "old-school", cash-only red-sauce joint "unburdened by pretention", this circa-1968 Ozone Park Italian is the place for "marvelous" meals that end with "sacks of leftovers"; the house wines might've been "made yesterday" and the digs "could use redecorating" – but then you "don't go for atmosphere."

Do or Dine ● *Eclectic* ▽ `25` `22` `24` `$32`

Bed-Stuy | 1108 Bedford Ave. (bet. Lexington Ave. & Quincy St.) |
Brooklyn | 718-684-2290

"Young, hip and full of creative flavor", this Bed-Stuy standout excels with "all kinds of crazy dishes and drinks" ("the foie gras donuts are a highlight") delivered by an "excellent staff"; the come-as-you-are space sporting a skull-and-bones mosaic, disco ball and "hip-hop" soundtrack can "get a little crowded" but most are too busy "having a really fun time" to care.

Dos Caminos *Mexican* `20` `19` `18` `$43`

E 50s | 825 Third Ave. (bet. 50th & 51st Sts.) | 212-336-5400
Meatpacking | 675 Hudson St. (bet. 13th & 14th Sts.) | 212-699-2400
(continued)

(continued)

Dos Caminos

Murray Hill | 373 Park Ave. S. (bet. 26th & 27th Sts.) | 212-294-1000
SoHo | 475 W. Broadway (bet. Houston & Prince Sts.) | 212-277-4300
www.doscaminos.com

"Killer" margs and guac made tableside highlight the "reliable", "affordable" Mexican offerings at these "lively" Steve Hanson joints; "harried" service and "generic" settings don't deter its "young, energetic" crowd from kicking up a "vibrant" "party scene."

Dos Toros *Mexican*   21 | 12 | 18 | $14

E 70s | 1111 Lexington Ave. (bet. 77th & 78th Sts.) | 212-535-4658
E Village | 137 Fourth Ave. (13th St.) | 212-677-7300
W Village | 11 Carmine St. (bet. Bleecker St. & 6th Ave.) | 212-627-2051
NEW **Williamsburg** | 189 Bedford Ave. (bet. N. 6th & 7th Sts.) |
Brooklyn | 718-384-8833
www.dostoros.com

"Legitimate" Mexican fare by way of the "Bay area" is the specialty of these "cheap, fab" taquerias, "eco-friendly" stops luring both bullish burrito buffs and Cali transplants; there's "always a line and never a table", but "fast delivery" is an option at most outlets.

Dovetail *American*   25 | 23 | 24 | $81

W 70s | 103 W. 77th St. (Columbus Ave.) | 212-362-3800 |
www.dovetailnyc.com

John Fraser's "suave" New American is a "memorable" UWS destination, offering an "exquisite symphony" of "original" dishes, "stunningly" presented by a "gracious" staff in a "serene", bi-level setting; such "perfection" is understandably expensive, though the $52 'Sunday suppa' is a "special treat."

Due ◑ *Italian*   21 | 16 | 21 | $51

E 70s | 1396 Third Ave. (bet. 79th & 80th Sts.) | 212-772-3331 |
www.duenyc.com

Locals tout the "simple", "satisfying" Northern Italian cooking and "feel-at-home" atmosphere at this longtime "low-profile" Upper Eastsider; "rustic" looks and "warm" service enhance its "unpretentious" air, and fair prices seal the deal.

DuMont *American*   23 | 18 | 20 | $30

Williamsburg | 432 Union Ave. (bet. Devoe St. & Metropolitan Ave.) |
Brooklyn | 718-486-7717 | www.dumontnyc.com

DuMont Burger ◑ *American*

Williamsburg | 314 Bedford Ave. (bet. S. 1st & 2nd Sts.) | Brooklyn |
718-384-6127 | www.dumontburger.com

A "neighborhood mainstay", this "casual" Williamsburg New American offers "mad delicious" grub sourced from "farmer's markets" and best savored in its "romantic" back garden; the burger-oriented Bedford branch aces the "perfect" patty, but is about as "small" as the bun.

Dumpling Man ◑⇆ *Chinese*   20 | 9 | 16 | $13

E Village | 100 St. Marks Pl. (bet. Ave. A & 1st Ave.) | 212-505-2121 |
www.dumplingman.com

Steamed or seared, the "scrumptious dumplings" at this East Village Chinese make for a "super-cheap", cash-only snack that's handmade "right in front of you" (a "show in itself"); many prefer to "stuff themselves" on the run since the premises "aren't much to look at."

The Dutch *American*

| 23 | 21 | 21 | $62 |

SoHo | 131 Sullivan St. (Prince St.) | 212-677-6200 | www.thedutchnyc.com

Chef Andrew Carmellini's "delish" riffs on American dishes draw "trendsetters" to this "fashionable" SoHo "winner"; critics cite "pricey" tariffs, "scene over substance" and "construction-zone decibel levels", but consensus says it's "well worth the investment" – "if only it were easier to get in."

E&E Grill House *Steak*

| 21 | 19 | 22 | $47 |

W 40s | Pearl Hotel | 233 W. 49th St. (bet. B'way & 8th Ave.) | 212-505-9909 | www.eegrillhouse.com

"Darn-good steaks" and seafood are the headliners at this "heart-of-Times Square" chophouse where a minimalist, "modern" setting and "eager-to-please" staffers set a "delightful" mood; throw in tabs that "won't break the bank", and showgoers say this baby's got star "potential."

East End Kitchen *American*

| 20 | 19 | 18 | $47 |

E 80s | 539 E. 81st St. (bet. East End & York Aves.) | 212-879-0450 | www.eastendkitchennyc.com

"Finally", "sleepy" Yorkville has a "neighborhood" haunt all its own in this "promising" place offering "homey" Americana, "casual" brunching and even a grab-and-go espresso bar; the "Hamptons"-esque decor is "stylish", but critics wish the servers would "get their act together."

East Pacific *Asian*

| 22 | 19 | 20 | $31 |

Murray Hill | 120 E. 34th St. (bet. Lexington & Park Aves.) | 212-696-2818
New Springville | Staten Island Mall | 2655 Richmond Ave. (Richmond Hill Rd.) | Staten Island | 718-370-2225

These "surprisingly good" Pan-Asians in Murray Hill and the Staten Island Mall offer menus running the gamut from sushi to dim sum and pad Thai, all "bursting with flavor"; "strive-to-please" service and "won't-break-the-bank" tabs complete the "palatable" picture.

E.A.T. *American*

| 20 | 12 | 15 | $40 |

E 80s | 1064 Madison Ave. (bet. 80th & 81st Sts.) | 212-772-0022 | www.elizabar.com

Before "Madison Avenue shopping" or hitting the "Museum Mile", "East Side ladies" and others drop by Eli Zabar's "high-style" American for "tastefully prepared" sandwiches and salads; despite "money-is-no-object" tabs, "rushed" service and "glamorized deli" digs, it's "always busy."

Eataly *Italian*

| 23 | 19 | 17 | $41 |

Flatiron | 200 Fifth Ave. (bet. 23rd & 24th Sts.) | 212-229-2560 | www.eataly.com

A "sprawling" "cornucopia of Italian delights", this "three-ring-circus" Flatiron food hall from the Batali-Bastianich team doles out "heavenly" pastas, pizzas, veggies, fish, cheese, coffee and gelato from stations set within a gourmet "mercato"; "victims of their own success", it's also a "daunting" "madhouse" with limited seating, but most agree "the B and B team did it right."

		FOOD	DECOR	SERVICE	COST

Eatery ◑ *American*

	21	17	19	$34

W 50s | 798 Ninth Ave. (53rd St.) | 212-765-7080 | www.eaterynyc.com
"Comfort food with a trendy twist" is the calling card of this Hell's Kitchen American where the midpriced chow arrives in "minimalist", "diner-chic" digs; "be-seen" types like the "gay-friendly" people-watching and tolerate the high-volume "hustle and bustle."

Ecco ⓢ *Italian*

	23	20	22	$58

TriBeCa | 124 Chambers St. (bet. Church St. & W. B'way) | 212-227-7074 | www.eccorestaurantny.com
"Still going strong", this "old-school" TriBeCan turns out "true-to-its-roots" Italian fare to the tune of a weekend "piano player"; "formal" staffers are also on key, leaving "Uptown prices" as the only off-notes.

Edi & The Wolf ◑ *Austrian*

	23	21	20	$48

E Village | 102 Ave. C (bet. 6th & 7th Sts.) | 212-598-1040 | www.ediandthewolf.com
"Unique" is the word on this "funky" East Village Austrian offering "rich", "authentic" fare paired with super suds and wines; the hipster "cozy-cottage" design seems straight out of a fractured fairy tale, while the "cute" garden is a quiet alternative to the "loud" goings-on inside.

Ed's Chowder House ◑ *Seafood*

	20	20	20	$57

W 60s | The Empire Hotel | 44 W. 63rd St. (bet. B'way & Columbus Ave.) | 212-956-1288 | www.chinagrillmgt.com
Perched in "classy digs" in the Empire Hotel, this "spiffy" seafooder is a catch for landlubbers seeking "expertly cooked" fish served "fast"; the "Cape Cod"–sounding moniker may be at odds with its "fancy", "pricey" identity, but fans like its "easy access to Lincoln Center."

Ed's Lobster Bar *Seafood*

	24	16	20	$43

NoLita | 222 Lafayette St. (bet. Broome & Spring Sts.) | 212-343-3236 | www.lobsterbarnyc.com
The "simple, whitewashed" setting gives this "upbeat" NoLita fish house a "New England" mood that goes well with its "pricey", "near-perfection" lobster rolls and bivalves; given the "cramped" table seating, regulars "eat at the bar" for "more attentive" service and added wiggle room.

Egg ⌀ *Southern*

	24	14	17	$23

Williamsburg | 135 N. Fifth St. (bet. Bedford Ave. & Berry St.) | Brooklyn | 718-302-5151 | www.pigandegg.com
Williamsburg's beloved "Southern egg palace" reigns as a "brunch favorite" where the "stellar", low-cost, down-home cooking is made from "fresh, local" ingredients ("nothing cures a hangover better"); it's no-frills with "relaxed" service and a cash-only rule, but to most the only real "drawback" is the "long line outside" on weekend mornings.

Eisenberg's Sandwich Shop *Sandwiches*

	18	10	16	$17

Flatiron | 174 Fifth Ave. (22nd St.) | 212-675-5096 | www.eisenbergsnyc.com
A "bygone" ode to the "greasy spoon", this circa-1929 Flatiron luncheonette is known for "basics" like tuna sandwiches and "old-style" egg creams; modernists may moan about "shabby" decor and "rickety" service, but for many, this remains a "sentimental" favorite.

	FOOD	DECOR	SERVICE	COST

El Centro ● *Mexican* | 21 | 18 | 20 | $27

W 50s | 824 Ninth Ave. (54th St.) | 646-763-6585 | www.elcentro-nyc.com
This "upbeat" Hell's Kitchen Mexican throws a "hip", "loud" fiesta ramped up by "awesome" margaritas and, oh yeah, "decently priced" south-of-the-border bites; the "quirky", "kitschy" setting is "always packed", though regulars wish the "music could be lowered a few decibels."

Eleven Madison Park *French* | 28 | 28 | 28 | $254

Flatiron | 11 Madison Ave. (24th St.) | 212-889-0905 | www.elevenmadisonpark.com
"Magical" is how admirers describe Daniel Humm's French "knockout" next to Madison Square Park, where "well-choreographed", "theatrical" tasting menus (think "card tricks") feature "exquisite" dishes and "memorable" wine pairings, served with "perfect precision" by an "amazing" pro staff in "spectacular" "landmark" digs; you may need to "take out a mortgage" first, but it "doesn't get much better" than this.

Eliá Ⓜ *Greek* | 25 | 20 | 23 | $53

Bay Ridge | 8611 Third Ave. (bet. 86th & 87th Sts.) | Brooklyn | 718-748-9891 | www.eliarestaurant.com
Bringing Bay Ridge an "exceptional" "taste of the Mediterranean", this Greek "neighborhood" fixture produces "perfectly cooked" whole fish and other "innovative" specials; sure, it's a "splurge", but the staff is "hospitable" and there are bonus "outdoor seats" on the garden deck.

Elias Corner ●❖ *Greek/Seafood* | 23 | 10 | 16 | $40

Astoria | 24-02 31st St. (24th Ave.) | Queens | 718-932-1510 | www.eliascorner.com
Grilled fish so fresh it tastes like it was "caught an hour ago" is the specialty of this "no-frills" Astoria Greek with not much decor and "no menus" (just check out the "cold case" and point); though it only accepts cash and service is "so-so", the tabs are sure "hard to beat."

Elio's ● *Italian* | 24 | 18 | 20 | $69

E 80s | 1621 Second Ave. (bet. 84th & 85th Sts.) | 212-772-2242
A magnet for "media" moguls, "Page Six regulars" and "monied" UES types, this "old-school" Italian dispenses food "delectable" enough to justify the "through-the-nose" tabs; expect the "cold shoulder" if you're not a "member of the club", but at least the "cheek-to-jowl" seating bolsters the chance of rubbing elbows with "Matt Lauer."

NEW **The Ellington** ● *Pub Food* | - | - | - | M

W 100s | 936 Amsterdam Ave. (106th St.) | 212-222-4050 | www.theellingtonny.com
The underserved Upper Upper West Side gets some action via this new arrival offering elevated pub grub in weathered, country-kitchen digs; the tabs are reasonable, while cocktails like the 'Sophisticated Lady' pay homage to its namesake, Duke Ellington.

NEW **The Elm** *French* | - | - | - | E

Williamsburg | King & Grove Hotel | 160 N. 12th St. (bet. Bedford Ave. & Berry St.) | Brooklyn | 718-218-1088 | www.theelmnyc.com
Top toque Paul Liebrandt (ex Corton) goes casual at this subterranean Modern French newcomer in Williamsburg's King & Grove

Hotel, though 'casual' to this chef are dishes like foie gras with spiced strawberry gelée; the upscale setting features high ceilings and an open kitchen, leaving the relatively approachable pricing as the most Brooklyn thing about it; P.S. an eight-seat chef's counter is in the works.

El Parador Cafe *Mexican*
23 | 18 | 21 | $45

Murray Hill | 325 E. 34th St. (bet. 1st & 2nd Aves.) | 212-679-6812 | www.elparadorcafe.com

A "devoted clientele" gets its "paella fix" at this '59-vintage Murray Hill vet that's known for "true-to-its-roots", "old-world" Mexican cooking; obscured by Midtown Tunnel traffic, it's a "hidden gem" – polished by "cordial" servers – that insiders want to keep "secret."

El Paso *Mexican*
24 | 16 | 19 | $28

E 100s | 1643 Lexington Ave. (104th St.) | 212-831-9831 | www.elpasony.com

E 90s | 64 E. 97th St. (bet. Madison & Park Aves.) | 212-996-1739

Harlem | 237 E. 116th St. (bet. 2nd & 3rd Aves.) | 212-860-4875

Eastsiders count on these "solid", unpretentious Uptown Mexicans for "terrific" tacos and other standards ("try the agua frescas") made "fresh" with "quality ingredients"; "tight quarters" and "so-so" service are offset by "unbelievable-value" prices.

El Porrón *Spanish*
23 | 19 | 22 | $48

E 60s | 1123 First Ave. (bet. 61st & 62nd Sts.) | 212-207-8349 | www.elporronnyc.com

Tapas "like you'd find in Barcelona" make for "real-thing" dining at this UES Spaniard sporting a "something-for-everyone" menu; "winning wine" arrives in the namesake pitcher, and the crowd's a mix of "lively" types who "come hungry, thirsty and often."

El Pote ⌧ *Spanish*
23 | 15 | 22 | $44

Murray Hill | 718 Second Ave. (bet. 38th & 39th Sts.) | 212-889-6680 | www.elpote.com

"Home away from home" for Murray Hill amigos since '77, this Spanish stalwart keeps business brisk with "fantastic paella" and other "first-rate" Iberian standards; maybe it's looking a bit "shabby", but locals count themselves "lucky" to have it.

El Quijote ● *Spanish*
21 | 15 | 19 | $44

Chelsea | 226 W. 23rd St. (bet. 7th & 8th Aves.) | 212-929-1855

"Old-school to the hilt", this "colorful" Chelsea octogenarian may be "faded" but is still "memorable" for Spanish food plated in "gut-buster portions"; the decor lies somewhere between "tacky" and "kitschy", but the prices are "decent" and that "lobster deal can't be beat."

El Quinto Pino ● *Spanish*
25 | 20 | 22 | $40

Chelsea | 401 W. 24th St. (bet. 9th & 10th Aves.) | 212-206-6900 | www.elquintopinonyc.com

Little plates "go a long way" at Alex Raij's "tiny", "adorable" Chelsea tapas bar, where the "rich", "gorgeous" Spanish bites – including that "wonderful", "nothing-like-it-on-this-planet" uni panini – pair well with the "solid" wines and "romantic" vibe; despite "limited" bar-style seating, it's a "come-back-to."

	FOOD	DECOR	SERVICE	COST

NEW El Toro Blanco *Mexican/Seafood* ▽ 22 | 21 | 18 | $50

W Village | 257 Sixth Ave. (bet. Bedford & Downing Sts.) | 212-645-0193 |
www.eltoroblanconyc.com

Elevating classic Mexican eats to "gourmet" levels, Josh Capon's slick
West Villager delivers dishes that "burst with flavor" amid a scene of
"trendy" "hustle and bustle"; though service can be "spotty", prices
that are relatively "reasonable" for the upscale milieu help make it a
"zesty addition to the 'hood."

Ember Room *Asian* 21 | 21 | 20 | $43

W 40s | 647 Ninth Ave. (bet. 45th & 46th Sts.) | 212-245-8880 |
www.emberroom.com

From consulting chef Ian Kittichai comes this "sleek" Hell's Kitchen eatery specializing in "exceptional" Asian fusion fare, including a plethora of
small plates, all served in a "dark", nightclub-ish setting; moderate pricing and service with "panache" complete the promising picture.

Embers *Steak* 22 | 16 | 20 | $47

Bay Ridge | 9519 Third Ave. (bet. 95th & 96th Sts.) | Brooklyn |
718-745-3700 | www.embersbayridge.com

A "working-class" Bay Ridge chophouse primed to "fill that steak
craving", this area "institution" sears tender, "juicy" cuts at nearly
"half the price" of the Midtown big boys; it remains "reliable" under
"new ownership", but when it's "too crowded", there's always the
"next-door meat store."

Emilia's *Italian* ▽ 22 | 18 | 22 | $36

Fordham | 2331 Arthur Ave. (Crescent Ave.) | Bronx | 718-364-0013 |
www.emiliasrestaurant.com

"In the heart of" Arthur Avenue's "food mecca", this longtime Italian
"mainstay" proffers "delicious" "red-sauce standards" in "generous
portions", including "wonderful daily specials"; happily there's "minimal frenzy" within its "cozy", nothing-fancy digs, which are presided
over by a "friendly" staff.

Empanada Mama ● *S American* 23 | 12 | 16 | $18

NEW LES | 189 E. Houston St. (bet. Ludlow & Orchard Sts.) | 212-673-0300
W 50s | 763 Ninth Ave. (bet. 51st & 52nd Sts.) | 212-698-9008
www.empmamanyc.com

Stuffing its "huge following" with "amazing" empanadas and arepas,
this 24/7 Hell's Kitchen "hole-in-the-wall" (with a new LES offshoot)
is the mother of all "cheap" South American "pocket"-food purveyors;
undersized, "overcrowded" and at times "disorganized", it "lends itself to takeout."

Empellón Cocina ⓜ *Mexican* 22 | 19 | 19 | $54

E Village | 105 First Ave. (bet. 6th & 7th Sts.) | 212-780-0999
Empellón Taqueria *Mexican*

W Village | 230 W. Fourth St. (W. 10th St.) | 212-367-0999
www.empellon.com

Chef Alex Stupak's "bold" detour from desserts at WD-50 to "high-
minded" Mexicana pays off at these "trendy" destinations; the original
West Village outlet "redefines the taco", while the "more upscale" East
Village spin-off aces "super-imaginative" small plates – between the
"killer" drinks and "fashionable" following, both enjoy crazy "buzz."

	FOOD	DECOR	SERVICE	COST

Empire Steakhouse *Steak*
24 | 20 | 23 | $68

E 50s | 36 W. 52nd St. (bet. 5th & 6th Aves.) | 212-582-6900 |
www.empiresteakhousenyc.com

Carnivores commend the "tender", "top-notch" steaks at this "busy"
chophouse from the Ben & Jack's folks, "conveniently located" near
Rock Center; "attentive" service contributes to the generally "pleasant" vibe, even if the decor doesn't rise above "standard Midtown."

Emporio *Italian*
23 | 20 | 19 | $45

NoLita | 231 Mott St. (bet. Prince & Spring Sts.) | 212-966-1234 |
www.emporiony.com

Aurora alums are behind this *"bellissimo"* NoLita trattoria, a "sublime"
option for "authentic" Neapolitan pizzas and "homemade pastas"
served in a rustic-industrial setting; when the front room gets too "tight",
regulars head for the "greenhouse"-like back room.

EN Japanese Brasserie *Japanese*
25 | 25 | 23 | $65

W Village | 435 Hudson St. (Leroy St.) | 212-647-9196 | www.enjb.com

"Excellent" Japanese cuisine – including "amazing" housemade tofu and
"wow"-worthy kaiseki menus – served within "beautiful" digs have made
a "favorite" of this "upscale" West Villager; a "tremendous sake list" and
"earnest" service are other reasons it's spot on for "date night."

Enzo's ●Ⓜ *Italian*
23 | 18 | 22 | $41

Morris Park | 1998 Williamsbridge Rd. (Neill Ave.) | Bronx | 718-409-3828 |
www.enzosbronxrestaurant.com

Enzo's of Arthur Avenue *Italian*

Fordham | 2339 Arthur Ave. (bet. 184th & 187th Sts.) | Bronx |
718-733-4455 | www.enzosofthebronx.com

These "blue-ribbon" "red-sauce palaces" in the Bronx dish out "down-
home" Italian standards in mammoth portions, and toss in some "old-
school charm" on the side; the "unpretentious" staff "treats you like
family", so embrace the "time warp" – and "don't fill up on the bread."

Eolo *Italian*
21 | 15 | 19 | $50

Chelsea | 190 Seventh Ave. (bet. 21st & 22nd Sts.) | 646-225-6606 |
www.eolonyc.com

There's "intelligent life in the kitchen" of this Sicilian "contender" offering "off-the-beaten-recipe-path" dishes paired with "exceptional
wines"; the "nondescript" trattoria setting may be at odds with the
"Chelsea prices", perhaps why there are "no struggles to get a table."

Erawan *Thai*
23 | 20 | 21 | $36

Bayside | 42-31 Bell Blvd. (bet. 42nd & 43rd Aves.) | Queens |
718-428-2112 | www.erawanthaibayside.com

Bayside locals tout this "go-to Thai" for its "aromatic" offerings with
"interesting modern twists", abetted by "gentle" service and a "fancy"
"Manhattan atmosphere"; though prices lie on the "premium" side for
the genre, it's ever "crowded" at prime times.

Erminia ☒ *Italian*
24 | 23 | 24 | $70

E 80s | 250 E. 83rd St. (bet. 2nd & 3rd Aves.) | 212-879-4284 |
www.erminiaristorante.com

If you're looking for "romance", try this "transporting" UES Roman
boîte where a "cavelike", candlelit setting sets the mood for "knock-

out" cooking, while "attentive" service and a "leisurely" pace do the rest; sure, it's "expensive", but there are "only a few tables", lending exclusivity to this "special experience."

Esca ● *Italian/Seafood* | 24 | 20 | 22 | $73 |

W 40s | 402 W. 43rd St. (bet. 9th & 10th Aves.) | 212-564-7272 | www.esca-nyc.com

The Batali-Bastianich-Pasternack gang "don't disappoint" at this "up-scale" Hell's Kitchen Italian seafooder presenting a "splendid repertoire" of "fabulous" fin fare, "excellent" pastas and more, matched with an "impressive" wine list and served by an "attentive" crew; some carp about "pricey" tabs and "tight" seating, but to the majority it's an "excellent pre- or post-theater" pick and an all-around "memorable experience."

NEW Estela ●☒ *Mediterranean* | – | – | – | M |

NoLita | 47 E. Houston St., upstairs (bet. Mott & Mulberry Sts.) | 212-219-7693 | estelanyc.com

Upstairs from NoLita's Botanica is this well-priced arrival from Ignacio Mattos, who has traded in the aggressive modernism of his Isa days for creative, farmer's market–driven small plates with a Med bent; there's an ambitious wine list emphasizing unusual French labels, a long front bar with plenty of room for walk-ins, and brunch is in the works.

Etcetera Etcetera *Italian* | 22 | 19 | 22 | $53 |

W 40s | 352 W. 44th St. (bet. 8th & 9th Aves.) | 212-399-4141 | www.etcetnyc.com

"Casual" but "lively", this Hell's Kitchen Italian features a "modern" menu that's a match for its "contemporary" looks; "splendid", "get-you-to-the-theater-on-time" service makes up for "noisy" acoustics, though regulars say it's "quieter upstairs."

Ethos *Greek* | 21 | 18 | 19 | $46 |

E 50s | 905 First Ave. (51st St.) | 212-888-4060
Murray Hill | 495 Third Ave. (bet. 33rd & 34th Sts.) | 212-252-1972
www.ethosrestaurants.com

"Fish is the star" at these "cheerful" Greek tavernas where the "always-fresh" catch arrives in "abundant portions" and is dispensed "with finesse" by a "friendly" crew; Sutton Place may be "much better" than the Murray Hill spin-offs lookswise, but all share "affordability."

Excellent Dumpling House *Chinese* | 22 | 6 | 13 | $18 |

Chinatown | 111 Lafayette St. (bet. Canal & Walker Sts.) | 212-219-0212

There's "no false advertising" at this Chinatowner where the "name-says-it-all" dumplings are served with equally "excellent" Shanghainese plates; true, there's "no atmosphere" and service is of the "rush-you-out" variety, but "at these prices, who cares?"

NEW Exchange Alley ● *American* | – | – | – | M |

E Village | 424 E. Ninth St. (bet. Ave. A & 1st Ave.) | 212-228-8525 | www.exchangealleynyc.com

Bringing a touch of the Big Easy to the East Village, this midpriced arrival plies New Orleans–influenced small and large plates washed down with upscale cocktails; the funky, candlelit space brims with tchotchkes and kitsch, including an oversize '40s-era painting of a pinup girl holding a raw steak.

	FOOD	DECOR	SERVICE	COST

Extra Fancy ● *Seafood* — ▽ 20 | 19 | 21 | $36

Williamsburg | 302 Metropolitan Ave. (Roebling St.) | Brooklyn | 347-422-0939 | www.extrafancybklyn.com

Ironic moniker to the contrary, this Williamsburg seafooder is "nothing too fancy", both in its "reasonably priced", "delicious" New England–inspired eats and clam-shack looks; "friendly, prompt" service, an impressive craft beer and cocktail list and a big backyard are other draws.

Extra Virgin *Mediterranean* — 23 | 19 | 19 | $42

W Village | 259 W. Fourth St. (Perry St.) | 212-691-9359 | www.extravirginrestaurant.com

The "young" and "glamorous" hobnob at this "fashionable" West Villager over "seasonal" Med fare that "won't break the bank"; although the place is usually "crowded" and the no-rez policy leads to "waits", amusing "people-watching" helps pass the time.

Fabio Piccolo Fiore *Italian* — 23 | 19 | 22 | $56

E 40s | 230 E. 44th St. (bet. 2nd & 3rd Aves.) | 212-922-0581 | www.fabiopiccolofiore.com

"Fab-u-lous" owner Fabio "works the room" at this "enjoyable" Italian situated between Grand Central and the U.N.; the "wonderful" food arrives in a "serene" setting enhanced by "welcoming" service, "well-spaced tables" and "quiet" acoustics.

F & J Pine Restaurant *Italian* — 23 | 21 | 21 | $38

Morris Park | 1913 Bronxdale Ave. (bet. Matthews & Muliner Aves.) | Bronx | 718-792-5956

"Gigantic portions" are the name of the game at this "doggy bag"–guaranteed Bronx Italian ladling out "loads of red sauce" for fans of "old-time" carbo-loading; "checkered" tablecloths, sports "memorabilia" decor and Yankee sightings are all part of the "colorful" proceedings.

Farm on Adderley *American* — 24 | 20 | 21 | $37

Ditmas Park | 1108 Cortelyou Rd. (bet. Stratford & Westminster Rds.) | Brooklyn | 718-287-3101 | www.thefarmonadderley.com

Ditmas Park denizens feel "lucky" to have this "worthwhile" New American and its "ambitious" meals made from "super-fresh" ingredients; a harvest like this could "cost twice as much in Manhattan", and insiders hint the food tastes even better from a "garden" seat.

The Fat Radish ❷ *British* — 24 | 22 | 19 | $48

LES | 17 Orchard St. (bet. Canal & Hester Sts.) | 212-300-4053 | www.thefatradishnyc.com

"Veggie fanatics" get the royal treatment at this "trendy" Lower Eastsider that "oozes cool" with its "creative" Modern British cooking and "hiptastic" "art-crowd" following; regulars allow extra time since the "slacker" servers are in no hurry to mete out the "pricey but princely" fare.

Fatty Crab *Malaysian* — 22 | 14 | 18 | $46

W Village | 643 Hudson St. (bet. Gansevoort & Horatio Sts.) | 212-352-3590 | www.fattycrew.com

"Sticky-salty-sweet" Malaysian street eats make for "delectable" dining at Zak Pelaccio's "buzzy" Villager that's a magnet for "adventurous" "heat"-seekers; however, it's "not for the faint of heart" given the "doing-you-a-favor" service, "pounding music" and "steadily climbing bills."

	FOOD	DECOR	SERVICE	COST

Fatty 'Cue *BBQ/SE Asian*
| 22 | 18 | 20 | $46 |

W Village | 50 Carmine St. (bet. Bedford & Bleecker Sts.) | 212-929-5050
Williamsburg | 91 S. Sixth St. (Berry St.) | Brooklyn | 718-599-3090 ●
www.fattycrew.com

"Delicious" 'cue with "exotic" SE Asian flair is the deal at these West Village–Williamsburg BBQ joints from chef Zak Pelaccio, also known for their "interesting, strong cocktails"; the settings and service are "casual" and the mood "festive", equally suited to "date" night or "with a group"; P.S. the "amazing drunk brunch" at Carmine Street packs serious "value."

Fatty Fish *Asian*
| 23 | 16 | 20 | $38 |

E 60s | 406 E. 64th St. (bet. 1st & York Aves.) | 212-813-9338 |
www.fattyfishnyc.com

Upper Eastsiders are hooked on this Asian-fusion practitioner boasting "surprisingly creative" cooking (and sushi) served by "solicitous" staffers who just "keep smiling"; a "Zen-like" mood and "beautiful outdoor patio" distract from the "small" dimensions.

Fedora ● *American/French*
| 23 | 20 | 21 | $55 |

W Village | 239 W. Fourth St., downstairs (bet. Charles & W. 10th Sts.) |
646-449-9336 | www.fedoranyc.com

Gabe Stulman's "low-key chic" relaunch of a longtime West Village basement earns a tip of the cap for its "interesting" Franco-American menu and "beautiful neon sign"; retaining the "speakeasy vibe" of the old haunt and tossing in some "Wisconsin hospitality", it's now "better than ever", except perhaps for the cost.

Felice *Italian*
| 21 | 20 | 20 | $47 |

E 60s | 1166 First Ave. (64th St.) | 212-593-2223 |
www.felicenyc.com
E 80s | 1593 First Ave. (83rd St.) | 212-249-4080 | www.felicenyc.com
NEW **Financial District** | Gild Hall Hotel | 15 Gold St. (bet. Maiden Ln. & Platt St.) | 212-785-5950 | www.felicewinebar.com

These "moderately hip" wine bars spice up "date nights" with "affordable", "well-chosen" vinos paired with "tasty" Italian small plates; the "gracious" service and "sexy" ambiance "appeal to multiple generations", though they mainly draw "younger" folks.

Felidia *Italian*
| 26 | 22 | 24 | $80 |

E 50s | 243 E. 58th St. (bet. 2nd & 3rd Aves.) | 212-758-1479 |
www.felidia-nyc.com

"Long live Lidia Bastianich" cheer fans of the "TV" chef and her "elegant" East Side "flagship", where "superb" Italian cuisine is ferried by a "professional" crew within a "truly charming", "old-world" townhouse setting; you may need to "check your bank account before going", but most agree the "wonderful experience" is "worth every penny."

Ferrara ● *Bakery*
| 23 | 17 | 18 | $21 |

Little Italy | 195 Grand St. (bet. Mott & Mulberry Sts.) | 212-226-6150 |
www.ferraracafe.com

Open 121 years "and counting", this Little Italy bakery is a "legend" famed for its "heaven-on-a-plate" cannoli and "pick-me-up" espresso; "crowds of tourists" and "expensive"-for-what-it-is tabs draw brickbats, yet most agree this NYC relic "still has charm."

	FOOD	DECOR	SERVICE	COST

Fette Sau ● *BBQ* — 26 | 16 | 15 | $31

Williamsburg | 354 Metropolitan Ave. (bet. Havemeyer & Roebling Sts.) | Brooklyn | 718-963-3404 | www.fettesaubbq.com

It's the "quintessential Williamsburg experience" to "join the hipsters" at this "serious foodie" "heaven" for "awesome" dry-rub, by-the-pound BBQ – voted "NYC's best" – that "matches so well" with the "artisan" beers and bourbons on offer; no rezzies means "crazy lines" for "cafeteria-style" service in a "former garage" outfitted with "communal picnic tables" – but to most it's so "worth it."

15 East ⓈJapanese — 26 | 22 | 24 | $81

Union Sq | 15 E. 15th St. (5th Ave.) | 212-647-0015 | www.15eastrestaurant.com

At this Union Square Japanese, the "top-notch" sushi "presented with art and love" by chef Masato Shimizu "might ruin you for the everyday" stuff, likewise the "exquisite" small plates and "incredible sakes"; it's "elegant all the way down the line", from the "tactful" service to the "calming", "minimalist" decor – paired with a predictably "maximalist bill."

57 Napoli Pizza e Vino *Pizza* — 23 | 19 | 20 | $29

E 50s | 120 E. 57th St., upstairs (bet. Lexington & Park Aves.) | 212-750-4586 | www.57napoli.com

Ok, the obscure second-floor address may be "easy to miss", but this East Midtown pizzeria is worth seeking out for "tasty" Neapolitan pies fired in a "wood-burning oven"; there's not much decor save for a floor-to-ceiling window "with a good view of 57th Street", but service is "friendly" and the tabs "affordable."

Fig & Olive *Mediterranean* — 21 | 21 | 19 | $48

E 50s | 10 E. 52nd St. (bet. 5th & Madison Aves.) | 212-319-2002
E 60s | 808 Lexington Ave. (bet. 62nd & 63rd Sts.) | 212-207-4555
Meatpacking | 420 W. 13th St. (bet. 9th Ave. & Washington St.) | 212-924-1200
www.figandolive.com

A "buzzy, glamorous" feel pervades these "trendy" Mediterraneans featuring "fresh, tasty", kinda "pricey" fare (with "cute" olive oil tastings), "lovely" decor and "uneven" service; the "huge" Meatpacking mother ship is "more hip" than its smaller East Side satellites, which make "classy" "after-shopping" options.

Fiorentino's ⓂItalian — 21 | 15 | 21 | $35

Gravesend | 311 Ave. U (bet. McDonald Ave. & West St.) | Brooklyn | 718-372-1445 | www.fiorentinosristorante.com

"Old-school Brooklyn" endures at this "bustling" Gravesend Italian best known for "grandma"-style Neapolitan food plated in "tremendous" portions; its *Goodfellas*-esque crowd doesn't mind the "no-frills" decor, "noisy" decibels and no-rez rule given the "astonishingly cheap" tabs.

Fiorini ⓈItalian — 21 | 19 | 21 | $57

E 50s | 209 E. 56th St. (bet. 2nd & 3rd Aves.) | 212-308-0830 | www.fiorinirestaurantnyc.com

Somewhat "off the beaten path" in East Midtown, Lello Arpaia's "neighborhood" Neapolitan offers "hearty", "traditional" fare in a "comfortable" milieu; "spacious" dimensions and "never-too-noisy" acoustics please its mature following, the "steep" tabs not so much.

	FOOD	DECOR	SERVICE	COST

FireBird Ⓜ *Russian* — 20 | 25 | 22 | $67

W 40s | 365 W. 46th St. (bet. 8th & 9th Aves.) | 212-586-0244 |
www.firebirdrestaurant.com

"Dining with the tsars" comes to Restaurant Row via this "ornate"
townhouse celebrating "imperial Russia" in an "antiques"-laden duplex that outsparkles the "tasty" mother-country cuisine; "excellent"
infused vodkas and "first-class" service burnish the "schmaltzy" mood
that ends with bills "too rich for peasant blood."

Firenze ❶ *Italian* — 21 | 20 | 23 | $53

E 80s | 1594 Second Ave. (bet. 82nd & 83rd Sts.) | 212-861-9368 |
www.firenzeny.com

"Candlelight and exposed-brick walls" set a "romantic" mood at this
longtime UES Italian that evokes Florence with "solid" Tuscan cooking
delivered by a "couldn't-be-nicer" crew; neighborly prices ice the cake.

Fish *Seafood* — 23 | 15 | 20 | $39

W Village | 280 Bleecker St. (Jones St.) | 212-727-2879 |
www.fishrestaurantnyc.com

Like the "simpleton name" implies, there's "nothing fancy" going on at
this West Village seafood shack, just "truly good" catch proffered with
great shuck for your buck (check out the $8 oyster special); trade-offs
include "funky" looks and "tight-squeeze" seating.

FishTag *Greek/Seafood* — 23 | 19 | 21 | $52

W 70s | 222 W. 79th St. (bet. Amsterdam Ave. & B'way) | 212-362-7470 |
www.fishtagrestaurant.com

Bringing a "downtown" vibe to the UWS, Michael Psilakis' "relaxed"
Greek is a "breath of fresh air" for "delectable" fish dispatched in "nice-
looking" digs by "enthusiastic" staffers; "decoding the menu" may re-
quire repeat visits, if you can abide the "din" and the "pricey" check.

5 & Diamond *American* — 22 | 20 | 21 | $36

Harlem | 2072 Frederick Douglass Blvd. (bet. 112th & 113th Sts.) |
646-684-4662 | www.5anddiamondrestaurant.com

Exemplifying Harlem's "burgeoning" restaurant scene, this "intimate"
New American lures an "eclectic crowd" with "fine", moderately priced
takes on familiar classics, including a "luscious mac 'n' cheese."

Five Leaves ❶ *American* — 26 | 22 | 19 | $31

Greenpoint | 18 Bedford Ave. (Lorimer St.) | Brooklyn | 718-383-5345 |
www.fiveleavesny.com

A "must-try" "signature burger" and "excellent pancakes" star on the
"fab" all-day New American menu at this "informal" Greenpoint bistro; its "casual", "nautical-themed" quarters get "packed", especially
during weekend brunch, when the wait can be "tough" – though
"friendly" service and "fair" prices compensate.

5 Napkin Burger *Burgers* — 21 | 17 | 18 | $28

E Village | 150 E. 14th St. (bet. 3rd & 4th Aves.) | 212-228-5500 ❶
W 40s | 630 Ninth Ave. (45th St.) | 212-757-2277 ❶
W 80s | 2315 Broadway (84th St.) | 212-333-4488 ❶
Astoria | 35-01 36th St. (35th Ave.) | Queens | 718-433-2727
www.5napkinburger.com

"You'll need all those napkins and a trip to the gym" after indulging in
the "giant", "delightfully juicy" patties that make this "kid-friendly"

chain a "solid contender" in the "gourmet burger" category; it's a "tribute to its quality" that the "rather retro settings" are "packed during peak hours", but "the downside" is "crazy noise levels."

508 ● *Italian/Mediterranean* | 22 | 19 | 20 | $42

Hudson Square | 508 Greenwich St. (bet. Canal & Spring Sts.) | 212-219-2444 | www.508nyc.com
"Better-than-expected" Italian-Mediterranean dishes are paired with a "nice assortment" of beers "brewed on the premises" at this Hudson Square boîte; the "out-of-the-way" address means the crowd's "mostly locals", but the "cozy", candlelit ambiance charms whoever drops in.

Five Points *American/Mediterranean* | 21 | 20 | 20 | $50

NoHo | 31 Great Jones St. (bet. Bowery & Lafayette St.) | 212-253-5700 | www.fivepointsrestaurant.com
"Simple yet sophisticated" Mediterranean–New Americana draws diners to this "off-the-beaten-track" NoHo "oasis of calm" where "helpful" staffers and a "hypnotic" babbling brook supply the "feng shui"; it's famed for an "out-of-this-world" brunch, when "reservations are an absolute must."

Flatbush Farm ● *American* | 21 | 18 | 17 | $38

Park Slope | 76 St. Marks Ave. (Flatbush Ave.) | Brooklyn | 718-622-3276 | www.flatbushfarm.com
"Farm-to-table" bounties are the draw at this affordable Park Slope American where the "solid" menu is assembled from "wholesome" local ingredients; the less-enthused cite "uneven" service, but it wins kudos for a "super brunch" and a "little-piece-of-heaven" garden.

NEW Fletcher's Brooklyn Barbecue *BBQ* | ▽ 22 | 16 | 21 | $31

Gowanus | 433 Third Ave. (bet. 7th & 8th Sts.) | Brooklyn | 347-763-2680 | www.fletchersbklyn.com
Former R.U.B. pitmaster Matt Fisher oversees the "real BBQ" at this locavore-friendly Gowanus arrival smoking the classics (St. Louis ribs, brisket) and more "unique items" (Asian-inspired char siu); the "super-casual" setup features "friendly" counter service, by-the-pound pricing and communal seating.

Flex Mussels *Seafood* | 23 | 18 | 20 | $45

E 80s | 174 E. 82nd St. (bet. Lexington & 3rd Aves.) | 212-717-7772
W Village | 154 W. 13th St. (bet. 6th & 7th Aves.) | 212-229-0222
www.flexmussels.com
Fans "flex their taste buds" at these "bustling" bivalve bastions imported from Prince Edward Island that "exceed expectations" with "plump" moules and "unusual" desserts (e.g. "boozy donuts", "deep-fried whoopie pies"); "price-is-right" tabs seal the deal, though the "cost of popularity" is a "maddening din."

Flor de Mayo ● *Chinese/Peruvian* | 21 | 10 | 18 | $25

W 80s | 484 Amsterdam Ave. (bet. 83rd & 84th Sts.) | 212-787-3388
W 100s | 2651 Broadway (bet. 100th & 101st Sts.) | 212-663-5520
"Widen your belt a notch" before approaching these UWS Chinese-Peruvian "favorites" where "flavorful" rotisserie chicken and other "bracing" eats are slung in "huge" portions for "bargain" sums; "zero" decor, "minimal" service and "hectic" digs make a strong case for "takeout."

	FOOD	DECOR	SERVICE	COST

NEW Flor de Sol ◐ Spanish — — — M

Chelsea | 100 10th Ave. (16th St.) | 212-366-1640 | www.flordesolnyc.com

Now conveniently located smack under the High Line, this reincarnated tapas bar supplies much the same Catalan bites and sangria but in roomier, jewel-toned West Chelsea digs; occasional flamenco dancers and live music add to the festive vibe for post-park nights.

Fonda Mexican 23 | 19 | 20 | $37

E Village | 40 Ave. B (3rd St.) | 212-677-4069
Park Slope | 434 Seventh Ave. (bet. 14th & 15th Sts.) | Brooklyn | 718-369-3144 Ⓜ
www.fondarestaurant.com

For "memorable Nuevo Mexican", these "festive" cantinas are "the place to go" for "upscale" (yet well-priced) cooking and "interesting cocktails"; the "small" Park Slope original can feel "cramped" ("go when the backyard is open") but the East Villager is roomier – and boasts a "fantastic happy hour."

Forcella Pizza 22 | 16 | 18 | $28

NEW Murray Hill | 377 Park Ave. S. (bet. 26th & 27th Sts.) | 212-448-1116 ◐
NoHo | 334 Bowery (bet. Bond & Great Jones Sts.) | 212-466-3300
Williamsburg | 485 Lorimer St. (bet. Grand & Powers Sts.) | Brooklyn | 718-388-8820
www.forcellaeatery.com

An "experience straight from Italy", these "real-deal" pizzerias feature "light-as-air" Neapolitan pies, many of which are "flash-fried", then oven-finished in brightly tiled stoves; the digs are plain and the service "could be more attentive", but at least they're "lively" and "affordable."

Forlini's ◐ Italian 19 | 14 | 19 | $45

Chinatown | 93 Baxter St. (bet. Bayard & Walker Sts.) | 212-349-6779

Whether you're on "jury duty" or "just got out of the Tombs", this circa-1943, courthouse-convenient Italian remains a "workmanlike" source for "red-sauce" cooking; some hold it in contempt for "tired" looks, but the final verdict is "satisfying" enough.

Fornino Pizza 24 | 17 | 20 | $27

NEW Greenpoint | 849 Manhattan Ave. (bet. Milton & Noble Sts.) | Brooklyn | 718-389-5300
Williamsburg | 187 Bedford Ave. (N. 7th St.) | Brooklyn | 718-384-6004 | www.forninopizza.com

In the eternal "NY pizza wars", this long-running Williamsburg pie "favorite" (with a new Greenpoint offshoot) is a "strong player" thanks to "decadent" toppings and "perfectly done" wood-fired crusts; P.S. a third outlet is on the way inside Brooklyn Bridge Park.

Forty Four American 20 | 23 | 21 | $56

W 40s | Royalton Hotel | 44 W. 44th St. (bet. 5th & 6th Aves.) | 212-944-8844 | www.royaltonhotel.com

This "swanky" Midtown New American has long been a favored "media" "power" player due to its "quiet" hotel location, "excellent cocktails" and "solid" cooking (especially at breakfast), which arrives via "very good" servers; it'll "cost a lot" to hang with the "Condé Nast" folks, but playing like an "insider" could be worth the "indulgence."

	FOOD	DECOR	SERVICE	COST

44 & X ● *American*
W 40s | 622 10th Ave. (bet. 44th & 45th Sts.) | 212-977-1170

| 22 | 20 | 21 | $45 |

44½ ● *American*
W 40s | 626 10th Ave. (bet. 44th & 45th Sts.) | 212-399-4450
www.heaveninhellskitchen.com

"Tasty" takes on American comfort classics play second fiddle to the "aspiring-actor" waiters clad in "double entendre" T-shirts at these "gay-friendly" Hell's Kitchen standbys; they're "uplifting" options in an otherwise "dreary part of town", earning bonus points for "formidable brunch" and proximity to the "Signature Theatre complex."

Four Seasons ⌧ *American*

| 27 | 28 | 27 | $103 |

E 50s | 99 E. 52nd St. (bet. Lexington & Park Aves.) | 212-754-9494 | www.fourseasonsrestaurant.com

Midtown's "gold standard" of "classic luxury" draws "elite" folks with "delectable" New American cuisine, a "timeless" midcentury modern setting and "flawless service" under the aegis of owners Alex von Bidder and Julian Niccolini; the Grill Room is a magnet for lunchtime "movers and shakers" while the Pool Room is best for "romance", but either way the tabs are "extravagant" and jackets are de rigueur for gents.

NEW The Fourth ● *American*

| - | - | - | M |

E Village | Hyatt Union Sq. | 132 Fourth Ave. (13th St.) | 212-432-1324

Tucked inside the Hyatt Union Square, this new all-day American brasserie from the Tocqueville team features a casual cafe area up front and a more formal dining room in the back, separated by a dangling sculpture of wooden bed frames; there's also a counter vending grab-and-go coffee and pastries in the AM.

Fragole *Italian*

| 24 | 17 | 21 | $35 |

Carroll Gardens | 394 Court St. (bet. Carroll St. & 1st Pl.) | Brooklyn | 718-522-7133 | www.fragoleny.com

This veteran Carroll Gardens Italian remains a "neighborhood favorite" for its "solid" cooking "with an eye toward authenticity", "quality wine list" and overall "charm"; "friendly" staffers and "affordable" tabs keep it filled with "happy" customers – but as it's "small" and takes no reservations, just "be prepared to wait" for a table at prime times.

Francisco's Centro Vasco *Seafood/Spanish*

| 23 | 13 | 20 | $52 |

Chelsea | 159 W. 23rd St. (bet. 6th & 7th Aves.) | 212-645-6224 | www.franciscoscentrovasco.com

"Monster-size" lobsters at "fair prices" are the highlight of this longtime Chelsea Spaniard that also offers "wonderful paella" and "potent sangria"; "dumpy" digs and "noisy, crowded" conditions don't deter fans who feel it's "cheaper to come here than to cook your own."

Frank ●⌿ *Italian*

| 23 | 14 | 18 | $37 |

E Village | 88 Second Ave. (bet. 5th & 6th Sts.) | 212-420-0202 | www.frankrestaurant.com

This cash-only East Villager is a longtime standby for "da best (other than mother's)" Italian "home cooking" at "solid-value" prices; it's a "jam-packed", no-frills joint with a "no-rez policy" that spells waits at prime times, but you can always pass the time at its next-door Vera Bar.

	FOOD	DECOR	SERVICE	COST

Frankie & Johnnie's ⊠ *Steak* | 22 | 16 | 21 | $68

Garment District | 32 W. 37th St. (bet. 5th & 6th Aves.) | 212-947-8940
W 40s | 269 W. 45th St., 2nd fl. (8th Ave.) | 212-997-9494 ◐
www.frankieandjohnnies.com

To experience "days long past", try this circa-1926 Theater District "throwback" accessed via "rickety stairs" and known for "delectable" steaks, "career" waiters and "rough-around-the-edges" decor; its Garment District sibling (set in John Barrymore's former townhouse) is similarly "old-fashioned", though prices are decidedly up to date.

Frankies Spuntino *Italian* | 23 | 18 | 20 | $44

W Village | 570 Hudson St. (11th St.) | 212-924-0818 ◐
Carroll Gardens | 457 Court St. (bet. 4th Pl. & Luquer St.) | Brooklyn |
718-403-0033
www.frankiesspuntino.com

"Terrific in all the ways that count", these "rustic Italians" with "pleasant vibes" and "huge buzz" are touted for "impressive" Tuscan cooking and "charming" settings; the Carroll Gardens original boasts a "beautiful garden", but both share "decent" prices, "noise" and no-rez rules.

Franny's *Italian/Pizza* | 25 | 18 | 20 | $40

Park Slope | 348 Flatbush Ave. (bet. 8th Ave. & Sterling Pl.) | Brooklyn |
718-230-0221 | www.frannysbrooklyn.com

Now in roomier, buzzier digs a few blocks down Flatbush from its original location, this longtime Park Slope favorite continues to turn out "second-to-none" artisanal pizzas - now from two wood-burning ovens in back - along with "exquisite" appetizers, pastas and other "simple"-yet-sophisticated Italian dishes; the bar is bigger too, with a broader wine and cocktail list, making the perfect perch when facing the inevitable "wait" (still no rezzies).

Fratelli *Italian* | 21 | 17 | 20 | $39

Pelham Gardens | 2507 Eastchester Rd. (Mace Ave.) | Bronx |
718-547-2489

"Where all the locals go", this "neighborhood" Pelham Gardens Italian has been plating "large portions" of "tasty" red-sauce chow for two decades now; "friendly" service and "decent" pricing trump the "nondescript" environs.

Fratelli la Bufala ◐ *Pizza* | ▽ 20 | 16 | 14 | $34

W 70s | 2161 Broadway (76th St.) | 212-496-5303 |
www.fratellilabufalanyc.com

Upper Westsiders who "don't feel like going downtown" for designer pizza but wouldn't mind a "Euro" vibe with their pie head to this "upbeat" outpost of the Naples-based trattoria chain; still, while the wood-fired handiwork earns praise, a few fret the asking price is "a bit steep" for what you get.

Fraunces Tavern ◐ *Pub Food* | 18 | 22 | 19 | $43

(aka The Porterhouse Brewing Co. at Fraunces Tavern)
Financial District | 54 Pearl St. (Broad St.) | 212-968-1776 |
www.frauncestavern.com

Have a side of "history" with dinner at this FiDi "landmark" where George Washington bid farewell to his troops in 1783; today, it's a "refurbished" tavern serving "decent" pub grub and "diverse" beers in a

| | FOOD | DECOR | SERVICE | COST |

"faux Revolutionary" setting; cynics snipe it's "all about the building – not the food."

Fred's at Barneys NY *American/Italian*
| 20 | 19 | 19 | $50 |

E 60s | Barneys NY | 660 Madison Ave., 9th fl. (61st St.) | 212-833-2200 | www.barneys.com

"Shopping is hard work" and "sustenance is necessary", so "well-Botoxed" types unwind and "pick at a salad" at this "chichi" department-store canteen in Barneys; the "consistently good" Italian-American fare may be "pricey for what it is", but no one cares – it's "fun to be chic" here.

Freemans ⏺ *American*
| 22 | 24 | 19 | $48 |

LES | Freeman Alley (off Rivington St., bet. Bowery & Chrystie St.) | 212-420-0012 | www.freemansrestaurant.com

"Tucked away" down a Lower East Side alley, this "hipster" magnet feels "miles from NY" given the "kooky" Colonial tavern decor replete with "taxidermy" and "creaky wooden floors"; "solid" American cuisine and "great drinks too" offset the "hit-or-miss" service and "killer waits", but mostly, it's about the "scene."

Fresco by Scotto ⧉ *Italian*
| 22 | 19 | 21 | $57 |

E 50s | 34 E. 52nd St. (bet. Madison & Park Aves.) | 212-935-3434 | www.frescobyscotto.com

Fresco on the Go ⧉ *Italian*
E 50s | 40 E. 52nd St. (bet. Madison & Park Aves.) | 212-754-2700 | www.frescoonthego.com

For "delicious", "dependable" Tuscan fare with *Today Show* people-watching on the side, try this "friendly" 20-plus-year-old Midtowner via the "dedicated" Scotto family; it's "pricey", and "always packed" for lunch, so many opt for "super-fast" takeout from the to-go outlet down the block.

Friedman's Lunch *American*
| 22 | 16 | 19 | $24 |

Chelsea | Chelsea Mkt. | 75 Ninth Ave. (bet. 15th & 16th Sts.) | 212-929-7100 | www.friedmanslunch.com

Name notwithstanding, they also whip up breakfast and brunch at this "pleasant" American inside "fun Chelsea Market" known for its "hearty", "delicious" sandwiches and other "gourmet comfort" fare (including "terrific gluten-free options"); "slow service" and "not much seating" explain the typical "waits" for a table.

Friend of a Farmer *American*
| 18 | 18 | 17 | $34 |

Gramercy | 77 Irving Pl. (bet. 18th & 19th Sts.) | 212-477-2188 | www.friendofafarmerny.com

"Cute rustic" comes to Gramercy Park via this "quaint" American "country kitchen" that has crowds crowing about its "farm-fresh" vittles and "hippie" air; citified pricing, "slow service" and weekend brunch "lines down the block" come with the territory.

NEW Fritzl's Lunch Box *American*
| – | – | – | I |

Bushwick | 173 Irving Ave. (bet. Stanhope & Stockholm Sts.) | Brooklyn | 929-210-9531 | www.fritzlslunchbox.com

From a Roberta's alum, this self-described 'real simple neighborhood restaurant' in Bushwick proffers inventive, crowd-pleasing spins on classic American sandwiches, burgers and pastas; its banquette-equipped space with a retro luncheonette feel and a back garden has been packing in locals since day one.

Fuleen Seafood ❶ *Chinese/Seafood*

| 22 | 10 | 17 | $34 |

Chinatown | 11 Division St. (Bowery) | 212-941-6888
"Squirmingly fresh", Hong Kong–style fish straight from a "saltwater tank" reels folks into this "cheap" Chinatown seafooder; despite a "boisterous", "fluorescent" setting, it remains a "dive worth diving into" whether on jury duty or painting the town red (it's open till 2 AM).

Fulton *Seafood*

| 22 | 18 | 20 | $56 |

E 70s | 205 E. 75th St. (bet. 2nd & 3rd Aves.) | 212-288-6600 | www.fultonnyc.com
It's from the "Citarella folks", so it's no surprise the fish is simply "delish" at this "memorable" Upper East Side dock – and so "fresh" it "just may jump off your plate"; "gracious service", a "charming", brick-walled setting and a "never-too-busy" atmosphere make the prices more palatable.

Fushimi *Japanese*

| 23 | 23 | 20 | $43 |

Bay Ridge | 9316 Fourth Ave. (bet. 93rd & 94th Sts.) | Brooklyn | 718-833-7788
Williamsburg | 475 Driggs Ave. (bet. N. 10th & 11th Sts.) | Brooklyn | 718-963-2555
Grant City | 2110 Richmond Rd. (bet. Colfax & Lincoln Aves.) | Staten Island | 718-980-5300
www.fushimigroup.com

These "sexy" outer-borough Japanese standouts are "an experience" complete with "sleek" settings, "fun, young atmosphere", "city-quality" sushi and "inventive" cocktails; maybe tabs are "not the cheapest", but then again these are "not your regular around-the-corner sushi" joints.

Fusia ⊠ *Asian*

| ∇ 22 | 16 | 20 | $30 |

E 50s | 677 Lexington Ave. (56th St.) | 212-308-2111 | www.fusiaasiancuisine.net
From sushi to stir-fry to pad Thai, this "friendly" East Midtown Pan-Asian "has it all under one roof", served up by an "eager-to-please" crew; "good-value" prices and a "pleasant", "quiet" vibe are further reasons area office types and others rely on it for everyday "quick lunches."

Gabriel's ⊠ *Italian*

| 23 | 19 | 23 | $63 |

W 60s | 11 W. 60th St. (bet. B'way & Columbus Ave.) | 212-956-4600 | www.gabrielsbarandrest.com
"Polished service" overseen by "natural host" Gabriel Aiello sets the "classy" tone at this "even-keeled" Columbus Circle Italian known for "delicious" cooking, a "comfortable" setting and proximity to Lincoln Center; given the rather "hefty" tabs, "media" types from nearby CBS and CNN prefer it for lunch.

Gahm Mi Oak ❶ *Korean*

| 20 | 14 | 15 | $26 |

Garment District | 43 W. 32nd St. (bet. B'way & 5th Ave.) | 212-695-4113 | www.gahmmioak.com
Renowned for its "lifesaving" *sollongtang* beef soup – especially "good when hung over" – this K-town Korean is also commended for its "delectable" kimchi; "rushed" service and a "hectic" atmosphere are counterbalanced by "cheap" tabs and 24/7 availability.

	FOOD	DECOR	SERVICE	COST

NEW Ganso 🗲 *Japanese/Noodle Shop* ▽ 22 | 18 | 18 | $22

Downtown Bklyn | 25 Bond St. (Livingston St.) | Brooklyn | 718-403-0900 | www.gansonyc.com

A "welcome addition" to Downtown Brooklyn, this "friendly", "priced-right" Japanese slurp shop ladles out ramen from chef Ryuji Irie (ex Matsuri), "wonderfully satisfying" bowls featuring "rich", meticulously made broth and "delicious noodles", alongside snacks like "awesome" chicken wings and pork buns; it all comes in "spare but comfortable" wood-lined digs.

NEW Gaonnuri ●🗲 *BBQ/Korean* ▽ 21 | 27 | 19 | $59

Garment District | 1250 Broadway, 39th fl. (32nd St.) | 212-971-9045 | www.gaonnurinyc.com

Its "biggest appeal" are its "amazing" "panoramic" vistas "over Midtown" from a "chic", 39th-floor space, but this "upscale" new player on the K-town scene also "holds its own" with "stylishly prepared" Korean fare, including "traditional" tabletop BBQ; service is variable and you "pay for the view", but that "sunset over the Hudson" is "worth it."

Garden Café *American* 20 | 18 | 20 | $28

Inwood | 4961 Broadway (bet. Isham & 207th Sts.) | 212-544-9480

"Solid" New Americana turns up at this "cozy" Inwood spot near the Cloisters that "feels like downtown without the downtown prices"; some shrug "nothing special", but all agree on the "friendly" service and "cute" back garden.

Gargiulo's *Italian* 22 | 19 | 22 | $48

Coney Island | 2911 W.15th St. (bet. Mermaid & Surf Aves.) | Brooklyn | 718-266-4891 | www.gargiulos.com

After a "swim at the beach", have a "swim in red sauce" at this circa-1907 Coney Island "time warp", a "catering hall"–size arena for good "old-fashioned" Neapolitan cooking ferried by "tuxedo-clad" waiters; the "colorful" crowd feels its "reputation is deserved", while a nightly raffle means "you could eat for free."

Gari ● *Japanese* 27 | 16 | 22 | $83

W 70s | 370 Columbus Ave. (bet. 77th & 78th Sts.) | 212-362-4816

Sushi of Gari *Japanese*

E 70s | 402 E. 78th St. (bet. 1st & York Aves.) | 212-517-5340 ●
NEW TriBeCa | 130 W. Broadway (Duane St.) | 212-285-0130 🗲
W 40s | 347 W. 46th St. (bet. 8th & 9th Aves.) | 212-957-0046 ●
W 50s | Plaza Food Hall | 1 W. 59th St. (5th Ave.) | 646-755-3230
www.sushiofgari.com

For an "unforgettable sensory journey", try the omakase at Gari Sugio's "off-the-charts" Japanese quintet, where the "jewel"-like sushi is simply "sublime"; despite "modest", "bento box"–size settings and "go-for-broke" tabs, finatics say these "bucket-list" destinations are the "last word" in raw-fish "bliss."

Gazala's *Mideastern* 21 | 14 | 18 | $31

W 40s | 709 Ninth Ave. (bet. 48th & 49th Sts.) | 212-245-0709
W 70s | 380 Columbus Ave. (78th St.) | 212-873-8880
www.gazalaplace.com

"Delectable" Druze dishes are delivered by these "casual" Mideasterns where the "solid" cooking and "inexpensive" tabs offset "modest" de-

| | FOOD | DECOR | SERVICE | COST |

cor and "hit-or-miss" service; the UWS spin-off is "more spacious" than the "cramped" Hell's Kitchen original (which boasts a BYO policy).

Gemma ◐ *Italian*
21 | 23 | 20 | $45

E Village | The Bowery Hotel | 335 Bowery (bet. 2nd & 3rd Sts.) | 212-505-7300 | www.theboweryhotel.com
Primo "people-watching" abounds at this "fun", all-day Bowery Hotel Italian that lures "scenesters" with a "romantic", "country-chic" setting festooned with "hundreds of candles"; "tasty" vittles, "attentive service" and "fair prices" make the "no-rez" policy (except for hotel guests) less of a drag.

NEW The General ◐ *Asian*
▽ 20 | 22 | 18 | $67

LES | 199 Bowery (Spring St.) | 212-271-7101 | www.emmgrp.com
"Pretty people" are all over this "trendy" Bowery arrival from the EMM folks (Catch) set in a sprawling space done up with reclaimed wood, exposed brick and funky wallpaper; the pricing's "premium", the service "lacking" and the shareable Asian menu via *Top Chef*'s Hung Huynh "delish", though some say it's "not about the food" but the "scene."

The General Greene *American*
20 | 17 | 18 | $33

Fort Greene | 229 DeKalb Ave. (Clermont Ave.) | Brooklyn | 718-222-1510 | www.thegeneralgreene.com
"Small plates win big" at this "casual" Fort Greene New American, where the grub's "local", "seasonal" and "affordable"; it's a natural for a "hipster" brunch or "before the Brooklyn Flea", and the "very Brooklyn" vibe extends to the "simple" decor and pleasant "outdoor seating."

Gennaro ⌿ *Italian*
24 | 14 | 18 | $43

W 90s | 665 Amsterdam Ave. (bet. 92nd & 93rd Sts.) | 212-665-5348 | www.gennaronyc.com
Be ready for a "long line" at this "durable" UWS Italian that takes "no reservations" and no plastic but does provide "wonderful", "hearty" fare for "non-gourmet prices"; even after a "third expansion", it's still "difficult to get a table after 7 PM."

Gigino at Wagner Park *Italian*
21 | 19 | 18 | $47

Financial District | 20 Battery Pl. (Little West St.) | 212-528-2228 | www.gigino-wagnerpark.com
Gigino Trattoria *Italian*
TriBeCa | 323 Greenwich St. (Duane St.) | 212-431-1112 | www.gigino-trattoria.com
It almost "feels like Florence" at this "affordable" TriBeCa Tuscan featuring "above-average" food, "friendly" service and a "high-ceilinged", "farmhouse-like" milieu; "outdoor dining" with a "one-of-a-kind view" of the harbor and Statue of Liberty is the thing at its "off-the-beaten-path" sibling in Wagner Park.

Gino's ⓜ *Italian*
24 | 18 | 20 | $35

Bay Ridge | 7414 Fifth Ave. (bet. Bay Ridge Pkwy. & 74th St.) | Brooklyn | 718-748-1698 | www.ginosbayridge.com
A "neighborhood" "staple" since 1964, this ever-"crowded" Bay Ridge Italian serves up "generous portions" of "fresh" classics "just like mom makes" in "casual" environs; "get ready to wait in line" at prime times, but the all-around "enjoyable" experience and "reasonable" tab ensure it's "well worth it."

	FOOD	DECOR	SERVICE	COST

Giorgio's of Gramercy *American/Italian*
| 21 | 18 | 22 | $47 |

Flatiron | 27 E. 21st St. (bet. B'way & Park Ave. S.) | 212-477-0007 |
www.giorgiosofgramercy.com

The epitome of a "true sleeper", this 20-plus-year-old Italian-American "class act" in the Flatiron features "consistently good" cooking that suggests "unsung talent in the kitchen"; "reasonable" rates, "gracious" service and "early brothel" decor are other incentives.

Giovanni Rana *Italian*
| ▽ 24 | 21 | 22 | $43 |

Chelsea | Chelsea Market | 75 Ninth Ave. (bet. 15th & 16th Sts.) |
212-601-2687 | www.rananyc.com

"Delicious", "über-fresh" noodles "dominate" the "superb" menu at this "warm, bright" Chelsea Market Italian from a pasta purveyor that's "an establishment in Italy"; "helpful" service, "reasonable" prices and sidewalk seating are further allures, though those on the go hit the "great take-out" section in back.

Giovanni Venticinque *Italian*
| 23 | 19 | 23 | $66 |

E 80s | 25 E. 83rd St. (bet. 5th & Madison Aves.) | 212-988-7300 |
www.giovanniventicinque.com

"Excellent" Tuscan fare and a "gracious" staff that "makes you feel welcome" keep this UES Italian popular with a "neighborhood" crowd; "intimate" and "hushed" enough for "real conversation", it boasts "proximity to the Met" and a $25 lunch prix fixe that offsets otherwise "pricey" tabs.

Girasole *Italian*
| 21 | 16 | 20 | $62 |

E 80s | 151 E. 82nd St. (bet. Lexington & 3rd Aves.) | 212-772-6690 |
www.girasolerestaurantnyc.com

This "above-average" UES "neighborhood" Italian has been hosting an "older crowd" since 1989; "reliably good" cooking and "efficient" service compensate for the somewhat "stodgy" air, though it earns bonus points since "you can actually hear your dining companion."

Glass House Tavern ● *American*
| 19 | 18 | 20 | $46 |

W 40s | 252 W. 47th St. (bet. B'way & 8th Ave.) | 212-730-4800 |
www.glasshousetavern.com

Something "calming" in the "hectic Theater District", this "solid performer" provides New Americana that tastes even better when Broadway "stars" are seated alongside you; "reasonable" rates and "cordial" service also draw applause, though insiders advise "eat upstairs."

Gnocco *Italian*
| 22 | 17 | 19 | $38 |

E Village | 337 E. 10th St. (bet. Aves. A & B) | 212-677-1913 |
www.gnocco.com

"Authentic Emilian fare" is the focus of this East Village Italian praised for its "tasty pizza", "lengthy wine list" and "excellent" namesake dish; the "most prized tables" are in its "lovely", all-seasons garden, though "modest" pricing and "helpful" service are available throughout.

Gobo *Vegan/Vegetarian*
| 23 | 19 | 20 | $36 |

E 80s | 1426 Third Ave. (81st St.) | 212-288-5099
W Village | 401 Sixth Ave. (bet. 8th St. & Waverly Pl.) | 212-255-3242
www.goborestaurant.com

Vegan food gets some "fancy" twists at this "non-preachy" duo offering an "unusually varied" menu of Asian-accented vittles that are

| | FOOD | DECOR | SERVICE | COST |

"wonderfully healthy"; the UES outpost may be more "upscale" than its "earthy" Village cousin, but both share good, "down-to-earth" service.

Go Burger *Burgers*
18 | 15 | 16 | $26

E 70s | 1448 Second Ave. (bet. 75th & 76th Sts.) | 212-988-9822
Garment District | 310 W. 38th St. (bet. 8th & 9th Aves.) | 212-290-8000
www.goburger.com

"Gourmet burgers" and "spiked shakes" are the specialty of these satellites of a national chain via the BLT Burger team; service may "need improvement", but "massive crowds" suggest it's doing something right; P.S. the Garment District outlet is a kiosk inside restaurant Casa Nonna.

Golden Unicorn *Chinese*
21 | 14 | 14 | $26

Chinatown | 18 E. Broadway (Catherine St.) | 212-941-0911 |
www.goldenunicornrestaurant.com

"Mobbed and noisy" is a given at this "huge" C-town Cantonese featuring "endless carts" stocked with "heavenly dim sum"; "hurried", "English"-challenged service and "basic Chinatown wedding party decor" are forgiven since it's a lot "cheaper than flying to Hong Kong."

Good *American*
21 | 17 | 20 | $43

W Village | 89 Greenwich Ave. (bet. Bank & W. 12th Sts.) | 212-691-8080 |
www.goodrestaurantnyc.com

"Should be named 'great'" say die-hard supporters of this West Village American "respite" that's still something of a "hidden gem" despite "simple", "hearty" cooking and "kind service"; aesthetes may find the decor "boring", but there's always a "weekend line" for its "amazing brunch."

Good Enough to Eat *American*
21 | 15 | 18 | $28

W 80s | 520 Columbus Ave. (85th St.) | 212-496-0163 |
www.goodenoughtoeat.com

It lost the white picket fence in the move to new nearby digs, but this "great-value" UWS "old favorite" continues to offer the same all-day dining à la "Vermont" with "simple" American comfort items; the new space retains the "cute", farmhousey feel but is roomier with more outdoor seating – but "painful waits" are still the norm at weekend brunch.

Good Fork 🅜 *Eclectic*
25 | 18 | 24 | $46

Red Hook | 391 Van Brunt St. (bet. Coffey & Van Dyke Sts.) | Brooklyn |
718-643-6636 | www.goodfork.com

"Rough Red Hook" gets its own "culinary outpost" via this "small" Eclectic where the "seriously good" Asian-accented menu is dispatched at a "fair price" point; "attractive" rustic looks, a back garden and "actually friendly hipster waiters" are further incentives.

Gordon Ramsay ●🅩🅜 *French*
23 | 22 | 22 | $102

W 50s | London NYC Hotel | 151 W. 54th St. (bet. 6th & 7th Aves.) |
212-468-8888 | www.gordonramsay.com

Though he's just a consultant now, Gordon Ramsay's "spirit" lives on at his namesake Midtown hotel dining room where the "first-rate", prix fixe–only French menu is "expertly crafted" and delivered by a "charming" crew; the "modern" setting is "elegantly decorated", but some feel the "high tariffs" could use "fine tuning" absent the star of the show.

| | FOOD | DECOR | SERVICE | COST |

Gotham Bar & Grill *American*

27 | 25 | 26 | $84

G Village | 12 E. 12th St. (bet. 5th Ave. & University Pl.) | 212-620-4020 | www.gothambarandgrill.com

"Still going strong" after 30 years, "cooking genius" Alfred Portale's "delightful" Village "destination" scores "high marks" all around, from the "towering", "wickedly delicious" New American cuisine and "professional" service to the "classy, airy" room; it's "a splurge sort of place" for sure, but the $25 prix fixe lunch is a "bargain."

Gottino ● *Italian*

▽ 20 | 20 | 21 | $41

W Village | 52 Greenwich Ave. (bet. Charles & Perry Sts.) | 212-633-2590

Fans love "getting into small-plate trouble" at this itty-bitty West Village enoteca where the food is "delicious" and the mood "hip"; if "courteous" service and moderate pricing aren't enough, there's also an "absolute-heaven" back garden.

Grace's Trattoria *Italian*

19 | 16 | 20 | $47

E 70s | 201 E. 71st St. (bet. 2nd & 3rd Aves.) | 212-452-2323 | www.gracestrattoria.com

For "no-nonsense", "well-prepared" Italiana, this longtime UES trattoria offers the same "great quality" as Grace's Marketplace next door; maybe the decor's a bit dull, but the "prompt service" and "fair prices" make for such an "easy night out" that its "graying crowd" doesn't mind.

Gradisca *Italian*

24 | 19 | 22 | $55

W Village | 126 W. 13th St. (bet. 6th & 7th Aves.) | 212-691-4886 | www.gradiscanyc.com

"Superb pastas" hand-rolled by the owner's mama are the "main attraction" at this "low-key" West Village Italian, but other "savory" dishes and a "strong wine list" further secure its standing as an area "favorite"; some say it's a bit "pricey" considering the "small portions" and "casual ambiance", but "friendly" service adds value.

Graffiti ☒ *Eclectic*

25 | 18 | 22 | $46

E Village | 224 E. 10th St. (bet. 1st & 2nd Aves.) | 212-677-0695 | www.graffitinyc.com

"Surprising flavor combinations" are the forte of this "super-inventive" East Village Eclectic showcasing chef Jehangir Mehta's "delectable" Indian-accented small plates; though the "communal"-tabled space is beyond "minuscule", the "value is big", the service "good-humored" and the mood "friendly."

Gramercy Tavern *American*

28 | 26 | 27 | $120

Flatiron | 42 E. 20th St. (bet. B'way & Park Ave. S.) | 212-477-0777 | www.gramercytavern.com

"A classic that seems to maintain its standing effortlessly", Danny Meyer's Flatiron "favorite" promises a "wow experience" featuring chef Michael Anthony's "top-of-the-line" New American cuisine, "superlative" pro service and a "beautiful", "flower-filled" atmosphere; while you'll spend a "handsome sum" to dine in the prix fixe–only main room, the "fabulous à la carte offerings" in the front tavern are a somewhat "more affordable" option.

Grand Sichuan *Chinese*

20 | 10 | 14 | $28

Chelsea | 172 Eighth Ave. (bet. 18th & 19th Sts.) | 212-243-1688

(continued)

Grand Sichuan

Chelsea | 229 Ninth Ave. (24th St.) | 212-620-5200 ◖
E 50s | 1049 Second Ave. (bet. 55th & 56th Sts.) | 212-355-5855
E Village | 19-23 St. Marks Pl. (bet. 2nd & 3rd Aves.) | 212-529-4800
Murray Hill | 227 Lexington Ave. (bet. 33rd & 34th Sts.) | 212-679-9770
W 40s | 368 W. 46th St. (bet. 8th & 9th Aves.) | 212-969-9001
W 70s | 307 Amsterdam Ave. (bet. 74th & 75th Sts.) | 212-580-0277
W Village | 15 Seventh Ave. S. (bet. Carmine & Leroy Sts.) | 212-645-0222
Rego Park | 98-108 Queens Blvd. (bet. 66th & 67th Aves.) | Queens |
718-268-8833
www.grandsichuan.com

"For those who like it hot", this "popular" Chinese chain promises "authentically fiery" Sichuan fare ordered from a "humongous menu"; "ignore" the "forgettable" decor and "so-so" service and just focus on the "reasonable" tabs that make for a "grand bargain" indeed.

Grand Tier ⊠ *American* | 20 | 25 | 23 | $84 |

W 60s | Metropolitan Opera House, 2nd fl. | Lincoln Center Plaza
(bet. 63rd & 65th Sts.) | 212-799-3400 | www.patinagroup.com
Those long opera nights have a "delightful" prelude at this Lincoln
Center American where the "tasty" if "limited" menu is served in a
"dramatic", chandeliered setting overlooking the Met foyer; not surprisingly, the crowd's "well dressed" and the tabs "expensive", but
payoffs include "efficiency" and "dessert at intermission."

Gran Electrica ◖ *Mexican* | ▽ 22 | 23 | 22 | $38 |

Dumbo | 5 Front St. (Old Fulton St.) | Brooklyn | 718-852-2789 |
www.granelectrica.com
"Delicate and simple but super-delicious", the midpriced Mexican
eats at this "pleasant" Dumbo taqueria pair well with an extensive list
of mescals, tequilas and specialty cocktails that regulars "love"; "Day
of the Dead–inspired wallpaper makes the ambiance" indoors, while
the "fun patio" is a "go-to for summertime drinking."

NEW Grape & Vine ◖ *American* | - | - | - | M |

G Village | Jade Hotel | 52 W. 13th St. (6th Ave.) | 212-300-4525 |
www.grapevine-nyc.com
An archway off the Jade Hotel lobby leads to this tavernlike Villager
whose artsy dining area dishes up American standards; a moodier front
bar pours cocktails with names like 'The Gossip', a nod to the 11th Street
saloon where the eponymous phrase supposedly originated.

Gray's Papaya ◖⊄ *Hot Dogs* | 20 | 6 | 14 | $7 |

G Village | 402 Sixth Ave. (8th St.) | 212-260-3532
W 70s | 2090 Broadway (72nd St.) | 212-799-0243
These 24/7 hot dog stands vend "surprisingly good" wieners washed
down with "frothy" papaya drinks; "quick" turnaround and "chump-change" tabs offset the "gruff" service, "what-a-dump" decor and lack
of seats that make them "quintessential" NY "institutions."

Great Jones Cafe ◖ *Cajun* | 21 | 15 | 19 | $29 |

NoHo | 54 Great Jones St. (bet. Bowery & Lafayette St.) | 212-674-9304 |
www.greatjones.com
"No-frills" says it all about this "friendly" NoHo Cajun where the "solid"
vittles arrive in a "dumpy", verging on "campy" setting; 30-plus years

on, the crowd's still "local", the vibe "downtown" and the jukebox as "great" as ever.

Great NY Noodle Town ◗⇗ *Noodle Shop* | 23 | 7 | 12 | $18 |

Chinatown | 28 Bowery (Bayard St.) | 212-349-0923 |
www.greatnynoodletown.com

"Surrender to the crowd experience" and "sit with strangers" at this "chaotic" C-town noodle shop known for "dirt-cheap" Cantonese chow (and notable salt-baked seafood) served into the wee hours; not so great is "no decor", "no credit cards" and "difficult" service.

Greek Kitchen *Greek* | 20 | 14 | 18 | $32 |

W 50s | 889 10th Ave. (58th St.) | 212-581-4300 | www.greekkitchennyc.com
Set on the fringes of Hell's Kitchen, this "local" Greek rolls out "solid" cooking at "moderate" tabs, then ups the ante with "convenience" to Fordham, John Jay College and Lincoln Center; it's more than "welcome" in an "area of limited culinary resources", though ultimately "nothing to write home about."

Greenhouse Café *American* | 20 | 19 | 21 | $36 |

Bay Ridge | 7717 Third Ave. (bet. 77th & 78th Sts.) | Brooklyn |
718-833-8200 | www.greenhousecafe.com
This circa-1979 Bay Ridge American presents a "reliable" menu of Americana that's best savored in its "lovely" greenhouse room; "family-friendly" atmospherics, "moderate prices" and "rapid" service tell the rest of the appealing story.

Grifone ☒ *Italian* | 25 | 18 | 24 | $67 |

E 40s | 244 E. 46th St. (bet. 2nd & 3rd Aves.) | 212-490-7275
A "tried-and-true" East Side option since '85, this "old-line" Northern Italian near the U.N. fields an "extensive" menu of "outstanding" dishes; "dated" decor and "captains-of-industry" price tags detract, but its mature following digs the "discreet" service and "calm, quiet" mien.

Grimaldi's ⇗ *Pizza* | 23 | 13 | 16 | $23 |

Flatiron | Limelight Mktpl. | 656 Sixth Ave. (bet. 20th & 21st Sts.) |
646-484-5665
NEW Murray Hill | 462 Second Ave. (26th St.) | 646-833-7076
Coney Island | 1215 Surf Ave. (bet. Stillwell Ave. & 12th St.) | Brooklyn |
718-676-2630
Dumbo | 1 Front St. (bet. Dock & Old Fulton Sts.) | Brooklyn |
718-858-4300
Douglaston | Douglaston Plaza | 242-02 61st Ave. (Douglaston Pkwy.) |
Queens | 718-819-2133
www.grimaldisnyc.com
Fans "pay their dues in line" for one of the "crisp", "craveable" pies out of the coal-fired oven at this "iconic" Dumbo pizzeria and its "easier-to-get-into" offshoots around town; they're "cash only" and sell "no slices", but the "affordable" tabs are "worth a quick trip to the ATM."

The Grocery ☒Ⓜ *American* | 27 | 18 | 25 | $64 |

Carroll Gardens | 288 Smith St. (bet. Sackett & Union Sts.) | Brooklyn |
718-596-3335 | www.thegroceryrestaurant.com
"Carefully sourced", "superbly executed" New American food served with a "warm, personal touch" makes this enduring Smith Street "jewel" one of "Brooklyn's finest culinary experiences"; given the "no-frills",

	FOOD	DECOR	SERVICE	COST

"closetlike" dining room, insiders say it's "best when you can sit in the back garden."

Guantanamera ◐ Cuban   20 | 16 | 19 | $36

W 50s | 939 Eighth Ave. (bet. 55th & 56th Sts.) | 212-262-5354 |
www.guantanamerany.com

"Jumping" is the word on this "fun" Midtown Cuban where the "tasty", "authentic" chow is nearly overwhelmed by the "amazing mojitos" and "ridiculously loud live music"; "reasonable" rates and hand-rolled cigars on weekend nights supply extra "oomph."

NEW Guy's American American   ∇ 17 | 17 | 16 | $37

W 40s | 220 W. 44th St. (bet. 7th & 8th Aves.) | 646-532-4897 |
www.guyfieri.com

"Relaxed, energetic" and "exactly what you'd expect" from Food Network star Guy Fieri, this "cavernous" Times Square "tourist" magnet dispenses "just-ok" midpriced American eats in "biiig" portions; a "chatty" staff works the tri-level, 500-seat space, which sports "fun" decor "matching Guy's personality" – think "tacky" Americana tchotchkes, hot-rod paintings and a huge merch counter.

Gwynnett St. American   ∇ 27 | 20 | 24 | $58

Williamsburg | 312 Graham Ave. (bet. Ainslie & Devoe Sts.) | Brooklyn |
347-889-7002 | www.gwynnettst.com

"Innovative choices match the hipster 'hood" at this Williamsburg "treasure", a deceptively "casual" setting for "cutting-edge" New American cuisine from a former WD-50 chef; an "out-of-this-world" tasting menu and "expert cocktails" ferried by an "accommodating" staff further make it "worth the trip."

Gyu-Kaku Japanese   21 | 19 | 19 | $43

E 40s | 805 Third Ave., 2nd fl. (bet. 49th & 50th Sts.) | 212-702-8816
E Village | 34 Cooper Sq. (bet. Astor Pl. & 4th St.) | 212-475-2989
W 40s | 321 W. 44th St. (bet. 8th & 9th Aves.) | 646-692-9115
www.gyu-kaku.com

"Novelty"-seekers hype this "delicious, do-it-yourself" Japanese yakiniku franchise where you "cook your own" BBQ on tabletop charcoal braziers; since the "small portions" can add up to "pricey" tabs, bargain-hunters show up for the "happy-hour specials."

Hakkasan Chinese   23 | 25 | 20 | $77

W 40s | 311 W. 43rd St. (bet. 8th & 9th Aves.) | 212-776-1818 |
www.hakkasan.com

"Over-the-top", "super-cool" Shanghai-chic decor sets the "glitzy" mood at this "upscale" Theater District outpost of the London-based chain turning out "fancy", "delicious" Cantonese-inspired dishes with Western accents; ornate latticework partitions make the "massive" space feel more intimate, but the super-"expensive" tabs are harder to disguise.

Hampton Chutney Co. Indian   21 | 10 | 16 | $17

SoHo | 68 Prince St. (bet. Crosby & Lafayette Sts.) | 212-226-9996
W 80s | 464 Amsterdam Ave. (bet. 82nd & 83rd Sts.) | 212-362-5050
www.hamptonchutney.com

Both "light and filling", the "delicious" dosas with "nonconventional" fillings add up to "exotic", "affordable" eating at these "casual" Indian standbys in SoHo and on the Upper West Side; it's a "cool concept", but the "basic" counter-service setups have many turning to them mostly for takeout.

Hanci Turkish Cuisine *Turkish*

FOOD	DECOR	SERVICE	COST
21	13	19	$35

W 50s | 854 10th Ave. (56th St.) | 212-707-8144 | www.hanciturkishcuisine.com

"Worth the walk" to way west 10th Avenue, this "low-key" Turk proffers "simple", "nicely prepared" plates for a modest price; not much decor is offset by "good service" and convenience to "John Jay College and Lincoln Center."

Hanco's *Sandwiches/Vietnamese*

FOOD	DECOR	SERVICE	COST
20	9	15	$12

Boerum Hill | 85 Bergen St. (Smith St.) | Brooklyn | 718-858-6818 | www.hancosny.com ⊘
Brooklyn Heights | 147 Montague St. (bet. Clinton & Henry Sts.) | Brooklyn | 347-529-5054
Park Slope | 350 Seventh Ave. (10th St.) | Brooklyn | 718-499-8081 | www.hancosny.com

"Addictive", "drool"-inducing banh mi sandwiches washed down with "excellent" bubble teas (plus pho in Park Slope and Brooklyn Heights) ensure these Vietnamese storefronts are "always busy"; "no frills" sums up both the decor and service, but few mind given the price.

Hangawi *Korean/Vegetarian*

FOOD	DECOR	SERVICE	COST
25	24	23	$51

Murray Hill | 12 E. 32nd St. (bet. 5th & Madison Aves.) | 212-213-0077 | www.hangawirestaurant.com

An "experience to be savored", this K-town vegetarian "revelation" offers "sublime" Korean food, "attention-to-detail" service and a "tranquil", "templelike" setting where "shoes come off at the door"; perhaps "you won't believe you spent so much for vegetables", but to most it's "worth every penny."

NEW Hanjan ●✉ *Korean*

FOOD	DECOR	SERVICE	COST
▽ 22	16	20	$52

Flatiron | 36 W. 26th St. (bet. B'way & 6th Ave.) | 212-206-7226 | www.hanjan26.com

On a "booming stretch of 26th Street" in the Flatiron is this upscale gastropub (a Danji sibling), where the "Korean soul food" small plates are "inventive and classic by turns", and pair well with "awesome" rice beer and "exotic cocktails"; the "long waits" to get into its "cozy", "minimalist" space speak for themselves.

NEW Harding's ● *American*

FOOD	DECOR	SERVICE	COST
–	–	–	M

Flatiron | 32 E. 21st St. (bet. B'way & Park Ave. S.) | 212-600-2105 | www.hardingsnyc.com

You can salute the flag and your steak and potatoes at this patriotic Flatironer that pays homage to all-American classics with its mid-priced menu of oysters Rockefeller, Waldorf salad and the like; antique stars-and-stripes, framed vintage front pages and other Americana touches provide a fitting backdrop.

NEW Harlem Shake *Burgers*

FOOD	DECOR	SERVICE	COST
–	–	–	I

Harlem | 100 W. 124th St. (Lenox Ave.) | 212-222-8300 | www.harlemshakenyc.com

This fast-casual joint evokes old-school Harlem with signed photos of neighborhood notables, a life-size picture of 'Miss Harlem Shake' and

| | FOOD | DECOR | SERVICE | COST |

vintage JET magazine covers decorating the walls; the signature burger is a blend of beef from Pat La Frieda that's cooked smash-style and served on a potato roll.

NEW Harlow ●☒ *Seafood*
▽ 19 | 28 | 23 | $80

E 50s | 111 E. 56th St. (bet. Lexington & Park Aves.) | 212-935-6600 | www.harlownyc.com

Swanky seafood surfaces in Midtown at this "snazzy" newcomer via restaurateur Richie Notar (Nobu) that's an out-of-the-box hit with "attractive" high-society types; no surprise, the prices are hefty, but payoffs include "excellent" service, a "fabulous" bar scene and a "gorgeous" setting replete with deco furniture and ornate plasterwork.

The Harrison *American*
22 | 21 | 22 | $63

TriBeCa | 355 Greenwich St. (Harrison St.) | 212-274-9310 | www.theharrison.com

By now a "TriBeCa standard", Jimmy Bradley's "time-honored favorite" keeps on keeping on with "excellent" New Americana, "welcoming" service and "comfortable" quarters filled with the "buzz of regulars"; while not cheap, it's so "relaxing" that the tabs seem incidental to the "consistently reliable" experience.

Harry Cipriani ● *Italian*
22 | 21 | 23 | $92

E 50s | Sherry-Netherland Hotel | 781 Fifth Ave. (bet. 59th & 60th Sts.) | 212-753-5566 | www.cipriani.com

"Billionaires" and "divorcées" nibble on "upscale" Venetian victuals at this Sherry-Netherland "one-percenter" refuge known for serving the "best Bellinis in town"; the "eye-popping" tabs may cause more of a stir than the food, but then again, "you're paying to see who's sitting next to you."

Harry's Cafe & Steak ●☒ *Steak*
22 | 21 | 21 | $53

Financial District | 1 Hanover Sq. (bet. Pearl & Stone Sts.) | 212-785-9200 | www.harrysnyc.com

Long "Wall Street's go-to eatery", this FiDi "throwback" in the historic India House attracts "captains of industry" with "mouthwatering" steaks and more backed by one of the best wine cellars in the city; it's "busy" for lunch, quieter at dinner and "expense account"–worthy all the time.

Harry's Italian *Italian*
21 | 18 | 19 | $33

Financial District | 2 Gold St. (Platt St.) | 212-747-0797 ●
Financial District | 225 Murray St. (West St.) | 212-608-1007 ●
W 40s | 30 Rockefeller Plaza, Concourse Level (bet. 49th & 50th Sts.) | 212-218-1450
www.harrysitalian.com

"Amazing" pizzas "star" on the menu of "standard Italian favorites" at these "welcoming" fallbacks from the Harry's Cafe folks; "ample portions" and "reasonable pricing" cement their "go-to" status for "less-than-formal lunches" at the FiDi locations or eats on the move from the "busy" takeout-only Rock Center outlet.

Haru *Japanese*
21 | 17 | 18 | $42

E 70s | 1327 Third Ave. (76th St.) | 212-452-1028 ●
E 70s | 1329 Third Ave. (76th St.) | 212-452-2230 ●
Financial District | 1 Wall Street Ct. (Pearl St.) | 212-785-6850

(continued)

(continued)

Haru

Flatiron | 220 Park Ave. S. (18th St.) | 646-428-0989
W 40s | 205 W. 43rd St. (bet. 7th & 8th Aves.) | 212-398-9810 ◗
W 80s | 433 Amsterdam Ave. (bet. 80th & 81st Sts.) | 212-579-5655 ◗
www.harusushi.com

"Delish fish" sliced in "large" pieces is the hook at this stylish Japanese mini-chain where the "premium" sushi "won't break the budget"; it may be "a bit of a factory" and "blasting music" puts it high on the "decibel meter", but its "young, vibrant" following doesn't seem to mind.

Hasaki *Japanese*

24 | 16 | 19 | $45

E Village | 210 E. Ninth St. (Stuyvesant St.) | 212-473-3327 |
www.hasakinyc.com

"Gourmet" sushi and "authentic" Japanese dishes are served for "reasonable" rates at this compact, '84-vintage East Villager; a no-rez rule makes for "long lines" at prime time, so regulars show up for the "can't-go-wrong" lunch specials.

Hatsuhana ☒ *Japanese*

25 | 17 | 22 | $57

E 40s | 17 E. 48th St. (bet. 5th & Madison Aves.) | 212-355-3345
E 40s | 237 Park Ave. (bet. 45th & 46th Sts.) | 212-661-3400
www.hatsuhana.com

"Serious", "old-school sushi" is the lure at these "long-established" Midtown Japanese twins where the "artful presentation" begins with "aim-to-please" service; "bland decor" that "needs refreshing" seems at odds with the rather "pricey" tabs, but you don't last this long without doing something right.

Havana Alma de Cuba *Cuban*

21 | 18 | 20 | $41

W Village | 94 Christopher St. (bet. Bedford & Bleecker Sts.) |
212-242-3800 | www.havananyc.com

"Good-humored" servers pass "pitchers of mojitos" and "substantial" portions of appealing Cuban comfort chow at this "festive" West Villager; "live music", "reasonable" rates and a "lovely rear garden" keep things "bustling" here, so be prepared for "noise" and "chair-bumping."

Havana Central *Cuban*

19 | 18 | 18 | $36

W 40s | 151 W. 46th St. (bet. 6th & 7th Aves.) | 212-398-7440 ◗
W 100s | 2911 Broadway (bet. 113th & 114th Sts.) |
212-662-8830
www.havanacentral.com

"Always a blast", these "lush-bordering-on-tacky" Cubans conjure up "Havana in a bygone era" via "satisfying" classic comestibles and "kick-butt" cocktails; both share "uneven" service, "reasonable" tabs and "noisy-as-all-get-out" decibels, though Midtown's "touristy" and Uptown more "collegiate."

Haveli ◗ *Indian*

21 | 16 | 20 | $33

E Village | 100 Second Ave. (bet. 5th & 6th Sts.) | 212-982-0533
A "reliable" East Village vet that "excels" with "satisfying" cooking, this comparatively "lovely" Indian around the corner from its Sixth Street competitors is among "the best of the bunch"; "welcoming" service and consistent "quality" help justify tabs slightly "pricier" than some in the zone.

	FOOD	DECOR	SERVICE	COST

Hearth *American/Italian*   24 | 20 | 23 | $66

E Village | 403 E. 12th St. (1st Ave.) | 646-602-1300 |
www.restauranthearth.com

An East Village "mecca for foodies", chef Marco Canora's Tuscan-American "old faithful" promises "delectable" fare from a "farm-based menu", complemented by a "fantastic", "amazingly eclectic" wine list; such "locavore goodness doesn't come cheap", but "sincere" service and a "warm", "bustling" atmosphere help ensure it's "worth the splurge."

Hecho en Dumbo ● *Mexican*   23 | 17 | 19 | $42

NoHo | 354 Bowery (bet. 4th & Great Jones Sts.) | 212-937-4245 |
www.hechoendumbo.com

"Inventive" Mexican small plates are "served with a side of hipster" at this "sceney", "sex-Mex" standout that's a prime example of the "Bowery renaissance"; sure, "service could be better", but tabs are "pretty reasonable" and insiders say the tasting menu–only "chef's table is the way to go" – and there's also a next-door bar/event space, Salón Hecho.

Heidelberg *German*   20 | 17 | 19 | $41

E 80s | 1648 Second Ave. (bet. 85th & 86th Sts.) | 212-628-2332 |
www.heidelbergrestaurant.com

When it comes to "classic", "stick-to-your-ribs" Germanica, this 75-plus-year-old Yorkville "time capsule" fields a "heavy", "no-apologies" menu washed down with "boots of beer"; "costumed" staffers and a "kitschy", "oompah-pah" setting are part of the "fun" package.

Hell's Kitchen *Mexican*   23 | 18 | 20 | $46

W 40s | 679 Ninth Ave. (bet. 46th & 47th Sts.) | 212-977-1588 |
www.hellskitchen-nyc.com

"Tasty modern" Mexican food draws "big crowds" to this "high-concept" Clinton cantina where the "margaritas keep flowing" as the "noise" levels rise; even "thoughtful service" can't ease the "pre-theater crush", yet the overall experience is "closer to heaven" than the name suggests.

Henry Public ●⊘⌿ *Pub Food*   20 | 21 | 18 | $31

Cobble Hill | 329 Henry St. (bet. Atlantic Ave. & Pacific St.) | Brooklyn |
718-852-8630 | www.henrypublic.com

"Trendy in a late-1800s sort of way", this "olde-timey" Cobble Hill pub serves a "limited" menu anchored by an "off-the-charts" turkey-leg sandwich; "cool", "suspendered" bartenders shake "sophisticated" cocktails, leaving the "cash-only", no-rez rules as the only downsides.

Henry's ● *American*   20 | 19 | 20 | $41

W 100s | 2745 Broadway (105th St.) | 212-866-0600 | www.henrysnyc.com

"Widely spaced tables", "high ceilings" and "conversation"-enabling alfresco seating are among the appeals at this Columbia-area bistro; the New American cooking is as "reliable" as the "good-value" tabs and "aim-to-please" service, hence its popularity with everyone from "families" to local "literati."

Henry's End *American*   25 | 17 | 23 | $48

Brooklyn Heights | 44 Henry St. (bet. Cranberry & Middagh Sts.) |
Brooklyn | 718-834-1776 | www.henrysend.com

"As good as the day it opened" in 1973, this "distinctive" Brooklyn Heights destination remains a "sentimental favorite" due to "inven-

| | FOOD | DECOR | SERVICE | COST |

tive" New American cooking, including its seasonal wild-game festival bringing "exotic critters" to the table; a "small-town" atmosphere and "efficient" service make the "sardine seating" feel almost "cozy."

Hibino *Japanese*   25 | 18 | 22 | $38

Cobble Hill | 333 Henry St. (Pacific St.) | Brooklyn | 718-260-8052 | www.hibino-brooklyn.com

"Fresh-as-one-can-get" sushi vies for the spotlight with the "daily changing" *obanzai* (small plates) and "amazing" housemade tofu at this "quirky" Cobble Hill Japanese; "budget-friendly" tabs and "unobtrusive" service embellish its "subdued", "unique" ambiance.

Hide-Chan *Japanese/Noodle Shop*   22 | 14 | 16 | $22

E 50s | 248 E. 52nd St., 2nd fl. (bet. 2nd & 3rd Aves.) | 212-813-1800 | www.hidechanramen.com

The sound of diners "noisily slurping" "cooked-to-perfection" noodles swimming in "flavorful" broth provides the background music at this "authentic" East Midtown Japanese ramen joint; alright, the service is "a bit rushed" and the setting "cramped", but "low costs" keep the trade brisk.

🆕 Hill & Dale ❶ *Gastropub*   - | - | - | M

LES | 115 Allen St. (Delancey St.) | 212-420-1115 | www.hillanddalenyc.com

From the Brooklyneer team, this LES gastropub turns out trumped-up, trendy American comfort bites like organic deviled eggs and sliders at gentle prices; the rustic, brick-walled space (ex Allen & Delancey, Mary Queen of Scots) has seats along the long bar, a few tables and several plush leather couches.

Hill Country *BBQ*   23 | 16 | 16 | $34

Flatiron | 30 W. 26th St. (bet. B'way & 6th Ave.) | 212-255-4544 | www.hillcountryny.com

Dishing up "fine Texas BBQ" in "NYC of all places", this bi-level Flatiron roadhouse is forever "mobbed" with fans of its "moist brisket", "excellent ribs" and other meaty "delights", plus "quality sides", offered up "cafeteria-style"; maybe the "by-the-pound" pricing is a bit steep "for a serve-yourself-on-paper-plate kind of place", but live bands downstairs "add to the appeal."

Hill Country Chicken *Southern*   20 | 14 | 16 | $20

Flatiron | 1123 Broadway (25th St.) | 212-257-6446 | www.hillcountrychicken.com

"Crispy-crunchy" fried chicken (including a "fabulous" skinless version) and "decent sides" make it hard to "save room for pie" at this low-budget Flatiron Southerner; regulars ignore the "service hiccups" and "groaninducing", "rec-room" decor, reporting it's "quieter" downstairs.

Hillstone *American*   23 | 21 | 21 | $43

E 50s | Citicorp Bldg. | 153 E. 53rd St. (enter on 3rd Ave. & 54th St.) | 212-888-3828
Murray Hill | NY Life Bldg. | 378 Park Ave. S. (27th St.) | 212-689-1090
www.hillstone.com

Young "corporate" guns frequent these "surprisingly good", "affordable" outlets of the national chain for "easy" American comfort items (i.e. its "famous" spinach-artichoke dip) served in "dark", "roomy" environs; "lively bar scenes" distract from the perennial "waits" at prime times.

Home *American*   22 | 17 | 21 | $45

W Village | 20 Cornelia St. (bet. Bleecker & W. 4th Sts.) | 212-243-9579 | www.homerestaurantnyc.com

A West Village "find", this under-the-radar vet serves up "comfort"-oriented Americana at a "fair price"; its "tiny" digs are "cozy" ("just like the name implies"), but "tables on top of each other" have many trying for seats in the "nice garden that takes you out of the city" for a while.

Hop Kee ●⇄ *Chinese*   21 | 7 | 15 | $22

Chinatown | 21 Mott St., downstairs (bet. Chatham Sq. & Mosco St.) | 212-964-8365 | www.hopkeenyc.com

"Old-guard", cash-only Chinatown cellar that's been slinging "traditional" Cantonese food – "and plenty of it" – since 1968; "dank" decor and "zombie" service are offset by "late"-night hours, "rock-bottom" tabs and an "Anthony Bourdain" endorsement.

Hospoda *American/Czech*   23 | 23 | 23 | $59

E 70s | Bohemian National Hall | 321 E. 73rd St. (bet. 1st & 2nd Aves.) | 212-861-1038 | www.hospodanyc.com

Ensconced in the UES Bohemian National Hall, this "chic", "upscale" contender incorporates "striking" modern decor and "accommodating" service to buttress its beer-friendly New American fare with "modern Czech" touches; various iterations of Pilsner Urquell on tap pleases, "tiny portions" and "pricey" tabs less so, but the general "prague-nosis is it's worth czeching out."

The House ● *American*   21 | 24 | 21 | $56

Gramercy | 121 E. 17th St. (bet. Irving Pl. & Park Ave. S.) | 212-353-2121 | www.thehousenyc.com

This tri-level Gramercy standout proffers "solid" New American cooking but "even better ambiance" given its "romantic", "candlelit" setting in a "gorgeous" 1854 carriage house; factor in "attentive" service, and obviously it's a "perfect" date place, though you pay to "impress" here.

Hudson Clearwater ● *American*   23 | 22 | 22 | $56

W Village | 447 Hudson St. (Morton St.) | 212-989-3255 | www.hudsonclearwater.com

A "hidden entrance" on Morton Street isn't deterring the crowds from this West Village "total scene", incidentally offering "first-rate" New American food backed up by "exceptional" cocktails; its "hip young" following doesn't seem to mind the "lively" acoustics and "tables on top of one another."

Hudson River Café *American*   20 | 20 | 18 | $41

Harlem | 697 W. 133rd St. (12th Ave.) | 212-491-9111 | www.hudsonrivercafe.com

There's "a lot going on" at this "indoor-outdoor" West Harlem venue, starting with its "outstanding views of the Hudson" and "delicious", Latin-accented Americana; as the evening progresses, it "turns into a club" complete with "live music" and "weekend pat-downs."

	FOOD	DECOR	SERVICE	COST

Hummus Kitchen *Kosher/Mediterranean* `20` `15` `18` `$22`

E 80s | 1613 Second Ave. (bet. 83rd & 84th Sts.) | 212-988-0090
Murray Hill | 444 Third Ave. (bet. 30th & 31st Sts.) | 212-696-0055
W 50s | 768 Ninth Ave. (bet. 51st & 52nd Sts.) | 212-333-3009 ◗
W 80s | 416 Amsterdam Ave. (80th St.) | 212-799-0003
www.hummuskitchen.com

These "casual" Med standbys whip up "quality" hummus with a "spe-cial zing" along with a raft of other vegetarian options; despite "smallish" settings and "disorganized" service, they're an "affordable" "fast-food alternative", especially for those who need it "kosher."

Hummus Place *Israeli/Kosher/Vegetarian* `22` `13` `17` `$18`

E Village | 109 St. Marks Pl. (bet. Ave. A & 1st Ave.) | 212-529-9198
W 70s | 305 Amsterdam Ave. (bet. 74th & 75th Sts.) | 212-799-3335
W Village | 71 Seventh Ave. S. (bet. Barrow & Bleecker Sts.) | 212-924-2022
www.hummusplace.com

Those who like their hummus "silky" and their pita bread "fresh" and "warm" kvell over the kosher vegetarian offerings at these "popular" Israelis; though decor is nearly "nonexistent", service is "pleasant", the grub "filling" and the tabs "terrific."

Hundred Acres *American* `20` `20` `18` `$51`

SoHo | 38 MacDougal St. (Prince St.) | 212-475-7500 |
www.hundredacresnyc.com

"Farm-fresh" New American "home cooking" arrives in an appropriately "country-road" setting at this SoHo charmer that's kin to Cookshop and Five Points; its "cult following" commends its "delicious brunch" and "awesome garden", only wishing there were "more menu options."

The Hurricane ☒ *Asian/Steak* `21` `26` `21` `$59`
(fka Hurricane Club)

Flatiron | 360 Park Ave. S. (26th St.) | 212-951-7111 |
www.thehurricaneclub.com

"Dressed-to-impress" types channel their "inner beachcomber" at this Flatiron "whirlwind" that recently changed its menu – it's now an Asian-accented steak-and-sushi place – but the "clever cocktails" still come in "giant fishbowls"; its big, "exotic" room is considered "less a restaurant" and more of a "club scene", complete with "loud" acous-tics and "pricey" tabs.

NEW Hybird *Chicken* `-` `-` `-` `I`

Chelsea | Chelsea Mkt. | 75 Ninth Ave. (bet. 15th & 16th Sts.) |
212-989-3332 | www.hybirdnyc.com

Taste Questlove's take on fried chicken at the Roots drummer's new grab-and-go stand inside Chelsea Market, a co-venture with restaura-teur Stephen Starr; the modestly priced bird is offered by the piece alongside a selection of steamed and fried dumplings and slushy drinks.

Il Bagatto ◗ Ⓜ *Italian* `25` `17` `20` `$45`

E Village | 192 E. Second St. (bet. Aves. A & B) | 212-228-0977 |
www.ilbagattonyc.com

A "diamond in the rough", this "no-frills" East Village Italian is known for its "top-notch" "homestyle" cooking, notably its "scrumptious" pastas; fair pricing and "warm" service make it "hard to get reservations" at prime times, so it's good that the next-door wine bar "rocks."

	FOOD	DECOR	SERVICE	COST

Il Bambino *Italian* | 27 | 19 | 23 | $22 |

Astoria | 34-08 31st Ave. (bet. 34th & 35th Sts.) | Queens | 718-626-0087 |
www.ilbambinonyc.com

Panini "addicts" rave about the "beyond-crispy" bread and "right ratio" of "fantastic ingredients" within in the "hearty", "bargain"-priced
pressed sandwiches at this "rustic" Astorian with Italian and Spanish
leanings; factor in "impeccable service" with "zero pretense" and a
"cozy" back garden, and it's a neighborhood "must try."

Il Buco ◐ *Italian/Mediterranean* | 25 | 22 | 21 | $63 |

NoHo | 47 Bond St. (bet. Bowery & Lafayette St.) | 212-533-1932 |
www.ilbuco.com

Il Buco Alimentari e Vineria ◐ *Italian/Mediterranean*

NoHo | 53 Great Jones St. (bet. Bowery & Lafayette St.) | 212-837-2622 |
www.ilbucovineria.com

"Phenomenal" Med-Italian fare and "impressive wines" are served in
"welcoming" fashion within "cozy"-yet-stylish "farmhouse" digs
at this "fabulous" longtime NoHo "hot spot"; the scene's just as
"buzzy" – and the tabs equally "pricey" – at its nearby market/wine
bar sibling, where "fun" communal seating is just the thing for sharing
"wonderful small plates."

Il Cantinori *Italian* | 23 | 23 | 22 | $69 |

G Village | 32 E. 10th St. (bet. B'way & University Pl.) | 212-673-6044 |
www.ilcantinori.com

Pastas to "write home to Italy about" star on the Tuscan menu at
this "classy" Village "favorite", which is "still going strong" after
more than three decades; it's known as a "celebrity hangout" with
the concordant "price factor", but mere mortals also tout it as a
"special-occasion" destination.

Il Cortile *Italian* | 23 | 20 | 21 | $56 |

Little Italy | 125 Mulberry St. (bet. Canal & Hester Sts.) | 212-226-6060 |
www.ilcortile.com

"*Buongusto* is an understatement" at this "memory-lane" Italian, a
"good bet on Mulberry" since 1975 thanks to its "hearty" food served
by waiters who have "been there forever"; though it's "a bit pricey" for
the area, regulars report a seat in the "delightful" garden atrium is
"worth the trip" alone.

Il Giglio ☒ *Italian* | 25 | 20 | 24 | $73 |

TriBeCa | 81 Warren St. (bet. Greenwich St. & W. B'way) | 212-571-5555 |
www.ilgigliorestaurant.com

An "empty stomach and a full wallet" are necessities at this "longtime"
TriBeCa Italian where a meal begins with complimentary antipasti fol-
lowed by a "luxurious" array of "old-world classics"; "outdated" decor,
"tight quarters" and high prices are offset by "attentive" service
and "generous portions."

Ilili *Lebanese* | 24 | 22 | 22 | $56 |

Chelsea | 236 Fifth Ave. (bet. 27th & 28th Sts.) | 212-683-2929 |
www.ililinyc.com

"Creative" Lebanese dishes take "deliciousness to a new level" at this
"hip", "high-energy" haunt in "cool", "spacious", wood-lined digs near
Madison Square Park; "noise" can be a "drawback" and "tabs can

mount", but "beautiful people abound", and "attentive" service helps make it "great for groups."

Il Mulino *Italian* · 26 | 18 | 23 | $94
G Village | 86 W. Third St. (bet. Sullivan & Thompson Sts.) | 212-673-3783

Il Mulino Uptown ⬧ *Italian*
E 60s | 37 E. 60th St. (bet. Madison & Park Aves.) | 212-750-3270
www.ilmulino.com

"Forget Little Italy" say fans of this "old-school" Village "must" (with an UES offshoot following in its footsteps), where "old-school waiters" "stuff you with freebies" before rolling out "outstanding" Italian cooking in "copious portions"; despite "crowded" conditions and "outdated" decor, it's an "expense-account paradise" – "if you can manage a reservation."

Il Postino ● *Italian* · 23 | 20 | 22 | $68
E 40s | 337 E. 49th St. (bet. 1st & 2nd Aves.) | 212-688-0033 | www.ilpostinony.com

Waiters inhale, then recite a "huge list of daily specials" at this "old-world" U.N.-area Italian that will also "cook anything you want"; an "intimate" "opera"-enhanced space further boosts the "wonderful dining experience", but value-seekers avoid the "reliably expensive" tabs by going for the lunchtime prix fixe.

Il Riccio ● *Italian* · 20 | 16 | 20 | $58
E 70s | 152 E. 79th St. (bet. Lexington & 3rd Aves.) | 212-639-9111 | www.ilriccioblu.com

UES denizens "of a certain age" (hello Mayor Bloomberg!) patronize this "clubby" Italian for its "above-average" Amalfi Coast food served in a "friendly", "white-tablecloth" room; if the compact main room gets "tight", there's a "lovely" "little" enclosed garden in back.

Il Tinello ⬧ *Italian* · 25 | 21 | 25 | $75
W 50s | 16 W. 56th St. (bet. 5th & 6th Aves.) | 212-245-4388 | www.iltinellony.com

"Serenity" reigns at this Midtown "grande dame" exuding "senior appeal" and patrolled by "conscientious" waiters in "black tie"; everyone agrees that the Northern Italian cooking is "superb", but given the "corporate-checkbook" tabs, many save it for "special occasions."

Il Vagabondo *Italian* · 20 | 16 | 19 | $51
E 60s | 351 E. 62nd St. (bet. 1st & 2nd Aves.) | 212-832-9221 | www.ilvagabondo.com

"Old-school" Italian fans find "all the favorites" at this 1965-vintage Upper Eastsider, where the food "sticks to your ribs" and the waiters have "been there for centuries"; the decor may be "nothing to write home about", but the "unique" indoor bocce court is.

Inakaya *Japanese* · 22 | 22 | 23 | $59
W 40s | NY Times Bldg. | 231 W. 40th St. (bet. 7th & 8th Aves.) | 212-354-2195 | www.inakayany.com

It's always "showtime" at this "high-drama" Japanese robatayaki specialist in the NY Times building, where "friendly" staffers dish out "grilled delights" (plus "swanky sushi") while engaging in ritualized "yelling and screaming"; however, all the "fun" – which is most intense at the robata counter – can add up to "big bucks."

	FOOD	DECOR	SERVICE	COST

Indochine *French/Vietnamese* | 21 | 22 | 19 | $57 |

E Village | 430 Lafayette St. (bet. Astor Pl. & 4th St.) | 212-505-5111 | www.indochinenyc.com

Ever "sexy" – even "timeless" – this "'80s hot spot" opposite the Public Theater still lures "attractive thin" folk with "on-target" French-Vietnamese fare served in "exotic" digs à la 1930s Saigon; perhaps its "elegance is slightly worn", but the "people-watching" is as stellar as ever.

Indus Valley *Indian* | 22 | 16 | 20 | $33 |

W 100s | 2636 Broadway (100th St.) | 212-222-9222 | www.indusvalleyus.com

Though the ambiance may be "average", the "intensely flavorful" eats at this UWS Indian are "a cut above", ditto the "solicitous" service; penny-pinchers find the $15 weekend lunch buffet "awesome", and allow it's "worth the few extra bucks" at dinner.

'Inoteca ● *Italian* | 21 | 17 | 19 | $39 |

LES | 98 Rivington St. (Ludlow St.) | 212-614-0473 | www.inotecanyc.com

It's "easy to get carried away" at this "lively" LES enoteca given the "right-on" Italian small plates and "dizzying" wine selection; "hit-or-miss" service, "over-the-top" decibels and a "challenging" non-English menu don't faze its "twentysomething" clientele.

Ipanema *Brazilian/Portuguese* | 23 | 17 | 20 | $41 |

W 40s | 13 W. 46th St. (bet. 5th & 6th Aves.) | 212-730-5848 | www.ipanemanyc.com

Under the radar "in the middle of Little Brazil", this "friendly" joint in the West 40s has been churning out "authentic" Brazilian-Portuguese dishes for more than a quarter-century; the kitschy "samba decor" may be "less spectacular" than the "tasty" grub, but the vibe's "relaxed" and the prices "better than fair."

Ippudo ● *Japanese/Noodle Shop* | 25 | 20 | 20 | $30 |

E Village | 65 Fourth Ave. (bet. 9th & 10th Sts.) | 212-388-0088
NEW **W 50s** | 321 W. 51st St. (bet. 8th & 9th Aves.) | 212-974-2500
www.ippudony.com

The East Village Japanese "ramen king" has been joined by a Hell's Kitchen outpost, and both ladle out "serious" noodles in the "richest, most complex" broth ("what heaven must taste like") along with "spectacular", "succulent pork buns"; "upscale" looks and "speedy" staffers who "cheer when you enter" distract from the "famously long waits."

Isabella's *American/Mediterranean* | 20 | 19 | 20 | $45 |

W 70s | 359 Columbus Ave. (77th St.) | 212-724-2100 | www.isabellas.com

"Convenience" to the Museum of Natural History and the New-York Historical Society is a draw at this veteran Steve Hanson "standby", where "reliable" Mediterranean-American meals are ferried by "friendly" folks; during its "mobbed" weekend brunch, regulars request sidewalk seats – the "traffic on Columbus Avenue is quieter than the noise inside."

	FOOD	DECOR	SERVICE	COST

Ise *Japanese* ▽ 22 | 12 | 18 | $42

Financial District | 56 Pine St. (bet. Pearl & William Sts.) |
212-785-1600 🖂
W 50s | 58 W. 56th St. (bet. 5th & 6th Aves.) | 212-707-8702
www.iserestaurant.com

Authentically Japanese with a "clientele to match", these "solid"
izakayas in Midtown and the Financial District provide "real-deal"
sushi and "legit" cooked dishes that result in "crowded" lunch
hours; "spare" digs and "perfunctory" service are offset by a
"reasonable" bottom line.

Island Burgers & Shakes *Burgers* 21 | 12 | 18 | $19

W 50s | 766 Ninth Ave. (bet. 51st & 52nd Sts.) | 212-307-7934
W 80s | 422 Amsterdam Ave. (80th St.) | 212-877-7934
www.islandburgersandshakes.com

"Huge burgers" on "big buns" accessorized with "every topping known
to man" are the raisons d'être of these "retro" West Side patty palaces
that "finally sell fries" too; "spoon-licking shakes" sweeten the sour
taste left by "sparse seating and service."

I Sodi *Italian* 25 | 18 | 22 | $60

W Village | 105 Christopher St. (bet. Bleecker & Hudson Sts.) |
212-414-5774 | www.isodinyc.com

Like a "little bit of Florence" in the West Village, this "small" Italian
supplies "generously sized" portions of "first-tier" Tuscan fare
lubricated by a "substantial wine list" and signature Negronis;
"charming" service makes the "tight squeeze" seem delightfully
"intimate", even "romantic."

Isola ● *Italian* - | - | - | E

SoHo | Mondrian SoHo Hotel | 9 Crosby St. (bet. Grand & Howard Sts.) |
212-389-0000 | www.isolasoho.com

A reboot of the Mondrian SoHo Hotel's Imperial No. 9, this under-
the-radar iteration serves coastal Italian dishes (with a focus on
crudo) in a striking, glass-lined greenhouse; no reservations are
accepted, save for guests of the hotel, and the upscale pricing is in
keeping with the tony mood.

Italianissimo *Italian* 22 | 18 | 22 | $54

E 80s | 307 E. 84th St. (bet. 1st & 2nd Aves.) | 212-628-8603 |
www.italianissimony.net

Its "jewel box" size reflects the neighborhood-"gem" status of this
"*bellissimo*" UES Italian where the "just-like-mama" cooking and
"brick-walled" setting seem right out of a "Woody Allen" movie; "solicitous" service and an "excellent" $27 early-bird make this one
a "great find."

Ithaka *Greek/Seafood* 19 | 16 | 19 | $50

E 80s | 308 E. 86th St. (bet. 1st & 2nd Aves.) | 212-628-9100 |
www.ithakarestaurant.com

"Neighborhood tavernas" don't get much more "relaxed" than this
"quiet" Yorkville Greek where the "honest" food and "wonderful
grilled fish" channel Santorini – or at least "Astoria"; maybe the whitewashed setting could be "spiffed up", but thankfully the tables are "far
enough apart" and service is "attentive."

	FOOD	DECOR	SERVICE	COST

I Trulli *Italian*   `22` `20` `21` `$62`

Murray Hill | 122 E. 27th St. (bet. Lexington & Park Ave. S.) | 212-481-7372 | www.itrulli.com

"Rustic but sophisticated", this Murray Hill Southern Italian purveys a trulli "special" Puglian menu paired with "outstanding" wines via its adjoining enoteca; an "expansive" garden and "roaring" fireplace are seasonal draws, though "helpful" service and "costly" tabs are part of the package year-round.

Jackson Diner *Indian*   `21` `12` `16` `$25`

G Village | 72 University Pl. (bet. 10th & 11th Sts.) | 212-466-0820 | www.jacksondinernyc.com
Jackson Heights | 37-47 74th St. (bet. 37th Ave. & 37th Rd.) | Queens | 718-672-1232 | www.jacksondiner.com

Jackson Heights' Little India is home to this 30-plus-year-old subcontinental that has a "winner" of a Village offshoot; the decor is "pure diner" at both, but the grub is "satisfying", the prices "low" and the service "laid-back" – and regulars say the lunchtime "buffet is the way to go."

Jackson Hole *Burgers*   `19` `12` `16` `$23`

E 60s | 232 E. 64th St. (bet. 2nd & 3rd Aves.) | 212-371-7187 ◗
E 80s | 1611 Second Ave. (bet. 83rd & 84th Sts.) | 212-737-8788 ◗
Murray Hill | 521 Third Ave. (35th St.) | 212-679-3264 ◗
W 80s | 517 Columbus Ave. (85th St.) | 212-362-5177
Bayside | 35-01 Bell Blvd. (35th Ave.) | Queens | 718-281-0330 ◗
Jackson Heights | 69-35 Astoria Blvd. (70th St.) | Queens | 718-204-7070 ◗
www.jacksonholeburgers.com

"Immense" burgers ("share or explode") and moderate prices are the calling cards of this longtime mini-chain; though the patties are "juicy" enough, "amateur" service and "jackson-hole-in-the-wall" decor make it an "average experience" for many.

Jack's Wife Freda ◗ *American*   ▽ `19` `15` `21` `$36`

SoHo | 224 Lafayette St. (bet. Broome & Spring Sts.) | 212-510-8550 | www.jackswifefreda.com

An "attentive, knowledgeable" crew doles out "delish" American fare with a "Middle Eastern twist" at this "friendly" SoHo cafe; affordable tabs and "bright", "simple" surrounds explain why it's a "bustling" neighborhood "go-to" – "be prepared to wait" at prime times.

Jack the Horse Tavern *American*   `23` `20` `21` `$45`

Brooklyn Heights | 66 Hicks St. (Cranberry St.) | Brooklyn | 718-852-5084 | www.jackthehorse.com

"Cozy, taverny" vibes prevail at this Brooklyn Heights "hideaway" where "upscale" American food (including "amazing mac 'n' cheese") is dispatched in a room conducive to "relaxed conversation"; "cheerful" service offsets the "small portions" and "slightly pricey" tabs.

Jacob's Pickles ◗ *American*   `20` `18` `19` `$34`

W 80s | 509 Amsterdam Ave. (bet. 84th & 85th Sts.) | 212-392-5407 | www.jacobspickles.com

An UWS "den of decadence", this "country-meets-city" tavern keeps 'em coming with "fantastic fried chicken" and other well-priced "Southern comfort" faves (including, yes, "divine pickles") dished up in "casual" surrounds; it all goes down well with suds from an "amazing" beer list – let the "knowledgeable" staff "help you choose."

Jaiya *Thai*

22 | 16 | 16 | $31

E 80s | 1553 Second Ave. (bet. 80th & 81st Sts.) | 212-717-8877
Murray Hill | 396 Third Ave. (28th St.) | 212-889-1330
www.jaiya.com

Whether you prefer "spicy" or "incendiary", these East Side Thais offer "authentic" Siamese food running the gamut from standard classics to "challenging, take-no-hostages" dishes; "decent" price points trump the "noisy" settings and less-than-stellar service.

Jake's Steakhouse *Steak*

24 | 19 | 22 | $55

Riverdale | 6031 Broadway (242nd St.) | Bronx | 718-581-0182 |
www.jakessteakhouse.com

"Scenic views of Van Cortlandt Park" make the "Manhattan-quality" steaks taste even juicier at this "neighborhood" Riverdale chophouse where the service is "professional" and the beer selection "vast"; although "expensive", it's "cheaper than the city", and there's "valet parking" to boot.

James *American*

24 | 22 | 22 | $45

Prospect Heights | 605 Carlton Ave. (St. Marks Ave.) | Brooklyn |
718-942-4255 | www.jamesrestaurantny.com

"Creative", "full-of-flavor" Americana with a "local" focus match with an "awesome" drink list at this "charming", upscale Prospect Heights haunt; quartered in "welcoming" whitewashed-brick digs, it's "convenient to BAM" and the Barclays Center, but also a local brunch magnet.

Jane *American*

21 | 17 | 19 | $42

G Village | 100 W. Houston St. (bet. LaGuardia Pl. & Thompson St.) |
212-254-7000 | www.janerestaurant.com

"Young, trendy" folk flock to this "upbeat" Village American for "quite tasty" cooking, with "moderate" tabs, "austere" decor and "generally good service" on the side; though "insanely busy", the weekend brunch is the scene to make, provided you can stomach "loud" decibels on top of your "hangover."

Japonica *Japanese*

23 | 15 | 20 | $49

G Village | 100 University Pl. (12th St.) | 212-243-7752 |
www.japonicanyc.com

An "old friend" in the Village since '78, this Japanese vet "never gets old" thanks to "enormous portions" of "delicate", "fresh" sushi that "tastes expensive"; the decor may be "long in the tooth", but service is "attentive" and the overall dining experience "solid."

Jean Georges *French*

28 | 27 | 28 | $153

W 60s | Trump Int'l Hotel | 1 Central Park W. (61st St.) | 212-299-3900 |
www.jean-georgesrestaurant.com

"Every bit deserving of its praise", Jean-Georges Vongerichten's CPW culinary "cathedral" persists as a "paragon" of "sophisticated" service and "marvelously inventive" New French cuisine, with "superb wines to match"; the "serene, civilized" (jackets required) setting rounds out the "top-notch dining experience" that's "priced accordingly" – though the $38 prix fixe lunch promises the same "high quality" without "breaking the bank."

| | FOOD | DECOR | SERVICE | COST |

Jean-Georges' Nougatine *French*   27 | 24 | 26 | $68

W 60s | Trump Int'l Hotel | 1 Central Park W. (61st St.) | 212-299-3900 | www.jean-georgesrestaurant.com

"Less formal" than Jean Georges, but "just as delicious", this "classy-casual" front-room alternative provides "perfectly prepared" New French food that puts a "lighter hit on the wallet"; it's best accessed for breakfast or after-work drinks and snacks, though that "marvelous" $32 prix fixe lunch may just be the "biggest bargain in the city."

NEW Jeepney *Filipino*   ▽ 23 | 14 | 19 | $35

E Village | 201 First Ave. (bet. 12th & 13th Sts.) | 212-533-4121 | www.jeepneynyc.com

The Maharlika team strikes again with this well-priced Filipino gastropub in the East Village, a "visit to Manila" where the hearty, "adventure-some" dishes are meant for sharing; it's named after highly decorated taxis from the WWII era, and the nothing-fancy, "kinda fun" space features large pin-up photos and colorful murals.

Jeffrey's Grocery *American*   22 | 20 | 21 | $48

W Village | 172 Waverly Pl. (Christopher St.) | 646-398-7630 | www.jeffreysgrocery.com

There's "Wisconsin" in the air at Gabe Stulman's "hip" Village American, a tiny, "homey" thing where the "tasty" menu is as limited as the square footage; "divine oysters" and "attention to detail" offset the "not-Midwestern prices", though a few feel it's "more scene than place to eat."

Jewel Bako ●☒ *Japanese*   25 | 22 | 23 | $80

E Village | 239 E. Fifth St. (bet. 2nd & 3rd Aves.) | 212-979-1012 | www.jewelbakosushi.com

"Casually elegant" and "expensively" priced, this bamboo-lined East Village Japanese slices a "flawless symphony" of "incredibly fresh fish"; for best results, aficionados "sit at the sushi bar" and go the "omakase" route, though no matter where you land, owners Jack and Grace Lamb "really take care of you."

J.G. Melon ●⇆ *Pub Food*   21 | 13 | 16 | $30

E 70s | 1291 Third Ave. (74th St.) | 212-744-0585

"Prep school" alumni and assorted "J.Crew" types populate this "no-fuss, no-muss" Upper East Side pub celebrated for "killer burgers" and "old-school" cottage fries; despite "rushed" service, a "cash-only" rule and digs in need of "freshening", it's "always mobbed."

Jing Fong *Chinese*   20 | 13 | 12 | $23

Chinatown | 20 Elizabeth St. (bet. Bayard & Canal Sts.) | 212-964-5256 | www.jingfongny.com

Set in a "football field–size" hall, this "bustling" C-town Cantonese rolls out "delectable" dim sum "à la Hong Kong" on "quickly moving carts" propelled by "brusque" staffers; it's "crowded at peak hours", a "hectic madhouse" on weekends and "affordable" all the time.

Joe Allen ● *American*   19 | 18 | 20 | $45

W 40s | 326 W. 46th St. (bet. 8th & 9th Aves.) | 212-581-6464 | www.joeallenrestaurant.com

Known for its "posters of Broadway bombs" and "serviceable" American grub, this "timeless" Theater District joint is still a magnet for "showbiz" types and those who love them; après-theater "stargazing" – "yes, that's who you think it is in that dark corner" – lends "glamour" to the proceedings.

Joe & Pat's *Italian/Pizza* | 23 | 13 | 19 | $23

Castleton Corners | 1758 Victory Blvd. (bet. Manor Rd. & Winthrop Pl.) | Staten Island | 718-981-0887 | www.joeandpatspizzany.com

It's "all about" the "deliciously thin, crispy", "darn good" pizzas at this Staten Island Italian "staple" that's been dishing up "delicious" "family meals" for "generations"; there's "not much atmosphere" to speak of, but "fast" service and modest tabs go a long way.

JoeDoe Ⓜ *American* | ▽ 24 | 19 | 24 | $50

E Village | 45 E. First St. (bet. 1st & 2nd Aves.) | 212-780-0262 | www.chefjoedoe.com

Parlaying "big ideas in a small space", this East Village American offers "distinctive", Jewish-accented dishes assembled from "quality ingredients"; the overall vibe is "cool-comfortable" and the staff "just the right amount of helpful" – only "uptown prices" give any pause.

Joe's Ginger ⊅ *Chinese* | 20 | 10 | 14 | $23

Chinatown | 25 Pell St. (Doyers St.) | 212-285-0999 | www.joeginger.com

"Slightly slicker" and "less crazy" than its nearby sibling, Joe's Shanghai, this C-town contender features the "same great soup dumplings", "rushed service" and lack of decor; "individual tables" and "less waiting on line" are additional benefits.

Joe's Pizza ● *Pizza* | 23 | 8 | 14 | $12

NEW **E Village** | 150 E. 14th St. (3rd Ave.) | 212-388-9474
W Village | 7 Carmine St. (bet. Bleecker St. & 6th Ave.) | 212-366-1182 | www.joespizzanyc.com

"Legendary to locals", this "grab-and-go" West Village pizzeria (with a new offshoot in the East Village) has been slinging "hot-out-of-the-oven" slices since 1975; "hole-in-the-wall" looks and "stand-up counter service" are part of this "quintessential NY" experience, but explain why some are "not impressed."

Joe's Shanghai *Chinese* | 22 | 10 | 14 | $27

Chinatown | 9 Pell St. (bet. Bowery & Doyers St.) | 212-233-8888 ⊅
W 50s | 24 W. 56th St. (bet. 5th & 6th Aves.) | 212-333-3868
Flushing | 136-21 37th Ave. (bet. Main & Union Sts.) | Queens | 718-539-3838 ⊅
www.joeshanghairestaurants.com

You may be "elbow to elbow with strangers" at these "popular" Shanghainese "standbys", but "who cares" when you're slurping "to-die-for" soup dumplings; "brusque" treatment and "no atmosphere" come with "bargain" prices that allow you to "eat till you burst."

John Dory Oyster Bar ● *Seafood* | 24 | 20 | 19 | $55

Chelsea | Ace Hotel | 1196 Broadway (29th St.) | 212-792-9000 | www.thejohndory.com

Berthed in Chelsea's Ace Hotel, this "airy" seafooder via April Bloomfield and Ken Friedman offers everything from "succulent oysters" to "inspired" small plates; "guppy-size portions", "hefty" tabs and "disinter-

	FOOD	DECOR	SERVICE	COST

ested" service are offset by a "happening vibe", kitschy-"cool" digs and "sublime" Parker House rolls.

John's of 12th Street ✍ *Italian* `22` `15` `19` `$35`

E Village | 302 E. 12th St. (2nd Ave.) | 212-475-9531 | www.johnsof12thstreet.com

"Upholding the art of Italian cooking" since 1908, this East Village "institution" endures thanks to "no-nonsense" red-sauce meals (plus recently added vegan selections), all at "fair prices"; "no credit cards" and "nothing-fancy" decor – think "Chianti bottles" and "melted candle wax" – add to the "time-warp" vibe.

John's Pizzeria *Pizza* `22` `15` `17` `$25`

E 60s | 408 E. 64th St. (bet. 1st & York Aves.) | 212-935-2895
W 40s | 260 W. 44th St. (bet. 7th & 8th Aves.) | 212-391-7560 | www.johnspizzerianyc.com ●
W Village | 278 Bleecker St. (Jones St.) | 212-243-1680 | www.johnsbrickovenpizza.com ●✍

"Classic" thin-crust pies ("no slices") served "super-hot" from the coal-fired brick oven explain the "perpetual crowds" at this "old-time Village institution" and its "convenient" spin-offs; if the decor is "nothing special", "quick" service and "affordable" tabs entice for a "casual" bite.

JoJo *French* `24` `21` `23` `$69`

E 60s | 160 E. 64th St. (bet. Lexington & 3rd Aves.) | 212-223-5656 | www.jean-georges.com

The "intimate rooms" at this East Side Jean-Georges Vongerichten French bistro lure "plutocrats" in the mood for "romance"; the cooking is "excellent", the service "courteous" and though the pricing's geared toward "one-percenters", prix fixe deals carry the day.

Jones Wood Foundry ● *British* `21` `21` `20` `$40`

E 70s | 401 E. 76th St. (bet. 1st & York Aves.) | 212-249-2700 | www.joneswoodfoundry.com

Bringing a bit of "jolly old England" to Yorkville, this wood-paneled British pub dispenses "wonderful fish 'n' chips" and other "simple" classics washed down with an "impressive" suds selection; "ambiance is what sells this place", along with "helpful" service and a "lovely garden."

Jordans Lobster Dock *Seafood* `22` `10` `16` `$32`

Sheepshead Bay | 3165 Harkness Ave. (Plumb 2nd St.) | Brooklyn | 718-934-6300 | www.jordanslobster.com

Locals "pretend they're in Maine" at this "salty" Sheepshead Bay seafooder where live lobsters in "big tanks" make for ultra-"fresh" eating; sure, the "decor's as minimal as the service", but tabs are "dirt-cheap" and an on-site retail market means you can "eat your goodies at home."

Joseph Leonard ● *American* `24` `20` `22` `$47`

W Village | 170 Waverly Pl. (Grove St.) | 646-429-8383 | www.josephleonard.com

"Original", "deeply satisfying" takes on New American standards draw "super-cool" folks to Gabe Stulman's West Village "hot spot" that ups the ante with "reasonable" tariffs and open-all-day hours; the "hiply rustic", "lumberjacky" setting is so "tiny" that "crowded" conditions and long "waits" are a given.

	FOOD	DECOR	SERVICE	COST

Josie's *Eclectic*
20 | 15 | 19 | $36

W 70s | 300 Amsterdam Ave. (74th St.) | 212-769-1212 | www.josiesnyc.com

They "do healthy right" at this "mostly organic" UWS Eclectic where the "meats are free-range", the pricing "midrange" and the overall experience "guilt-free"; too bad about the "diner" looks and "hit-or-miss" service, but the "upbeat" mood still draws lots of "chicks" and "children."

Joya ⊄ *Thai*
23 | 18 | 19 | $23

Cobble Hill | 215 Court St. (bet. Warren & Wyckoff Sts.) | Brooklyn | 718-222-3484

Scenes don't get much more "boisterous" or "fun" than at this Cobble Hill Thai where a mix of "awesome" food, "cheap" tabs and "sleek" design attracts "young, hip" throngs; "dance-club" acoustics send regulars to the "more peaceful" back garden, but there's no sidestepping the "so-so service" and "cash-only" rule.

Jubilee *French/Seafood*
21 | 18 | 18 | $55

E 50s | 948 First Ave. (bet. 52nd & 53rd Sts.) | 212-888-3569 | www.jubileeny.net

That it "moved to a larger location" a while back "is a plus" according to loyal Francophiles who frequent this longtime UES neighborhood bistro, a haven of "relaxed sophistication" in which to enjoy a "quick trip to Paris"; the seafood-oriented French fare (including those "tasty" moules) also continues to please, so it's no wonder reservations remain highly recommended.

NEW Juliana's *Pizza*
∇ 27 | 19 | 22 | $27

Dumbo | 19 Old Fulton St. (bet. Front & Water Sts.) | Brooklyn | 718-596-6700 | www.julianaspizza.com

"Welcome back, Patsy!" cheer fans of the original owner of the famed Grimaldi's and his latest pizzeria under the Brooklyn Bridge (this one named for his mother); it serves up "superb, thin-crust", "coal oven"-fired pies in "crisp, clean", jukebox-equipped digs, and allows eaters to "skip the lines" found elsewhere – at least until the word gets out.

Jungsik ⊠ *Korean*
26 | 25 | 27 | $120

TriBeCa | 2 Harrison St. (Hudson St.) | 212-219-0900 | www.jungsik.kr

A "marriage of delicate flavors and bold, heartier ones" distinguishes the "inventive", "exquisitely presented" Korean cuisine at this high-end TriBeCan; the "clean"-lined space is as "elegant and artful as the food", and "attentive" pro service completes the "unforgettable" experience that's "just wow on every note."

Junior's *Diner*
19 | 14 | 17 | $27

E 40s | Grand Central | 89 E. 42nd St., Lower Dining Concourse (Vanderbilt Ave.) | 212-983-5257
W 40s | 1515 Broadway (7th Ave.) | 212-302-2000 ●
Downtown Bklyn | 386 Flatbush Avenue Ext. (DeKalb Ave.) | Brooklyn | 718-852-5257 ●
www.juniorscheesecake.com

"Nationally known" as a "cheesecake paradise", this "dependable" diner trio also delivers "basic" American eats that "don't break the bank"; from the original "Brooklyn institution" "greasy spoon" to the more modern Midtown offshoots, the "touristy" digs may be "mobbed", but the staff will "get you in and out in a hurry."

Junoon *Indian*

FOOD	DECOR	SERVICE	COST
24	25	23	$67

Flatiron | 27 W. 24th St. (bet. 5th & 6th Aves.) | 212-490-2100 | www.junoonnyc.com

"Out-of-this-world haute Indian" dining in "elegant" environs makes this "fantastic" Flatironer a "destination", whether the main room with its "well-spaced tables" or the "dark", "intriguing" front lounge; you can really "rack up a bill", but staffers who "go out of their way to make you feel special" add value.

Juventino *Eclectic*

FOOD	DECOR	SERVICE	COST
∇ 25	22	22	$40

Park Slope | 370 Fifth Ave. (bet. 5th & 6th Sts.) | Brooklyn | 718-360-8469 | www.juventinonyc.com

Park Slope locals can't pay enough "compliments" to this "neighborhood" "favorite" proffering "dazzling" Eclectic fare and "affordable wine selections" within "simple", "airy" surrounds; it can be "hard to get a table", but the "welcoming" staff "tries hard to please" and the back patio adds elbow room in warmer months.

Kajitsu ⊠ *Japanese/Vegetarian*

FOOD	DECOR	SERVICE	COST
-	-	-	VE

Murray Hill | 125 E. 39th St. (bet. Lexington & Park Aves.) | 212-228-4873 | kajitsunyc.com

Newly ensconced in a second-floor Murray Hill space that's an airy step up from its former East Village basement digs, this wood-lined, Zen-like Japanese vegetarian remains a practitioner of the ancient Buddhist shojin cuisine, served kaiseki-style at dinner (tasting menus start at $55); at lunchtime it goes by the name Kokage, and adds seafood and eggs to the set-menu offerings.

Kang Suh ● *Korean*

FOOD	DECOR	SERVICE	COST
22	12	15	$37

Garment District | 1250 Broadway (32nd St.) | 212-564-6845 | www.kangsuh.com

"After-hours" types tout this 30-plus-year-old Garment Center Korean for its "authentic" BBQ, low tabs and "24/7" open-door policy; since it's "not much to look at" and "you'll smell like it when you leave", maybe it's good that the staff "rushes you through your meal."

Kanoyama *Japanese*

FOOD	DECOR	SERVICE	COST
25	15	18	$55

E Village | 175 Second Ave. (bet. 11th & 12th Sts.) | 212-777-5266 | www.kanoyama.com

"Artfully arranged" sushi, including "varieties you don't often see", is the hook at this East Village Japanese "adventure" that seals the deal with tabs that are "reasonable" vis-a-vis the "high quality"; maybe the place "doesn't look like much", but an adjacent sake/oyster bar allows room to spread out.

Kashkaval *Mediterranean*

FOOD	DECOR	SERVICE	COST
22	15	17	$29

W 50s | 856 Ninth Ave. (56th St.) | 212-581-8282 | www.kashkavalfoods.com
NEW Kashkaval Garden *Mediterranean*
W 50s | 852 Ninth Ave. (bet. 55th & 56th Sts.) | 212-245-1758 | www.kashkavalgarden.com

Despite "small" dimensions, this Hell's Kitchen Med features a "gourmet cheese market" up front plus a "secret", "candlelit" rear wine bar dispensing "quality" fondues and small plates; its new nearby sibling shares a similar menu and equally welcome "cheap" tabs, but adds a small garden to the list of endearments.

Kati Roll Company · Indian

22 | **9** | **14** | **$12**

E 50s | 229 E. 53rd St. (bet. 2nd & 3rd Aves.) | 212-888-1700
Garment District | 49 W. 39th St. (bet. 5th & 6th Aves.) | 212-730-4280
G Village | 99 MacDougal St. (Bleecker St.) | 212-420-6517 ◗
www.thekatirollcompany.com

"Grab-and-go" Indian street food is the concept at this trio rolling out "mouthwatering" kati wraps assembled from "fragrant ingredients"; "exceptional value" keeps them as "busy as Bombay" at lunchtime, "tacky" settings and "slow" service to the contrary.

Katsu-Hama · Japanese

22 | **13** | **16** | **$30**

E 40s | 11 E. 47th St. (bet. 5th & Madison Aves.) | 212-758-5909
W 50s | 45 W. 55th St., 2nd fl. (bet. 5th & 6th Aves.) | 212-541-7145 ◗
www.matsuyafoods-usa.com

"Deep-fried comfort food" in pork-cutlet form is the specialty of these Midtown Japanese tonkatsu parlors where the goods are "tender and juicy" and "most of the customers speak the language"; "easy-on-the-pocketbook" tabs trump "not much decor" and "indifferent" service.

Katz's Delicatessen ⊘ Deli

24 | **11** | **14** | **$25**

LES | 205 E. Houston St. (Ludlow St.) | 212-254-2246 |
www.katzsdelicatessen.com

Slinging "piled-high" pastrami sandwiches and other "old-time Jewish deli" staples since 1888, this cash-only LES "legend" is generally "packed" with "tourists and locals alike"; the "cafeteria-style" digs evoke a "bygone period" while the "surly-but-lovable" staff is a slice of "real NY", but "for the ultimate" experience, movie buffs suggest "sit at the *When Harry Met Sally* table."

Keens Steakhouse · Steak

26 | **24** | **24** | **$76**

Garment District | 72 W. 36th St. (bet. 5th & 6th Aves.) | 212-947-3636 |
www.keens.com

You don't have to be a carnivore to appreciate the "rich history" of this circa-1885 Garment District "meat house", though "outstanding" steaks and "glorious" mutton chops ("yeah, you read that right") are key to its "charm"; with "seamless" service, a "superb" scotch selection and thousands of antique clay pipes "adorning the ceiling", it "doesn't get more old NY."

Kellari Taverna ◗ Greek

22 | **21** | **21** | **$55**

W 40s | 19 W. 44th St. (bet. 5th & 6th Aves.) | 212-221-0144 |
www.kellari.us

Seafood seemingly "fresh from Poseidon's trident" and other "superb" Greek specialties make this "attractive, upscale" Midtowner a "popular" pick pre- and post-performance; "knowledgeable, efficient" service and "decent portions" help justify "pricey" tabs, though the $32 pre-theater prix fixe packs serious "value."

Keste Pizza e Vino · Pizza

25 | **15** | **19** | **$27**

W Village | 271 Bleecker St. (Morton St.) | 212-243-1500 |
www.kestepizzeria.com

"Regulars" find themselves "yearning" for the "sensational" Neapolitan pies ("oh, that crust!") with "fresh, flavorful toppings" at this "popular" West Village pizzeria; but while the goods may be "hard to beat", "go at off hours" unless you're "willing to stand in line" for a seat in the "sparse", "elbow-to-elbow" space.

NEW Khe-Yo ⑤ *Laotian*   – | – | – | M

TriBeCa | 157 Duane St. (bet. Hudson St. & W. B'way) | 212-587-1089 | www.kheyo.com

Marc Forgione partners with his longtime executive chef, Soulayphet Schwader, at this new TriBeCa Southeast Asian whose succinct, well-priced menu spotlights the rare-in-these-parts flavors of Laos; the brick-walled, banquette-lined room has an industrial feel, and in the works is a kiosk, Khe-Yosk (get it?), that will offer take-out sandwiches.

NEW King Noodle *Noodle Shop/Pan-Asian*   – | – | – | I

Bushwick | 1405 Flushing Ave. (Morgan Ave.) | Brooklyn | 718-456-6543 | www.kingnoodlebk.com

An alum of Roberta's and Do or Dine is behind this new Bushwick noodle joint whose over-the-top Pan-Asian wok dishes (kimchi carbonara topped with Doritos, anyone?) are matched with tiki-inspired cocktails; equally trippy is its kaleidoscopically hued interior, complete with a coral reef–themed mural, LED lighting and a disco ball.

Kings' Carriage House Ⓜ *American*   21 | 25 | 23 | $64

E 80s | 251 E. 82nd St. (bet. 2nd & 3rd Aves.) | 212-734-5490 | www.kingscarriagehouse.com

Best known for its "lovely setting", this Upper East Side "hidden treasure" is nestled in a "romantic" duplex suggesting an "English country house"; the prix fixe–only New American menu is also "top-drawer", with "gracious" service, "quiet" decibels and "dainty" afternoon tea as bonuses.

King Yum *Chinese/Polynesian*   20 | 17 | 20 | $27

Fresh Meadows | 181-08 Union Tpke. (bet. Kent St. & Surrey Pl.) | Queens | 718-380-1918 | www.kingyumrestaurant.com

At this 1953-vintage Fresh Meadows "institution", dishes ordered from a "standard suburban" Chinese-Polynesian menu are dispatched in a "hokey", tiki-fied setting replete with "bamboo walls" and "umbrella drinks"; other winning features include "friendly service" and "old-timey" tabs.

Kin Shop *Thai*   24 | 17 | 21 | $49

W Village | 469 Sixth Ave. (bet. 11th & 12th Sts.) | 212-675-4295 | www.kinshopnyc.com

"Taking Thai in new directions", chef Harold Dieterle's "high-end" West Villager "knocks it out of the park" with "vibrant", "inventive" dishes delivered by a "helpful" team; loyalists insist the "unique" flavors trump the "serene" but somewhat "pedestrian" space.

Ki Sushi *Japanese*   25 | 19 | 21 | $39

Boerum Hill | 122 Smith St. (bet. Dean & Pacific Sts.) | Brooklyn | 718-935-0575

"Pristine sushi", "innovative rolls" and "clean", minimal looks keep business booming at this Boerum Hill Japanese that clinches the deal with "reasonable" prices; throw in "pleasant" service and it's "pretty much what you want in a neighborhood restaurant."

	FOOD	DECOR	SERVICE	COST

Kitchenette *Southern*

19 | **15** | **17** | **$24**

TriBeCa | 156 Chambers St. (bet. Greenwich St. & W. B'way) | 212-267-6740
W 100s | 1272 Amsterdam Ave. (bet. 122nd & 123rd Sts.) | 212-531-7600
www.kitchenetterestaurant.com

Southern "comfort" cooking is the specialty of these "kitschy" "country farmhouse"–inspired standbys where both the menus and the portions are "big"; the "cutesy", "small-town" decor earns mixed response, but all agree on the "rushed" service and low tabs.

Kittichai *Thai*

24 | **26** | **21** | **$61**

SoHo | 60 Thompson Hotel | 60 Thompson St. (bet. Broome & Spring Sts.) | 212-219-2000 | www.kittichairestaurant.com

"Exotic" decor with a "mesmerizing", "lily-laden pool" sets the backdrop for "innovative Thai cooking" at this "chic" Siamese in SoHo's 60 Thompson Hotel; while "expensive" tabs are part of the package, there's always the $38 dinner prix fixe if you're "watching pennies."

Knickerbocker Bar & Grill ● *American*

20 | **18** | **20** | **$51**

G Village | 33 University Pl. (9th St.) | 212-228-8490 | www.knickerbockerbarandgrill.com

"Time warps" don't get more "lovable" than this 1977-vintage Villager, an "old-school" source of "no-surprises" Americana that's "solid" but "won't knock your socks off"; though the room's a tad "tattered", "warm" service and "surprisingly good" weekend jazz make this one a keeper.

Koi *Japanese*

24 | **23** | **21** | **$64**

NEW **SoHo** | Trump SoHo Hotel | 246 Spring St. (bet. 6th Ave. & Varick St.) | 212-842-4550
W 40s | Bryant Park Hotel | 40 W. 40th St. (bet. 5th & 6th Aves.) | 212-921-3330
www.koirestaurant.com

"Fashionistas" and other "trendy" types nibble "Japanese delicacies" (including "designer" sushi) at these "plush" retreats in the Bryant Park Hotel and now in the Trump SoHo; the "LA vibe" and "wonderfully snooty" service are a "bit too Beverly Hills" for some, but even enthusiasts agree it's best to "avoid getting stuck with the bill."

Ko Sushi *Japanese*

21 | **16** | **20** | **$33**

E 70s | 1329 Second Ave. (70th St.) | 212-439-1678
E 80s | 1619 York Ave. (85th St.) | 212-772-8838
www.newkosushi.com

These "No-frills", separately owned Japanese Upper Eastsiders furnish a "neighborhood" following with "tasty" raw fish that's "priced right"; "quick" service makes the "cafeteria"-like settings more palatable, though aesthetes recommend "reliable delivery."

Kotobuki *Japanese*

▽ **25** | **18** | **19** | **$42**

E Village | 56 Third Ave. (bet. 10th & 11th Sts.) | 212-353-5088 | www.kotobukimanhattan.com

Venerated Long Island sushi chainlet takes on Manhattan at this East Village beachhead, where "outstanding" cuts of fish as well as "innovative" entrees are ferried by an "attentive" crew in sleek minimalist environs; given its avid fan base ("count on a satisfying experience every time"), making a reservation is a good idea.

	FOOD	DECOR	SERVICE	COST

Kouzan ● Japanese
19 | 18 | 19 | $35

W 90s | 685 Amsterdam Ave. (93rd St.) | 212-280-8099 |
www.kouzanny.com

Starting with its "dim lighting" and "serene" feeling, this "pretty" Upper
West Side Japanese "raises expectations" that are met by "quality"
sushi and cooked items, all delivered by a "bend-over-backwards"
team; throw in tabs geared to the "99%" and no wonder it's such
a "neighborhood asset."

Kuma Inn ⊅ Filipino/Thai
25 | 13 | 19 | $35

LES | 113 Ludlow St., 2nd fl. (bet. Delancey & Rivington Sts.) |
212-353-8866 | www.kumainn.com

One of NYC's "best hidden gems", this "obscure" Filipino-Thai accessed up a flight of LES stairs puts out an "avant-garde" small-plates
menu "exploding with flavor"; the "hole-in-the-wall" digs are "tight",
but the "price is right" and "BYO makes it even better."

Kum Gang San ● Korean
21 | 16 | 17 | $34

Garment District | 49 W. 32nd St. (bet. B'way & 5th Ave.) | 212-967-0909
Flushing | 138-28 Northern Blvd. (bet. Bowne & Union Sts.) | Queens |
718-461-0909
www.kumgangsan.net

These 24/7 "kitsch" palaces sling Korean BBQ in "cavernous" settings
equipped with waterfalls and pianos; the "traditional" food is "solid",
the decor "age worn" and the service "rush-rush", but it's still "good
for first-timers" and "out-of-towners."

Kunjip ● Korean
22 | 12 | 13 | $26

Garment District | 9 W. 32nd St. (5th Ave.) | 212-216-9487 |
www.kunjip.net

Always open and almost "always crowded", this "popular" 24/7
Garment Districter plies an "extensive menu" of "traditional Korean
cooking" in a "no-frills" atmosphere; while seating's "cramped" and
servers "rush you out the door", the "solid" chow largely redeems all.

Kurumazushi ⊠ Japanese
28 | 15 | 24 | $151

E 40s | 7 E. 47th St., 2nd fl. (bet. 5th & Madison Aves.) | 212-317-2802 |
www.kurumazushi.com

"Year after year", the "quality and selection of fresh fish" results in
"ethereal, next-level" sushi at chef Toshihiro Uezu's pioneering
Midtowner, perched in a "peaceful", second-floor space; tabs may be
"extravagant", but prices are "warranted" for a "traditional experience" on par with "high-end places in Japan."

Kutsher's Tribeca American/Jewish
20 | 20 | 20 | $51

TriBeCa | 186 Franklin St. (bet. Greenwich & Hudson Sts.) | 212-431-0606 |
www.kutsherstribeca.com

"TriBeCa meets the Borscht Belt" at this "Catskills-inspired" eatery
from Jeffrey Chodorow, purveying "upscale versions" of "heartburn-
worthy" Jewish-American soul food in "hip", "modern" digs; although
it's "noisy" and "not kosher", even traditionalists call it a "nice try."

Kyochon Chicken ● Chicken
20 | 16 | 16 | $19

Murray Hill | 319 Fifth Ave. (bet. 32nd & 33rd Sts.) | 212-725-9292

(continued)

(continued)

Kyochon Chicken

Flushing | 156-50 Northern Blvd. (bet. 156th & 157th Sts.) | Queens | 718-939-9292
www.kyochonus.com

Fried chicken gets an "oh-so-spicy" Korean spin – and some "soy-garlic" inflections – at these "addictive" Murray Hill–Flushing satellites of the global poultry chain; "modern" food-court design distracts from the "small portions" and tabs that are "a bit pricey for wings."

Kyo Ya ● *Japanese*

27 | 24 | 25 | $99

E Village | 94 E. Seventh St., downstairs (1st Ave.) | 212-982-4140

With "stunningly good" Kyoto-style dishes "meticulously arranged" on an "array of pottery", the "presentation alone is worth the trip" to this East Village "temple to kaiseki"; "attentive" service helps justify "expensive" tabs, but reservations are a must, given the "intimate" setting.

La Baraka *French*

23 | 18 | 26 | $45

Little Neck | 255-09 Northern Blvd. (2 blocks east of Little Neck Pkwy.) | Queens | 718-428-1461 | www.labarakarest.com

Renowned for the "hospitality" of "lovely hostess" Lucette, this longstanding Little Neck venue follows through with "terrific" Tunisian-accented French fare; though the "cheesy" decor "needs an update", tabs are "reasonable" and the overall mood definitely "enjoyable."

La Bergamote *Bakery/French*

24 | 16 | 16 | $22

Chelsea | 177 Ninth Ave. (20th St.) | 212-627-9010
W 50s | 515 W. 52nd St. (bet. 10th & 11th Aves.) | 212-586-2429
www.labergamotenyc.com

These "buttery" patisserie/cafes supply "high-quality" French pastries that are "gorgeous to look at and just as delicious to taste", plus other savory "light meals"; granted, the service "could use a little help", but "more seating" at the casual Chelsea original and outdoor seating at the Hell's Kitchen offshoot draw applause.

La Boîte en Bois *French*

21 | 16 | 21 | $56

W 60s | 75 W. 68th St. (bet. Columbus Ave. & CPW) | 212-874-2705 | www.laboitenyc.com

A longtime "pre-theater favorite" near Lincoln Center, this "tiny", "sweet" French boîte turns out "classic" bistro dishes in a "congenial" setting overseen by "fast-moving" staffers; "sardine"-can dimensions, "old-fashioned" decor and kinda "pricey" tabs come with the territory.

La Bonne Soupe *French*

19 | 13 | 16 | $33

W 50s | 48 W. 55th St. (bet. 5th & 6th Aves.) | 212-586-7650 | www.labonnesoupe.com

"Serviceable" enough for a "quick bite", this 40-plus-year-old Midtown "pinch hitter" is best known for its "divine onion soup", though the rest of its French bistro menu is certainly "reliable"; "brusque" service, "crowded" conditions and "no-frills" looks are blunted by good "value."

La Bottega ● *Italian/Pizza*

21 | 20 | 18 | $43

Chelsea | Maritime Hotel | 88 Ninth Ave. (17th St.) | 212-243-8400 | www.themaritimehotel.com

It's all about the "amazing outdoor terrace" at this lazy-day Italian in the Maritime Hotel where the "simple but delicious" offerings take a backseat to the "trendy" people–watching and "happening" scene; "loud" acoustics and "slow" service are the price of its popularity.

L'Absinthe *French*
21 | 22 | 21 | $67

E 60s | 227 E. 67th St. (bet. 2nd & 3rd Aves.) | 212-794-4950 | www.labsinthe.com

"Toulouse-Lautrec" would feel at home in this "classic" UES brasserie where the "fine food", "attentive service" and "*très* Gallic" ambiance evoke a "midnight-in-Paris" mood; *bien sûr,* it's "expensive" to "pretend you're in France", but its "upscale crowd" doesn't seem to care.

Lady Mendl's *Teahouse*
22 | 26 | 23 | $44

Gramercy | Inn at Irving Pl. | 56 Irving Pl. (bet. 17th & 18th Sts.) | 212-533-4466 | www.ladymendls.com

Ladies live it up à la *Downton Abbey* at this "mahvelous" Gramercy tearoom where "excellent" servers present "tasty" sandwiches and sweets along with "wonderful" brews in an "elegant" Victorian setting; it's "pricey" whether "your boyfriend" comes or not, but a "pampered afternoon" is the reward.

La Esquina ● *Mexican*
23 | 22 | 18 | $42

Little Italy | 114 Kenmare St. (bet. Cleveland Pl. & Lafayette St.) | 646-613-7100 | www.esquinanyc.com

Cafe de la Esquina Ⓜ *Mexican*
Williamsburg | 225 Wythe Ave. (N. 3rd St.) | Brooklyn | 718-393-5500 | www.esquinabk.com

"Straight-up *delicioso*" describes both the food and the scene at this ever-"trendy" Little Italy Mexican comprised of a "dive"-like taqueria, casual indoor/outdoor cafe and "ultracool", hard-to-access underground grotto; the Williamsburg spin-off set in a "futuristic retro diner" comes equipped with a moody back room and "huge outdoor patio."

NEW Lafayette *French*
∇ 19 | 22 | 17 | $72

NoHo | 380 Lafayette St. (Great Jones St.) | 212-533-3000 | www.lafayetteny.com

This much anticipated newcomer from chef Andrew Carmellini (The Dutch, Locanda Verde) offers "classic" French country cooking in the NoHo space that was formerly Chinatown Brasserie (the sprawling setting done up in "pseudo belle epoque style" also includes an on-site bakery and several private rooms); all-day hours make access a bit easier, but brace yourself for crowds and waits at prime times.

La Follia *Italian*
22 | 18 | 21 | $40

Gramercy | 226 Third Ave. (19th St.) | 212-477-4100 | www.lafollianyc.com

Whether you land in the up-front enoteca or the rear dining room, the same "terrific" Italian small plates and pastas are available at this "casual" Gramercy "neighborhood place"; fans like the "sincere" service and "affordable" rates, the "no-reservations policy" not so much.

La Fonda del Sol Ⓩ *Spanish*
22 | 21 | 20 | $57

E 40s | MetLife Bldg. | 200 Park Ave. (enter on 44th St. & Vanderbilt Ave.) | 212-867-6767 | www.patinagroup.com

Conveniently sited above Grand Central, this reincarnation of a "classic" '60s Spaniard offers both a "lively after-work bar" serving "upscale tapas" and a "soothing", more "sophisticated" back room; it's "a bit high-priced", but at least the service is "professional."

		FOOD	DECOR	SERVICE	COST

La Gioconda *Italian*

22 | 17 | 21 | $40

E 50s | 226 E. 53rd St. (bet. 2nd & 3rd Aves.) | 212-371-3536 |
www.lagiocondany.com

"Neighborhood" cognoscenti claim this "tiny" Turtle Bay "hideaway"
is worth a visit for "fine Italian" fare at moderate tabs served up by a
"warm", "attentive" team; it's rather "undiscovered" despite many
years in business, and regulars relish the "unrushed" pace.

La Grenouille ⊠Ⓜ *French*

28 | 28 | 28 | $113

E 50s | 3 E. 52nd St. (bet. 5th & Madison Aves.) | 212-752-1495 |
www.la-grenouille.com

With "lavish flower displays" amid "magnificent", "artfully decorated"
environs ("where Truman Capote entertained his swans"), the "visual
feast is beyond compare" at Charles Masson's "transporting" East Side
"NYC classic", which is equally beloved for its "exquisite" haute French
cuisine and "seamless" service; the "first-class" experience is "worth
your last dollar" – though the $38 upstairs lunch deal is a "bargain."

La Lanterna di Vittorio ⏺ *Italian*

20 | 23 | 20 | $30

G Village | 129 MacDougal St. (bet. 3rd & 4th Sts.) | 212-529-5945 |
www.lalanternacaffe.com

It's all about the "romantic feel" at this Village Italian "slice of heaven"
purveying "enjoyable", "affordable" light bites in "quaint" quarters lit
by a fireplace and "lantern-filled" garden; "live jazz" in the adjoining
bar adds further "first-date" appeal.

La Lunchonette *French*

21 | 15 | 20 | $45

Chelsea | 130 10th Ave. (18th St.) | 212-675-0342

"It hasn't changed much in all these years, and that's a good thing" say
supporters of this "low-key", "fair-priced" West Chelsea bistro; its "divey charm" is just the thing post–"High Line" – and on Sunday night
there's a "chanteuse/accordionist."

La Mangeoire *French*

22 | 21 | 21 | $56

E 50s | 1008 Second Ave. (bet. 53rd & 54th Sts.) | 212-759-7086 |
www.lamangeoire.com

If you "can't get to Provence", check out this next-best-thing
Midtowner where chef Christian Delouvrier whips up "imaginative takes
on traditional country French dishes"; its longevity (since 1975) may be
due to the "warm" service and "transporting" South-of-France decor.

La Masseria ⏺ *Italian*

23 | 20 | 21 | $57

W 40s | 235 W. 48th St. (bet. B'way & 8th Ave.) | 212-582-2111 |
www.lamasserianyc.com

Showgoers tout this "quick-pace" Hell's Kitchen Italian for its "hearty"
cooking, "sweet farmhouse" setting and "fast" service that "gets you
to the theater on time"; "crowded" conditions and "pricey-but-worth-
the-money" tabs complete the overall appealing picture.

Lambs Club *American*

22 | 25 | 23 | $73

W 40s | Chatwal Hotel | 132 W. 44th St. (bet. 6th & 7th Aves.) |
212-997-5262 | www.thelambsclub.com

You may be "looking around for Nick and Nora Charles" what with the
"red leather" deco decor at Geoffrey Zakarian's "sophisticated" Theater
District charmer; the New American food is just as "fabulous", the ser-

vice "super-attentive" and the fireplace usually "roaring", but if the pricing's too "dear", have smart cocktails instead in the upstairs lounge.

La Mediterranée *French*

20	17	19	$50

E 50s | 947 Second Ave. (bet. 50th & 51st Sts.) | 212-755-4155 | www.lamediterraneeny.com

"Delicious", "no-surprises" cooking, "friendly service" and "fair prices" have kept this "old-fashioned" Midtown Provençal a "neighborhood favorite" for more than 30 years; few notice the "dated" decor when the nightly pianist is "taking requests."

La Mela ● *Italian*

21	14	19	$39

Little Italy | 167 Mulberry St. (bet. Broome & Grand Sts.) | 212-431-9493 | www.lamelarestaurant.com

"Belly-busting, multicourse" meals are the backbone of this "old-school Little Italy" vet where the "solid" Southern Italian cooking can be ordered either à la carte or in family-style prix fixes; maybe the decor "leaves much to be desired", but "service is "prompt" and the pricing "fair."

Landbrot Bakery & Bar ● *Bakery/German*

▽ 20	18	19	$27

LES | 185 Orchard St. (bet. Houston & Stanton Sts.) | 212-260-2900
W Village | 137 Seventh Ave. S. (Charles St.) | 212-255-7300
www.landbrotbakery.com

These German bakery/cafes (named for their signature, twice-baked rye loaf) offer everything from pretzels and "killer" breads to sausages and a "great beer selection"; the double-decker West Village original is larger than its LES sibling, but both share early opening and late closing hours.

L & B Spumoni Gardens *Dessert/Pizza*

24	13	17	$22

Bensonhurst | 2725 86th St. (bet. W. 10th & 11th Sts.) | Brooklyn | 718-449-6921 | www.spumonigardens.com

A "tradition" for "pizza-lovers" since 1939, the "crispy" Sicilian square pies are as "reliable as the sunset" at this "lively" Bensonhurst landmark, and having spumoni for dessert adds up to the "perfect dinner"; despite "dated" decor and so-so service, it's "worth the trip" for the "nostalgia" alone.

Landmarc *French*

21	20	20	$48

TriBeCa | 179 W. Broadway (bet. Leonard & Worth Sts.) | 212-343-3883
W 60s | Time Warner Ctr. | 10 Columbus Circle, 3rd fl. (60th St. at B'way) | 212-823-6123 ●
www.landmarc-restaurant.com

Marc Murphy's "credible" French bistros are "popular" options thanks to "straightforward, well-prepared" food, "bargain" wine lists and "saving-grace" late-night hours; despite "no reservations", the 10-year-old TriBeCa original has become a neighborhood institution, while the considerably larger TWC offshoot draws the "stroller crowd" with its "casual" air and "reasonable" pricing.

Landmark Tavern ● *Pub Food*

18	20	19	$39

W 40s | 626 11th Ave. (46th St.) | 212-247-2562 | www.thelandmarktavern.org

Around for 140-plus years, this "off-the-beaten-path" Hell's Kitchen tavern is deemed "worth the detour" for its "cozy olde NY" atmosphere alone; grab a pint and some "standard" pub grub delivered by a "caring" crew – "they don't make 'em like this anymore."

Land Thai Kitchen Thai
| 23 | 14 | 17 | $29 |

W 80s | 450 Amsterdam Ave. (bet. 81st & 82nd Sts.) | 212-501-8121 | www.landthaikitchen.com

"Big on flavor" but not in decor or size, this UWS "neighborhood Thai" dispenses "top-notch" standards "quick" at "wallet-friendly" rates; since "waits" are the norm at peak times, many elect for "takeout/delivery."

NEW L & W Oyster Co. Seafood
| ∇ 20 | 16 | 20 | $50 |

Chelsea | 254 Fifth Ave. (bet. 28th & 29th Sts.) | 212-203-7772 | www.landwoyster.com

A "find" near Madison Square Park, this new seafooder dispenses "informal beach-style" favorites ("go for the lobster roll" and "fresh oysters, natch") in airy, urban-clam-shack environs; solid service and an overall "fun atmosphere" have most plotting to "go back again" soon.

La Palapa ● Mexican
| 22 | 18 | 21 | $36 |

E Village | 77 St. Marks Pl. (bet. 1st & 2nd Aves.) | 212-777-2537 | www.lapalapa.com

"High-class Mexican" cuisine "cooked with love" is offered "cheap" and served with "courtesy" at this East Village cantina; the "luscious margaritas" that pack "plenty of punch" take your mind off "scrunched" seating, but "bring ear protection" at peak times.

La Piazzetta Italian
| ∇ 23 | 21 | 22 | $41 |

Williamsburg | 442 Graham Ave. (bet. Frost & Richardson Sts.) | Brooklyn | 718-349-1627 | www.lapiazzettany.com

This "charm"-filled trattoria transports diners away from the "craziness of Williamsburg" and "back to Italy" with "old-world" comfort dishes so "authentic" that locals worry the "secret will get out"; it's a natural for "date night", with "pre-hip prices" heightening the appeal.

NEW L'Apicio Italian
| 22 | 22 | 21 | $61 |

E Village | 13 E. First St. (bet. Bowery & 2nd Ave.) | 212-533-7400 | www.lapicio.com

An "early hit" with "fashionable" folk, this "wonderful" new East Village Italian from the Dell'anima/L'Artusi team offers a "refined", pasta-centric menu in a big, "glam" room; "appreciative" service, an "amazing bar scene" and a "bustling" mood complete the "trendy" picture.

La Pizza Fresca Italian/Pizza
| 22 | 17 | 17 | $41 |

Flatiron | 31 E. 20th St. (bet. B'way & Park Ave. S.) | 212-598-0141 | www.lapizzafrescaristorante.com

It was a "granddaddy of the artisan pizza trend", and this Flatiron "favorite" continues to turn out "superior" Neapolitan pies along with "terrific pasta"; "attentive" staffers with "smiles on all faces" help maintain the "relaxed" mood.

NEW La Pulperia ● Pan-Latin
| - | - | - | M |

W 40s | 371 W. 46th St. (bet. 8th & 9th Aves.) | 212-956-3055 | www.pulperianyc.com

This compact arrival to Restaurant Row presents a seafood-centric Pan-Latin menu from an ex-Toloache chef, plus a raw bar; its name means 'general store', and its rustic interior is done up with Mexican floor tiles and shelves brimming with wine and liquor bottles and colorful produce.

L'Artusi   *Italian*
27 | 23 | 24 | $61

W Village | 228 W. 10th St. (bet. Bleecker & Hudson Sts.) | 212-255-5757 | www.lartusi.com

"Something special" from the Dell'anima team, this West Village Italian "justifiably lures throngs" with "top-notch" cooking matched with an "impressive" wine list (the "hip vibe", "pretty" decor and "snap-to-it" service don't hurt, either); sure, it's pricey and sometimes "over-crowded", but the payoff is "stylish" dining.

La Silhouette   *French*
24 | 19 | 24 | $74

W 50s | 362 W. 53rd St. (bet. 8th & 9th Aves.) | 212-581-2400 | www.la-silhouettenyc.com

"Off the beaten path" in Hell's Kitchen, this "serious" French "destination restaurant" wins raves thanks to "terrific" food and an "able" staff; critics cite "stark" decor, a "labyrinthine" layout and "Le Bernardin prices", but still like that it's "close to the theaters."

La Sirène ⊬ *French*
24 | 16 | 22 | $52

Hudson Square | 558 Broome St. (Varick St.) | 212-925-3061 | www.lasirenenyc.com

"Decadent" preparations of "traditional" French cuisine shuttled by "charming" staffers are the lures at this "cozy" (read: "small") Hudson Square bistro; "tight" seating and a no-plastic policy are offset by a no-corkage-fee BYO policy that helps keep the tabs more bearable.

NEW La Slowteria Ⓜ *Mexican*
‒ | ‒ | ‒ | I

Carroll Gardens | 548 Court St. (9th St.) | Brooklyn | 718-858-2222 | www.laslowteria.com

Its name is a tribute to Slow Food and the Mexican card game Lotería, and this affordable Carroll Gardens taquería – a sequel to the Tulum original – sources its ingredients locally and offers a few surprises like raw bar–style oysters; fresh juices and NY State beers wash it all down.

Las Ramblas ❶ *Spanish*
23 | 17 | 20 | $38

W Village | 170 W. Fourth St. (bet. Cornelia & Jones Sts.) | 646-415-7924 | www.lasramblasnyc.com

Like "spending a couple of hours in Barcelona" without the airfare, this "tiny" Village tapas joint offers "fantastic" tidbits and "delicious san-gria" for little *dinero*; staffers "make sure everyone's happy" despite "noisy", crowded conditions, so just "grab a table and start ordering."

La Superior ❶⊬ *Mexican*
∇ 25 | 14 | 16 | $22

Williamsburg | 295 Berry St. (bet. S. 2nd & 3rd Sts.) | Brooklyn | 718-388-5988 | www.lasuperiornyc.com

"Fantastic tiny tacos" and offbeat takes on Mexican street food hit the trifecta for "tasty, authentic, cheap" satisfaction at this Williamsburg "standout"; the "cramped", undistinguished setting and cash-only policy don't keep the neighborhood masses from queuing up.

La Taza de Oro Ⓩ⊬ *Puerto Rican*
22 | 10 | 20 | $16

Chelsea | 96 Eighth Ave. (bet. 14th & 15th Sts.) | 212-243-9946

"Stick-to-your-ribs" Puerto Rican chow washed down with signature cafe con leche comes at an "unbeatable price" at this Chelsea "old-timer"; the neighborhood may have gone "fancy", but there's been "no decor" here since it opened in 1957.

Lattanzi ● *Italian* | 22 | 19 | 21 | $58 |

W 40s | 361 W. 46th St. (bet. 8th & 9th Aves.) | 212-315-0980 | www.lattanzinyc.com

Something "special" on Restaurant Row, this "better-than-average" Italian separates itself from the pack with an unusual post-theater menu of Roman-Jewish specialties; otherwise, it's a strictly "old-guard" experience with "gracious" service and a "charming" setting featuring lots of "dining nooks and crannies."

Laut *Malaysian/Thai* | 22 | 14 | 19 | $32 |

Union Sq | 15 E. 17th St. (bet. B'way & 5th Ave.) | 212-206-8989 | www.lautnyc.com

Southeast Asia's "vast variety of flavors" get their due at this Union Square purveyor of "authentic", "crazy-good" dishes from Malaysia, Thailand and beyond; there's "no ambiance" to speak of, but "affordable" tabs and "friendly" service keep things copacetic.

Lavagna *Italian* | 24 | 18 | 21 | $49 |

E Village | 545 E. Fifth St. (bet. Aves. A & B) | 212-979-1005 | www.lavagnanyc.co

At this "unassuming" yet "polished" Alphabet City "gem", "terrific" Tuscan cooking, "attentive" staffers and "cozy, brick-walled" digs work "romantic" wonders; factor in "affordable" prices, and it's no wonder the "tight" digs are "always crowded."

La Vara *Spanish* | ∇ 27 | 22 | 25 | $53 |

Cobble Hill | 268 Clinton St. (bet. Verandah Pl. & Warren St.) | Brooklyn | 718-422-0065 | www.lavarany.com

Alex Raij and Eder Montero (Txikito, El Quinto Pino) "have done it again" with this Cobble Hill tapas champ where the "innovative, balanced", "deeply tasty" Southern Spanish cuisine is matched with "unique" cocktails and wines; its "simple" yet "elegant" interior and tiny patio are presided over by a "super-friendly", "knowledgeable" staff.

La Vigna *Italian* | 23 | 18 | 23 | $41 |

Forest Hills | 100-11 Metropolitan Ave. (70th Ave.) | Queens | 718-268-4264 | www.lavignany.com

Merging "local charm" and "big-city quality", this Forest Hills "standout" rolls out "excellent" Italian food conveyed by "nice-to-see-you-again" staffers; the "simple" setting is similarly in keeping with the "down-home" neighborhood feel.

La Villa Pizzeria *Pizza* | 23 | 17 | 20 | $28 |

Mill Basin | Key Food Plaza | 6610 Ave. U (66th St.) | Brooklyn | 718-251-8030

Park Slope | 261 Fifth Ave. (bet. 1st St. & Garfield Pl.) | Brooklyn | 718-499-9888

Howard Bch | Lindenwood Shopping Ctr. | 8207 153rd Ave. (82nd St.) | Queens | 718-641-8259
www.lavillaparkslope.com

These "basic neighborhood red-sauce" joints dish out "first-rate" pizzas along with a "lengthy" roster of "comfort" Italian items; nondescript settings and "loud" acoustics are offset by "modest" tabs.

	FOOD	DECOR	SERVICE	COST

Lavo ● *Italian*
E 50s | 39 E. 58th St. (bet. Madison & Park Aves.) | 212-750-5588 | www.lavony.com

21 | 21 | 19 | $64

It's one "crazy" scene at this "pricey" Midtown Italian that rivals nearby sibling Tao as a "meet-and-mingle" hub for the "Botox-and-high-heels" set and the "expense-account suits" who love them; just bring "earplugs" and an appetite – the "garlicky" fare is "surprisingly good" – and then "go party" in the "thumping" downstairs club.

Lazzara's ⊠ *Pizza*
Garment District | 221 W. 38th St. (bet. 7th & 8th Aves.) | 212-944-7792 | www.lazzaraspizza.com

∇ 24 | 12 | 16 | $21

"Square and superb" sums up the thin-crust pizzas produced by this "under-the-radar" Garment Distict "staple"; its second-floor "hole-in-the-wall" setting is a "busy" scene at lunch, so plenty procure pies to go.

NEW The LCL ● *American*
E 40s | Westin New York Grand Central | 212 E. 42nd St. (bet. 2nd & 3rd Aves.) | 212-405-4399 | www.thelclnyc.com

- | - | - | M

Accessible from breakfast through late-night, this Gerber Group new-comer in the Westin New York Grand Central furnishes straightforward American bites at a fair price; the spacious, contemporary setting is loungey enough to also work for drinks and nibbles after dark.

Le Bernardin ⊠ *French/Seafood*
W 50s | 155 W. 51st St. (bet. 6th & 7th Aves.) | 212-554-1515 | www.le-bernardin.com

29 | 28 | 28 | $169

Dining doesn't get much more "blissful" than at this "sublime" Midtown French seafooder via Maguy Le Coze and chef Eric Ripert, a near "religious experience" where "exquisite" meals, "meticulous" service and an "impressive", revamped room have again earned it Top Food and Most Popular honors in NYC; granted, the tabs are equally "extraordinary" – the prix fixe-only dinners start at $130 – but then again, it's "fabulous in every way"; P.S. a no-reserving lounge offers small plates, while a neighboring wine bar and private dining room in the former Palio/Piano Due spaces are in the works.

Le Cirque ⊠ *French*
E 50s | One Beacon Ct. | 151 E. 58th St. (bet. Lexington & 3rd Aves.) | 212-644-0202 | www.lecirque.com

25 | 26 | 25 | $96

"Old-time grandeur" endures at Sirio Maccioni's "time-tested" Midtown "dining icon", now in its 40th year thanks to a combination of "sumptuous" French cuisine, "exquisite" service and a "posh", Adam Tihany-designed setting with an "imaginative" circus motif; though both "jackets and deep pockets are required" in the main room, its cafe adjunct is less formal and more casually priced.

L'Ecole *French*
SoHo | International Culinary Ctr. | 462 Broadway (Grand St.) | 212-219-3300 | www.lecolenyc.com

24 | 20 | 23 | $56

"Eager students" cook for you at this "charming" International Culinary Center trainer French restaurant in SoHo; with "delicious" execution that's "often as good as the pros" and prix fixe menus proffering "excellent value", its "occasional slip-ups" are easy to overlook.

	FOOD	DECOR	SERVICE	COST

Le Colonial *French/Vietnamese* | 21 | 23 | 21 | $62 |

E 50s | 149 E. 57th St. (bet. Lexington & 3rd Aves.) | 212-752-0808 |
www.lecolonialnyc.com

At this "gorgeous" Midtowner, you'll be "transported to an exotic
place" where the spirit of 1920s "colonial Indochine" is in the air and
on the plate in the form of "terrific" French-Vietnamese fare; the "old
Saigon" sensibility extends to a "comfortable upstairs lounge", though
prices are strictly modern day.

Left Bank *American*   ▽ | 20 | 20 | 22 | $51 |

W Village | 117 Perry St. (Greenwich St.) | 212-727-1170 |
www.leftbankmanhattan.com

European-influenced New American fare is "served with care" at this
West Villager where the "attractive" space is suitable for conversation;
"decent prices" further its status as a solid "neighborhood hangout."

Legend *Chinese* | 21 | 14 | 15 | $33 |

Chelsea | 88 Seventh Ave. (bet. 15th & 16th Sts.) | 212-929-1778 |
www.legendrestaurant88.com ❶

NEW **W 70s** | 127 W. 72nd St. (bet. Amsterdam & Columbus Aves.) |
917-441-4793

NEW **W 100s** | 258 W. 109th St. (bet. Amsterdam Ave. & B'way) |
212-222-4800 ❶

"Your mouth won't feel the same" after sampling the "super-hot",
"super-good" Sichuan fare at these affordable Chinese venues; happy-
hour deals at the "A-1 bar" draw a "vibrant crowd", and timid palates
should know that it also offers less fiery dishes.

Le Gigot Ⓜ *French* | 24 | 19 | 24 | $59 |

W Village | 18 Cornelia St. (bet. Bleecker & W. 4th Sts.) | 212-627-3737 |
www.legigotrestaurant.com

"Everything's right" at this "petite" West Village bistro, a "Francophile's
dream" where "meticulously prepared" Provençal dishes come via a
"superb" staff; granted, the seating's "tight" and the tabs "pricey", but
it's hard to beat for a "romantic dinner for two."

Le Grainne Cafe ❶ *French* | 20 | 16 | 17 | $30 |

Chelsea | 183 Ninth Ave. (21st St.) | 646-486-3000 | www.legrainnecafe.com
A "charming breath of France" blows your way at this "cozy" Chelsea
French cafe where "delightful vittles" and birdbath-size café au laits supply "simple" comfort; habitués say the "crowded" digs and "occasionally
distracted" service are the trade-offs for feeling "transported."

Le Marais *French/Kosher/Steak* | 20 | 16 | 18 | $55 |

W 40s | 150 W. 46th St. (bet. 6th & 7th Aves.) | 212-869-0900 |
www.lemarais.net

"If you're a kosher carnivore", this Theater District French "staple"
comes across with "excellent steaks" that pass muster with the highest authority; though the service "doesn't match" the food quality and
the surrounds are "forgettable", it's generally "packed" all the same.

Lemongrass Grill *Thai* | 19 | 16 | 18 | $26 |

Cobble Hill | 156 Court St. (bet. Amity & Pacific Sts.) | Brooklyn |
718-522-9728 | www.lemongrassnyc.com

"Pretty standard" is the word on this "acceptable" if "predictable"
Cobble Hill Thai turning out "consistently ok" chow at "affordable"

rates; maybe the interior "could use refurbishing", but who cares when you can get so much for so little?

Leopard at des Artistes ● *Italian*   21 | 25 | 22 | $76

W 60s | 1 W. 67th St. (bet. Columbus Ave. & CPW) | 212-787-8767 | www.theleopardnyc.com

The UWS space that once housed Café des Artistes has been "beautifully updated" and "reenergized" with the "beloved" Howard Chandler Christy murals "looking brighter than ever"; given the "honest" Italian food served by "skilled" staffers, no wonder "well-heeled" locals and the "Lincoln Center" crowd have returned in droves.

Leo's Latticini ⊠Ⓜ *Deli/Italian*   26 | 12 | 23 | $15
(aka Mama's of Corona)

Corona | 46-02 104th St. (46th Ave.) | Queens | 718-898-6069
Mama's of Corona ⊠Ⓜ *Deli/Italian*

Flushing | Citi Field | 126th St. & Roosevelt Ave. (behind the scoreboard) | Queens

"Nobody makes a sandwich" like this Corona "old-school Italian deli" where the subs are "fit for royalty" and the mozz is among the "best in the boroughs"; its Citi Field stand services Mets fans on game days, but unfortunately without those "adorable ladies" behind the counter.

Le Pain Quotidien *Bakery/Belgian*   18 | 14 | 15 | $25

E 60s | 833 Lexington Ave. (bet. 63rd & 64th Sts.) | 212-755-5810
E 70s | 252 E. 77th St. (bet. 2nd & 3rd Aves.) | 212-249-8600
E 80s | 1131 Madison Ave. (bet. 84th & 85th Sts.) | 212-327-4900
Flatiron | 931 Broadway (bet. 21st & 22nd Sts.) | 646-395-9926
G Village | 10 Fifth Ave. (8th St.) | 212-253-2324
G Village | 801 Broadway (11th St.) | 212-677-5277
SoHo | 100 Grand St. (bet. Greene & Mercer Sts.) | 212-625-9009
W 50s | 922 Seventh Ave. (58th St.) | 212-757-0775
W 60s | 60 W. 65th St. (bet. B'way & CPW) | 212-721-4001
W 70s | 50 W. 72nd St. (bet. Columbus Ave. & CPW) | 212-712-9700
www.lepainquotidien.com
Additional locations throughout the NY area

For an "unfussy" "coffee-shop alternative", try this "quickie" Belgian bakery/cafe chain patronized for its "easy" menus (with "many organic choices") served in "rustic, woody" rooms at "elbow-to-elbow" communal tables; "predictability" and "disorganized" service are a pain, but "inexpensive" tabs and "all-around-town" locations compensate.

Le Parisien *French*   22 | 17 | 21 | $41

Murray Hill | 163 E. 33rd St. (bet. Lexington & 3rd Aves.) | 212-889-5489 | www.leparisiennyc.com

"Teleport" to the "banks of the Seine" via this "cozy", "Paris-in-Murray-Hill" French bistro offering "excellent", "well-priced" renditions of "all the classics"; "charming" staffers compensate for "tiny" dimensions and help seal its standing as a local "winner."

Le Perigord *French*   25 | 21 | 25 | $82

E 50s | 405 E. 52nd St. (bet. FDR Dr. & 1st Ave.) | 212-755-6244 | www.leperigord.com

"Classic to the core", this 50-year-old exemplar of "the way fine dining used to be" offers "true French haute cuisine" in a "calm" Sutton Place room overseen by "pampering" staffers under the watchful eye of owner Georges Briguet; its "old-money" following calls it "pure pleasure", the ooh-la-la tabs notwithstanding.

Le Pescadeux ●Ⓜ *Seafood*　　22 | 18 | 22 | $53

SoHo | 90 Thompson St. (bet. Prince & Spring Sts.) | 212-966-0021 | www.lepescadeux.com

A slice of Quebec in SoHo, this "relaxed" French-Canadian seafood specialist offers "delicious" midpriced dishes in pairable half-orders, a "catchy" hook that diversifies your meal; "congenial" hospitality and occasional live music enhance the "inviting" ambiance.

🆕 Le Philosophe *French*　　▽ 24 | 17 | 19 | $57

NoHo | 55 Bond St. (bet. Bowery & Lafayette St.) | 212-388-0038 | www.lephilosophe.us

"Delicious", age-old Gallic dishes – think frogs' legs, lobster Thermidor, duck à l'orange – turn up at this new NoHo French bistro that's a hit with "locals" despite "tiny" dimensions and "humble" decor; "getting a table can be a challenge", but if you can identify all of the philosophers on the wall mural, your meal's free.

Le Relais de Venise L'Entrecôte *French/Steak*　　20 | 17 | 19 | $43

E 50s | 590 Lexington Ave. (52nd St.) | 212-758-3989 | www.relaisdevenise.net

It's all about "value" at this "unique" Midtown French brasserie where the "one-trick-pony" menu consists only of steak frites and salad for a $27 fixed price; fans find it "quick and easy", though the no-reservations rule makes for waits at prime times.

Le Rivage *French*　　21 | 18 | 22 | $48

W 40s | 340 W. 46th St. (bet. 8th & 9th Aves.) | 212-765-7374 | www.lerivagenyc.com

"Old-school" French dining is alive and well at this circa-1958 Restaurant Row survivor where the "middle-of-the-road" Gallic offerings are "consistent" and the service "understands curtain time"; the digs may be "dated", but the post-theater $25 prix fixe is quite the "deal."

Les Halles ● *French/Steak*　　20 | 17 | 18 | $48

Financial District | 15 John St. (bet. B'way & Nassau St.) | 212-285-8585
Murray Hill | 411 Park Ave. S. (bet. 28th & 29th Sts.) | 212-679-4111
www.leshalles.net

Ever "popular", these "vibrant" French brasseries are known for their "first-rate" steak frites, "dark" lighting and "noisy" decibels; though the "people-watching" can be "fun", "don't count on seeing" long-gone chef-at-large Anthony Bourdain.

Le Veau d'Or 🖺 *French*　　19 | 16 | 21 | $59

E 60s | 129 E. 60th St. (bet. Lexington & Park Aves.) | 212-838-8133

"Forgotten" French bistro classics work their "throwback" magic on loyal patrons of this circa-1937 Eastsider; though it's "had a full life" – and it shows – here's hoping it may "continue forever."

Lexington Brass *American*　　18 | 17 | 17 | $45

E 40s | Hyatt 48 Lex Hotel | 517 Lexington Ave. (48th St.) | 212-392-5976 | www.lexingtonbrass.com

Just north of Grand Central, this airy, "casual" brasserie from the EMM Group (Catch) vends midpriced New American standards to a

	FOOD	DECOR	SERVICE	COST

"business"-oriented crowd from morning till late; its "cool bar" is a magnet for "after-work" sorts and "tourists" resting their feet.

Le Zie 2000 ❶ *Italian* — 22 | 15 | 20 | $44

Chelsea | 172 Seventh Ave. (bet. 20th & 21st Sts.) | 212-206-8686 | www.lezie.com

"High-end in quality but not in price" sums up the Venetian cuisine at this "lively" Chelsea Italian; regulars suggest the "back room" if quiet dining is preferred, and say "beware" the "daily specials" that sell for "much more" than the regular fare.

NEW The Library at the Public ❶ *American* — ▽ 18 | 21 | 18 | $51

E Village | Public Theater | 425 Lafayette St., 2nd fl. (bet. Astor Pl. & 4th St.) | 212-539-8777 | www.thelibraryatthepublic.com

This "welcome addition" upstairs at the Public Theater bows in with American fare from chef Andrew Carmellini that's "creative without being over the top"; though on the "expensive" side, it "couldn't be easier before the show", and the "dark", "clubby" quarters include a "vibrant" bar scene.

Lido *Italian* — 22 | 20 | 21 | $38

Harlem | 2168 Frederick Douglass Blvd. (117th St.) | 646-490-8575 | www.lidoharlem.com

Harlem denizens declare you "don't need to go Downtown for first-rate Italian food" thanks to this "solid" Uptown player; its "skillfully prepared" dishes are served in "relaxed" environs by "friendly" staffers, with no letup in "quality" during the popular "bottomless-mimosa" brunch.

Liebman's Delicatessen *Deli/Kosher* — 23 | 12 | 19 | $24

Riverdale | 552 W. 235th St. (Johnson Ave.) | Bronx | 718-548-4534 | www.liebmansdeli.com

For a "corned beef on rye, hold the cardiogram", check out this Bronx kosher Jewish deli that's been plating "overstuffed" sandwiches since 1953; though it "hasn't changed in years" – as evidenced in the "faded" decor and "slapdash" service – fans feel it "never disappoints."

Lil' Frankie's Pizza ❶⊟ *Pizza* — 24 | 18 | 18 | $32

E Village | 19 First Ave. (bet. 1st & 2nd Sts.) | 212-420-4900 | www.lilfrankies.com

Really "solid" Italian fare "without frills" at an "affordable price" is the signature of this "casual", cash-only East Villager (sibling of Frank, Sauce and Supper); it offers "standout" Neapolitan pizzas, late hours and a "garden room", with way-"crowded" peak times as the main detraction.

Lincoln *Italian* — 24 | 26 | 25 | $81

W 60s | Lincoln Ctr. | 142 W. 65th St. (bet. Amsterdam Ave. & B'way) | 212-359-6500 | www.lincolnristorante.com

"Luxury fine dining" is yours at this "sophisticated" charmer in the Lincoln Center campus, where chef Jonathan Benno's "sumptuous" Modern Italian food arrives in a "dramatic", glass-walled, grass-roofed space; "impeccable" service, "serious mixology" and a "fascinating open kitchen" justify the "exorbitant" tabs, and followers say it's "worth the trip even if you're not going to the opera."

	FOOD	DECOR	SERVICE	COST

The Lion ● *American*

21 | 24 | 21 | $68

G Village | 62 W. Ninth St. (bet. 5th & 6th Aves.) | 212-353-8400 | www.thelionnyc.com

Chef-owner John DeLucie conjures up "old-school" NY at this "fashionable" Village American where a "huge skylight, eclectic art and photos" provide the backdrop for a "happening", "celeb"-centric scene; the "homey-yet-upscale" fare takes a backseat to the "exciting" buzz, but it's just as "delicious."

Littleneck ⊅ *Seafood*

▽ 24 | 18 | 21 | $41

Gowanus | 288 Third Ave. (bet. Carroll & President Sts.) | Brooklyn | 718-522-1921 | www.littleneckbrooklyn.com

Who knew a clam shack could "thrive" a block from the Gowanus, but this New England–style seafooder boasts a loyal local following for its well-priced shore classics; "friendly" service and a "cute" rough-hewn setting balance the "lack of reservations" and cash-only "pains" in the neck.

Little Owl *American/Mediterranean*

25 | 19 | 23 | $58

W Village | 90 Bedford St. (Grove St.) | 212-741-4695 | www.thelittleowlnyc.com

"Little" is an understatement at this 28-seat West Village "gem", where chef Joey Campanaro whips up "fantastic" Med–New Americana in a "cramped", "big-windowed" space; reservations are notoriously "hard to get" – even "if you can eat at 5:30" – so regulars make sure to "mark the calendar" and call 30 days ahead.

Little Poland *Diner/Polish*

20 | 8 | 18 | $19

E Village | 200 Second Ave. (bet. 12th & 13th Sts.) | 212-777-9728

"Heaping portions" of "filling" Polish "diner food" comes "cheap as can be" at this "old-time" East Village "greasy spoon"; "drab" the interior may be, but wait till you taste those "perfect pierogi" – you couldn't do better in Gdansk.

Lobster Box ● *Seafood*

20 | 16 | 18 | $48

City Island | 34 City Island Ave. (bet. Belden & Rochelle Sts.) | Bronx | 718-885-1952 | www.lobsterboxrestaurant.com

City Island's veteran dockside seafooder offers a "super view" of Long Island Sound as a backdrop for shore meals that are "decent" but "not fine dining"; prepare to "wait on line" because both "tourists" and locals like being netted here.

Locale *Italian*

▽ 21 | 21 | 20 | $37

Astoria | 33-02 34th Ave. (33rd St.) | Queens | 718-729-9080 | www.localeastoria.com

Set in a "residential" Astoria neighborhood, this midpriced Italian serves "cut-above-normal" fare in a "pleasant", "SoHo"-like space; its "friendly" staff, enticing bar and weekend brunch are additional assets rendering it "worth a try."

Locanda Verde *Italian*

25 | 22 | 21 | $63

TriBeCa | Greenwich Hotel | 377 Greenwich St. (N. Moore St.) | 212-925-3797 | www.locandaverdenyc.com

Andrew Carmellini's "happening" TriBeCa Italian draws a "star-studded", "masters-of-the-universe" crowd with an irresistible mix of "heavenly" cooking and "hip" vibrations; too bad it's "consistently crowded" with "tight" seating, variable service and "ear-shattering" decibels, but the fact that reservations are virtually "impossible" to get speaks for itself.

Locanda Vini & Olii Ⓜ *Italian*   26 | 25 | 25 | $54

Clinton Hill | 129 Gates Ave. (bet. Cambridge Pl. & Grand Ave.) | Brooklyn | 718-622-9202 | www.locandany.com

"Marvelous" Northern Italian food is served in a "converted" former drugstore at this Clinton Hill "find" run by a "knowledgeable" team that "takes pride" in its work; in short, the "lovely" vintage setting, "really friendly" staff and "eclectic" eats are a prescription for "top-notch" dining.

Loi *Greek*   22 | 22 | 22 | $60

W 70s | 208 W. 70th St. (bet. Amsterdam & West End Aves.) | 212-875-8600 | www.restaurantloi.com

"High-quality", "high-priced" Greek cuisine with a "healthy" spin and "gracious" chef-owner Maria Loi's signature "personal touch" is the hook at this "classy addition" to the Upper West Side dining scene; "spacious", "comfortable" quarters "close to Lincoln Center" seal the deal.

Lombardi's ⊄ *Pizza*   24 | 15 | 18 | $25

NoLita | 32 Spring St. (bet. Mott & Mulberry Sts.) | 212-941-7994 | www.firstpizza.com

This NoLita pizza "shrine" (which claims to be America's first pizzeria) still draws throngs with its ultra-"authentic" coal-fired, thin-crust goods; it doesn't take plastic or reservations, and you may have to "tussle with the tourists to get a table", but for many it's a real "slice of NY" – even though it "doesn't do slices."

Lomzynianka ⊄ *Polish*   ▽ 22 | 12 | 17 | $19

Greenpoint | 646 Manhattan Ave. (bet. Nassau & Norman Aves.) | Brooklyn | 718-389-9439 | www.lomzynianka.com

It's "classic Greenpoint" all the way at this local "treasure" dishing out "wonderful" Polish home cooking that rises above the "modest" decor; the BYO policy and "astonishingly reasonable prices" mean "you can't go wrong" here – except when you try to pronounce the name.

London Lennie's *Seafood*   23 | 18 | 21 | $45

Rego Park | 63-88 Woodhaven Blvd. (bet. Fleet Ct. & Penelope Ave.) | Queens | 718-894-8084 | www.londonlennies.com

A "longtime resident" of Rego Park, this circa-1959 fishmonger fields a "wide selection" of "fresh", "unfussy" seafood in "big", "nothing-fancy" digs; "fast" service and quite reasonable pricing keep it "always crowded."

Lorenzo's *Italian*   ▽ 22 | 23 | 22 | $49

Bloomfield | Hilton Garden Inn | 1100 South Ave. (Lois Ln.) | Staten Island | 718-477-2400 | www.lorenzosdining.com

"Food and entertainment" go hand in hand at this Staten Island Italian in Bloomfield, where the "weekend cabarets" and "jazz brunch" are big hits with "locals" looking for a "classy" outing "without city hassles"; service also rates high, but grumbles about "uneven" cuisine persist.

Loukoumi Taverna *Greek*

▽ 24 | 20 | 22 | $35

Astoria | 45-07 Ditmars Blvd. (bet. 45th & 46th Sts.) | Queens | 718-626-3200 | www.loukoumitaverna.com

"Excellent", "authentic" taverna fare leads the charge at this "warm, inviting" Astoria Greek; it's located "a bit away" from the main neighborhood action, but "affordable" tabs and a back garden clinch the "good-on-all-counts" endorsement.

NEW Louro *American/Portuguese*

▽ 21 | 18 | 22 | $65

W Village | 142 W. 10th St. (bet. Greenwich Ave. & Waverly Pl.) | 212-206-0606 | www.louronyc.com

"Love and care" inform the "creative" cooking at this new West Villager where the American menu sports a decided Portuguese accent; the understated room is busiest on Monday nights, when it morphs into the Nossa Mesa Supper Club, featuring "delicious", intriguingly themed tasting menus.

Lucali ⌻ *Pizza*

27 | 19 | 19 | $27

Carroll Gardens | 575 Henry St. (bet. Carroll St. & 1st Pl.) | Brooklyn | 718-858-4086

"If you can get in", the pies and calzones are mighty darn "awesome" at this Carroll Gardens "neighborhood" pizzeria, again voted No. 1 in NYC; it takes neither credit cards nor reservations, and "long waits" are the norm, but the BYO policy is "pretty cool."

Lucien ◐ *French*

23 | 17 | 20 | $49

E Village | 14 First Ave. (1st St.) | 212-260-6481 | www.luciennyc.com

"Charming" owner Lucien Bahaj's East Village French "favorite" rolls out "first-rate bistro" classics and a "convivial" vibe that will "take you to Paris in a flash"; ok, it's on the "cramped" side, but tell that to its regulars who "leave with a smile every time."

Lucky's Famous Burgers ◐ *Burgers*

20 | 11 | 18 | $14

Chelsea | 264 W. 23rd St. (bet. 7th & 8th Aves.) | 212-242-4900
LES | 147 E. Houston St. (bet. Eldridge & Forsyth Sts.) | 212-254-4900
W 50s | 370 W. 52nd St. (bet. 8th & 9th Aves.) | 212-247-6717
www.luckysfamousburgers.com

For a "decent" burger that will "fill you up" on a "budget" at just about any hour, this "fast food–type" franchise "does the trick"; most say "takeout" is the way to go, unless "tacky", "bright-red-and-yellow" interiors are your thing.

Luke's Lobster *Seafood*

23 | 11 | 17 | $24

E 80s | 242 E. 81st St. (bet. 2nd & 3rd Aves.) | 212-249-4241
E Village | 93 E. Seventh St. (bet. Ave. A & 1st Ave.) | 212-387-8487
Financial District | 26 S. William St. (bet. Beaver & Broad Sts.) | 212-747-1700
W 50s | Plaza Food Hall | 1 W. 59th St. (5th Ave.) | 646-755-3227
W 80s | 426 Amsterdam Ave. (bet. 80th & 81st Sts.) | 212-877-8800
NEW Dumbo | Brooklyn Bridge Park | 11 Water St. (New Dock St.) | Brooklyn | 917-882-7516
www.lukeslobster.com

"Less is more" at these "simple" seafood shacks where the "limited" menus are highlighted by "sublime" lobster rolls that they "don't over-mayo" – and "don't come cheap"; the "funky" setups suggest "Cape

166

	FOOD	DECOR	SERVICE	COST

Cod minus the ocean", but "tiny" dimensions and "cramped" conditions lead many to opt for takeout.

NEW Luksus 🗟Ⓜ *American* | - | - | - | VE |

Greenpoint | 615 Manhattan Ave. (Nassau Ave.) | Brooklyn | 718-389-6034 | www.luksusnyc.com
Set in the back room of Greenpoint's beer bar Tørst, this ambitious New American nook offers $75 prix fixe-only tasting menus featuring cutting-edge dishes with a distinct Scandinavian bent; despite the name ('luxury' in Danish), the spare, open-kitchened space has but 26 seats, and great word of mouth is making reservations a challenge.

Luna Piena *Italian* | 20 | 16 | 20 | $50 |

E 50s | 243 E. 53rd St. (bet. 2nd & 3rd Aves.) | 212-308-8882 | www.lunapienanyc.com
Midtown "office" folk and "locals" alike say "you can't go wrong" at this midpriced Italian where "winning" dishes arrive via "attentive" staffers who "go out of their way" to please; maybe the garden-equipped setting's a bit "unprepossessing", but most call the overall experience "genuinely nice."

Lunetta Ⓜ *Italian* | ▽ 21 | 16 | 20 | $39 |

Boerum Hill | 116 Smith St. (bet. Dean & Pacific Sts.) | Brooklyn | 718-488-6269 | www.lunetta-ny.com
This "cozy" Boerum Hill Italian "keeps things interesting" with a menu of "seasonal" midpriced small plates that are "crafted with care"; the accommodations feature a food bar where you can "watch the chef" work, as well as a garden in back.

Lupa *Italian* | 25 | 18 | 21 | $57 |

G Village | 170 Thompson St. (bet. Bleecker & Houston Sts.) | 212-982-5089 | www.luparestaurant.com
Just "like home – with incredible food" – this "informal" Villager is a showcase for Mario Batali's "simple" yet "flavorful" Roman dishes dispatched in "rustic" digs by a "good-humored" crew; "reasonable prices" offset the "seating squeeze" and "boisterous" decibels ("lunch is quieter"), and regulars report that "advance reservations" are a must.

Lure Fishbar *Seafood* | 23 | 23 | 21 | $59 |

SoHo | 142 Mercer St. (Prince St.) | 212-431-7676 | www.lurefishbar.com
It's "quite the scene" at this "packed" SoHo cellar seafooder where the "fresh" catch is "perfectly cooked" and on par with the "classy", "cruise-ship" decor; though tabs are steep and the "ebullient", "mixed-age" crowd makes a lot of racket, it's generally considered an "all-around winner."

Lusardi's ❶ *Italian* | 23 | 19 | 22 | $65 |

E 70s | 1494 Second Ave. (bet. 77th & 78th Sts.) | 212-249-2020 | www.lusardis.com
"Friendly" owner Mario Lusardi oversees the "vintage poster"-lined room at this longtime UES "institution" where the Tuscan food is as "terrific" as the "gracious" service and "old-fashioned style"; its "adult", "high-end crowd" doesn't mind the "expensive" checks, given that it has "maintained its quality over the years."

	FOOD	DECOR	SERVICE	COST

Luz *Nuevo Latino*
∇ 23 | 19 | 21 | $37

Fort Greene | 177 Vanderbilt Ave. (bet. Myrtle & Willoughby Aves.) | Brooklyn | 718-246-4000 | www.luzrestaurant.com

Nuevo Latino dishes sporting "interesting flavor combos" team up with "great" cocktails to deliver "reasonably priced" good times at this Fort Greene find; granted, it's "slightly out of the way", but fans say it's "worth the trip" for a "zesty" meal in "cool", "unpretentious" environs.

Luzzo's *Pizza*
26 | 15 | 18 | $30

E Village | 211 First Ave. (bet. 12th & 13th Sts.) | 212-473-7447 | www.luzzospizza.com

In an "area rich with good pizzerias", the "outstanding" Neapolitan-style pies proffered at this East Villager have the distinction of being fired in one of the few remaining coal-burning ovens in NYC; despite "waits" and not much decor, purists "highly recommend" it.

Lychee House *Chinese*
22 | 16 | 20 | $38

E 50s | 141 E. 55th St. (bet. Lexington & 3rd Aves.) | 212-753-3900 | www.lycheehouse.com

Ranking a "notch above most", this Midtown Chinese offers a "wide variety" of "well-prepared", well-priced items including "fine Shanghainese and Malaysian" dishes and "inventive dim sum", backed by libations from a full bar; since ambiance ain't the focus here, some opt for takeout.

Mable's Smokehouse *BBQ*
∇ 23 | 18 | 20 | $26

Williamsburg | 44 Berry St. (N. 11th St.) | Brooklyn | 718-218-6655 | www.mablessmokehouse.com

Get your "BBQ fix" at this "spacious", "laid-back" Williamsburg joint where the "plentiful" ribs, brisket and pulled pork pack "bold and robust flavors" and are "priced just right"; "cafeteria-style ordering" and "shared tables" bolster the "transports-you-to-Tennessee" vibe.

Macao Trading Co. ❶ *Chinese/Portuguese*
20 | 24 | 18 | $52

TriBeCa | 311 Church St. (bet. Lispenard & Walker Sts.) | 212-431-8750 | www.macaonyc.com

Channeling a "1940s" "Macao gambling parlor", this "dazzling", bi-level TriBeCan offers plentiful "eye candy" to go with its Chinese-Portuguese chow; late-night, it turns "club"-like – "loud and crowded" with uneven service – but most are having too much "fun" to care.

Macelleria ❶ *Italian/Steak*
21 | 20 | 20 | $57

Meatpacking | 48 Gansevoort St. (bet. Greenwich & Washington Sts.) | 212-741-2555 | www.macelleria.com

"When you want some pasta with your steak", try this "buzzy" Meatpacking Italian chophouse whose "unadorned" fare "doesn't disappoint" but also "doesn't come cheap"; it boasts a "witty butcher theme" indoors, while alfresco seats afford prime "MPD crowd"-watching.

Macondo ❶ *Pan-Latin*
∇ 22 | 22 | 21 | $39

LES | 157 E. Houston St. (bet. Allen & Eldridge Sts.) | 212-473-9900 | www.macondonyc.com

Pan-Latin "street food at its best" comes in "lively" environs at this "friendly" Lower Eastsider where small plates "packed with flavor" meet "tropical" cocktails "made to perfection"; it hosts a *muy* "happening bar scene", so be ready for "crowds and noise."

	FOOD	DECOR	SERVICE	COST

Madangsui *Korean*

22 | 13 | 17 | $34

Garment District | 35 W. 35th St. (bet. 5th & 6th Aves.) | 646-873-6470 | www.madangsui.com

Koreatown cognoscenti "head straight for the BBQ" at this "authentic" Seoul-fooder where the meat hits the grill at your table and an "efficient" crew keeps the proceedings on track; there's "not much" decor, but the "long waits" on weekends aren't for the scenery.

Mad Dog & Beans ● *Mexican*

19 | 18 | 16 | $32

Financial District | 83 Pearl St. (bet. Broad St. & Hanover Sq.) | 212-269-1177 | www.maddogandbeans.com

Among the FiDi's few Mexican options, this "festive after-work scene" serves up "fab guac" and "even better margaritas", plus other "decent" standards; it's "dark and noisy" with "so-so service", but all's forgiven during summer when you can sit out on the "Stone Street strip."

Madiba ● *S African*

23 | 24 | 21 | $32

Fort Greene | 195 DeKalb Ave. (bet. Adelphi St. & Carlton Ave.) | Brooklyn | 718-855-9190 | www.madibarestaurant.com

For a "real taste of South Africa", hit this "unassuming, relaxed" Fort Greene "hangout" that feels "like a vacation" thanks to its "cool" eclectic look, "comforting", "affordable" fare and "warm" service (just "don't be in a rush"); regulars note it's "*the* place to watch futbol/ World Cup games."

Madison Bistro *French*

20 | 16 | 20 | $50

Murray Hill | 238 Madison Ave. (bet. 37th & 38th Sts.) | 212-447-1919 | www.madisonbistro.com

"Every neighborhood should have a local bistro" like this Murray Hill "sleeper" that's appreciated for its "quality" French classics and prix fixe deals; "well-behaved" locals are drawn to its "friendly" vibe and "relaxing" (if "generic") room that's "conducive to conversation."

Madison's ● *Italian*

20 | 17 | 19 | $39

Riverdale | 5686 Riverdale Ave. (bet. 258th & 259th Sts.) | Bronx | 718-543-3850

"One of the more upscale" options on Riverdale's "main drag", this "popular" Italian fallback features "fresh, well-prepared" fare delivered by an "attentive" crew; those who "don't want to go" to Manhattan call it a "safe" bet.

Maggie Brown ●⇗ *American*

∇ 23 | 19 | 20 | $24

Clinton Hill | 455 Myrtle Ave. (bet. Washington & Waverly Aves.) | Brooklyn | 718-643-7001 | www.maggiebrownrestaurant.com

"Dinner's not bad", but it's the "brunch done right" – "comfort"-oriented Americana "recalling mom, if she went to culinary school" – that draws "mobs" to this "relaxed", cash-only Clinton Hill "hangout"; the "clever package" includes "spot-on" prices, "retro-homey" digs and "friendly" "bohemian" service.

Maharlika ⇗ *Filipino*

25 | 20 | 22 | $36

E Village | 111 First Ave. (bet. 6th & 7th Sts.) | 646-392-7880 | www.maharlikanyc.com

Filipino food gets "redefined" at this "hip" East Villager that jump-starts the "not-mainstream" cuisine with some modern "twists" (Spam fries, anyone?); its "enthusiastic audience" reports that its "cozy" mood, bargain tabs and "warm" service distract from the "tight seating" and cash-only policy.

Maialino ● Italian · 26 | 23 | 25 | $67

Gramercy | Gramercy Park Hotel | 2 Lexington Ave. (21st St.) | 212-777-2410 | www.maialinonyc.com

Everything "comes together perfectly" at Danny Meyer's "busy" Gramercy Italian, a near-"flawless" take on a Roman trattoria with a "delicious" menu highlighted by a "heavenly" namesake roast suckling pig; its "genuine hospitality", "bright country setting" and attention to "detail" signal a restaurant "at the top of its game" – no wonder it's so "hard to get a reservation."

NEW Maison O ●⊠ Japanese · - | - | - | M

Little Italy | 98 Kenmare St. (bet. Lafayette & Mulberry Sts.) | 212-274-9898 | www.maisononyc.com

Chef Tadashi Ono (ex Matsuri) is behind this Little Italy Japanese izakaya purveying a menu that runs the gamut from sushi to yakitori grill items; formerly known as Kenmare, the duplex setting feels more like a club than an eatery (the cult movie posters help), and late-night the action moves to its karaoke-friendly basement lounge.

Malagueta M Brazilian · ∇ 24 | 16 | 20 | $37

Astoria | 25-35 36th Ave. (28th St.) | Queens | 718-937-4821 | www.malaguetany.com

"You'll have to search" to find this family-owned "gem" in "residential" Astoria, but its "delicious", "real-deal" Brazilian fare is deemed "well worth the effort"; the "small storefront" digs are "nothing fancy", but "friendly" service and "reasonable" prices add value.

Malatesta Trattoria ●⊅ Italian · 24 | 16 | 20 | $38

W Village | 649 Washington St. (Christopher St.) | 212-741-1207

"Wonderful" trattoria-style staples at "reasonable", cash-only rates make this "friendly" way West Village Italian "popular" enough to justify "long waits"; the "simple" interior gets "crowded and noisy", but in summer there's "sidewalk dining."

Malecon ● Dominican · 21 | 12 | 16 | $20

Washington Heights | 4141 Broadway (175th St.) | 212-927-3812
W 90s | 764 Amsterdam Ave. (bet. 97th & 98th Sts.) | 212-864-5648
Kingsbridge | 5592 Broadway (231st St.) | Bronx | 718-432-5155
www.maleconrestaurants.com

Churning out "super-good" Dominican chow, this trio is famed for "finger-lickin' chicken" slathered in so much "garlicky goodness" it's best to "wear a bib"; given the mega-portions and mini-prices, fans excuse "hole-in-the-wall" looks and service as "slow" as the rotisserie.

Maloney & Porcelli Steak · 23 | 20 | 23 | $72

E 50s | 37 E. 50th St. (bet. Madison & Park Aves.) | 212-750-2233 | www.maloneyandporcelli.com

"Expense accounts" were made for Alan Stillman's Midtown chophouse, a "class operation all the way" where the steaks are "prepared to perfection" (and the signature pork shank "may be even better"); "clubby" decor and "friendly" service keep regulars regular, while its weekend wine dinners are an "exceptional value."

Mama Joy's ● *Southern* | - | - | - | I |

Bushwick | 1084 Flushing Ave. (Porter Ave.) | Brooklyn | 347-295-2227 |
www.mamajoys.com

Inhabiting a Bushwick block short on dining options, this modern Southern gastropub dishes out a small, modestly priced roster of belt-busting Dixie fare, washed down with beer, wine and cocktails; the down-home space features distressed brick walls lined with vintage photographs.

Mamajuana Cafe *Dominican/Nuevo Latino* | 21 | 20 | 19 | $41 |

Inwood | 247 Dyckman St. (Seaman Ave.) | 212-304-0140 ●
W 80s | 570 Amsterdam Ave. (bet. 87th & 88th Sts.) | 212-362-1514
Woodside | 33-15 56th St. (B'way) | Queens | 718-565-6454 ●
www.mamajuana-cafe.com

Admirers advise "go hungry" to these "inviting" Dominican-Nuevo Latino cafes serving "huge portions" of "delish" fare with "modern flair"; a "lively" scene fueled by "fantastic" sangria makes for "fun times", especially in summer in the Inwood original's sidewalk seats.

Mamoun's ●⇥ *Mideastern* | 23 | 7 | 16 | $8 |

E Village | 22 St. Marks Pl. (bet. 2nd & 3rd Aves.) | 212-387-7747
G Village | 119 MacDougal St. (bet. Bleecker & W. 3rd Sts.)
www.mamouns.com

This Middle Eastern Village duo vends "some of the best falafel" and shawarma around for beyond-"affordable" prices; indeed, it's such a "late-night munchies heaven" that few notice the so-so service and "hole-in-the-wall" settings.

Mandoo Bar *Korean* | 20 | 10 | 15 | $21 |

Garment District | 2 W. 32nd St. (bet. B'way & 5th Ave.) | 212-279-3075

"Man oh mandoo" – the "freshest", "fast and fab" dumplings made right in front of you are the main event at this "reliable" Garment District Korean; its "no-decor" digs are "small" and "often crowded", but "cheap" prices compensate.

Manducatis *Italian* | 23 | 16 | 21 | $45 |

LIC | 13-27 Jackson Ave. (47th Ave.) | Queens | 718-729-4602 |
www.manducatis.com

Manducatis Rustica *Italian*

LIC | 46-33 Vernon Blvd. (bet. 46th & 47th Sts.) | Queens | 718-937-1312 |
www.manducatisrustica.com

Like a "visit to the old country", this "warm", "family-run" LIC Italian supplies "wonderful" "homestyle" fare and wines from a "deep" list (pizza and gelato are the highlights of the "scaled-down" Rustica offshoot); yes, the look may be "dated", but loyalists say that only "adds to the charm."

Manetta's ⊠ *Italian* | 23 | 18 | 22 | $38 |

LIC | 10-76 Jackson Ave. (11th St.) | Queens | 718-786-6171

"Delish" Italiana "straight out of nonna's kitchen" – including "fantastic" wood-fired pizza – and service that's "all smiles" have locals calling this LIC "mainstay" the "perfect neighborhood restaurant"; "family-run" and kid-friendly, it "exudes comfort", especially in winter before the fireplace.

	FOOD	DECOR	SERVICE	COST

NEW Manon ●⊠ American — — — E
Meatpacking | 407 W. 14th St. (bet. 9th & 10th Aves.) | 212-596-7255 |
www.manon-nyc.com

Bringing some Vegas glitz to the Meatpacking District, this flashy new bar/lounge/restaurant rolls out a modern American menu in a soaring, brick- and velvet-lined space arranged over three levels; the tabs are as lofty as the ceilings, but its young, party-hearty crowd doesn't seem to mind.

NEW Manzanilla Spanish ▽ 23 22 23 $69
Murray Hill | 345 Park Ave. S. (26th St.) | 212-477-9400 |
www.manzanillanyc.com

This NYC version of the Malaga original brings "not-typical", cutting-edge Spanish cooking to Park Avenue South via modernist chef Dani Garcia; an "airy" setting and "efficient" service offset the pricey tariffs, and though a few fret it "tries too hard", most see lots of "potential."

Manzo Italian/Steak 25 16 21 $70
Flatiron | Eataly | 200 Fifth Ave. (bet. 23rd & 24th Sts.) | 212-229-2180 |
www.eataly.com

The sole "white-tablecloth" option within Eataly, the Batali-Bastianich team's Flatiron "foodie mecca", this "carnivore heaven" presents a "*delizioso*" beef-centric Italian menu that also features "wonderful fresh pastas"; being located in a "bustling", "noisy" market is "not the sexiest", and "you pay for the privilege" – but to most it's "worth every hard-earned penny."

Maoz Vegetarian Mideastern/Vegetarian 21 10 15 $12
E 100s | Central Park | Harlem Meer, 5th Ave. & 106th St.
G Village | 59 E. Eighth St. (bet. B'way & University Pl.) | 212-420-5999
Union Sq | 38 Union Sq. E. (bet. 16th & 17th Sts.) | 212-260-1988
W 40s | 558 Seventh Ave. (40th St.) | 212-777-0820 ●
W 40s | 683 Eighth Ave. (bet. 43rd & 44th Sts.) | 212-265-2315 ●
W 70s | 2047 Broadway (bet. 70th & 71st Sts.) | 212-362-2622 ●
W 100s | 2857 Broadway (bet. 110th & 111th Sts.) | 212-222-6464
www.maozusa.com

"Quick and easy" is the word on this Mideastern-vegetarian franchise where the falafel is "respectable", the tabs "economical" and the salads customizable at a "self-serve topping bar"; little decor and service lead many to reserve it "strictly for takeout."

Má Pêche American 23 18 20 $61
W 50s | Chambers Hotel | 15 W. 56th St. (bet. 5th & 6th Aves.) |
212-757-5878 | www.momofuku.com

Bringing a "welcome twist" to "corporate-dining" Midtown, David Chang's "urbane" New American offers an "inspired" menu and "interesting", large-format group meals; "lackadaisical" service, a "blasting soundtrack" and a "stark" setting may detract, but the "amazing" treats from the upstairs Momofuku Milk Bar help sweeten the experience.

Marble Lane ● Steak ▽ 21 25 20 $67
Chelsea | Dream Downtown Hotel | 355 W. 16th St. (bet. 8th & 9th Aves.) |
212-229-2559 | www.dreamdowntown.com

"Chic", nightclub-esque digs and *Top Chef* alum Manuel Treviño's "fine aged" meat draw "models and scenesters" to this under-the-radar

	FOOD	DECOR	SERVICE	COST

steakhouse in Chelsea's "trendy" Dream Downtown Hotel; the only beefs are variable service and "high prices."

Marc Forgione *American* | 26 | 23 | 24 | $72 |

TriBeCa | 134 Reade St. (bet. Greenwich & Hudson Sts.) | 212-941-9401 | www.marcforgione.com

Iron Chef Marc Forgione "takes comfort food to a new level" at this "candlelit, characterful" TriBeCa New American with an "upscale lodge" feel, patrolled by a "thoughtful" staff; it's a "perfect date" place – just book far ahead, plan on a "pricey" tab and know that the "crowded bar" can be "noisy."

Marcony ● *Italian* | 25 | 22 | 25 | $66 |

Murray Hill | 184 Lexington Ave. (bet. 31st & 32nd Sts.) | 646-837-6020 | www.marconyusa.com

When an "Italian vacation" isn't in the cards, there's always this Murray Hill "standout" whose "fantastic" classic dishes and "service to match" arrive in "transporting", "Capri-comes-to-NY" quarters; it's an "all-around wonderful dining experience" that justifies the "pricey" tab and the trip to an out-of-the-way block.

Marco Polo *Italian* | 20 | 17 | 20 | $44 |

Carroll Gardens | 345 Court St. (Union St.) | Brooklyn | 718-852-5015 | www.marcopoloristorante.com

They "treat you like family" at this circa-1983 Carroll Gardens Italian that serves an "upscale red-sauce" bill of fare; the "updated", tablecloth-free decor gets mixed reviews, but the fireplace and Marco Polo murals remain, along with the "friendly" service and moderate pricing.

Marea *Italian/Seafood* | 28 | 26 | 26 | $105 |

W 50s | 240 Central Park S. (bet. B'way & 7th Ave.) | 212-582-5100 | www.marea-nyc.com

"Memorable" is putting it mildly at chef Michael White's Columbus Circle "stunner", again voted NYC's No. 1 Italian thanks to "exquisite" seafood and pasta dispatched in a "quiet", "contemporary" setting by a "skilled, unobtrusive" team; it draws a "dressed-up" crowd of "celebs" and "one-percenters" who bring an "extra credit card" to settle the "astronomical" checks – though lunch is a "more affordable" option.

Maria Pia *Italian* | 19 | 16 | 19 | $41 |

W 50s | 319 W. 51st St. (bet. 8th & 9th Aves.) | 212-765-6463 | www.nycrg.com

"Geared to the pre-theater crowd", this "reliable" Hell's Kitchen "red-sauce joint" keeps 'em coming back with "quick" service, a "charming garden" and "reasonable" rates (especially the $26 dinner prix fixe); non-showgoers hit it "off-hours" to avoid the "noisy" crush.

Mario's Ⓜ *Italian* | 22 | 16 | 21 | $43 |

Fordham | 2342 Arthur Ave. (bet. Crescent Ave. & 184th St.) | Bronx | 718-584-1188 | www.mariosrestarthurave.com

An "iconic red-sauce" Bronx "home away from home", this 95-year-old Neapolitan on the "bustling" Arthur Avenue "tourist strip" "never steers you wrong"; "old-time waiters" working the "no-pretense" digs ensure regulars remain in their "comfort zone."

	FOOD	DECOR	SERVICE	COST

Mari Vanna ● *Russian* | 21 | 24 | 22 | $62 |

Flatiron | 41 E. 20th St. (bet. B'way & Park Ave. S.) | 212-777-1955 |
www.marivanna.ru

Like "stepping into your grandmother's house in Moscow" – but with a
"party" vibe fueled by "flowing vodka" – this "fabulous" Flatiron magnet for "expats" and "beautiful young things" serves up "hearty"
Russian staples; "attentive" service and a "unique-in-NY" experience
help justify the "pricey" tab.

Market Table *American* | 23 | 20 | 21 | $54 |

W Village | 54 Carmine St. (Bedford St.) | 212-255-2100 |
www.markettablenyc.com

As the name implies, this West Villager spotlights "farmer's market-
fresh" ingredients on its "up-to-date" New American menu; the "bustling" room with "huge windows" overlooking the passing scene skews
"tight" and "noisy", but "friendly" staffers help keep things "comfy."

MarkJoseph Steakhouse *Steak* | 24 | 19 | 22 | $77 |

Financial District | 261 Water St. (bet. Dover St. & Peck Slip) |
212-277-0020 | www.markjosephsteakhouse.com

Pack a "huuuge appetite" and "corporate card" to best enjoy this "out-of-
the-way" FiDi chop shop where "lunch is a better value"; "no-frills",
"standard steakhouse" digs put the focus on the "outstanding" beef (and
"even better" bacon appetizer) delivered by "knowledgeable" staffers.

The Mark Restaurant ● *American* | 22 | 24 | 23 | $79 |

E 70s | Mark Hotel | 25 E. 77th St. (bet. 5th & Madison Aves.) |
212-606-3030 | www.themarkrestaurantnyc.com

"Another dining coup" by Jean-Georges Vongerichten, this "very UES"
enclave is "always on the mark" with "top-notch" New American fare
and "deferential" service at predictably "high prices"; since the
"lovely" dining room is usually on the "quiet" side, go-getters head for
the "vibrant bar."

Markt *Belgian* | 20 | 17 | 18 | $44 |

Flatiron | 676 Sixth Ave. (21st St.) | 212-727-3314 |
www.marktrestaurant.com

There's "nothing fishy" about this "busy", all-day Flatiron brasserie,
just "mussels in excelsis" and other "simple", "tasty" Belgian staples
backed up by a "gazillion excellent beers"; the acoustics are "loud"
and service can be "hurried", but that's just part of the "fun" package.

Marlow & Sons ● *American* | 24 | 19 | 21 | $43 |

Williamsburg | 81 Broadway (bet. Berry St. & Wythe Ave.) | Brooklyn |
718-384-1441 | www.marlowandsons.com

"Pitch-perfect", "farm-fresh" New Americana from a "limited", "daily
changing" lineup is the lure at this all-day Williamsburg pioneer that
still packs plenty of "hipster" cred; the "rustic", micro-size confines
can be "cramped", so many angle to "sit outside."

NEW The Marrow *German/Italian* | ∇ 23 | 20 | 22 | $67 |

W Village | 99 Bank St. (Greenwich St.) | 212-428-6000 |
www.themarrownyc.com

Top Chef winner Harold Dieterle (Kin Shop, Perilla) pays homage to his
Italian/German heritage at his latest West Village "hot spot", where

the "hearty", meat-centric menu is accompanied by a "brilliant" European wine list; service is "excellent" and the window-lined room "airy", and despite "loud" decibels and "expensive" tabs, this newcomer already looks like "another hit."

Marseille *French/Mediterranean*   21 | 19 | 20 | $49

W 40s | 630 Ninth Ave. (44th St.) | 212-333-2323 | www.marseillenyc.com
"Like being in Paris – but with better service" – this Hell's Kitchen French-Med brasserie serves a "well-priced", "quality" menu in a rather "hectic" room that suggests "Casablanca"; its trump card is "convenience" to Broadway theaters, and they know how to "get you out in time for your curtain."

Maruzzella ● *Italian*   20 | 15 | 20 | $49

E 70s | 1483 First Ave. (bet. 77th & 78th Sts.) | 212-988-8877 | www.maruzzellanyc.com
There's "nothing fancy" about this UES "quintessential neighborhood Italian", just "surprisingly good" cooking brought to table by "old-school" servers; "friendly owners" on the scene and "reasonable"-for-the-zip-code rates make the "modest" decor easy to overlook.

Mary's Fish Camp ⊠ *Seafood*   25 | 14 | 20 | $45

W Village | 64 Charles St. (4th St.) | 646-486-2185 | www.marysfishcamp.com
"Like a visit to Cape Cod", this "funky" Village seafood shack is famed for its "kicking lobster rolls" served in a "primitive" room by a "heavily tattooed" crew; sinkers include "cramped" seats and a "no-rez" rule that leads to "long waits", but ultimately the "hard-to-beat" fish triumphs.

Mas (Farmhouse) ● *American*   27 | 25 | 26 | $96

W Village | 39 Downing St. (bet. Bedford & Varick Sts.) | 212-255-1790 | www.masfarmhouse.com
"Everything you could ask for in a dining experience", this "cozy" West Village American is a "foodie must", showcasing the "amazing", "farm-to-table" skills of chef Galen Zamarra; "polished" service and an "intimate" ambiance set the stage for "romantic" dalliances, and although decidedly pricey, it's "worth every penny."

Mas (La Grillade) ● *American*   23 | 22 | 24 | $78

W Village | 28 Seventh Ave. S. (bet. Leroy & Morton Sts.) | 212-255-1795 | www.maslagrillade.com
From "talented" chef Galen Zamarra comes this "special" West Village follow-up to Mas (Farmhouse) that specializes in "interesting" Americana prepared on a wood-fired grill; partisans praise the "relaxed" service, "magical smell" and attention to "detail", though a few fault the "pricey" tariffs and decor that "leaves a bit to be desired."

Masa ⊠ *Japanese*   27 | 24 | 25 | $585

W 60s | Time Warner Ctr. | 10 Columbus Circle, 4th fl. (60th St. at B'way) | 212-823-9800
Bar Masa ⊠ *Japanese*
W 60s | Time Warner Ctr. | 10 Columbus Circle, 4th fl. (60th St. at B'way) | 212-823-9800
www.masanyc.com
Chef Masayoshi Takayama's "transcendent" skills yield "superlative sushi" worthy of a "last meal" at this "tranquil" Time Warner Center

Japanese, though the notorious $450-and-up prix fixes leave a massive "hole in your wallet"; "a bargain compared" to the main room, the adjacent bar is an "excellent way to sample" the wares à la carte.

Max *Italian*

▽ 18	16	18	$35

TriBeCa | 181 Duane St. (bet. Greenwich & Hudson Sts.) | 212-966-5939 | www.max-ny.com

"Amazing housemade pastas" and other "hearty" Italian basics offered at some of the "best prices in Manhattan" keep locals loyal to this "friendly" TriBeCa eatery; it's "not the most elegant place", but regulars report it's "enjoyable" overall.

Max Caffe ● *Italian*

23	17	16	$29

W 100s | 1262 Amsterdam Ave. (bet. 122nd & 123rd Sts.) | 212-531-1210

Max SoHa ●⊄ *Italian*

W 100s | 1274 Amsterdam Ave. (123rd St.) | 212-531-2221 | www.maxsoha.com

"Popular with the Columbia crowd", these "friendly", low-cost UWS spots have two distinct personalities: cash-only SoHa offers "rustic" Italian staples in a "cozy" space with the option to "eat outside", while the Caffe features "comfy couches and chairs for relaxing and eating."

Maya *Mexican*

23	19	20	$53

E 60s | 1191 First Ave. (bet. 64th & 65th Sts.) | 212-585-1818 | www.richardsandoval.com

The words "upscale" and "refined" are "not usually associated with a Mexican restaurant", but this "sophisticated" Upper Eastsider is just that, serving "delectable" food in a "remodeled" room that includes an adjacent tequileria; sure, it's "noisy" as heck and the tabs skew "expensive", but it's still considered a "special treat."

NEW Maysville *American*

▽ 22	20	20	$62

Flatiron | 17 W. 26th St. (bet. B'way & 6th Ave.) | 646-490-8240 | www.maysvillenyc.com

From the team behind Brooklyn's Char No. 4 comes this new Flatiron spot offering "solid" New Americana paired with an "amazing whiskey selection"; "loud" acoustics and "overcrowded" conditions detract, but "strong drinks" and just the "right amount of trendiness" compensate.

Maze *French*

24	21	21	$69

W 50s | London NYC Hotel | 151 W. 54th St. (bet. 6th & 7th Aves.) | 212-468-8889 | www.gordonramsay.com

This New French eatery proffers "simple, elegant" small plates in a "bustling" space off the lobby of Midtown's "fashionable" London NYC Hotel; those who find it "too noisy" and "pricey" at dinner note it's "terrific" for a quieter lunch, when there's a "wonderful" $29 prix fixe.

Maz Mezcal *Mexican*

20	18	20	$40

E 80s | 316 E. 86th St. (bet. 1st & 2nd Aves.) | 212-472-1599 | www.mazmezcal.com

"Hits all the right spots" say Yorkville locals of this "family-owned" Mexican "standby" where a "lively neighborhood crowd" assembles for "tasty" classics; "reasonable prices" and "friendly" service are two more reasons it's "still packed after all these years."

	FOOD	DECOR	SERVICE	COST

McCormick & Schmick's *Seafood/Steak* | 18 | 18 | 19 | $54 |

W 50s | 1285 Sixth Ave. (bet. 51st & 52nd Sts.) | 212-459-1222 |
www.mccormickandschmicks.com

There are "no surprises" at this Rock Center–area "corporate" surf 'n'
turf house – and "sometimes that's exactly what you want"; "reliable"
fresh fare and "solid" service in "publike" environs are what's on offer,
along with one of the "best happy hours" in these parts.

Meatball Shop ● *Sandwiches* | 24 | 17 | 19 | $24 |

NEW **Chelsea** | 200 Ninth Ave. (22nd St.) | 212-257-4363
NEW **E 70s** | 1462 Second Ave. (bet. 76th & 77th Sts.) | 212-257-6121
LES | 84 Stanton St. (bet. Allen & Orchard Sts.) | 212-982-8895
W Village | 64 Greenwich Ave. (Perry St.) | 212-982-7815
Williamsburg | 170 Bedford Ave. (bet. N. 7th & 8th Sts.) | Brooklyn |
718-551-0520
www.themeatballshop.com

"So many choices, so little time" is the dilemma at these "hipster"
sandwich shops specializing in "mouthwatering", "super-cheap"
meatballs (finished off with "must-have" ice cream sandwiches);
since the "cramped" locations are "small" and "well known", "long
waits" come with the territory.

Megu *Japanese* | 24 | 26 | 22 | $91 |

TriBeCa | 62 Thomas St. (bet. Church St. & W. B'way) | 212-964-7777
Megu Midtown *Japanese*
E 40s | Trump World Tower | 845 United Nations Plaza (bet. 47th &
48th Sts.) | 212-964-7777
www.megurestaurants.com

"Impressive", "over-the-top" decor centered around a "giant Buddha"
ice sculpture sets the stage for "delectable" modern Japanese "fine
dining" at these TriBeCa-Midtown East "stunners", where "meticulous"
service takes the edge off "steep" tabs; they're perfect for a "power
meal", "date" or any time "someone else is paying."

Mehtaphor ⬧ *Eclectic* | ∇ 24 | 18 | 22 | $57 |

TriBeCa | Duane Street Hotel | 130 Duane St. (Church St.) | 212-542-9440 |
www.mehtaphornyc.com

"Super-talented" chef Jehangir Mehta turns out "terrific, original"
Eclectic small plates at this "cool" TriBeCan in the Duane Street Hotel;
"accommodating" service is another reason to "love the place"
despite "shoeboxlike" dimensions.

Melba's *American/Southern* | 24 | 20 | 21 | $32 |

Harlem | 300 W. 114th St. (8th Ave.) | 212-864-7777 |
www.melbasrestaurant.com

"Divine chicken 'n' waffles" and other "Southern"-accented American
comfort classics "done right" are the thing at this "warm" Harlem retreat; its "small" setting is "chill and homey" by day, "hopping and groov-
ing" come evening (especially on Tuesdays when there's live music).

NEW **Meli** ⬧ *Greek* | – | – | – | M |

Murray Hill | 1 E. 35th St. (5th Ave.) | 212-481-6354 |
www.melinyc.com

Updated Aegean classics star at this midpriced Murray Hill Greek that
offers seafood and meat entrees matched with fruity cocktails and old-

school ouzos; the modern, white-on-white space is decorated with an elaborate chandelier and large photomurals of Greek landscapes.

Mémé ● *Mediterranean/Moroccan* | 22 | 16 | 20 | $41

W Village | 581 Hudson St. (Bank St.) | 646-692-8450 | www.memeonhudson.com

It's the "Mediterranean on Hudson Street" at this "affordable" West Villager dispensing "wonderful" small plates and entrees with "Moroccan flair"; "friendly" service and an appealing "bohemian" vibe will "keep you returning", unless the "tight-packed tables" make you feel like you're "flying coach."

Menchanko-tei *Japanese/Noodle Shop* | 19 | 12 | 16 | $23

E 40s | 131 E. 45th St. (bet. Lexington & 3rd Aves.) | 212-986-6805
W 50s | 43 W. 55th St., 2nd fl. (bet. 5th & 6th Aves.) | 212-541-7145
www.menchankotei.com

"Big bowls" brimming with "delicious broth and slurpy noodles" come out "lightning fast" at these "no-frills" Midtown ramen joints that are "packed during lunch"; ok, they're "tiny, cramped" "holes-in-the-wall" with "brusque" service, but at least the "price is right."

Menkui Tei *Japanese/Noodle Shop* | 20 | 10 | 17 | $18

E Village | 63 Cooper Sq. (bet. 7th St. & St Marks Pl.) | 212-228-4152 ●⌿
W 50s | 58 W. 56th St. (bet. 5th & 6th Aves.) | 212-707-8702

"Hang out with Japanese salarymen" at these low-budget "real ramen bars" ladling out "slurp-worthy noodles" and other "quick", "delicious" classics; despite decidedly "unpretentious" settings, they're on the "regular rotation" for many folks.

Mercadito ● *Mexican* | 24 | 16 | 18 | $34

E Village | 179 Ave. B (bet. 10th & 11th Sts.) | 212-529-6490
W Village | 100 Seventh Ave. S. (Grove St.) | 212-647-0830
www.mercaditorestaurants.com

To "quench taco cravings", hit these crosstown Mexican "favorites" where the "fair-priced", "authentic tastes" are best washed down with a "terrific margarita" or two; both the service and the "tight" quarters are "undistinguished", but in warm weather, the West Villager's patio is the "spot to be."

Mercato ● *Italian* | 21 | 17 | 19 | $43

Garment District | 352 W. 39th St. (bet. 8th & 9th Aves.) | 212-643-2000 | www.mercatonyc.com

A "pleasant surprise" in the restaurant-"barren" zone near Port Authority, this "well-kept secret" slings "genuine homestyle" Italian food at "reasonable" rates; its "cozy", "brick-walled" room tended by a "warm" staff is "worth seeking out" if you're in the area.

Mercer Kitchen ● *American/French* | 22 | 22 | 20 | $54

SoHo | Mercer Hotel | 99 Prince St. (Mercer St.) | 212-966-5454 | www.themercerkitchen.com

Ever "chic", Jean-Georges Vongerichten's "still buzzy" SoHo vet in the Mercer Hotel is touted for "enjoyable" Franco-American cooking offered in "dimly lit" subterranean digs; given the "social" atmospherics and servers who "don't rush you", it's "easy to talk and linger" here.

	FOOD	DECOR	SERVICE	COST

Mermaid Inn *Seafood*　　　　　21 | 17 | 20 | $46

E Village | 96 Second Ave. (bet. 5th & 6th Sts.) | 212-674-5870
W 80s | 568 Amsterdam Ave. (bet. 87th & 88th Sts.) | 212-799-7400
Mermaid Oyster Bar *Seafood*

G Village | 79 MacDougal St. (bet. Bleecker & Houston Sts.) | 212-260-0100
www.themermaidnyc.com

"Like being in Nantucket", these "neighborly" seafooders provide "well-
seasoned" catch (including a "lovely" lobster roll) in funky nautical
settings; "jolly" vibes, "good-humored" service and "bargain" oysters
at the "happy hour-and-a-half" are further reasons why it's often
"packed to the gills."

Mesa Coyoacan *Mexican*　　　∇ 24 | 20 | 20 | $35

Williamsburg | 372 Graham Ave. (bet. Conselyea St. & Skillman Ave.) |
Brooklyn | 718-782-8171 | www.mesacoyoacan.com

"Why fly to Mexico City" when there's this Williamsburg standout
proffering "incredible tacos" and other "authentic", "damn fine" dishes
in "hip, fun" digs; "amazing margaritas" and "inexpensive" tabs are additional reasons why locals declare "you will not be disappointed."

Meskerem *Ethiopian*　　　　　23 | 12 | 17 | $26

G Village | 124 MacDougal St. (bet. Bleecker & W. 3rd Sts.) | 212-777-8111
If you're "looking for something different", this "hole-in-the-wall",
"no-fork-necessary" Village Ethiopian offers "delicious" traditional
dishes "eaten with the hands" using "spongy" injera bread; wallet-
friendly rates trump "no decor" and "lackadaisical" service.

Meson Sevilla *Spanish*　　　　20 | 15 | 21 | $42

W 40s | 344 W. 46th St. (bet. 8th & 9th Aves.) | 212-262-5890 |
www.mesonsevilla.com

Theater ticket–holders seeking a paella fix turn to this "popular"
Restaurant Row Spaniard (with Italian dishes too) for "pleasant" prov-
ender and sangria; the room's "a bit tatty" and gets "elbow-to-elbow"
pre-curtain, but it's hard to beat the rates or location.

MexiBBQ ● *BBQ/Mexican*　　　21 | 21 | 19 | $27

Astoria | 37-11 30th Ave. (bet. 37th & 38th Sts.) | Queens | 718-626-0333 |
www.mexiqny.com

"Dozens of beers on tap" are the claim to fame of this "high-energy"
Astorian, which also earns olés for its "*muy bueno*" low-cost Mexican
BBQ; "friendly" servers work the "industrial-chic" interior – "now if
they would just take reservations."

Mexicana Mama Ⓜ *Mexican*　　23 | 15 | 19 | $34

G Village | 47 E. 12th St. (bet. B'way & University Pl.) | 212-253-7594
W Village | 525 Hudson St. (bet. Charles & W. 10th Sts.) | 212-924-4119
"*Pequeño* place", *grande* taste sums up these "minuscule" Village
Mexicans doling out "addictive" eats at "fair prices"; they're "always
packed" with "long waits", so regulars either go "early" or do delivery.

Mexican Radio ● *Mexican*　　　21 | 16 | 18 | $33

NoLita | 19 Cleveland Pl. (bet. Kenmare & Spring Sts.) | 212-343-0140 |
www.mexrad.com

This "casual" NoLita longtimer "comes in loud and clear" thanks to
"better-than-average" Mexican "standards" washed down with some

of the "best margaritas"; the decor's "not very impressive", but the "party" people don't seem to mind.

Mexico Lindo   *Mexican*
▽ 22 | 17 | 22 | $35

Gramercy | 459 Second Ave. (26th St.) | 212-679-3665 | www.mexicolindonyc.com

A Gramercy Park "fixture", this circa-1972 "neighborhood" Mexican is touted for its "truly authentic", "down-to-earth" cooking, "friendly" service and "best-buy" prices; maybe it "needs a makeover", but no one cares "after a margarita or two."

Mexicue   *BBQ/Mexican*
19 | 13 | 17 | $17

Chelsea | 345 Seventh Ave. (bet. 29th & 30th Sts.) | 212-244-0002 ⌧
LES | 106 Forsyth St. (bet. Broome & Grand Sts.) | 646-559-4100
www.mexicue.com

It's the "popular food truck" gone "brick-and-mortar" at these LES-Chelsea spin-offs offering the same "fresh", Mexican-meets-BBQ fare served "quick" in "small", colorful settings; "very reasonable prices" compensate for the "just satisfactory" ambiance.

Mezzaluna ● *Italian*
21 | 15 | 18 | $47

E 70s | 1295 Third Ave. (bet. 74th & 75th Sts.) | 212-535-9600 | www.mezzalunanyc.com

Pizza Mezzaluna   *Pizza*

G Village | 146 W. Houston St. (MacDougal St.) | 212-533-1242 | www.pizzamezzalunanyc.com

Despite the "tiniest" of dimensions, this 30-year-old UES Italian "staple" boasts a "strong" track record, "swiftly" sending out wood-oven pizzas ("the highlight") and other "soulful" standards in "crowded" digs; its Village sibling supplies a similar menu geared toward takeout.

Mezzogiorno   *Italian*
21 | 18 | 20 | $47

SoHo | 195 Spring St. (Sullivan St.) | 212-334-2112 | www.mezzogiorno.com

"Authentic, ample" Italiana is the forte of this "cute little" SoHo stalwart, an "old reliable" whose "cheerful" atmosphere and "attentive" service keep the "locals and tourists" coming back for more; insiders angle for a table outside or by the "open French doors."

Michael Jordan's The Steak House NYC ● *Steak*
21 | 21 | 20 | $67

E 40s | Grand Central | 23 Vanderbilt Ave. (43rd St.) | 212-655-2300 | www.michaeljordansnyc.com

It's the "unusual location" – a balcony overlooking the "scurrying" masses in Grand Central's Main Concourse – that's the hook at this "reliable" chophouse, where the beef is "aged" and the prices "high"; critics find "nothing original" going on, but the "wonderful" views provide ample distraction.

Michael's ⌧ *Californian*
22 | 23 | 23 | $69

W 50s | 24 W. 55th St. (bet. 5th & 6th Aves.) | 212-767-0555 | www.michaelsnewyork.com

"Media titans" are drawn to this "classy", 25-year-old Midtowner that's known more for its breakfast and lunch "power" scenes than its "fresh", "premium-priced" Californian fare and "pro" service; "relaxed" dinner comes "without the hot crowd", but no matter when you dine, the "lovely" room's "fresh flowers and art" are a constant.

	FOOD	DECOR	SERVICE	COST

NEW Mighty Quinn's Barbecue *BBQ*   `24` `13` `16` `$23`

E Village | 103 Second Ave. (6th St.) | 212-677-3733 |
www.mightyquinnsbbq.com

An "awesome addition" to NYC's BBQ wars, this new East Villager specializes in slow-cooked 'cue, combining techniques from Texan and Carolinian pitmasters; "phenomenal prices", an "industrial-cool" design and the "self-serve, slap-it-on-a-platter" process draw "young" types who don't mind the "mob-scene" atmosphere.

Mike's Bistro *American/Kosher*   `24` `18` `22` `$56`

W 70s | 228 W. 72nd St. (bet. B'way & West End Ave.) | 212-799-3911 |
www.mikesbistro.com

Kosher food gets the "gourmet" treatment at this Upper Westsider where the eponymous chef-owner turns out "delicious" New American dishes; yes, "you pay" for the privilege, but "wonderful service" and "Mike going from table to table" add value – "his mother must be kvelling."

Mile End *Deli*   `23` `13` `18` `$25`

Boerum Hill | 97 Hoyt St. (bet. Atlantic Ave. & Pacific St.) | Brooklyn |
718-852-7510

Mile End Sandwich Shop *Sandwiches*

NoHo | 53 Bond St. (bet. Bowery & Lafayette St.) | 212-529-2990
www.mileenddeli.com

For a "novel take on traditional deli food", check out these "quirky" joints offering Montreal-style Jewish classics made with "amazing" meats cured and smoked in-house; despite "tight-squeeze" dimensions, "small tables" and variable service, both locations are "wildly popular", especially with the "hipster" set.

Mill Basin Deli *Deli/Kosher*   `22` `16` `19` `$26`

Mill Basin | 5823 Ave. T (bet. 58th & 59th Sts.) | Brooklyn | 718-241-4910 |
www.millbasindeli.com

"Memories of delis past come alive" when noshing on a "what-could-be-better pastrami on rye" at this circa-1972 Mill Basin vet; given such "rich Jewish delicacies" and a setting dressed up with "gallery"-worthy fine art, mavens tolerate the no-frills service and "Manhattan prices."

Millesime *Seafood*   `19` `20` `18` `$64`

Murray Hill | Carlton Hotel | 92 Madison Ave. (29th St.) | 212-889-7100 |
www.millesimerestaurant.com

"Tucked away" in the Carlton Hotel, this "pretty" Murray Hill seafooder is appreciated as much for its "enchanting" stained-glass skylight as for its "fresh", pricey fin fare; a "quiet oasis" by day, it "comes alive" after dark with occasional live jazz.

Milos ◑ *Greek/Seafood*   `27` `24` `24` `$87`

W 50s | 125 W. 55th St. (bet. 6th & 7th Aves.) | 212-245-7400 |
www.milos.ca

"Absolutely delectable" seafood arrives in a "sleek", "airy" room at this "gold-standard" Midtown Hellenic, where the "just-caught" catch is as "impeccable" as the "brisk" service; "by-the-pound pricing" adds up to "sky-high" tabs, but the lunch and pre-theater prix fixes are "experiments in Greek austerity."

	FOOD	DECOR	SERVICE	COST

Mimi's Hummus *Mideastern*
24 | 15 | 20 | $22

Ditmas Park | 1209 Cortelyou Rd. (bet. Argyle & Westminster Rds.) | Brooklyn | 718-284-4444 | www.mimishummus.com

"Phenomenal housemade hummus" and the "fluffiest" pita are highlights of the "limited menu" of "delicious" Middle Eastern eats at this "modest" Ditmas Park standout; "inexpensive" prices and "friendly" vibrations make up for the "teeny-tiny" dimensions and "cramped" conditions.

Minca ●⊄ *Japanese/Noodle Shop*
▽ 23 | 10 | 18 | $19

E Village | 536 E. Fifth St. (bet. Aves. A & B) | 212-505-8001 | www.newyorkramen.com

There are "no pretenses" at this "basic" East Village noodle shop, just the "charming simplicity" of "excellent" ramen with the "most slurp-worthy broth"; the "tiny" space is "perpetually packed", but at least the service is "fast" and the prices "affordable."

Minetta Tavern ● *French*
24 | 21 | 21 | $67

G Village | 113 MacDougal St. (Minetta Ln.) | 212-475-3850 | www.minettatavernny.com

Channeling "long-gone better times", Keith McNally's "retro" remodel of a classic 1937 Village tavern is still "sceney" thanks to French cooking that's as "delicious" as the "Madonna-Gwyneth-Sting" celeb-sightings; the "back room" is the place to sit and the "epic" Black Label burger the thing to order, provided you can snag a "difficult reservation."

Miranda *Italian/Pan-Latin*
23 | 21 | 24 | $44

Williamsburg | 80 Berry St. (N. 9th St.) | Brooklyn | 718-387-0711 | www.mirandarestaurant.com

The "food is full of love, as is the service" at this Williamsburg "neighborhood gem" dishing out an "inspired" mix of Italian and Pan-Latin dishes; "hidden in an old saloon" space, it offers a rare-for-the-area "minimal noise level", further inspiring first-timers to "become regulars."

NEW Mira Sushi & Izakaya ⊠ *Japanese*
▽ 28 | 26 | 27 | $37

Flatiron | 46 W. 22nd (5th & 6th Aves.) | 212-989-7889 | www.mirasushi.com

"Trendy vibes" emanate from this new Japanese izakaya–cum–sushi bar in the Flatiron, offering "creative", street food–inspired small plates and raw items in low-lit, brick-walled digs; "friendly" service and "fair prices" ice the cake.

Miriam *Israeli/Mediterranean*
21 | 17 | 19 | $33

Park Slope | 79 Fifth Ave. (Prospect Pl.) | Brooklyn | 718-622-2250 | www.miriamrestaurant.com

"Dinner is a pleasure" but "brunch is the meal" that has Park Slopers flocking to this "affordable" Israeli-Med, whose narrow space is a "mob scene" on weekends, but happily service remains "prompt"; "go at off times" for a calmer taste of its "tasty" fare.

Misdemeanor ● *Eclectic*
- | - | - | M

Downtown Bklyn | NU Hotel | 85 Smith St. (bet. Atlantic Ave. & State St.) | Brooklyn | 718-852-8585 | www.nuhotelbrooklyn.com

Consulting chef Jehangir Mehta (Graffiti, Mehtaphor) has put together a limited menu of Eclectic small plates at this cafe in Downtown

Brooklyn's NU Hotel, where the biggest draw may be the expansive sidewalk seating running along Smith Street.

Mission Chinese Food ❶ *Chinese*

| 23 | 13 | 17 | $34 |

LES | 154 Orchard St. (bet. Rivington & Stanton Sts.) | 212-529-8800 | www.missionchinesefood.com

"When they say spicy, they mean it" at this Lower East Side "cult hit", where chef Danny Bowien's "Californian Sichuan" cooking features "intense", "thermonuclear" spicing that's "not for the masses"; "crazy waits", "hole-in-the-wall" looks and "elbow-to-elbow" seating aren't deterring the crowds, and regulars are thrilled that it's now accepting limited reservations.

Miss Korea BBQ ❶🅭Ⓜ *Korean*

| 22 | 19 | 20 | $36 |

Garment District | 10 W. 32nd St. (bet. B'way & 5th Ave.) | 212-594-4963 | www.misskoreabbq.com

Ok, the "name is odd", but the food's "delicious" at this "busy" Korean BBQ specialist; its Zen-like quarters are "lovely" and "spacious compared to others" in K-town, and the prices are "competitive", so no surprise it's "always packed."

Miss Lily's ❶ *Jamaican*

| 21 | 20 | 20 | $38 |

G Village | 132 W. Houston St. (Sullivan St.) | 646-588-5375 | www.misslilysnyc.com

"*The* place to be" for "cool" cats, Serge Becker's "sexy" Village Jamaican features a clever "diner"-like interior pulsing with "hip" island tunes and overseen by an "utterly beautiful" staff; the well-priced Caribbean chow is "delicious" (especially at "killer brunch"), but it's really more about the "bumping" scene.

Miss Mamie's *Soul Food/Southern*

| 22 | 13 | 18 | $26 |

Harlem | 366 W. 110th St. (bet. Columbus & Manhattan Aves.) | 212-865-6744

Miss Maude's *Soul Food/Southern*

Harlem | 547 Lenox Ave. (bet. 137th & 138th Sts.) | 212-690-3100 | www.spoonbreadinc.com

"Real Southern comfort food" in "tremendous portions" keeps the crowds coming to these Harlem soul fooders; ok, the decor is "kind of plain" and the "friendly" servers "can be slow", but no one minds given the "tasty" eats and "fair prices."

The Modern *American/French*

| 26 | 26 | 25 | $127 |

W 50s | Museum of Modern Art | 9 W. 53rd St. (bet. 5th & 6th Aves.) | 212-333-1220 | www.themodernnyc.com

"Pure class all the way", this Danny Meyer "triumph" is a "truly special" MoMA showcase for "inspired" French–New American cooking served by a "choreographed" team; the "exquisite" view of the sculpture garden helps justify the "steep" prix fixe–only tabs, though "more affordable" small plates are available à la carte in the "busy" front bar.

Moim Ⓜ *Korean*

| 23 | 23 | 20 | $39 |

Park Slope | 206 Garfield Pl. (7th Ave.) | Brooklyn | 718-499-8092 | www.moimrestaurant.com

"Creative" Korean cookery comes to Park Slope via this "unique" spot where the "high-class" food belies the moderate costs; "modern" decor and a "lovely" garden add to its allure, and since it's "not the big new thing" anymore, there are "no more ridiculous waits" for a table.

Mojave ● *Southwestern* 22 | 23 | 20 | $32

Astoria | 22-36 31st St. (bet. Ditmars Blvd. & 23rd Ave.) | Queens | 718-545-4100 | www.mojaveny.com

A place for "good times" with friends or family, this spacious Astorian plies "flavorful" Southwestern grub and "fabulous margaritas" in a "beautiful" hacienda with a pleasant patio out back; low prices and "welcoming" service cement its standing as a solid "neighborhood spot."

Móle *Mexican* 21 | 16 | 17 | $37

E 80s | 1735 Second Ave. (bet. 89th & 90th Sts.) | 212-289-8226
LES | 205 Allen St. (Houston St.) | 212-777-3200 ⊞
W Village | 57 Jane St. (Hudson St.) | 212-206-7559
Williamsburg | 178 Kent Ave. (N. 4th St.) | Brooklyn | 347-384-2300
www.molenyc.com

"Tasty", "authentic" Mexican food turns up at this "everyday" mini-chain that seals the deal with "even better" margaritas; "tight" confines, "loud music" and "hurried" service are trumped by fair prices and a "good happy hour."

Molly's ● *Pub Food* 22 | 19 | 21 | $29

Gramercy | 287 Third Ave. (bet. 22nd & 23rd Sts.) | 212-889-3361 | www.mollysshebeen.com

A burger that "could vie for best in town", the "freshest pints" and "lovely Colleens waiting on you" make this "step-back-in-time" Irish pub a Gramercy "favorite"; it's the "real deal" with a "like-in-Dublin" feel that includes a "sawdust-covered floor" and "wood-burning fireplace."

Molyvos *Greek* 23 | 20 | 21 | $59

W 50s | 871 Seventh Ave. (bet. 55th & 56th Sts.) | 212-582-7500 | www.molyvos.com

An "oh-so-convenient location" to Carnegie Hall and City Center is one of the draws at this "perennial favorite" that follows through with "delicious" Greek grub and "amiable" service; "nice decor", "bearable" acoustics and a "spacious-by-Manhattan-standards" setting complete the "solid" picture.

Momofuku Ko ● *American* 27 | 19 | 23 | $163

E Village | 163 First Ave. (bet. 10th & 11th Sts.) | 212-500-0831 | www.momofuku.com

"Creativity" thrives at David Chang's East Village "blast", where "avant-garde", Asian-accented American plates are served in a tasting format at a 12-seat chef's counter; sure, the online-only rezzies are "tough" to get and the $125 set price is not for every budget, but the payoff is "truly memorable" dining.

Momofuku Noodle Bar *American* 24 | 16 | 18 | $35

E Village | 171 First Ave. (bet. 10th & 11th Sts.) | 212-777-7773 | www.momofuku.com

The "original David Chang establishment", this 10-year-old East Village American is renowned for its "juicy" pork buns and "gold-standard" ramen; the setting's "nothing fancy" with "bench seating" and "in-and-out service", but "excellent value" makes for the "crazy crowds" and "long lines."

	FOOD	DECOR	SERVICE	COST

Momofuku Ssäm Bar ❶ *American* | 25 | 17 | 20 | $50 |

E Village | 207 Second Ave. (13th St.) | 212-254-3500 | www.momofuku.com

"Truly creative", David Chang's "cool" East Villager rolls out a "mad-value", Asian-accented American menu that's highlighted by a "to-die-for" bo ssäm pork shoulder feast; "stark" looks and "loud" decibels come with the territory, as do "long lines."

Momo Sushi Shack ✍ *Japanese* | ▽ 27 | 22 | 25 | $31 |

Bushwick | 43 Bogart St. (Moore St.) | Brooklyn | 718-418-6666 | www.momosushishack.com

"Definitely not a shack", this "trendy", cash-only Bushwick Japanese serves "interesting, delicious" small plates and sushi at "wooden communal tables" geared toward the "hipster" trade; it "fills up fast" despite an "unexpected location", so "get there early."

Momoya *Japanese* | 23 | 19 | 20 | $44 |

Chelsea | 185 Seventh Ave. (21st St.) | 212-989-4466
W 80s | 427 Amsterdam Ave. (bet. 80th & 81st Sts.) | 212-580-0007
www.momoyanyc.com

Sushi sophisticates head to this "unassuming" Chelsea-UWS Japanese duo for "generous portions" of "amazingly fresh" fish plus "top-notch entrees" at "won't-break-the-bank" prices; "modern" decor and "helpful" service are other reasons why it's "always bustling."

Monkey Bar ❶⛔ *American* | 20 | 23 | 20 | $68 |

E 50s | Elysée Hotel | 60 E. 54th St. (bet. Madison & Park Aves.) | 212-308-2950 | www.monkeybarnewyork.com

"Jazz-age ambiance" endures at Graydon Carter's Midtown canteen festooned with "fun" murals of 1920s-era celebs monkeying around; the "better-than-it-needs-to-be" American grub is accompanied by "creative" cocktails, but a few say what used to be a "see-and-be-seen" scene now "lacks excitement."

Mon Petit Cafe *French* | 19 | 15 | 19 | $43 |

E 60s | 801 Lexington Ave. (62nd St.) | 212-355-2233 | www.monpetitcafe.com

A "little bit of Paris in the shadow of Bloomingdale's", this 30-year-old vet offers "homey French" staples that are a great break "in the middle of an intense shopping day"; the tearoom-style room "may not meet the standards of the Designers Guild", but "sweet" service lends a "cozy" vibe.

Mont Blanc ❶ *Austrian/Swiss* | 23 | 15 | 23 | $42 |

W 40s | 315 W. 48th St. (bet. 8th & 9th Aves.) | 212-582-9648 | www.montblancrestaurant.com

Fondue freaks plug this "cozy" Theater District "time capsule" that's been serving "delicious" Swiss-Austrian staples since 1982; "gracious" staffers overseen by a "charming" owner "get you to the show on time", so it's a "win-win all around" – even if it "could use a face-lift."

Montebello ⛔ *Italian* | 24 | 20 | 24 | $57 |

E 50s | 120 E. 56th St. (bet. Lexington & Park Aves.) | 212-753-1447 | www.montebellonyc.com

One of the "best-kept secrets in Midtown" is this "oasis of peace and quiet" where "personalized" service and "fantastic" Northern Italian fare keep its "older" client base returning; it's "a bit on the expensive side", but hey, at least "you can linger."

	FOOD	DECOR	SERVICE	COST

Monte's Ⓜ *Italian* — 20 | 18 | 22 | $40

Gowanus | 451 Carroll St. (bet. Nevins St. & 3rd Ave.) | Brooklyn | 718-852-7800 | www.montesnyc.com

This circa-1906 Gowanus Italian boasts "accommodating new owners" and turns out a "step-back-in-time", "like-home" menu highlighted by "wonderful" pizza; a "warm Brooklyn welcome" and "solid value" sweeten the deal.

NEW Montmartre *French* — ▽ 19 | 15 | 23 | $61

Chelsea | 158 Eighth Ave. (18th St.) | 646-596-8838 | www.montmartrenyc.com

Restaurateur Gabe Stulman and chef Tien Ho (Má Pêche) are the minds behind this "jammed" Chelsea bistro that originally featured an old-school French menu that's been recently tweaked with "delicious" SE Asian and North African accents; early visitors report it's "still getting it together", though a new back garden has doubled the seating capacity.

Mooncake Foods Ⓩ⇥ *Asian* — 20 | 10 | 17 | $21

Chelsea | 263 W. 30th St. (bet. 7th & 8th Aves.) | 212-268-2888
NEW Financial District | 111 John St. (bet. Cliff & Pearl Sts.) | 212-233-8808
SoHo | 28 Watts St. (bet. 6th Ave. & Thompson St.) | 212-219-8888
W 50s | 359 W. 54th St. (bet. 8th & 9th Aves.) | 212-262-9888
www.mooncakefoods.com

The "healthy cheap eats" come "quickly and without fuss" at this "cool", cash-only Pan-Asian quartet; it's "loud" and "crowded" with "nonexistent decor", but "great value for the money", inspiring many to "keep it in the rotation" – especially for delivery and takeout.

Morandi *Italian* — 23 | 21 | 20 | $53

W Village | 211 Waverly Pl. (Charles St.) | 212-627-7575 | www.morandiny.com

A somewhat under-the-radar "jewel in Keith McNally's crown", this all-day West Village trattoria rolls out an "off-the-hook" Italian menu served in "rustic", "perennially buzzy" confines; the "energy is contagious" – but if the "noise overwhelms", "sit out on the sidewalk and people-watch."

The Morgan Dining Room Ⓜ *American* — 19 | 22 | 19 | $40

Murray Hill | The Morgan Library & Museum | 225 Madison Ave. (bet. 36th & 37th Sts.) | 212-683-2130 | www.themorgan.org

For a "civilized" repast while taking in the "wonders of the Morgan Library", this lunch-only museum cafe offers "limited" but quite "good" American bites served in a "light-filled" atrium or J. Pierpont's "elegant" former dining room; it's all very "genteel" – with "prices to match."

Morimoto *Japanese* — 26 | 27 | 24 | $87

Chelsea | 88 10th Ave. (bet. 15th & 16th Sts.) | 212-989-8883 | www.morimotonyc.com

"More than a restaurant", this "showy" West Chelsea "experience" reveals the "creative juices" of *Iron Chef* Masaharu Morimoto via an "ethereal" Japanese menu, served by an "exceptional" team; the "chic", white-on-white setting is "calming" and the tabs "shocking", though the "fantastic" omakase is "worth every penny"; P.S. the "restrooms are not to be missed."

	FOOD	DECOR	SERVICE	COST

Morton's The Steakhouse Steak   22 | 21 | 23 | $79

E 40s | 551 Fifth Ave. (45th St.) | 212-972-3315
NEW **Financial District** | Club Quarters WTC | 136 Washington St.
(bet. Albany & Cedar Sts.) | 212-608-0171
www.mortons.com

"Go hungry" to these "corporate" chophouses where "huge" steaks with "just the right char" arrive with bountiful sides; it's predictably "expensive" (the "bar bites are the best deal"), but "classy" service and "upmarket", wood-paneled looks keep its "expense-account" crowd content.

Moti Mahal Delux Indian   ▽ 23 | 14 | 18 | $41

E 60s | 1149 First Ave. (63rd St.) | 212-371-3535 | www.motimahaldelux.us
The UES is home to this first U.S. outpost of the "unusual" international chain specializing in "quality" Indian tandoor cooking (the "delicious" butter chicken is its signature dish); tabs are "reasonable", the decor "simple" and the service "efficient" – many report being "pleasantly surprised" here.

Motorino ● Pizza   25 | 13 | 17 | $27

E Village | 349 E. 12th St. (bet. 1st & 2nd Aves.) | 212-777-2644
NEW **Williamsburg** | 139 Broadway (bet. Bedford & Driggs Aves.) |
Brooklyn | 718-599-8899
www.motorinopizza.com

The "gold standard" for "artsy pizza", this "delicious" duo builds Neapolitan-style pies with "superb ingredients" on "sublime thin crusts" that may "haunt your dreams"; news flash: the temporarily closed Brooklyn original is back at a new address near the Williamsburg Bridge.

Moustache ● Mideastern   23 | 14 | 18 | $27

E 100s | 1621 Lexington Ave. (102nd St.) | 212-828-0030
E Village | 265 E. 10th St. (bet. Ave. A & 1st Ave.) | 212-228-2022
W Village | 90 Bedford St. (bet. Barrow & Grove Sts.) | 212-229-2220 🗲
www.moustachepitza.com

"Straightforward", "delicious" Middle Eastern staples come at a "low price" at this "popular" trio; service is "nonchalant" and the "no-decor" setups tilt "tiny and cramped", but the minute that "just-baked pita" arrives, "all is forgiven."

NEW MP Taverna ● Greek   – | – | – | M

Astoria | 31-29 Ditmars Blvd. (33rd St.) | Queens | 718-777-2187 |
www.mptaverna.com

Chef Michael Psilakis (FishTag) lands in Astoria with this modern take on a Greek tavern, offering everything from whole fish to a Hellenic spin on paella; the industrial-chic duplex setting includes a casual street level with floor-to-ceiling windows and a more polished dining room above.

Mr. Chow ● Chinese   22 | 22 | 21 | $77

E 50s | 324 E. 57th St. (bet. 1st & 2nd Aves.) | 212-751-9030
Mr. Chow Tribeca ● Chinese
TriBeCa | 121 Hudson St. (N. Moore St.) | 212-965-9500
www.mrchow.com

"Upper-crust dining" endures at this longtime East Side Chinese (and its younger TriBeCa sibling) offering a "delicious", "classic" menu; voters split on its buzz factor – "still glamorous" vs. "lost its luster" – but there's agreement on the "elegant" settings and "super-high" price tags.

	FOOD	DECOR	SERVICE	COST

Mr. K's *Chinese* — 23 | 24 | 23 | $63

E 50s | 570 Lexington Ave. (51st St.) | 212-583-1668 | www.mrksny.com
An "opulent" pink art deco interior is the backdrop for "sumptuous"
Chinese dining at this "high-class" East Side "throwback" overseen by
a "ritzy, tuxedoed" staff; yes, prices run "high", but there's always the
$28 prix fixe lunch.

Mughlai *Indian* — 20 | 14 | 17 | $37

W 70s | 320 Columbus Ave. (75th St.) | 212-724-6363 |
www.mughlainyc.com
"Save yourself a trip to Sixth Street" at this "quiet" UWS "mainstay"
that's been supplying "delish" Indian standards for more than three
decades; "often disinterested" service and "slightly more-than-average
prices" for the genre don't deter devotees.

NEW Murray's Cheese Bar ● *American* — 24 | 16 | 19 | $31

W Village | 264 Bleecker St. (bet. Leroy & Morton Sts.) | 646-476-8882 |
www.murrayscheesebar.com
Spun off from the popular West Village fromage shop a few doors
down, this equally "busy" American offers a "limited", cheese-centric
menu ranging from "amazing flights" to "fabulous" fondue; "knowledgeable cheesemongers" keep the pace brisk in the "cramped",
white-tiled space.

NEW Musket Room ● *New Zealand* — - | - | - | M

NoLita | 265 Elizabeth St. (bet. Houston & Prince Sts.) | 212-219-0764 |
www.musketroom.com
An Auckland-born chef is behind the burners at this new NoLita venture dispatching New Zealand cuisine in a rustic setting heavy on the
exposed brick and distressed wood; up front there's a walnut bar,
while the back dining room overlooks a garden where herbs are grown
for the kitchen.

NEW M. Wells Dinette *Québécois* — ∇ 27 | 18 | 21 | $40

LIC | MoMA PS1 | 22-25 Jackson Ave. (46th Ave.) | Queens |
718-786-1800 | www.magasinwells.com
French-Canadian chef Hugue Dufour's latest, this lunch-only LIC cafeteria in MoMA PS1 offers "rich, delicious" Québécois fusion fare in a former schoolhouse space that's appropriately designed like a "classroom"
with "chalkboard menus" and cubbyhole desks; P.S. closed on Tuesdays
and Wednesdays; museum admission not required for entry.

Nanni ⊠ *Italian* — 24 | 14 | 22 | $64

E 40s | 146 E. 46th St. (bet. Lexington & 3rd Aves.) | 212-697-4161 |
www.nanninyc.com
"Loyal regulars" populate this "old-world" Northern Italian near Grand
Central, where "excellent" classic dishes "like grandma's" are ferried
by beloved, "been-there-forever" waiters; yes, it's "expensive" given
the "ancient surroundings", but you'll "not leave disappointed."

Naples 45 ⊠ *Italian/Pizza* — 19 | 16 | 18 | $37

E 40s | MetLife Bldg. | 200 Park Ave. (45th St.) | 212-972-7001 |
www.naples45.com
This "handy", "commuter"-friendly venue near Grand Central knocks
out a "solid", if "unspectacular" Southern Italian menu led by "authen-

| | FOOD | DECOR | SERVICE | COST |

tic" Neapolitan pizza; "serviceable" service and relatively "inexpensive" tabs offset the "loud" acoustics and crazy "bustle" at lunchtime, when it fills up with "non-CEO" types; P.S. closed weekends.

Naruto Ramen ⊄ *Japanese/Noodle Shop* | 22 | 12 | 17 | $16

E 80s | 1596 Third Ave. (bet. 89th & 90th Sts.) | 212-289-7803 | www.narutoterakawa.com

Slurpaholics "line up outside" this low-cost, cash-only Upper East Side noodle shop to snag one of its 14 bar seats and watch the cooks concoct "delicious", "traditional" ramen soups "right in front of you"; even though "not the most comfortable" spot, it's still "hard to beat on a cold day."

The National ● *American* | 20 | 19 | 18 | $53

E 50s | Benjamin Hotel | 557 Lexington Ave. (50th St.) | 212-715-2400 | www.thenationalnyc.com

"Crazy-busy for lunch, quieter and more relaxed at dinner", Geoffrey Zakarian's "business" nexus in Midtown's Benjamin Hotel presents a "comfortable" setting for "solid", "simple" American cooking; noise levels are "loud" and the service "spotty", but the crowds keep coming.

Natsumi ● *Japanese* | 24 | 19 | 22 | $46

W 50s | Amsterdam Court Hotel | 226 W. 50th St. (bet. B'way & 8th Ave.) | 212-258-2988 | www.natsuminyc.com

Amid the Theater District "madness" lies this Japanese "sleeper" that "exceeds expectations" with its "delectable sushi", "helpful" service and "reasonable" rates; other endearments include a "sleek" room "not filled to the brim with tourists" and a "tolerable noise level."

Naya *Lebanese* | 22 | 18 | 20 | $38

E 50s | 1057 Second Ave. (bet. 55th & 56th Sts.) | 212-319-7777
Naya Express ⊠ *Lebanese*
E 40s | 688 Third Ave. (43rd St.) | 212-557-0007
www.nayarestaurants.com

Meze mavens dig into "marvelous" Lebanese dishes at this "classy" Eastsider where the "staff treats you like family", but the "striking", "all-white" interior feels more "futuristic railway car" than homey taverna; the "lunchtime lines" at the counter-service Grand Central–area offshoot "say it all."

Neary's ● *Pub Food* | 17 | 16 | 21 | $48

E 50s | 358 E. 57th St. (1st Ave.) | 212-751-1434 | www.nearys.com

"Consummate host" Jimmy Neary and his "welcoming" "old-school staff" keep loyal "seniors" coming back to this "frozen-in-time" Midtown watering hole; it's a "cozy place" to relax and have a drink, with "dependable" Irish bar food in a supporting role.

Negril *Caribbean/Jamaican* | 23 | 21 | 20 | $38

G Village | 70 W. Third St. (bet. La Guardia Pl. & Thompson St.) | 212-477-2804 | www.negrilvillage.com

"Hot food, hot crowd" sums up this "modern" Village Jamaican where the "lively" scene is fueled by "phenomenal" cocktails and "flavorful", "dressed-up" Caribbean fare; sure, other competitors are "less expensive", but you're paying for the "upscale" milieu here.

	FOOD	DECOR	SERVICE	COST

Nello ◑ *Italian* — 18 | 17 | 16 | $108

E 60s | 696 Madison Ave. (bet. 62nd & 63rd Sts.) | 212-980-9099 |
www.nellorestaurantnyc.com

Money is no object at this one-of-a-kind UES Italian, famed for serving "nothing-out-of-this-world" food for "mortgage-the-house" sums; habitués jockey for the "sidewalk seats" on Madison Avenue ("*the* place to be seen"), overlooking the "pretentious" crowd and "undeserved attitude" from staffers who "think they're celebs."

NEW Nerai ⑤ *Greek* — - | - | - | E

E 50s | 55 E. 54th St. (bet. Madison & Park Aves.) | 212-759-5554 |
www.nerainyc.com

Elevated Greek dining comes to Midtown via this sophisticated new Hellenic set in the former Oceana digs; a swanky, high-ceilinged setting and ultrafresh seafood priced by the pound help explain price tags aimed at the power-lunch crowd.

Neta ⑤ *Japanese* — ▽ 27 | 18 | 23 | $114

G Village | 61 W. Eighth St. (6th Ave.) | 212-505-2610 | www.netanyc.com

"Living up to its billing", this "intriguing" Village Japanese from two Masa alums offers everything from "exceptional" small plates to "generous omakase", served in an "austere" room by "helpful" staffers who make the expensive tabs easier to swallow; for best results, "sit at the sushi bar."

New Leaf Ⓜ *American* — 21 | 24 | 21 | $44

Washington Heights | Fort Tryon Park | 1 Margaret Corbin Dr. (190th St.) |
212-568-5323 | www.newleafrestaurant.com

Almost "like a country inn", this "charming" American "getaway" in "lovely" Fort Tryon Park offers "appealing" locavore-friendly fare matched with equally "pleasant" service; profits go to Bette Midler's NY Restoration Project, so few mind if it's "a bit pricey" – especially if they're dining on the "magical" terrace.

New Malaysia *Malaysian* — ▽ 23 | 13 | 16 | $22

Chinatown | Chinatown Arcade | 46-48 Bowery (bet. Bayard & Canal Sts.) |
212-964-0284

Despite an "awkward location" in a "Chinatown alley", this Malaysian mainstay has been "packing in the locals" for nearly 40 years; given its "huge menu" of "delicious", seriously "inexpensive" dishes, "flavor" junkies overlook its "not-up-to-snuff" service.

New WonJo ◑ *Korean* — 22 | 14 | 18 | $35

Garment District | 23 W. 32nd St. (bet. B'way & 5th Ave.) | 212-695-5815 |
www.newwonjo.com

"Korean awesomeness, 24 hours a day" is the deal at this K-town vet whose low-cost, "crave"-worthy specialties include tableside BBQ; service can be "harried", but following a renovation, the room wins "bonus points" because "you won't smell like the grill."

NEW New York Sushi Ko ◑⑤ *Japanese* — - | - | - | VE

LES | 91 Clinton St. (bet. Delancey & Rivington Sts.) | 917-734-5857 |
www.newyorksushiko.com

Intimate and informal, this new LES Japanese via a chef who's a Masa and 15 East alum offers omakase-only dinners made from fish flown in

| | | FOOD | DECOR | SERVICE | COST |

from around the world; the 10-seat nook may be strictly minimalist, but the pricing's maximal – the fixed-price meals start at $75.

Ngam ❶ *Thai*

▽ 22 | 17 | 21 | $37

E Village | 99 Third Ave. (bet. 12th & 13th Sts.) | 212-777-8424 | www.ngamnyc.com

"Worth a try" for its "imaginative" twists on Thai comfort fare, this "bright" East Villager is also favored for its "value" pricing and "personable" service; while "giant plates" on "small tables" add to the "tight" feel of its rough-hewn space, sidewalk seating eases the crush.

Nha Trang *Vietnamese*

22 | 8 | 16 | $20

Chinatown | 148 Centre St. (bet. Walker & White Sts.) | 212-941-9292
Chinatown | 87 Baxter St. (bet. Bayard & Canal Sts.) | 212-233-5948

The "wonderful pho" and other "honest" Vietnamese fare dished out at this Chinatown twosome is "so good", it's almost a "reason to love jury duty"; sure, service is "get-'em-in-and-out" and the settings "totally charmless", but no one minds – it's "so cheap, you could treat 10 friends."

Nice Green Bo ⊄ *Chinese*

22 | 6 | 11 | $18

Chinatown | 66 Bayard St. (bet. Elizabeth & Mott Sts.) | 212-625-2359

"Hungry hordes" hit this Chinatown "hole-in-the-wall" to nosh on "some of NY's best soup dumplings" and other "first-rate, bargain-priced" Shanghai specialties; "dumpy" digs and "grumpy" staffers are part of the experience.

Nice Matin ❶ *French/Mediterranean*

19 | 18 | 18 | $46

W 70s | 201 W. 79th St. (Amsterdam Ave.) | 212-873-6423 | www.nicematinnyc.com

"Always running full throttle", this all-day UWS "hive" features "reliable" French-Med eats dispatched in an atmospheric space channeling the "south of France"; it somehow manages to "feel upscale and informal at the same time", but given the prime-time "noise" and "crush", regulars report it's "best off-peak."

Nick & Toni's Cafe *Mediterranean*

19 | 16 | 18 | $49

W 60s | 100 W. 67th St. (bet. B'way & Columbus Ave.) | 212-496-4000 | www.nickandtoniscafe.com

Just a "short walk" from Lincoln Center, this "low-key" offshoot of the "popular" East Hampton standby plies "enjoyable", "straightforward" Mediterranean fare via a "quick" team; "reasonable" rates make it a good bet "pre-movie or -show", with the chance of spotting "journalists from nearby ABC."

Nick's *Pizza*

23 | 14 | 19 | $26

E 90s | 1814 Second Ave. (94th St.) | 212-987-5700 | www.nicksnyc.com
Forest Hills | 108-26 Ascan Ave. (bet. Austin & Burns Sts.) | Queens | 718-263-1126 ⊄

A "step above your everyday pizza place", this UES–Forest Hills duo specializes in "charred", thin-crust pies with "perfect sauce" and some "gourmet flair"; true, both the decor and service "could be a bit better", but the "neighborhood feel" is fine as is.

	FOOD	DECOR	SERVICE	COST

Nicky's Vietnamese
Sandwiches ∅ *Sandwiches*

21 | 9 | 17 | $12

Financial District | 99-C Nassau St. (bet. Ann & Fulton Sts.) | 212-766-3388 🗷
Boerum Hill | 311 Atlantic Ave. (bet. Hoyt & Smith Sts.) | Brooklyn | 718-855-8838

"Crusty baguettes" and "tasty" fillings make for some of the "best banh mi outside of Vietnam" at this "cheap", cash-only, "bare-bones" Boerum Hill storefront, which also ladles out "fantastic" pho; the FiDi sibling is roomier but equally "plain-Jane", so many "grab and go."

Nicola's ● *Italian*

21 | 17 | 20 | $63

E 80s | 146 E. 84th St. (bet. Lexington & 3rd Aves.) | 212-249-9850 | www.nicolasnyc.com

"Yes, it's like a private club" admit the "well-heeled" regulars drawn to this "unhurried" Upper Eastsider by its "scrumptious", "old-time" Italian cooking and "warm welcomes"; despite being "expensive" and "a wee bit dated", it's good to know that you can "develop membership status" with return visits.

Nicoletta ● *Italian/Pizza*

▽ 19 | 19 | 19 | $30

E Village | 160 Second Ave. (10th St.) | 212-432-1600 | www.nicolettanyc.com

Superstar chef Michael White (Marea, Osteria Morini) does the "lower-price" thing at this East Village pizzeria where the thick-crusted, "Wisconsin-style" pies arrive in a big-windowed, brick-walled setting; still, critics find the goods "inconsistent" and say there are "better" choices nearby.

NEW Nightingale 9 *Noodle Shop/Vietnamese*

- | - | - | M

Carroll Gardens | 345 Smith St. (Carroll St.) | Brooklyn | 347-689-4699 | www.nightingale9.com

This new Smith Street noodle shop from the Seersucker folks features a pared-down, sharing-style Vietnamese menu inspired by the food found at native stalls and street vendors; the understated interior is an exercise in uncluttered Brooklyn cool, ditto the moderate prices.

99 Miles to Philly *Cheesesteaks*

21 | 11 | 17 | $15

NEW E 40s | 300 E. 45th St. (2nd Ave.) | 212-297-9500
E Village | 94 Third Ave. (bet. 12th & 13th Sts.) | 212-253-2700 ●∅
www.99milestophilly.com

The closest you'll get to Philly that "doesn't involve a Chinatown bus", these East Village–Midtown cheesesteak palaces proffer a marquee sandwich that's a "solid", "satisfying", "gooey mess"; "late-night" availability trumps "grungy" looks and minimal seating, but aesthetes advise "get it to go."

Ninja *Japanese*

19 | 26 | 23 | $61

TriBeCa | 25 Hudson St. (bet. Duane & Reade Sts.) | 212-274-8500 | www.ninjanewyork.com

With "jumping ninjas and a roaming magic act", they really "go all out" at this "gimmicky" TriBeCa theme joint done up "like a Japanese village" in feudal times; it's "fun for kids", but grown-ups' opinions vary ("naff" vs. a "blast") – most agree you'll "shell out" for only "so-so" eats.

	FOOD	DECOR	SERVICE	COST

Nino's *Italian* — 21 | 19 | 21 | $58

E 70s | 1354 First Ave. (bet. 72nd & 73rd Sts.) | 212-988-0002 |
www.ninosnyc.com

Nino's Tuscany Steak House *Italian/Steak*

W 50s | 117 W. 58th St. (bet. 6th & 7th Aves.) | 212-757-8630 |
www.ninostuscany.com

Nino's Positano *Pizza*

E 40s | 890 Second Ave. (bet. 47th & 48th Sts.) | 212-355-5540 |
www.ninospositano.com

"More than a typical neighborhood Italian", this "civilized" mini-chain
is touted for its "delicious food" and "friendly" staffers; the "old-
world-cozy" settings are reflected in the "old-school" menus, and if
the tariffs are "a little pricey", "smiling" host Nino always "enhances
the dining experience."

Nippon ☒ *Japanese* — ▽ 23 | 18 | 23 | $63

E 50s | 155 E. 52nd St. (bet. Lexington & 3rd Aves.) | 212-758-0226 |
www.restaurantnippon.com

"One of NYC's oldest" Japanese restaurants, this circa-1963 Midtown
"favorite" still turns out "delicious", "traditional" fare - including
sushi - with "no glitz, no glam", just "gracious" attention; maybe it's a
tad "pricey" and the decor "hasn't been updated" of late, but overall
it's a "treat."

Nirvana *Indian* — 22 | 20 | 20 | $40

Murray Hill | 346 Lexington Ave. (bet. 39th & 40th Sts.) | 212-983-0000 |
www.nirvanany.com

"Perfectly seasoned" classics at moderate rates draw curryphiles
to this "upscale", lesser-known Murray Hill Indian where they "tai-
lor the spice to taste"; "attentive" staffers tend the "contemporary", brick-walled setting featuring a lively lounge and "inviting"
upstairs dining room.

Nizza ◐ *French/Italian* — 19 | 16 | 18 | $38

W 40s | 630 Ninth Ave. (bet. 44th & 45th Sts.) | 212-956-1800 |
www.nizzanyc.com

"Won't-break-the-bank" prices for "solid" classics ensure this
"casual" Hell's Kitchen French-Italian is plenty "popular" pre- or
post-theater; the noise level can be "a bit much", but "cheerful"
staffers and sidewalk seating take the edge off; P.S. the gluten-free
options are "impressive."

Nobu *Japanese* — 27 | 23 | 24 | $84

TriBeCa | 105 Hudson St. (Franklin St.) | 212-219-0500

Nobu 57 *Japanese*

W 50s | 40 W. 57th St. (bet. 5th & 6th Aves.) | 212-757-3000

Nobu, Next Door *Japanese*

TriBeCa | 105 Hudson St. (Franklin St.) | 212-334-4445
www.noburestaurants.com

Nobu Matsuhisa's 20-year-old TriBeCa flagship "has lost none of its
luster", still offering "exceptional" Japanese-Peruvian fare to an "attractive" crowd in a "theatrical", David Rockwell-designed space; its
"more casual" next-door offshoot and more "touristy" Midtown outlet
are "just as delicious" - and just as "expensive."

	FOOD	DECOR	SERVICE	COST

Nocello *Italian*
22 | **18** | **22** | **$52**

W 50s | 257 W. 55th St. (bet. B'way & 8th Ave.) | 212-713-0224 | www.nocello.net

"Enduring and endearing" – not to mention "convenient" if you're bound for Carnegie Hall or City Center – this "cozy" Tuscan turns out "plentiful" platefuls of "fine" fare; "charming owners" who "take pride" add an "intimate" feel to the "unassuming" digs.

Noche Mexicana *Mexican*
22 | **11** | **17** | **$21**

W 100s | 842 Amsterdam Ave. (bet. 101st & 102nd Sts.) | 212-662-6900 | www.noche-mexicana.com

"Come hungry" to this Upper Westsider dishing out *"muy autentico"* Mexican cooking; "unbeatable prices" trump the "divey" decor, and as for service, it "improves if you speak Spanish – even just a little."

NoHo Star ● *American/Asian*
19 | **16** | **18** | **$36**

NoHo | 330 Lafayette St. (Bleecker St.) | 212-925-0070 | www.nohostar.com

The "offbeat" menu "should just say 'everything, plus Chinese'" at this "long-standing" NoHo "favorite" that "cheerfully" offers Asian specialties side by side with "kicked-up" American eats; tabs "priced right" and a "comfy" setting are other reasons this "star keeps shining."

NoMad *American/European*
27 | **26** | **24** | **$89**

Chelsea | NoMad Hotel | 1170 Broadway (28th St.) | 347-472-5660 | www.thenomadhotel.com

"All the hype is justified" at Daniel Humm and Will Guidara's NoMad Hotel "stunner", offering a "first-rate" American-European menu led by what may be the "best chicken dish on the planet"; the multiroom setting is "stylish", the service "suave" and the bar scene "sexy", so even though it's "definitely not cheap", it's still virtually "impossible to get a table" here.

Nom Wah Tea Parlor *Chinese*
21 | **13** | **17** | **$22**

Chinatown | 13 Doyers St. (bet. Chatham Sq. & Pell St.) | 212-962-6047 | www.nomwah.com

You may "need Google Maps" to find it, but this "quintessential" Chinatown parlor is worth seeking out for its "dazzling array" of "real-deal", "made-to-order" dim sum; around since 1920 but recently "revitalized", it also gets a "bravo" for its "fire-sale prices."

Noodle Bar ⊅ *Asian/Noodle Shop*
21 | **13** | **18** | **$21**

W Village | 26 Carmine St. (bet. Bedford & Bleecker Sts.) | 212-524-6800 | www.noodlebarnyc.com

"Fast and satisfying" noodle soups and wok dishes are yours at this "unassuming" West Village Asian; it "warms you up" and "fills you up" for "cheap", so most don't mind the "no-frills" setting and service with some "rough" edges.

Noodle Pudding Ⓜ ⊅ *Italian*
25 | **18** | **21** | **$39**

Brooklyn Heights | 38 Henry St. (bet. Cranberry & Middagh Sts.) | Brooklyn | 718-625-3737

A "beacon" in Brooklyn Heights, this "boisterous" Italian is usually "hopping by 6:30" thanks to a "loyal local following" that loves its "fantastic food" and "delightful" staff; cash-only, no-rez hassles are offset by the "convivial" mood and "more-than-fair" prices.

| | FOOD | DECOR | SERVICE | COST |

Nook ⊅ *Eclectic* | 23 | 12 | 19 | $33 |

W 50s | 746 Ninth Ave. (bet. 50th & 51st Sts.) | 212-247-5500
Only "slightly bigger than a walk-in closet", this "aptly named" Hell's Kitchen "neighborhood hangout" compensates for its "cramped setting" and "sometimes gruff" service with "well-prepared" Eclectic eats; the cash-only policy hardly matters since "BYO makes it a super bargain."

Norma's *American* | 25 | 19 | 20 | $44 |

W 50s | Le Parker Meridien | 119 W. 56th St. (bet. 6th & 7th Aves.) | 212-708-7460 | www.normasnyc.com
Folks "serious about breakfast" tout this Parker Meridien American that satisfies early-rising "hearty eaters" with portions so "huge" that you "may never eat again"; alright, the tabs are "crazy expensive" – i.e. the "zillion-dollar lobster frittata" (ok, only $1,000) – but the setting is "sleek", the service "professional" and the brunches "quintessential."

North End Grill *American/Seafood* | 24 | 23 | 24 | $70 |

Financial District | 104 North End Ave. (bet. Murray & Vesey Sts.) | 646-747-1600 | www.northendgrillnyc.com
Finally, there's "destination dining in Battery Park City" via Danny Meyer's "spacious" American yearling, where "maestro" chef Floyd Cardoz prepares an "imaginative", seafood-centric menu delivered by a "couldn't-be-nicer" crew; the "airy", "contemporary" room is "reasonably quiet", so lively sorts join the "Wall Street overachievers" at the bar.

Northern Spy Food Co. *American* | 24 | 18 | 21 | $43 |

E Village | 511 E. 12th St. (bet. Aves. A & B) | 212-228-5100 | www.northernspyfoodco.com
This "wonderfully eccentric" East Village "locavore destination" turns out "savory", "farm-to-table" American food at "moderate" rates; "warm and fuzzy" service makes up for the "very small space" that's usually "crammed" at prime times.

North Square *American* | 23 | 19 | 22 | $49 |

G Village | Washington Sq. Hotel | 103 Waverly Pl. (MacDougal St.) | 212-254-1200 | www.northsquareny.com
Apart from the "Washington Square regulars" and "half of NYU", few know about this "swell little neighborhood place", a "favorite" of "grown-ups" who show up for its "superior", "value"-priced New American cuisine and "cordial" service; "easy" decibels – i.e. you "can talk without going hoarse" – seal the deal.

No. 7 ●Ⓜ *American* | 22 | 15 | 17 | $25 |

Fort Greene | 7 Greene Ave. (bet. Cumberland & Fulton Sts.) | Brooklyn | 718-522-6370 | www.no7restaurant.com

No. 7 Sub *Sandwiches*

Chelsea | Ace Hotel | 1188 Broadway (bet. 28th & 29th Sts.) | 212-532-1680 Ⓢ

W 50s | Plaza Food Hall | 1 W. 59th St., lower level (5th Ave.) | 646-755-3228

NEW Dumbo | Brooklyn Bridge Park | 11 Water St. (New Dock St.) | Brooklyn

(continued)

(continued)

No. 7 Sub

Greenpoint | 931 Manhattan Ave. (bet. Java & Kent Sts.) | Brooklyn | 718-389-7775
www.no7sub.com

Fort Greene locals and BAM-goers seeking something "original" head for this "relaxed", "hipster"-friendly New American known for "inventive" combos that "hit the flavor Lotto"; similarly "odd pairings work magic" in sandwich form at its "laid-back" counter-service spin-offs.

Nove ⓜ *Italian*

∇ 24 | 22 | 23 | $57

Eltingville | 3900 Richmond Ave. (Amboy Rd.) | Staten Island | 718-227-3286 | www.noveitalianbistro.com

"Not your typical SI Italian", this "trendy" trattoria "fills a void" with its "excellent" cuisine served in "fancy" environs by staffers who treat you "really well"; yes, it's "high-priced" for the borough, but it's "crowded" nonetheless – be sure to "make a reservation."

Novitá ● *Italian*

25 | 19 | 23 | $62

Gramercy | 102 E. 22nd St. (bet. Lexington Ave. & Park Ave. S.) | 212-677-2222 | www.novitanyc.com

The "definition of 'neighborhood gem'", this 20-year-old Gramercy staple serves Northern Italian fare so "scrumptious" that no one seems to mind the "cheek-to-jowl" seating and "concomitant noise levels"; "highly efficient" service and "modestly priced wines" are other reasons regulars plead "please keep this a secret."

Numero 28 ⊯ *Pizza*

24 | 13 | 18 | $28

E 70s | 1431 First Ave. (bet. 74th & 75th Sts.) | 212-772-8200
E Village | 176 Second Ave. (bet. 11th & 12th Sts.) | 212-777-1555 ●
NEW **W 90s** | 660 Amsterdam Ave. (92nd St.) | 212-706-7282
W Village | 28 Carmine St. (bet. Bedford & Bleecker Sts.) | 212-463-9653
www.numero28.com

"Real Italians" are responsible for the "perfectly crisp"–crusted "rectangular" pies from wood-fired brick ovens at this pizzeria mini-chain; the "reasonable cost" pleases the wallet-conscious, while a general "nonchalant" attitude boosts the "authentic" dolce vita vibe.

Num Pang *Cambodian/Sandwiches*

25 | 7 | 16 | $13

NEW **Chelsea** | Chelsea Mkt. | 75 Ninth Ave. (bet. 15th & 16th Sts.) | 212-390-8851
E 40s | 140 E. 41st St. (bet. Lexington & 3rd Aves.) | 212-867-8889
NEW **Flatiron** | 1129 Broadway (bet. 25th & 26th Sts.) | 212-647-8889
G Village | 21 E. 12th St. (bet. 5th Ave. & University Pl.) | 212-255-3271 ⊯
www.numpangnyc.com

"Cambodia's answer" to the banh mi craze, this quartet dispenses "damn good" sandwiches "worth standing in line" for, with "more-than-fair" prices and "speedy service" sweetening the deal; despite an overall "no-frills" feel, most report "you can't go wrong" here.

Nurnberger Bierhaus *German*

∇ 23 | 19 | 20 | $34

New Brighton | 817 Castleton Ave. (bet. Davis & Pelton Aves.) | Staten Island | 718-816-7461 | www.nurnbergerbierhaus.com

Staten Islanders in the mood for Wiener schnitzel and beer "meet the gang" at this "festive" New Brighton take on Bavaria, where the

	FOOD	DECOR	SERVICE	COST

German grub is matched with "wonderful" brews on tap; it's "authentic" down to the "hokey decor", dirndl-clad staff and back biergarten.

Nyonya ⊅ *Malaysian* — 23 | 15 | 16 | $24

Little Italy | 199 Grand St. (bet. Mott & Mulberry Sts.) | 212-334-3669 ●
Bensonhurst | 2322 86th St. (Bay 34th St.) | Brooklyn | 718-265-0888
Borough Park | 5323 Eighth Ave. (54th St.) | Brooklyn | 718-633-0808 ●
www.ilovenyonya.com

When you crave "spice and exotic flavors", this "amazing" Malaysian trio fills the bill with "generous" servings of "fresh", "delicious" food at "ridiculously good" rates (just "bring cash"); "assembly-line" service and "packed", basic quarters only "add to the experience."

NYY Steak ⊠Ⓜ *Steak* — 22 | 22 | 20 | $66

Yankee Stadium | Yankee Stadium | 1 E. 161st St., Gate 6 (River Ave.) | Bronx | 646-977-8325 | www.nyysteak.com

"Heaven" for Bronx Bombers fans, this year-round steakhouse inside Yankee Stadium is a carnivore's "home run" given "surprisingly good" beef served in "baseball-themed" digs; "you'll pay" for the privilege, but "you can't beat the atmosphere" – especially when the team "just won."

Oaxaca ⊅ *Mexican* — 21 | 11 | 17 | $16

E Village | 16 Extra Pl. (bet. Bowery & 2nd Ave.) | 212-677-3340
NEW **W 80s** | 424 Amsterdam Ave. (bet. 80th & 81st Sts.) | 212-580-4888 ●
W Village | 48 Greenwich Ave. (bet. Charles & Perry Sts.) | 212-366-4488
Park Slope | 250 Fourth Ave. (bet. Carroll & President Sts.) | Brooklyn | 718-222-1122 ●
www.oaxacatacos.com

"Addictive", "legit" tacos keep 'em coming to these "casual" Mexicans where the "unbeatable prices" also "hit the mark"; "no-frills" settings and "don't-hold-your-breath" service lead regulars to get it to go.

Oceana *American/Seafood* — 24 | 23 | 23 | $77

W 40s | McGraw Hill Bldg. | 120 W. 49th St. (bet. 6th & 7th Aves.) | 212-759-5941 | www.oceanarestaurant.com

"Business folk" flock to this "cavernous" Rock Center American seafooder for its "pristine fish", "gorgeous raw bar" and "classy" service; though opinions split on the decor ("upper-class" vs. "over-engineered"), all agree on the "hefty" tabs and "habit-forming" cooking.

Ocean Grill *Seafood* — 24 | 21 | 21 | $57

W 70s | 384 Columbus Ave. (bet. 78th & 79th Sts.) | 212-579-2300 | www.oceangrill.com

"There's always a buzz" at Steve Hanson's "popular" UWS seafooder, where crowds pile in for "tasty", "simply grilled" marine cuisine served by a "competent" staff in a "white-tablecloth", "Hamptons-esque" setting; when the "noise level gets too high", insiders escape to the "pleasant" sidewalk seats.

The Odeon *American/French* — 19 | 18 | 19 | $51

TriBeCa | 145 W. Broadway (Thomas St.) | 212-233-0507 | www.theodeonrestaurant.com

"Historical hipness" clings to this "iconic" '80s-era bistro, once a happening scene and now a "favorite mainstay" for TriBeCa locals seeking "well-prepared" Franco-American meals; the "relaxed vibe" and "great people-watching" make it "still fun" for everything from brunch to "late-night" snacking.

Ofrenda *Mexican*

∇ 23 | 16 | 20 | $39

W Village | 113 Seventh Ave. S. (bet. Christopher & W. 10th Sts.) | 212-924-2305 | www.ofrendanyc.com

A "cut above" your corner Mexican joint, this "informal" Village cantina cooks up *fabuloso* fare delivered by a "terrific" staff; yes, the "cozy" space skews "tight", but given "affordable" tabs, most hardly notice.

Okeanos *Greek/Seafood*

21 | 18 | 21 | $40

Park Slope | 314 Seventh Ave. (8th St.) | Brooklyn | 347-725-4162 | www.okeanosnyc.com

Ok, it may look like a "glorified diner", but this "welcoming" Park Slope Hellenic produces relatively "upscale" takes on Greek staples, including flapping "fresh seafood"; an "eager-to-please" staff and "reasonable" prices are other reasons neighbors call it "a keeper."

Old Homestead *Steak*

25 | 19 | 21 | $80

Meatpacking | 56 Ninth Ave. (bet. 14th & 15th Sts.) | 212-242-9040 | www.theoldhomesteadsteakhouse.com

"Old-style NY" dining doesn't get much more authentic than this steakhouse "original" that's been grilling "perfectly seared" chops in the Meatpacking since 1868; the "huge prices" don't faze its core crowd of "men spending too much", though the "massive" portions leave them as "overstuffed" as the furniture.

NEW Old School Brooklyn Ⓜ *American*

- | - | - | M

Carroll Gardens | 520 Court St. (bet. Huntington & Nelson Sts.) | Brooklyn | 718-407-0047 | www.oldschoolbk.com

Living up to its name, this Carroll Gardens newcomer takes diners back in time with a homestyle Italian-American menu heavy on the red gravy; the appropriately vintage setting comes complete with framed family photos, a china cabinet and an antique Singer sewing machine.

Olea *Mediterranean*

23 | 22 | 21 | $34

Fort Greene | 171 Lafayette Ave. (Adelphi St.) | Brooklyn | 718-643-7003 | www.oleabrooklyn.com

"Delicious", "ambitious" tapas and a "dream"-worthy brunch "bring the Mediterranean" – and "the masses" – to this "inviting" Fort Greene "mainstay"; it boasts a "BAM-convenient" address, "charming" service and "gentle" live music – but just go "off-peak" to avoid a "wait."

Olives *Mediterranean*

22 | 21 | 21 | $58

Union Sq | W Hotel Union Sq. | 201 Park Ave. S. (17th St.) | 212-353-8345 | www.olivesnewyork.com

"Singles" mingle at Todd English's "fun" W Union Square Med plying an "inventive" (if "pricey") menu spotlighting "marvelous" flatbreads; an "attentive staff" oversees the "modern" dining room, though the "noise" issuing from the "crowded" bar can be "the pits."

Omai *Vietnamese*

24 | 17 | 20 | $41

Chelsea | 158 Ninth Ave. (bet. 19th & 20th Sts.) | 212-633-0550 | www.omainyc.com

"For a change of pace", this "pleasant" Chelsea Vietnamese fills the bill with "delicious", "delicate" fare, "spiced just right"; "pleasant prices" are a plus, but since they "added the sign" outside, insiders lament that the "tight", "low-key" space has become "crowded."

Omen A Zen ● *Japanese* ▽ 25 | 20 | 23 | $61

SoHo | 113 Thompson St. (bet. Prince & Spring Sts.) | 212-925-8923
"Outstanding" Kyoto-style fare is the hallmark of this "classic SoHo" Japanese vet offering "excellent" cooked dishes plus sashimi (but no sushi); "efficient" staffers oversee the "serene setting" where "celeb sightings" are a "good omen" – if also a prediction of "expensive" tabs.

Omonia Cafe ● *Coffeehouse/Greek* 20 | 17 | 17 | $21

Bay Ridge | 7612-14 Third Ave. (bet. 76th & 77th Sts.) | Brooklyn | 718-491-1435
Astoria | 32-20 Broadway (33rd St.) | Queens | 718-274-6650
www.omoniacafe.com
A "mind-boggling array" of "heavenly" sweets awaits at these Greek coffeehouses also serving savory "comfort food"; the "neon lights" and "disco vibe" suit "teenagers" who "hang out and socialize" late-night, but everyone appreciates prices that don't "break your piggy bank."

1 Bite Mediterranean *Mediterranean* 22 | 20 | 21 | $34

E 50s | 875 Third Ave. (bet. 52nd & 53rd Sts.) | 212-888-0809 | www.1bitenyc.com
Plan on consuming more than the name suggests at this East Side Med, because the kitchen's "authentic" small plates are "very tasty" and "healthy" to boot; a "friendly" staff, affordable tabs and "pleasing" ambiance round out the "enjoyable" package.

One if by Land, Two if by Sea *American* 24 | 27 | 25 | $117

W Village | 17 Barrow St. (bet. 7th Ave. S. & W. 4th St.) | 212-228-0822 | www.oneifbyland.com
"Steeped in history" and "romance", this "historic" Village "rendezvous" set in Aaron Burr's former carriage house offers "superb" American food (i.e. that "signature beef Wellington"), delivered by staffers who "take their job seriously"; seductive touches like a piano bar, "candlelit rooms" and four fireplaces distract from the "very expensive", prix fixe–only tabs.

101 *American/Italian* 22 | 20 | 21 | $42

Bay Ridge | 10018 Fourth Ave. (100th St.) | Brooklyn | 718-833-1313 | www.101bayridge.com
It's "still tough to find a table" on prime nights at this longtime Bay Ridge "local joint" whose "quality" midpriced Italian-American fare, "wonderful location overlooking the Verrazano" and convenient valet parking keep 'em coming; a "busy, loud" atmosphere is part of the package.

1 or 8 Ⓜ *Japanese* 24 | 22 | 23 | $49

Williamsburg | 66 S. Second St. (Wythe Ave.) | Brooklyn | 718-384-2152 | www.oneoreightbk.com
"Unique style" permeates this "off-the-beaten-path" Williamsburg sushi standout spinning "unconventional" takes on Japanese fare in a "sleek white" setting that's a "minimalist's" "heaven"; along with the "high-quality" fare, regulars single out the "delightful staff" as key to the "consistently solid" experience.

	FOOD	DECOR	SERVICE	COST

107 West *Eclectic* | 20 | 18 | 19 | $34 |

W 100s | 2787 Broadway (bet. 107th & 108th Sts.) | 212-864-1555 | www.107west.com

A "longtime haunt" near Columbia, this no-frills "favorite" plies a "decent" "do-all" Eclectic menu spanning the gamut from Cajun and Tex-Mex "basics" to pastas and sushi; maybe it's "nothing too exciting", but the "happy-to-have you" service and "fair prices" keep the seats full.

Oriental Garden *Chinese/Seafood* | 22 | 12 | 15 | $34 |

Chinatown | 14 Elizabeth St. (bet. Bayard & Canal Sts.) | 212-619-0085 | www.orientalgardenny.com

"Don't let the drab decor fool you" at this vintage C-town Cantonese, because the "wonderful dim sum" and fresh seafood, straight from the tanks in front, just might "knock your socks off"; the mood may be "manic", but the "banquet" comes "without an insane price."

Orsay ◗ *French* | 18 | 21 | 18 | $57 |

E 70s | 1057 Lexington Ave. (75th St.) | 212-517-6400 | www.orsayrestaurant.com

An UES re-creation of "bygone France" by way of "Balthazar", this Gallic brasserie offers the "expected" French dishes (at "unexpectedly high prices") to a "boisterous", "multigenerational" crowd; "indifferent" service and a "lovely" art nouveau setting add authenticity.

Orso ◗ *Italian* | 23 | 19 | 22 | $58 |

W 40s | 322 W. 46th St. (bet. 8th & 9th Aves.) | 212-489-7212 | www.orsorestaurant.com

A "Theater District standard" since 1983, this "enjoyable" Restaurant Row Italian is touted for "delicious" dishes dispatched by a time-sensitive "staff of would-be actors"; while the interior is rather "plain" and reservations can be a "problem", the chance of "seeing Liza Minnelli" keeps the crowds coming.

Osso Buco *Italian* | 20 | 16 | 20 | $43 |

E 90s | 1662 Third Ave. (93rd St.) | 212-426-5422 | www.ossobuco2go.com

It's "not adventurous" and the digs are "nothing special", but this "trusty" Italian is a "satisfying option" for Upper Eastsiders and 92nd Street Y visitors, thanks to its "tasty" red-sauce fare served "family-style"; "accommodating" service, a "relaxed" vibe and "easy prices" seal the deal.

Osteria al Doge ◗ *Italian* | 20 | 18 | 20 | $50 |

W 40s | 142 W. 44th St. (bet. B'way & 6th Ave.) | 212-944-3643 | www.osteria-doge.com

Exuding "old-world charm", this Times Square duplex rolls out "tasty" Venetian victuals at a "reasonable-for-Midtown" price; regulars request the balcony to "avoid the noise of the bar crowd", but wherever you land, the "well-orchestrated" service will "get you to the theater on time, no matter what."

Osteria Laguna ◗ *Italian* | 21 | 18 | 19 | $48 |

E 40s | 209 E. 42nd St. (bet. 2nd & 3rd Aves.) | 212-557-0001 | www.osteria-laguna.com

Offering a "welcome" "neighborhood feel in a non-neighborhood area", this "busy" Italian between Grand Central and the U.N. serves

| | FOOD | DECOR | SERVICE | COST |

"straight-ahead" Venetian eats at fair rates; it's a "perfect lunch spot for on-the-go execs", with a "people-watching" bonus when the French doors are open.

Osteria Morini *Italian*
24 | 19 | 21 | $59

SoHo | 218 Lafayette St. (bet. Broome & Spring Sts.) | 212-965-8777 | www.osteriamorini.com

Chef Michael White "goes bohemian" at this "casual" SoHo Italian where the "simple, rustic" Emilia-Romagna menu is highlighted by "amazing" pastas; the pricing's "reasonable" if "not cheap", and "earplugs are necessary at prime times", but ultimately this one stays "always busy" for a reason.

Otto ● *Italian/Pizza*
23 | 19 | 20 | $40

G Village | 1 Fifth Ave. (8th St.) | 212-995-9559 | www.ottopizzeria.com

"Energetic" is an understatement at this "happening" enoteca/pizzeria from the Batali-Bastianich juggernaut, where "lots of families" and "mobs of NYU students" turn up the volume to "rock concert–like levels"; "mouthwatering" pizza, a "huge wine list" and "decent prices" are the draws, and the "railway terminal–themed" space is always "running on schedule."

Ouest *American*
24 | 21 | 22 | $67

W 80s | 2315 Broadway (84th St.) | 212-580-8700 | www.ouestny.com

"Special-night-out" celebrants tout chef Tom Valenti's "civilized" New American, "one of the few classy places" on the "Upper Ouest Side"; "seriously wonderful" food, "exemplary" service and "comfortable", red leather–lined environs justify the somewhat "expensive" tabs, though the $34 early-bird is "highly recommended."

Our Place *Chinese*
18 | 15 | 18 | $36

E 70s | 242 E. 79th St. (bet. 2nd & 3rd Aves.) | 212-288-4888 | www.ourplace79.com

At this 25-year-old UES Chinese "standby", "reasonably good" Cantonese standards – plus dim sum on weekends – satisfy locals who "don't want to travel" Downtown; "usually smooth service" and slightly "nicer digs" following a relocation make it "worth the few extra yuan."

Ovelia *Greek*
23 | 20 | 20 | $32

Astoria | 34-01 30th Ave. (34th St.) | Queens | 718-721-7217 | www.ovelia-ny.com

A "go-to" for Astorians seeking "Greek chic", this bar/eatery offers "fresh" Hellenic specialties with a "modern twist", including housemade sausages; "hospitable" owners, modest tabs and a "casual", "pleasant" setting with "outdoor seating" help keep it "popular."

Oyster Bar ⓩ *Seafood*
22 | 18 | 17 | $50

E 40s | Grand Central | 89 E. 42nd St., lower level (Park Ave.) | 212-490-6650 | www.oysterbarny.com

Serving up "history on the half shell" amid the "hustle of Grand Central", this "casual" seafood "institution" has been a "lively" "good time" for more than a century; whether you snare a table in the "tiled" dining room, "at the counter for a quick commuter nosh" or "stick to the quieter saloon", "brusque" service and "noise levels" as "high" as the tabs come with the territory; P.S. an outlet in Park Slope's ex-Fornino space is in the works.

Pachanga Patterson ● *Mexican* ▽ 23 | 21 | 21 | $28

Astoria | 33-17 31st Ave. (bet. 33rd & 34th Sts.) | Queens | 718-554-0525 | www.pachangapatterson.com

Putting a "cool spin" on Mexican classics, this "hip" Astoria joint from the Vesta folks offers "reasonably priced" tacos, small plates and a few mains; the colorful quarters work well for "low-key" hanging out, while the "sunny" backyard is another reason it's a "wonderful find."

Pacificana *Chinese* 23 | 15 | 18 | $27

Sunset Park | 813 55th St. (8th Ave.) | Brooklyn | 718-871-2880

"Delicious" dim sum at "pleasing" prices draws "throngs" to this Hong Kong–style 500-seater in Sunset Park, where a roster of Cantonese classics backs up what's on the "rolling carts"; although service is generally "quick", the "huge" digs are often a "madhouse", so "be patient" – it's "worth the wait."

Padre Figlio ☒ *Italian/Steak* 22 | 17 | 21 | $62

E 40s | 310 E. 44th St. (bet. 1st & 2nd Aves.) | 212-286-4310 | www.padrefiglio.com

A "welcoming" vibe prevails at this "unheralded" U.N.-area Italian steakhouse, where a "father-and-son team" makes you "feel at home" as you dine on "reliable" fare; live entertainment on weekends is a bonus, as is the $39 prix fixe.

The Palm *Steak* 24 | 18 | 22 | $78

E 40s | 837 Second Ave. (45th St.) | 212-687-2953 ☒
TriBeCa | 206 West St. (bet. Chambers & Warren Sts.) | 646-395-6393
W 50s | 250 W. 50th St. (bet. B'way & 8th Ave.) | 212-333-7256
Palm Too *Steak*
E 40s | 840 Second Ave. (bet. 44th & 45th Sts.) | 212-697-5198
www.thepalm.com

"Everything's big" at this "macho" steakhouse chain – from the "brontosaurus"-size chops and "monstrous lobsters" to the "high prices"; it's a natural "when you just want to eat a lot", but be prepared for "gruff" service and not much decor, save for "fun" caricatures on the walls (the 1926 original at 837 Second Avenue is best ambiancewise).

Palma *Italian* 24 | 20 | 21 | $60

W Village | 28 Cornelia St. (bet. Bleecker & W. 4th Sts.) | 212-691-2223 | www.palmanyc.com

Sicilian cooking made with "loving care" tastes like "nonna's homemade" at this "charming" West Villager, where "friendly attention" from the staff enhances the "true neighborhood" feel; the "lovely garden" adds appeal, while the private party–only back carriage house is "perfect for a special occasion."

Palm Court *American* 21 | 26 | 22 | $65

W 50s | Plaza Hotel | 768 Fifth Ave. (59th St.) | 212-546-5300 | www.theplaza.com

It doesn't "come much more elegant" than this Plaza Hotel American "icon", where a "gracious" staff glides through the "gilded" palm-lined setting to offer the "royal" treatment at breakfast, lunch and afternoon

	FOOD	DECOR	SERVICE	COST

tea; sure, it's a "splurge", but it's "not just for tourists"; P.S. star chef Geoffrey Zakarian has just been named its culinary director.

Pampano *Mexican/Seafood* | 24 | 21 | 21 | $55 |

E 40s | 209 E. 49th St., 2nd fl. (bet. 2nd & 3rd Aves.) | 212-751-4545

Pampano Taqueria *Mexican*

E 40s | Crystal Pavilion | 805 Third Ave. (bet. 49th & 50th Sts.) | 212-751-5257

www.modernmexican.com

Mexican "hits the high notes" at this "top-drawer" seafooder from chef Richard Sandoval and tenor Plácido Domingo, where "unobtrusive" servers tend the "lovely" upstairs dining room; the more casual ground-floor space offers "interesting tapas", while the lunch-only Taqueria continues to do "gangbuster business."

Pam Real Thai Food ⊄ *Thai* | 22 | 9 | 18 | $23 |

W 40s | 404 W. 49th St. (bet. 9th & 10th Aves.) | 212-333-7500 | www.pamrealthaifood.com

"Real-deal" Thai, "spiced to your taste", comes via "speedy" staffers at this cash-only Hell's Kitchen joint considered an "excellent pre-theater" choice; the digs are "kinda dumpy" but no one cares given pricing that's "one of the best deals in town."

Paola's *Italian* | 23 | 19 | 22 | $62 |

E 90s | Wales Hotel | 1295 Madison Ave. (92nd St.) | 212-794-1890 | www.paolasrestaurant.com

As a "sophisticated" haunt for "ritzy" Upper Eastsiders, this "attractive" Carnegie Hill Italian wins favor with *delizioso* cuisine and "hospitality" via the "gracious" eponymous owner and her "tip-top" staff; wallet-watching wags dub it "Payola's" – but it's "thriving" (and "loud") for a reason.

Papaya King ●⊄ *Hot Dogs* | 21 | 6 | 14 | $9 |

E 80s | 179 E. 86th St. (3rd Ave.) | 212-369-0648
NEW E Village | 3 St. Marks Pl. (3rd Ave.) | 646-692-8482
www.papayaking.com

"Easier than a trip to Coney Island", these weiner wonderlands supply "happiness in a tube" via "damn fine" hot dogs washed down with "yummy" papaya drinks; ok, there's "no atmosphere", not much service and "no star chef attached", but ultra-"cheap" tabs keep the trade brisk.

Pappardella ● *Italian* | 20 | 16 | 19 | $43 |

W 70s | 316 Columbus Ave. (75th St.) | 212-595-7996 | www.pappardella.com

This "inviting" UWS "neighborhood joint" is a "not-too-expensive" option for "tasty pastas" and other "solid" Italian standards delivered by an "efficient" team; whether you relax indoors or "sit outside" and scope out the Columbus Avenue scene, count on "no pressure."

Paradou *French* | 22 | 18 | 19 | $49 |

Meatpacking | 8 Little W. 12th St. (bet. Greenwich & Washington Sts.) | 212-463-8345 | www.paradounyc.com

Something rather "charming" in the "yuppie theme park" that is the Meatpacking District, this "informal" bistro bats out "solid" French grub for "reasonable" dough; it's best known for its "great" all-seasons garden and "energetic" brunches fueled by "unlimited champagne cocktails."

	FOOD	DECOR	SERVICE	COST

The Park ● *Mediterranean* — 17 | 24 | 16 | $40
Chelsea | 118 10th Ave. (bet. 17th & 18th Sts.) | 212-352-3313 | www.theparknyc.com

"Beautiful" multitiered surroundings are the draw at this Chelsea eatery-cum-nightery near the High Line, best known for a year-round garden "dressed up like Central Park"; despite only "ok" Med fare and service "hiccups", it's "attractive" enough to "make for a good time."

Park Side ● *Italian* — 25 | 20 | 22 | $50
Corona | 107-01 Corona Ave. (bet. 51st Ave. & 108th St.) | Queens | 718-271-9321 | www.parksiderestaurantny.com

"Local color" abounds at this longtime "Corona landmark" much revered for its "excellent", "old-school" Italian fare and "energetic" fan base, everyone from "politicians" to "goodfellas"; regulars feel it "rivals Arthur Avenue", what with the "valet parking", "plentiful" portions and "classy" service from a "tuxedoed" team.

Parlor Steakhouse *Steak* — 21 | 21 | 20 | $60
E 90s | 1600 Third Ave. (90th St.) | 212-423-5888 | www.parlorsteakhouse.com

"One of the few decent options above 86th Street", this "much-needed" Carnegie Hill steakhouse serves "quality" surf 'n' turf in a "lovely" modern setting; a "hopping bar scene" and convenience to the 92nd Street Y compensate for the "pricey" tabs.

Parm *Italian/Sandwiches* — 23 | 15 | 18 | $30
NoLita | 248 Mulberry St. (bet. Prince & Spring Sts.) | 212-993-7189 | www.parmnyc.com

They "elevate" chicken, meatball or eggplant parm to "dizzying heights" at this NoLita adjunct of Torrisi, turning out "signature sandwiches" and other "just-right" Italian dishes; it's already too "popular" for the "tiny", diner-esque space, so be prepared for "lengthy waits"

Parma *Italian* — 21 | 14 | 21 | $60
E 70s | 1404 Third Ave. (bet. 79th & 80th Sts.) | 212-535-3520 | www.parmanyc.com

This "longtime" UES Italian is a bastion of "hearty" cooking delivered by a seasoned staff that's clearly "there to please"; maybe it's "pricey" and "not much to look at", but it just "feels right" to loyal patrons.

Pascalou *French* — 21 | 15 | 19 | $44
E 90s | 1308 Madison Ave. (bet. 92nd & 93rd Sts.) | 212-534-7522 | www.pascalou.info

So long as you don't mind sitting "elbow-to-elbow", this UES vet is "dependable" for "authentic" French fare served in the "tiniest" space; a "welcoming" vibe and "cost-conscious" tabs – "especially the early-bird" – are additional bonuses.

Pasha *Turkish* — 20 | 18 | 19 | $43
W 70s | 70 W. 71st St. (bet. Columbus Ave. & CPW) | 212-579-8751 | www.pashanewyork.com

It's a bit like being "magically transported" to the "Bosphorus" at this "sedate" UWS retreat where "fine" Turkish staples are enhanced by "attentive" service and "civilized" surroundings; adherents applaud it as a "fairly priced" change of pace en route to Lincoln Center.

	FOOD	DECOR	SERVICE	COST

Pasquale's Rigoletto *Italian*
21 | 16 | 19 | $45

Fordham | 2311 Arthur Ave. (Crescent Ave.) | Bronx | 718-365-6644
For an "authentic Bronx experience", try this Arthur Avenue "landmark" offering "generous" helpings of "real Italian" classics seasoned with "a lot of local color"; it's a post–Yankee game "favorite", though it might be time for a decor "makeover."

Pastis ● *French*
22 | 21 | 19 | $51

Meatpacking | 9 Ninth Ave. (Little W. 12th St.) | 212-929-4844 | www.pastisny.com
"As much a scene as a restaurant", Keith McNally's "morning-to-evening" French bistro brings a "real Parisian feel" to the Meatpacking with its "adept" Gallic fare and atmospheric setting; "mechanical" service and "sky-high noise" are downsides, but no one notices as it's "mostly about people-watching anyway."

Pastrami Queen *Deli/Kosher*
21 | 6 | 14 | $26

E 70s | 1125 Lexington Ave. (78th St.) | 212-734-1500 | www.pastramiqueen.com
"Outstanding pastrami" is the claim to fame of this UES deli "staple" that's the "real thing" for "overstuffed sandwiches" and other kosher "basics done right"; seating is "almost an afterthought" in the "cramped, dingy" space, so "takeout is best."

Patricia's *Italian*
24 | 21 | 22 | $36

Morris Park | 1082 Morris Park Ave. (bet. Haight & Lurting Aves.) | Bronx | 718-409-9069 | www.patriciasnyc.com
Bronx-based boosters of this Morris Park Italian say it "satisfies" any hankering for "solid" "homestyle cooking" and "excellent" wood-fired pizzas; "beautiful decor", "friendly" service and good "bang for the buck" complete the "dependable" picture.

Patsy's *Italian*
22 | 18 | 22 | $57

W 50s | 236 W. 56th St. (bet. B'way & 8th Ave.) | 212-247-3491 | www.patsys.com
It "doesn't get more old-school" than this 70-year-old Midtown "throwback", a "favorite of Sinatra's" that still purveys "delicious" Neapolitan cooking and "quality service"; some say it could stand a "refresh", but the "heaping" portions and Theater District proximity are fine as is.

Patsy's Pizzeria *Pizza*
20 | 13 | 16 | $27

Chelsea | 318 W. 23rd St. (bet. 8th & 9th Aves.) | 646-486-7400 | www.patsyspizzeria.us
NEW E 40s | 801 Second Ave. (bet. 42nd & 43rd Sts.) | 212-878-9600 | www.patsyspizzeria.us
E 60s | 1279 First Ave. (69th St.) | 212-639-1000 | www.patsyspizzeria.us
E 60s | 206 E. 60th St. (bet. 2nd & 3rd Aves.) | 212-688-9707 | www.patsyspizzeria.us
G Village | 67 University Pl. (bet. 10th & 11th Sts.) | 212-533-3500 | www.patsyspizzeria.us
Harlem | 2287 First Ave. (bet. 117th & 118th Sts.) | 212-534-9783 | www.thepatsyspizza.com ⊖
W 70s | 61 W. 74th St. (bet. Columbus Ave. & CPW) | 212-579-3000 | www.patsyspizzeria.us
A "long-standing entry in the NY pizza wars", this circa-1933 East Harlem pie parlor offers a "solid" menu of "yummy, thin-crust"

items at "easy-on-the-wallet" tabs; its separately owned spin-offs share "generic" decor and barely "decent service", so diehards stick to the original.

Paul & Jimmy's *Italian*

| 20 | 18 | 20 | $48 |

Gramercy | 123 E. 18th St. (bet. Irving Pl. & Park Ave. S.) | 212-475-9540 | www.paulandjimmys.com

"It's been there for ages", meaning "they know what they're doing" at this "family-owned" Gramercy Italian supplying "solid", "old-school" staples via a "welcoming" crew; it's "appreciated" hereabouts, not least because the lunch and dinner prix fixes are quite the "deal."

Paulie Gee's Ⓜ *Pizza*

| 26 | 22 | 21 | $28 |

Greenpoint | 60 Greenpoint Ave. (bet. Franklin & West Sts.) | Brooklyn | 347-987-3747 | www.pauliegee.com

There's "never a boring pizza" at this Greenpoint "standout", whose "exquisite" Neapolitan pies marry a "perfect" "wood-fired" crust with "innovative", locavore-oriented toppings (including "lots of vegan options"); "omnipresent owner" Paulie himself "loves to schmooze" in the "cool, rustic room."

Peacefood Café *Kosher/Vegan/Vegetarian*

| 23 | 16 | 17 | $23 |

NEW **G Village** | 41 E. 11th St. (University Pl.) | 212-979-2288
W 80s | 460 Amsterdam Ave. (82nd St.) | 212-362-2266
www.peacefoodcafe.com

"Imaginative" (and kosher) "vegan deliciousness" attracts an "unpretentious" crunchy crowd to these "casual", "Woodstock-like" joints; "earnest" if "lackadaisical" service is a downside, but "guilt-free" grub at "affordable" rates makes it hard not to "feel at peace."

Peaches *Southern*

| 23 | 19 | 22 | $28 |

Bed-Stuy | 393 Lewis Ave. (MacDonough St.) | Brooklyn | 718-942-4162 | www.bcrestaurantgroup.com

Peaches HotHouse *Southern*

Bed-Stuy | 415 Tompkins Ave. (Hancock St.) | Brooklyn | 718-483-9111 | www.bcrestaurantgroup.com

This Bed-Stuy duo boasts a "no-nonsense" Southern comfort-food menu that's a "win-win" when paired with its "buoyant" vibe and "sincere" service; in sum, "your palate will be pleased", and so will your wallet.

Peanut Butter & Co. *Sandwiches*

| 21 | 14 | 18 | $14 |

G Village | 240 Sullivan St. (bet. Bleecker & W. 3rd Sts.) | 212-677-3995 | www.ilovepeanutbutter.com

"Kitschy and creative", this Village niche "celebrates peanut butter in all its glory" with sandwiches spanning the "classics" to "concoctions you'd never think of"; it's a surefire hit with the kids, though the "bare-bones" digs are "tight if you eat in."

NEW Pearl & Ash 🌑 *American*

| - | - | - | M |

NoLita | 220 Bowery (bet. Prince & Spring Sts.) | 212-837-2370 | www.pearlandash.com

Chef Richard Kuo (ex Corton, Frej, WD-50) turns out boundary-pushing American small plates at this new Bowery arrival, where a vast wine list complements the carefully composed menu; the latticed-walled rectangular space features lots of hip tchotchkes, and is already experiencing the crowds and clamor that come with an instant hit.

	FOOD	DECOR	SERVICE	COST

Pearl Oyster Bar ⊠ *New England/Seafood*   26 | 16 | 20 | $49
W Village | 18 Cornelia St. (bet. Bleecker & W. 4th Sts.) | 212-691-8211 |
www.pearloysterbar.com

"Delish" lobster rolls to "dream about" and other seafood dishes with
"New England flair" leave regulars "happy as clams" at Rebecca
Charles' "lively" West Village "gem"; given the "close quarters" and
"no-rez policy", it helps to "get there early."

Pearl Room *Seafood*   23 | 21 | 21 | $51
Bay Ridge | 8201 Third Ave. (82nd St.) | Brooklyn | 718-833-6666 |
www.thepearlroom.com

"As fancy as it gets in Bay Ridge", this seafaring "surprise" provides
"excellent preparations" of "fresh" fin fare served by an "attentive"
crew in a fetching setting suitable for "romantic" encounters; the only
catch is that it can be "pretty pricey."

Peasant Ⓜ *Italian*   24 | 21 | 20 | $61
NoLita | 194 Elizabeth St. (bet. Prince & Spring Sts.) | 212-965-9511 |
www.peasantnyc.com

From the "warm, inviting space" to the "fabulous", "wood-fired" cuisine and "professional" service, this "unforgettable" Italian "outshines" many of its NoLita neighbors; it's not cheap, but romeos bent
on "romance" head for the cellar wine bar for after-dinner drinks.

Peels ❶ *American*   20 | 20 | 17 | $36
E Village | 325 Bowery (2nd St.) | 646-602-7015 | www.peelsnyc.com
Staked somewhere "between retro and the new hip", this East Village
duplex from the "creators of Freemans" caters to the "discerning
nosher" with "well-executed" takes on Southern-style American
"comfort" classics; the "warm", whitewashed space hosts a "fantastic", "buttery" brunch – "if you can get in."

Peking Duck House *Chinese*   22 | 14 | 17 | $42
Chinatown | 28 Mott St. (bet. Chatham Sq. & Pell St.) | 212-227-1810
E 50s | 236 E. 53rd St. (bet. 2nd & 3rd Aves.) | 212-759-8260
www.pekingduckhousenyc.com

With its "juicy" meat and "savory, crispy skin", the signature Peking duck
"carved tableside" is a "real treat" at this "old-fashioned" Chinese duo; if
the decor seems "lacking" and service somewhat "lackadaisical", "wine
lovers" applaud the BYO policy at the Chinatown location.

Pellegrino's *Italian*   24 | 20 | 24 | $47
Little Italy | 138 Mulberry St. (bet. Grand & Hester Sts.) | 212-226-3177
"High-quality" traditional Italian cooking and "personal service" from
tuxedoed "pros" foster the "happy ambiance" at this "consistent"
"winner" in the heart of Little Italy; regulars prefer sitting outside and
taking in the only-in-NY Mulberry Street "scene."

Penelope *American*   22 | 18 | 18 | $25
Murray Hill | 159 Lexington Ave. (30th St.) | 212-481-3800 |
www.penelopenyc.com

Murray Hill locals tout this "adorable" neighborhood "favorite" for
"fab", "comfort"-oriented New American plates served in "country
cafe" digs at a "reasonable cost"; the "amazing brunch" is in "high de-
mand", so have "patience" with the inevitable "waits."

	FOOD	DECOR	SERVICE	COST

The Penrose ● *American*
▽ 20 | 21 | 15 | $34

E 80s | 1590 Second Ave. (bet. 82nd & 83rd Sts.) | 212-203-2751 |
www.penrosebar.com

Almost "too hip for the neighborhood", this "happening" UES gastro-pub plies "tasty cocktails" and a "limited" lineup of "solid" American bar food (including a notable LaFrieda burger); it also stands out thanks to "homey" vintage decor and a "downtown vibe."

Pepe Giallo *Italian*
22 | 14 | 17 | $25

Chelsea | 253 10th Ave. (bet. 24th & 25th Sts.) | 212-242-6055 |
www.pepegiallo.com

Pepe Rosso To Go *Italian*

SoHo | 149 Sullivan St. (bet. Houston & Prince Sts.) | 212-677-4555 |
www.peperossotogo.com

For a "budget-conscious" "quick bite", this "friendly" duo slings "lotsa pasta" and other "pretty good" Italian staples that are "easy on the wallet"; just be prepared for "totally unassuming" "joints" where service is "almost DIY."

Pepolino *Italian*
26 | 19 | 24 | $61

TriBeCa | 281 W. Broadway (bet. Canal & Lispenard Sts.) | 212-966-9983 |
www.pepolino.com

"Hiding in plain sight" on the fringes of TriBeCa, this "charming" trattoria delivers a "magic combination" of "savory" Tuscan farm cuisine and "attentive" service amid "rustic" surrounds; the experience is "not cheap", but given the "high quality", insiders still consider it a "deal."

Pequena ⊅ *Mexican*
▽ 21 | 18 | 18 | $24

Fort Greene | 86 S. Portland Ave. (bet. Fulton St. & Lafayette Ave.) |
Brooklyn | 718-643-0000
Prospect Heights | 601 Vanderbilt Ave. (Bergen St.) | Brooklyn |
718-230-5170
www.pequenarestaurant.com

"Authentic zing" makes up for "tiny" dimensions at this "funky" Fort Greene "micro"-*cucina*, where the "delicious" Mexican "favorites" come at "decent prices"; those who say the original is "suffocating" find the roomier Prospect Heights spin-off a relief.

Pera *Mediterranean*
20 | 20 | 18 | $50

E 40s | 303 Madison Ave. (bet. 41st & 42nd Sts.) | 212-878-6301
SoHo | 54 Thompson St. (bet. Broome & Spring Sts.) | 212-878-6305
www.peranyc.com

This "attractive" pair is a "solid" bet for Turkish-accented Mediterranean fare – including a "lovely range" of meze – served in "modern" surrounds; the Midtown original is a "no-brainer for business", while the stylin' SoHo spin-off sports a "stunning outdoor deck."

Perbacco ● *Italian*
23 | 17 | 21 | $52

E Village | 234 E. Fourth St. (bet. Aves. A & B) | 212-253-2038 |
www.perbacconyc.com

"Not your mama's Italian", this "itty-bitty" East Villager specializes in "creatively prepared" versions of familiar favorites set down by "enthusiastic servers"; maybe the "high prices" don't jibe with the "unassuming" setting, but baccers say foodwise it "outshines" many of its neighbors.

	FOOD	DECOR	SERVICE	COST

Perilla *American*

26 | 20 | 24 | $63

W Village | 9 Jones St. (bet. Bleecker & W. 4th Sts.) | 212-929-6868 |
www.perillanyc.com

Harold Dieterle's West Village American "fully delivers on its star-
chef reputation" with "creative" American standards (witness the
"glory that is the spicy duck meatball") served by a "polished" staff; an
"intimate" atmosphere and tabs that are "well priced for the quality"
make it a "spot-on" choice for "inspired" dining.

Periyali *Greek*

23 | 20 | 23 | $60

Flatiron | 35 W. 20th St. (bet. 5th & 6th Aves.) | 212-463-7890 |
www.periyali.com

"Dependably rewarding" since 1987, this Flatiron "Greek classic" remains a "refined" refuge for "superb fresh fish" and "gracious service" in "soothing" surrounds where a "low noise level" enables "good
conversation"; its "upscale" admirers attest it's more than "worth
the high price."

Perla ⏺ *Italian*

24 | 21 | 23 | $66

G Village | 24 Minetta Ln. (bet. MacDougal St. & 6th Ave.) | 212-933-1824 |
www.perlanyc.com

"Righteous" pastas and other "rustic" plates are a "pure delight" at
this "cozy" Village Italian from restaurateur Gabe Stulman (Chez
Sardine, Montmartre); "celebrities mixed in with the hoi polloi" make
for a "crazy-busy" scene, but with a "charming" crew to boost the
"warm feelings", it's "worth the try" to snag a table.

Per Lei ⏺ *Italian*

20 | 18 | 19 | $55

E 70s | 1347 Second Ave. (71st St.) | 212-439-9200 | www.perleinyc.com
"Young" Eurocentric sorts kick up a "fun vibe" at this Upper East Side
hangout where the Italian classics are "well prepared", but the "happening" scene is far tastier; conversationalists head for the sidewalk
seats to "avoid the loud bar", but there's no getting around tabs that
run "a bit high."

Perry St. *American*

26 | 25 | 24 | $69

W Village | 176 Perry St. (West St.) | 212-352-1900 |
www.perrystreetrestaurant.com

"Another Jean-Georges gem", this "exquisite" West Village New
American sees chef Cedric Vongerichten continue the family legacy
("like father, like son") with "innovative" cooking in a "serene",
Richard Meier–designed space along the Hudson; perhaps it's "expensive and a little out of the way", but the "smooth" service alone ensures a "memorable" experience.

Per Se *American/French*

28 | 28 | 29 | $325

W 60s | Time Warner Ctr. | 10 Columbus Circle (60th St. at B'way) |
212-823-9335 | www.perseny.com

"Unpretentious perfection" starts with the "superb" nine-course tasting menu at chef Thomas Keller's "flawless" French–New American in
the Time Warner Center and continues with "inspiring" Central Park
views and "approachable", "amazingly well-orchestrated" service
(again voted No. 1 in NYC); granted, the $295 set price may be "astro-
nomical", but overall this jackets-required destination is "hard to top"
for a "bucket-list" indulgence.

	FOOD	DECOR	SERVICE	COST

Persepolis *Persian*

22 | 16 | 20 | $41

E 70s | 1407 Second Ave. (bet. 73rd & 74th Sts.) | 212-535-1100 | www.persepolisnewyork.com

A "standout" among the "few Persians" in town, this Upper Eastsider offers "interesting", "well-spiced" Iranian dishes (the signature "sour-cherry rice is a treat") in an "understated" milieu; given the "personal service" and overall "value", it's "easy to relax and enjoy" here.

Pescatore ● *Italian/Seafood*

20 | 16 | 20 | $47

E 50s | 955 Second Ave. (bet. 50th & 51st Sts.) | 212-752-7151 | www.pescatorerestaurant.com

Eastsiders count on this "reliable" "local Italian" thanks to its "plentiful" portions of fish and pasta that are "surprisingly good for the price"; with its "pleasant" service, "homey" feel and "alfresco" tables upstairs and down, some call it a "sleeper" date place.

Petaluma *Italian*

18 | 16 | 18 | $50

E 70s | 1356 First Ave. (73rd St.) | 212-772-8800 | www.petalumarestaurant.com

A "longtime" UES "local", this standby supplies brick-oven pizzas and other Italian basics that are "consistently good" if "not particularly distinctive"; the "open" space is "appealing", though critics contend it's an "upscale wannabe" that's gotten "a little too pricey."

Peter Luger Steak House ⊅ *Steak*

27 | 16 | 21 | $83

Williamsburg | 178 Broadway (Driggs Ave.) | Brooklyn | 718-387-7400 | www.peterluger.com

Voted NYC's No. 1 steakhouse for the 30th year in a row, this circa-1887 Williamsburg "landmark" offers a "classic, straightforward" menu (highlighted by a "terrific" aged porterhouse) that "hasn't changed" in eons but still draws big "crowds"; "gruff" service and a "no-frills, boys'-club" ambiance are "part of the experience", and don't forget to bring "plenty of cash" – it doesn't accept credit cards.

Peter's Since 1969 *American*

▽ 20 | 15 | 19 | $30

E 50s | 667 Lexington Ave. (bet. 55th & 56th Sts.) | 212-308-1969 🛢
Williamsburg | 168 Bedford Ave. (bet. N. 7th & 8th Sts.) | Brooklyn | 718-388-2811
www.peterssince.com

For "comforting" chow "done right", these cross-borough joints dispense "awesome" rotisserie chicken and other "hearty" American dishes for "reasonable" sums; with "nothing-fancy" counter-service setups staffed by a "sweet" crew, they're "easy, filling" options.

Petite Abeille *Belgian*

19 | 16 | 17 | $32

Flatiron | 44 W. 17th St. (bet. 5th & 6th Aves.) | 212-727-2989
Gramercy | 401 E. 20th St. (1st Ave.) | 212-727-1505
TriBeCa | 134 W. Broadway (bet. Duane & Thomas Sts.) | 212-791-1360
W Village | 466 Hudson St. (Barrow St.) | 212-741-6479
www.petiteabeille.com

"Fresh, tasty" mussels, "crispy" frites and other "hearty" Belgian classics pair with a "vast" beer selection at this "charming" chainlet of "neighborhood" bistros; service might be "hit-or-miss", but given the "reasonable" prices, it fits the bill for "casual, low-key dining."

	FOOD	DECOR	SERVICE	COST

Petrossian *Continental/French* | 24 | 24 | 23 | $75 |

W 50s | 182 W. 58th St. (7th Ave.) | 212-245-2214 | www.petrossian.com
"Caviar is king" at this "formal" art deco "classic" near Carnegie Hall
where the staff "never rushes you" and the "very expensive" French-
Continental menu also features "reasonable prix fixe offerings"; for a
"quick bite", there's also a "little cafe next door."

Philip Marie ●Ⓜ *American* | 19 | 17 | 19 | $44 |

W Village | 569 Hudson St. (W. 11th St.) | 212-242-6200 |
www.philipmarie.com
A Village "standby" for "homestyle cooking", this "laid-back" New
American does a "solid" job with its "unpretentious" menu; admittedly,
it's "not quite fine dining", but the "fair value" keeps regulars regular.

Philippe ● *Chinese* | 23 | 20 | 20 | $68 |

E 60s | 33 E. 60th St. (bet. Madison & Park Aves.) | 212-644-8885 |
www.philippechow.com
"Low-lit and high-class", this East Side Chinese channels "Mr. Chow"
with "well-crafted" cuisine served in a "cacophonous" setting to a
"glamorous" crowd; the $20 prix fixe lunch dodges the "sky-high"
tabs – but while you may "run into Lil' Kim", skeptics shrug the scene's
"better than the food."

Pho Bang ⇰ *Noodle Shop/Vietnamese* | 22 | 8 | 14 | $16 |

Little Italy | 157 Mott St. (bet. Broome & Grand Sts.) | 212-966-3797
Elmhurst | 82-90 Broadway (bet. 45th & Whitney Aves.) | Queens |
718-205-1500
Flushing | 41-07 Kissena Blvd. (bet. Barclay & 41st Aves.) | Queens |
718-939-5520
Phollowers endorse this Vietnamese trio as a "legit" source for "substantial" bowls of the "mmm-mmm" namesake soup; regulars ignore
the "tacky" decor and waiters who "communicate in grunts", and focus instead on the "super-deal" tabs.

Phoenix Garden ⇰ *Chinese* | 23 | 10 | 14 | $31 |

Murray Hill | 242 E. 40th St. (bet. 2nd & 3rd Aves.) | 212-983-6666 |
www.thephoenixgarden.com
A "real find" in Murray Hill, this "unassuming" BYO may be "as good
as" Chinatown for "genuine Cantonese" specialties led by an "excellent salt-and-pepper shrimp"; fans overlook the "attitude", "dreary
decor" and cash-only policy because you can't beat the "value."

Piccola Venezia *Italian* | 25 | 17 | 24 | $58 |

Astoria | 42-01 28th Ave. (42nd St.) | Queens | 718-721-8470 |
www.piccola-venezia.com
"You name it, they prepare it" at this venerable Astoria "charmer", where
the "menu's only a suggestion" and the "traditional" Italian dishes are
"impeccably" rendered; it's "a little pricey" given the "dated" decor, but
"personalized service" ensures everyone feels "like family."

Piccolo Angolo Ⓜ *Italian* | 26 | 14 | 22 | $47 |

W Village | 621 Hudson St. (Jane St.) | 212-229-9177 |
www.piccoloangolo.com
Owner and "character" Renato Migliorini puts "heart and soul"
into this "homey" West Village vet, where the "ample portions" of

"wonderful" Northern Italian fare and "amiable" service inspire many a "permanent smile"; it's a "tiny" place with "lines outside", so insiders reserve ahead.

Picholine *French/Mediterranean*

FOOD	DECOR	SERVICE	COST
27	25	26	$103

W 60s | 35 W. 64th St. (bet. B'way & CPW) | 212-724-8585 | www.picholinenyc.com

Thanks to "sophisticated" French-Med fare dispatched in a "classy" setting by an "impeccable" team, Terry Brennan's "oasis of calm" near Lincoln Center continues to draw a "loyal clientele", especially among "cheese lovers" who save room for the "unusual" selections; granted, the tabs will cost you "big bucks", but the payoff is a "thoroughly elegant dining experience."

Pies-N-Thighs ● *Soul Food*

FOOD	DECOR	SERVICE	COST
24	14	18	$22

Williamsburg | 166 S. Fourth St. (Driggs Ave.) | Brooklyn | 347-529-6090 | www.piesnthighs.com

As a "front-runner" for "succulent" fried chicken and sides topped off with "damn good" pie, this Williamsburg soul food specialist is an "artery-clogging" "treat"; maybe the "snug" space is "not so special", but the "amiable" service and "even friendlier prices" earn a "thumbs-up."

Pietro's ⊠ *Italian/Steak*

FOOD	DECOR	SERVICE	COST
24	14	22	$68

E 40s | 232 E. 43rd St. (bet. 2nd & 3rd Aves.) | 212-682-9760

In the Grand Central area since 1932, this "old-school" holdout rests its rep on "excellent steaks" and Italian basics served in "copious amounts" by a "gracious", "been-there-for-years" staff; no, the room's "not glamorous", but its "loyal following" savors the "quiet conversation."

Pig and Khao ●Ⓜ *SE Asian*

FOOD	DECOR	SERVICE	COST
▽ 23	15	18	$45

LES | 68 Clinton St. (bet. Rivington & Stanton Sts.) | 212-920-4485 | www.pigandkhao.com

Former *Top Chef* contestant Leah Cohen is behind the burners of this "innovative" LES Southeast Asian that incorporates Thai and Filipino flavors (and "amazing pork dishes") in its "good-value" menu; set in the former Falai space, it features communal tables, an open kitchen with a chef's counter and a "cute little" back garden.

Pig Heaven *Chinese*

FOOD	DECOR	SERVICE	COST
21	14	19	$36

E 80s | 1540 Second Ave. (bet. 80th & 81st Sts.) | 212-744-4333 | www.pigheavennyc.com

"When nothing but pig will do", "sweetheart" hostess Nancy Lee's "aptly named" UES Chinese vet comes in handy as a "relaxed" option for affordable "hog-inspired dishes" led by "superior spare-ribs"; the "cheesy" pink decor gets a few grunts, but for devotees, it's "all about taste."

Pinche Taqueria *Mexican*

FOOD	DECOR	SERVICE	COST
21	11	15	$15

NEW Chelsea | 103 W. 14th St. (bet. 6th & 7th Aves.) | 212-989-1289
NoHo | 333 Lafayette St. (Bleecker St.) | 212-343-9977
NoLita | 227 Mott St. (bet. Prince & Spring Sts.) | 212-625-0090
www.pinchetaqueria.com

Pedigreed via a Tijuana original, these "no-frills" taquerias "hit the spot" with "pretty authentic" tacos and other "tasty" West Coast–style Mexican eats; the quarters may be "cramped", but for peso-pinchers the prices are "worth an elbow or two."

	FOOD	DECOR	SERVICE	COST

NEW The Pines American
▽ 23 | 16 | 20 | $49

Gowanus | 284 Third Ave. (bet. Carroll & President Sts.) | Brooklyn |
718-596-6560 | www.thepinesbrooklyn.com

The team behind Gowanus' Littleneck strikes again with this "hip"
nook serving "creative" New American vittles in artfully lived-in digs
outfitted with church pews and lodge-appropriate knickknacks; in
warm weather, the "lovely" back patio offers grill dishes and ciders.

Ping's Seafood Chinese/Seafood
21 | 12 | 14 | $30

Chinatown | 22 Mott St. (bet. Chatham Sq. & Mosco St.) | 212-602-9988
Elmhurst | 83-02 Queens Blvd. (Goldsmith St.) | Queens | 718-396-1238
www.pingsnyc.com

With "first-rate" seafood backed by "varied", "flavorful" dim sum,
these Chinatown-Elmhurst Cantonese contenders stay "ping on tar-
get"; despite "simple" settings and "not-that-welcoming" service,
they "pack 'em in", especially for that "madhouse" Sunday brunch.

Pinocchio Ⓜ Italian
24 | 17 | 24 | $49

E 90s | 1748 First Ave. (bet. 90th & 91st Sts.) | 212-828-5810

"Really fine" for a "local place", this "tiny" UES Italian offers a "robust"
menu with "special attention" from its "true gentleman" of an owner;
the space is "a bit close", but that doesn't deter "devoted" regulars.

Pintaile's Pizza Pizza
▽ 20 | 7 | 13 | $18

E 80s | 1573 York Ave. (bet. 83rd & 84th Sts.) | 212-396-3479 |
www.pintailespizza.com

Proof that pizza can "actually be healthy", this Yorkville "neighborhood haunt" produces "well-crafted pies" featuring "unusually thin"
whole-wheat crusts and "fresh", "inventive" toppings; it's a "real hole-
in-the-wall", though, so many go "carryout."

Pio Pio Peruvian
23 | 15 | 18 | $28

E 90s | 1746 First Ave. (bet. 90th & 91st Sts.) | 212-426-5800
Murray Hill | 210 E. 34th St. (bet. 2nd & 3rd Aves.) | 212-481-0034
W 40s | 604 10th Ave. (bet. 43rd & 44th Sts.) | 212-459-2929
W 90s | 702 Amsterdam Ave. (94th St.) | 212-665-3000
Mott Haven | 264 Cypress Ave. (bet. 138th & 139th Sts.) | Bronx |
718-401-3300
Jackson Heights | 84-02 Northern Blvd. (bet. 84th & 85th Sts.) |
Queens | 718-426-4900 ◐
Jackson Heights | 84-21 Northern Blvd. (85th St.) | Queens | 718-426-1010
Rego Park | 62-30 Woodhaven Blvd. (bet. Dry Harbor Rd. & 62nd Dr.) |
Queens | 718-458-0606 ⊟
www.piopio.com

Dishing out "huge portions" of "juicy" rotisserie chicken with "addicting" green sauce, these "no-frills" Peruvians prove you can indulge in
a "satisfying" meal without "breaking the bank"; some warn service
might be "rushed" and noise levels "outrageous", but they're "fun with
a group" and "family-friendly" to boot.

Piper's Kilt ◑ Burgers/Pub Food
21 | 14 | 20 | $22

Inwood | 4946 Broadway (bet. Isham & 207th Sts.) | 212-569-7071 |
www.piperskiltofinwood.com
Kingsbridge | 170 W. 231st St. (Albany Crescent) | Bronx | 347-602-7880

"Locals" gather for some of the "best burgers around" at these Bronx-
Inwood "mainstays", where the "satisfying" pub fare is best chased

with a "mug of beer" or three; their "throwback" Irish bar setups accommodate "everyone from toddlers to drunken Jets fans."

Pisticci *Italian*

25 | 20 | 22 | $36

W 100s | 125 La Salle St. (B'way) | 212-932-3500 | www.pisticcinyc.com

It "doesn't get much better for local Italian" dining than this "warm, welcoming" Columbia-area "favorite", home to "scrumptious" food at "reasonable prices" and free "jazz on Sundays"; the "no-reservations" rule can be "a drag", yet the "long lines" deter few.

PizzArte *Pizza*

21 | 20 | 19 | $37

W 50s | 69 W. 55th St. (bet. 5th & 6th Aves.) | 212-247-3936 | www.pizzarteny.com

"True" Neapolitan specialties make this "authentic" Italian a "wonderful addition to Midtown", serving "perfectly charred" pizzas from a "wood-burning oven" as well as other "well-priced" Italiana; what's more, this "cool", "modern" duplex is lined with art, all for sale.

P.J. Clarke's ● *Pub Food*

17 | 16 | 17 | $39

E 50s | 915 Third Ave. (55th St.) | 212-317-1616

P.J. Clarke's at Lincoln Square ● *Pub Food*

W 60s | 44 W. 63rd St. (Columbus Ave.) | 212-957-9700

P.J. Clarke's on the Hudson ⊠ *Pub Food*

Financial District | 4 World Financial Ctr. (Vesey St.) | 212-285-1500

www.pjclarkes.com

A bastion of "old NY coolness", this circa-1884 Midtown saloon is renowned for its "super-duper" burgers, "historic ambiance" and "fun bar scene"; while the newer spin-offs "don't have the charm" of the original, the Lincoln Center outpost offers pre-theater convenience, while the FiDi branch boasts "lovely water views."

The Place *American/Mediterranean*

23 | 24 | 24 | $57

W Village | 310 W. Fourth St. (bet. Bank & W. 12th Sts.) | 212-924-2711 | www.theplaceny.com

"Nestled" below sidewalk level, this "quintessential West Village date spot" is "sure to impress" with its "romantic", fireplace-equipped setting, "decadent" Med–New American cooking and "warm" service; the only quibble is with the "boring name", which fans complain "doesn't do it justice."

Plaza Food Hall *Eclectic*

22 | 21 | 18 | $43

W 50s | Plaza Hotel | 1 W. 59th St., lower level (5th Ave.) | 212-986-9260 | www.theplazafoodhall.com

A "great way to graze", this "vibrant" "one-stop shop" below The Plaza provides "outstanding" Eclectic options via "varying food stations" issuing sushi, pizza, grill grub and much more; partly run by Todd English and recently expanded to add more vendors, it's plenty "popular" despite "so-so" service and "lunch counter–style" seating.

Pó *Italian*

25 | 17 | 22 | $54

W Village | 31 Cornelia St. (bet. Bleecker & W. 4th Sts.) | 212-645-2189 | www.porestaurant.com

Pocket-size but "charming", this "longtime" Villager remains an "absolute gem" furnishing "first-quality" Italian fare "without an ounce of pretense"; "repeat customers" confirm the "tight squeeze" is "so worth it" for "amazing" dining that "won't break the bank."

Poke ⊠⊅ *Japanese* | 24 | 14 | 18 | $44 |

E 80s | 343 E. 85th St. (bet. 1st & 2nd Aves.) | 212-249-0569 | www.pokesushinyc.com

The "finest fish" lures UES sushiphiles to this cash-only Japanese BYO, a modest standby touted for its "creative" rolls and "off-menu" items; "affordable" rates ensure it's "always busy", even if critics take a poke at the "no-reservations policy" and "long lines."

Pok Pok Ny *Thai* | ∇ 24 | 13 | 19 | $35 |

Red Hook | 127 Columbia St. (bet. Degraw & Kane Sts.) | Brooklyn | 718-923-9322 | www.pokpokpdx.com

"No frills, but all thrills" is the word on Andy Ricker's "bold" Columbia Waterfront yearling that lures throngs with its "affordable", "delectable" takes on "real Thai" classics; despite a "cramped" setting, no-rez rule and "crazy" waits, aficionados say "believe the hype"; P.S. it's poised to move to bigger digs at 117 Columbia Street.

Pok Pok Phat Thai ●⊅ *Thai* | - | - | - | I |

LES | 137 Rivington St. (bet. Norfolk & Suffolk Sts.) | 718-923-9322 | www.pokpokwing.com

Pad Thai is the specialty of this noodle-centric LES den from chef Andy Ricker, a sibling of his Red Hook wonder, Pok Pok Ny; maybe the cash-only offerings are limited and the setting ultratiny, but no one cares given the low tabs and high quality.

Pommes Frites ● *Belgian* | 24 | 10 | 16 | $10 |

E Village | 123 Second Ave. (7th St.) | 212-674-1234 | www.pommesfrites.ws

"Crispy outside yet tender inside", the "world-class" Belgian fries arrive with a "crazy array of dipping sauces" at this East Village one-trick pony where there's often "a line out the door" (especially for a "late-night snack"); since the "tiny" digs are usually "packed", most get it "to go."

Pomodoro Rosso *Italian* | 21 | 17 | 21 | $43 |

W 70s | 229 Columbus Ave. (bet. 70th & 71st Sts.) | 212-721-3009 | www.pomodororossonyc.com

It's like "mama's in the kitchen" cooking up "hearty" Italian "comfort" classics at this "quaint" UWS longtimer near Lincoln Center; it's run with "loving care", but "no reservations" mean "big waits" – "get there early" if you're going pre-performance.

Pongal *Indian/Kosher/Vegetarian* | ∇ 24 | 16 | 18 | $25 |

Murray Hill | 110 Lexington Ave. (bet. 27th & 28th Sts.) | 212-696-9458 | www.pongalnyc.com

Home to South Indian specialties "not easily found elsewhere", this Curry Hill "dosa nirvana" pleases fans with its "delicious" kosher-vegetarian bounty; service can be "slow" and there's "no decor" to speak of, so most focus on the "unbeatable" cost.

Pongsri Thai *Thai* | 21 | 13 | 18 | $29 |

Chelsea | 165 W. 23rd St. (bet. 6th & 7th Aves.) | 212-645-8808
Chinatown | 106 Bayard St. (Baxter St.) | 212-349-3132

(continued)

(continued)

Pongsri Thai

W 40s | 244 W. 48th St. (bet. B'way & 8th Ave.) | 212-582-3392
www.pongsri.net

"Authentic curries" and other "quality" Thai eats are "delivered with real spice" at these "bargain-priced" veterans; the decor's "not fancy", but "convenient" locations and "fast" service make them a "good choice" when you're "pressed for time."

Ponticello *Italian*   24 | 21 | 23 | $54

Astoria | 46-11 Broadway (bet. 46th & 47th Sts.) | Queens | 718-278-4514 |
www.ponticelloristorante.com

Ever "reliable" since 1982, this Astoria Northern Italian boasts a "terrific" roster of "classics" served by seasoned waiters who ensure you'll be "well taken care of"; if it seems "slightly overpriced" for the "old-world" ambiance, habitués still "feel completely at home."

Ponty Bistro ● *African/French*   22 | 14 | 19 | $45

Gramercy | 218 Third Ave. (bet. 18th & 19th Sts.) | 212-777-1616 |
www.pontybistro.com

"Sparking your taste buds", this all-day Gramercy "find" offers "original" French-Senegalese dishes livened up with African spices and "charming" service; it's also "well priced" (notably the $25 early-bird), but word's "getting out" and the "narrow" room fills up fast.

Porchetta *Italian*   24 | 10 | 18 | $18

E Village | 110 E. Seventh St. (bet. Ave. A & 1st Ave.) | 212-777-2151 |
www.porchettanyc.com

"Hog heaven" in the East Village, chef Sara Jenkins' "one-trick pony" vends only Italian roast pork – whether as "scrumptious" signature sandwiches or platters – plus a few sides; given the six-seat, "hole-in-the-wall" setup, it's "basically a take-out place."

Porsena *Italian*   22 | 15 | 19 | $50

E Village | 21 E. Seventh St. (bet. 2nd & 3rd Aves.) | 212-228-4923 |
www.porsena.com

The "knowing hand" of chef-owner Sara Jenkins elevates the "heavenly pastas" and other "delicious, straightforward" Italian staples at this "friendly" East Villager; it works as a "down-to-earth" "date spot", albeit one that's apt to be "busy" and "uninteresting" to look at.

Porter House New York *Steak*   26 | 25 | 25 | $77

W 60s | Time Warner Ctr. | 10 Columbus Circle (60th St. at B'way) |
212-823-9500 | www.porterhousenewyork.com

From "fabulous" cuts of meat to "interesting" sides, a "feast awaits" at Michael Lomonaco's TWC "destination steakhouse" where "impeccable" service helps justify the "expensive" prices; indeed, the Central Park views from the "elegant" dining room are as "impressive" as the food.

Portofino *Italian/Seafood*   22 | 19 | 22 | $49

City Island | 555 City Island Ave. (Cross St.) | Bronx | 718-885-1220 |
www.portofinocityisland.com

A "throwback" to "old-style" dining, this "steady", circa-1975 City Island Italian is a "staple" for "enjoyable", if familiar, fare focusing on "fresh" seafood; longtime loyalists agree it's "worth the price" alone for the alfresco deck seating and its "view of the water."

	FOOD	DECOR	SERVICE	COST

Posto *Pizza*
24 | 14 | 18 | $29

Gramercy | 310 Second Ave. (18th St.) | 212-716-1200 |
www.postothincrust.com

The "thinnest", "winningest" crust is the hallmark of this Gramercy
pizzeria, a "local hot spot" cranking out "splendid" pies at "accessible
prices"; it's a "tight space" with "no decor" and "not-so-courteous"
service, so the to-go trade stays brisk.

Pranna ● *SE Asian*
18 | 23 | 19 | $47

Murray Hill | 79 Madison Ave. (bet. 28th & 29th Sts.) | 212-696-5700 |
www.prannarestaurant.com

With its "lovely" design, this "spacious" Murray Hill Southeast Asian offers a "modern" backdrop for its "tasty" plates; there's also a "lively bar"
that takes on a "club vibe" as the night wears on, so never mind if it's
"expensive" for what some term "style over substance."

NEW Preserve 24 ● *American*
- | - | - | M

LES | 177 E. Houston St. (bet. Allen & Orchard Sts.) | 646-837-6100 |
www.preserve24.com

One of the year's quirkiest newcomers, this rustic LES restaurant-
cum–art installation is done up like an explorer's club, with off-the-
wall design elements like piano-pedal beer-tap handles, fans made
from oars and a bar with a built-in rowboat; a big, wood-burning pot-
belly stove is the source of much of the hearty American grub on offer.

Press 195 ● *Sandwiches*
24 | 17 | 20 | $22

Bayside | 40-11 Bell Blvd. (bet. 40th & 41st Aves.) | Queens |
718-281-1950 | www.press195.com

The "hardest part is choosing" from the "extensive list" of "creative,
satisfying" panini capably pressed at this "affordable" Bayside "casual-
eats" standout; "addicting" fries complete the "perfect combination."

NEW Prime Grill *Kosher/Steak*
- | - | - | E

W 50s | 25 W. 56th St. (bet. 5th & 6th Aves.) | 212-692-9292 |
www.primehospitalityny.com

Relocated to new Midtown digs in the former Beacon space, this glatt
kosher steakhouse now sprawls over two levels arranged around a
happening bar; its observant movers-and-shakers crowd likes the upscale menu and vibrant atmosphere, the pricey tabs not so much.

Prime KO *Kosher/Steak*
23 | 22 | 20 | $63

W 80s | 217 W. 85th St. (bet. Amsterdam Ave. & B'way) | 212-496-1888 |
www.primehospitalityny.com

Steaks "cooked to perfection" plus "delicious" sushi keep this "swank"
Upper West Side kosher steakhouse "crowded", even though the tabs
are decidedly "not cheap"; service gets mixed marks, but most consider it a "fun venue", especially if you factor in "fancy cocktails" and
occasional DJ nights.

Prime Meats ● *American/Steak*
23 | 21 | 21 | $54

Carroll Gardens | 465 Court St. (Luquer St.) | Brooklyn | 718-254-0327 |
www.frankspm.com

The "name says it" about this carnivore-oriented Frankies Spuntino
spin-off in Carroll Gardens, where "delicious", "German-inspired"
American steakhouse fare arrives via a "whiskered", "über-hip" staff;

| | FOOD | DECOR | SERVICE | COST |

the "cool, Prohibition-style" digs get "packed" and it "doesn't take reservations", so "arrive early."

Primola ● Italian
23 | 18 | 20 | $65

E 60s | 1226 Second Ave. (bet. 64th & 65th Sts.) | 212-758-1775

No stranger to "Page Six" mentions, this "clubby" Italian satisfies its "moneyed UES" clientele with "dependable" pastas at "steep prices"; count on service "with a smile" if you're a regular, a "celebrity" or "wearing dark glasses", but for first-timers the "attitude" can be "intimidating."

Print American
22 | 23 | 23 | $64

W 40s | Ink48 Hotel | 653 11th Ave. (bet. 47th & 48th Sts.) | 212-757-2224 | www.printrestaurant.com

Way "out of the way" in West Hell's Kitchen, this "yet-to-be-discovered" New American is "first rate" for "locavoracious" fare and "smart" service in "stylish" environs; insiders have cocktails after dinner on the "rooftop lounge" with its drop-dead, 360-degree "skyline view."

Prosperity Dumpling Chinese
26 | 4 | 14 | $6

LES | 46 Eldridge St. (bet. Canal & Hester Sts.) | 212-343-0683 | www.prosperitydumpling.com

"Frugal foodies" rave about the "awesome", "meaty dumplings" and other "tasty" items at this "bang-for-your-buck" LES Chinese; "long lines" and "haphazard" service in "utterly cramped" surrounds make for a strong case for takeout.

Prune American
25 | 16 | 22 | $53

E Village | 54 E. First St. (bet. 1st & 2nd Aves.) | 212-677-6221 | www.prunerestaurant.com

Chef Gabrielle Hamilton's "idiosyncratic" 15-year-old East Villager remains as "fascinating" as ever thanks to "inspired" New American "food for thought" that's "graciously served" in a "tiny", "cheek-by-jowl" space; habitués report it "can't be beat" for weekend brunch, despite the "enormously long lines."

Public Eclectic
23 | 24 | 22 | $66

NoLita | 210 Elizabeth St. (bet. Prince & Spring Sts.) | 212-343-7011 | www.public-nyc.com

"Sure to impress" with its "genius", "library"-like AvroKO interior, this "cool" NoLita Eclectic follows through with a "unique" Australian/New Zealand–inspired menu ("kangaroo appetizer", anyone?); the "hospitality" keeps its "energetic" fan base coming back, especially for the "outstanding brunch."

Pulino's ● Pizza
20 | 19 | 18 | $38

NoLita | 282 Bowery (E. Houston St.) | 212-226-1966 | www.pulinosny.com

Keith McNally's "buzzy", all-day pizzeria is a "boon" to the Bowery for "solid" pies that "range from classic to inventive" ("breakfast pizza" – "why not?"); the "efficient service" and "cool" bottles-and-tile interior pull in an "energetic" crowd, though "your hearing may pay the price."

Pulqueria ● Mexican
▽ 20 | 21 | 17 | $46

Chinatown | 11 Doyers St., downstairs (bet. Bowery & Pell St.) | 212-227-3099 | www.pulquerianyc.com

You'd "never expect it" given the "hidden" Chinatown basement locale, but this "speakeasy-style" Mexican joint from the Apothéke folks

	FOOD	DECOR	SERVICE	COST

"authentically" musters regional eats that venture well "beyond the ordinary"; "interesting cocktails" based on pulque, the "namesake spirit", ease the pain of paying.

Pure Food & Wine *Vegan/Vegetarian* | 24 | 22 | 24 | $53 |

Gramercy | 54 Irving Pl. (bet. 17th & 18th Sts.) | 212-477-1010 | www.purefoodandwine.com

Granted, it's "very different", but this Gramercy vegan "revelation" deserves recognition for the "unexpected" "flavor and flair" of its "dazzling" raw cuisine; "capable service" and a "lovely" garden enhance the "pure pleasure", even if it's a "quite expensive" way to "feel virtuous."

Pure Thai Cookhouse *Thai* | 25 | 16 | 19 | $24 |

W 50s | 766 Ninth Ave. (bet. 51st & 52nd Sts.) | 212-581-0999 | www.purethaishophouse.com

Purists plug this Hell's Kitchen "hole-in-the-wall" for the "authenticity" of its "full-flavored" Thai dishes, many starring "homemade egg noodles" in "perfectly spiced" soups (just "watch out for the heat"); the pace is "fast", the prices "decent" and the ambiance "elbow-to-elbow."

Purple Yam *Asian* | 22 | 18 | 20 | $35 |

Ditmas Park | 1314 Cortelyou Rd. (bet. Argyle & Rugby Rds.) | Brooklyn | 718-940-8188 | www.purpleyamnyc.com

A "delicate touch" distinguishes the "creative" cookery at this Ditmas Park Pan-Asian, best known for its "tasty" takes on traditional Filipino fare; customers are tended by the "nicest" staff, and the prices are no less agreeable.

Pylos ⦿ *Greek* | 27 | 23 | 22 | $52 |

E Village | 128 E. Seventh St. (bet. Ave. A & 1st Ave.) | 212-473-0220 | www.pylosrestaurant.com

The "refined" Greek menu is "creative in wonderful ways" at this "higher-end" East Village Hellenic tucked into a "tight" but "lively" space decorated with clay pots suspended overhead; "attentive" service "with a smile" makes it all the more "charming."

Qi *Thai* | 22 | 22 | 19 | $29 |

Union Sq | 31 W. 14th St. (bet. 5th & 6th Aves.) | 212-929-9917
W 40s | 675 Eighth Ave. (43rd St.) | 212-247-8991
NEW **Qi Thai Grill** *Thai*

Williamsburg | 176 N. Ninth St. (bet. Bedford & Driggs Aves.) | Brooklyn | 718-302-1499
www.qirestaurant.com

Chef Pichet Ong delivers "beautifully presented", "beyond-the-ordinary" Asian-Thai dishes in "high-energy" settings at this "trendy" trio, where service can be "spotty", but "decent" prices compensate; P.S. the Williamsburg outpost, a collaboration with Queens stalwart Sripraphai, is the latest arrival.

NEW Quality Italian ⦿ *Italian/Steak* | - | - | - | E |

W 50s | 57 W. 57th St., 2nd fl. (enter on 6th Ave. bet. 57th & 58th Sts.) | 212-390-1111 | www.qualityitalian.com

Sibling to Quality Meats around the corner, this new Midtown steakhouse via Michael Stillman offers a variety of pricey chops accompanied by Italian-American favorites; the multiroom, AvroKO-designed space feels like Brooklyn with its distressed industrial look, and

	FOOD	DECOR	SERVICE	COST

there's a bonus walk-up, stand-up-only bar on the street level behind a retractable garage door.

Quality Meats *American/Steak*

| 26 | 24 | 24 | $75 |

W 50s | 57 W. 58th St. (bet. 5th & 6th Aves.) | 212-371-7777 | www.qualitymeatsnyc.com

In a city populated by "classic" chop shops, this "sexy", "modern" Midtowner is a "breath of fresh air", teaming "skilled" service with a "creative" American steakhouse menu that runs the gamut from "fabulous" cuts of beef to "killer ice cream"; sure, it's something of a "splurge", but it certainly "lives up to its name."

Quantum Leap *Health Food/Vegetarian*

| 21 | 12 | 18 | $22 |

G Village | 226 Thompson St. (bet. Bleecker & W. 3rd Sts.) | 212-677-8050 | www.quantumleaprestaurant.com

"One of the original" Greenwich Village health-food havens, this "small" '70s survivor still supplies "tasty" vegetarian specialties and a few fish options; in keeping with the "low-key", "collegey" atmosphere, expect "laid-back" service and "affordable" tabs.

Quatorze Bis *French*

| 20 | 19 | 20 | $62 |

E 70s | 323 E. 79th St. (bet. 1st & 2nd Aves.) | 212-535-1414

"Steady" and "essential", this "longtime" UES French bistro remains a local "favorite" for its "delicious" "Left Bank menu" and "welcoming" atmosphere; it's "not cheap" and could "use a face-lift", but its "prosperous clientele" still deems it a "pleasant experience."

Quattro Gatti *Italian*

| 21 | 18 | 21 | $51 |

E 80s | 205 E. 81st St. (3rd Ave.) | 212-570-1073

Though "not fancy", this "cozy" UES stalwart is favored as a "predictable" fallback for "pretty good" homestyle Italian food served by "old-school types"; "sleepy" but "affordable", it's "worth repeat business."

Queen *Italian*

| 24 | 16 | 22 | $45 |

Brooklyn Heights | 84 Court St. (bet. Livingston & Schermerhorn Sts.) | Brooklyn | 718-596-5955 | www.queenrestaurant.com

A circa-1958 "Brooklyn Heights institution" near the courthouses, this "homey" Italian continues its reign as an area "favorite" for "true redsauce" fare minus culinary gimmicks; given the "gracious service" and "reasonable" tabs, most pardon the "dated" decor.

Queen of Sheba ❂ *Ethiopian*

| 22 | 16 | 17 | $29 |

W 40s | 650 10th Ave. (bet. 45th & 46th Sts.) | 212-397-0610 | www.shebanyc.com

"Hidden" in Hell's Kitchen, this "real-thing" Ethiopian offers "flavorful" fare – "numerous" veggie dishes included – that's eaten with your hands and "a heap of injera" bread; even with "small" quarters and "slow" pacing, it's a "repeater" for the cost-conscious crowd.

Queens Kickshaw ❂ *Coffeehouse/Sandwiches*

| 23 | 19 | 21 | $21 |

Astoria | 40-17 Broadway (bet. 41st & Steinway Sts.) | Queens | 718-777-0913 | www.thequeenskickshaw.com

"Specializing in grilled cheese", this saloonish, all-day Astoria sandwich shop kicks the "gooey" staple "to another level" and also features other fromage-focused eats served by "friendly" hipsters; its specialty coffees and craft beers are a "huge plus", as is the "cheap" cost.

	FOOD	DECOR	SERVICE	COST

Radiance Tea House *Teahouse* | 21 | 22 | 21 | $32 |

W 50s | 158 W. 55th St. (bet. 6th & 7th Aves.) | 212-217-0442 |
www.radiancetea.com

Radiating "calm" amid the "Midtown madness", this "delightful"
teahouse matches a "huge" selection of "exotic" brews with an affordable menu of "light", Chinese-accented bites; the "very Zen" surroundings (which also house a gift shop) lend some "spiritual quietude."

Rai Rai Ken ● ⊄ *Japanese/Noodle Shop* | 20 | 11 | 16 | $16 |

E Village | 218 E. 10th St. (bet. 1st & 2nd Aves.) | 212-477-7030

Now in "bigger digs" down the block, this "Tokyo-style" East Village
noodle bar features a few tables in addition to the counter; it's still
cash only and "not the fanciest" joint, but it remains as "quick", "authentic" and "budget"-friendly as ever.

Ramen Setagaya *Japanese/Noodle Shop* | 20 | 11 | 14 | $19 |

E Village | 34 St. Marks Pl. (bet. 2nd & 3rd Aves.) | 212-387-7959 |
www.ramensetagayany.com

"Reliable" ramen is served "hot and fast" with "no pretension" at this
"fulfilling" East Village branch of a Japan-based noodle-shop outfit; regulars "ignore the decor" and focus instead on the "inexpensive" tabs.

Randazzo's *Seafood* | 21 | 11 | 17 | $34 |

Sheepshead Bay | 2017 Emmons Ave. (21st St.) | Brooklyn | 718-615-0010 |
www.randazzosclambar.com

A "friendly" crew dishes up "simple", "fresh" seafood plus random
"red-sauce" classics at this "iconic" Sheepshead Bay clam shop; even
though there's "no decor" to speak of, locals are thrilled it's back after
"taking a beating from Hurricane Sandy."

Rao's ⊠ ⊄ *Italian* | 22 | 17 | 22 | $82 |

Harlem | 455 E. 114th St. (Pleasant Ave.) | 212-722-6709 | www.raos.com

It practically "takes an act of Congress" to score a "coveted table", but
if you "get lucky", Frank Pellegrino's East Harlem Italian lives up to the
"mystique" with its "terrific" cooking and "central-casting" crowd;
short of VIP connections, ordinary folks can visit the "one in Las Vegas" or just "buy the sauce in jars."

Raoul's ● *French* | 25 | 21 | 22 | $65 |

SoHo | 180 Prince St. (bet. Sullivan & Thompson Sts.) | 212-966-3518 |
www.raouls.com

The "'it' factor" endures at this "classic", circa-1975 SoHo bistro that
stays "true to itself" and its arty admirers with "surprisingly serious"
French fare served in a "sexy" setting that includes a "magical" garden
accessed through the kitchen; though it can be "noisy and crowded",
few rue its "popularity" or high price.

Rare Bar & Grill *Burgers* | 21 | 17 | 18 | $33 |

Chelsea | Fashion 26 Hotel | 152 W. 26th St. (bet. 6th & 7th Aves.) |
212-807-7273
Murray Hill | Affinia Shelburne Hotel | 303 Lexington Ave. (37th St.) |
212-481-1999
www.rarebarandgrill.com

Given their "top-notch" burgers and french fry samplers, these "mid-
scale" patty purveyors are rarely less than "bustling"; if the Murray

Hill original is too "packed", the Chelsea spin-off has a "ton of space" – and "hoppin'" rooftop bars await at both.

Ravagh *Persian*
23 | 15 | 19 | $31

E 60s | 1237 First Ave. (bet. 66th & 67th Sts.) | 212-861-7900
Murray Hill | 11 E. 30th St. (bet. 5th & Madison Aves.) | 212-696-0300
www.ravaghpersiangrill.com

Persian pundits pronounce this "authentic" East Side pair "spot-on" for "succulent kebabs" and other "delicious" Iranian standards; "generous" portions and "nominal" pricing offset the "lacking decor."

Rayuela *Pan-Latin*
23 | 24 | 21 | $56

LES | 165 Allen St. (bet. Rivington & Stanton Sts.) | 212-253-8840 | www.rayuelanyc.com

Besides being an eyeful, this "snazzy" Lower Eastsider "wows the palate" with "bold" Pan-Latin tapas served in a "lovely" duplex setting centered around an "amazing" live olive tree; "gracious" staffers oversee a milieu that's "sceney" – and accordingly "pricey."

Real Madrid *Spanish*
21 | 15 | 19 | $40

Mariners Harbor | 2075 Forest Ave. (bet. Bruckner & Union Aves.) | Staten Island | 718-447-7885 | www.realmadridrestaurant.com

"You get what you pay for" at this Spanish vet in Staten Island's Mariners Harbor that scores with lobster specials and other "dependable" dishes in "hungry man–size" helpings; "satisfying meals" at "decent prices" help realists disregard decor that seems to have been kicked around a bit.

Recette ● *American*
24 | 18 | 21 | $75

W Village | 328 W. 12th St. (Greenwich St.) | 212-414-3000 | www.recettenyc.com

"Expertly prepared" if "exceptionally small" servings pack a "punch" that may "make you want to lick the plate" at this "neighborhoody" Village New American; "cacophonic" acoustics, "high prices" and "cramped" quarters don't deter the "elbow-to-elbow" crush of "hipster foodies."

Red Cat *American/Mediterranean*
23 | 19 | 21 | $57

Chelsea | 227 10th Ave. (bet. 23rd & 24th Sts.) | 212-242-1122 | www.theredcat.com

The "Chelsea art-world vibe" thrives at this "lively" nexus near the High Line that's been dispensing "top-notch" Med-American fare for 15 years; "solid service" and a "charming" (if "loud") ambiance keep its "gallery-hopping" clientele content, and while "a bit expensive", it still "feels like a treat."

Red Egg *Chinese*
20 | 17 | 18 | $31

Little Italy | 202 Centre St. (Howard St.) | 212-966-1123 | www.redeggnyc.com

"Not nearly as hectic" as the usual dim sum specialists, this "contemporary" Little Italy Chinese dispenses "high-quality" tidbits that are "made to order" and served by a "competent" crew with "no carts" in sight; despite the "lounge"-like setting, prices remain egg-ceptably "low."

Redeye Grill ● *American/Seafood*
21 | 19 | 20 | $59

W 50s | 890 Seventh Ave. (56th St.) | 212-541-9000 | www.redeyegrill.com

Steadily "busy" since 1996, Shelly Fireman's "classy" Midtowner fields a "dependable" American menu offering "tons of seafood";

	FOOD	DECOR	SERVICE	COST

"prompt" service, a "dramatic" setting and "pretty-penny" pricing are all part of the "vibrant" experience – and that location directly opposite Carnegie Hall sure is "handy."

RedFarm ● *Chinese* | 25 | 17 | 21 | $53 |

W Village | 529 Hudson St. (bet. Charles & W. 10th Sts.) | 212-792-9700 | www.redfarmnyc.com

Famed for its "elevated" dim sum and "creative" locavore cooking, this "innovative" West Village Chinese is perpetually "packed" with "hip" young types; "tight" tables, a no-rez rule and "noisy" decibels can make the experience a bit "hectic", but it's popular enough to have an UWS spin-off in the works.

NEW Red Gravy *Italian* | ▽ 20 | 17 | 19 | $45 |

Brooklyn Heights | 151 Atlantic Ave. (bet. Clinton & Henry Sts.) | Brooklyn | 718-855-0051 | www.redgravynyc.com

A "welcome addition" to Brooklyn Heights, this "neighborhood" trattoria via chef Saul Bolton (The Vanderbilt) features "delicious" Italian food crafted from seasonal ingredients; tabs are "reasonable", the staff "eager to please" and the brick-lined, wooden-beamed setting is as casually hip as the crowd.

The Redhead ● *Southern* | 22 | 15 | 19 | $41 |

E Village | 349 E. 13th St. (bet. 1st & 2nd Aves.) | 212-533-6212 | www.theredheadnyc.com

"Outrageously good" Southern comfort classics (including a particularly "nice fried chicken") and "perfectly made" cocktails keep this "unassuming" East Village bar/eatery always "crowded"; despite a "no-frills" "bar atmosphere", it packs serious "value" – "if you can score" a table, that is.

Red Hook Lobster Pound Ⓜ *Seafood* | 24 | 10 | 18 | $27 |

Red Hook | 284 Van Brunt St. (bet. Pioneer St. & Visitation Pl.) | Brooklyn | 718-858-7650 | www.redhooklobsterpound.com

"Back from the floods", this "cool" Red Hook seafooder specializes in "mouthwatering" lobster rolls prepared Maine-style (cold) or Connecticut-style (warm); the "picnic-area" decor makes it clear that eating is the "only thing they care about", but it's worth venturing over for the "deal" pricing alone.

Red Rooster *American* | 22 | 22 | 22 | $52 |

Harlem | 310 Lenox Ave. (bet. 125th & 126th Sts.) | 212-792-9001 | www.redroosterharlem.com

"Cock of the walk" Marcus Samuelsson rolls out an "outstanding", Southern-accented American menu at this "jumping Harlem joint" where the scene's "lively" and the people-watching "superb"; "efficient" service and frequent live music in Ginny's Supper Club downstairs are other reasons why it's perpetually "crowded."

Regional *Italian* | 19 | 15 | 17 | $37 |

W 90s | 2607 Broadway (bet. 98th & 99th Sts.) | 212-666-1915 | www.regionalnyc.com

"Neighborhood" regulars like this "friendly" UWS Italian for its "solid" regional lineup featuring pasta-centric choices from all over The Boot; even better, it's quite "affordable", with "special deals" on Monday and Tuesday nights.

	FOOD	DECOR	SERVICE	COST

Remi *Italian*
22 | **22** | **21** | **$63**

W 50s | 145 W. 53rd St. (bet. 6th & 7th Aves.) | 212-581-4242 | www.remi-ny.com

"Reliable" "all-around quality" marks this "upscale" Midtown Italian vet, where "outstanding" Venetian specialties are "served with panache" to "pre-theater" and "business" types; the "serene" space with its "impressive" Grand Canal mural is so "pretty" that you may forget the "expense account"–ready prices.

Republic *Asian*
19 | **15** | **16** | **$24**

Union Sq | 37 Union Sq. W. (bet. 16th & 17th Sts.) | 212-627-7172 | www.thinknoodles.com

Long a "Union Square standby", this Asian "mess hall" still "does the trick" with "filling" bowls of noodles and more at "bargain-basement prices"; the "communal-style" setup is "awkward" and "noisy as all get-out", but its "young" followers eat and exit "in a flash."

Resto ◑ *Belgian*
21 | **17** | **18** | **$43**

Murray Hill | 111 E. 29th St. (bet. Lexington Ave. & Park Ave. S.) | 212-685-5585 | www.restonyc.com

A "hedonist's delight", this Murray Hill gastropub offers a "refreshing" chance to chow down on "really tasty" Belgian eats à la burgers and moules frites, chased with a "tremendous beer selection"; the "low roar" in the room testifies to its "appreciative" following.

Reynard ◑ *American*
▽ **23** | **25** | **22** | **$55**

Williamsburg | Wythe Hotel | 80 Wythe Ave. (N. 11th St.) | Brooklyn | 718-460-8004 | www.reynardsnyc.com

A "beautifully repurposed space" inside a circa-1901 factory near Williamsburg's waterfront, this "hip" Wythe Hotel New American provides an artfully weathered setting for its "superb" seasonal cuisine; sure, the tabs run a tad "expensive", but payoffs include "classy" atmospherics and a "lively" crowd.

Ricardo Steak House *Steak*
▽ **25** | **19** | **21** | **$41**

Harlem | 2145 Second Ave. (bet. 110th & 111th Sts.) | 212-289-5895 | www.ricardosteakhouse.com

East Harlem has a "real gem" in this "well-done" steakhouse where "simply delicious" chops are served with "flair" to a crowd with "energy" to spare; its art-lined room and "quiet patio" also draw applause, as does the good-"value" pricing.

Rice 'n' Beans ◑ *Brazilian*
21 | **11** | **19** | **$26**

W 50s | 744 Ninth Ave. (bet. 50th & 51st Sts.) | 212-265-4444

They "don't have many seats", but this Hell's Kitchen "hole-in-the-wall" furnishes Brazilian staples "flavorful" enough to offset the "humble" surroundings and "laconic service"; with "more than reasonable" tabs, it does the trick as a "casual" pre-theater "find."

Riposo 46 ◑ *Italian*
21 | **18** | **21** | **$34**

W 40s | 667 Ninth Ave. (bet. 46th & 47th Sts.) | 212-247-8018

Riposo 72 ◑ *Italian*

W 70s | 50 W. 72nd St. (Columbus Ave.) | 212-799-4140

"Welcoming all around", these "above-average" wine bars offer "priced-right" Italian bites that are "well matched" with a "good selection" of

	FOOD	DECOR	SERVICE	COST

vino; both the "cute little" Hell's Kitchen original and its "roomier" UWS sequel promote "romantic" meet-ups.

Risotteria *Italian*
| 22 | 12 | 19 | $27 |

W Village | 270 Bleecker St. (Morton St.) | 212-924-6664 | www.risotteria.com

A "celiac's delight", this Village Italian works "gluten-free magic" with a "delish" menu showcasing the "art of risotto" plus wheatless pizza; the "tiny", "crammed" space may be "not much to look at", but fans still "squeeze in" for the "fair prices" alone.

River Café *American*
| 26 | 27 | 26 | $130 |

Dumbo | 1 Water St. (bet. Furman & Old Fulton Sts.) | Brooklyn | 718-522-5200 | www.rivercafe.com

The "million-dollar views" of Lower Manhattan are "indispensable" at Buzzy O'Keeffe's "true NY classic" on the Dumbo waterfront, refurbished following Hurricane Sandy and still maintaining the "highest standards" via "glorious" New American cuisine from a "professional staff" in a "romantic" setting; granted, the prix fixe–only dinners are a "splurge", but then again, the dining here is truly "memorable."

Riverpark *American*
| 24 | 26 | 24 | $65 |

Murray Hill | Alexandria Ctr. | 450 E. 29th St. (bet. FDR Dr. & 1st Ave.) | 212-729-9790 | www.riverparknyc.com

Sure, it's "out of the way" in a remote Kip's Bay office complex, yet chef Tom Colicchio sure "knows how to put a restaurant on the map" with "excellent" New American food served in a cool, "contemporary" setting; "warm" service and "lovely" East River views from its outdoor terrace make the experience all the more "delightful."

NEW River Styx Ⓜ *American*
| - | - | - | M |

Greenpoint | 21 Greenpoint Ave. (bet. East River & West St.) | Brooklyn | 718-383-8833 | www.riverstyxny.com

Floating ashore in West Greenpoint, this stylish New American from the folks behind Williamsburg's Roebling Tea Room offers moderately priced, seafood-focused American fare, much of it cooked in a wood-fired brick oven; the space nods to the area's nautical past with wharf-chic decor and whimsically named cocktails.

Riverview ◐ *American*
| 21 | 24 | 20 | $59 |

LIC | 2-01 50th Ave. (bet. Center Blvd. & 49th Ave.) | Queens | 718-392-5000 | www.riverviewny.com

Anchored alongside the East River, this spacious LIC New American purveys a solid menu that skews "pricey" for the location; for a complimentary "romantic" fillip, a walk along the water after dinner affords "breathtaking views of the Manhattan skyline."

Rizzo's Pizza *Pizza*
| 23 | 13 | 19 | $15 |

E 90s | 1426 Lexington Ave. (93rd St.) | 212-289-0500
NEW LES | 17 Clinton St. (bet. Houston & Stanton Sts.) | 646-454-1262
Astoria | 30-13 Steinway St. (bet. 30th & 31st Aves.) | Queens | 718-721-9862
www.rizzosfinepizza.com

The thin, "tasty" square pies come with a "tangy sauce" at this enduring "local pizza joint" in Astoria, now joined by Carnegie Hill/LES annexes; the economical tabs are in line with the strictly functional setups.

| | FOOD | DECOR | SERVICE | COST |

Robataya *Japanese*   `23` `22` `22` `$55`
E Village | 231 E. Ninth St. (bet. 2nd & 3rd Aves.) | 212-979-9674 |
www.robataya-ny.com
It's all about the "authentic" robata counter at this "transporting" East
Village Japanese where patrons are "entertained" by chefs grilling "high-
quality" veggies, meats and fish served on "long wooden paddles";
while a bit "expensive", it's "something different" and "so much fun."

Robert *American*   `20` `26` `21` `$57`
W 50s | Museum of Arts and Design | 2 Columbus Circle, 9th fl.
(bet. B'way & 8th Ave.) | 212-299-7730 | www.robertnyc.com
High "above the fray", this museum American boasts such "wondrous"
views of Columbus Circle and Central Park that the "pricey" fare is "almost an afterthought"; insiders note that the experience is just as "striking" over cocktails in the lounge, but either way, a window table is "key."

Roberta's ● *Italian/Pizza*   `26` `17` `18` `$36`
Bushwick | 261 Moore St. (Bogart St.) | Brooklyn | 718-417-1118 |
www.robertaspizza.com
Redefining the "Brooklyn aesthetic", this "super-popular" Bushwick
Italian draws "throngs of hipsters" with its "phenomenal" wood-fired pizzas, as well as other "smashing" dishes crafted with "ingredients picked
from their own garden"; despite "hit-or-miss service", "communal tables" and "long waits", most agree it's "worth the extended trip on the L."

Roberto ⊠ *Italian*   `26` `19` `22` `$57`
Fordham | 603 Crescent Ave. (Hughes Ave.) | Bronx | 718-733-9503 |
www.roberto089.com
For a "true Arthur Avenue experience", fans of "old-world" cooking
head to this "busy" Bronx Italian where chef Roberto Paciullo prepares
"Manhattan"-worthy dishes delivered by a "gracious" staff; given the
"small" setting, "sophisticated" mood and no-rez policy, there's almost "always a wait."

Roc *Italian*   `22` `20` `21` `$56`
TriBeCa | 190 Duane St. (Greenwich St.) | 212-625-3333 |
www.rocrestaurant.com
"Year after year", this TriBeCa "standby" remains roc-"solid" for "fancy"
Italian classics courtesy of "delightful owners" who ensure that regulars are "treated like family"; a "peaceful setting" with "outdoor seating" distracts from prices that slant "expensive."

Rock Center Café *American*   `19` `21` `19` `$51`
W 50s | Rockefeller Ctr. | 20 W. 50th St. (bet. 5th & 6th Aves.) |
212-332-7620 | www.patinagroup.com
With its "rink-side" view of skaters during the winter and open-air tables
in front of the Prometheus statue in summer, this Rock Center American
is an "undeniable draw" for "tourists" and "holiday guests"; "only average" food proves that you're paying for "location, location, location."

Rocking Horse Cafe *Mexican*   `22` `16` `18` `$38`
Chelsea | 182 Eighth Ave. (bet. 19th & 20th Sts.) | 212-463-9511 |
www.rockinghorsecafe.com
"Handy" in the neighborhood, this "buoyant" Chelsea veteran "rocks on"
with "flavorful" Mexican grub offered at "sure-value" tabs (i.e. that

	FOOD	DECOR	SERVICE	COST

"best-kept-secret" $15 brunch); rowdy crowds fueled by "fab" margaritas make for a "lively scene" and mucho "noise."

Rolf's *German*

| 17 | 21 | 17 | $43 |

Gramercy | 281 Third Ave. (22nd St.) | 212-477-4750 | www.rolfsnyc.com
Best experienced "around the holidays", this circa-1968 Gramercy German "time warp" is a "sight to see" when the "jaw-droppingly" "gaudy" Oktoberfest and Christmas decorations go up ("bring your sunglasses"); too bad the "run-of-the-mill" food makes a case for just a "drink at the bar."

Roll-n-Roaster ● *Sandwiches*

| 22 | 12 | 16 | $15 |

Sheepshead Bay | 2901 Emmons Ave. (bet. Nostrand Ave. & 29th St.) | Brooklyn | 718-769-5831 | www.rollnroaster.com
"Retro fast-food" fans roll into this "busy" Sheepshead Bay "institution" to chow down on "bangin'" roast beef sandwiches and "must-have" cheese fries served into the wee hours; the aging digs are pretty "beat up", but "there's a reason why they've been in business" since 1970.

Roman's *Italian*

| ∇ 24 | 19 | 21 | $45 |

Fort Greene | 243 DeKalb Ave. (bet. Clermont & Vanderbilt Aves.) | Brooklyn | 718-622-5300 | www.romansnyc.com
Its "locally sourced" Italian small plates "change every day, but the quality doesn't" at this "hip" Fort Greene sibling of Marlow & Sons that's a "memorable" blend of culinary "passion" and "neighborhoody" vibes; no reservations means a "standard" wait, providing time to size up the bar's "talented mixologists."

Room Service *Thai*

| 21 | 22 | 18 | $27 |

Chelsea | 166 Eighth Ave. (bet. 18th & 19th Sts.) | 212-691-0299
W 40s | 690 Ninth Ave. (bet. 47th & 48th Sts.) | 212-582-0999 ●
www.roomservicerestaurant.com
"Decked out with mirrors and chandeliers", these "eye-popping" eateries are "jazzy" destinations for "spot-on" Thai bites and "ultrafast" service at a "fair price"; "upbeat" vibrations, "cool cocktails" and "fun-loving" crowds are all part of the "like-a-nightclub" milieu.

Rosa Mexicano *Mexican*

| 22 | 21 | 20 | $49 |

E 50s | 1063 First Ave. (58th St.) | 212-753-7407 ●
Flatiron | 9 E. 18th St. (bet. B'way & 5th Ave.) | 212-533-3350
W 60s | 61 Columbus Ave. (62nd St.) | 212-977-7700 ●
www.rosamexicano.com
From the "terrific" tableside guacamole to the "habit-forming" pomegranate margaritas, the fare's "reliably delicious" at this "always enjoyable" Mexican trio; while tabs can be on the "pricey" side, "attentive" service and "lively", colorful settings make dining here "feel like a party."

Rosanjin ⧆ *Japanese*

| ∇ 25 | 22 | 25 | $136 |

TriBeCa | 141 Duane St. (bet. Church St. & W. B'way) | 212-346-0664 | www.rosanjintribeca.com
Aesthetically "amazing", this "petite" TriBeCa Japanese is a "top-end" kaiseki specialist showcasing the "heavenly" tastes and textures of "exquisitely presented" set menus deferentially served by a kimono-clad staff; the "serene" setting makes for a "transporting" experience that's (predictably) "expensive."

	FOOD	DECOR	SERVICE	COST

Rosemary's ● *Italian*
21 **22** **19** **$51**

W Village | 18 Greenwich Ave. (W. 10th St.) | 212-647-1818 |
www.rosemarysnyc.com

Taking "locally sourced" food to the next level with a rooftop garden,
this "trendy" West Village Italian offers "flavorful" plates in an "open",
"airy" room; given the "packed", "zoo"-like scene and "ridiculous
waits" due to the no-reservation rule, insiders say it's best experienced
during "off-hours."

Rose Water *American*
25 **20** **24** **$47**

Park Slope | 787 Union St. (bet. 5th & 6th Aves.) | Brooklyn |
718-783-3800 | www.rosewaterrestaurant.com

Park Slope's own "locavore heaven", this way-"cozy" New American vet
remains "consistently fabulous" with its "inventive", "seasonally driven"
menu and service "like a finely oiled machine"; it's a "favorite" brunch
pick, where the only thorn is "bumping elbows" in the "tight space."

Rossini's ● *Italian*
23 **18** **24** **$64**

Murray Hill | 108 E. 38th St. (bet. Lexington & Park Aves.) | 212-683-0135 |
www.rossinisrestaurant.com

The "good old days" endure at this 1978-vintage Murray Hill Italian
touted for its "excellent" Tuscan fare and "seamless" service from
"tuxedo"-attired staffers; the nightly piano player and live "opera music" on Saturdays help soothe any "sticker shock."

Rothmann's *Steak*
23 **20** **22** **$73**

E 50s | 3 E. 54th St. (bet. 5th & Madison Aves.) | 212-319-5500 |
www.rothmannssteakhouse.com

Centrally sited for the suits crowd, this "clubby" Midtown steakhouse
provides "wonderful" chops and "dependable" service "without fuss and
drama"; ok, it's "costly", but the "comfort level" holds whether you're
there to "clinch a deal" or throw back some "cocktails after work."

Rouge et Blanc Ⓜ *French/Vietnamese*
▽ **25** **20** **22** **$63**

SoHo | 48 MacDougal St. (bet. Houston & Prince Sts.) | 212-260-5757 |
www.rougeetblancnyc.com

This SoHo "sleeper" achieves "subtlety" with a "brilliant" French-
Vietnamese lineup that "marries perfectly" with its "wonderful" wine
list; a "low-key" space ("think *The Quiet American*") and "never-rushed"
service make it a "hidden gem" – at least until the "masses catch on."

Rouge Tomate Ⓢ *American*
24 **25** **23** **$69**

E 60s | 10 E. 60th St. (bet. 5th & Madison Aves.) | 646-237-8977 |
www.rougetomatenyc.com

Upper Eastsiders "eat without guilt" at this "elegant" New American
where the "market-driven" "spa food" is "calorie conscious" but nonetheless "delicious"; though a few quibble about "minuscule" portions,
it's ultimately a "place to recommend" for "trim waistline" types with
"money to burn."

Rubirosa *Italian/Pizza*
23 **15** **19** **$38**

NoLita | 235 Mulberry St. (bet. Prince & Spring Sts.) | 212-965-0500 |
www.rubirosanyc.com

"Perfecto" pizzas and "soulful" pastas offered at a "fair price" keep
this tolerably "trendy" NoLita Italian on "solid footing" with its "funky

| | FOOD | DECOR | SERVICE | COST |

downtown" crowd; it's "friendly enough" and "rocks with energy" at prime times, so expect a "wait" for entree into its "cramped" quarters.

Ruby Foo's Asian
18 | 20 | 18 | $45

W 40s | 1626 Broadway (49th St.) | 212-489-5600 | www.rubyfoos.com
Theatergoers, tourist "throngs" and "kids galore" pile into this "cavernous" Times Square Asian serving "better-than-expected" eats with a side of "kitsch"; the "'50s Hollywood Chinese" decor and "spotty" service lead some to sigh that "better choices abound."

Rucola ◑ Italian
24 | 21 | 21 | $41

Boerum Hill | 190 Dean St. (Bond St.) | Brooklyn | 718-576-3209 |
www.rucolabrooklyn.com
This "wonderful" all-day option in Boerum Hill fields a rustic, "farm-to-table" Italian menu that's "decently priced" enough to appeal to "hipsters and family groups" alike; the lumber-lined space is "tight", so prepare for "close contact" and a "challenge" getting in.

Rue 57 ◑ French
19 | 18 | 18 | $49

W 50s | 60 W. 57th St. (6th Ave.) | 212-307-5656 | www.rue57.com
"Convenience is key" at this 15-year-old brasserie that's "well located" in the heart of Midtown, turning out "reliable" if "not outstanding" French eats plus sushi; despite "uneven" service, "noisy" decibels and a "tourist"-centric crowd, it's usually "bustling" – verging on "hectic."

NEW Runner & Stone American/Bakery
∇ 23 | 23 | 20 | $43

Gowanus | 285 Third Ave. (bet. Carroll & President Sts.) | Brooklyn |
718-576-3360 | www.runnerandstone.com
Gowanus' bustling Third Avenue is home to this "pleasant" all-day bakery/eatery from Smorgasburg vets; the concise, seasonal New American menu features one of the "best bread baskets in Brooklyn", served in a "nicely detailed" space adorned with heavy wood tables and whitewashed brick walls.

Russian Samovar ◑ Continental/Russian
20 | 18 | 19 | $53

W 50s | 256 W. 52nd St. (bet. B'way & 8th Ave.) | 212-757-0168 |
www.russiansamovar.com
"Home away from home" for "Russian-speakers", this "cheerful" Theater District stalwart serves "well-prepared" Russo-Continental staples amid live piano–led "festivity" that gets louder as the night progresses; tasty "infused vodkas" distract from the "lackluster" decor.

Russian Tea Room ◑ Continental/Russian
20 | 25 | 22 | $69

W 50s | 150 W. 57th St. (bet. 6th & 7th Aves.) | 212-581-7100 |
www.russiantearoomnyc.com
Its "glamorously ostentatious" decor intact, this "legendary" Russo-Continental alongside Carnegie Hall still provides a "glitzy" czarist backdrop for "posh" noshing built around caviar and blini; "outrageous" prices for "so-so" food have fans lamenting its "former glory", though some say it works best as a "theatrical experience" for "out-of-towners."

Ruth's Chris Steak House Steak
23 | 20 | 22 | $74

W 50s | 148 W. 51st St. (bet. 6th & 7th Aves.) | 212-245-9600 |
www.ruthschris.com
A slather of "melted butter" adds some "extra-fab" sizzle to the "big cuts" of beef at this "first-rate" Theater District link of the New Orleans-

| | FOOD | DECOR | SERVICE | COST |

based steakhouse chain; likewise, the "personalized" service and "upscale" woodwork are as "impressive" as the tabs are "high."

Rye *American*
25 | 22 | 22 | $44

Williamsburg | 247 S. First St. (bet. Havemeyer & Roebling Sts.) | Brooklyn | 718-218-8047 | www.ryerestaurant.com

A "speakeasy-style" setting complete with a vintage bar sets the scene for "fine cocktails" paired with "first-rate" grub at this somewhat "hidden" Williamsburg American; "low-key" vibrations, "charming" service and "no airs" keep its "hipster" crowd content.

Sacred Chow *Vegan/Vegetarian*
▽ 22 | 14 | 20 | $24

G Village | 227 Sullivan St. (bet. Bleecker & W. 3rd Sts.) | 212-337-0863 | www.sacredchow.com

For a "lifestyle change", try this "wee" Village health food niche, where "ingenious" kosher vegan recipes yield "wholesome" grub with "creative flair"; "earthy" enthusiasts find it "laid-back" and "reasonably priced", though nonbelievers note it's "very impressed with itself."

Sagaponack *Seafood*
18 | 18 | 18 | $43

Flatiron | 4 W. 22nd St. (bet. 5th & 6th Aves.) | 212-229-2226 | www.sagaponacknyc.com

Those hankering for "the Hamptons" settle for the "simple" but "solid" catch served in "beachfront"-esque surrounds at this Flatiron seafooder; it's a "nice little taste of the East Coast", and at a "reasonable" cost to boot.

Sahara ● *Turkish*
22 | 15 | 18 | $31

Gravesend | 2337 Coney Island Ave. (bet. Aves. T & U) | Brooklyn | 718-376-8594 | www.saharapalace.com

It's "old-school at this point", but this durable Gravesend Turk is "hard to beat" for "seriously good" grilled fare ("kebab is king") at the right price; the "huge" space may be "short on ambiance", but that doesn't hurt its "popularity" with "groups and families."

Saju Bistro ● *French*
20 | 19 | 21 | $44

W 40s | Mela Hotel | 120 W. 44th St. (bet. B'way & 6th Ave.) | 212-997-7258 | www.sajubistro.com

A "slice of Paree" in Times Square, this "very French" bistro is "spot-on" for "traditional Provençal dishes" offered at "fair" prices; it's especially "convenient" pre-theater with an "engaging" staff to get you in and out.

Sakagura ● *Japanese*
25 | 22 | 22 | $53

E 40s | 211 E. 43rd St., downstairs (bet. 2nd & 3rd Aves.) | 212-953-7253 | www.sakagura.com

"Like Tokyo" but "minus the 14-hour plane ride", this "relaxing" Japanese izakaya tucked beneath a "nondescript" office building near Grand Central is the "real deal" for "incredible" small plates matched with "exceptional" sakes; naturally, its "high quality" comes with a "price tag to match."

NEW SakaMai ●▣ *Japanese*
- | - | - | E

LES | 157 Ludlow St. (Stanton St.) | 646-590-0684 | www.sakamai.com

This new LES sake lounge backs up its "amazing" rice-wine list with a "refined" menu of Japanese dishes that are "perfectly matched" to the liquids; the dimly lit room exudes downtown cool, thanks to equal parts of distressed brick, votive lights and filmy curtains.

Salinas *Spanish*   22 | 21 | 20 | $61

Chelsea | 136 Ninth Ave. (bet. 18th & 19th Sts.) | 212-776-1990 | www.salinasnyc.com

"Charmed" Chelsea dwellers hail this "creative" Spaniard for its "terrific tapas" served in an "unusually elegant" space complete with a "retractable roof" sheltering a "fabulous garden"; sure, it's on the "pricey" side, but this is "one to reckon with."

Salt & Fat Ⓜ *American/Asian*   26 | 16 | 22 | $36

Sunnyside | 41-16 Queens Blvd. (bet. 41st & 42nd Sts.) | Queens | 718-433-3702 | www.saltandfatny.com

The name shows a "sense of humor", but they "take the food seriously" at this Sunnyside "rising star" where "inventive" small plates showcase a "delectable" blend of New American and Asian flavors; given the "super-helpful" staff and "Queens prices", it's definitely one to "look out for."

Salumeria Rosi Parmacotto *Italian*   25 | 19 | 21 | $48

W 70s | 283 Amsterdam Ave. (bet. 73rd & 74th Sts.) | 212-877-4800
NEW Il Ristorante Rosi Ⓢ *Italian*
E 70s | 903 Madison Ave. (bet. 72nd & 73rd Sts.) | 212-517-7700
www.salumeriarosi.com

The "quality shines" at chef Cesare Casella's *molto Italiano* UWS enoteca/salumeria, where the cured meats, Tuscan small plates and wines seem like a gift from "the mother country"; the roomier Madison Avenue spin-off serves much of the same in a more upscale, white-tableclothed room.

NEW Salvation Taco ● *Mexican*   ▽ 22 | 18 | 16 | $34

Murray Hill | Pod 39 Hotel | 145 E. 39th St. (bet. Lexington & 3rd Aves.) | 212-865-5800 | www.salvationtaco.com

Hitmakers April Bloomfield and Ken Friedman (The Breslin, Spotted Pig) are behind this "wildly popular" new Murray Hill Mexican offering "inventive" if "comically small" tacos plus "not-for-everyone" items like pig ears and chicken feet; the "quirky" setting mixes religious iconography with Ping-Pong tables, but it's so "noisy" few notice.

Sambuca *Italian*   19 | 17 | 19 | $42

W 70s | 20 W. 72nd St. (bet. Columbus Ave. & CPW) | 212-787-5656 | www.sambucanyc.com

"Italian cooking, family-style" sums up the scene at this "trustworthy" Upper West Side fixture, where the "gigantic" platters of "typical" dishes (plus a gluten-free menu) are "meant for sharing"; "reasonable" tabs compensate for "dated" decor, and it's "a lot easier to get into" than Carmine's.

Sammy's Fishbox ● *Seafood*   21 | 18 | 20 | $45

City Island | 41 City Island Ave. (Rochelle St.) | Bronx | 718-885-0920 | www.sammysfishbox.com

"You will not leave hungry" could be the motto of this "huge" City Island vet, which has been churning out "generous" servings of seafood since 1966; though not cheap, it's something of a "tourist" magnet, so count on it being "crowded in summer months."

	FOOD	DECOR	SERVICE	COST

Sammy's Noodle Shop & Grill ● *Chinese/Noodle Shop*

20 | 10 | 17 | $27

G Village | 453 Sixth Ave. (bet.10th & 11th Sts.) | 212-924-6688
"Bring your appetite" to this "efficient" Village Chinese that rolls out a
"wide menu" of "inexpensive" comfort items, notably noodle soups;
seriously "worn-out" digs and service "without a smile" explain why
it's mostly a "neighborhood take-out" option.

Sammy's Roumanian *Jewish*

20 | 10 | 18 | $58

LES | 157 Chrystie St. (Delancey St.) | 212-673-0330
This LES "heartburn city" brings on "old-fashioned" Jewish staples
"covered in schmaltz" and vodka in ice blocks in a "grungy basement"
setting where a keyboardist spouts "nonstop shtick"; like being in a
"perpetual bar mitzvah", the clamorous "cavorting" could cause "car-
diac arrest" – but it's a "great way to go."

Sammy's Shrimp Box ● *Seafood*

23 | 19 | 21 | $40

City Island | 64 City Island Ave. (Horton St.) | Bronx | 718-885-3200 |
www.sammysshrimpbox.com
Docked at the end of the strip near its Fish Box forerunner, this "casual" City Islander dispenses "down-to-earth" fried seafood – and
"lots of it" – at a "nice price"; it's a standard "summer hang", where
you can expect "crowded" conditions.

Sandro's *Italian*

25 | 16 | 21 | $67

E 80s | 306 E. 81st St. (bet. 1st & 2nd Aves.) | 212-288-7374 |
www.sandrosnyc.com
Almost "better than a ticket to Rome", this "cozy" UES Italian "rises
above the ordinary" with "lovely" Italian cuisine via "mercurial" chef-
owner Sandro Fioriti, who sometimes greets diners in his "pajama bot-
toms"; even if the "high prices" don't jibe with the "simple setting",
fans feel it's "difficult to beat."

Sanford's ● *American*

22 | 20 | 20 | $26

Astoria | 30-13 Broadway (bet. 30th & 31st Sts.) | Queens | 718-932-9569 |
www.sanfordsnyc.com
In business since 1922 but now flaunting a "contemporary" makeover, this "friendly" Astoria diner serves "higher-caliber" American
comfort food at "reasonable" rates 24 hours a day; the formula is
"deservedly popular", especially at brunch when the "only drawback
is the wait."

San Matteo *Italian/Pizza*

25 | 13 | 18 | $29

E 90s | 1739 Second Ave. (90th St.) | 212-426-6943 |
www.sanmatteopanuozzo.com
This UES Italian "find" lures locals with "quality" Neapolitan pizzas
and "wonderful" *panuozzi,* panini-esque creations; it's "cheap" and
"charming", but the tradeoffs include "tiny" dimensions, "shoehorned"
seating and rather "lackluster" service.

San Pietro ⊠ *Italian*

24 | 20 | 24 | $88

E 50s | 18 E. 54th St. (bet. 5th & Madison Aves.) | 212-753-9015 |
www.sanpietrorestaurant.us
"Filled with CEOs" and "older sophisticates" at lunch, this "top-notch"
Southern Italian is a Midtown "class act" offering "sumptuous" cuisine

and "treat-you-like-royalty" service; it's "wildly costly", however, so it helps if "money is no object."

Sant Ambroeus *Italian*   21 | 19 | 19 | $61

E 70s | 1000 Madison Ave. (bet. 77th & 78th Sts.) | 212-570-2211
W Village | 259 W. Fourth St. (Perry St.) | 212-604-9254
www.santambroeus.com

"Sophisticated" sorts are drawn to these "Milano-in-NY" cafes where "chichi" Italian nibbles are served in a "civilized" milieu; the crowd runs the gamut from "past-due trophy wives" to "first-rate Eurotrash" who don't mind the "snooty" service and "splurge"-worthy tabs.

Sapphire Indian Cuisine *Indian*   21 | 19 | 19 | $41

W 60s | 1845 Broadway (bet. 60th & 61st Sts.) | 212-245-4444 |
www.sapphireny.com

A "welcome retreat" off Columbus Circle, this "quiet" Indian is touted for its "reliable" kitchen, "courteous" service and "comfortable" quarters; though it's a tad "more expensive" than some, the $16 buffet lunch is a "best bargain", and it's particularly "pleasurable" prior to Lincoln Center.

Sarabeth's *American*   20 | 17 | 19 | $37

Chelsea | Chelsea Mkt. | 75 Ninth Ave. (bet. 15th & 16th Sts.) |
212-989-2424 | www.sarabeth.com
E 90s | 1295 Madison Ave. (92nd St.) | 212-410-7335 | www.sarabeth.com
Garment District | Lord & Taylor | 424 Fifth Ave., 5th fl. (bet. 38th & 39th Sts.) | 212-827-5068 | www.sarabeth.com
NEW Murray Hill | 381 Park Ave. S. (bet. 27th & 28th Sts.) | 212-335-0093 |
www.sarabeth.com Ⓢ Ⓜ
TriBeCa | 339 Greenwich St. (bet. Harrison & Jay Sts.) | 212-966-0421 |
www.sarabeth.com
W 50s | 40 Central Park S. (bet. 5th & 6th Aves.) | 212-826-5959 |
www.sarabethscps.com
W 80s | 423 Amsterdam Ave. (bet. 80th & 81st Sts.) | 212-496-6280 |
www.sarabeth.com

Longtime "favorites" for breakfast and brunch, these "charming" all-day eateries draw devotees with "hearty" American comfort food and baked goods; though the morning's "festive chaos" can be too "bracing" for some, at night a quieter, "grown-up" vibe prevails.

Saraghina ⊄ *Pizza*   ▽ 26 | 24 | 22 | $26

Bed-Stuy | 435 Halsey St. (Lewis Ave.) | Brooklyn | 718-574-0010 |
www.saraghinabrooklyn.com

Pizzaphiles salute this multiroomed Bed-Stuy "hidden treasure" run by a "superb" staff, where the "excellent", wood-fired Neapolitan pies are a "real steal" given the "amazing" quality; the pleasingly "rustic" premises also house a coffee bar – another reason it's counted as a "savior in this neighborhood."

Saravanaa Bhavan *Indian/Vegetarian*   23 | 12 | 15 | $24

Murray Hill | 81 Lexington Ave. (26th St.) | 212-679-0204
W 70s | 413 Amsterdam Ave. (bet. 79th & 80th Sts.) |
212-721-7755
www.saravanabhavan.com

"Packed" at prime times, these UWS–Curry Hill national chain links sling "absolutely delicious" South Indian veggie fare, including "must-try" dosas; "brusque" service and interiors that "need an upgrade" are offset by "interesting flavors" and "value" pricing.

Sardi's ●Ⓜ *Continental*   18 | 22 | 21 | $57

W 40s | 234 W. 44th St. (bet. 7th & 8th Aves.) | 212-221-8440 | www.sardis.com

Sure, it's mainly a "tourist joint", but this circa-1921 Theater District "showbiz institution" is best known for its celeb caricatures on the walls and (occasional) Broadway stars in the seats; if its Continental fare and career waiters seem "passionately outdated", fans insist that's part of the "charm."

Sasabune ⓈⓂ *Japanese*   28 | 11 | 21 | $115

E 70s | 401 E. 73rd St. (bet. 1st & York Aves.) | 212-249-8583

"Trust the chefs" at Kenji Takahashi's "outstanding" UES Japanese offering "unforgettable", omakase-only meals featuring "delicate", "skillfully prepared" sushi; even though the digs are "cramped" and the service "rushed", devotees happily shell out "bank loan"–worthy sums for such a "high-quality" experience.

Sauce ●⇟ *Italian*   ▽ 26 | 20 | 22 | $36

LES | 78 Rivington St. (Allen St.) | 212-420-7700 | www.saucerestaurant.com

Red gravy and red meat are the focus at this "booming" Lower Eastsider, where the "homestyle" Southern Italian eats are served in a "low-key" setting; a butcher shop (Tiberio Custom Meats) in full view of the dining room makes it a saucier version of siblings Lil' Frankie's and Supper, but with the same "reasonable" prices and cash-only policy.

Saxon & Parole *American*   22 | 23 | 20 | $58

NoHo | 316 Bowery (Bleecker St.) | 212-254-0350 | www.saxonandparole.com

"Lively and energetic", this "stylish" NoHo "scene" from the AvroKO team "oozes cool", drawing deep-pocketed "beautiful people" into its "happening", equestrian-themed digs; look for a "sophisticated", meat-centric American menu backed up by "eye-opening cocktails."

Sazon *Puerto Rican*   23 | 21 | 21 | $47

TriBeCa | 105 Reade St. (bet. Church St. & W. B'way) | 212-406-1900 | www.sazonnyc.com

"High-class" Puerto Rican fare draws both "down-home and beautiful" types to this "sexy" TriBeCa spot, where the popular pernil is "as good as your *abuela*'s"; "upbeat" music and sangria with the "right amount of flair" ratchet up the "fun" (albeit "noisy") vibe.

Scaletta *Italian*   21 | 19 | 21 | $55

W 70s | 50 W. 77th St. (bet. Columbus Ave. & CPW) | 212-769-9191 | www.scalettaristorante.com

Inventive it's not, but this "dependable" UWS "favorite" has been serving "solid", "old-style" Northern Italiana with "simple elegance" for 25 years; the "spacious seating" and "blissful quiet" make conversation here a "pleasure", and "no one pushes you out the door."

Scalinatella ● *Italian*   24 | 17 | 21 | $89

E 60s | 201 E. 61st St., downstairs (3rd Ave.) | 212-207-8280

"Exceptional" Capri-style dishes draw a moneyed crowd to this "private club"–like UES Italian, situated downstairs in an "intimate" grotto; service is as "impressive" as the "fabulous" food, but if your server steers you toward the specials, brace yourself for "sticker shock."

Scalini Fedeli ⊠ *Italian* 27 | 25 | 26 | $93

TriBeCa | 165 Duane St. (bet. Greenwich & Hudson Sts.) | 212-528-0400 | www.scalinifedeli.com

"Abundant with marvelous choices", the prix fixe–only menus at Michael Cetrulo's TriBeCa Italian feature "outstanding" dishes bolstered by an "equally lavish" wine cellar; "dedicated" staffers, "old-world" decor and "very expensive" tabs are all part of the "la dolce vita" package.

Scarpetta *Italian* 26 | 22 | 22 | $75

Chelsea | 355 W. 14th St. (bet. 8th & 9th Aves.) | 212-691-0555 | www.scarpettanyc.com

Fans say it's all about the "rightfully hyped" spaghetti at Scott Conant's "sleek" 14th Street Italian, where the "modern" bill of fare consists of "elegantly simple" dishes; sure, you'll "pay dearly" for the privilege, but "top-notch" service and a "beautiful" setting are compensations.

Schiller's ◐ *Eclectic* 19 | 19 | 18 | $38

LES | 131 Rivington St. (Norfolk St.) | 212-260-4555 | www.schillersny.com

Balthazar's younger, "lower-priced" cousin, this "cool" LES bistro from Keith McNally is an ever-"packed" nexus for "solid" Eclectic fare delivered by a "well-meaning" team; even though the "noisy" room is "a place to be seen, not heard", it remains a perennial downtown "favorite."

Schnipper's Quality Kitchen *American* 19 | 13 | 16 | $17

Flatiron | 23 E. 23rd St. (bet. Madison & Park Ave. S.) | 212-233-1025
W 40s | 620 Eighth Ave. (41st St.) | 212-921-2400
www.schnippers.com

"Stick-to-your-ribs" diner fare is the specialty of this American duo vending "tasty" burgers, "thick" shakes and "just-right" sloppy joes; "fair prices" and counter-service, "cafeteria"-style settings are also part of the "cheap-and-cheerful" picture.

Schnitzel Haus *German* ▽ 23 | 18 | 21 | $34

Bay Ridge | 7319 Fifth Ave. (74th St.) | Brooklyn | 718-836-5600 | www.schnitzelhausny.com

"Real", "no-apologies" German home cooking and "excellent" tap beers make it "impossible to leave hungry" from this Bay Ridge Bohemian; "nice prices", "laid-back" vibrations and live music on weekends further endear it to locals.

Scottadito Osteria Toscana Ⓜ *Italian* ▽ 22 | 19 | 22 | $40

Park Slope | 788 Union St. (bet. 6th & 7th Aves.) | Brooklyn | 718-636-4800 | www.scottadito.com

It's been "overlooked for too long" insist Park Slope partisans of this "quiet" spot offering "hearty" Northern Italiana in "rustic", "fireplace"-enhanced digs; "affordable" tabs, "attentive" service" and an "unlimited-mimosa brunch" strengthen their argument.

SD26 *Italian* 25 | 24 | 23 | $74

Murray Hill | 19 E. 26th St. (bet. 5th & Madison Aves.) | 212-265-5959 | www.sd26ny.com

From the "dynamic" father-daughter team of Tony and Marisa May, this "chic" Madison Square Park "destination" rolls out "exceptional"

Italian fare accompanied by a "killer" wine list; of course, "deep pockets" come in handy, but further payoffs include a "glamorous", "soaring" setting and "gracious" service.

Sea *Thai*

22 | **24** | **19** | **$30**

Meatpacking | 835 Washington St. (Little W. 12th St.) | 212-243-3339
Williamsburg | 114 N. Sixth St. (Berry St.) | Brooklyn | 718-384-8850 ●
www.seathainyc.com

It's all about the "awe-inspiring interiors" at these "nightclub"-like Thai eateries resembling "dreamy temples" replete with "huge Buddhas"; "party" people swaying to the "techno" soundtrack report that the "served-fast" chow is as "delicious" as the "bargain" tabs.

NEW Sea Fire Grill *Seafood*

∇ **28** | **25** | **27** | **$74**

E 40s | 158 E. 48th St. (bet. Lexington & 3rd Aves.) | 212-935-3785 |
www.theseafiregrill.com

The Benjamin Steak House crew has a "terrific" handle on seafood at this "up-and-coming" Midtowner where "beautifully prepared" fish and equally "exceptional" meats are set down with "old-school flair" in suitably tony surrounds; while "not cheap" – "quality never is" – "everything works here."

Sea Grill ⊠ *Seafood*

23 | **24** | **23** | **$73**

W 40s | Rockefeller Ctr. | 19 W. 49th St. (bet. 5th & 6th Aves.) |
212-332-7610 | www.theseagrillnyc.com

With a "prime setting" overlooking the skating rink and holiday Christmas tree, this "iconic" Rock Center piscatorium is a "treat" that's "not just for tourists"; despite "special-occasion" pricing, the "excellent" food and service are "worth the occasional splurge."

Sea Shore ● *Seafood*

∇ **21** | **19** | **21** | **$46**

City Island | 591 City Island Ave. (Cross St.) | Bronx | 718-885-0300 |
www.seashorerestaurant.com

A City Island "place to be" since 1920, this "friendly" seafooder dishes up "tastes-just-caught" catch in an "old-fashioned", shore-side setting; it's "noisy", but the outdoor dining and marina views are compelling attractions for "families" and "weekend" visitors, likewise the relatively moderate prices.

Seäsonal *Austrian*

25 | **20** | **23** | **$70**

W 50s | 132 W. 58th St. (bet. 6th & 7th Aves.) | 212-957-5550 |
www.seasonalnyc.com

"Classic" Austrian cuisine gets "playful twists" and "seasonal" spins at this "refined" Midtowner overseen by a "knowledgeable" staff; some wonder "why it's not more beloved" given its "convenient location" near Carnegie Hall and City Center – "expensive" tabs may be a clue.

2nd Ave Deli ● *Deli/Kosher*

22 | **13** | **17** | **$29**

E 70s | 1442 First Ave. (75th St.) | 212-737-1700
Murray Hill | 162 E. 33rd St. (bet. Lexington & 3rd Aves.) | 212-689-9000
www.2ndavedeli.com

"Forgo your diet" for a "cholesterol high" at these "real-deal" kosher delis, which "bring back memories" with their "super-size sandwiches" and other "belt-busting" classics; despite "minimal" decor, "variable" service and "sticker shock", they're "a keeper" – just pack a "shoehorn to fit" into the Murray Hill digs (the UES site's roomier).

Visit zagat.com

	FOOD	DECOR	SERVICE	COST

Seersucker *Southern*   23 | 21 | 23 | $43

Carroll Gardens | 329 Smith St. (bet. Carroll & President Sts.) | Brooklyn | 718-422-0444 | www.seersuckerbrooklyn.com
Bringing the "best of the South up north", this Carroll Gardens "escape" turns "wonderful" local products into "soul-pleasing" Southern dishes with "modern twists"; "sweet" staffers and down-to-earth prices keep the "minimalist-chic" setting "buzzy."

NEW Sen ⧄ *Japanese*   ∇ 23 | 21 | 18 | $62

Flatiron | 12 W. 21st St. (bet. 5th & 6th Aves.) | 212-388-5736 | www.senrestaurant.com
Spun off from a longtime Sag Harbor favorite, this "creative" new Flatiron Japanese offers "quite good" sushi as well as noodles, sumiyaki and more; a dim, sexy interior and striking steel-and-bamboo bar area make the pricey tabs more tolerable.

Serafina *Italian*   18 | 16 | 17 | $44

E 50s | 38 E. 58th St. (bet. Madison & Park Aves.) | 212-832-8888 ●⧄
E 60s | 33 E. 61st St. (bet. Madison & Park Aves.) | 212-702-9898 ●
E 70s | 1022 Madison Ave., 2nd fl. (79th St.) | 212-734-2676 ●
Meatpacking | 7 Ninth Ave. (Little W. 12th St.) | 646-964-4494 ●
W 40s | Time Hotel | 224 W. 49th St. (bet. B'way & 8th Ave.) | 212-247-1000 ●
W 50s | Dream Hotel | 210 W. 55th St. (bet. B'way & 7th Ave.) | 212-315-1700 ●
W 70s | On the Ave Hotel | 2178 Broadway (77th St.) | 212-595-0092
www.serafinarestaurant.com
Everyone from "families" to "fashionistas" turns up at this "easy" Italian mini-chain that's renowned for its "super" thin-crust pizzas, backed up with "satisfying" if "basic" pastas and salads; expect a "hectic" scene and "rushed" service, but also a "good buy for your buck."

Serendipity 3 ● *Dessert*   20 | 21 | 17 | $31

E 60s | 225 E. 60th St. (bet. 2nd & 3rd Aves.) | 212-838-3531 | www.serendipity3.com
"Must-try" frozen hot chocolate is the signature dish ("everything else is a prelude") at this "whimsical" East Side sweets 'n' gifts shop that's been around since 1954; despite "pricey" rates, "sassy" service and "crazy crowds", it's still a magnet for "tourists" and "grandchildren" alike.

Sette Mezzo ⧄ *Italian*   24 | 17 | 21 | $74

E 70s | 969 Lexington Ave. (bet. 70th & 71st Sts.) | 212-472-0400
The "simple" Italian fare is "excellent" but almost beside the point at this UES "cognoscenti" clubhouse, where "upscale" regulars get "house accounts" and "personable" service, but for everyone else it's cash only and "snark, snark, snark"; either way, expect "tight tables" and a "steep" tab.

Settepani *Bakery*   ∇ 23 | 21 | 24 | $38

Harlem | 196 Lenox Ave. (120th St.) | 917-492-4806
Williamsburg | 602 Lorimer St. (bet. Conselyea St. & Skillman Ave.) | Brooklyn | 718-349-6524
www.settepani.com
Both this "stylish" Harlem cafe and its Billyburg bakery sibling are known for "fabulous" desserts, but the former also boasts a "fantastic" menu

of Italian bites and a "wonderful wine list"; "friendly" staffers add to the "inviting", "relaxed" vibe at these neighborhood "gems."

Seva Indian Cuisine Indian

▽ 24 | 16 | 20 | $21

Astoria | 30-07 34th St. (30th Ave.) | Queens | 718-626-4440 | www.sevaindianrestaurant.com

Not your average curry house, this "small but cozy" Astoria standout spotlights "flavorful" Northern Indian cuisine that can be made "as spicy as you want"; everyone leaves "happily full", and the prix fixes and all-you-can-eat weekend brunch supply amazing "bang for the buck."

Seven's Turkish Grill Turkish

20 | 15 | 19 | $35

W 70s | 158 W. 72nd St. (bet. Amsterdam & Columbus Aves.) | 212-724-4700 | www.seventurkishgrill.com

At this "pleasant" UWS Turk, the "just-baked" bread and "subtlely spiced" dishes make it a "favorite" with locals; perhaps the plain setting feels a bit "anonymous", but the "warm", "attentive" service and "fair prices" more than compensate.

Sevilla ● Spanish

23 | 15 | 21 | $42

W Village | 62 Charles St. (W. 4th St.) | 212-929-3189 | www.sevillarestaurantandbar.com

"They know what they're doing" at this 1941-vintage Village "garlic haven" delivering "fabulous paellas" and other low-cost Spanish classics via "efficient" staffers; maybe the decor's getting "worn", but patrons downing "out-of-this-world sangria" are having too much "fun" to notice.

Sezz Medi' Mediterranean/Pizza

22 | 18 | 17 | $30

W 100s | 1260 Amsterdam Ave. (122nd St.) | 212-932-2901 | www.sezzmedi.com

It's all about the "famous" brick-oven pizzas and other Med staples at this "inexpensive" Columbia hangout; service can be "inattentive" and the rustic digs are nothing fancy, but this "popular" spot is still considered a "plus for the neighborhood."

Sfoglia Italian

23 | 19 | 21 | $65

E 90s | 1402 Lexington Ave. (92nd St.) | 212-831-1402 | www.sfogliarestaurant.com

Widely praised for "authentic" Italian cooking, "knowledgeable" servers and "romantic" faux farmhouse digs, this Carnegie Hill standby near the 92nd Street Y is an "oasis of class"; though "pricey", most agree it's "worth the money" – "getting a table" is the real problem.

Shabu-Shabu 70 Japanese

21 | 13 | 21 | $40

E 70s | 314 E. 70th St. (bet. 1st & 2nd Aves.) | 212-861-5635 | www.shabushabu70.com

"Fun" shabu-shabu cooked at the table backed up with "very good" sushi are the draws at this 35-year-old UES "neighborhood" Japanese; affordable rates and "congenial" service outshine the "simple" verging on "shabby" setting.

Shake Shack Burgers

21 | 13 | 15 | $16

E 80s | 154 E. 86th St. (bet. Lexington & 3rd Aves.) | 646-237-5035
Financial District | 215 Murray St. (bet. North End Ave. & West St.) | 646-545-4600

(continued)

Shake Shack

Flatiron | Madison Square Park | E. 23rd St. (bet. B'way & Madison Ave.) | 212-889-6600

W 40s | 691 Eighth Ave. (44th St.) | 646-435-0135 ◑

W 70s | 366 Columbus Ave. (77th St.) | 646-747-8770

Downtown Bklyn | Fulton Street Mall | 409 Fulton St. (Adams St.) | Brooklyn | 718-307-7590

Flushing | Citi Field | 12301 Roosevelt Ave. (126th St.) | Queens 🚇 Ⓜ www.shakeshack.com

Slinging "crowd-pleasing", "old-school" burgers and "creamy smooth" shakes, Danny Meyer's "über-popular" mini-chain is a "fast-food revelation" thanks to "cheap, high-quality" eats; "outrageous" lines and "musical-chairs" seating come with the territory, so regulars prefer the less frenzied "off hours."

Shalezeh *Persian* 22 | 18 | 22 | $44

E 80s | 1420 Third Ave. (bet. 80th & 81st Sts.) | 212-288-0012 | www.shalezeh.com

"As close as you can get to authentic Persian dining in NYC", this "refined", moderately priced Upper Eastsider presents "fragrant, richly flavored" cuisine (notably the rice dishes) in "comfortable" quarters; "gracious" service burnishes the overall "pleasant" experience.

Shanghai Café *Chinese* 24 | 10 | 12 | $19

Little Italy | 100 Mott St. (bet. Canal & Hester Sts.) | 212-966-3988 | www.shanghaicafenyc.com

This "tiny" Little Italy Chinese churns out its signature "succulent" soup dumplings and other Shanghai treats "fast" and "dirt-cheap"; indeed, the "flavorful" eats distract from the "barking" service and inauspicious "fluorescent-light-and-Formica" setting.

Shanghai Pavilion *Chinese* 21 | 19 | 21 | $35

E 70s | 1378 Third Ave. (bet. 78th & 79th Sts.) | 212-585-3388 | www.shanghaipavillion.com

It's hard to say what's most surprising about this "comfortable" UES Chinese: the "better-than-expected" Shanghainese cooking, "service with a smile" or "quiet", "upscale atmosphere"; whatever the case, it's a "welcome combination", especially given the modest price.

Shi *Asian* 24 | 25 | 21 | $38

LIC | 47-20 Center Blvd. (Vernon Blvd.) | Queens | 347-242-2450 | www.shilic.com

"Fantastic views of the NYC skyline" combine with "delicious" Pan-Asian cuisine, "amazing cocktails" and a "lovely staff" for a winning overall experience at this "upscale" LIC high-rise dweller; since it's "stronger than most in the area", insiders advise making "reservations" in advance.

Shorty's ◑ *Cheesesteaks* 22 | 13 | 17 | $18

NEW Financial District | 62 Pearl St. (bet. Broad St. & Coenties Slip) | 212-480-3900

Murray Hill | 66 Madison Ave. (bet. 27th & 28th Sts.) | 212-725-3900

W 40s | 576 Ninth Ave. (bet. 41st & 42nd Sts.) | 212-967-3055

www.shortysnyc.com

When "homesick for Philly", these "specialty" joints come in handy for "darn good impersonations of classic cheesesteaks" washed down with craft suds; just be aware they're "basically bars" that are particularly "earsplitting" when Eagles games are on the tube.

Shula's Steak House *Steak*

21 | 19 | 22 | $75

W 40s | Westin New York Times Square Hotel | 270 W. 43rd St. (bet. B'way & 8th Ave.) | 212-201-2776 | www.westinny.com

Not surprisingly, a "football" theme prevails at this Times Square outlet of gridiron coach Don Shula's steakhouse chain; it scores with "tasty" beef and "efficient" service, but while its memorabilia may appeal to "Dolphins fans", for Jets and Giants supporters "nothing's remarkable" enough to come "running back."

Shun Lee Cafe ⬤ *Chinese*

21 | 18 | 19 | $49

W 60s | 43 W. 65th St. (bet. Columbus Ave. & CPW) | 212-769-3888

"Convenient" pre- or post–Lincoln Center, this "been-there-for-ages" Chinese is still renowned for "good Uptown dim sum", even if its "old-school" menu and checkerboard decor may be "due for an update"; still, it's more "casual" and "less expensive" than its next-door sibling.

Shun Lee Palace ⬤ *Chinese*

24 | 21 | 22 | $60

E 50s | 155 E. 55th St. (bet. Lexington & 3rd Aves.) | 212-371-8844

Michael Tong's "venerable" Eastsider remains a "grande dame" of "fine Chinese dining", delivering "exceptional" dishes via "outstanding" staffers in an "elegant" room since 1971; just bring a "fat wallet" – it's among the "classiest" of its kind, but "you'll pay for it."

Shun Lee West ⬤ *Chinese*

22 | 20 | 21 | $56

W 60s | 43 W. 65th St. (bet. Columbus Ave. & CPW) | 212-595-8895

At Michael Tong's UWS exemplar of "upscale" dining, "fancy" Chinese food is dispatched by a "top-drawer" team in an "exotic", black-lacquered space festooned with gilded dragons; sure, it's "high priced" and a bit "old-fashioned", but there's a reason why it's been a neighborhood "cornerstone" since the '80s.

Siam Square Ⓜ *Thai*

▽ 22 | 18 | 20 | $31

Riverdale | 564 Kappock St. (Knolls Crescent) | Bronx | 718-432-8200 | www.siamsq.com

Riverdale spice-hounds tout the "creative specials" and other "well-flavored" Thai dishes served at this reasonably priced find; the decor isn't much, but it's "quiet", the staff's "welcoming" and locals know they're "lucky to have such quality dining" nearby.

Sidecar ⬤Ⓜ *American*

23 | 20 | 22 | $39

Park Slope | 560 Fifth Ave. (bet. 15th & 16th Sts.) | Brooklyn | 718-369-0077 | www.sidecarbrooklyn.com

The barkeeps "mix a mean drink" at this "bustling" Park Slope purveyor of "original" cocktails and "tasty" American comfort fare that's prepared in an open kitchen visible from the copper-topped bar; the ultimate "local haunt", it also gets a "thumbs-up" for its late-night hours.

Sik Gaek ⬤ *Korean*

22 | 14 | 19 | $36

Flushing | 161-29 Crocheron Ave. (162nd St.) | Queens | 718-321-7770 Ⓜ
Woodside | 49-11 Roosevelt Ave. (50th St.) | Queens | 718-205-4555
www.sikgaekusa.com

"Adventurous" types crowd these low-budget Flushing-Woodside Koreans, where "attentive" servers dole out "authentic" oceanic fare to the tune of "blaring hip-hop"; though the sight of seafood "still wriggling in the pot" can be "off-putting", it's "fun" for "big groups" and high on "exotic excitement."

Sinigual *Mexican*

FOOD	DECOR	SERVICE	COST
21	20	19	$42

E 40s | 640 Third Ave. (41st St.) | 212-286-0250 |
www.sinigualrestaurants.com

"Delicious" Mexican standards and "potent margaritas" get a "modern spin" at this "convivial" contender near Grand Central; the "cavernous" space can get "noisy" (especially after work at the bar), but the "tableside guac" alone justifies the "price of admission."

Sip Sak *Turkish*

FOOD	DECOR	SERVICE	COST
20	14	17	$38

E 40s | 928 Second Ave. (bet. 49th & 50th Sts.) | 212-583-1900 |
www.sip-sak.com

"Solid" Turkish specialties full of flavor come at "fair" rates at this 10-year-old U.N.-area "standby"; the "Montparnasse-meets-the-Dardanelles" decor is considered "just ok", but the food and service shore up an overall "satisfying" experience.

NEW Sirio ❶ *Italian*

FOOD	DECOR	SERVICE	COST
▽ 22	23	25	$81

E 60s | Pierre Hotel | 795 Fifth Ave. (61st St.) | 212-940-8195 |
www.siriony.com

Legendary restaurateur Sirio Maccioni (Le Cirque) brings "classy" sophistication to the UES via this Vegas import transplanted to the Pierre Hotel; targeted toward "society" movers and shakers, it features a "delicious" Tuscan menu – highlighted by a signature spaghetti carbonara – served in an "elegant", Adam Tihany–designed setting.

Sistina *Italian*

FOOD	DECOR	SERVICE	COST
25	19	23	$79

E 80s | 1555 Second Ave. (bet. 80th & 81st Sts.) | 212-861-7660

"Adult" diners gather at this "civilized" UES "white-tablecloth" Italian, where "inspired" cuisine is matched with an "outstanding" wine list; "impeccable" service and attractive, "old-world" decor make the "mind-blowing" pricing easier to swallow.

606 R&D *American*

FOOD	DECOR	SERVICE	COST
23	22	22	$37

Prospect Heights | 606 Vanderbilt Ave. (bet. Prospect Pl. & St. Marks Ave.) |
Brooklyn | 718-230-0125 | www.606vanderbiltbklyn.com

A "popular" pick along "Vanderbilt Avenue's growing Restaurant Row", this "charming" Prospect Heights yearling plies "delectible" midpriced American "farm-to-table" fare within a "bright", narrow space augmented with a roomy backyard; everyone "loves watching them" crank up the resident machine to make the "amazing donuts in the morning", and the prix fixe Sunday supper is "a steal."

67 Burger *Burgers*

FOOD	DECOR	SERVICE	COST
21	17	19	$19

Fort Greene | 67 Lafayette Ave. (bet. Elliott Pl. & Fulton St.) | Brooklyn |
718-797-7150
Park Slope | 234 Flatbush Ave. (bet. Bergen St. & 6th Ave.) | Brooklyn |
718-399-6767
www.67burger.com

These "cafeteria"-style Brooklyn "burger havens" supply "cooked-to-order" patties plus "all manner of fixin's" to locals as well as BAM and Barclays Center attendees; no one minds the "sterile" settings what with the "reasonable" tabs and "kid-friendly" vibes.

	FOOD	DECOR	SERVICE	COST

S'MAC *American*
23 | 11 | 15 | $15

E Village | 345 E. 12th St. (bet. 1st & 2nd Aves.) | 212-358-7912
NEW **Murray Hill** | 157 E. 33rd St. (bet. Lexington & 3rd Aves.) | 212-683-3900
www.smacnyc.com

"Fancy", "delicious" mac 'n' cheese is the specialty of these "affordable" "pleasure palaces" that offer vegan, gluten-free and customized variants; given "minimal seating", "cheesy" decor and service that's "less than caring", many opt for the "take-and-bake" option.

The Smile ● *Mediterranean*
▽ 21 | 20 | 19 | $30

NoHo | 26 Bond St., downstairs (bet. Bowery & Lafayette St.) | 646-329-5836 | www.thesmilenyc.com

Smile to Go *Mediterranean*

SoHo | 22 Howard St. (bet. Crosby & Lafayette Sts.) | 646-863-3893 | www.smiletogonyc.com

"Hipsters abound" at this "sweet" little NoHo nook (and its SoHo take-out satellite) that flies a bit under the radar with its "charming", "rustic" basement locale and "basic" Med bites; by day, it's an "ideal" stop for coffee, and if the staff can be "spacey", at least they "always smile."

The Smith ● *American*
19 | 17 | 18 | $43

E 50s | 956 Second Ave. (51st St.) | 212-644-2700
E Village | 55 Third Ave. (bet. 10th & 11th Sts.) | 212-420-9800
NEW **W 60s** | 1900 Broadway (63rd St.) | 212-496-5700
www.thesmithnyc.com

"Don't expect an intimate conversation" at this "million-decibel" mini-chain that supplies "basic" but "appealing" American grub to "under-35" throngs out to "eat and be merry"; "especially popular for brunch", they're routinely "bustling" thanks to "good value" and "upbeat" vibes.

Smith & Wollensky ● *Steak*
23 | 19 | 21 | $78

E 40s | 797 Third Ave. (49th St.) | 212-753-1530 | www.smithandwollenskynyc.com

"Get your year's quota" of beef at this "classic" Midtown steakhouse where "enormous", "juicy" cuts and "powerful" libations arrive in a "boys'-club" milieu packed with "chummy" suits "bonding over business"; staffers "straight out of the '50s" run the show, dispensing bills best settled by "expense account."

Smoke Joint *BBQ*
22 | 14 | 19 | $25

Fort Greene | 87 S. Elliott Pl. (bet. Fulton St. & Lafayette Ave.) | Brooklyn | 718-797-1011 | www.thesmokejoint.com

The "sauce is boss" at this cheap Fort Greene BBQ specialist, a "funky" standby for "outstanding", "smoky" ribs and "on-point" wings; true, it's "rough around the edges", but service is "solid", and the crowds happily "eat while standing" – "'cuz it's so packed."

Smorgasburg Ⓜ⇵ *Eclectic*
27 | 15 | 17 | $22

NEW **Dumbo** | Brooklyn Bridge Park | 30 Water St. (Dock St.) | Brooklyn | 718-928-6603
Williamsburg | East River State Park | 90 Kent Ave. (N. 7th St.) | Brooklyn | 718-928-6603 Ⓢ
www.smorgasburg.com

This roaming, seasonal food market – Saturdays in Williamsburg, Sundays in Dumbo – features "fantastic", "deliciously cheap" eats

| | FOOD | DECOR | SERVICE | COST |

from local food purveyors along with bonus views of the "Manhattan skyline"; the "sheer variety" of eclectic offerings makes the trip "essential", but be prepared for "crazy crowds."

Smorgas Chef *Scandinavian*
20 | 17 | 19 | $38

Financial District | 53 Stone St. (William St.) | 212-422-3500
Murray Hill | Scandinavia House | 58 Park Ave. (bet. 37th & 38th Sts.) | 212-847-9745
W Village | 283 W. 12th St. (4th St.) | 212-243-7073
www.smorgas.com

Admirers would return "just for the meatballs", but these "reliable" Scandinavians offer plenty of other "traditional" dishes as well, brought to table by a "lovely" staff; the surroundings are "spare" but "relaxing", and better still the check won't "break the bank."

Snack *Greek*
23 | 16 | 20 | $37

SoHo | 105 Thompson St. (bet. Prince & Spring Sts.) | 212-925-1040 | www.snacksoho.com

Snack Taverna *Greek*

W Village | 63 Bedford St. (Morton St.) | 212-929-3499 | www.snacktaverna.com

"Delectable" Hellenic dishes in "large portions" are the draws at this "friendly" Greek duo; the slightly roomier West Village outlet is "a step up" from its "teeny", 12-seat SoHo sibling, but both exude "rustic charm" – and the "price is just right."

sNice *Sandwiches/Vegetarian*
20 | 16 | 17 | $16

SoHo | 150 Sullivan St. (bet. Houston & Prince Sts.) | 212-253-5405
W Village | 45 Eighth Ave. (bet. Horatio & Jane Sts.) | 212-645-0310
Park Slope | 315 Fifth Ave. (3rd St.) | Brooklyn | 718-788-2121
www.snicecafe.com

These "chill" sandwich spots prove that vegetarian fare can be both "delicious" and "healthy"; everyone from "moms-to-be" to "laptop" users finds the "diverse" menus and "friendly community spirit" soNice.

Soba Nippon *Japanese/Noodle Shop*
22 | 16 | 21 | $40

W 50s | 19 W. 52nd St. (bet. 5th & 6th Aves.) | 212-489-2525 | www.sobanippon.com

They "grow their own buckwheat" to make the noodles at this "good-value" Midtown Japanese soba standout, where "personal" service and "calm" atmospherics make it "perfect for stressed-out afternoons"; "worn decor" seems to be the sole downside.

Soba Totto *Japanese/Noodle Shop*
24 | 19 | 19 | $46

E 40s | 211 E. 43rd St. (bet. 2nd & 3rd Aves.) | 212-557-8200 | www.sobatotto.com

"Stunning" housemade soba and "fresh" yakitori – but no sushi – beckon Grand Central commuters to this "dimly lit" Midtown Japanese; the prices may be a bit "expensive" for the genre, but it's a pleasure to "sit at the bar and watch the charcoal pros work their magic."

Soba-ya *Japanese/Noodle Shop*
23 | 18 | 20 | $31

E Village | 229 E. Ninth St. (bet. 2nd & 3rd Aves.) | 212-533-6966 | www.sobaya-nyc.com

At this "low-key" East Village Japanese, the "perfectly made" soba features "refreshing broths" and "delicious noodles"; the no-reservations policy can cause "weekend waits", but "affordable" price tags and "pleasant" environs more than compensate.

Socarrat Paella Bar *Spanish*

22 | 17 | 18 | $49

Chelsea | 259 W. 19th St. (bet. 7th & 8th Aves.) | 212-462-1000
E 50s | 953 Second Ave. (bet. 50th & 51st Sts.) | 212-759-0101
NoLita | 284 Mulberry St. (bet. Houston & Prince Sts.) |
212-219-0101
www.socarratpaellabar.com

These "low-key" Spaniards plate some of the best paella "this side of Valencia", along with "hard-to-resist" tapas and "fruit-laden" sangria; communal seating at the "cramped" Chelsea original isn't everyone's bag, but there's more room at the Midtown and NoLita spin-offs.

Sofrito ● *Puerto Rican*

24 | 21 | 19 | $50

E 50s | 400 E. 57th St. (bet. 1st Ave. & Sutton Pl.) | 212-754-5999 |
www.sofritony.com

"To-die-for" mofongo and pernil get washed down with "fruity vacation drinks" at this "clubby" Sutton Place Puerto Rican, where "loud Latin music" booms and someone's always "celebrating something"; the "enormous" repasts are "surprisingly affordable", but "bring your earplugs."

Sojourn ● *Eclectic*

23 | 20 | 20 | $46

E 70s | 244 E. 79th St. (bet. 2nd & 3rd Aves.) | 212-537-7745 |
www.sojournrestaurant.com

This "sexy" UES Eclectic dispatches a "wide range" of "creative" small plates and "unusual beers" to an "attractive clientele"; the "dimly lit" setting exudes "downtown" vibrations and the staff is certainly "knowledgeable", but "order carefully" or the bill may be a "shock."

Solera ⊠ *Spanish*

24 | 20 | 23 | $55

E 50s | 216 E. 53rd St. (bet. 2nd & 3rd Aves.) | 212-644-1166 |
www.solerany.com

"Civilized" is the word on this longtime East Midtown Spaniard where "terrific" tapas, "plenty of paella" and Iberian wines are dispensed by a "friendly" crew; prices are somewhat "high", but the payoff is a "comfortable" setting where "conversation is easily possible."

Solo *Italian/Kosher*

25 | 22 | 22 | $68

E 50s | 550 Madison Ave. (bet. 55th & 56th Sts.) | 212-833-7800 |
www.solonyc.com

It's the "crème de la crème" of glatt kitchens say fans of this "quiet" Midtowner offering an "expansive" menu of "splendid" kosher Italian dishes; the "pretty" place and its "unpretentious" staff exude "refinement", but its "captive audience" has to "part with a lot of shekels."

Son Cubano ⊠ *Cuban*

22 | 21 | 19 | $47

Chelsea | 544 W. 27th St. (bet. 10th & 11th Aves.) | 212-366-1640 |
www.soncubanonyc.com

Reopened in Way West Chelsea, this "upbeat" eatery/nightclub retains its "old Havana" supper-club vibe, from the glitzy chandeliers to the checkerboard dance floor; the kitchen turns out midpriced Cuban favorites, best paired with tropical cocktails, and later on the scene turns into a "Latin dance party."

	FOOD	DECOR	SERVICE	COST

Song ⌷ *Thai* | 24 | 18 | 18 | $23 |

Park Slope | 295 Fifth Ave. (bet. 1st & 2nd Sts.) | Brooklyn | 718-965-1108
Park Slopers sing the praises of this "family-friendly" Joya sibling, where the "fantastic" Thai dishes are so "inexpensive" and "generously portioned" that most take the no-credit-card policy in stride; if the high "volume of music and chatter" inside rankles, there's always the "rear garden."

Sons of Essex ● *American* | ▽ 20 | 22 | 19 | $50 |

LES | 133 Essex St. (bet. Rivington & Stanton Sts.) | 212-674-7100 | www.sonsofessexles.com
Expect a "vintage" vibe – starting with a "cool" delicatessen entrance – at this somewhat "pricey" Lower Eastsider; "service suffers" at times and the "happening bar scene" threatens to overshadow the "decadent" New American fare, but most are having too much "fun" to notice.

Sookk *Thai* | 21 | 19 | 20 | $26 |

W 100s | 2686 Broadway (bet. 102nd & 103rd Sts.) | 212-870-0253
UWS locals leave this "reliable" neighborhood Thai with a "full stomach" thanks to its "generous portions" of "innovative", Bangkok-inspired street eats; the "calm" setting may be "tiny", but few mind given the "super-cheap" tariffs.

Sorella ● M *Italian* | ▽ 24 | 20 | 23 | $58 |

LES | 95 Allen St. (bet. Broome & Delancey Sts.) | 212-274-9595 | www.sorellanyc.com
It's "love at first bite" for many at this "hidden" LES Italian praised for its "consistently exciting" Piedmontese small plates paired with regional wines; "helpful" service and a "cool", "inviting" setting take the edge off of the pricey tabs.

Sosa Borella ● *Argentinean/Italian* | 20 | 16 | 20 | $46 |

W 50s | 832 Eighth Ave. (50th St.) | 212-262-7774 | www.sosaborella.com
This West 50s vet "just keeps rolling along" with "simple", "tasty" Argentinean-Italian fare served in "friendly" environs; "value" rates and a "pleasant" rooftop are other reasons it's an "excellent choice" pre- or post-theater.

Soto ● 图 *Japanese* | 27 | 19 | 21 | $104 |

W Village | 357 Sixth Ave. (bet. Washington Pl. & W. 4th St.) | 212-414-3088
It's "uni heaven" at this West Village Japanese, where chef Sotohiro Kosugi turns out "wonderfully creative" urchin dishes plus "beyond-all-expectations" sushi and "amazing" omakase; "efficient" service and a "tranquil", "minimalist" setting help calm nerves jangled by the "splurge" pricing.

SottoVoce *Italian* | 21 | 17 | 20 | $39 |

Park Slope | 225 Seventh Ave. (4th St.) | Brooklyn | 718-369-9322 | www.sottovocerestaurant.com
"Reliable pastas" and other Italian basics "done right" keep this "unpretentious" Park Sloper "popular", as do the "can't-be-beat" $11 prix fixe lunch and "unlimited-mimosa" brunch; "familial service" and "pleasant" sidewalk seating ice the cake.

				FOOD	DECOR	SERVICE	COST

South Brooklyn Pizza ● *Pizza*
| 23 | 15 | 17 | $14 |

E Village | 122 First Ave. (bet. 7th St. & St. Marks Pl.) |
212-533-2879
Boerum Hill | 63 Fourth Ave. (bet. Bergen St. & St. Marks Pl.) | Brooklyn |
718-399-7770
Carroll Gardens | 451 Court St. (bet. 4th Pl. & Luquer St.) | Brooklyn |
718-852-4038 Ⓜ☞
Park Slope | 447 First St. (bet. 6th & 7th Aves.) | Brooklyn |
718-832-1022
www.southbrooklynpizza.com
This burgeoning mini-chain of "funky" pizzerias dishes up "incredibly
fresh" "NYC-style" thin-crust pies; you can also get slices – which
many take on the run given the no-frills, "hole-in-the-wall" setups.

South Gate ● *American*
| 21 | 25 | 20 | $72 |

W 50s | JW Marriott Essex House | 154 Central Park S. (bet. 6th & 7th Aves.) |
212-484-5120 | www.154southgate.com
Somewhat "under the radar" despite an "unbeatable" Essex House location, this "quiet CPS find" offers Kerry Heffernan's "delightful" New
Americana in "glam" quarters; ok, "you'd expect better service" given
the "stiff price", but most just focus on the "view of Central Park."

Sparks Steak House ☒ *Steak*
| 25 | 20 | 23 | $85 |

E 40s | 210 E. 46th St. (bet. 2nd & 3rd Aves.) | 212-687-4855 |
www.sparkssteakhouse.com
"Carnivores with expense accounts" descend on this circa-1966
Midtown chophouse for "succulent" steaks and an "endless" wine list
proffered by "career waiters" in "clubby" surrounds; maybe the vibe's
"anachronistic", but tradition is "what they're selling" here, and regulars think it's "worth every penny."

Spasso ● *Italian*
| 23 | 19 | 21 | $53 |

W Village | 551 Hudson St. (Perry St.) | 212-858-3838 | www.spassonyc.com
"Innovative" Italian fare and "excellent" wines come via "friendly"
staffers at this slightly "sceney" West Villager; locals who note it becomes "loud and tight" at prime times "hope it doesn't get more
popular" – prices "on the expensive side" may keep crowds in check.

Speedy Romeo *Italian/Pizza*
| ▽ 22 | 21 | 19 | $34 |

Clinton Hill | 376 Classon Ave. (Greene Ave.) | Brooklyn | 718-230-0061 |
www.speedyromeo.com
Housed in a former body shop, this "high-quality" Clinton Hill Italian
specializes in "top-notch" wood-fired pizzas topped with "housemade
mozz" and other "fresh" ingredients, but it also serves grill dishes; the
"casual", brick-lined space centered around an open kitchen is done
up in old-school Brooklyn style.

Spice *Thai*
| 19 | 15 | 17 | $29 |

Chelsea | 199 Eighth Ave. (bet. 20th & 21st Sts.) | 212-989-1116
Chelsea | 236 Eighth Ave. (22nd St.) | 212-620-4585
E 70s | 1479 First Ave. (77th St.) | 212-744-6374
E Village | 104 Second Ave. (6th St.) | 212-533-8900
E Village | 77 E. 10th St. (4th Ave.) | 212-388-9006
G Village | 39 E. 13th St. (bet. B'way & University Pl.) | 212-982-3758
W 80s | 435 Amsterdam Ave. (81st St.) | 212-362-5861
Park Slope | 61 Seventh Ave. (Lincoln Pl.) | Brooklyn | 718-622-6353

| | FOOD | DECOR | SERVICE | COST |

(continued)

Spice

NEW LIC | 47-45 Vernon Ave. (48th Ave.) | Queens | 718-392-7888 | www.spicethainyc.com

"Generous" helpings of "straightforward" Thai fare offered "cheap" keep this chain "popular" among "college" types and others "on a budget"; "lively" but "noisy" environs and "unenthusiastic" service are part of the package, but there's always "reliable" delivery.

Spice Market ● *SE Asian* 　　23 | 26 | 21 | $61

Meatpacking | 403 W. 13th St. (9th Ave.) | 212-675-2322 | www.spicemarketnewyork.com

Now in its 10th year, Jean-Georges Vongerichten's ever-"trendy" Southeast Asian offers "inventive" haute street food and "different" cocktails in an "exotic" Meatpacking "fantasy palace" setting complete with "special" private rooms downstairs; "deafening noise" and "steep prices" to the contrary, most report an "overall great time" here.

Spicy & Tasty 🍽 *Chinese* 　　24 | 11 | 15 | $25

Flushing | 39-07 Prince St. (Roosevelt Ave.) | Queens | 718-359-1601

The "name says it all" about this cash-only Flushing Chinese where the "hot, hot, hot" Sichuan cooking will "open your sinuses" but won't scorch your wallet; overlook the "nonexistent" decor, no-rez rule and any "communication problems" with the staff – it's "all about the food" here.

Spiga *Italian* 　　23 | 18 | 21 | $54

W 80s | 200 W. 84th St. (bet. Amsterdam Ave. & B'way) | 212-362-5506 | www.spiganyc.com

Among the "best-kept secrets on the UWS", this "off-the-beaten-path" trattoria is a "tiny sanctuary" of "rich", "refined" Italian cooking; ok, the "romantic" setting skews "tight" and the tabs may be "a little pricey", but "gracious" service helps make up for it.

Spigolo *Italian* 　　24 | 16 | 20 | $62

E 80s | 1561 Second Ave. (81st St.) | 212-744-1100 | www.spigolonyc.com

Upper Eastsiders squeeze into this "closet-size" trattoria for "fantastic" (if "pricey") Italian classics delivered by a "thoughtful" crew; snagging a reservation can be "tough", but first come, first served outside seats ease the process in summer.

Spina *Italian* 　　25 | 19 | 22 | $45

E Village | 175 Ave. B (11th St.) | 212-253-2250 | www.spinarestaurant.com

"Fresh pastas like nonna makes" are the draw at this "cute", midpriced East Village Italian where the noodles are "made right in front of you"; a "relaxing" ambiance and "gracious" service help cement its reputation as an "inviting" neighborhood nexus.

Spotted Pig ● *European* 　　24 | 20 | 19 | $49

W Village | 314 W. 11th St. (Greenwich St.) | 212-620-0393 | www.thespottedpig.com

Famed for April Bloomfield's "brilliant" Modern European cooking (including an "awesome" burger), this 10-year-old West Village gastropub remains a bona fide "scene" complete with "hopping" atmospherics and "celeb sightings"; a no-rez policy and "tight" dimensions lead to "inevitable" waits, but overall it's more than "worthwhile."

	FOOD	DECOR	SERVICE	COST

Spring Street Natural ❶ *Health Food* | 20 | 17 | 18 | $31

NoLita | 62 Spring St. (Lafayette St.) | 212-966-0290 |
www.springstreetnatural.com

Spring Natural Kitchen ❶ *Health Food*

W 80s | 474 Columbus Ave (83rd St.) | 646-596-7434 |
www.springnaturalkitchen.com

"Not just for the granola crowd", this "affordable" NoLita longtimer
and its Upper West Side offshoot sling "wholesome" dishes featuring
veggies, fish and fowl that suit everyone from "vegans to carnivores";
given the "relaxing" "hippie" ambiance, "you can sit forever and
won't be bothered."

Sripraphai ⌗ *Thai* | 27 | 14 | 17 | $27

Woodside | 64-13 39th Ave. (bet. 64th & 65th Sts.) | Queens |
718-899-9599 | www.sripraphairestaurant.com

"Still the champ", this Queens "gem" is again ranked NYC's top Thai
thanks to a "staggeringly vast" choice of "legit" dishes that "burn with
flavor" and incendiary spice; despite "pedestrian" decor, "unremark-
able" service and a cash-only rule, the "fair" prices alone make it worth
the "schlep to Woodside."

Stage Door *Deli* | 19 | 13 | 17 | $25

Financial District | 26 Vesey St. (bet. B'way & Church St.) | 212-791-5252 |
www.stagedoordeli.net

Garment District | 5 Penn Plaza (bet. 33rd & 34th Sts.) | 212-868-9655 |
www.stagedoordeli.com ❶

"Deli food served diner-style" sums up these separately owned "basic" Jewish delis, where the sandwiches are "piled high" with corned
beef and pastrami; popular with both "tourists and locals", they offer
a taste of the "good old days" in settings with "not much character."

Stamatis ❶ *Greek* | 23 | 14 | 18 | $35

Astoria | 29-09 23rd Ave. (bet. 29th & 31st Sts.) | Queens | 718-932-8596 |
www.stamatisrestaurant.com

"If you can't get to Greece", this "well-established", "family-oriented"
Astoria taverna provides an "authentic" alternative with its "reliable"
Hellenic cooking; "stark" decor and somewhat "indifferent" service
are less transporting, but "reasonable prices" take the edge off.

Standard Grill ❶ *American* | 22 | 22 | 20 | $59

Meatpacking | Standard Hotel | 848 Washington St. (bet. Little W. 12th &
13th Sts.) | 212-645-4100 | www.thestandardgrill.com

"Happening" folks gravitate to this "festive" Meatpacking District
American, drawn by its "reliably good" food, "fun people-watching"
and front cafe "pickup scene"; but "deafening" decibels and
"shoulder-to-shoulder" crowds lead some to dub it a "place more to be
seen than fed."

St. Andrews ❶ *Seafood/Steak* | 19 | 18 | 19 | $42

W 40s | 140 W. 46th St. (bet. B'way & 6th Ave.) | 212-840-8413 |
www.standrewsnyc.com

A "scotch-drinker's heaven", this atmospheric Theater District pub
pours a "tremendous" selection of single malts and draft beers paired
with "traditional" surf 'n' turf; the staff's "accents" and "cute kilts" enhance the "little bit of Scotland" mood.

	FOOD	DECOR	SERVICE	COST

St. Anselm *American*
27 | 20 | 24 | $43

Williamsburg | 355 Metropolitan Ave. (Havemeyer St.) | Brooklyn |
718-384-5054

A "meat-lover's paradise", this Williamsburg American vends
"amazing", "affordable" steaks along with other "farm-fresh" fare;
the "rugged", brick-walled interior may be "bare-bones", the clientele "a bit too hip" and no reservations leads to "long waits", yet it
remains ever "popular."

Stanton Social ● *Eclectic*
24 | 22 | 20 | $55

LES | 99 Stanton St. (bet. Ludlow & Orchard Sts.) | 212-995-0099 |
www.thestantonsocial.com

"Young" things flock to this "energetic" Lower Eastsider to graze on
"delicious" Eclectic share plates and "yummy" tipples in a "chic" duplex setting; what with the "extreme decibels" and "ridiculous waits",
its "bachelorette"-heavy crowd calls it "quite the scene", though some
cynics yawn it's "played out."

Steak Frites *French/Steak*
20 | 18 | 19 | $48

Union Sq | 9 E. 16th St. (bet. 5th Ave. & Union Sq. W.) | 212-675-4700 |
www.steakfritesnyc.com

"Like the name says", steak frites is the main attraction at this Union
Square French bistro, where the rest of the menu's considered "just
ok" and priced a "bit on the high side"; when the "barn"-size room gets
too "noisy", regulars sit outside for some prime people-watching.

Steak 'n Shake ● *Burgers*
20 | 14 | 17 | $13

W 50s | 1695 Broadway (bet. 53rd & 54th Sts.) | 212-247-6584 |
www.steaknshake.com

Boosters brave the "Times Square crowds" for "juicy burgers" and
"unbeatable" shakes at this Midwestern chain link housed in the Ed
Sullivan Theater; given "unbelievably cheap" tabs, "seating's at a premium" in its retro-diner digs – especially when the audience is lined up
for the Letterman show.

STK *Steak*
23 | 24 | 21 | $75

Meatpacking | 26 Little W. 12th St. (bet. 9th Ave. & Washington St.) |
646-624-2444 ●
W 40s | 1114 Sixth Ave. (bet. 42nd & 43rd Sts.) |
646-624-2455 ⑤
www.stkhouse.com

Merging a nightclub and a chop shop into one "trendy" package, this
"chic" duo plates "very good" steaks in "glamorous", loungelike environs full of "beautiful people" and "thumping" DJ'd sounds; the pricing's "steep", so "bring the black card" and remember "you're paying
for the vibe."

Stonehome Wine Bar ● *American*
21 | 19 | 20 | $39

Fort Greene | 87 Lafayette Ave. (S. Portland Ave.) | Brooklyn |
718-624-9443 | www.stonehomewinebar.com

"Unpretentious" but "romantic", this "cozy" Fort Greene wine bar
boasts a 200-strong selection of "fairly priced" vintages paired
with an "ever-changing" menu of "solid" New Americana; equipped
with a "pretty back garden", it's close to BAM and "perfect" pre-
or post-show.

FOOD	DECOR	SERVICE	COST

Stone Park Café *American*

24 | **20** | **22** | **$49**

Park Slope | 324 Fifth Ave. (3rd St.) | Brooklyn | 718-369-0082 |
www.stoneparkcafe.com

"Inventive" seasonal cooking in a "moderately upscale" milieu earns
"neighborhood favorite" status for this Park Slope New American; a
"wonderful" staff, outdoor tables and a "fantastic brunch" are further
endearments, and if tabs are "a bit pricey", it's well worth the "splurge."

NEW The Strand ●⑤ *BBQ*

▽ **21** | **17** | **15** | **$30**

Astoria | 25-27 Broadway (bet. Crescent & 29th Sts.) | Queens |
718-440-3231 | www.thestrandsmokehouse.com

"Solid" smokehouse eats are accompanied by whiskey and craft suds
at this "hip" Astoria BBQ where live bands on weekends provide a
"raucous" soundtrack; the sprawling, "counter-service" setting lies
somewhere between a "cafeteria" and a "glorified college beer hall."

Strip House *Steak*

25 | **22** | **22** | **$79**

G Village | 13 E. 12th St. (bet. 5th Ave. & University Pl.) | 212-328-0000
NEW **W 40s** | 15 W. 44th St. (bet. 5th & 6th Aves.) | 212-336-5454
www.striphouse.com

Strip House Next Door *American*

G Village | 11 E. 12th St., downstairs (bet. 5th Ave. & University Pl.) |
212-838-9197 | www.striphousegrill.com

"Red velvet walls" and vintage burlesque star photos lend a "fun,
bordello-esque" feel to these "sexy" Steve Hanson chop shops that
follow through with "sumptuous" steaks and "stellar" sides; "old-
school" vibrations, "outstanding" service and "expensive" price tags
complete the "quality" picture.

Sueños ⓜ *Mexican*

23 | **19** | **20** | **$48**

Chelsea | 311 W. 17th St. (bet. 8th & 9th Aves.) | 212-243-1333 |
www.suenosnyc.com

"Superior" progressive Mexican fare with "innovative twists" keeps
chef Sue Torres' "cozy", "off-the-beaten-path" Chelsea favorite busy
with fans of "made-to-order guacamole" paired with "excellent" margaritas; tabs may be a touch "expensive", but it's a "friendly place to
explore new flavors."

Sugar Freak *Cajun/Creole*

▽ **22** | **24** | **22** | **$29**

Astoria | 36-18 30th Ave. (bet. 36th & 37th Sts.) | Queens |
718-726-5850 | www.sugarfreak.com

A change of pace on the busy 30th Avenue strip, this "bit of N'Awlins
in Astoria" traffics in "real-deal" Cajun-Creole favorites, "kickass
cocktails" and "desserts that'll make a sugar freak out of anyone";
"kitschy-cute" decor with a "DIY feel" and "swift", "friendly" service
seal the deal.

Sugiyama ●⑤ⓜ *Japanese*

28 | **20** | **27** | **$102**

W 50s | 251 W. 55th St. (bet. B'way & 8th Ave.) | 212-956-0670 |
www.sugiyama-nyc.com

"You'd swear you were in Tokyo" at this "serene", underknown
Midtown Japanese where "skillful" chef Nao Sugiyama's "outstanding" kaiseki meals are ferried by "warm", "wonderful" servers; the
"unforgettable experience" comes at a "steep" prix fixe-only tab, but
the pre-theater deal packs "value."

| | FOOD | DECOR | SERVICE | COST |

Super Linda ● *S American* ▽ 17 | 16 | 15 | $48
TriBeCa | 109 W. Broadway (Reade St.) | 212-227-8998 |
www.superlindanyc.com

Scenesters pack this "hip" TriBeCan via Matt Abramcyk (ex Beatrice
Inn) and Serge Becker (Miss Lily's), where the South American chow
is "flavorful" – if "not quite super" – and served in atmospheric surrounds, including a "sexy" basement lounge; despite "snotty" service,
it's still pretty "popular."

Supper ●⇄ *Italian* 25 | 19 | 20 | $43
E Village | 156 E. Second St. (bet. Aves. A & B) | 212-477-7600 |
www.supperrestaurant.com

At this "low-key" East Villager from the Frank crew, "comfort"-oriented
Italiana is dispensed by a "pleasant" team at easy prices; despite "tight"
communal tables, "long waits" and a cash-only policy, the "rustic"
digs are "always bustling"; P.S. it now accepts reservations.

SushiAnn ⊠ *Japanese* 25 | 19 | 23 | $67
E 50s | 38 E. 51st St. (bet. Madison & Park Aves.) | 212-755-1780 |
www.sushiann.net

"Business-oriented" types converge on this "consistently excellent"
Midtown Japanese for "simple", "high-quality" sushi, competently delivered; the traditionally decorated digs are less notable and tabs are
high, but its "CEOs-in-training" crowd doesn't seem to mind.

Sushi Damo *Japanese* 23 | 19 | 21 | $42
W 50s | 330 W. 58th St. (bet. 8th & 9th Aves.) | 212-707-8609 |
www.sushidamo.com

With "quality" sushi, "prompt" service and "median" prices, this "under-
the-radar" Japanese near the Time Warner Center "ticks off all the
boxes"; maybe the somewhat "stark" digs "could use an update", but
ultimately it's "reliable" enough for an "easy" meal.

Sushiden *Japanese* 24 | 17 | 22 | $63
E 40s | 19 E. 49th St. (bet. 5th & Madison Aves.) | 212-758-2700
W 40s | 123 W. 49th St. (bet. 6th & 7th Aves.) | 212-398-2800 ⊠
www.sushiden.com

"Catering to the Japanese businessman crowd", these "no-frills"
Midtown vets vend "exquisite" sushi and sashimi in "serene" settings;
"attentive" service compensates for the "wallet-capturing" tabs,
though they're decidedly cheaper than "going to Tokyo."

NEW Sushi Dojo ⊠Ⓜ *Japanese* – | – | – | E
E Village | 110 First Ave. (bet. 6th & 7th Sts.) | 646-692-9398 |
www.sushidojonyc.com

From a Morimoto alum comes this new East Village Japanese that's
making a name for itself with bargain-priced omakase starting at $45;
the slim setting has but 36 seats, so reservations are a must.

SushiSamba ● *Brazilian/Japanese* 22 | 20 | 19 | $53
Flatiron | 245 Park Ave. S. (bet. 19th & 20th Sts.) | 212-475-9377
W Village | 87 Seventh Ave. S. (Barrow St.) | 212-691-7885
www.sushisamba.com

"Youthful" admirers salute this "fun" Flatiron–West Village duo for its
"unique" Brazilian-Japanese fusion menu that's well matched with

| | FOOD | DECOR | SERVICE | COST |

"wonderful" libations; "lethargic service" can be a letdown given the "premium prices", but their "cool" quarters are typically "hopping."

Sushi Seki ●🔲 *Japanese* | 28 | 14 | 22 | $80 |

E 60s | 1143 First Ave. (bet. 62nd & 63rd Sts.) | 212-371-0238
Transforming "pristine fish" into "phenomenal sushi", "master-of-his-art" chef Seki "never disappoints" at this "something-special" East Side Japanese; "late-night" hours draw night owls who don't mind the "costly" tabs and "needs-a-face-lift" decor.

Sushi Sen-nin 🔲 *Japanese* | 25 | 17 | 21 | $56 |

Murray Hill | 30 E. 33rd St. (bet. Madison Ave. & Park Ave S.) | 212-889-2208 | www.sushisennin.com
Though a "neighborhood favorite", this Murray Hill Japanese remains an "under-the-radar" source for "some of the freshest sushi" around at prices "accessible" enough for "semi-regular" dining; "friendly" service is another plus, but don't expect much in the way of decor.

Sushiya *Japanese* | 22 | 16 | 22 | $38 |

W 50s | 28 W. 56th St. (bet. 5th & 6th Aves.) | 212-247-5760 | www.sushiya56.com
"Solid" sushi at "affordable" rates keeps the lunch hour "busy" at this Midtown Japanese "business" standby; ok, it's "not hoity-toity", but the "fanfare-free" milieu makes for a "pleasant" everyday repast, and you can't beat the "great location."

Sushi Yasuda 🔲 *Japanese* | 28 | 22 | 24 | $88 |

E 40s | 204 E. 43rd St. (bet. 2nd & 3rd Aves.) | 212-972-1001 | www.sushiyasuda.com
Even though "chef Yasuda is gone", the "raw talent" in the kitchen perseveres at this "top-of-the-line" Japanese near Grand Central known for its "succulent" sushi; don't be misled by the "austere decor", it's "not inexpensive" – though the $28 prix fixe is a big-time bargain and there's now a no-tipping policy.

Sushi Zen 🔲 *Japanese* | 26 | 20 | 22 | $66 |

W 40s | 108 W. 44th St. (bet. B'way & 6th Ave.) | 212-302-0707 | www.sushizen-ny.com
It's "less touted" than some, but supporters say this Japanese "island of calm" is "one of the Theater District's best" given its "pristine", "beautifully presented" sushi; "excellent" service and "small" but "Zen"-like digs help justify the "expensive" tabs.

Sweet Melissa *Dessert/Sandwiches* | 20 | 17 | 18 | $20 |

Park Slope | 175 Seventh Ave. (bet. 1st & 2nd Sts.) | Brooklyn | 718-788-2700 | www.sweetmelissapatisserie.com
The "pastries rock" at this "cute" Park Slope bakery/cafe where "decadent desserts", afternoon tea and "pleasing" soups and salads win favor; a "casual" vibe and a "nice garden" offset "so-so service" and prices slightly "expensive" for the genre.

Swifty's *American* | 17 | 18 | 19 | $66 |

E 70s | 1007 Lexington Ave. (bet. 72nd & 73rd Sts.) | 212-535-6000 | www.swiftysnyc.com
"If you don't own a house in the Hamptons", you probably "won't feel at home" at this UES "neighborhood club" where "the elite meet for

meatloaf" and other "flatline" American standards; outsiders are exiled to the front of the house, but the choicest "social x-ray" people-watching is in the back room.

	FOOD	DECOR	SERVICE	COST

Sylvia's *Soul Food/Southern*

20 | 15 | 19 | $32

Harlem | 328 Lenox Ave. (bet. 126th & 127th Sts.) | 212-996-0660 | www.sylviasrestaurant.com

A "true icon of Harlem", this circa-1962 soul food "mainstay" warms hearts with "generous" helpings of Southern classics and a "fun" Sunday gospel brunch; old-timers opine it's "not what it used to be" but allow it's still "worth a visit", as the "tour buses out front" suggest.

Symposium *Greek*

20 | 16 | 21 | $27

W 100s | 544 W. 113th St. (bet. Amsterdam Ave. & B'way) | 212-865-1011 | www.symposiumnyc.com

Serving "students and absentminded Columbia profs" for 45 years, this "friendly" Morningside Heights Greek slings "large portions" of "hearty" traditional dishes at "rock-bottom prices"; "kitschy" decor (including "paintings on the ceiling") only bolsters its charm.

Szechuan Gourmet *Chinese*

23 | 12 | 16 | $28

E 70s | 1395 Second Ave. (bet. 72nd & 73rd Sts.) | 212-737-1838 | www.szechuangourmetny.info
Garment District | 21 W. 39th St. (bet. 5th & 6th Aves.) | 212-921-0233
W 50s | 242 W. 56th St. (bet. B'way & 8th Ave.) | 212-265-2226 | www.szechuangourmet.net
Flushing | 135-15 37th Ave. (bet. Main & Prince Sts.) | Queens | 718-888-9388 | www.szechuangourmetnyc.com

"If you can take the heat", head for these "real Sichuans" where the "fiery" cuisine "beats the wontons off" typical Chinese joints; although the "brusque" service and "dumpy" decor aren't nearly as sizzling, the "low prices" compensate.

Table d'Hôte *American/French*

19 | 13 | 18 | $55

E 90s | 44 E. 92nd St. (bet. Madison & Park Aves.) | 212-348-8125 | www.tabledhote.info

If you're "unable to take that trip to Paris", check out this Carnegie Hill "tradition" (since 1978) plying "delicious" French-American fare in "neighborly" confines; given the *très* "petite" dimensions, however, you might consider packing a "shoehorn."

Taboon *Mediterranean/Mideastern*

24 | 19 | 21 | $52

W 50s | 773 10th Ave. (52nd St.) | 212-713-0271 | www.taboononline.com

Taboonette *Mediterranean/Mideastern*

G Village | 30 E. 13th St. (bet. 5th Ave. & University Pl.) | 212-510-7881 | www.taboonette.com

It's "out of the way", but this West Hell's Kitchen outpost is often "jammed" thanks to its "delectable" Med–Middle Eastern cuisine, including "fresh, hot" bread from the namesake oven; its quick-service Village spin-off specializes in flatbread sandwiches with hearty fillings.

Taci's Beyti *Turkish*

25 | 15 | 21 | $32

Midwood | 1955 Coney Island Ave. (bet. Ave. P & Kings Hwy.) | Brooklyn | 718-627-5750 | www.tacisbeyti.com

In a refreshingly "hipster-free corner of Brooklyn", this long-standing BYO Turk is a Midwood "favorite" for "huge portions" of "delicious" classic dishes, including "juicy" kebabs; the staff "couldn't be nicer", ditto the prices, and the plain-Jane digs are "more appealing" following a spiff-up.

Tacombi at Fonda Nolita ◐ *Mexican*

FOOD	DECOR	SERVICE	COST
23	19	17	$22

NoLita | 267 Elizabeth St. (bet. Houston & Prince Sts.) | 917-727-0179 | www.tacombi.com

Taking the "concept of a food truck" indoors, this "real-deal" NoLita taqueria plies "delicious" "mini-me-size" tacos from a vintage VW van parked in an "industrial garage"; it's a "fun", "kitschy" experience, even if the "picniclike" seating "could be nicer."

Taïm *Israeli/Vegetarian*

26	9	16	$13

NoLita | 45 Spring St. (Mulberry St.) | 212-219-0600
W Village | 222 Waverly Pl. (bet. 11th & Perry Sts.) | 212-691-1287
www.taimfalafel.com

"Basically a take-out counter" with a few stools, this West Village vegetarian Israeli draws "100-mile-long" lines with its "sublime" falafel and "amazing" smoothies; its NoLita sibling offers a bit more elbow room with the same "value" pricing.

Takahachi *Japanese*

25	17	22	$40

E Village | 85 Ave. A (bet. 5th & 6th Sts.) | 212-505-6524 ◐
TriBeCa | 145 Duane St. (bet. Church St. & W. B'way) | 212-571-1830
www.takahachi.net

"Creative sushi" and "tasty" Japanese home-cooking basics at a favorable "quality-to-price ratio" earn these TriBeCa-East Village twins "favorite-in-the-'hood" status; a "helpful" staff adds warmth to the "nothing-fancy" setups, which "bustle" at prime times.

Takashi *Japanese*

26	18	22	$69

W Village | 456 Hudson St. (bet. Barrow & Morton Sts.) | 212-414-2929 | www.takashinyc.com

"Fantastic" yakiniku ("cook-your-own" Japanese BBQ) is the draw at this West Villager where "daring", "every-piece-of-the-cow" offerings have "adventurous" carnivores enthusing "welcome to the offal house"; "attentive" service and "pleasantly minimalist" decor keep the focus on the "amazing cuts."

Talde ◐ *Asian*

25	20	23	$47

Park Slope | 369 Seventh Ave. (11th St.) | Brooklyn | 347-916-0031 | www.taldebrooklyn.com

Top Chef contender Dale Talde oversees this "high-energy" Park Slope Pan-Asian where the "creative", pork and seafood-heavy menu is rated a "triumph"; it's no-rez and the "tavern"-like digs are usually "jammed" – good thing the staff is so "patient and helpful."

Tamarind ◐ *Indian*

26	24	24	$58

Flatiron | 41-43 E. 22nd St. (bet. B'way & Park Ave. S.) | 212-674-7400
TriBeCa | 99 Hudson St. (bet. Franklin & Harrison Sts.) | 212-775-9000
www.tamarind22.com

This "civilized" duo, again rated NYC's top Indian, provides "exceptional" gourmet cuisine and "gracious" service both at the "warm" Flatiron original and the more expansive TriBeCa spin-off; while it's "not cheap", the overall "superior" performance is "worth the rupees" – and the $25 prix fixe lunch works for those "on a budget."

	FOOD	DECOR	SERVICE	COST

Tang Pavilion *Chinese*
23 | 18 | 22 | $40

W 50s | 65 E. 55th St. (bet. 5th & 6th Aves.) | 212-956-6888 |
www.tangpavilionchinese.com

"Terrific" traditional Shanghai cooking makes this "sophisticated"
Midtown Chinese a "top choice" near City Center and Carnegie Hall;
some aesthetes note its once-"classy" decor is "getting a little frayed",
but the service remains "polished" as ever, and "reasonable prices"
are the crowning touch.

Tanoreen Ⓜ *Mediterranean/Mideastern*
26 | 19 | 23 | $41

Bay Ridge | 7523 Third Ave. (76th St.) | Brooklyn | 718-748-5600 |
www.tanoreen.com

It's "worth the trip" to this "out-of-the-way" Bay Ridge "find" for "artfully prepared", "beautifully seasoned" Med–Middle Eastern home
cooking; some say it's getting "a bit pricey", but the "warm welcome"
compensates – "charismatic" chef-owner Rawia Bishara "makes a
point of stopping at every table."

NEW Tanoshi Sushi Ⓢ Ⓜ *Japanese*
- | - | - | M

E 70s | 1372 York Ave. (bet. 73rd & 74th Sts.) | 646-727-9056 |
www.tanoshisushi.com

NEW Tanoshi Bento Ⓢ *Japanese*
E 70s | 1372 York Ave. (bet. 73rd & 74th Sts.) | 917-265-8254 |
www.tanoshibento.com

This under-the-radar Yorkville Japanese has attracted a fervent fan
base thanks to its real-deal sushi and wallet-friendly omakase (around
$50); trade-offs include a funky storefront setting and super-tough
reservations – there are only 10 seats, and three seatings a night; P.S. its
new, next-door sibling offers everything from soba to bento boxes.

Tao ● *Asian*
24 | 27 | 21 | $61

E 50s | 42 E. 58th St. (bet. Madison & Park Aves.) | 212-888-2288 |
www.taorestaurant.com

"Flashy" Eastern decor featuring a "giant Buddha" is the main draw at
this "huge" Midtown Pan-Asian where the "delish" chow competes
with the "club atmosphere", and though the check can quickly "ratchet
up", its "upbeat crowd" doesn't seem to care; P.S. an equally mega
spin-off is in the works in Chelsea's Maritime Hotel.

Tarallucci e Vino *Italian*
20 | 18 | 19 | $38

E Village | 163 First Ave. (10th St.) | 212-388-1190
Flatiron | 15 E. 18th St. (bet. B'way & 5th Ave.) | 212-228-5400
W 80s | 475 Columbus Ave. (83rd St.) | 212-362-5454
www.taralluccievino.net

When you seek a "drop-in spot for a glass of wine" and a "step-up-
from-your-standard-Italian" bite, this "relaxed" trio is a "safe" bet;
"quality" espresso and pastries (the mainstays of the East Village original) make it a morning "favorite" as well.

Tartine ⊅ *French*
22 | 15 | 18 | $33

W Village | 253 W. 11th St. (4th St.) | 212-229-2611
At this cash-only West Village bistro, "delectable" French basics and
a "could-be-in-Paris" vibe come at an "affordable" price, helped along
by the BYO policy; the "tiny" space can be "tight", and "long waits" are
a given, so regulars try for one of the sidewalk tables.

	FOOD	DECOR	SERVICE	COST

Taste American
▽ 21 | 16 | 20 | $55

E 80s | 1413 Third Ave. (bet. 80th & 81st Sts.) | 212-717-9798 |
www.elizabar.com

A self-service cafe "without frills" by day, Eli Zabar's UES American makes a chameleonlike evening transition into an "intimate dining room", rolling out seasonal "home cooking for grown-ups"; deep-pocketed locals don't mind paying for the "civilized" experience given the "top-quality" ingredients.

Tasty Hand-Pulled Noodles ⊅ Noodle Shop
22 | 6 | 15 | $12

Chinatown | 1 Doyers St. (Bowery) | 212-791-1817

Soups brimming with "springy, chewy" noodles and "excellent" dumplings are the stars at this tiny Chinatown "hole-in-the-wall"; "quick" service and "cheap" tabs – plus a view of the chefs at work "slamming and pulling" dough – help distract from the seriously "sketchy" decor.

Tatiana ● Russian
20 | 17 | 15 | $57

Brighton Bch | 3152 Brighton Sixth St. (Brightwater Ct.) | Brooklyn |
718-891-5151 | www.tatianarestaurant.com

The "vodka flows like the Volga" at this 20-year-old Brighton Beach nightclub offering "surprisingly good" Russian grub that takes a backseat to the "over-the-top" "Vegas-style" floor show; alfresco fans prefer the "beautiful" Atlantic Ocean scenery from a boardwalk table.

Taverna Kyclades Greek/Seafood
26 | 13 | 19 | $36

Astoria | 33-07 Ditmars Blvd. (33rd St.) | Queens | 718-545-8666 |
www.tavernakyclades.com

"Super-fresh" seafood worthy of the "Greek gods" draws "persistent crowds" to this Astoria Hellenic where the "can't-go-wrong" prices offset the "tight, noisy" setting; the real rub is the no-rez policy and attendant "horrendous lines" – "go early" or "fight for a place to stand outside"; P.S. an East Village branch is in the works.

T-Bar Steak & Lounge Steak
21 | 20 | 20 | $61

E 70s | 1278 Third Ave. (73rd St.) | 212-772-0404 | www.tbarnyc.com

Tony Fortuna's "tony" steakhouse tenders "delicious", "not-frightfully-overpriced" beef in "pleasant" surrounds via a "gracious" crew; the "UES-housewives-of-NY" crowd at the bar kicks up a "noisy" scene, so "if you want to hear yourself talk", opt for the back room.

Tea & Sympathy British
22 | 19 | 20 | $28

W Village | 108 Greenwich Ave. (Jane St.) | 212-807-8329 |
www.teaandsympathy.com

"Anglophiles and expat Brits" make a beeline for this "tiny" West Village teahouse where English comfort food arrives on "charmingly varied china"; "helpful"-but-"cheeky" service is a "hallmark" and a "long wait" de rigueur, but satisfied sippers say it's the "perfect place for afternoon tea."

Telepan American
26 | 22 | 25 | $73

W 60s | 72 W. 69th St. (bet. Columbus Ave. & CPW) | 212-580-4300 |
www.telepan-ny.com

Greenmarket cuisine "wizard" Bill Telepan oversees this "high-level" UWS New American, where "perfectionist" plates are served in a "soothing" townhouse setting by "first-rate" staffers; granted, it's "costly" (the $28 prix fixe lunch aside), but the "serious foodies" and "Lincoln Centric" types who love it "don't mind paying the price."

Telly's Taverna ● *Greek/Seafood*   21 | 15 | 18 | $38

Astoria | 28-13 23rd Ave. (bet. 28th & 29th Sts.) | Queens | 718-728-9056 | www.tellystaverna.com

"Simple perfection" via the "freshest" grilled fish is yours at this "old-time" Astoria Greek taverna, where the nothing-fancy digs are "large", "relaxing" and overseen by a "friendly, never rushed" staff; factor in "fair prices", and no wonder it's a local "favorite."

Tenzan *Japanese*   21 | 16 | 18 | $35

E 50s | 988 Second Ave. (bet. 52nd & 53rd Sts.) | 212-980-5900 | www.tenzanrestaurants.com ●
E 80s | 1714 Second Ave. (89th St.) | 212-369-3600 | www.tenzansushi89.com
W 70s | 285 Columbus Ave. (73rd St.) | 212-580-7300 | www.tenzanrestaurants.com
Bensonhurst | 7117 18th Ave. (71st St.) | Brooklyn | 718-621-3238

"Local" loyalists make these separately owned Japanese spots a natural for "good-sized portions" of "solid sushi"; since the decor's "nothing to write home about", most focus on the "bang-for-your-buck" price points.

Teodora *Italian*   20 | 15 | 20 | $52

E 50s | 141 E. 57th St. (bet. Lexington & 3rd Aves.) | 212-826-7101 | www.teodorarestaurant.com

It "almost gets lost" in the Midtown "hustle", but this "charming" Northern Italian can be counted on for "authentic", pasta-centric cooking; it may be "a bit costly", but "pleasant" service and "no-pretenses" digs make it a safe bet for a "quiet evening out."

Teresa's *Diner*   20 | 13 | 17 | $23

Brooklyn Heights | 80 Montague St. (Hicks St.) | Brooklyn | 718-797-3996

Sited steps from the Promenade, this 25-year-old Brooklyn Heights "institution" keeps the neighbors coming with "hearty" diner staples (plus some Polish dishes) plated in "massive portions"; all appreciate the "incredible prices", though "standoffish" service and basic "coffee-shop" decor are also part of the "bargain."

Terroir ● *Italian*   20 | 20 | 21 | $41

E Village | 413 E. 12th St. (bet. Ave. A & 1st Ave.) | 646-602-1300
Murray Hill | 439 Third Ave. (bet. 30th & 31st Sts.) | 212-481-1920
TriBeCa | 24 Harrison St. (bet. Greenwich & Hudson Sts.) | 212-625-9463
NEW Park Slope | 284 Fifth Ave. (1st St.) | Brooklyn | 718-832-9463
www.wineisterroir.com

These "unstuffy" enotecas are touted for "enormous" wine lists paired with "tasty" Italian small plates; "well-versed", "down-to-earth" service is another plus, but "don't forget the credit card" as all those nibbles can quickly "add up."

Tertulia *Spanish*   24 | 19 | 20 | $61

W Village | 359 Sixth Ave. (Washington Pl.) | 646-559-9909 | www.tertulianyc.com

"Northern Spain" comes to "Nuevo York" via this Villager from Seamus Mullen (ex Boqueria), where "fabulous" tapas and Basque cider on tap are dispensed in "rustic", stone-walled digs; it's a "*muy caliente*" scene with "high prices" and a no-rez policy that can make for "long waits", but fans insist it's "worth it."

Testaccio *Italian*
▽ 22 | 21 | 20 | $46

LIC | 47-30 Vernon Blvd. (47th Rd.) | Queens | 718-937-2900 |
www.testacciony.com

"Well worth the trip to LIC", this brick-walled, multilevel Italian serves "excellent" Roman cuisine in a "snazzy" former warehouse space manned by an "attentive" staff; if tabs are "high for the neighborhood", that's the price of "sophistication."

Tevere *Italian/Kosher*
▽ 24 | 21 | 22 | $64

E 80s | 155 E. 84th St. (bet. Lexington & 3rd Aves.) | 212-744-0210 |
www.teverenyc.com

Providing "consistent quality" since 1982, this UES Italian delights its orthodox following with "delicious" kosher Roman fare served by a staff that knows how to "take care of you"; while not cheap, there's no denying "it fits a need."

Thai Market *Thai*
23 | 17 | 17 | $25

W 100s | 960 Amsterdam Ave. (bet. 107th & 108th Sts.) | 212-280-4575 |
www.thaimarketny.net

"Authentic" dishes that go way "beyond pad Thai" make this "no-frills" UWS Siamese "fill up quick"; the "funky" decor evokes "street carts in Bangkok", as do the "very reasonable" prices – no surprise, it's a hit with the "college crowd."

Thalassa ◐ ☒ *Greek/Seafood*
24 | 25 | 23 | $68

TriBeCa | 179 Franklin St. (bet. Greenwich & Hudson Sts.) | 212-941-7661 |
www.thalassanyc.com

"Elegant" Greek seafood is the specialty of this "high-end" TriBeCa "special-occasion" option; of course, such "fine" fish comes at a price ("you help pay its airfare"), but "first-rate" service and an "expansive", "Santorini"-esque setting soften any sticker shock.

Thalia ◐ *American*
20 | 20 | 20 | $48

W 50s | 828 Eighth Ave. (50th St.) | 212-399-4444 |
www.restaurantthalia.com

"Perfect" before or after the theater, this "reliable" Hell's Kitchen vet plies "solid", "well-priced" Americana ferried by "pleasant" staffers who ensure that you'll "make your show"; its "lively crowd" can kick up some "noise", but that's all part of the "open, friendly atmosphere."

Thistle Hill Tavern ◐ *American*
20 | 19 | 19 | $38

Park Slope | 441 Seventh Ave. (15th St.) | Brooklyn | 347-599-1262 |
www.thistlehillbrooklyn.com

Already a "neighborhood stalwart", this midpriced Park Slope American rolls out "reliable" gastropub fare in "bustling" corner tavern digs; alright, it can feel a tad "tight" at prime times, but the "accommodating" staff and kickin' specialty drinks keep things "comfortable."

Tía Pol *Spanish*
25 | 16 | 20 | $46

Chelsea | 205 10th Ave. (bet. 22nd & 23rd Sts.) | 212-675-8805 |
www.tiapol.com

Now in its 10th year, this West Chelsea Spaniard is "still amazing" (and still "perpetually packed") thanks to "delectable" tapas and "well-chosen" Iberian wines served in a beyond-"cozy" space; most take the "cramped" quarters in stride – it stays "crowded for good reason."

Tiella *Italian*   25 | 15 | 23 | $58

E 60s | 1109 First Ave. (bet. 60th & 61st Sts.) | 212-588-0100 | www.tiellanyc.com

"Marvelous" little namesake pizzas, "housemade pastas" and other "delectable" Neapolitan dishes lure Eastsiders to this "informal", pricey Italian; it's "about the size and shape of a Pullman dining car", but "caring" service makes it feel more "charming" than "crowded."

Tiffin Wallah *Indian/Vegetarian/Kosher*   22 | 14 | 18 | $23

Murray Hill | 127 E. 28th St. (bet. Lexington Ave. & Park Ave. S.) | 212-685-7301 | www.tiffindelivery.us

"Tasty", "deliciously cheap" South Indian fare keeps the trade brisk at this "unassuming" Curry Hill veggie-kosher standby; the $7 lunch buffet is such a "deal" that the diminutive digs are usually "mobbed" at midday, but "fast" service keeps things moving.

Tiny's ● *American*   21 | 21 | 19 | $41

TriBeCa | 135 W. Broadway (bet. Duane & Thomas Sts.) | 212-374-1135 | www.tinysnyc.com

"As the name would imply", this "cool" TriBeCan from nightlife czar Matt Abramcyk and former NY Ranger Sean Avery is indeed "tiny", though the "rustic, bohemian" interior tilts more "cute" than "cramped"; the American menu is equally compact, but showcases an "awesome" lunchtime burger.

Tipsy Parson ● *Southern*   21 | 20 | 20 | $44

Chelsea | 156 Ninth Ave. (bet. 19th & 20th Sts.) | 212-620-4545 | www.tipsyparson.com

"Too cute for words", this midpriced Chelsea "standout" near the High Line dishes up "decadent" Southern "country cooking" backed by "lovely cocktails"; the "homey" interior and "easy-with-a-smile" service keep the crowd "happy."

Tocqueville *American/French*   27 | 25 | 26 | $87

Union Sq | 1 E. 15th St. (bet. 5th Ave. & Union Sq. W.) | 212-647-1515 | www.tocquevillerestaurant.com

A "quiet refuge" for "grown-ups", this "refined" Union Square French-New American offers a "most sophisticated" dining experience via "artful" chef Marco Moreira's "exquisite" cuisine served by staffers "who take pride in their work"; of course, the "high standard" commands "upscale" pricing, but there's a $29 prix fixe lunch for bargain-hunters.

Tolani ● *Eclectic*   20 | 18 | 20 | $47

W 70s | 410 Amsterdam Ave. (bet. 79th & 80th Sts.) | 212-873-6252 | www.tolaninyc.com

Global comfort food served tapas-style is paired with "diverse" wines at this "charming" UWS "hideaway"; along with the "well-prepared" Eclectic bites, the "dark, relaxing" vibe and "friendly" service have earned it "neighborhood favorite" status.

Toloache *Mexican*   24 | 18 | 21 | $48

E 80s | 166 E. 82nd St. (bet. Lexington & 3rd Aves.) | 212-861-4505

(continued)

(continued)

Toloache
W 50s | 251 W. 50th St. (bet. B'way & 8th Ave.) | 212-581-1818
Toloache Taqueria 🅱 *Mexican*
Financial District | 83 Maiden Ln. (bet. Gold & William Sts.) |
212-809-9800
www.toloachenyc.com
"Distinctive" takes on Mexican standards, "memorable" margaritas
and "enthusiastic" service are the draws at this "appealing" (if "noisy")
Theater District "find" and its "slightly fancier" UES sibling; downtown, the Taqueria is "hard to beat" for a fast FiDi lunch.

Tommaso *Italian*
23 | 18 | 21 | $48
Dyker Heights | 1464 86th St. (bet. Bay 8th St. & 15th Ave.) | Brooklyn |
718-236-9883 | www.tommasoinbrooklyn.com
Although touted for its "old-world" red-sauce favorites the "way you
remember them", the real draw at this 45-year-old Dyker Heights Italian
is the "opera floor show" on certain nights; beyond the "festive" vibe
and "loving" service, it also boasts an "amazing" wine cellar.

Tomoe Sushi *Japanese*
26 | 10 | 16 | $48
G Village | 172 Thompson St. (bet. Bleecker & Houston Sts.) | 212-777-9346
"Go early" or be prepared for "lines out the door" at this "tiny" Village
Japanese where the lure is "entertainingly big" slabs of "wonderful" sushi at "value" tabs; "tight" digs, "nonexistent" decor and
so-so service are the trade-offs, but no one cares given the "quality-
for-the-dollar" ratio.

Tom's ⇕ *Diner*
21 | 18 | 23 | $18
Prospect Heights | 782 Washington Ave. (Sterling Pl.) | Brooklyn |
718-636-9738 | www.tomsbrooklyn.com
NEW Tom's Coney Island *Diner*
Coney Island | 1229 Boardwalk W. (Stillwell Ave.) | Brooklyn |
718-942-4200
On weekend mornings the lines wrap "around the block" at this circa-
1936 Prospect Heights diner beloved as much for its "second-to-none"
service and "old-school kitschy vibe" as for its "to-die-for" pancakes
and "even better prices"; it slings breakfast and lunch only, though the
new Coney Island spin-off stays open later in the summer.

Tony's Di Napoli *Italian*
22 | 18 | 21 | $41
E 60s | 1081 Third Ave. (bet. 63rd & 64th Sts.) | 212-888-6333
W 40s | Casablanca Hotel | 147 W. 43rd St. (bet. 6th & 7th Aves.) |
212-221-0100 ◗
www.tonysnyc.com
Made for "large groups", this "welcoming" Italian duo takes a page
from the "Carmine's" playbook, purveying "heaping" portions of "reliable" red-sauce standards at "affordable" prices; "tons of people"
turn up to kick up a "din" and leave "completely satiated."

Topaz *Thai*
22 | 14 | 17 | $30
W 50s | 127 W. 56th St. (bet. 6th & 7th Aves.) | 212-957-8020 |
www.topazthai.com
Near Carnegie Hall and City Center, this "simple" Thai slings "flavorful" classics priced way "low" for the zip code; "drab" digs with "no el-

| | FOOD | DECOR | SERVICE | COST |

"bow room" and variable service offset the "bargain" tabs, but still it's "always packed."

Torrisi Italian Specialties *Italian* 27 | 19 | 24 | $80

NoLita | 250 Mulberry St. (bet. Prince & Spring Sts.) | 212-965-0955 | www.torrisinyc.com

"Exceptional dining" awaits at this "real-deal" NoLita nook, where "original" takes on Italian-American eats are "done to perfection" and presented by an "attentive" staff at a $60 prix fixe–only price; the "cozy" setting may verge on "cramped", but it's "worth the work to get a reservation" – the overall experience is "amazing."

Tortilleria Nixtamal *Mexican* 26 | 13 | 20 | $16

Corona | 104-05 47th Ave. (bet. 104th & 108th Sts.) | Queens | 718-699-2434 | www.tortillerianixtamal.com

It's "all about the masa" ground in-house at this Corona Mexican renowned for the freshest tortillas "this side of the Rio Grande", as well as "authentic" tacos and "melt-in-your-mouth" tamales; sure, it's a "hole-in-the-wall", but compensations include "friendly" service and budget pricing.

Tosca Café ● *Italian* 23 | 23 | 23 | $36

Throgs Neck | 4038 E. Tremont Ave. (bet. Miles & Sampson Aves.) | Bronx | 718-239-3300 | www.toscanyc.com

"Eat and be seen" at this "nightclub"-like Throgs Neck spot, whose array of "quite good", "straightforward" Italian eats also features sushi ("quite the combination"); the "large", "loungey" setup includes a "cool roofdeck" and "happening" bar, and hosts what may be the Bronx's "best brunch."

Totonno's Pizzeria Napolitano Ⓜ☞ *Pizza* 25 | 11 | 16 | $21

Coney Island | 1524 Neptune Ave. (bet. 15th & 16th Sts.) | Brooklyn | 718-372-8606

Surviving a recent flood and fire, this seemingly indestructible 90-year-old pizzeria remains a Coney Island "legend" thanks to "incredible" coal-oven pies dispatched in a no-frills, "family-run" milieu; despite no slices, no plastic and "slow" service, fans say it's "classic Brooklyn" at its best.

Totto Ramen ●☞ *Japanese/Noodle Shop* 26 | 11 | 17 | $19

W 50s | 366 W. 52nd St. (bet. 8th & 9th Aves.) | 212-582-0052 | www.tottoramen.com

"Insanely delicious" ramen soups sold "cheap" inspire "ridiculous waits" at this teeny, "takes-you-back-to-Tokyo" Hell's Kitchen nook, again voted NYC's No. 1 noodle shop; skeptics shrug it's over-"hyped", but "there's a reason people stand on line for hours" here – and it's not the "bare-bones" decor.

Tournesol *French* 24 | 16 | 20 | $42

LIC | 50-12 Vernon Blvd. (bet. 50th & 51st Aves.) | Queens | 718-472-4355 | www.tournesolnyc.com

Just like finding "Paris in Queens", this "convivial" LIC bistro offers "*magnifique*" French fare at "easy-on-the-pocketbook" rates; yes, the "cramped space" means "you really have to like your neighbor", but the "warm welcome" from a "most pleasant" staff compensates.

	FOOD	DECOR	SERVICE	COST

Tra Di Noi Ⓜ *Italian* — ▽ 24 | 14 | 24 | $42

Fordham | 622 E. 187th St. (bet. Belmont & Hughes Sts.) | Bronx |
718-295-1784
"Like a meal at grandma's house", this family-run "jewel" off Arthur
Avenue might have "not much decor" but is warmed by "truly accommodating" service; still, it's the "fresh", "cooked-just-right" Italian
classics that make it "worth the trip."

Traif ❶Ⓜ *Eclectic* — 26 | 18 | 22 | $45

Williamsburg | 229 S. Fourth St. (bet. Havemeyer & Roebling Sts.) |
Brooklyn | 347-844-9578 | www.traifny.com
The name alone (which roughly translates as 'non-kosher') is a "surefire way to attract buzz" in the Hasidic Williamsburg vicinity, and this
"pork-lover's paradise" delivers an array of "dynamite" Eclectic small
plates at a "reasonable" price; "helpful" service and snug quarters
with an all-seasons patio round out this "great find."

Trattoria Dell'Arte ❶ *Italian* — 22 | 20 | 21 | $59

W 50s | 900 Seventh Ave. (bet. 56th & 57th Sts.) | 212-245-9800 |
www.trattoriadellarte.com
A "perennial favorite" opposite Carnegie Hall, this "bustling" Tuscan
is ever a "safe bet" with its "terrific" pizza, "requisite" antipasti bar
and "amusing" body-parts decor; it's a "convenient" work lunch or
"pre-theater" choice, so "bring your appetite – and your credit card."

Trattoria L'incontro Ⓜ *Italian* — 26 | 21 | 25 | $59

Astoria | 21-76 31st St. (Ditmars Blvd.) | Queens | 718-721-3532 |
www.trattorialincontro.com
Upholding its "well-deserved reputation", this "destination" Astoria
Italian is renowned for chef-owner Rocco Sacramone's "outstanding"
cooking paired with a "great wine list"; the "spot-on service" is a "show
in itself" as the waiters rattle off the "voluminous" list of specials.

Trattoria Pesce & Pasta *Italian/Seafood* — 20 | 15 | 20 | $37

E 80s | 1562 Third Ave. (bet. 87th & 88th Sts.) | 212-987-4696 |
www.trattoriapescepasta.com
W 90s | 625 Columbus Ave. (bet. 90th & 91st Sts.) | 212-579-7970
W Village | 262 Bleecker St. (Leroy St.) | 212-645-2993 |
www.pesce-pasta.com ❶
"Simple, well-done" seafood and pastas at a "fair price" is the "satisfying" formula at these "cozy, old-fashioned" neighborhood Italians;
they're "not night-out-on-the-town" picks, but they fill the bill when
you "don't want a fuss."

Trattoria Romana *Italian* — 25 | 17 | 23 | $48

Dongan Hills | 1476 Hylan Blvd. (Benton Ave.) | Staten Island | 718-980-3113
"First-rate" Southern cuisine makes this 20-year-old Dongan Hills
"mainstay" a "worthwhile" Staten Island destination; "attentive" service, "reasonable" prices and a chef-owner who "treats his guests like
family" help explain the "throngs" waiting in line.

Trattoria Toscana *Italian* — 25 | 16 | 23 | $47

W Village | 64 Carmine St. (bet. Bedford St. & 7th Ave. S.) | 212-675-8736
"Flavorful", "well-priced" Tuscan cooking has made this "totally unpretentious" West Village Italian a "long-standing" neighborhood hit;

maybe it's "nothing unusual", but they "don't cram diners cheek-by-jowl", and a "warm, friendly" vibe prevails.

	FOOD	DECOR	SERVICE	COST

Trattoria Trecolori *Italian*   21 | 18 | 21 | $44

W 40s | 254 W. 47th St. (bet. B'way & 8th Ave.) | 212-997-4540 | www.trattoriatrecolori.com

The staffers "make everyone feel at home" at this "inviting" Theater District Italian, a "red-sauce" joint that earns ovations for its "value" pricing and "lively" atmosphere; it "gets packed" pre- and post-curtain, so rezzies are "a must."

Tre Dici ⧆ *Italian*   23 | 19 | 22 | $53

Chelsea | 128 W. 26th St. (bet. 6th & 7th Aves.) | 212-243-8183

Tre Dici Steak ⧆ *Steak*

Chelsea | 128 W. 26th St., 2nd fl. (bet. 6th & 7th Aves.) | 212-243-2085
www.tredicinyc.com

"Delicious" Italian fare prepared with "hip flair" is the draw at this "genial" Chelsea standby with a "modern" look; upstairs, a steakhouse with a "mysterious entryway" serves "tasty" beef in "seductive" crimson red digs that look one part "speakeasy", one part "bordello."

Tre Otto *Italian*   21 | 17 | 18 | $41

E 90s | 1408 Madison Ave. (bet. 97th & 98th Sts.) | 212-860-8880 | www.treotto.com

"Solid" Italiana at "fair prices" makes this "small", "no-pretenses" Upper Eastsider an "acceptable" asset in an area with "few options" (talk about an "escape from Mount Sinai!"); when the weather's warm, the "pretty patio" is the place to be.

NEW Tre Stelle ◐ *Italian*   - | - | - | M

Flatiron | Wyndham Garden Hotel | 37 W. 24th St. (bet. 5th & 6th Aves.) | 212-255-4655 | www.trestelleny.com

This Flatiron Italian serves a midpriced menu of antipasti, salads and pastas (made slightly more healthful by the omission of cream from their sauces) washed down with a Boot-heavy list of wines; the slick, modern setting features a slotted wooden garage door that separates the bar from the dining room.

Trestle on Tenth *American*   22 | 18 | 21 | $48

Chelsea | 242 10th Ave. (24th St.) | 212-645-5659 | www.trestleontenth.com

"Rustic" New American cuisine with Swiss inflections and an "intelligent" wine list appeal to gallery-goers and High Line hoofers alike at this "exposed-brick" Chelsea "oasis"; a "lovely" garden out back and "accommodating" staffers take the edge off of the slightly "pricey" tabs.

Tribeca Grill *American*   22 | 21 | 22 | $60

TriBeCa | 375 Greenwich St. (Franklin St.) | 212-941-3900 | www.myriadrestaurantgroup.com

"Still a winner", Drew Nieporent and Robert De Niro's long-standing TriBeCa New American maintains its "high standards" with "delicious" vittles and a "great wine list"; the "focused" service and "airy", "upbeat" milieu keep it a "popular" option, and the $25 prix fixe lunch offers a break from the otherwise "expensive" tabs.

	FOOD	DECOR	SERVICE	COST

Triomphe *French*
23 | 21 | 23 | $69

W 40s | Iroquois Hotel | 49 W. 44th St. (bet. 5th & 6th Aves.) | 212-453-4233 | www.triompheny.com

A "real find" in the Theater District, this all-day French "jewel box" in the Iroquois Hotel turns out "excellent, innovative" cuisine in a "tiny" setting; the "quiet atmosphere" and "superb service" help take the sting out of the "expensive" tariffs.

Tulsi *Indian*
24 | 22 | 23 | $57

E 40s | 211 E. 46th St. (bet. 2nd & 3rd Aves.) | 212-888-0820 | www.tulsinyc.com

"Inspired" chef Hemant Mathur (ex Dévi) is "fully engaged" at this "tranquil" dining room near Grand Central dispensing "innovative" Indian fare with "fusion flair"; "attentive" service and a "beautiful" room with "sheer curtains separating tables" help justify the "pricey" tabs.

Turkish Cuisine ❶ *Turkish*
20 | 14 | 19 | $36

W 40s | 631 Ninth Ave. (bet. 44th & 45th Sts.) | 212-397-9650 | www.turkishcuisinenyc.com

"Consistent", "tasty" Turkish fare at moderate rates make this long-time Theater District storefront a worthwhile "pre-curtain choice"; fans appreciate the "pleasant" staff, and overlook the "unassuming" decor by heading for the back garden.

Turkish Grill *Turkish*
∇ 22 | 16 | 20 | $30

Sunnyside | 42-03 Queens Blvd. (bet. 42nd & 43rd Sts.) | Queens | 718-392-3838 | www.turkishgrillnyc.com

"Excellent", "delicately spiced" kebabs, salads and meze are menu highlights at this "authentic" Sunnyside Turkish "find"; "polite" service and eminently "reasonable" rates compensate for "lackluster" surrounds.

Turkish Kitchen *Turkish*
22 | 18 | 20 | $42

Murray Hill | 386 Third Ave. (bet. 27th & 28th Sts.) | 212-679-6633 | www.turkishkitchen.com

"As real as it gets", this "tried-and-true" Murray Hill Turk earns "undying loyalty" with "high-quality" traditional eats at "modest" prices; "courteous" staffers oversee the "comfortable" setting, and the "lavish" Sunday brunch "defeats all efforts at self-control."

Turkuaz *Turkish*
20 | 20 | 20 | $38

W 100s | 2637 Broadway (100th St.) | 212-665-9541 | www.turkuazrestaurant.com

"Tasty", well-priced Turkish food served by "costumed" waiters amid decor right out of a "sultan's private tent" draw "armchair travelers" and "belly-dancing" buffs to this "amenable" Upper Westsider; the "plentiful" Sunday buffet is an additional lure.

Tuscany Grill *Italian*
25 | 19 | 22 | $47

Bay Ridge | 8620 Third Ave. (bet. 86th & 87th Sts.) | Brooklyn | 718-921-5633 | www.tuscanygrillbrooklyn.com

Beloved in Bay Ridge for "excellent" contemporary Tuscan food at mid-range prices, this "lovely" neighborhood Italian caters to a "mature, upscale" crowd; valet parking and "welcoming" service are further reasons why it's "been around for years."

	FOOD	DECOR	SERVICE	COST

12th Street Bar & Grill ● *American* | 22 | 20 | 21 | $39 |

Park Slope | 1123 Eighth Ave. (12th St.) | Brooklyn | 718-965-9526 |
www.12thstreetbarandgrill.com

A locals' "go-to", this South Sloper is an "old reliable" for "well-prepared"
yet "affordable" New Americana delivered by an "accommodating"
crew; the "pretty" main dining room is fit for a casual "date", while the
round-the-corner pub offers the same menu with "sports on the telly."

12 Chairs *American/Mideastern* | 22 | 18 | 20 | $32 |

SoHo | 56 MacDougal St. (bet. Houston & Prince Sts.) | 212-254-8640 |
www.12chairscafe.com

The kind of "nice cheapie" that "high-rent" SoHo "could use more of",
this "chill" cafe dishes up "value"-priced, "lovingly made" American-
Mideastern noshes in "cozy, familial" digs (though it does have "more
than 12 chairs"); with so many "basic pleasures", most "can't wait
to go back."

21 Club ⊠ *American* | 23 | 25 | 25 | $75 |

W 50s | 21 W. 52nd St. (bet. 5th & 6th Aves.) | 212-582-7200 |
www.21club.com

"Dine surrounded by history" at this circa-1929 Midtown former speakeasy, a "NY icon" where tuxedoed "career waiters" make you "feel like
one of the *Mad Men*" within "delightful" "throwback" digs including a
"legendary" barroom hung with "model planes and miscellaneous
knickknacks" and private rooms upstairs that are "outstanding" for
parties; just "dress up" (jackets required) and expect a "hefty bill" for
American "country club cuisine (but better)" – though there's always
the "best-in-town" deal of a $42 pre-theater prix fixe.

26 Seats Ⓜ *French* | 22 | 18 | 21 | $41 |

E Village | 168 Ave. B (bet. 10th & 11th Sts.) | 212-677-4787 |
www.26seatsbistro.com

A "date night" to remember kicks into gear at this "romantic"
Alphabet City "fave", a "cozy" French bistro featuring "delightful"
classics, "lovely" service and endearingly "mismatched decor"; yes,
it's as "minuscule" as the name implies, but skimpy square footage
aside, "great value" abounds.

Two Boots *Pizza* | 19 | 12 | 15 | $16 |

E 40s | Grand Central Station | 89 E. 42nd St., Lower Dining Concourse
(Vanderbilt Ave.) | 212-557-7992 | www.twoboots.com
E 80s | 1617 Second Ave. (84th St.) | 212-734-0317 | www.twoboots.com ●
E Village | 42 Ave. A (bet. 3rd & 4th Sts.) | 212-254-1919 |
www.twoboots.com ●
NoHo | 74 Bleecker St. (B'way) | 212-777-1033 | www.twoboots.com ●
W 40s | 625 Ninth Ave. (bet. 44th & 45th Sts.) | 212-956-2668 |
www.twoboots.com ●
W 90s | 2547 Broadway (bet. 95th & 96th Sts.) | 212-280-2668 |
www.twoboots.com ●
W Village | 201 W. 11th St. (7th Ave. S.) | 212-633-9096 |
www.twoboots.com ●
Park Slope | 514 Second St. (bet. 7th & 8th Aves.) | Brooklyn |
718-499-3253 | www.twobootsbrooklyn.com ●

"Nontraditional" is the word on these "Cajun-inspired" pizzerias where a
"crunchy" cornmeal crust, "yummy" toppings and "provocative" names

add some "N'Awlins" flavor; the settings and service are "casual" but "great for kids" – just ask the "mommy brigade" at the separately owned, full-menu Park Slope outlet.

2 West ● *American* | 22 | 21 | 22 | $53 |

Financial District | Ritz-Carlton Battery Park | 2 West St. (Battery Pl.) | 917-790-2525 | www.ritzcarlton.com

This Battery Park New American may be "low-key" for a Ritz-Carlton resident, but business types value its "peaceful" vibe, not to mention its "delicious" food and "excellent" service; a "beautiful" Hudson River panorama is part of the package, as is an "expensive" tab.

Txikito *Spanish* | 24 | 17 | 21 | $52 |

Chelsea | 240 Ninth Ave. (bet. 24th & 25th Sts.) | 212-242-4730 | www.txikitonyc.com

Each dish is a "new adventure" at this "crowded" Basque "gem" in Chelsea, where the pintxos pack "big flavor" and the wines may transport you to "San Sebastián"; the vibe is "cool" and the service "friendly", and while prices "vary depending on your order", most agree the "cost-benefit ratio is high."

NEW Umami Burger *Burgers* | - | - | - | I |

G Village | 432 Sixth Ave. (bet. 9th & 10th Sts.) | 212-677-8626 | www.umamiburger.com

The East Coast's first outpost of the LA-based sensation, this new Villager slings patties topped with umami-rich items like Parmesan crisps, roasted tomatoes and caramelized onions; upscale price tags – the burgers range from $10 to $15 – are offset by waiter service, a full bar and industrial-chic digs.

Umberto's Clam House ● *Italian/Seafood* | 21 | 15 | 18 | $42 |

Little Italy | 132 Mulberry St. (bet. Grand & Hester Sts.) | 212-431-7545 | www.umbertosclamhouse.com

Linguine-lovers "dig the clams" and pastas "like mamma used to make" at this "casual" Italian seafooder on Mulberry Street; purists "miss the original location" and knock its "tourist" tendencies, but all appreciate the "fair" pricing.

NEW Uncle Boons Ⓜ *Thai* | - | - | - | M |

NoLita | 7 Spring St. (bet. Bowery & Elizabeth Sts.) | 646-370-6650 | www.uncleboons.com

Forward-thinking Thai food via Per Se vets has folks flocking to this NoLita entry fielding a menu that includes both casual and elaborate dishes, chased with beer slushies; Bangkok flea-market finds on the walls and Thai takes on American pop on the stereo lend a festive feel, while a back room with a mirrored ceiling has private party written all over it.

Uncle Jack's Steakhouse *Steak* | 23 | 21 | 22 | $70 |

Garment District | 440 Ninth Ave. (bet. 34th & 35th Sts.) | 212-244-0005

W 50s | 44 W. 56th St. (bet. 5th & 6th Aves.) | 212-245-1550

Bayside | 39-40 Bell Blvd. (40th Ave.) | Queens | 718-229-1100
www.unclejacks.com

They "don't skimp on the portions" at this "old-fashioned" steakhouse trio, where the beef is "delicious" and the service "engag-

| | FOOD | DECOR | SERVICE | COST |

ing"; expect the genre's "usual clubby atmosphere", and if "nothing sets it apart" from the competition, it's their equal when it comes to "expensive" pricing.

Uncle Nick's *Greek*   21 | 12 | 18 | $35

Chelsea | 382 Eighth Ave. (29th St.) | 212-609-0500
W 50s | 747 Ninth Ave. (bet. 50th & 51st Sts.) | 212-245-7992
www.unclenicksgreekrestaurant.com

Fans say there's "no need to venture to Astoria" given the "tasty", "stick-to-your-ribs" chow and "affordable" tabs at this "casual" Greek duo famed for its "fun" flaming cheese signature dish; sure, the settings skew "shabby" and service can be "rushed", but they stay "busy" nonetheless.

Union Square Cafe *American*   27 | 23 | 26 | $72

Union Sq | 21 E. 16th St. (bet. 5th Ave. & Union Sq. W.) | 212-243-4020 | www.unionsquarecafe.com

"Still going strong", this Union Square "tent pole in Danny Meyer's restaurant empire" bases its "well-earned reputation" on "stellar", Greenmarket-fresh New American food served by "engaging" staffers in a "refined" setting made for "intimate conversation"; it's a "special-occasion" place with appropriately "costly" tabs, and though scoring a reservation can be tough, insiders advise "dining at the bar."

Untitled Ⓜ *American*   21 | 18 | 19 | $38

E 70s | Whitney Museum | 945 Madison Ave., downstairs (75th St.) | 212-570-3670 | www.untitledatthewhitney.com

A "good restaurant in an art museum" is not an oxymoron thanks to Danny Meyer's "upscale" take on the classic coffee shop inside the Whitney; "attractive" and starkly "modern", it vends "comforting" sandwiches, "terrific" java and other light breakfast and lunch items from its "small menu."

Ushiwakamaru Ⓩ *Japanese*   28 | 18 | 23 | $89

G Village | 136 W. Houston St. (bet. MacDougal & Sullivan Sts.) | 212-228-4181

Even if they "can't pronounce the name", "serious" sushiphiles tout this Village Japanese sleeper for "exquisite", "high-end" raw fish and particularly "sublime omakase"; some find the "tiny", no-frills interior "disappointing for the price", but hey, it costs "less than a flight to Tokyo."

Uskudar *Turkish*   21 | 12 | 19 | $38

E 70s | 1405 Second Ave. (bet. 73rd & 74th Sts.) | 212-988-4046 | www.uskudarnyc.com

Although "cramped" and "narrow", this "tiny" Upper East Side Turk does a brisk business thanks to "surprisingly tasty" cooking and "friendly" staffers; "easy-on-the-wallet" prices seal the deal.

Utsav *Indian*   21 | 19 | 19 | $42

W 40s | 1185 Sixth Ave., 2nd fl. (enter on 46th St. bet. 6th & 7th Aves.) | 212-575-2525 | www.utsavny.com

Although somewhat "difficult to find", this Theater District Indian de-livers "above-average" classics in "civilized" modern digs manned by a "gracious" crew; if prices seem a "little high", the $32 pre-theater prix fixe pleases bargain-hunters.

	FOOD	DECOR	SERVICE	COST

Uva ● *Italian* | 22 | 21 | 20 | $43 |

E 70s | 1486 Second Ave. (bet. 77th & 78th Sts.) | 212-472-4552 |
www.uvanyc.com

"Beautiful food" and "beautiful people" collide at this "noisy" UES
"date destination" trading in "delicious" Italian small plates and "wonderful wines"; an "enchanting" back garden, "decent" price tags and
"attentive" service have earned it "neighborhood-favorite" status.

Valbella ☒ *Italian* | 24 | 24 | 23 | $84 |

E 50s | 11 E. 53rd St. (bet. 5th & Madison Aves.) | 212-888-8955 |
www.valbellamidtown.com

Meatpacking | 421 W. 13th St. (bet. 9th Ave. & Washington St.) |
212-645-7777 | www.valbellanyc.com

Thanks to "excellent" Northern Italian cuisine, "terrific" wines, "lavish" settings and "solicitous" service, this "classy" twosome draws a
"mix of ages" in the mood to "celebrate"; just "bring an appetite" and
your "expense account" – and don't forget their "perfect" private
rooms for special events.

The Vanderbilt ● *American* | 21 | 20 | 20 | $42 |

Prospect Heights | 570 Vanderbilt Ave. (Bergen St.) | Brooklyn |
718-623-0570 | www.thevanderbiltnyc.com

Already a "standby" on Prospect Heights' burgeoning Vanderbilt
Avenue strip, Saul Bolton's "stylish", midpriced American gastropub trades in "delightful", "strictly in-season" small plates
washed down with "delicious cocktails"; locals rate it "friendly",
"no-hassles" experience.

Vanessa's Dumpling House *Chinese* | 21 | 8 | 12 | $10 |

E Village | 220 E. 14th St. (bet. 2nd & 3rd Aves.) | 212-529-1329 |
LES | 118 Eldridge St. (bet. Broome & Grand Sts.) | 212-625-8008 |
Williamsburg | 310 Bedford Ave. (bet. S. 1st & 2nd Sts.) | Brooklyn |
718-218-8806

These "always busy" dumpling dispensers offer a "yummy" namesake
specialty that's fried or steamed while you wait; the barely "utilitarian" setups feature minimal seating and service is "insouciant" at
best, but they're hard to beat for a "fast, filling", "dirt-cheap" nosh.

Vareli ● *American* | 23 | 20 | 19 | $41 |

W 100s | 2869 Broadway (bet. 111th & 112th Sts.) | 212-678-8585 |
www.varelinyc.com

Bringing much-needed "sophistication" to the "sea of college bars
and restaurants" around Columbia, this "adult" New American offers an "inventive" menu served in "wine barrel"–themed digs;
checks run a bit high for the area, so bargain-hunters "ask for
the bar menu."

Vatan Ⓜ *Indian/Vegetarian* | 23 | 24 | 23 | $41 |

Murray Hill | 409 Third Ave. (29th St.) | 212-689-5666 |
www.vatanny.com

An "incredible variety of flavors" from "delicate" to "spicy" emerges
from the kitchen of this Murray Hill vegetarian Indian where the "authentic Gujarati" specialties come in an all-you-can-eat Thali format
for $30; "accommodating" service and a transporting "village" setting
complete the "totally unique experience."

	FOOD	DECOR	SERVICE	COST

Veatery ◐ *Vietnamese* ▽ 22 | 14 | 20 | $27

E 80s | 1700 Second Ave. (88th St.) | 212-722-0558 | www.veatery.com
"Excellent renditions" of Vietnamese standards make this "under-the-radar" Upper Eastsider a "delightful" find for classic satays and noodle dishes; "satisfying" service and "good-value" prices seal the deal – locals are "so glad to have it" in the neighborhood.

Veritas *American* 25 | 22 | 25 | $93

Flatiron | 43 E. 20th St. (bet. B'way & Park Ave. S.) | 212-353-3700 | www.veritas-nyc.com
"Masterful" New American cuisine, a "biblical" wine list and "exceptional" service are the hallmarks of this Flatiron "gem", now in its second incarnation under chef Sam Hazen; "true oenophiles" praise the "romantic", "contemporary" setting, the "expense account"–worthy price tags not so much.

Veselka ◐ *Ukrainian* 20 | 12 | 16 | $23

E Village | 144 Second Ave. (9th St.) | 212-228-9682 | www.veselka.com
The "belly-filling" Ukrainian comfort food recalls "great-grandmother's kitchen" at this 24/7 East Villager known for its borscht, pierogi and other "budget" foods; the decor's "long in the tooth" and service "could be better", but it's usually "bustling" with a "diverse crowd."

Vesta *Italian* 26 | 19 | 23 | $35

Astoria | 21-02 30th Ave. (21st St.) | Queens | 718-545-5550 | www.vestavino.com
Among the "besta" in its "residential" corner of Astoria, this local "favorite" serves a "limited menu" of pizzas and other "simple" Italian dishes with a "sustainable", "seasonal" bent at "remarkably fair" prices; the unpretentious digs can be "cramped" at peak hours, but an "engaging" staff keeps things simpatico.

Vesuvio ◐ *Italian* 20 | 17 | 19 | $32

Bay Ridge | 7305 Third Ave. (bet. 73rd & 74th Sts.) | Brooklyn | 718-745-0222 | www.vesuviobayridge.com
It may "not have the name recognition" of other Brooklyn pizza stalwarts, but this "comfortable" neighborhood Italian in Bay Ridge has been slinging "delicious" pies since 1953, along with an "abundance" of pastas; "friendly" staffers, "fair" tabs and "never a long wait" keep regulars regular.

Vezzo *Pizza* 23 | 15 | 17 | $24

Murray Hill | 178 Lexington Ave. (31st St.) | 212-839-8300 | www.vezzothincrust.com
"Paper-thin", "crispy"-crusted pies with "toppings to suit any taste" are the specialty of this "busy", "bargain-priced" Murray Hill pizzeria; the digs are "tight" and service can be "slooow", but all's forgiven after a bite of that "outstanding" Shroomtown pie.

Via Brasil *Brazilian/Steak* 21 | 16 | 20 | $40

W 40s | 34 W. 46th St. (bet. 5th & 6th Aves.) | 212-997-1158 | www.viabrasilrestaurant.com
A "mainstay" of 46th Street's "Little Brazil" strip, this circa-1978 stalwart turns out "traditional" meat-centric Brazilian fare chased

with "strong drinks"; if the "dark" surroundings are on the "charmless" side, "personable" staffers and "reasonable-for-Midtown" tabs more than compensate.

Via Emilia ⬙ *Italian*   23 | 16 | 20 | $43

Flatiron | 47 E. 21st St. (bet. B'way & Park Ave. S.) | 212-505-3072 | www.viaemilianyc.net

"Delectable" Emilia-Romagnan food paired with "excellent Lambruscos" is the lure at this "overlooked" Flatiron Italian that follows through with "friendly" service and "low prices" (it's now accepting credit cards); the "over-modern" setting may be on the "stark" side, but at least there's some "elbow room" between tables.

Via Quadronno *Italian*   23 | 17 | 19 | $40

E 70s | 25 E. 73rd St. (bet. 5th & Madison Aves.) | 212-650-9880 | www.viaquadronno.com

"Practice your air-kissing" with "chic Euro moms" while enjoying "to-die-for" Italian panini and espresso at this "seriously clubby" UES rendition of a Milanese bar; the price of admission skews high and the quarters can be "tight", but it's open all day and perfect "before shopping or the museums."

ViceVersa *Italian*   22 | 21 | 23 | $57

W 50s | 325 W. 51st St. (bet. 8th & 9th Aves.) | 212-399-9291 | www.viceversanyc.com

At this "vibrant" Theater District staple, the "top-notch" Italian cooking garners as much praise as the "attentive" staffers who will "get you out in time" for your curtain; factor in a "sleek" interior augmented with a "delightful" back patio, and it's an all-around "pleasant" dining experience.

Victor's Cafe *Cuban*   22 | 20 | 21 | $53

W 50s | 236 W. 52nd St. (bet. B'way & 8th Ave.) | 212-586-7714 | www.victorscafe.com

Around since 1963, this Theater District Cuban "doesn't rest on its laurels", supplying "solid" food and "fantastic" mojitos in "energetic" environs exuding classic "Havana style – ceiling fans and all"; "old-world" service and live music enhance this "welcome respite", but be prepared for "noise" and "tourists."

The View ◐ *American*   16 | 24 | 19 | $87

W 40s | Marriott Marquis Hotel | 1535 Broadway, 47th fl. (bet. 45th & 46th Sts.) | 212-704-8880 | www.theviewnyc.com

"As the name implies", it's all about the "second-to-none" 360-degree views of Manhattan at this "revolving" Times Square hotel eatery; just "be prepared to spend" to dine on "so-so" American grub with "lots of tourists", though even jaded natives admit it can be a "fun experience."

Villa Berulia *Italian*   24 | 21 | 26 | $55

Murray Hill | 107 E. 34th St. (bet. Lexington & Park Aves.) | 212-689-1970 | www.villaberulia.com

"Warm hospitality" is the hallmark of this longtime Murray Hill "fall-back" that "strives for perfection" with "excellent" Italian fare served by a "top-notch" crew; maybe the "old-fashioned" room "could use an update", but to its "mature" fan base it feels "like coming home."

	FOOD	DECOR	SERVICE	COST

Villa Mosconi ⊠ *Italian*

23 | 17 | 22 | $49

G Village | 69 MacDougal St. (bet. Bleecker & Houston Sts.) | 212-673-0390 | www.villamosconi.com

Red-sauce fanciers endorse this "old-school" Village Italian "throwback" (since 1976) for its "generous portions" of "smack-your-lips-good" classics delivered by "delightful" staffers; maybe the "old-world" digs could "use updating", but "decent prices" please its "longtime" regulars.

Vincent's ● *Italian*

22 | 15 | 19 | $38

Little Italy | 119 Mott St. (Hester St.) | 212-226-8133

A Little Italy fixture since "before you were born", this 1904-vintage Italian is renowned for its "incredible" hot marinara that "makes the dishes sing"; "quick" service, comfy "old-school" digs and "price-is-right" tabs cement its "standby" status.

Vinegar Hill House *American*

24 | 21 | 20 | $51

Vinegar Hill | 72 Hudson Ave. (bet. Front & Water Sts.) | Brooklyn | 718-522-1018 | www.vinegarhillhouse.com

"Brooklyn to its core", this New American "hipster magnet" in "middle-of-nowhere" Vinegar Hill is "worth seeking out" for "incredibly crafted" meals served in "cozy" digs complete with the "most romantic garden"; the only rubs are "cramped" conditions and "long waits" – though the latter is less of an issue now that it takes reservations.

Virgil's Real Barbecue ● *BBQ*

20 | 15 | 18 | $36

W 40s | 152 W. 44th St. (bet. B'way & 6th Ave.) | 212-921-9494 | www.virgilsbbq.com

"Decent" BBQ turns up in Times Square at this 20-year-old "crowd-pleaser" that rolls out "huge portions" of "greasy" grub in "massive" digs; ok, it's "not Texas" and the decor and service are "nothing memorable", but you'd never know it from the hordes of "tourists" in attendance.

Vivolo ⊠ *Italian*

20 | 17 | 20 | $53

E 70s | 140 E. 74th St. (bet. Lexington & Park Aves.) | 212-737-3533

Cucina Vivolo ⊠ *Italian*

E 70s | 138 E. 74th St. (bet. Lexington & Park Aves.) | 212-717-4700 www.vivolonyc.com

An "old-school" enclave set in a fireplace-equipped townhouse, this circa-1977 UES Italian seduces its mature fan base with "simple", "satisfying" repasts, "clubby" looks and "welcoming" service; its spin-off cafe is more casual and less expensive.

V-Note *Vegan*

23 | 20 | 22 | $40

E 70s | 1522 First Ave. (bet. 79th & 80th Sts.) | 212-249-5009 | www.v-notenyc.com

A "varied" menu of "inventive" vegan dishes with "flair" draws crunchy types to this UES herbivore hangout, a Blossom sibling that's also praised for its gluten-free menu and "wonderful wines"; the "modern", banquette-lined setting hints at the "pricey" tabs to come.

Wa Jeal *Chinese*

24 | 14 | 18 | $35

E 80s | 1588 Second Ave. (bet. 82nd & 83rd Sts.) | 212-396-3339 | www.wajealrestaurant.com

For a "10-alarm fire" of the taste buds, diners turn to this "excellent" UES Chinese praised for "incendiary" Sichuan dishes that are "hot but amazingly nuanced"; too bad about the "drab" decor, but "quick service" and "comfortable prices" make it "worth a visit."

Walker's ● *Pub Food*
19 | 15 | 20 | $33

TriBeCa | 16 N. Moore St. (Varick St.) | 212-941-0142

"As local as it gets in TriBeCa", this "quintessential" neighborhood pub is populated by everyone from area "families" and "bankers" to "film people shooting nearby"; "welcoming" vibes, a "funky" setting and "quality" bar food at "value" rates keep the place humming.

Wall & Water *American*
21 | 22 | 20 | $55

Financial District | Andaz Wall St. Hotel | 75 Wall St. (Water St.) | 212-699-1700 | www.wallandwaterny.com

This hotel-based "business-lunch" haven draws FiDi denizens with a "good" (if "limited") American lineup served in "contemporary" surrounds complete with a display kitchen; don't forget your "expense account", and if the dining room mood is too sedate, there's always the "hopping bar."

Wallsé *Austrian*
26 | 22 | 24 | $78

W Village | 344 W. 11th St. (Washington St.) | 212-352-2300 | www.kg-ny.com

"Top-notch" Modern Austrian fare keeps "schnitzel fans" coming to Kurt Gutenbrunner's "welcoming" "Vienna-in-NYC" Villager that's hung with "Julian Schnabel artwork"; "impeccable" service ensures that the "sophisticated" experience measures up to the steep tab.

Walter Foods ● *American*
23 | 21 | 22 | $40

Williamsburg | 253 Grand St. (Roebling St.) | Brooklyn | 718-387-8783 | www.walterfoods.com

Walter's ● *American*

Fort Greene | 166 DeKalb Ave. (Cumberland St.) | Brooklyn | 718-488-7800 | www.waltersbrooklyn.com

Brooklyn's "Socratic ideal of a neighborhood place", this Williamsburg-Fort Greene duo dispenses spiffed-up American comfort dishes accompanied by "killer" cocktails; "reasonable" prices and "comfortable" interiors are other pluses – they "care about the details here and it shows."

Water Club ⓜ *American*
22 | 26 | 24 | $71

Murray Hill | East River & 30th St. (enter on 23rd St.) | 212-683-3333 | www.thewaterclub.com

"Inspiring water views" from a barge docked on the East River lend a "romantic" aura to this "charming" venue that survived Hurricane Sandy, where a "pro" staff serves "excellent" American fare (and a "terrific" Sunday brunch); granted, it's best enjoyed "when your rich uncle is in town", but it's an automatic choice when it comes to "special-occasion" dining.

Water's Edge ⓩ *American/Seafood*
22 | 25 | 22 | $65

LIC | 401 44th Dr. (East River) | Queens | 718-482-0033 | www.watersedgenyc.com

"Romantic" is the word on this Long Island City "special-occasion" favorite where the "magnificent" Manhattan skyline views induce swoons; the "great tasting" American seafood may be "expensive for what you get", but not considering the "exceptional ambiance."

	FOOD	DECOR	SERVICE	COST

Waverly Inn ● *American* | 21 | 23 | 20 | $71

W Village | 16 Bank St. (Waverly Pl.) | 917-828-1154 | www.waverlynyc.com
Maybe the "celebrity buzz has slowed", but Graydon Carter's "clubby" West Villager still offers "high-end" spins on American "home-cooking" favorites in "cozy", fireplace-enhanced confines (complete with Edward Sorel murals); a "more democratic reservations system" makes it more "neighborly" than ever.

WD-50 *American/Eclectic* | 25 | 20 | 25 | $117

LES | 50 Clinton St. (bet. Rivington & Stanton Sts.) | 212-477-2900 | www.wd-50.com
Bring an "open mind" to chef Wylie Dufresne's "cutting-edge" Lower Eastsider, where the "work-of-art" American-Eclectic menu is composed of "thoughtful", "unconventional" dishes; "skilled" staffers oversee the "appealing", open-kitchen space, and while the prix fixe-only format is "not cheap", it's definitely an "experience."

West Bank Cafe ● *American* | 19 | 16 | 19 | $45

W 40s | Manhattan Plaza | 407 W. 42nd St. (bet. 9th & 10th Aves.) | 212-695-6909 | www.westbankcafe.com
Convenient to 42nd Street's Theater Row, this American "standby" earns applause for "satisfying" chow served in "congenial" environs; the menu "may not be the most exciting", but the prices are "affordable" and they get you "out on time" for your show.

Westville *American* | 23 | 14 | 18 | $26

Chelsea | 246 W. 18th St. (8th Ave.) | 212-924-2223
E Village | 173 Ave. A (11th St.) | 212-677-2033
Hudson Square | 333 Hudson St. (bet. Charlton & Vandam Sts.) | 212-776-1404 🅢 Ⓜ
W Village | 210 W. 10th St. (Bleecker St.) | 212-741-7971
www.westvillenyc.com
This "homey" American quartet draws fans with a "wonderful", market-oriented menu that includes many "interesting vegetable dishes" at "super-value" tabs; overseen by a "courteous" crew, they're predictably "busy", but the waits are "well worth it."

Whym *American* | 19 | 17 | 20 | $39

W 50s | 889 Ninth Ave. (bet. 57th & 58th Sts.) | 212-315-0088 | www.whymnyc.com
The "name says it all" about the "whimsical takes" on New American classics at this "pleasant" eatery not far from Lincoln Center; fans say it "hits the sweet spot" of "decent prices" and "friendly" service, meriting many a "return" visit.

'Wichcraft *Sandwiches* | 17 | 11 | 15 | $17

Chelsea | 269 11th Ave. (bet. 27th & 28th Sts.) | 212-780-0577 🅢
Chelsea | 601 W. 26th St. (bet. 11th & 12th Aves.) | 212-780-0577 🅢
E 40s | 245 Park Ave. (47th St.) | 212-780-0577 🅢
E 40s | 555 Fifth Ave. (46th St.) | 212-780-0577 🅢
Flatiron | 11 E. 20th St. (B'way) | 212-780-0577
G Village | 60 E. Eighth St. (Mercer St.) | 212-780-0577
TriBeCa | 397 Greenwich St. (Beach St.) | 212-780-0577
W 40s | Rockefeller Ctr. | 1 Rockefeller Plaza (bet. 5th & 6th Aves.) | 212-780-0577

(continued)

(continued)
'Wichcraft
W 40s | 11 W. 40th St. (6th Ave.) | 212-780-0577
W 60s | David Rubenstein Atrium at Lincoln Ctr. | 61 W. 62nd St.
(Columbus Ave.) | 212-780-0577
www.wichcraftnyc.com
Additional locations throughout the NY area

"Original" sandwiches and "on-the-go" snacks made from "quality"
ingredients justify the "premium" price tags at this ever-expanding
chain from *Top Chef*'s Tom Colicchio; "no-frills" setups and "inconsistent" service don't deter the lunchtime "masses."

Wild Ginger   *Asian/Vegetarian*   `22` `18` `21` `$26`
Little Italy | 380 Broome St. (bet. Mott & Mulberry Sts.) | 212-966-1883 |
www.wildgingeronline.com
Cobble Hill | 112 Smith St. (bet. Dean & Pacific Sts.) | Brooklyn |
718-858-3880 | www.wildgingeronline.com
Williamsburg | 212 Bedford Ave. (bet. N. 5th & 6th Sts.) | Brooklyn |
718-218-8828 | www.wildgingerny.com

For a "healthy change of pace", it's "vegan paradise" at these separately
owned Pan-Asians where the "creative", "flavorful" dishes feature
"mock meat" that "even carnivores can enjoy"; "accommodating" service and "cheap" prices complete the virtuous picture.

Wildwood Barbeque   *BBQ*   `19` `17` `17` `$38`
Flatiron | 225 Park Ave. S. (bet. 18th & 19th Sts.) | 212-533-2500 |
www.wildwoodbbq.com

The intoxicating "smell of smoky barbecue" pervades this "cavernous"
Flatironer dishing up "tasty" 'cue at "decent prices"; however, purists
dismiss it as "BBQ for beginners", citing "impersonal" service, a
"chain-restaurant" feel with "flat-screens everywhere" and "loud",
"frat-boy" crowds.

NEW Willow Road ● *American*   ▽ `23` `19` `19` `$53`
Chelsea | 85 10th Ave. (bet. 15th & 16th Sts.) | 646-484-6566 |
www.willowroadnyc.com

Right off the High Line, this "fun" Chelsea gastropub offers a
"better-than-expected" variety of American small plates and
cocktails in a slickly rustic room heavy on the reclaimed wood and
subway tile; the crowd's young, the decibels loud and the price
point a bit spendy.

Wo Hop   ⊉ *Chinese*   `22` `7` `16` `$20`
Chinatown | 17 Mott St. (bet. Mosco & Worth Sts.) | 212-267-2536 |
www.wohopnyc.com

"Old-school" is an understatement at this 1938-vintage Chinatown
double-decker known for "tried-and-true" Cantonese cooking at
"rock-bottom", cash-only tabs; despite "abrupt" service and "dingy"
digs decorated with a "zillion photos", "long lines" are the norm –
especially "late-night."

Wolfgang's Steakhouse   *Steak*   `25` `21` `23` `$79`
E 50s | 200 E. 54th St. (3rd Ave.) | 212-588-9653
Murray Hill | 4 Park Ave. (33rd St.) | 212-889-3369
TriBeCa | 409 Greenwich St. (bet. Beach & Hubert Sts.) |
212-925-0350

(continued)

Wolfgang's Steakhouse

W 40s | NY Times Bldg. | 250 W. 41st St. (bet. 7th & 8th Aves.) |
212-921-3720
www.wolfgangssteakhouse.net

"Real NY steakhouses at real NY prices", this "fast-paced" chainlet is
a "steady contender" for "succulent" cuts delivered in a "brusque but
professional" style; their "manly" milieus can be "noisy and crowded",
but overall they "do it well" here.

Wollensky's Grill ● *Steak*   23 | 17 | 21 | $62

E 40s | 201 E. 49th St. (3rd Ave.) | 212-753-0444 |
www.smithandwollenskynyc.com

"Less highfalutin'" and somewhat "cheaper" than its next-door big
brother, Smith & Wollensky, this "casual" Midtowner serves "dynamite" steaks and burgers in "high-energy" environs; it's especially beloved for its "late-dining" hours, open nightly till 2 AM.

Wondee Siam *Thai*   21 | 12 | 18 | $24

W 50s | 792 Ninth Ave. (bet. 52nd & 53rd Sts.) | 212-459-9057
W 50s | 813 Ninth Ave. (bet. 53rd & 54th Sts.) | 917-286-1726
W 100s | 969 Amsterdam Ave. (bet. 107th & 108th Sts.) |
212-531-1788 ●

"Consistently delicious" Thai fare brings back "memories of Bangkok"
at these "hole-in-the-wall" Westsiders; ok, they're "not fancy" and
"seating is limited", but service is "fast" and regulars say the "rock-
bottom prices" are the key to their enduring "popularity."

Wong 🗷 *Asian*   24 | 16 | 19 | $55

W Village | 7 Cornelia St. (bet. Bleecker & W. 4th Sts.) | 212-989-3399 |
www.wongnewyork.com

Simpson Wong (Cafe Asean) has a "winner" in this midpriced West
Villager where the "inventive" small plates combine Pan-Asian flavors
with "farm-fresh ingredients"; regulars say the "tight squeeze" doesn't
seem so bad after a few "fun cocktails."

Wu Liang Ye *Chinese*   23 | 12 | 14 | $35

W 40s | 36 W. 48th St. (bet. 5th & 6th Aves.) | 212-398-2308

Just off Rock Center and "one of the best Chinese restaurants north of
C-town" is this source for "real-deal", "tingly" Sichuan cooking ("bring
tissues to deal with your runny nose"); "bargain prices" outweigh the
"glum" digs and "rushed" service.

Xi'an Famous Foods ⊄ *Chinese*   24 | 6 | 13 | $12

Chinatown | 67 Bayard St. (bet. Bowery & Mott St.) |
718-885-7788
E Village | 81 St. Marks Pl. (1st Ave.) | 212-786-2068
NEW Greenpoint | 86 Beadel St. (bet. Morgan & Vandervoort Aves.) |
Brooklyn | 212-786-2068
Flushing | Golden Shopping Mall | 41-28 Main St. (41st Rd.) | Queens |
718-888-7713
www.xianfoods.com

"Freakin' awesome" hand-pulled noodles and "famous" cumin-lamb
burgers are menu "standouts" at these "seriously no-frills" purveyors
of "spicy" Western Chinese food; seats are "lacking" and service is
"pretty much nonexistent", but "low, low prices" keep them "popular."

	FOOD	DECOR	SERVICE	COST

NEW Xixa ● M _Mexican_ | - | - | - | M

Williamsburg | 241 S. Fourth St. (Havemeyer St.) | Brooklyn |
718-388-8860 | www.xixany.com

This "terrific" sibling of Williamsburg's Traif makes its mark with an extensive selection of "surreally inventive" Mexicana served in a funky cantina below the BQE; eclectic wines and tequilas, plus a staff that's "good about not rushing" the pace add to the "profound eating experience."

Yakitori Totto ● _Japanese_ | 25 | 16 | 18 | $47

W 50s | 251 W. 55th St. (bet. B'way & 8th Ave.) | 212-245-4555 |
www.tottonyc.com

"If it can be put on a skewer, they'll do it" at this "small" Midtown yakitori den where meats, veggies and "chicken parts that you never knew existed" are grilled on sticks; it's a real "excursion to Tokyo" complete with "cramped", "noisy" digs and tabs that can "add up quickly."

Yama ⓧ _Japanese_ | 23 | 14 | 18 | $43

E 40s | 308 E. 49th St. (bet. 1st & 2nd Aves.) | 212-355-3370
Gramercy | 122 E. 17th St. (Irving Pl.) | 212-475-0969 |
www.yamasushinyc.com
W Village | 38-40 Carmine St. (bet. Bedford & Bleecker Sts.) |
212-989-9330

"Bigger is better" declare sushiphiles who report that these Japanese triplets roll out "monster-size" slabs of the "freshest fish" at a "decent price"; even with "hit-or-miss" service, "crowded" conditions and "drab" quarters, there are usually "long waits at prime times."

Yefsi Estiatorio ● _Greek_ | 25 | 19 | 22 | $52

E 70s | 1481 York Ave. (bet. 78th & 79th Sts.) | 212-535-0293 |
www.yefsiestiatorio.com

A "great addition to the Far East Side", this instantly "popular" Yorkville yearling features "excellent" Greek cooking via a "talented" ex-Milos chef, with "wonderful" mezes as a focus; the "rustic", "like-in-Athens" setting includes the added bonus of a "charming garden."

Yerba Buena _Pan-Latin_ | 24 | 19 | 22 | $49

E Village | 23 Ave. A (bet. 1st & 2nd Sts.) | 212-529-2919 ●
W Village | 1 Perry St. (Greenwich Ave.) | 212-620-0808
www.ybnyc.com

Chef Julian Medina delivers "delectable", "inventive" Pan-Latin fare matched with "creative drinks" at these "stylish" crosstown siblings manned by a "helpful" crew; just be aware that the space is "tight" and the "noise level rises a few decibels" as the night wears on.

Yuba _Japanese_ | ▽ 23 | 18 | 21 | $48

E Village | 105 E. Ninth St. (bet. 3rd & 4th Aves.) | 212-777-8188 |
www.yubarestaurant.com

"Easily overlooked" in the East Village, this "small" Japanese is worth seeking out for "outstanding" sushi and cooked items made with "first-rate" luxe ingredients; fans overlook the "nondescript" setting and focus instead on its favorable "quality-to-price ratio."

Yuca Bar ● _Pan-Latin_ | 21 | 16 | 18 | $31

E Village | 111 Ave. A (7th St.) | 212-982-9533 | www.yucabarnyc.com
"Lively" and full of "good-looking" folks, this "colorful" East Villager mixes "delicious", well-priced Pan-Latin fare with "killer" drinks; it

| | FOOD | DECOR | SERVICE | COST |

gets "loud" and service can lag, but for "people-watching" by the open doors and windows, it's hard to beat.

Yuka *Japanese*

| 22 | 11 | 16 | $31 |

E 80s | 1557 Second Ave. (bet. 80th & 81st Sts.) | 212-772-9675 | www.yukasushi.com

"Talk about a bargain", this "busy" Yorkville Japanese veteran offers "super-fresh", all-you-can-eat sushi for just $21 per person; the space and service are pretty basic, so most diners focus on the "amazing deal."

Yunnan Kitchen *Chinese*

| ∇ 21 | 17 | 18 | $52 |

LES | 79 Clinton St. (bet. Delancey & Rivington Sts.) | 212-253-2527 | www.yunnankitchen.com

Offering a "fun take on Modern Chinese" cooking, this Lower Eastsider's market-driven fare focuses on the "tasty" cuisine of the eponymous province; the "cramped" space is outfitted with vintage Chinese jewelry and a tiger-skin rug, and "loud" acoustics come with the territory.

Yura on Madison *Sandwiches*

| 20 | 12 | 14 | $23 |

E 90s | 1292 Madison Ave. (92nd St.) | 212-860-1598 | www.yuraonmadison.com

A neighborhood haunt for nearby "prep school girls" and their "Madison Avenue moms", this "pricey" Carnegie Hill corner cafe turns out "consistently delicious" sandwiches, salads and baked goods; it "needs more seating" and service is merely "adequate", so "takeout" is an attractive option.

Yuva *Indian*

| 23 | 18 | 19 | $41 |

E 50s | 230 E. 58th St. (bet. 2nd & 3rd Aves.) | 212-339-0090 | www.yuvanyc.com

"Perfectly spiced" cooking, including "excellent tandoori" specialties, makes this "comfortable", "upscale" Indian stand out among its East 58th Street brethren; "modest" prices, "sweet" servers and a "reasonably quiet setting" encourage comers to "linger."

Zabb Elee *Thai*

| 22 | 12 | 17 | $25 |

E Village | 75 Second Ave. (bet. 4th & 5th Sts.) | 212-505-9533
Jackson Heights | 71-28 Roosevelt Ave. (72nd St.) | Queens | 718-426-7992 ●♥
www.zabbelee.com

"Complex flavors" – some of them "blistering hot" – distinguish these "delicious", "affordable" Thais in the East Village and Jackson Heights supplying "unusual" Northeastern Isan cooking to "adventurous" diners; "friendly" staffers add warmth to the otherwise "sterile" environs.

Zaitzeff *Burgers*

| ∇ 21 | 10 | 15 | $18 |

Financial District | 72 Nassau St. (John St.) | 212-571-7272 | www.zaitzeff.com

"Tasty" patties of all persuasions – Kobe beef, sirloin, turkey, vegetable – made with "quality" ingredients and served on "terrific Portuguese rolls" are the draw at this FiDi burger-and-beer purveyor; "small" dimensions make it more enjoyable either before or after the "lunch crush."

	FOOD	DECOR	SERVICE	COST

Zaytoons *Mideastern*

Carroll Gardens | 283 Smith St. (Sackett St.) | Brooklyn |
718-875-1880
Fort Greene | 472 Myrtle Ave. (bet. Hall St. & Washington Ave.) |
Brooklyn | 718-623-5522
Prospect Heights | 594 Vanderbilt Ave. (St. Marks Ave.) | Brooklyn |
718-230-3200 ⊟
www.zaytoonsrestaurant.com

20 | **14** | **17** | **$21**

For "tasty", "reliable" Middle Eastern fare, stay tooned to this Brooklyn
trio staffed by a "pleasant" crew; "tables are close", but the pricing's
"terrific" – and Carroll Gardens and Fort Greene are BYO, while Prospect
Heights boasts an "attractive garden."

Zebú Grill *Brazilian*

E 90s | 305 E. 92nd St. (bet. 1st & 2nd Aves.) | 212-426-7500 |
www.zebugrill.com

▽ **23** | **17** | **21** | **$45**

Upper Eastsiders on a meat binge hit this "relaxed" Brazilian specializing in "fantastic" churrasco dishes; "solicitous" service and "a caip-
irinha or two" confirm that this somewhat "out-of-the-way" contender
is a "pleasant" enough respite for a "quiet evening" out.

Ze Café *French/Italian*

E 50s | 398 E. 52nd St. (bet. FDR Dr. & 1st Ave.) | 212-758-1944 |
www.zecafe.com

21 | **23** | **20** | **$52**

You almost "feel like you're in a flower shop" – and that's no surprise
since this French-Italian Sutton Place "jewel box" is run by Zezé, one
of NYC's top florists; service is "charming" and the "tasty" light meals
are perfect for "lunch with the ladies" ("dah-ling!"), so no one seems
to mind the "steep" pricing.

Zengo Ⓩ *Pan-Latin*

E 40s | 622 Third Ave. (40th St.) | 212-808-8110 |
www.richardsandoval.com

22 | **23** | **20** | **$50**

A "beautiful" tri-level space designed by AvroKO sets the stage for a
"special" experience at this Grand Central–area Pan-Latin presenting
Richard Sandoval's "imaginative" Asian-accented cuisine; "pricey"
tabs and "tiny portions" annoy, but "welcoming" service and a downstairs tequila lounge tip the balance.

Zenkichi ●Ⓜ *Japanese*

Williamsburg | 77 N. Sixth St. (Wythe Ave.) | Brooklyn | 718-388-8985 |
www.zenkichi.com

26 | **25** | **25** | **$60**

A "hidden treasure", this "unique" Williamsburg Japanese izakaya
features "artfully prepared" small plates – but no sushi – served in a
"dark", "date-night-nirvana" triplex by "superb" staffers summoned
via "push button"; just "be prepared to splurge" for the privilege.

Zen Palate *Vegetarian*

Gramercy | 115 E. 18th St. (bet. Irving Pl. & Park Ave. S.) |
212-387-8885
Murray Hill | 516 Third Ave. (34th St.) | 212-685-6888
W 40s | 663 Ninth Ave. (46th St.) | 212-582-1669
www.zenpalate.com

19 | **14** | **17** | **$30**

It's "amazing what they do with tofu" at these Asian-influenced
vegetarian standbys featuring a variety of "fake-meat" dishes that
"even a carnivore can love"; foes pronounce them "stereotypical",

but at least the "fair pricing" outweighs the "harried" service and "dingy" decor.

	FOOD	DECOR	SERVICE	COST

Zero Otto Nove *Italian/Pizza*
24 | 21 | 22 | $43

Flatiron | 15 W. 21st St. (bet. 5th & 6th Aves.) | 212-242-0899
Fordham | 2357 Arthur Ave. (186th St.) | Bronx | 718-220-1027 Ⓜ
www.roberto089.com

The homemade dishes are a "pasta lover's dream" at this "authentic" Southern Italian duo, where "attentive servers" deliver an "old-world menu" that also highlights "terrific pizza"; the original Arthur Avenue enclave recalls a "courtyard in Sicily", though the newer Flatiron branch is an equally "worthy" follow-up.

Zito's Sandwich
21 | 16 | 18 | $17

Shoppe *Italian/Sandwiches*
Park Slope | 195 Fifth Ave. (bet. Berkeley Pl. & Union St.) | Brooklyn | 718-857-1950
Park Slope | 300 Seventh Ave. (bet. 7th & 8th Sts.) | Brooklyn | 718-499-2800
www.zitossandwichshoppe.com

The "old-time Brooklyn" submarine sandwich shop gets an update via these counter-service Park Slope venues vending "tasty" classic Italian heros made with "quality ingredients", accompanied by NY beer and wine; the "simple" setups feature back patios that add warm-weather appeal.

Zoma *Ethiopian*
▽ 24 | 20 | 20 | $30

Harlem | 2084 Frederick Douglass Blvd. (113th St.) | 212-662-0620 | www.zomanyc.com

Mavens say "some of the best" Ethiopian food in the city is served at this "upscale" Harlem contender offering "delicious", "authentic" stews eaten with injera bread; "modern" decor and "friendly" service enhance the experience, as do the affordable checks.

Zum Schneider ●⊭ *German*
21 | 18 | 19 | $32

E Village | 107 Ave. C (7th St.) | 212-598-1098 | www.zumschneider.com

It's all about the "humongous" Bavarian steins of beer and German brats at this affordable East Village "slice of Munich" that's a "boisterous" "haus away from home" where "every day's a party"; hit the ATM since it's "cash only", and prepare to wait during "Oktoberfest."

Zum Stammtisch *German*
24 | 20 | 21 | $40

Glendale | 69-46 Myrtle Ave. (bet. 69th Pl. & 70th St.) | Queens | 718-386-3014 | www.zumstammtisch.com

Bring your appetite to this Glendale German doling out "hearty" classics in "you-won't-leave-hungry" portions; "pleasant frauleins in Alpine costume" toting steins of "frosty beer" bolster the kitschy "hofbrauhaus-in-Bavaria" vibe, while affordable prices ensure it won't "bring out the wurst in you."

Zuzu Ramen Ⓜ⊭ *Japanese/Noodle Shop*
▽ 23 | 16 | 21 | $26

Park Slope | 173 Fourth Ave. (Degraw St.) | Brooklyn | 718-398-9898 | www.zuzuramen.com

"First-rate" Japanese noodles will make you forget the "ramen of your college-dorm days" at this "local favorite" on the Park Slope–Gowanus border; it's an "affordable", "friendly" standby that just might have you "watching *Tampopo* again."

NEW ZZ's Clam Bar ●☒Ⓜ *Seafood*   − | − | − | VE

G Village | 169 Thompson St. (bet. Bleecker & Houston Sts.) | 212-254-3000 | www.zzsclambar.com

From the Torrisi boys (owners of Carbone just down the street) comes this new Greenwich Village raw bar, an intimate, 12-seat venue vending seafood crudo along with oysters, clams, caviar and fancy libations; despite pricing not for the faint of heart – starting with those $20 cocktails – it's an immediate hit, so reservations are a must.

INDEXES

LOCATION MAPS

Special Features

Listings cover the best in each category and include names, locations and Food ratings. Multi-location restaurants' features may vary by branch.

BAR/SINGLES SCENES

A.G. Kitchen | **W 70s**	18
NEW Arlington Club | **E 70s**	21
Atlantic Grill | **E 70s**	22
Bagatelle | **Meatpacking**	20
Baraonda | **E 70s**	19
Beauty & Essex | **LES**	22
Bill's Bar | **Meatpacking**	19
Blue Ribbon | **multi.**	25
Blue Water | **Union Sq**	24
Bobo | **W Vill**	23
Bowery Diner | **LES**	18
Breslin | **Chelsea**	23
Brother Jimmy's | **multi.**	17
Bryant Park Grill/Cafe | **W 40s**	19
Buddakan | **Chelsea**	25
Cabana | **multi.**	22
Cafe Noir | **SoHo**	20
Catch | **Meatpacking**	23
Citrus B&G | **W 70s**	20
Coffee Shop | **Union Sq**	17
Corner Social | **Harlem**	17
Crave Fishbar | **E 50s**	25
DBGB | **E Vill**	24
Del Frisco's | **W 40s**	25
Delicatessen | **NoLita**	19
Dos Caminos | **multi.**	20
Dutch | **SoHo**	23
NEW El Toro Blanco | **W Vill**	22
Freemans | **LES**	22
NEW General | **LES**	20
NEW Harlow | **E 50s**	19
Hillstone | **multi.**	23
Hudson Clearwater | **W Vill**	23
Hurricane | **Flatiron**	21
'Inoteca | **LES**	21
Joya | **Cobble Hill**	23
Koi | **W 40s**	24
La Esquina | **L Italy**	23
NEW Lafayette | **NoHo**	19
Lavo | **E 50s**	21
NEW LCL | **E 40s**	-
Lion | **G Vill**	21
Lure Fishbar | **SoHo**	23
Macao Trading | **TriBeCa**	20
NEW Manon | **Meatpacking**	-
NEW Maysville | **Flatiron**	22
Miss Lily's | **G Vill**	21
Otto | **G Vill**	23
Pastis | **Meatpacking**	22
Peels | **E Vill**	20
Penrose | **E 80s**	20
Perla | **G Vill**	24
Pulino's | **NoLita**	20
Pulqueria | **Chinatown**	20
Rosemary's | **W Vill**	21
NEW Salvation Taco | **Murray Hill**	22
Saxon & Parole | **NoHo**	22
Smith | **multi.**	19
Sons of Essex | **LES**	20
Spice Market | **Meatpacking**	23
Standard Grill | **Meatpacking**	22
Stanton Social | **LES**	24
STK | **Meatpacking**	23
Tao | **E 50s**	24
NEW Willow Road | **Chelsea**	23

BREAKFAST

Balthazar | **SoHo**	24
Barney Greengrass | **W 80s**	24
Brasserie | **E 50s**	22
Breslin | **Chelsea**	23
Bubby's | **TriBeCa**	20
Buvette | **W Vill**	24
Cafe Luxembourg | **W 70s**	21
Cafe Mogador | **E Vill**	23
Café Sabarsky/Fledermaus | **E 80s**	22
Carnegie Deli | **W 50s**	22
Casa Lever | **E 50s**	23
City Bakery | **Flatiron**	22
Clinton St. Baking | **LES**	25
Coppelia | **Chelsea**	23
E.A.T. | **E 80s**	20
Egg | **W'burg**	24
Five Leaves | **Greenpt**	26
Forty Four | **W 40s**	20
Friedman's Lunch | **Chelsea**	22
Jean-Georges' Noug. | **W 60s**	27
Jeffrey's Grocery | **W Vill**	22

Joseph Leonard | **W Vill**	24
Katz's Deli | **LES**	24
Kitchenette | **multi.**	19
🆕 Lafayette | **NoHo**	19
Lambs Club | **W 40s**	22
Landmarc | **W 60s**	21
🆕 LCL | **E 40s**	-
Le Pain Q. | **multi.**	18
Locanda Verde | **TriBeCa**	25
Maialino | **Gramercy**	26
Marlow/Sons | **W'burg**	24
Michael's | **W 50s**	22
Morandi | **W Vill**	23
Nice Matin | **W 70s**	19
NoHo Star | **NoHo**	19
Norma's | **W 50s**	25
Palm Court | **W 50s**	21
Pastis | **Meatpacking**	22
Peels | **E Vill**	20
Penelope | **Murray Hill**	22
Pulino's | **NoLita**	20
Reynard | **W'burg**	23
Rosemary's | **W Vill**	21
Rue 57 | **W 50s**	19
Sant Ambroeus | **multi.**	21
Sarabeth's | **multi.**	20
Standard Grill | **Meatpacking**	22
Tartine | **W Vill**	22
Taste | **E 80s**	21
Teresa's | **Bklyn Hts**	20
Tom's | **Prospect Hts**	21
Untitled | **E 70s**	21
Veselka | **E Vill**	20
Wall/Water | **Financial**	21

BRUNCH

ABC Kitchen | **Flatiron**	26
Almond | **Flatiron**	20
Americano | **Chelsea**	22
Amy Ruth's | **Harlem**	22
A.O.C. | **W Vill**	20
Applewood | **Park Slope**	25
Aquagrill | **SoHo**	26
Artisanal | **Murray Hill**	23
Atlantic Grill | **multi.**	22
A Voce | **W 60s**	24
Back Forty | **E Vill**	22
Balaboosta | **NoLita**	23
Balthazar | **SoHo**	24
Bar Americain | **W 50s**	23

Beaumarchais | **Meatpacking**	22
Blue Ribbon Bakery | **W Vill**	24
Blue Water | **Union Sq**	24
Bocca Lupo | **Cobble Hill**	23
Brasserie 8½ | **W 50s**	22
Bubby's | **TriBeCa**	20
Buttermilk | **Carroll Gdns**	25
Cafe Cluny | **W Vill**	22
Café d'Alsace | **E 80s**	21
Cafe Luluc | **Cobble Hill**	21
Cafe Luxembourg | **W 70s**	21
Cafe Mogador | **E Vill**	23
Cafe Ronda | **W 70s**	20
Cafeteria | **Chelsea**	21
Calle Ocho | **W 80s**	21
Carlyle | **E 70s**	23
Cascabel Taqueria | **multi.**	21
Cebu | **Bay Ridge**	20
Celeste | **W 80s**	23
Clinton St. Baking | **LES**	25
Colicchio/Sons | **Chelsea**	25
Colonie | **Bklyn Hts**	25
Community Food | **W 100s**	23
Cookshop | **Chelsea**	23
Cornelia St. Cafe | **W Vill**	19
David Burke Townhse. | **E 60s**	25
db Bistro Moderne | **W 40s**	25
DBGB | **E Vill**	24
Delicatessen | **NoLita**	19
Dell'anima | **W Vill**	25
Delta Grill | **W 40s**	20
Diner | **W'burg**	24
Dutch | **SoHo**	23
Eatery | **W 50s**	21
Edi & The Wolf | **E Vill**	23
Ed's Chowder | **W 60s**	20
Empellón | **W Vill**	22
Extra Virgin | **W Vill**	23
Fat Radish | **LES**	24
Fatty Crab | **W Vill**	22
FishTag | **W 70s**	23
Five Leaves | **Greenpt**	26
5 Points | **NoHo**	21
44 & X/44½ | **W 40s**	22
Friend/Farmer | **Gramercy**	18
Good | **W Vill**	21
Great Jones Cafe | **NoHo**	21
Hearth | **E Vill**	24
Home | **W Vill**	22

Hundred Acres | **SoHo**	20
Ilili | **Chelsea**	24
Isabella's | **W 70s**	20
Jack Horse | **Bklyn Hts**	23
Jane | **G Vill**	21
JoeDoe | **E Vill**	24
JoJo | **E 60s**	24
Jones Wood Foundry | **E 70s**	21
Joseph Leonard | **W Vill**	24
Kitchenette | **multi.**	19
NEW Lafayette | **NoHo**	19
La Follia | **Gramercy**	22
Lambs Club | **W 40s**	22
NEW L'Apicio | **E Vill**	22
La Silhouette | **W 50s**	24
Lavo | **E 50s**	21
Le Gigot | **W Vill**	24
Leopard/des Artistes | **W 60s**	21
NEW Le Philosophe | **NoHo**	24
Les Halles | **multi.**	20
Lexington Brass | **E 40s**	18
Lido | **Harlem**	22
Lion | **G Vill**	21
Locale | **Astoria**	21
Locanda Verde | **TriBeCa**	25
Lorenzo's | **Bloomfield**	22
Maggie Brown | **Clinton Hill**	23
Maialino | **Gramercy**	26
Mark | **E 70s**	22
NEW Marrow | **W Vill**	23
Mercadito | **multi.**	24
Mesa Grill | **Flatiron**	23
Mile End | **Boerum Hill**	23
Minetta Tavern | **G Vill**	24
Miriam | **Park Slope**	21
Miss Lily's | **G Vill**	21
Miss Mamie/Maude | **Harlem**	22
Mon Petit Cafe | **E 60s**	19
NEW Montmartre | **Chelsea**	19
NEW Murray's Cheese | **W Vill**	24
NEW Musket Room | **NoLita**	–
Nice Matin | **W 70s**	19
Norma's | **W 50s**	25
Northern Spy | **E Vill**	24
No. 7 | **Ft Greene**	22
Ocean Grill | **W 70s**	24
Odeon | **TriBeCa**	19
Ofrenda | **W Vill**	23
Olea | **Ft Greene**	23

Ouest | **W 80s**	24
Palm Court | **W 50s**	21
Paradou | **Meatpacking**	22
Pastis | **Meatpacking**	22
Peels | **E Vill**	20
Penelope | **Murray Hill**	22
Perilla | **W Vill**	26
Petrossian | **W 50s**	24
NEW Preserve 24 | **LES**	–
Prune | **E Vill**	25
Public | **NoLita**	23
NEW Red Gravy | **Bklyn Hts**	20
Red Rooster | **Harlem**	22
Resto | **Murray Hill**	21
River Café | **Dumbo**	26
Riverpark | **Murray Hill**	24
Rocking Horse | **Chelsea**	22
Rose Water | **Park Slope**	25
Sanford's | **Astoria**	22
Sarabeth's | **multi.**	20
Saxon & Parole | **NoHo**	22
Schiller's | **LES**	19
Scottadito | **Park Slope**	22
Seersucker | **Carroll Gdns**	23
Spasso | **W Vill**	23
Spotted Pig | **W Vill**	24
Stanton Social | **LES**	24
Stone Park | **Park Slope**	24
Sylvia's | **Harlem**	20
Tartine | **W Vill**	22
Taste | **E 80s**	21
Telepan | **W 60s**	26
Tertulia | **W Vill**	24
Thistle Hill | **Park Slope**	20
Tipsy Parson | **Chelsea**	21
Tom's | **Prospect Hts**	21
Tribeca Grill | **TriBeCa**	22
Turkish Kitchen | **Murray Hill**	22
Union Sq. Cafe | **Union Sq**	27
Untitled | **E 70s**	21
Vanderbilt | **Prospect Hts**	21
Wallsé | **W Vill**	26
Water Club | **Murray Hill**	22
Waverly Inn | **W Vill**	21
NEW Willow Road | **Chelsea**	23

BUFFET

(Check availability)

Bombay Palace | **W 50s**	20
Bukhara Grill | **E 40s**	21

Chola | **E 50s**	23
Darbar | **multi.**	21
Dhaba | **Murray Hill**	23
Indus Valley | **W 100s**	22
Jackson Diner | **multi.**	21
Sapphire Indian | **W 60s**	21
Tiffin Wallah | **Murray Hill**	22
Turkuaz | **W 100s**	20
View | **W 40s**	16
Yuva | **E 50s**	23

BYO

Afghan Kebab | **multi.**	20
Azuri Cafe | **W 50s**	25
Baluchi's | **Murray Hill**	19
Buddha Bodai | **Chinatown**	23
Butcher Bar | **Astoria**	24
Di Fara | **Midwood**	26
Gazala's | **W 40s**	21
Hampton Chutney | **multi.**	21
Kuma Inn | **LES**	25
La Sirène | **Hudson Square**	24
Legend | **W 100s**	21
Little Poland | **E Vill**	20
Lomzynianka | **Greenpt**	22
Lucali | **Carroll Gdns**	27
Mezzaluna/Pizza | **G Vill**	21
Nicky's | **multi.**	21
Nook | **W 50s**	23
Oaxaca | **Park Slope**	21
Padre Figlio | **E 40s**	22
Pho Bang | **L Italy**	22
Phoenix Gdn. | **Murray Hill**	23
Poke | **E 80s**	24
Qi | **W'burg**	22
Red Hook Lobster | **Red Hook**	24
sNice | **W Vill**	20
Taci's Beyti | **Midwood**	25
NEW Tanoshi | **E 70s**	-
Tartine | **W Vill**	22
Tea & Sympathy | **W Vill**	22
Wondee Siam | **W 50s**	21
Zaytoons | **multi.**	20

CELEBRITY CHEFS

Alain Allegretti
Bistro La Promenade | **Chelsea**	23

Michael Anthony
Gramercy Tavern | **Flatiron**	28

Julieta Ballesteros
Crema | **Chelsea**	23

Dan Barber
Blue Hill | **G Vill**	27

Lidia Bastianich
Felidia | **E 50s**	26
Manzo | **Flatiron**	25

Mario Batali
Babbo | **G Vill**	27
Casa Mono | **Gramercy**	25
Del Posto | **Chelsea**	26
Esca | **W 40s**	24
Lupa | **G Vill**	25
Manzo | **Flatiron**	25
Otto | **G Vill**	23

Jonathan Benno
Lincoln | **W 60s**	24

April Bloomfield
Breslin | **Chelsea**	23
John Dory Oyster Bar | **Chelsea**	24
NEW Salvation Taco | **Murray Hill**	22
Spotted Pig | **W Vill**	24

Saul Bolton
NEW Red Gravy | **Bklyn Hts**	20
Vanderbilt | **Prospect Hts**	21

David Bouley
Bouley | **TriBeCa**	29
Brushstroke/Ichimura | **TriBeCa**	26

Daniel Boulud
Bar Boulud | **W 60s**	24
Boulud Sud | **W 60s**	25
Café Boulud | **E 70s**	27
Daniel | **E 60s**	28
db Bistro Moderne | **W 40s**	25
DBGB | **E Vill**	24

Antoine Bouterin
Le Perigord | **E 50s**	25

Danny Bowien
Mission Chinese | **LES**	23

Jimmy Bradley
Harrison | **TriBeCa**	22

Terrance Brennan
Artisanal | **Murray Hill**	23
Picholine | **W 60s**	27

Scott Bryan
Apiary | **E Vill**	23

SPECIAL FEATURES

David Burke
  David Burke/Bloom. | **E 50s** — 19
  David Burke Fishtail | **E 60s** — 24
  David Burke Kitchen | **SoHo** — 24
  David Burke Townhse. | **E 60s** — 25
Joey Campanaro
  Little Owl | **W Vill** — 25
Marco Canora
  Hearth | **E Vill** — 24
  Terroir | **multi.** — 20
Floyd Cardoz
  North End Grill | **Financial** — 24
Andrew Carmellini
  Dutch | **SoHo** — 23
  NEW Lafayette | **NoHo** — 19
  NEW Library/Public | **E Vill** — 18
  Locanda Verde | **TriBeCa** — 25
Michael Cetrulo
  Scalini Fedeli | **TriBeCa** — 27
David Chang
  Má Pêche | **W 50s** — 23
  Momofuku Ko | **E Vill** — 27
  Momofuku Noodle | **E Vill** — 24
  Momofuku Ssäm | **E Vill** — 25
Rebecca Charles
  Pearl Oyster | **W Vill** — 26
Amanda Cohen
  Dirt Candy | **E Vill** — 25
Tom Colicchio
  Colicchio/Sons | **Chelsea** — 25
  Craft | **Flatiron** — 26
  Craftbar | **Flatiron** — 23
  Riverpark | **Murray Hill** — 24
  'Wichcraft | **multi.** — 17
Scott Conant
  Scarpetta | **Chelsea** — 26
Christian Delouvrier
  La Mangeoire | **E 50s** — 22
John DeLucie
  Bill's Food & Drink | **E 50s** — 18
  Crown | **E 80s** — 21
  Lion | **G Vill** — 21
Alain Ducasse
  Benoit | **W 50s** — 21
Wylie Dufresne
  NEW Alder | **E Vill** — 20
  WD-50 | **LES** — 25

Todd English
  Ça Va | **W 40s** — 21
  Château Cherbuliez | **Flatiron** — -
  Olives | **Union Sq** — 22
  Plaza Food Hall | **W 50s** — 22
Elizabeth Falkner
  NEW Corvo Bianco | **W 80s** — -
Guy Fieri
  NEW Guy's American | **W 40s** — 17
Sandro Fioriti
  Sandro's | **E 80s** — 25
Bobby Flay
  Bar Americain | **W 50s** — 23
  Mesa Grill | **Flatiron** — 23
Marc Forgione
  NEW Khe-Yo | **TriBeCa** — -
  Marc Forgione | **TriBeCa** — 26
Alex Garcia
  A.G. Kitchen | **W 70s** — 18
Alex Guarnaschelli
  Butter | **E Vill** — 23
Kurt Gutenbrunner
  Blaue Gans | **TriBeCa** — 22
  Café Sabarsky/Fledermaus | **E 80s** — 22
  Wallsé | **W Vill** — 26
Gabrielle Hamilton
  Prune | **E Vill** — 25
Kerry Heffernan
  South Gate | **W 50s** — 21
Peter Hoffman
  Back Forty | **multi.** — 22
Daniel Humm
  Eleven Madison | **Flatiron** — 28
  NoMad | **Chelsea** — 27
Hung Hyunh
  Catch | **Meatpacking** — 23
  NEW General | **LES** — 20
Eiji Ichimura
  Brushstroke/Ichimura | **TriBeCa** — 26
Sara Jenkins
  Porchetta | **E Vill** — 24
  Porsena | **E Vill** — 22
Gavin Kaysen
  Café Boulud | **E 70s** — 27
Thomas Keller
  Per Se | **W 60s** — 28

Mark Ladner
  Del Posto | **Chelsea** — 26

Paul Liebrandt
  NEW Elm | **W'burg** — _

Anita Lo
  Annisa | **W Vill** — 27

Maria Loi
  Loi | **W 70s** — 22

Michael Lomonaco
  Porter House | **W 60s** — 26

Nobu Matsuhisa
  Nobu | **multi.** — 27

Jehangir Mehta
  Graffiti | **E Vill** — 25
  Mehtaphor | **TriBeCa** — 24
  Misdemeanor |
    Downtown Bklyn — _

Carlo Mirarchi
  Blanca | **Bushwick** — 29
  Roberta's | **Bushwick** — 26

Marco Moreira
  15 East | **Union Sq** — 26
  Tocqueville | **Union Sq** — 27

Masaharu Morimoto
  Morimoto | **Chelsea** — 26

Charlie Palmer
  Aureole | **W 40s** — 26

David Pasternack
  Esca | **W 40s** — 24

Zak Pelaccio
  Fatty Crab | **W Vill** — 22
  Fatty 'Cue | **multi.** — 22

Alfred Portale
  Gotham B&G | **G Vill** — 27

Michael Psilakis
  FishTag | **W 70s** — 23
  NEW MP Taverna | **Astoria** — _

Cesar Ramirez
  Chef's/Brooklyn Fare |
    Downtown Bklyn — 27

Mary Redding
  Brooklyn Fish | **Park Slope** — 22
  Mary's Fish | **W Vill** — 25

Mads Refslund
  Acme | **NoHo** — 22

Andy Ricker
  Pok Pok Ny | **Red Hook** — 24
  Pok Pok Phat Thai | **LES** — _

Eric Ripert
  Le Bernardin | **W 50s** — 29

Marcus Samuelsson
  Red Rooster | **Harlem** — 22

Richard Sandoval
  Maya | **E 60s** — 23
  Pampano | **E 40s** — 24
  Zengo | **E 40s** — 22

Suvir Saran
  Dévi | **Flatiron** — 23

Angelo Sosa
  Añejo Tequileria | **W 40s** — 22

Alex Stupak
  Empellón | **E Vill** — 22

Gari Sugio
  Gari | **multi.** — 27

Nao Sugiyama
  Sugiyama | **W 50s** — 28

Masayoshi Takayama
  Masa/Bar Masa | **W 60s** — 27

Dale Talde
  Talde | **Park Slope** — 25

Bill Telepan
  Telepan | **W 60s** — 26

Sue Torres
  Sueños | **Chelsea** — 23

Laurent Tourondel
  NEW Arlington Club | **E 70s** — 21

Tom Valenti
  Ouest | **W 80s** — 24

Jean-Georges Vongerichten
  NEW ABC Cocina | **Flatiron** — _
  ABC Kitchen | **Flatiron** — 26
  Jean Georges | **W 60s** — 28
  JoJo | **E 60s** — 24
  Mark | **E 70s** — 22
  Mercer Kitchen | **SoHo** — 22
  Perry St. | **W Vill** — 26
  Spice Market | **Meatpacking** — 23

Jonathan Waxman
  Barbuto | **W Vill** — 24

Michael White
  Ai Fiori | **Garment** — 26
  NEW Butterfly | **TriBeCa** — _
  NEW Costata | **SoHo** — _
  Marea | **W 50s** — 28
  Nicoletta | **E Vill** — 19
  Osteria Morini | **SoHo** — 24

Jody Williams
Buvette | W Vill — 24

Geoffrey Zakarian
Lambs Club | W 40s — 22
National | E 50s — 20
Palm Court | W 50s — 21

Galen Zamarra
Mas | W Vill — 27
Mas (La Grillade) | W Vill — 23

CHILD-FRIENDLY

(* children's menu available)

Alice's Tea* | multi. — 20
Amorina* | Prospect Hts — 23
Amy Ruth's | Harlem — 22
Arirang Hibachi* | multi. — 21
Back Forty | multi. — 22
Bamonte's | W'burg — 22
Bark | Park Slope — 22
Beecher's Cellar | Flatiron — 23
BLT Burger* | G Vill — 22
Blue Ribbon* | multi. — 25
Blue Smoke* | Murray Hill — 22
Boathouse* | E 70s — 18
Bocca Lupo | Cobble Hill — 23
Bowery Diner* | LES — 18
Brennan | Sheepshead — 22
Brooklyn Farmacy | Carroll Gdns — 23
Brooklyn Fish* | Park Slope — 22
Bubby's* | TriBeCa — 20
Buttermilk* | Carroll Gdns — 25
Café Habana/Outpost | Ft Greene — 23
Carmine's* | W 40s — 21
ChipShop* | multi. — 20
Cowgirl* | W Vill — 17
DBGB* | E Vill — 24
Farm/Adderley* | Ditmas Pk — 24
Flatbush Farm | Park Slope — 21
Friend/Farmer* | Gramercy — 18
Gargiulo's | Coney Is — 22
Hill Country | Flatiron — 23
Hill Country Chicken* | Flatiron — 20
Jackson Hole* | multi. — 19
Joe & Pat's | Castleton Corners — 23
Josie's* | W 70s — 20
Junior's* | multi. — 19
L&B Spumoni* | Bensonhurst — 24
Landmarc* | multi. — 21
La Villa Pizzeria | multi. — 23
London Lennie* | Rego Pk — 23

Max* | TriBeCa — 18
Miss Mamie/Maude* | Harlem — 22
Nick's | multi. — 23
Ninja | TriBeCa — 19
Noodle Pudding | Bklyn Hts — 25
Osso Buco | E 90s — 20
Otto | G Vill — 23
Peanut Butter Co. | G Vill — 21
Pig Heaven | E 80s — 21
Pinche Taqueria | NoHo — 21
Pulino's* | NoLita — 20
Riverview* | LIC — 21
Rock Ctr.* | W 50s — 19
Rosa Mexicano* | multi. — 22
Ruby Foo's* | W 40s — 18
Sambuca* | W 70s — 19
Sarabeth's | multi. — 20
Serendipity 3 | E 60s — 20
Shabu-Shabu 70 | E 70s — 21
Shake Shack* | multi. — 21
S'MAC | multi. — 23
Sylvia's* | Harlem — 20
Tony's Di Napoli | W 40s — 22
Two Boots* | multi. — 19
Veselka | E Vill — 20
View* | W 40s — 16
Virgil's BBQ* | W 40s — 20
Zero Otto | Fordham — 24
Zum Stammtisch | Glendale — 24

COLLEGE-CENTRIC

Columbia
Cafe Du Soleil | W 100s — 19
Community Food | W 100s — 23
NEW Ellington | W 100s — -
Havana Central | multi. — 19
Kitchenette | multi. — 19
Maoz | W 100s — 21
Max SoHa/Caffe | W 100s — 23
Miss Mamie/Maude | Harlem — 22
Pisticci | W 100s — 25
Sezz Medi' | W 100s — 22
Symposium | W 100s — 20
Thai Market | W 100s — 23
NYU
Angelica Kit. | E Vill — 22
Artichoke Basille | E Vill — 22
BaoHaus | E Vill — 23
Café Habana/Outpost | NoLita — 23
Café Henri | W Vill — 20

Caracas	**E Vill**	24
Crif Dogs	**E Vill**	23
Dos Toros	**E Vill**	21
Gyu-Kaku	**E Vill**	21
Ippudo	**E Vill**	25
John's/12th St.	**E Vill**	22
La Esquina	**L Italy**	23
Mamoun's	**multi.**	23
99 Mi. to Philly	**E Vill**	21
Num Pang	**G Vill**	25
Otto	**G Vill**	23
Republic	**Union Sq**	19
S'MAC	**E Vill**	23
Smith	**E Vill**	19
Spice	**G Vill**	19
Vanessa's Dumpling	**E Vill**	21
Veselka	**E Vill**	20

COMMUTER OASIS

Grand Central

Ammos	**E 40s**	21
Aretsky's Patroon	**E 40s**	22
Benjamin Steak	**E 40s**	25
Bobby Van's	**E 40s**	23
Cafe Centro	**E 40s**	21
Capital Grille	**E 40s**	24
Cipriani Dolci	**E 40s**	22
Docks Oyster	**E 40s**	20
Fabio Piccolo	**E 40s**	23
Hatsuhana	**E 40s**	25
Junior's	**E 40s**	19
La Fonda/Sol	**E 40s**	22
NEW LCL	**E 40s**	-
Lexington Brass	**E 40s**	18
Menchanko-tei	**E 40s**	19
Michael Jordan	**E 40s**	21
Morton's	**E 40s**	22
Nanni	**E 40s**	24
Naples 45	**E 40s**	19
Naya	**E 40s**	22
Num Pang	**E 40s**	25
Oyster Bar	**E 40s**	22
Pera	**E 40s**	20
Pietro's	**E 40s**	24
Sakagura	**E 40s**	25
Sinigual	**E 40s**	21
Soba Totto	**E 40s**	24
Sparks	**E 40s**	25
Sushi Yasuda	**E 40s**	28
Tulsi	**E 40s**	24

Two Boots	**E 40s**	19
Zengo	**E 40s**	22

Penn Station

Biricchino	**Chelsea**	21
Brother Jimmy's	**Garment**	17
Casa Nonna	**Garment**	21
Chef Yu	**Garment**	21
NEW Gaonnuri	**Garment**	21
Keens	**Garment**	26
Lazzara's	**Garment**	24
Mooncake	**Chelsea**	20
Stage Door	**Garment**	19
Uncle Jack's	**Garment**	23
Uncle Nick's	**Chelsea**	21

Port Authority

Ça Va	**W 40s**	21
Chez Josephine	**W 40s**	20
Chimichurri Grill	**W 40s**	23
Dafni Greek	**W 40s**	19
Don Giovanni	**W 40s**	20
Esca	**W 40s**	24
Etc. Etc.	**W 40s**	22
5 Napkin Burger	**W 40s**	21
John's Pizzeria	**W 40s**	22
Shorty's	**W 40s**	22
Marseille	**W 40s**	21
Mercato	**Garment**	21
Qi	**W 40s**	22
Schnipper's	**W 40s**	19
Shake Shack	**W 40s**	21
Shula's	**W 40s**	21
West Bank	**W 40s**	19

DANCING/ ENTERTAINMENT

(Call for types and times
of performances)

Blue Fin	**W 40s**	23
Blue Smoke	**Murray Hill**	22
Blue Water	**Union Sq**	24
Cafe Steinhof	**Park Slope**	18
Cávo	**Astoria**	21
Chez Josephine	**W 40s**	20
Cornelia St. Cafe	**W Vill**	19
Delta Grill	**W 40s**	20
NEW Flor de Sol	**Chelsea**	-
Knickerbocker	**G Vill**	20
La Lanterna	**G Vill**	20
River Café	**Dumbo**	26
Sofrito	**E 50s**	24

Son Cubano	**Chelsea**	22
Sylvia's	**Harlem**	20
Tommaso	**Dyker Hts**	23

FIREPLACES

A Casa Fox	**LES**	23
Alberto	**Forest Hills**	23
Alta	**G Vill**	25
NEW Antica Pesa	**W'burg**	23
Applewood	**Park Slope**	25
Asellina	**Murray Hill**	20
Battery Gdns.	**Financial**	20
NEW Beatrice Inn	**W Vill**	17
Benjamin Steak	**E 40s**	25
Black Duck	**Murray Hill**	22
Boathouse	**E 70s**	18
Bouley	**TriBeCa**	29
Blossom	**W Vill**	23
Ça Va	**W 40s**	21
Cebu	**Bay Ridge**	20
Christos	**Astoria**	25
Club A Steak	**E 50s**	24
Cornelia St. Cafe	**W Vill**	19
Delta Grill	**W 40s**	20
Donovan's	**Woodside**	20
Dutch	**SoHo**	23
E&E Grill House	**W 40s**	21
F & J Pine	**Morris Park**	23
FireBird	**W 40s**	20
Forty Four	**W 40s**	20
Friend/Farmer	**Gramercy**	18
Glass House	**W 40s**	19
House	**Gramercy**	21
I Trulli	**Murray Hill**	22
Keens	**Garment**	26
Lady Mendl's	**Gramercy**	22
La Lanterna	**G Vill**	20
Lambs Club	**W 40s**	22
Lobster Box	**City Is**	20
Locanda Verde	**TriBeCa**	25
Lorenzo's	**Bloomfield**	22
Marco Polo	**Carroll Gdns**	20
McCormick/Schmick	**W 50s**	18
Molly's	**Gramercy**	22
NoMad	**Chelsea**	27
One if by Land	**W Vill**	24
Per Se	**W 60s**	28
Place	**W Vill**	23
Public	**NoLita**	23
Quality Meats	**W 50s**	26

NEW SakaMai	**LES**	-
Salinas	**Chelsea**	22
Scottadito	**Park Slope**	22
Sea Shore	**City Is**	21
St. Andrews	**W 40s**	19
Telly's Taverna	**Astoria**	21
Triomphe	**W 40s**	23
21 Club	**W 50s**	23
Vareli	**W 100s**	23
Vinegar Hill Hse.	**Vinegar Hill**	24
Vivolo/Cucina	**E 70s**	20
Water Club	**Murray Hill**	22
Waverly Inn	**W Vill**	21
WD-50	**LES**	25

GLUTEN-FREE OPTIONS

(Call to discuss specific needs)

NEW Betony	**W 50s**	-
Bistango	**Murray Hill**	21
Candle 79	**E 70s**	25
Caracas	**multi.**	24
Don Antonio	**W 50s**	24
Etc. Etc.	**W 40s**	22
5 Napkin Burger	**multi.**	21
Friedman's Lunch	**Chelsea**	22
Hill Country	**Flatiron**	23
Hummus Pl.	**multi.**	22
Keste Pizza	**W Vill**	25
Nice Matin	**W 70s**	19
Nizza	**W 40s**	19
Nom Wah Tea	**Chinatown**	21
Pappardella	**W 70s**	20
Risotteria	**W Vill**	22
Rubirosa	**NoLita**	23
Sambuca	**W 70s**	19
S'MAC	**E Vill**	23
V-Note	**E 70s**	23

GREEN/LOCAL/ ORGANIC

NEW ABC Cocina	**Flatiron**	-
ABC Kitchen	**Flatiron**	26
Aldea	**Flatiron**	25
Amali	**E 60s**	21
Angelica Kit.	**E Vill**	22
Applewood	**Park Slope**	25
Aroma Kitchen	**NoHo**	24
Arthur on Smith	**Boerum Hill**	21
Aureole	**W 40s**	26
Aurora	**multi.**	23

Babbo | **G Vill**	27
Back Forty | **E Vill**	22
Bar Boulud | **W 60s**	24
Barbuto | **W Vill**	24
BareBurger | **multi.**	22
Bark | **Park Slope**	22
Bell Book/Candle | **W Vill**	20
NEW Betony | **W 50s**	-
Blossom | **Chelsea**	23
Blue Hill | **G Vill**	27
Brooklyn Farmacy | **Carroll Gdns**	23
Buttermilk | **Carroll Gdns**	25
Café Habana/Outpost | **Ft Greene**	23
Cafe Loup | **W Vill**	19
Candle Cafe | **E 70s**	24
Candle 79 | **E 70s**	25
Caravan/Dreams | **E Vill**	23
City Bakery | **Flatiron**	22
Clinton St. Baking | **LES**	25
Colicchio/Sons | **Chelsea**	25
Colonie | **Bklyn Hts**	25
Community Food | **W 100s**	23
Cookshop | **Chelsea**	23
Craft | **Flatiron**	26
Degustation | **E Vill**	28
Dell'anima | **W Vill**	25
Del Posto | **Chelsea**	26
Diner | **W'burg**	24
Dirt Candy | **E Vill**	25
Egg | **W'burg**	24
Eleven Madison | **Flatiron**	28
Esca | **W 40s**	24
Farm/Adderley | **Ditmas Pk**	24
Fat Radish | **LES**	24
Fette Sau | **W'burg**	26
5 Points | **NoHo**	21
Flatbush Farm | **Park Slope**	21
NEW Fletcher's | **Gowanus**	22
Forcella | **NoHo**	22
Fornino | **W'burg**	24
Frankies | **multi.**	23
Franny's | **Park Slope**	25
General Greene | **Ft Greene**	20
Gobo | **multi.**	23
Good Fork | **Red Hook**	25
Gotham B&G | **G Vill**	27
Gramercy Tavern | **Flatiron**	28
Grocery | **Carroll Gdns**	27
Hearth | **E Vill**	24

Home | **W Vill**	22
Hundred Acres | **SoHo**	20
Il Buco | **NoHo**	25
Isabella's | **W 70s**	20
Jack Horse | **Bklyn Hts**	23
James | **Prospect Hts**	24
Josie's | **W 70s**	20
Juventino | **Park Slope**	25
Kin Shop | **W Vill**	24
L'Artusi | **W Vill**	27
NEW La Slowteria | **Carroll Gdns**	-
La Vara | **Cobble Hill**	27
Le Pain Q. | **Flatiron**	18
Lincoln | **W 60s**	24
Locanda Verde | **TriBeCa**	25
Lunetta | **Boerum Hill**	21
Lupa | **G Vill**	25
Marc Forgione | **TriBeCa**	26
Market Table | **W Vill**	23
Marlow/Sons | **W'burg**	24
NEW Marrow | **W Vill**	23
Mas | **W Vill**	27
Momofuku Ko | **E Vill**	27
Momofuku Noodle | **E Vill**	24
Momofuku Ssäm | **E Vill**	25
New Leaf | **Wash. Hts**	21
NEW Nightingale 9 | **Carroll Gdns**	-
NoMad | **Chelsea**	27
Northern Spy | **E Vill**	24
Paulie Gee's | **Greenpt**	26
Peaches | **Bed-Stuy**	23
Pearl Oyster | **W Vill**	26
Per Se | **W 60s**	28
NEW Preserve 24 | **LES**	-
Prime Meat | **Carroll Gdns**	23
Print | **W 40s**	22
Prune | **E Vill**	25
Pure Food/Wine | **Gramercy**	24
Redhead | **E Vill**	22
Riverpark | **Murray Hill**	24
Roberta's | **Bushwick**	26
Roman's | **Ft Greene**	24
Rosemary's | **W Vill**	21
Rose Water | **Park Slope**	25
Rouge Tomate | **E 60s**	24
Rucola | **Boerum Hill**	24
Seersucker | **Carroll Gdns**	23
Sfoglia | **E 90s**	23
606 R&D | **Prospect Hts**	23

Smoke Joint	**Ft Greene**	22
Stone Park	**Park Slope**	24
Telepan	**W 60s**	26
Thistle Hill	**Park Slope**	20
Tía Pol	**Chelsea**	25
Tortilleria Nixtamal	**Corona**	26
Trestle on 10th	**Chelsea**	22
Txikito	**Chelsea**	24
Union Sq. Cafe	**Union Sq**	27
Vanderbilt	**Prospect Hts**	21
Veselka	**E Vill**	20
Vesta	**Astoria**	26
Wong	**W Vill**	24
Zito's	**Park Slope**	21
Zum Schneider	**E Vill**	21

GROUP DINING

Almayass	**Flatiron**	22
Almond	**Flatiron**	20
Alta	**G Vill**	25
Arirang Hibachi	**multi.**	21
Artisanal	**Murray Hill**	23
Atlantic Grill	**multi.**	22
Balthazar	**SoHo**	24
Bar Americain	**W 50s**	23
Beauty & Essex	**LES**	22
Becco	**W 40s**	22
Blaue Gans	**TriBeCa**	22
BLT Prime	**Gramercy**	25
BLT Steak	**E 50s**	25
Blue Fin	**W 40s**	23
Blue Smoke	**multi.**	22
Blue Water	**Union Sq**	24
Boathouse	**E 70s**	18
Bond 45	**W 40s**	19
Brasserie 8½	**W 50s**	22
Breslin	**Chelsea**	23
Buddakan	**Chelsea**	25
Cabana	**multi.**	22
Calle Ocho	**W 80s**	21
Capital Grille	**multi.**	24
Carmine's	**multi.**	21
Casa Nonna	**Garment**	21
China Grill	**W 50s**	23
Churrascaria	**multi.**	23
Cilantro	**multi.**	19
Citrus B&G	**W 70s**	20
Colicchio/Sons	**Chelsea**	25
Congee	**LES**	20
Craftbar	**Flatiron**	23

Crispo	**W Vill**	23
DBGB	**E Vill**	24
Del Frisco's	**multi.**	25
Dinosaur BBQ	**multi.**	23
Dominick's	**Fordham**	23
Don Peppe	**Ozone Pk**	25
Dos Caminos	**multi.**	20
F & J Pine	**Morris Park**	23
Fette Sau	**W'burg**	26
Fig & Olive	**multi.**	21
Golden Unicorn	**Chinatown**	21
Gyu-Kaku	**multi.**	21
Havana Central	**multi.**	19
Hill Country	**Flatiron**	23
Hill Country Chicken	**Flatiron**	20
Hurricane	**Flatiron**	21
Ilili	**Chelsea**	24
Jing Fong	**Chinatown**	20
Kuma Inn	**LES**	25
Kum Gang San	**multi.**	21
L&B Spumoni	**Bensonhurst**	24
Landmarc	**multi.**	21
Má Pêche	**W 50s**	23
Momofuku Ssäm	**E Vill**	25
Morimoto	**Chelsea**	26
Ninja	**TriBeCa**	19
Nobu	**multi.**	27
Osso Buco	**E 90s**	20
Otto	**G Vill**	23
Oyster Bar	**E 40s**	22
Pacificana	**Sunset Pk**	23
Palm	**multi.**	24
Pastis	**Meatpacking**	22
Peking Duck	**multi.**	22
Peter Luger	**W'burg**	27
Public	**NoLita**	23
Quality Meats	**W 50s**	26
Redeye Grill	**W 50s**	21
Red Rooster	**Harlem**	22
Republic	**Union Sq**	19
Rosa Mexicano	**multi.**	22
Ruby Foo's	**W 40s**	18
Sahara	**Gravesend**	22
Sambuca	**W 70s**	19
Sammy's Roumanian	**LES**	20
Sik Gaek	**multi.**	22
Smith/Wollensky	**E 40s**	23
Sparks	**E 40s**	25
Spice Market	**Meatpacking**	23

Visit zagat.com

Standard Grill | **Meatpacking**	22
Stanton Social | **LES**	24
Tamarind | **multi.**	26
Tanoreen | **Bay Ridge**	26
Tao | **E 50s**	24
Tony's Di Napoli | **W 40s**	22
Tribeca Grill | **TriBeCa**	22
Victor's Cafe | **W 50s**	22
Wildwood BBQ | **Flatiron**	19
Wolfgang's | **multi.**	25
Zengo | **E 40s**	22

HIPSTER

Allswell | **W'burg**	23
NEW Aska | **W'burg**	23
BaoHaus | **E Vill**	23
Breslin | **Chelsea**	23
NEW BrisketTown | **W'burg**	25
Café Habana/Outpost | **NoLita**	23
NEW Charlie Bird | **SoHo**	-
Crif Dogs | **multi.**	23
Diner | **W'burg**	24
Do or Dine | **Bed-Stuy**	25
Egg | **W'burg**	24
Fatty 'Cue | **multi.**	22
Fette Sau | **W'burg**	26
Five Leaves | **Greenpt**	26
NEW Fritzl's Lunch | **Bushwick**	-
General Greene | **Ft Greene**	20
Hecho en Dumbo | **NoHo**	23
NEW Jeepney | **E Vill**	23
NEW King Noodle | **Bushwick**	-
La Superior | **W'burg**	25
Littleneck | **Gowanus**	24
NEW Luksus | **Greenpt**	-
Marlow/Sons | **W'burg**	24
Mile End | **multi.**	23
Mission Chinese | **LES**	23
Momo Sushi Shack | **Bushwick**	27
Motorino | **E Vill**	25
Nom Wah Tea | **Chinatown**	21
No. 7 | **multi.**	22
Pok Pok Ny | **Red Hook**	24
Roberta's | **Bushwick**	26
Smile | **multi.**	21
St. Anselm | **W'burg**	27
Vinegar Hill Hse. | **Vinegar Hill**	24
Walter | **multi.**	23
NEW Xixa | **W'burg**	-

HISTORIC PLACES

(Year opened; * building)

1763 | Fraunces Tavern* | **Financial**	18
1787 | One if by Land* | **W Vill**	24
1863 | City Hall* | **TriBeCa**	22
1868 | Landmark Tavern* | **W 40s**	18
1870 | Kings' Carriage* | **E 80s**	21
1884 | P.J. Clarke's | **E 50s**	17
1885 | Keens | **Garment**	26
1887 | Peter Luger | **W'burg**	27
1888 | Katz's Deli | **LES**	24
1892 | Ferrara | **L Italy**	23
1896 | Rao's | **Harlem**	22
1900 | Bamonte's | **W'burg**	22
1902 | Angelo's/Mulberry | **L Italy**	23
1904 | Vincent's | **L Italy**	22
1905 | Morgan* | **Murray Hill**	19
1906 | Barbetta | **W 40s**	22
1906 | Monte's | **Gowanus**	20
1907 | Gargiulo's | **Coney Is**	22
1908 | Barney Greengrass | **W 80s**	24
1908 | John's/12th St. | **E Vill**	22
1910 | Wolfgang's* | **Murray Hill**	25
1911 | Commerce* | **W Vill**	23
1913 | Oyster Bar | **E 40s**	22
1917 | Leopard/des Artistes* | **W 60s**	21
1919 | Mario's | **Fordham**	22
1920 | Leo's Latticini/Corona | **Corona**	26
1920 | Nom Wah Tea | **Chinatown**	21
1920 | Sea Shore | **City Is**	21
1920 | Waverly Inn | **W Vill**	21
1921 | Sardi's | **W 40s**	18
1922 | Defonte's | **Red Hook**	24
1922 | Sanford's | **Astoria**	22
1924 | Totonno Pizza | **Coney Is**	25
1926 | Frankie & Johnnie's | **W 40s**	22
1926 | Palm | **E 40s**	24
1927 | Ann & Tony's | **Fordham**	21
1927 | Russian Tea | **W 50s**	20
1929 | Eisenberg's | **Flatiron**	18
1929 | John's Pizzeria | **W Vill**	22
1929 | 21 Club | **W 50s**	23
1930 | Carlyle | **E 70s**	23
1930 | El Quijote | **Chelsea**	21

SPECIAL FEATURES

1932 | Papaya King | **E 80s**	21
1932 | Pietro's | **E 40s**	24
1933 | Patsy's | **Harlem**	20
1936 | Heidelberg | **E 80s**	20
1936 | Monkey Bar* | **E 50s**	20
1936 | Tom's | **Prospect Hts**	21
1937 | Carnegie Deli | **W 50s**	22
1937 | Denino | **Port Richmond**	26
1937 | Le Veau d'Or | **E 60s**	19
1937 | Minetta Tavern* | **G Vill**	24
1938 | Wo Hop | **Chinatown**	22
1939 | L&B Spumoni | **Bensonhurst**	24
1941 | Sevilla | **W Vill**	23
1942 | B & H Dairy | **E Vill**	22
1942 | Lobster Box | **City Is**	20
1943 | Forlini's | **Chinatown**	19
1944 | Patsy's | **W 50s**	22
1945 | Ben's Best | **Rego Pk**	23
1950 | Junior's | **Downtown Bklyn**	19
1950 | Paul & Jimmy's | **Gramercy**	20
1953 | King Yum | **Fresh Meadows**	20
1953 | Liebman's Deli | **Riverdale**	23
1953 | Vesuvio | **Bay Ridge**	20
1954 | Serendipity 3 | **E 60s**	20
1954 | Veselka | **E Vill**	20
1957 | Arturo's | **G Vill**	23
1957 | La Taza de Oro | **Chelsea**	22
1958 | Queen | **Bklyn Hts**	24
1959 | Brasserie | **E 50s**	22
1959 | El Parador | **Murray Hill**	23
1959 | Four Seasons | **E 50s**	27
1959 | London Lennie | **Rego Pk**	23
1959 | Rizzo's Pizza | **Astoria**	23
1960 | Bull & Bear | **E 40s**	22
1960 | Chez Napoléon | **W 50s**	22
1960 | Joe & Pat's | **Castleton Corners**	23
1960 | Molly's | **Gramercy**	22
1961 | Corner Bistro | **W Vill**	22
1962 | La Grenouille | **E 50s**	28
1962 | Sylvia's | **Harlem**	20
1963 | Joe Allen | **W 40s**	19
1963 | Victor's Cafe | **W 50s**	22
1964 | Di Fara | **Midwood**	26
1964 | Le Perigord | **E 50s**	25

HOTEL DINING

Ace Hotel	
Breslin | **Chelsea**	23
John Dory Oyster Bar | **Chelsea**	24
No. 7 | **Chelsea**	22
Affinia Shelburne Hotel	
Rare B&G | **Murray Hill**	21
Americano Hotel	
Americano | **Chelsea**	22
Amsterdam Court Hotel	
Natsumi | **W 50s**	24
Andaz Wall St. Hotel	
Wall/Water | **Financial**	21
Benjamin Hotel	
National | **E 50s**	20
Blakely Hotel	
Abboccato | **W 50s**	21
Bowery Hotel	
Gemma | **E Vill**	21
Bryant Park Hotel	
Koi | **W 40s**	24
Carlton Hotel	
Millesime | **Murray Hill**	19
Carlyle Hotel	
Carlyle | **E 70s**	23
Casablanca Hotel	
Tony's Di Napoli | **W 40s**	22
Chambers Hotel	
Má Pêche | **W 50s**	23
Chatwal Hotel	
Lambs Club | **W 40s**	22
City Club Hotel	
db Bistro Moderne | **W 40s**	25
Club Quarters WTC	
Morton's | **Financial**	22
Dream Downtown Hotel	
NEW Cherry | **Chelsea**	-
Marble Lane | **Chelsea**	21
Dream Hotel	
Serafina | **W 50s**	18
Duane Street Hotel	
Mehtaphor | **TriBeCa**	24
Dylan Hotel	
Benjamin Steak | **E 40s**	25
Elysée Hotel	
Monkey Bar | **E 50s**	20
Empire Hotel	
Ed's Chowder | **W 60s**	20

SPECIAL FEATURES

Thompson LES Hotel	
Blue Ribbon/Izakaya	**LES**	21
Time Hotel	
Serafina	**W 40s**	18
Trump Int'l Hotel	
Jean Georges	**W 60s**	28
Jean-Georges' Noug.	**W 60s**	27
Trump SoHo Hotel	
Koi	**SoHo**	24
Waldorf-Astoria	
Bull & Bear	**E 40s**	22
Wales Hotel	
Paola's	**E 90s**	23
Washington Sq. Hotel	
North Sq.	**G Vill**	23
Westin New York Grand Central	
NEW LCL	**E 40s**	⎤
Westin NY Times Square Hotel	
Shula's	**W 40s**	21
W Hotel Downtown	
BLT B&G	**Financial**	22
W Hotel Times Sq.	
Blue Fin	**W 40s**	23
W Hotel Union Sq.	
Olives	**Union Sq**	22
Wyndham Garden Hotel	
NEW Tre Stelle	**Flatiron**	⎤
Wythe Hotel	
Reynard	**W'burg**	23

HOT SPOTS

NEW ABC Cocina	**Flatiron**	⎤
NEW Alder	**E Vill**	20
NEW Antica Pesa	**W'burg**	23
NEW Arlington Club	**E 70s**	21
NEW Aska	**W'burg**	23
Bagatelle	**Meatpacking**	20
Beauty & Essex	**LES**	22
NEW Butterfly	**TriBeCa**	⎤
NEW Carbone	**G Vill**	21
Catch	**Meatpacking**	23
NEW Charlie Bird	**SoHo**	⎤
Corner Social	**Harlem**	17
DBGB	**E Vill**	24
Dutch	**SoHo**	23
NEW Elm	**W'burg**	⎤
NEW El Toro Blanco	**W Vill**	22
NEW General	**LES**	20
NEW Harlow	**E 50s**	19
Hudson Clearwater	**W Vill**	23

Hurricane	**Flatiron**	21
NEW Lafayette	**NoHo**	19
NEW L'Apicio	**E Vill**	22
Lavo	**E 50s**	21
NEW Le Philosophe	**NoHo**	24
NEW Luksus	**Greenpt**	⎤
NEW Manon	**Meatpacking**	⎤
NEW Marrow	**W Vill**	23
NEW Maysville	**Flatiron**	22
Minetta Tavern	**G Vill**	24
Mission Chinese	**LES**	23
Miss Lily's	**G Vill**	21
NEW Montmartre	**Chelsea**	19
NEW Murray's Cheese	**W Vill**	24
NoMad	**Chelsea**	27
NEW Pearl & Ash	**NoLita**	⎤
Penrose	**E 80s**	20
Perla	**G Vill**	24
Pok Pok Ny	**Red Hook**	24
Pulqueria	**Chinatown**	20
Red Rooster	**Harlem**	22
Reynard	**W'burg**	23
Rosemary's	**W Vill**	21
Rubirosa	**NoLita**	23
NEW Salvation Taco	**Murray Hill**	22
Saxon & Parole	**NoHo**	22
Smith	**multi.**	19
Standard Grill	**Meatpacking**	22
NEW Umami Burger	**G Vill**	⎤
NEW Uncle Boons	**NoLita**	⎤
NEW Willow Road	**Chelsea**	23

JACKET REQUIRED

Carlyle	**E 70s**	23
Daniel	**E 60s**	28
Four Seasons	**E 50s**	27
Jean Georges	**W 60s**	28
La Grenouille	**E 50s**	28
Le Bernardin	**W 50s**	29
Le Cirque	**E 50s**	25
Le Perigord	**E 50s**	25
Per Se	**W 60s**	28
River Café	**Dumbo**	26
21 Club	**W 50s**	23

LATE DINING

(Weekday closing hour)

NEW Aamanns-Copenhagen		20
varies	**TriBeCa**	
Aburiya Kinnosuke	12 AM		26
E 40s	

ABV | varies | **E 90s** 20

Adrienne's | 12 AM | **Financial** 23

NEW Alameda | 2 AM | **Greenpt** –

Alison Eighteen | 2 AM | **Flatiron** 21

Allswell | varies | **W'burg** 23

Añejo Tequileria | varies | **W 40s** 22

NEW Angolo SoHo | varies | **SoHo** 24

A.O.C. | varies | **W Vill** 20

Arirang Korean | 12 AM | **Garment** 22

Artichoke Basille | varies | **multi.** 22

Arturo's | 1 AM | **G Vill** 23

NEW Atrium Dumbo | varies | **Dumbo** –

Avra | 12 AM | **E 40s** 25

Ayza Wine | varies | **multi.** 20

Bagatelle | varies | **Meatpacking** 20

Bahari Estiatorio | 12 AM | **Astoria** 24

Balthazar | 1 AM | **SoHo** 24

B&B Winepub | varies | **SoHo** 22

BaoHaus | varies | **E Vill** 23

Baraonda | 1 AM | **E 70s** 19

Barbès | 12 AM | **Murray Hill** 20

Barbetta | 12 AM | **W 40s** 22

Bar Italia | varies | **E 60s** 19

Bar Jamón | 2 AM | **Gramercy** 23

Bar Pitti | 12 AM | **G Vill** 23

NEW Barraca | varies | **W Vill** 15

Barrio Chino | 1 AM | **LES** 24

Beaumarchais | varies | **Meatpacking** 22

Beauty & Essex | 1 AM | **LES** 22

Becco | 12 AM | **W 40s** 22

Beco | varies | **W'burg** 23

Bell Book/Candle | varies | **W Vill** 20

Best Pizza | 12 AM | **W'burg** 24

Bice | 12 AM | **E 50s** 21

Bill's Bar | 12 AM | **multi.** 19

Bistro Les Amis | varies | **SoHo** 22

Black Iron Burger | varies | **E Vill** 21

BLT B&G | 1 AM | **Financial** 22

Blue Fin | varies | **W 40s** 23

Blue 9 Burger | varies | **E Vill** 19

Blue Ribbon | varies | **multi.** 25

Blue Ribbon Bakery | varies | **W Vill** 24

NEW Blue Ribbon Fried Chicken | 2 AM | **E Vill** –

Blue Ribbon Sushi | varies | **SoHo** 26

Blue Ribbon Sushi B&G | 2 AM | **W 50s** 25

Blue Ribbon/Izakaya | 2 AM | **LES** 21

Bocca/Bacco | varies | **multi.** 21

Bocca Lupo | varies | **Cobble Hill** 23

Bohemian | 1 AM | **NoHo** 25

Bombay Palace | 12 AM | **W 50s** 20

BonChon | varies | **multi.** 21

Bond St | varies | **NoHo** 25

Boukiés | varies | **E Vill** 23

Braai | varies | **W 50s** 20

Brasserie Cognac | 12 AM | **W 50s** 19

Bread | varies | **NoLita** 21

Brennan | 1 AM | **Sheepshead** 22

Breslin | 12 AM | **Chelsea** 23

Brother Jimmy's | varies | **multi.** 17

Bubby's | 24 hrs. | **TriBeCa** 20

Buddakan | 12 AM | **Chelsea** 25

Buenos Aires | varies | **E Vill** 24

Bull & Bear | 12 AM | **E 40s** 22

NEW Butterfly | varies | **TriBeCa** –

Buvette | 2 AM | **W Vill** 24

BXL | 4 AM | **Flatiron** 19

Cafe Cluny | 12 AM | **W Vill** 22

Cafe Espanol | varies | **multi.** 20

Cafe Fiorello | 1 AM | **W 60s** 20

Cafe Gitane | varies | **multi.** 21

Café Habana/Outpost | 12 AM | **multi.** 23

Café Henri | 12 AM | **multi.** 20

Cafe Lalo | 2 AM | **W 80s** 20

Cafe Loup | varies | **W Vill** 19

Cafe Luluc | 12 AM | **Cobble Hill** 21

Cafe Mogador | varies | **multi.** 23

Cafe Noir | 2 AM | **SoHo** 20

Cafe Orlin | 1:30 AM | **E Vill** 22

Cafeteria | 24 hrs. | **Chelsea** 21

Calexico | varies | **multi.** 21

Camaje | 12 AM | **G Vill** 20

Campagnola | 12 AM | **E 70s** 23

Carmine's | 12 AM | **W 40s** 21

Carnegie Deli | 3:30 AM | **W 50s** 22

Casa Enrique | 12 AM | **LIC** 24

Listing	Rating
Casa Mono | 12 AM | **Gramercy**	25
Cascabel Taqueria | 12 AM | **multi.**	21
NEW Cata | 12 AM | **LES**	-
Cávo | 2 AM | **Astoria**	21
Cebu | 3 AM | **Bay Ridge**	20
Cercle Rouge | varies | **TriBeCa**	19
Chai Home | varies | **W'burg**	22
Char No. 4 | 1 AM | **Cobble Hill**	22
Château Cherbuliez | 2 AM | **Flatiron**	-
NEW Cherry | 12 AM | **Chelsea**	-
Chez Josephine | 1 AM | **W 40s**	20
Chez Oskar | 12 AM | **Ft Greene**	20
ChikaLicious | 12 AM | **E Vill**	25
Chimichurri Grill | varies | **W 40s**	23
Churrascaria | 12 AM | **multi.**	23
Cilantro | 12 AM | **multi.**	19
Cipriani D'twn | 12 AM | **SoHo**	23
NEW Clarkson | 1:30 AM | **W Vill**	20
NEW Cleveland | 12 AM | **NoLita**	-
NEW Cocotte | 12 AM | **SoHo**	-
Coffee Shop | varies | **Union Sq**	17
Colonie | varies | **Bklyn Hts**	25
Congee | varies | **LES**	20
Coppelia | 24 hrs. | **Chelsea**	23
Coppola's | 12 AM | **Murray Hill**	21
Corkbuzz | varies | **G Vill**	22
Corner Bistro | varies | **multi.**	22
Corner Social | 2 AM | **Harlem**	17
Corsino | 2 AM | **W Vill**	21
Courgette | 12 AM | **W 50s**	26
Covo | 12 AM | **Harlem**	23
Crab Shanty | varies | **City Is**	23
Creperie | 4 AM | **multi.**	22
Crif Dogs | varies | **multi.**	23
Danji | varies | **W 50s**	25
Da Silvano | varies | **G Vill**	22
DBGB | varies | **E Vill**	24
Del Frisco's | 12 AM | **W 40s**	25
Delicatessen | 1 AM | **NoLita**	19
Dell'anima | 2 AM | **W Vill**	25
Delta Grill | 12 AM | **W 40s**	20
Diner | 12 AM | **W'burg**	24
NEW Distilled | 12 AM | **TriBeCa**	-
Don Giovanni | varies | **multi.**	20
Donovan's | varies | **Woodside**	20
Due | varies | **E 70s**	21
DuMont | 2 AM | **W'burg**	23
Eatery | varies | **W 50s**	21
Edi & The Wolf | 12 AM | **E Vill**	23
El Centro | varies | **W 50s**	21
Elias Corner | 12 AM | **Astoria**	23
Elio's | varies | **E 80s**	24
NEW Ellington | varies | **W 100s**	-
El Quijote | varies | **Chelsea**	21
El Quinto Pino | varies | **Chelsea**	25
Empanada Mama | varies | **multi.**	23
Enzo's | 12 AM | **Morris Park**	23
NEW Estela | varies | **NoLita**	-
NEW Exchange Alley | varies | **E Vill**	-
Extra Fancy | 4 AM | **W'burg**	20
Fat Radish | 12 AM | **LES**	24
Fatty 'Cue | varies | **W'burg**	22
Fedora | varies | **W Vill**	23
Ferrara | varies | **L Italy**	23
Fette Sau | varies | **W'burg**	26
Five Leaves | 12 AM | **Greenpt**	26
5 Napkin Burger | 12 AM | **multi.**	21
508 | 12 AM | **Hudson Square**	22
Flatbush Farm | 1 AM | **Park Slope**	21
Flor/Mayo | 12 AM | **multi.**	21
Forcella | 12 AM | **Murray Hill**	22
Forlini's | 12 AM | **Chinatown**	19
NEW Fourth | 12 AM | **E Vill**	-
Frank | 1 AM | **E Vill**	23
Frankies | varies | **W Vill**	23
Fraunces Tavern | 1 AM | **Financial**	18
Fuleen Seafood | 2:30 AM | **Chinatown**	22
Gahm Mi Oak | 24 hrs. | **Garment**	20
NEW Gaonnuri | 12 AM | **Garment**	21
Gemma | varies | **E Vill**	21
Glass House | 12 AM | **W 40s**	19
Gordon Ramsay | 12 AM | **W 50s**	23
Gottino | 2 AM | **W Vill**	20
Gran Electrica | 12 AM | **Dumbo**	22
NEW Grape & Vine | 2 AM | **G Vill**	-
Gray's Papaya | 24 hrs. | **multi.**	20

Great Jones Cafe | varies | **NoHo** | 21

Great NY Noodle | 4 AM | **Chinatown** | 23

Guantanamera | varies | **W 50s** | 20

NEW Hanjan | 1 AM | **Flatiron** | 22

NEW Harlow | 1 AM | **E 50s** | 19

Harry Cipriani | 12 AM | **E 50s** | 22

Harry's Cafe | 12 AM | **Financial** | 22

Harry's Italian | varies | **Financial** | 21

Haru | 12 AM | **multi.** | 21

Havana Central | varies | **W 40s** | 19

Haveli | 12 AM | **E Vill** | 21

Hecho en Dumbo | varies | **NoHo** | 23

Henry Public | 1 AM | **Cobble Hill** | 20

Henry's | 4 AM | **W 100s** | 20

NEW Hill & Dale | varies | **LES** | -

Hop Kee | varies | **Chinatown** | 21

Hudson Clearwater | 12 AM | **W Vill** | 23

Hummus Kitchen | 12 AM | **W 50s** | 20

'Inoteca | 3 AM | **LES** | 21

Isola | varies | **SoHo** | -

Jackson Hole | varies | **multi.** | 19

Jack's Wife Freda | 12 AM | **SoHo** | 19

Jacob's Pickles | varies | **W 80s** | 20

J.G. Melon | 2:30 AM | **E 70s** | 21

Joe's Pizza | varies | **multi.** | 23

John Dory Oyster Bar | 12 AM | **Chelsea** | 24

Jones Wood Foundry | varies | **E 70s** | 21

Joseph Leonard | 2 AM | **W Vill** | 24

Junior's | varies | **multi.** | 19

Kang Suh | 24 hrs. | **Garment** | 22

Kashkaval | 4 AM | **W 50s** | 22

Kati Roll Company | varies | **G Vill** | 22

Kellari | 12 AM | **W 40s** | 22

NEW King Noodle | varies | **Bushwick** | -

Knickerbocker | 1 AM | **G Vill** | 20

Kum Gang San | 24 hrs. | **multi.** | 21

Kunjip | 24 hrs. | **Garment** | 22

Kyochon | varies | **multi.** | 20

La Esquina | 2 AM | **L Italy** | 23

La Lanterna | 3 AM | **G Vill** | 20

La Masseria | 12 AM | **W 40s** | 23

La Mela | 2 AM | **L Italy** | 21

Landbrot | varies | **multi.** | 20

Landmarc | 2 AM | **W 60s** | 21

Landmark Tavern | varies | **W 40s** | 18

La Palapa | 12 AM | **E Vill** | 22

NEW La Pulperia | varies | **W 40s** | -

Las Ramblas | 1 AM | **W Vill** | 23

La Superior | varies | **W'burg** | 25

Lavo | 1 AM | **E 50s** | 21

NEW LCL | varies | **E 40s** | -

Le Grainne Cafe | 12 AM | **Chelsea** | 20

NEW Le Philosophe | 1:30 AM | **NoHo** | 24

Les Halles | 12 AM | **multi.** | 20

NEW Library/Public | varies | **E Vill** | 18

Lil' Frankie | 2 AM | **E Vill** | 24

Shorty's | varies | **multi.** | 22

Lion | varies | **G Vill** | 21

Lobster Box | varies | **City Is** | 20

Lucien | 1 AM | **E Vill** | 23

Lucky's Famous | varies | **multi.** | 20

Macao Trading | 4 AM | **TriBeCa** | 20

Macelleria | 12 AM | **Meatpacking** | 21

Macondo | varies | **LES** | 22

Mad Dog | 2 AM | **Financial** | 19

Madiba | varies | **Ft Greene** | 23

Madison's | 2 AM | **Riverdale** | 20

Maggie Brown | 12 AM | **Clinton Hill** | 23

Maialino | 12:30 PM | **Gramercy** | 26

NEW Maison O | 12 AM | **L Italy** | -

Malecon | varies | **multi.** | 21

Mama Joy's | 1 AM | **Bushwick** | -

Mamajuana/Taina | varies | **multi.** | 21

Mamoun's | varies | **multi.** | 23

NEW Manon | varies | **Meatpacking** | -

Maoz | varies | **multi.** | 21

Marble Lane | varies | **Chelsea** | 21

Marcony | 12:30 PM | **Murray Hill** | 25

Mari Vanna | 1 AM | **Flatiron** | 21

Mark | 1 AM | **E 70s** | 22

Marlow/Sons | 12 AM | **W'burg** | 24

Maruzzella | varies | **E 70s** | 20

Max SoHa/Caffe | 12 AM | **W 100s** | 23

Meatball Shop | varies | **multi.** 24

Mémé | 12 AM | **W Vill** 22

Mercadito | varies | **multi.** 24

Mercato | 1 AM | **Garment** 21

Mercer Kitchen | varies | **SoHo** 23

MexiBBQ | varies | **Astoria** 21

Michael Jordan | 12 AM | **E 40s** 21

Minetta Tavern | 2 AM | **G Vill** 24

Misdemeanor | 12 AM | **Downtown Bklyn** -

Mission Chinese | 12 AM | **LES** 23

Miss Korea | 24 hrs. | **Garment** 22

Mojave | varies | **Astoria** 22

Molly's | 12 AM | **Gramercy** 22

Momofuku Ko | 1 AM | **E Vill** 27

Momofuku Ssäm | 2 AM | **E Vill** 25

Monkey Bar | 12 AM | **E 50s** 20

Mont Blanc | varies | **W 40s** 23

Motorino | varies | **multi.** 25

Moustache | 12 AM | **multi.** 23

NEW MP Taverna | varies | **Astoria** -

NEW Murray's Cheese | 1 AM | **W Vill** 24

NEW Musket Room | varies | **NoLita** -

National | 1 AM | **E 50s** 20

Natsumi | 11:30 PM | **W 50s** 24

Neary's | 1 AM | **E 50s** 17

New WonJo | 24 hrs. | **Garment** 22

NEW NY Sushi Ko | varies | **LES** -

Ngam | 12 AM | **E Vill** 22

Nice Matin | 12 AM | **W 70s** 19

Nicola's | 12 AM | **E 80s** 21

Nicoletta | 3 AM | **E Vill** 19

99 Mi. to Philly | 1 AM | **E Vill** 21

Nizza | 2 AM | **W 40s** 19

No. 7 | 12 AM | **Ft Greene** 22

Numero 28 | 12 AM | **E Vill** 24

Oaxaca | varies | **multi.** 21

Omen A Zen | 1 AM | **SoHo** 25

Omonia | 4 AM | **multi.** 20

Pachanga Patterson | varies | **Astoria** 23

Papaya King | varies | **multi.** 21

Park | 1 AM | **Chelsea** 17

Pastis | varies | **Meatpacking** 22

NEW Pearl & Ash | 12 AM | **NoLita** -

Penrose | 4 AM | **E 80s** 20

Perbacco | 1 AM | **E Vill** 23

Perla | varies | **G Vill** 24

Per Lei | 12 AM | **E 70s** 20

Philippe | 12 AM | **E 60s** 23

Pies-N-Thighs | 12 AM | **W'burg** 24

Pig and Khao | 12 AM | **LES** 23

Pio Pio | 12 AM | **Jackson Hts** 23

Piper's Kilt | 12:30 AM | **multi.** 21

P.J. Clarke's | varies | **multi.** 17

Pok Pok Phat Thai | varies | **LES** -

Pommes Frites | varies | **E Vill** 24

Ponty Bistro | 12 AM | **Gramercy** 22

Pranna | varies | **Murray Hill** 18

NEW Preserve 24 | 2 AM | **LES** -

Press 195 | 12 AM | **Bayside** 24

Prime Meat | 2 AM | **Carroll Gdns** 23

Primola | 12 AM | **E 60s** 23

Pulino's | 2 AM | **NoLita** 20

Pulqueria | 2 AM | **Chinatown** 20

NEW Quality Italian | 12 AM | **W 50s** -

Queens Kickshaw | 1 AM | **Astoria** 23

Rai Rai Ken | 2:30 AM | **E Vill** 20

Raoul's | 1 AM | **SoHo** 25

Redhead | 1 AM | **E Vill** 22

Reynard | 12 AM | **W'burg** 23

Rice 'n' Beans | 12 AM | **W 50s** 21

Riposo | varies | **multi.** 21

Riverview | 12 AM | **LIC** 21

Rizzo's Pizza | varies | **LES** 23

Roberta's | 12 AM | **Bushwick** 26

Roll-n-Roaster | 1 AM | **Sheepshead** 22

Rosemary's | 12 AM | **W Vill** 21

Rucola | 12 AM | **Boerum Hill** 24

Rue 57 | 12 AM | **W 50s** 19

Russian Samovar | 2 AM | **W 50s** 20

Sahara | 2 AM | **Gravesend** 22

Sakagura | varies | **E 40s** 25

NEW SakaMai | 12 AM | **LES** -

NEW Salvation Taco | varies | **Murray Hill** 22

Sammy's Fishbox | 2 AM | **City Is** 21

Sammy's Shrimp | varies | **City Is** 23

Sanford's | 24 hrs. | **Astoria** 22

Sauce | 2 AM | **LES** 26

Schiller's | 1 AM | **LES** 19

MEET FOR A DRINK

SPECIAL FEATURES

Atlantic Grill | **multi.**	22
NEW Atrium Dumbo | **Dumbo**	–
Aurora | **W'burg**	23
Back Forty | **SoHo**	22
Bar Boulud | **W 60s**	24
Barbounia | **Flatiron**	21
NEW Betony | **W 50s**	–
Bill's Food & Drink | **E 50s**	18
Blue Fin | **W 40s**	23
Blue Water | **Union Sq**	24
Bond St | **NoHo**	25
Boqueria | **Flatiron**	23
Brick Cafe | **Astoria**	21
Bryant Park Grill/Cafe | **W 40s**	19
Buddakan | **Chelsea**	25
Bull & Bear | **E 40s**	22
NEW Butterfly | **TriBeCa**	–
Cafe Luxembourg | **W 70s**	21
Cafe Steinhof | **Park Slope**	18
Casa Lever | **E 50s**	23
Catch | **Meatpacking**	23
Char No. 4 | **Cobble Hill**	22
City Hall | **TriBeCa**	22
Colicchio/Sons | **Chelsea**	25
Corner Social | **Harlem**	17
Crown | **E 80s**	21
Daniel | **E 60s**	28
DBGB | **E Vill**	24
Del Frisco's | **W 40s**	25
Dos Caminos | **multi.**	20
Dutch | **SoHo**	23
NEW El Toro Blanco | **W Vill**	22
NEW Estela | **NoLita**	–
Flatbush Farm | **Park Slope**	21
Four Seasons | **E 50s**	27
Freemans | **LES**	22
Glass House | **W 40s**	19
Gotham B&G | **G Vill**	27
Gramercy Tavern | **Flatiron**	28
Gran Electrica | **Dumbo**	22
NEW Harlow | **E 50s**	19
Harry's Cafe | **Financial**	22
Henry's | **W 100s**	20
Hillstone | **multi.**	23
House | **Gramercy**	21
Hudson River | **Harlem**	20
Jean Georges | **W 60s**	28
J.G. Melon | **E 70s**	21
Keens | **Garment**	26
Kellari | **W 40s**	22
Koi | **W 40s**	24
La Fonda/Sol | **E 40s**	22
Lambs Club | **W 40s**	22
Landmarc | **W 60s**	21
Lavo | **E 50s**	21
Le Cirque | **E 50s**	25
Le Colonial | **E 50s**	21
NEW Library/Public | **E Vill**	18
Lincoln | **W 60s**	24
Macao Trading | **TriBeCa**	20
Mad Dog | **Financial**	19
Maialino | **Gramercy**	26
Maloney/Porcelli | **E 50s**	23
NEW Manon | **Meatpacking**	–
Mari Vanna | **Flatiron**	21
Mark | **E 70s**	22
Markt | **Flatiron**	20
Masa/Bar Masa | **W 60s**	27
NEW Maysville | **Flatiron**	22
Maze | **W 50s**	24
Michael Jordan | **E 40s**	21
Minetta Tavern | **G Vill**	24
Modern | **W 50s**	26
Monkey Bar | **E 50s**	20
Morimoto | **Chelsea**	26
Natsumi | **W 50s**	24
Nobu | **W 50s**	27
NoMad | **Chelsea**	27
North End Grill | **Financial**	24
Odeon | **TriBeCa**	19
Orsay | **E 70s**	18
Ouest | **W 80s**	24
Park | **Chelsea**	17
Pastis | **Meatpacking**	22
Penrose | **E 80s**	20
Pies-N-Thighs | **W'burg**	24
P.J. Clarke's | **multi.**	17
Pulqueria | **Chinatown**	20
NEW Quality Italian | **W 50s**	–
Rayuela | **LES**	23
Red Rooster | **Harlem**	22
Reynard | **W'burg**	23
Roberta's | **Bushwick**	26
Rucola | **Boerum Hill**	24
Saxon & Parole | **NoHo**	22
SD26 | **Murray Hill**	25
NEW Sirio | **E 60s**	22
South Gate | **W 50s**	21

Spice Market | **Meatpacking**	23
Standard Grill | **Meatpacking**	22
St. Andrews | **W 40s**	19
Stanton Social | **LES**	24
STK | **Meatpacking**	23
Stone Park | **Park Slope**	24
Tao | **E 50s**	24
21 Club | **W 50s**	23
Wollensky's | **E 40s**	23
Zengo | **E 40s**	22

NEWCOMERS

Aamanns-Copenhagen | **TriBeCa**	20
ABC Cocina | **Flatiron**	-
Alameda | **Greenpt**	-
Alchemy, TX | **Jackson Hts**	-
Alder | **E Vill**	20
Amsterdam Burger | **W 90s**	25
Anassa Taverna | **E 60s**	-
Andanada 141 | **W 60s**	21
Angolo SoHo | **SoHo**	24
Antica Pesa | **W'burg**	23
Arlington Club | **E 70s**	21
Aska | **W'burg**	23
Atrium Dumbo | **Dumbo**	-
Barraca | **W Vill**	15
Beatrice Inn | **W Vill**	17
Betony | **W 50s**	-
Blue Ribbon Fried Chicken | **E Vill**	-
BrisketTown | **W'burg**	25
Bunker Vietnamese | **Ridgewood**	-
Butcher's Daughter | **NoLita**	-
Butterfly | **TriBeCa**	-
Cantine Paris. | **Financial**	-
Carbone | **G Vill**	21
Casa Pomona | **W 80s**	-
Cata | **LES**	-
Charlie Bird | **SoHo**	-
Cherry | **Chelsea**	-
Chez Sardine | **W Vill**	20
Clarke's Standard | **multi.**	20
Clarkson | **W Vill**	20
Cleveland | **NoLita**	-
Cocina Economica | **W 80s**	22
Cocotte | **SoHo**	-
Cole's | **W Vill**	21
Corvo Bianco | **W 80s**	-
Costata | **SoHo**	-

Cull & Pistol | **Chelsea**	-
Distilled | **TriBeCa**	-
Ellington | **W 100s**	-
Elm | **W'burg**	-
El Toro Blanco | **W Vill**	22
Estela | **NoLita**	-
Exchange Alley | **E Vill**	-
Fletcher's | **Gowanus**	22
Flor de Sol | **Chelsea**	-
Fourth | **E Vill**	-
Fritzl's Lunch | **Bushwick**	-
Ganso | **Downtown Bklyn**	22
Gaonnuri | **Garment**	21
General | **LES**	20
Grape & Vine | **G Vill**	-
Guy's American | **W 40s**	17
Hanjan | **Flatiron**	22
Harding's | **Flatiron**	-
Harlem Shake | **Harlem**	-
Harlow | **E 50s**	19
Hill & Dale | **LES**	-
Hybird | **Chelsea**	-
Jeepney | **E Vill**	23
Juliana's | **Dumbo**	27
Khe-Yo | **TriBeCa**	-
King Noodle | **Bushwick**	-
Lafayette | **NoHo**	19
L & W Oyster | **Chelsea**	20
L'Apicio | **E Vill**	22
La Pulperia | **W 40s**	-
La Slowteria | **Carroll Gdns**	-
LCL | **E 40s**	-
Le Philosophe | **NoHo**	24
Library/Public | **E Vill**	18
Louro | **W Vill**	21
Luksus | **Greenpt**	-
Maison O | **L Italy**	-
Manon | **Meatpacking**	-
Manzanilla | **Murray Hill**	23
Marrow | **W Vill**	23
Maysville | **Flatiron**	22
Meli | **Murray Hill**	-
Mighty Quinn's | **E Vill**	24
Mira Sushi | **Flatiron**	28
Montmartre | **Chelsea**	19
MP Taverna | **Astoria**	-
Murray's Cheese | **W Vill**	24
Musket Room | **NoLita**	-
M. Wells Dinette | **LIC**	27

NOTEWORTHY CLOSINGS (42)

OUTDOOR DINING

Flatbush Farm	**Park Slope**	21
44 & X/44½	**W 40s**	22
Frankies	**Carroll Gdns**	23
Gigino	**Financial**	21
Gnocco	**E Vill**	22
Gran Electrica	**Dumbo**	22
Grocery	**Carroll Gdns**	27
Home	**W Vill**	22
Isabella's	**W 70s**	20
Juventino	**Park Slope**	25
La Bottega	**Chelsea**	21
La Lanterna	**G Vill**	20
La Mangeoire	**E 50s**	22
L&B Spumoni	**Bensonhurst**	24
New Leaf	**Wash. Hts**	21
NEW Pines	**Gowanus**	23
Portofino	**City Is**	22
Pure Food/Wine	**Gramercy**	24
Roberta's	**Bushwick**	26
Salinas	**Chelsea**	22
San Pietro	**E 50s**	24
Sripraphai	**Woodside**	27
Tartine	**W Vill**	22
Trestle on 10th	**Chelsea**	22
ViceVersa	**W 50s**	22
Vinegar Hill Hse.	**Vinegar Hill**	24
Water Club	**Murray Hill**	22
Water's Edge	**LIC**	22

PEOPLE-WATCHING

Acme	**NoHo**	22
Amaranth	**E 60s**	21
NEW Antica Pesa	**W'burg**	23
Bagatelle	**Meatpacking**	20
Balthazar	**SoHo**	24
NEW Beatrice Inn	**W Vill**	17
Bice	**E 50s**	21
Breslin	**Chelsea**	23
Café Boulud	**E 70s**	27
Cafe Fiorello	**W 60s**	20
Cafe Gitane	**NoLita**	21
Carnegie Deli	**W 50s**	22
Casa Lever	**E 50s**	23
Cipriani D'twn	**SoHo**	23
Crown	**E 80s**	21
Da Silvano	**G Vill**	22
David Burke Townhse.	**E 60s**	25
Elio's	**E 80s**	24
Four Seasons	**E 50s**	27
Fred's at Barneys	**E 60s**	20

NEW Harlow	**E 50s**	19
Harry Cipriani	**E 50s**	22
Indochine	**E Vill**	21
Isabella's	**W 70s**	20
Joe Allen	**W 40s**	19
Katz's Deli	**LES**	24
Lavo	**E 50s**	21
Le Cirque	**E 50s**	25
Leopard/des Artistes	**W 60s**	21
Lion	**G Vill**	21
Marea	**W 50s**	28
Michael's	**W 50s**	22
Minetta Tavern	**G Vill**	24
Nello	**E 60s**	18
Nicola's	**E 80s**	21
NoMad	**Chelsea**	27
Orsay	**E 70s**	18
Orso	**W 40s**	23
Pastis	**Meatpacking**	22
Philippe	**E 60s**	23
Rao's	**Harlem**	22
Red Rooster	**Harlem**	22
Roberta's	**Bushwick**	26
Rosemary's	**W Vill**	21
Sant Ambroeus	**multi.**	21
Sette Mezzo	**E 70s**	24
Sparks	**E 40s**	25
Spice Market	**Meatpacking**	23
Spotted Pig	**W Vill**	24
Standard Grill	**Meatpacking**	22
Swifty's	**E 70s**	17
21 Club	**W 50s**	23
Via Quadronno	**E 70s**	23
Ze Café	**E 50s**	21

POWER SCENES

Ai Fiori	**Garment**	26
Aretsky's Patroon	**E 40s**	22
Bar Americain	**W 50s**	23
Bice	**E 50s**	21
BLT Prime	**Gramercy**	25
BLT Steak	**E 50s**	25
Bobby Van's	**E 40s**	23
Bull & Bear	**E 40s**	22
Carlyle	**E 70s**	23
Casa Lever	**E 50s**	23
China Grill	**W 50s**	23
Cipriani Club 55	**Financial**	23
City Hall	**TriBeCa**	22
Daniel	**E 60s**	28

Del Frisco's | **W 40s** — 25
Del Posto | **Chelsea** — 26
Elio's | **E 80s** — 24
Forty Four | **W 40s** — 20
Four Seasons | **E 50s** — 27
Fresco | **E 50s** — 22
Gotham B&G | **G Vill** — 27
Harry's Cafe | **Financial** — 22
Jean Georges | **W 60s** — 28
Keens | **Garment** — 26
La Grenouille | **E 50s** — 28
Le Bernardin | **W 50s** — 29
Le Cirque | **E 50s** — 25
Lion | **G Vill** — 21
Marea | **W 50s** — 28
Megu | **multi.** — 24
Michael's | **W 50s** — 22
Morton's | **E 40s** — 22
Nobu | **multi.** — 27
Norma's | **W 50s** — 25
North End Grill | **Financial** — 24
Peter Luger | **W'burg** — 27
Rao's | **Harlem** — 22
Russian Tea | **W 50s** — 20
San Pietro | **E 50s** — 24
Sant Ambroeus | **multi.** — 21
NEW Sirio | **E 60s** — 22
Smith/Wollensky | **E 40s** — 23
Solo | **E 50s** — 25
Sparks | **E 40s** — 25
21 Club | **W 50s** — 23

PRIVATE ROOMS/ PARTIES

Ai Fiori | **Garment** — 26
Arabelle | **E 60s** — 24
Aretsky's Patroon | **E 40s** — 22
Aroma Kitchen | **NoHo** — 24
A Voce | **W 60s** — 24
Barbetta | **W 40s** — 22
Battery Gdns. | **Financial** — 20
BLT Fish | **Flatiron** — 23
BLT Prime | **Gramercy** — 25
BLT Steak | **E 50s** — 25
Blue Hill | **G Vill** — 27
Blue Smoke | **Murray Hill** — 22
Blue Water | **Union Sq** — 24
Breslin | **Chelsea** — 23
Buddakan | **Chelsea** — 25
Capital Grille | **E 40s** — 24

Casa Lever | **E 50s** — 23
Cellini | **E 50s** — 22
City Hall | **TriBeCa** — 22
Craft | **Flatiron** — 26
Daniel | **E 60s** — 28
Del Frisco's | **W 40s** — 25
Delmonico's | **Financial** — 23
Del Posto | **Chelsea** — 26
Eleven Madison | **Flatiron** — 28
EN Japanese | **W Vill** — 25
Felidia | **E 50s** — 26
FireBird | **W 40s** — 20
Four Seasons | **E 50s** — 27
Fresco | **E 50s** — 22
Gabriel's | **W 60s** — 23
Gramercy Tavern | **Flatiron** — 28
Harry's Cafe | **Financial** — 22
Hurricane | **Flatiron** — 21
Il Buco | **NoHo** — 25
Il Cortile | **L Italy** — 23
Ilili | **Chelsea** — 24
'Inoteca | **LES** — 21
Jean Georges | **W 60s** — 28
Jungsik | **TriBeCa** — 26
Keens | **Garment** — 26
NEW Lafayette | **NoHo** — 19
La Grenouille | **E 50s** — 28
Landmark Tavern | **W 40s** — 18
Le Bernardin | **W 50s** — 29
Le Cirque | **E 50s** — 25
Le Perigord | **E 50s** — 25
Le Zie | **Chelsea** — 22
Lincoln | **W 60s** — 24
Maialino | **Gramercy** — 26
Maloney/Porcelli | **E 50s** — 23
Marea | **W 50s** — 28
Megu | **TriBeCa** — 24
Michael's | **W 50s** — 22
Milos | **W 50s** — 27
Modern | **W 50s** — 26
Mr. Chow | **E 50s** — 22
Mr. K's | **E 50s** — 23
Nobu | **multi.** — 27
NoMad | **Chelsea** — 27
Oceana | **W 40s** — 24
Palma | **W Vill** — 24
Park | **Chelsea** — 17
Parlor Steak | **E 90s** — 21
Periyali | **Flatiron** — 23

Per Se | **W 60s**	28
Picholine | **W 60s**	27
Public | **NoLita**	23
Raoul's | **SoHo**	25
Redeye Grill | **W 50s**	21
Remi | **W 50s**	22
River Café | **Dumbo**	26
Rock Ctr. | **W 50s**	19
Sambuca | **W 70s**	19
SD26 | **Murray Hill**	25
Shun Lee Palace | **E 50s**	24
Solo | **E 50s**	25
Sparks | **E 40s**	25
Spice Market | **Meatpacking**	23
Tao | **E 50s**	24
Thalassa | **TriBeCa**	24
Tocqueville | **Union Sq**	27
Tribeca Grill | **TriBeCa**	22
21 Club | **W 50s**	23
Valbella | **Meatpacking**	24
Water Club | **Murray Hill**	22

QUICK BITES

Arepas | **Astoria**	24
A Salt & Battery | **W Vill**	22
Azuri Cafe | **W 50s**	25
Baoguette | **multi.**	22
Bark | **Park Slope**	22
Calexico | **multi.**	21
Caracas | **multi.**	24
City Bakery | **Flatiron**	22
NEW Clarke's Standard | **multi.**	20
Creperie | **multi.**	22
Crif Dogs | **multi.**	23
Daisy May's | **W 40s**	21
David Burke/Bloom. | **E 50s**	19
Dos Toros | **multi.**	21
Dumpling Man | **E Vill**	20
El Quinto Pino | **Chelsea**	25
Empanada Mama | **W 50s**	23
Fresco | **E 50s**	22
Gray's Papaya | **multi.**	20
Hampton Chutney | **SoHo**	21
NEW Harlem Shake | **Harlem**	-
Hummus Kitchen | **multi.**	20
Hummus Pl. | **multi.**	22
Island Burgers | **multi.**	21
Joe's Pizza | **W Vill**	23
Kati Roll Company | **multi.**	22

La Bonne Soupe | **W 50s**	19
La Esquina | **L Italy**	23
NEW La Slowteria | **Carroll Gdns**	-
Shorty's | **multi.**	22
Luke's Lobster | **multi.**	23
Mamoun's | **multi.**	23
Maoz | **multi.**	21
Meatball Shop | **LES**	24
Miss Lily's | **G Vill**	21
Mooncake | **multi.**	20
Naruto Ramen | **E 80s**	22
Nice Green Bo | **Chinatown**	22
Nicky's | **Boerum Hill**	21
99 Mi. to Philly | **E Vill**	21
Noodle Bar | **W Vill**	21
Oaxaca | **Park Slope**	21
Papaya King | **E 80s**	21
Pepe Giallo/Rosso | **multi.**	22
Peter's 1969 | **multi.**	20
Pinche Taqueria | **multi.**	21
Pok Pok Phat Thai | **LES**	-
Pommes Frites | **E Vill**	24
Porchetta | **E Vill**	24
Press 195 | **Bayside**	24
Schnipper´s | **multi.**	19
Shake Shack | **multi.**	21
Smile | **SoHo**	21
Taïm | **multi.**	26
Tarallucci | **multi.**	20
Two Boots | **multi.**	19
Untitled | **E 70s**	21
Vanessa's Dumpling | **multi.**	21
Westville | **Hudson Square**	23
Zito's | **Park Slope**	21

QUIET CONVERSATION

Alison Eighteen | **Flatiron**	21
Annisa | **W Vill**	27
Arabelle | **E 60s**	24
Aroma Kitchen | **NoHo**	24
Asiate | **W 60s**	25
Aureole | **W 40s**	26
Basso56 | **W 50s**	23
Bombay Palace | **W 50s**	20
Brasserie 8½ | **W 50s**	22
Canaletto | **E 60s**	21
Cellini | **E 50s**	22
Chef's/Brooklyn Fare | **Downtown Bklyn**	27

Circus | **E 60s**	22
Da Umberto | **Chelsea**	25
Dawat | **E 50s**	23
EN Japanese | **W Vill**	25
Fiorini | **E 50s**	21
Giovanni | **E 80s**	23
Henry's | **W 100s**	20
Il Tinello | **W 50s**	25
Jean Georges | **W 60s**	28
Jungsik | **TriBeCa**	26
Kings' Carriage | **E 80s**	21
La Gioconda | **E 50s**	22
La Grenouille | **E 50s**	28
Le Bernardin | **W 50s**	29
Left Bank | **W Vill**	20
Madison Bistro | **Murray Hill**	20
Marea | **W 50s**	28
Mas | **W Vill**	27
Masa/Bar Masa | **W 60s**	27
Montebello | **E 50s**	24
Mr. K's | **E 50s**	23
North Sq. | **G Vill**	23
Palm Court | **W 50s**	21
Paul & Jimmy's | **Gramercy**	20
Periyali | **Flatiron**	23
Perry St. | **W Vill**	26
Per Se | **W 60s**	28
Petrossian | **W 50s**	24
Picholine | **W 60s**	27
Pietro's | **E 40s**	24
Remi | **W 50s**	22
Rosanjin | **TriBeCa**	25
Sfoglia | **E 90s**	23
Solera | **E 50s**	24
Teodora | **E 50s**	20
Tocqueville | **Union Sq**	27
12 Chairs | **SoHo**	22
Villa Berulia | **Murray Hill**	24
Ze Café | **E 50s**	21
Zenkichi | **W'burg**	26

RAW BARS

Agora Taverna | **Forest Hills**	21
Ammos | **E 40s**	21
NEW Anassa Taverna | **E 60s**	-
Aquagrill | **SoHo**	26
Atlantic Grill | **multi.**	22
Balthazar | **SoHo**	24
Bar Americain | **W 50s**	23

BLT Fish | **Flatiron**	23
Blue Fin | **W 40s**	23
Blue Ribbon | **SoHo**	25
Blue Water | **Union Sq**	24
Bowery Diner | **LES**	18
Catch | **Meatpacking**	23
City Crab | **Flatiron**	19
City Hall | **TriBeCa**	22
City Lobster | **W 40s**	20
NEW Cull & Pistol | **Chelsea**	-
David Burke Fishtail | **E 60s**	24
Docks Oyster | **E 40s**	20
Dutch | **SoHo**	23
Ed's Chowder | **W 60s**	20
Ed's Lobster | **NoLita**	24
Esca | **W 40s**	24
Fish | **W Vill**	23
Flex Mussels | **multi.**	23
Fulton | **E 70s**	22
Jeffrey's Grocery | **W Vill**	22
John Dory Oyster Bar | **Chelsea**	24
Jordans Lobster | **Sheepshead**	22
NEW L & W Oyster | **Chelsea**	20
NEW La Pulperia | **W 40s**	-
Littleneck | **Gowanus**	24
Lobster Box | **City Is**	20
London Lennie | **Rego Pk**	23
Lure Fishbar | **SoHo**	23
Má Pêche | **W 50s**	23
Mark | **E 70s**	22
Markt | **Flatiron**	20
McCormick/Schmick | **W 50s**	18
Mercer Kitchen | **SoHo**	22
Mermaid | **multi.**	21
Millesime | **Murray Hill**	19
Oceana | **W 40s**	24
Ocean Grill | **W 70s**	24
Oyster Bar | **E 40s**	22
Parlor Steak | **E 90s**	21
Pearl Oyster | **W Vill**	26
Pearl Room | **Bay Ridge**	23
P.J. Clarke's | **multi.**	17
Plaza Food Hall | **W 50s**	22
Riverview | **LIC**	21
Standard Grill | **Meatpacking**	22
SushiSamba | **Flatiron**	22
Thalia | **W 50s**	20
21 Club | **W 50s**	23
Uncle Jack's | **W 50s**	23

Walter | **multi.**	23
NEW ZZ's Clam Bar | **G Vill**	–

ROMANTIC PLACES

Alma | **Carroll Gdns**	20
Alta | **G Vill**	25
Asiate | **W 60s**	25
August | **W Vill**	22
Aureole | **W 40s**	26
Aurora | **multi.**	23
Balthazar | **SoHo**	24
Barbetta | **W 40s**	22
Battery Gdns. | **Financial**	20
Blue Hill | **G Vill**	27
Blue Ribbon Bakery | **W Vill**	24
Boathouse | **E 70s**	18
Bottino | **Chelsea**	21
Bouley | **TriBeCa**	29
Camaje | **G Vill**	20
Caviar Russe | **E 50s**	26
NEW Cherry | **Chelsea**	–
Chez Josephine | **W 40s**	20
Conviv. Osteria | **Park Slope**	25
Daniel | **E 60s**	28
David Burke Townhse. | **E 60s**	25
Del Posto | **Chelsea**	26
Eleven Madison | **Flatiron**	28
Erminia | **E 80s**	24
FireBird | **W 40s**	20
Firenze | **E 80s**	21
Four Seasons | **E 50s**	27
Gemma | **E Vill**	21
Gigino | **Financial**	21
House | **Gramercy**	21
Il Buco | **NoHo**	25
I Trulli | **Murray Hill**	22
James | **Prospect Hts**	24
JoJo | **E 60s**	24
Kings' Carriage | **E 80s**	21
L'Absinthe | **E 60s**	21
Lady Mendl's | **Gramercy**	22
La Grenouille | **E 50s**	28
La Lanterna | **G Vill**	20
La Mangeoire | **E 50s**	22
Lambs Club | **W 40s**	22
Le Gigot | **W Vill**	24
Locale | **Astoria**	21
Maria Pia | **W 50s**	19
Mari Vanna | **Flatiron**	21
Mas | **W Vill**	27

Mr. K's | **E 50s**	23
Nino's | **E 70s**	21
Olea | **Ft Greene**	23
One if by Land | **W Vill**	24
Ovelia | **Astoria**	23
Paola's | **E 90s**	23
Pasha | **W 70s**	20
Peasant | **NoLita**	24
Periyali | **Flatiron**	23
Perry St. | **W Vill**	26
Petrossian | **W 50s**	24
Philip Marie | **W Vill**	19
Piccola Venezia | **Astoria**	25
Pinocchio | **E 90s**	24
Place | **W Vill**	23
Raoul's | **SoHo**	25
River Café | **Dumbo**	26
Riverview | **LIC**	21
Roc | **TriBeCa**	22
Rye | **W'burg**	25
Sacred Chow | **G Vill**	22
Scalini Fedeli | **TriBeCa**	27
Sistina | **E 80s**	25
Spice Market | **Meatpacking**	23
Spiga | **W 80s**	23
Teodora | **E 50s**	20
Tocqueville | **Union Sq**	27
Tre Dici | **Chelsea**	23
26 Seats | **E Vill**	22
Uva | **E 70s**	22
View | **W 40s**	16
Wallsé | **W Vill**	26
Water Club | **Murray Hill**	22
Water's Edge | **LIC**	22
Zenkichi | **W'burg**	26
NEW ZZ's Clam Bar | **G Vill**	–

SENIOR APPEAL

Artie's | **City Is**	22
Aureole | **W 40s**	26
Bamonte's | **W'burg**	22
Barbetta | **W 40s**	22
Barney Greengrass | **W 80s**	24
Chez Napoléon | **W 50s**	22
Dawat | **E 50s**	23
DeGrezia | **E 50s**	24
Delmonico's | **Financial**	23
Del Posto | **Chelsea**	26
Due | **E 70s**	21
Embers | **Bay Ridge**	22

Fabio Piccolo | **E 40s**	23
Felidia | **E 50s**	26
Fiorini | **E 50s**	21
Gabriel's | **W 60s**	23
Giovanni | **E 80s**	23
Grifone | **E 40s**	25
Il Tinello | **W 50s**	25
Ithaka | **E 80s**	19
Kings' Carriage | **E 80s**	21
La Bonne Soupe | **W 50s**	19
La Mangeoire | **E 50s**	22
Lattanzi | **W 40s**	22
Leopard/des Artistes | **W 60s**	21
Le Perigord | **E 50s**	25
Lusardi's | **E 70s**	23
Mark | **E 70s**	22
Mr. K's | **E 50s**	23
NEW Nerai | **E 50s**	-
Nicola's | **E 80s**	21
Nippon | **E 50s**	23
Palm Court | **W 50s**	21
Piccolo Angolo | **W Vill**	26
Pietro's | **E 40s**	24
Ponticello | **Astoria**	24
Primola | **E 60s**	23
Quatorze Bis | **E 70s**	20
Quattro Gatti | **E 80s**	21
Remi | **W 50s**	22
Rossini's | **Murray Hill**	23
Russian Tea | **W 50s**	20
San Pietro | **E 50s**	24
Sardi's | **W 40s**	18
Scaletta | **W 70s**	21
Shanghai Pavilion | **E 70s**	21
Shun Lee West | **W 60s**	22
NEW Sirio | **E 60s**	22
Triomphe | **W 40s**	23

STARGAZING

NEW Antica Pesa | **W'burg**	23
Balthazar | **SoHo**	24
Bar Pitti | **G Vill**	23
NEW Beatrice Inn | **W Vill**	17
Bill's Food & Drink | **E 50s**	18
Bond St | **NoHo**	25
Cafe Luxembourg | **W 70s**	21
NEW Carbone | **G Vill**	21
Catch | **Meatpacking**	23
Crown | **E 80s**	21
Da Silvano | **G Vill**	22

Elio's | **E 80s**	24
Joe Allen | **W 40s**	19
Leopard/des Artistes | **W 60s**	21
Lion | **G Vill**	21
Marea | **W 50s**	28
Michael's | **W 50s**	22
Minetta Tavern | **G Vill**	24
Omen A Zen | **SoHo**	25
Orso | **W 40s**	23
Perla | **G Vill**	24
Philippe | **E 60s**	23
Rao's | **Harlem**	22
Spotted Pig | **W Vill**	24
Waverly Inn | **W Vill**	21

THEME RESTAURANTS

Cowgirl | **W Vill**	17
Ninja | **TriBeCa**	19
Ruby Foo's | **W 40s**	18

TOUGH TICKETS

NEW ABC Cocina | **Flatiron**	-
ABC Kitchen | **Flatiron**	26
NEW Aska | **W'burg**	23
Blanca | **Bushwick**	29
NEW Carbone | **G Vill**	21
Chef's/Brooklyn Fare | **Downtown Bklyn**	27
Dutch | **SoHo**	23
NEW Luksus | **Greenpt**	-
Minetta Tavern | **G Vill**	24
Momofuku Ko | **E Vill**	27
NoMad | **Chelsea**	27
NEW Pearl & Ash | **NoLita**	-
Red Rooster | **Harlem**	22
NEW Tanoshi | **E 70s**	-
NEW ZZ's Clam Bar | **G Vill**	-

TRANSPORTING EXPERIENCES

Asiate | **W 60s**	25
Balthazar | **SoHo**	24
Beauty & Essex | **LES**	22
Boathouse | **E 70s**	18
Buddakan | **Chelsea**	25
Cafe China | **Murray Hill**	24
FireBird | **W 40s**	20
Il Buco | **NoHo**	25
Ilili | **Chelsea**	24
Keens | **Garment**	26

SPECIAL FEATURES

Restaurant	Rating
Babbo | **G Vill**	27
Balthazar | **SoHo**	24
Barbetta | **W 40s**	22
Bar Boulud | **W 60s**	24
Becco | **W 40s**	22
BLT Fish | **Flatiron**	23
BLT Prime | **Gramercy**	25
BLT Steak | **E 50s**	25
Blue Fin | **W 40s**	23
Blue Hill | **G Vill**	27
Bobby Van's | **multi.**	23
Bottega Del Vino | **E 50s**	22
Bouley | **TriBeCa**	29
Café Boulud | **E 70s**	27
Capital Grille | **E 40s**	24
NEW Carbone | **G Vill**	21
Casa Mono | **Gramercy**	25
'Cesca | **W 70s**	23
Chef's/Brooklyn Fare | **Downtown Bklyn**	27
City Hall | **TriBeCa**	22
NEW Cocotte | **SoHo**	–
NEW Costata | **SoHo**	–
Craft | **Flatiron**	26
Daniel | **E 60s**	28
David Burke Townhse. | **E 60s**	25
db Bistro Moderne | **W 40s**	25
Del Frisco's | **W 40s**	25
Dell'anima | **W Vill**	25
Del Posto | **Chelsea**	26
Eleven Madison | **Flatiron**	28
Esca | **W 40s**	24
NEW Estela | **NoLita**	–
Felidia | **E 50s**	26
Frankies | **multi.**	23
Franny's | **Park Slope**	25
Gotham B&G | **G Vill**	27
Gramercy Tavern | **Flatiron**	28
Harry's Cafe | **Financial**	22
Hearth | **E Vill**	24
Il Buco | **NoHo**	25
'Inoteca | **LES**	21
I Trulli | **Murray Hill**	22
Jean Georges | **W 60s**	28
Junoon | **Flatiron**	24
NEW Lafayette | **NoHo**	19
Landmarc | **multi.**	21
La Pizza Fresca | **Flatiron**	22
La Vara | **Cobble Hill**	27
Le Bernardin | **W 50s**	29
Le Cirque | **E 50s**	25
Lupa | **G Vill**	25
Maialino | **Gramercy**	26
Marea | **W 50s**	28
Mas | **W Vill**	27
Megu | **TriBeCa**	24
Michael's | **W 50s**	22
Milos | **W 50s**	27
Modern | **W 50s**	26
Nice Matin | **W 70s**	19
NoMad | **Chelsea**	27
Oceana | **W 40s**	24
Osteria Morini | **SoHo**	24
Otto | **G Vill**	23
Ouest | **W 80s**	24
NEW Pearl & Ash | **NoLita**	–
Per Se | **W 60s**	28
Picholine | **W 60s**	27
Porter House | **W 60s**	26
Raoul's | **SoHo**	25
River Café | **Dumbo**	26
Rothmann's | **E 50s**	23
Rouge Tomate | **E 60s**	24
Salumeria/Ristoranti Rosi | **W 70s**	25
San Pietro | **E 50s**	24
Scalini Fedeli | **TriBeCa**	27
Scarpetta | **Chelsea**	26
SD26 | **Murray Hill**	25
NEW Sirio | **E 60s**	22
Smith/Wollensky | **E 40s**	23
Solera | **E 50s**	24
Sparks | **E 40s**	25
Terroir | **multi.**	20
Thalassa | **TriBeCa**	24
Tía Pol | **Chelsea**	25
Tommaso | **Dyker Hts**	23
Trestle on 10th | **Chelsea**	22
Tribeca Grill | **TriBeCa**	22
21 Club | **W 50s**	23
Txikito | **Chelsea**	24
Union Sq. Cafe | **Union Sq**	27
Uva | **E 70s**	22
Valbella | **Meatpacking**	24
Veritas | **Flatiron**	25
Vinegar Hill Hse. | **Vinegar Hill**	24
Wallsé | **W Vill**	26
Water's Edge | **LIC**	22

Cuisines

Includes names, locations and Food ratings.

AFGHAN

Afghan Kebab | **multi.** 20

AFRICAN

Ponty Bistro | **Gramercy** 22

AMERICAN

ABC Kitchen | **Flatiron** 26
ABV | **E 90s** 20
Acme | **NoHo** 22
A.G. Kitchen | **W 70s** 18
NEW Alameda | **Greenpt** -
NEW Alder | **E Vill** 20
Alice's Tea | **multi.** 20
Alison Eighteen | **Flatiron** 21
Allswell | **W'burg** 23
Annisa | **W Vill** 27
Apiary | **E Vill** 23
Applewood | **Park Slope** 25
Arabelle | **E 60s** 24
Aretsky's Patroon | **E 40s** 22
Arthur on Smith | **Boerum Hill** 21
Asiate | **W 60s** 25
Astor Room | **Astoria** 20
Atera | **TriBeCa** 25
NEW Atrium Dumbo | **Dumbo** -
Aureole | **W 40s** 26
Back Forty | **multi.** 22
B&B Winepub | **SoHo** 22
Bar Americain | **W 50s** 23
Battersby | **Carroll Gdns** 27
Battery Gdns. | **Financial** 20
NEW Beatrice Inn | **W Vill** 17
Beauty & Essex | **LES** 22
Beecher's Cellar | **Flatiron** 23
Bell Book/Candle | **W Vill** 20
Benchmark | **Park Slope** 22
NEW Betony | **W 50s** -
Bill's Food & Drink | **E 50s** 18
Bistro Ten 18 | **W 100s** 19
Black Duck | **Murray Hill** 22
Black Whale | **City Is** 22
Blanca | **Bushwick** 29
BLT B&G | **Financial** 22
Blue Hill | **G Vill** 27
Blue Ribbon | **multi.** 25
Blue Ribbon Bakery | **W Vill** 24

NEW Blue Ribbon Fried Chicken | **E Vill** -
Boathouse | **E 70s** 18
Bowery Diner | **LES** 18
Bryant Park Grill/Cafe | **W 40s** 19
Bubby's | **TriBeCa** 20
Butter | **E Vill** 23
NEW Butterfly | **TriBeCa** -
Buttermilk | **Carroll Gdns** 25
Cafe Cluny | **W Vill** 22
Cafe Orlin | **E Vill** 22
Cafeteria | **Chelsea** 21
Camaje | **G Vill** 20
Caviar Russe | **E 50s** 26
Chadwick's | **Bay Ridge** 24
NEW Charlie Bird | **SoHo** -
Cibo | **E 40s** 20
NEW Clarke's Standard | **multi.** 20
NEW Clarkson | **W Vill** 20
NEW Cleveland | **NoLita** -
Clinton St. Baking | **LES** 25
Coffee Shop | **Union Sq** 17
NEW Cole's | **W Vill** 21
Colicchio/Sons | **Chelsea** 25
Colonie | **Bklyn Hts** 25
Commerce | **W Vill** 23
Community Food | **W 100s** 23
Cookshop | **Chelsea** 23
Cornelia St. Cafe | **W Vill** 19
Corner Bistro | **multi.** 22
Corner Social | **Harlem** 17
Craft | **Flatiron** 26
Craftbar | **Flatiron** 23
Crown | **E 80s** 21
David Burke/Bloom. | **E 50s** 19
David Burke Fishtail | **E 60s** 24
David Burke Kitchen | **SoHo** 24
David Burke Townhse. | **E 60s** 25
Delicatessen | **NoLita** 19
Diner | **W'burg** 24
NEW Distilled | **TriBeCa** -
Donovan's | **multi.** 20
Dovetail | **W 70s** 25
DuMont | **W'burg** 23
Dutch | **SoHo** 23
East End Kitchen | **E 80s** 20

CUISINES

E.A.T.	**E 80s**	20
Eatery	**W 50s**	21
Ed's Lobster	**NoLita**	24
NEW Ellington	**W 100s**	-
Empanada Mama	**W 50s**	23
NEW Exchange Alley	**E Vill**	-
Farm/Adderley	**Ditmas Pk**	24
Fedora	**W Vill**	23
5 & Diamond	**Harlem**	22
Five Leaves	**Greenpt**	26
5 Points	**NoHo**	21
Flatbush Farm	**Park Slope**	21
Forty Four	**W 40s**	20
44 & X/44½	**W 40s**	22
Four Seasons	**E 50s**	27
NEW Fourth	**E Vill**	-
Fraunces Tavern	**Financial**	18
Fred's at Barneys	**E 60s**	20
Freemans	**LES**	22
Friedman's Lunch	**Chelsea**	22
Friend/Farmer	**Gramercy**	18
NEW Fritzl's Lunch	**Bushwick**	-
Garden Café	**Inwood**	20
General Greene	**Ft Greene**	20
Giorgio's	**Flatiron**	21
Glass House	**W 40s**	19
Good	**W Vill**	21
Good Enough/Eat	**W 80s**	21
Good Fork	**Red Hook**	25
Gotham B&G	**G Vill**	27
Gramercy Tavern	**Flatiron**	28
Grand Tier	**W 60s**	20
NEW Grape & Vine	**G Vill**	-
Greenhouse	**Bay Ridge**	20
Grocery	**Carroll Gdns**	27
NEW Guy's American	**W 40s**	17
Gwynnett St.	**W'burg**	27
NEW Harding's	**Flatiron**	-
NEW Harlem Shake	**Harlem**	-
Harrison	**TriBeCa**	22
Hearth	**E Vill**	24
Henry Public	**Cobble Hill**	20
Henry's	**W 100s**	20
Henry's End	**Bklyn Hts**	25
Hillstone	**multi.**	23
Home	**W Vill**	22
Hospoda	**E 70s**	23
House	**Gramercy**	21
Hudson Clearwater	**W Vill**	23

Hudson River	**Harlem**	20
Hundred Acres	**SoHo**	20
Isabella's	**W 70s**	20
Jackson Hole	**multi.**	19
Jack's Wife Freda	**SoHo**	19
Jack Horse	**Bklyn Hts**	23
Jacob's Pickles	**W 80s**	20
James	**Prospect Hts**	24
Jane	**G Vill**	21
Jeffrey's Grocery	**W Vill**	22
Joe Allen	**W 40s**	19
JoeDoe	**E Vill**	24
Joseph Leonard	**W Vill**	24
Kings' Carriage	**E 80s**	21
King Yum	**Fresh Meadows**	20
Knickerbocker	**G Vill**	20
Kutsher's	**TriBeCa**	20
Lambs Club	**W 40s**	22
Landmark Tavern	**W 40s**	18
La Silhouette	**W 50s**	24
NEW LCL	**E 40s**	-
Left Bank	**W Vill**	20
Lexington Brass	**E 40s**	18
NEW Library/Public	**E Vill**	18
Lion	**G Vill**	21
Little Owl	**W Vill**	25
NEW Louro	**W Vill**	21
NEW Luksus	**Greenpt**	-
Maggie Brown	**Clinton Hill**	23
NEW Manon	**Meatpacking**	-
Má Pêche	**W 50s**	23
Marble Lane	**Chelsea**	21
Marc Forgione	**TriBeCa**	26
Mark	**E 70s**	22
Market Table	**W Vill**	23
Marlow/Sons	**W'burg**	24
Mas	**W Vill**	27
Mas (La Grillade)	**W Vill**	23
NEW Maysville	**Flatiron**	22
Melba's	**Harlem**	24
Mercer Kitchen	**SoHo**	22
Mike's Bistro	**W 70s**	24
Modern	**W 50s**	26
Momofuku Ko	**E Vill**	27
Momofuku Noodle	**E Vill**	24
Momofuku Ssäm	**E Vill**	25
Monkey Bar	**E 50s**	20
Morgan	**Murray Hill**	19
NEW Murray's Cheese	**W Vill**	24

National	**E 50s**	20
Neary's	**E 50s**	17
New Leaf	**Wash. Hts**	21
NoHo Star	**NoHo**	19
NoMad	**Chelsea**	27
Norma's	**W 50s**	25
North End Grill	**Financial**	24
Northern Spy	**E Vill**	24
North Sq.	**G Vill**	23
Oceana	**W 40s**	24
Odeon	**TriBeCa**	19
NEW Old School Brooklyn	**Carroll Gdns**	–
One if by Land	**W Vill**	24
101	**Bay Ridge**	22
Ouest	**W 80s**	24
Palm Court	**W 50s**	21
NEW Pearl & Ash	**NoLita**	–
Peels	**E Vill**	20
Penelope	**Murray Hill**	22
Penrose	**E 80s**	20
Perilla	**W Vill**	26
Perry St.	**W Vill**	26
Per Se	**W 60s**	28
Peter's 1969	**multi.**	20
Philip Marie	**W Vill**	19
NEW Pines	**Gowanus**	23
Place	**W Vill**	23
NEW Preserve 24	**LES**	–
Prime Meat	**Carroll Gdns**	23
Print	**W 40s**	22
Prune	**E Vill**	25
Quality Meats	**W 50s**	26
Queens Kickshaw	**Astoria**	23
Recette	**W Vill**	24
Red Cat	**Chelsea**	23
Redeye Grill	**W 50s**	21
Red Rooster	**Harlem**	22
Reynard	**W'burg**	23
River Café	**Dumbo**	26
Riverpark	**Murray Hill**	24
NEW River Styx	**Greenpt**	–
Riverview	**LIC**	21
Robert	**W 50s**	20
Rock Ctr.	**W 50s**	19
Rose Water	**Park Slope**	25
Rouge Tomate	**E 60s**	24
Rue 57	**W 50s**	19
NEW Runner & Stone	**Gowanus**	23
Rye	**W'burg**	25
Salt & Fat	**Sunnyside**	26
Sanford's	**Astoria**	22
Sarabeth's	**multi.**	20
Saxon & Parole	**NoHo**	22
Schnipper´s	**multi.**	19
Serendipity 3	**E 60s**	20
Sidecar	**Park Slope**	23
606 R&D	**Prospect Hts**	23
S'MAC	**multi.**	23
Smile	**NoHo**	21
Smith	**multi.**	19
Sons of Essex	**LES**	20
South Gate	**W 50s**	21
Standard Grill	**Meatpacking**	22
St. Anselm	**W'burg**	27
Stonehome	**Ft Greene**	21
Stone Park	**Park Slope**	24
Strip House	**G Vill**	25
Swifty's	**E 70s**	17
Table d'Hôte	**E 90s**	19
Taste	**E 80s**	21
Telepan	**W 60s**	26
Thalia	**W 50s**	20
Thistle Hill	**Park Slope**	20
Tiny's	**TriBeCa**	21
Tocqueville	**Union Sq**	27
Trestle on 10th	**Chelsea**	22
Tribeca Grill	**TriBeCa**	22
12th St. B&G	**Park Slope**	22
12 Chairs	**SoHo**	22
21 Club	**W 50s**	23
2 West	**Financial**	22
Union Sq. Cafe	**Union Sq**	27
Untitled	**E 70s**	21
Vanderbilt	**Prospect Hts**	21
Vareli	**W 100s**	23
Veritas	**Flatiron**	25
View	**W 40s**	16
Vinegar Hill Hse.	**Vinegar Hill**	24
Walker's	**TriBeCa**	19
Wall/Water	**Financial**	21
Walter	**multi.**	23
Water Club	**Murray Hill**	22
Water's Edge	**LIC**	22
Waverly Inn	**W Vill**	21
WD-50	**LES**	25
West Bank	**W 40s**	19
Westville	**multi.**	23

CUISINES

Whym | **W 50s** — 19

NEW Willow Road | **Chelsea** — 23

ARGENTINEAN

Buenos Aires | **E Vill** — 24

Chimichurri Grill | **W 40s** — 23

Sosa Borella | **W 50s** — 20

ARMENIAN

Almayass | **Flatiron** — 22

ASIAN

Amber | **E 80s** — 19

Asiate | **W 60s** — 25

Betel | **W Vill** — 21

Buddakan | **Chelsea** — 25

Cafe Asean | **W Vill** — 22

China Grill | **W 50s** — 23

Citrus B&G | **W 70s** — 20

East Pacific | **multi.** — 22

Ember Room | **W 40s** — 21

Fatty 'Cue | **multi.** — 22

Fatty Fish | **E 60s** — 23

Fusia | **E 50s** — 22

NEW General | **LES** — 20

Mooncake | **multi.** — 20

Pig and Khao | **LES** — 23

Pranna | **Murray Hill** — 18

Purple Yam | **Ditmas Pk** — 22

Ruby Foo's | **W 40s** — 18

Salt & Fat | **Sunnyside** — 26

Shi | **LIC** — 24

Spice Market | **Meatpacking** — 23

Talde | **Park Slope** — 25

Tao | **E 50s** — 24

Wild Ginger | **multi.** — 22

Wong | **W Vill** — 24

Zengo | **E 40s** — 22

AUSTRIAN

Blaue Gans | **TriBeCa** — 22

Café Sabarsky/Fledermaus | **E 80s** — 22

Cafe Steinhof | **Park Slope** — 18

Edi & The Wolf | **E Vill** — 23

Mont Blanc | **W 40s** — 23

Seäsonal | **W 50s** — 25

Wallsé | **W Vill** — 26

BAKERIES

Andre's Café | **E 80s** — 19

Bouchon Bakery | **multi.** — 24

Cafe Dada | **Park Slope** — 22

City Bakery | **Flatiron** — 22

Clinton St. Baking | **LES** — 25

Ferrara | **L Italy** — 23

La Bergamote | **multi.** — 24

Landbrot | **multi.** — 20

Le Pain Q. | **multi.** — 18

NEW Runner & Stone | **Gowanus** — 23

Settepani | **W'burg** — 23

Sweet Melissa | **Park Slope** — 20

BARBECUE

NEW Alchemy, TX | **Jackson Hts** — -

Blue Smoke | **multi.** — 22

NEW BrisketTown | **W'burg** — 25

Brother Jimmy's | **multi.** — 17

Butcher Bar | **Astoria** — 24

Daisy May's | **W 40s** — 21

Dinosaur BBQ | **multi.** — 23

Fatty 'Cue | **multi.** — 22

Fette Sau | **W'burg** — 26

NEW Fletcher's | **Gowanus** — 22

Hill Country | **Flatiron** — 23

Mable's Smokehouse | **W'burg** — 23

MexiBBQ | **Astoria** — 21

Mexicue | **multi.** — 19

NEW Mighty Quinn's | **E Vill** — 24

Smoke Joint | **Ft Greene** — 22

NEW Strand | **Astoria** — 21

Virgil's BBQ | **W 40s** — 20

Wildwood BBQ | **Flatiron** — 19

BELGIAN

B. Café | **multi.** — 21

BXL | **multi.** — 19

Cannibal | **Murray Hill** — 24

Le Pain Q. | **multi.** — 18

Markt | **Flatiron** — 20

Petite Abeille | **multi.** — 19

Pommes Frites | **E Vill** — 24

Resto | **Murray Hill** — 21

BRAZILIAN

Beco | **W'burg** — 23

Churrascaria | **multi.** — 23

Circus | **E 60s** — 22

Coffee Shop | **Union Sq** — 17

Ipanema | **W 40s** — 23

Malagueta | **Astoria** — 24

Rice 'n' Beans | **W 50s** — 21

SushiSamba | **multi.** — 22

Via Brasil | **W 40s**	21
Zebú Grill | **E 90s**	23

BRITISH

A Salt & Battery | **W Vill**	22
Breslin | **Chelsea**	23
ChipShop | **multi.**	20
Fat Radish | **LES**	24
Jones Wood Foundry | **E 70s**	21
Tea & Sympathy | **W Vill**	22

BURGERS

NEW Amsterdam Burger | **W 90s**	25
Back Forty | **multi.**	22
BareBurger | **multi.**	22
Bill's Bar | **multi.**	19
Black Iron Burger | **E Vill**	21
BLT Burger | **G Vill**	22
Blue 9 Burger | **multi.**	19
Bonnie's Grill | **Park Slope**	22
Brgr | **multi.**	19
Burger Bistro | **multi.**	22
Burger Joint | **multi.**	24
NEW Clarke's Standard | **multi.**	20
Corner Bistro | **multi.**	22
Counter | **W 40s**	20
db Bistro Moderne | **W 40s**	25
DuMont | **W'burg**	23
5 Napkin Burger | **multi.**	21
Go Burger | **multi.**	18
NEW Harlem Shake | **Harlem**	–
Island Burgers | **multi.**	21
Jackson Hole | **multi.**	19
J.G. Melon | **E 70s**	21
Lucky's Famous | **multi.**	20
Minetta Tavern | **G Vill**	24
Molly's | **Gramercy**	22
Piper's Kilt | **multi.**	21
P.J. Clarke's | **multi.**	17
Rare B&G | **multi.**	21
Schnipper´s | **multi.**	19
Shake Shack | **multi.**	21
67 Burger | **multi.**	21
Spotted Pig | **W Vill**	24
Steak 'n Shake | **W 50s**	20
NEW Umami Burger | **G Vill**	–
Zaitzeff | **Financial**	21

CAJUN/CREOLE

Bayou | **Rosebank**	23
Delta Grill | **W 40s**	20

Great Jones Cafe | **NoHo**	21
Sugar Freak | **Astoria**	22

CALIFORNIAN

Michael's | **W 50s**	22

CAMBODIAN

Num Pang | **multi.**	25

CARIBBEAN

Ali's Roti | **multi.**	25

CAVIAR

Caviar Russe | **E 50s**	26
Petrossian | **W 50s**	24
Russian Tea | **W 50s**	20

CHEESE SPECIALISTS

Artisanal | **Murray Hill**	23
Ayza Wine | **multi.**	20
Beecher's Cellar | **Flatiron**	23
NEW Murray's Cheese | **W Vill**	24
Picholine | **W 60s**	27

CHEESESTEAKS

Shorty's | **multi.**	22
99 Mi. to Philly | **multi.**	21

CHICKEN

NEW Blue Ribbon Fried Chicken | **E Vill**	–
BonChon | **multi.**	21
Coco Roco | **multi.**	21
Hill Country Chicken | **Flatiron**	20
NEW Hybird | **Chelsea**	–
Kyochon | **multi.**	20
Malecon | **multi.**	21
Peter's 1969 | **W'burg**	20
Pies-N-Thighs | **W'burg**	24
Pio Pio | **multi.**	23
Pok Pok Phat Thai | **LES**	–
Yakitori Totto | **W 50s**	25

CHINESE

(* dim sum specialist)

Amazing 66 | **Chinatown**	22
BaoHaus | **E Vill**	23
Biang! | **Flushing**	24
Big Wong | **Chinatown**	22
Bo-Ky | **multi.**	22
Buddha Bodai* | **Chinatown**	23
Cafe China | **Murray Hill**	24
Chef Ho's | **E 80s**	22
Chef Yu | **Garment**	21

Chin Chin | **E 40s** 23
Chop-Shop | **Chelsea** 22
Congee | **LES** 20
Dim Sum Go Go* | **Chinatown** 21
Dumpling Man | **E Vill** 20
Excellent Dumpling* | **Chinatown** 22
Flor/Mayo | **multi.** 21
Fuleen Seafood | **Chinatown** 22
Golden Unicorn* | **Chinatown** 21
Grand Sichuan | **multi.** 20
Great NY Noodle | **Chinatown** 23
Hakkasan | **W 40s** 23
Hop Kee | **Chinatown** 21
Jing Fong* | **Chinatown** 20
Joe's Shanghai | **multi.** 22
Joe's | **Chinatown** 20
King Yum | **Fresh Meadows** 20
Legend | **multi.** 21
Lychee Hse.* | **E 50s** 22
Macao Trading | **TriBeCa** 20
Mission Chinese | **LES** 23
Mr. Chow | **multi.** 22
Mr. K's | **E 50s** 23
Nice Green Bo | **Chinatown** 22
NoHo Star | **NoHo** 19
Nom Wah Tea* | **Chinatown** 21
Oriental Gdn.* | **Chinatown** 22
Our Place* | **E 70s** 18
Pacificana | **Sunset Pk** 23
Peking Duck | **multi.** 22
Philippe | **E 60s** 23
Phoenix Gdn. | **Murray Hill** 23
Pig Heaven | **E 80s** 21
Ping's Seafood* | **multi.** 21
Prosperity Dumpling | **LES** 26
Red Egg | **L Italy** 20
RedFarm* | **W Vill** 25
Sammy's Noodle | **G Vill** 20
Shanghai Café | **L Italy** 24
Shanghai Pavilion | **E 70s** 21
Shun Lee Cafe* | **W 60s** 21
Shun Lee Palace | **E 50s** 24
Shun Lee West | **W 60s** 22
Spicy & Tasty | **Flushing** 24
Szechuan Gourmet | **multi.** 23
Tang Pavilion | **W 50s** 23
Tasty Hand-Pulled | **Chinatown** 22
Vanessa's Dumpling | **multi.** 21
Wa Jeal | **E 80s** 24

Wo Hop | **Chinatown** 22
Wu Liang Ye | **W 40s** 23
Xi'an | **multi.** 24
Yunnan Kitchen | **LES** 21

COFFEEHOUSES

Andre's Café | **E 80s** 19
Cafe Dada | **Park Slope** 22
Cafe Lalo | **W 80s** 20
Café Sabarsky/Fledermaus | **E 80s** 22
Le Pain Q. | **multi.** 18
Omonia | **multi.** 20
Queens Kickshaw | **Astoria** 23
Saraghina | **Bed-Stuy** 26
Smile | **multi.** 21
Tarallucci | **multi.** 20
Untitled | **E 70s** 21
Via Quadronno | **E 70s** 23

CONTINENTAL

Astor Room | **Astoria** 20
Battery Gdns. | **Financial** 20
Cebu | **Bay Ridge** 20
Petrossian | **W 50s** 24
Russian Samovar | **W 50s** 20
Russian Tea | **W 50s** 20
Sardi's | **W 40s** 18

CRÊPES

Creperie | **multi.** 22

CUBAN

Amor Cubano | **Harlem** 23
Café Habana/Outpost | **multi.** 23
Cuba | **G Vill** 23
Cubana Café | **Park Slope** 21
Guantanamera | **W 50s** 20
Havana Alma | **W Vill** 21
Havana Central | **multi.** 19
Son Cubano | **Chelsea** 22
Victor's Cafe | **W 50s** 22

CZECH

Hospoda | **E 70s** 23

DANISH

NEW Aamanns-Copenhagen | **TriBeCa** 20

DELIS

B & H Dairy | **E Vill** 22
Barney Greengrass | **W 80s** 24
Ben's Best | **Rego Pk** 23

Ben's Kosher | **multi.**	19
Carnegie Deli | **W 50s**	22
Katz's Deli | **LES**	24
Leo's Latticini/Corona | **Corona**	26
Liebman's Deli | **Riverdale**	23
Mile End | **Boerum Hill**	23
Mill Basin Deli | **Mill Basin**	22
Pastrami Queen | **E 70s**	21
2nd Ave Deli | **multi.**	22
Stage Door | **multi.**	19

DESSERT

Andre's Café | **E 80s**	19
Bouchon Bakery | **multi.**	24
Brooklyn Farmacy | **Carroll Gdns**	23
Cafe Lalo | **W 80s**	20
Café Sabarsky/Fledermaus | **E 80s**	22
ChikaLicious | **E Vill**	25
Chocolate Room | **multi.**	25
City Bakery | **Flatiron**	22
Ferrara | **L Italy**	23
La Bergamote | **multi.**	24
Junior's | **multi.**	19
Lady Mendl's | **Gramercy**	22
L&B Spumoni | **Bensonhurst**	24
Omonia | **multi.**	20
Sant Ambroeus | **multi.**	21
Serendipity 3 | **E 60s**	20
Settepani | **multi.**	23
Sweet Melissa | **Park Slope**	20
Tarallucci | **multi.**	20

DINER

Bowery Diner | **LES**	18
Brooklyn Farmacy | **Carroll Gdns**	23
Coppelia | **Chelsea**	23
Junior's | **multi.**	19
La Taza de Oro | **Chelsea**	22
Little Poland | **E Vill**	20
Schnipper´s | **multi.**	19
Teresa's | **Bklyn Hts**	20
Tom's | **multi.**	21

DOMINICAN

Malecon | **multi.**	21
Mamajuana/Taina | **multi.**	21

EASTERN EUROPEAN

Sammy's Roumanian | **LES**	20

ECLECTIC

Abigail's | **Garment**	20
NEW Alder | **E Vill**	20
Carol's | **Dongan Hills**	25
Corkbuzz | **G Vill**	22
Do or Dine | **Bed-Stuy**	25
Good Fork | **Red Hook**	25
Graffiti | **E Vill**	25
Josie's | **W 70s**	20
Juventino | **Park Slope**	25
Mehtaphor | **TriBeCa**	24
Misdemeanor | **Downtown Bklyn**	-
Nook | **W 50s**	23
107 West | **W 100s**	20
Plaza Food Hall | **W 50s**	22
Public | **NoLita**	23
Schiller's | **LES**	19
Smorgasburg | **multi.**	27
Sojourn | **E 70s**	23
Stanton Social | **LES**	24
Tolani | **W 70s**	20
Traif | **W'burg**	26
WD-50 | **LES**	25

ETHIOPIAN

Awash | **multi.**	22
Meskerem | **G Vill**	23
Queen of Sheba | **W 40s**	22
Zoma | **Harlem**	24

EUROPEAN

August | **W Vill**	22
Danny Brown | **Forest Hills**	26
Fushimi | **multi.**	23
NoMad | **Chelsea**	27
Spotted Pig | **W Vill**	24

FILIPINO

NEW Jeepney | **E Vill**	23
Kuma Inn | **LES**	25
Maharlika | **E Vill**	25

FONDUE

Artisanal | **Murray Hill**	23
Chocolate Room | **multi.**	25
Kashkaval | **W 50s**	22
Mont Blanc | **W 40s**	23

FRENCH

Americano | **Chelsea**	22
Arabelle | **E 60s**	24

Ayza Wine | **multi.**	20
Bagatelle | **Meatpacking**	20
Barbès | **Murray Hill**	20
Bistro S K | **City Is**	26
Bobo | **W Vill**	23
Bouchon Bakery | **multi.**	24
Bouley | **TriBeCa**	29
Brasserie 8½ | **W 50s**	22
Brass. Ruhlmann | **W 50s**	19
Breeze | **W 40s**	21
Brick Cafe | **Astoria**	21
Buvette | **W Vill**	24
Café Boulud | **E 70s**	27
Cafe Centro | **E 40s**	21
Cafe Du Soleil | **W 100s**	19
Cafe Gitane | **multi.**	21
Café Henri | **multi.**	20
Calliope | **E Vill**	22
NEW Cantine Paris. | **Financial**	–
Carlyle | **E 70s**	23
Cercle Rouge | **TriBeCa**	19
Château Cherbuliez | **Flatiron**	–
Chef's/Brooklyn Fare | **Downtown Bklyn**	27
Creperie | **LES**	22
Daniel | **E 60s**	28
DBGB | **E Vill**	24
Degustation | **E Vill**	28
Eleven Madison | **Flatiron**	28
NEW Elm | **W'burg**	–
Fedora | **W Vill**	23
FireBird | **W 40s**	20
Gordon Ramsay | **W 50s**	23
Indochine | **E Vill**	21
Jean Georges | **W 60s**	28
Jean-Georges' Noug. | **W 60s**	27
La Baraka | **Little Neck**	23
La Bergamote | **multi.**	24
La Boîte en Bois | **W 60s**	21
NEW Lafayette | **NoHo**	19
La Grenouille | **E 50s**	28
La Mangeoire | **E 50s**	22
La Mediterranée | **E 50s**	20
Le Bernardin | **W 50s**	29
Le Cirque | **E 50s**	25
L'Ecole | **SoHo**	24
Le Colonial | **E 50s**	21
Le Gigot | **W Vill**	24
Le Grainne Cafe | **Chelsea**	20

Le Marais | **W 40s**	20
Le Perigord | **E 50s**	25
Le Pescadeux | **SoHo**	22
NEW Le Philosophe | **NoHo**	24
Le Relais/Venise | **E 50s**	20
Le Rivage | **W 40s**	21
Le Veau d'Or | **E 60s**	19
Marseille | **W 40s**	21
Maze | **W 50s**	24
Mercer Kitchen | **SoHo**	22
Minetta Tavern | **G Vill**	24
Modern | **W 50s**	26
NEW Montmartre | **Chelsea**	19
Nizza | **W 40s**	19
Odeon | **TriBeCa**	19
Pascalou | **E 90s**	21
Per Se | **W 60s**	28
Petrossian | **W 50s**	24
Picholine | **W 60s**	27
Ponty Bistro | **Gramercy**	22
Rouge et Blanc | **SoHo**	25
Steak Frites | **Union Sq**	20
Tocqueville | **Union Sq**	27
Triomphe | **W 40s**	23
Ze Café | **E 50s**	21

FRENCH (BISTRO)

Almond | **Flatiron**	20
A.O.C. | **multi.**	20
Bacchus | **Boerum Hill**	20
Bar Boulud | **W 60s**	24
Benoit | **W 50s**	21
Bistro Cassis | **W 70s**	20
Bistro Chat Noir | **E 60s**	20
Bistro Citron | **W 80s**	20
Bistro La Promenade | **Chelsea**	23
Bistro Les Amis | **SoHo**	22
Bistro Le Steak | **E 70s**	18
Bistro 61 | **E 60s**	19
Bistro Vendôme | **E 50s**	22
Cafe Cluny | **W Vill**	22
Cafe Dada | **Park Slope**	22
Cafe Loup | **W Vill**	19
Cafe Luluc | **Cobble Hill**	21
Cafe Luxembourg | **W 70s**	21
Camaje | **G Vill**	20
Chez Jacqueline | **G Vill**	19
Chez Josephine | **W 40s**	20
Chez Lucienne | **Harlem**	21
Chez Napoléon | **W 50s**	22

Chez Oskar | **Ft Greene**	20
Cornelia St. Cafe | **W Vill**	19
db Bistro Moderne | **W 40s**	25
Deux Amis | **E 50s**	20
JoJo | **E 60s**	24
Jubilee | **E 50s**	21
La Bonne Soupe | **W 50s**	19
La Lunchonette | **Chelsea**	21
Landmarc | **multi.**	21
La Silhouette | **W 50s**	24
La Sirène | **Hudson Square**	24
Le Parisien | **Murray Hill**	22
Les Halles | **multi.**	20
Lucien | **E Vill**	23
Madison Bistro | **Murray Hill**	20
Mon Petit Cafe | **E 60s**	19
Nice Matin | **W 70s**	19
Paradou | **Meatpacking**	22
Pastis | **Meatpacking**	22
Quatorze Bis | **E 70s**	20
Raoul's | **SoHo**	25
Saju Bistro | **W 40s**	20
Table d'Hôte | **E 90s**	19
Tartine | **W Vill**	22
Tournesol | **LIC**	24
26 Seats | **E Vill**	22

FRENCH (BRASSERIE)

Artisanal | **Murray Hill**	23
Balthazar | **SoHo**	24
Beaumarchais | **Meatpacking**	22
Brasserie | **E 50s**	22
Brasserie Cognac East | **E 70s**	19
Café d'Alsace | **E 80s**	21
Ça Va | **W 40s**	21
L'Absinthe | **E 60s**	21
Orsay | **E 70s**	18
Rue 57 | **W 50s**	19

GASTROPUB

B&B Winepub | Amer. | **SoHo**	22
Cannibal | Belgian | **Murray Hill**	24
DBGB | Amer. | **E Vill**	24
NEW Hill & Dale | Amer. | **LES**	-
Penrose | Amer. | **E 80s**	20
Resto | Belgian | **Murray Hill**	21
Spotted Pig | Euro. | **W Vill**	24

GERMAN

Blaue Gans | **TriBeCa**	22
Heidelberg | **E 80s**	20
Landbrot | **multi.**	20
NEW Marrow | **W Vill**	23
Nurnberger | **New Brighton**	23
Rolf's | **Gramercy**	17
Schnitzel Haus | **Bay Ridge**	23
Seäsonal | **W 50s**	25
Zum Schneider | **E Vill**	21
Zum Stammtisch | **Glendale**	24

GREEK

Agnanti | **Astoria**	24
Agora Taverna | **Forest Hills**	21
Ammos | **E 40s**	21
NEW Anassa Taverna | **E 60s**	-
Avra | **E 40s**	25
Bahari Estiatorio | **Astoria**	24
Boukiés | **E Vill**	23
Cávo | **Astoria**	21
Dafni Greek | **W 40s**	19
Eliá | **Bay Ridge**	25
Elias Corner | **Astoria**	23
Ethos | **multi.**	21
FishTag | **W 70s**	23
Greek Kitchen | **W 50s**	20
Ithaka | **E 80s**	19
Kellari | **W 40s**	22
Loi | **W 70s**	22
Loukoumi | **Astoria**	24
NEW Meli | **Murray Hill**	-
Milos | **W 50s**	27
Molyvos | **W 50s**	23
NEW MP Taverna | **Astoria**	-
NEW Nerai | **E 50s**	-
Okeanos | **Park Slope**	21
Omonia | **multi.**	20
Ovelia | **Astoria**	23
Periyali | **Flatiron**	23
Pylos | **E Vill**	27
Snack | **multi.**	23
Stamatis | **Astoria**	23
Symposium | **W 100s**	20
Taverna Kyclades | **Astoria**	26
Telly's Taverna | **Astoria**	21
Thalassa | **TriBeCa**	24
Uncle Nick's | **multi.**	21
Yefsi Estiatorio | **E 70s**	25

HEALTH FOOD

(See also Vegetarian)

Community Food | **W 100s**	23
Josie's | **W 70s**	20

Mooncake | **multi.**	20
Spring/Natural | **multi.**	20

HOT DOGS

Bark | **Park Slope**	22
Crif Dogs | **multi.**	23
Go Burger | **multi.**	18
Gray's Papaya | **multi.**	20
Papaya King | **multi.**	21
Shake Shack | **multi.**	21

HUNGARIAN

Andre's Café | **E 80s**	19
Cafe Dada | **Park Slope**	22

ICE CREAM PARLORS

Brooklyn Farmacy | **Carroll Gdns**	23
Serendipity 3 | **E 60s**	20

INDIAN

Amma | **E 50s**	25
Baluchi's | **multi.**	19
Banjara | **E Vill**	23
Bombay Palace | **W 50s**	20
Bombay Talkie | **Chelsea**	20
Brick Ln. Curry | **multi.**	21
Bukhara Grill | **E 40s**	21
Chola | **E 50s**	23
Darbar | **multi.**	21
Dawat | **E 50s**	23
Dévi | **Flatiron**	23
Dhaba | **Murray Hill**	23
Hampton Chutney | **multi.**	21
Haveli | **E Vill**	21
Indus Valley | **W 100s**	22
Jackson Diner | **multi.**	21
Junoon | **Flatiron**	24
Kati Roll Company | **multi.**	22
Moti Mahal | **E 60s**	23
Mughlai | **W 70s**	20
Nirvana | **Murray Hill**	22
Pongal | **Murray Hill**	24
Sapphire Indian | **W 60s**	21
Saravanaa Bhavan | **multi.**	23
Seva Indian | **Astoria**	24
Tamarind | **multi.**	26
Tiffin Wallah | **Murray Hill**	22
Tulsi | **E 40s**	24
Utsav | **W 40s**	21
Vatan | **Murray Hill**	23
Yuva | **E 50s**	23

IRISH

Molly's | **Gramercy**	22

ISRAELI

Azuri Cafe | **W 50s**	25
Hummus Pl. | **multi.**	22
Miriam | **Park Slope**	21
Taïm | **multi.**	26

ITALIAN
(N=Northern; S=Southern)

Abboccato | **W 50s**	21
Acappella | N | **TriBeCa**	24
Acqua | S | **W 90s**	20
Ai Fiori | **Garment**	26
Alberto | N | **Forest Hills**	23
Al Di La | **Park Slope**	27
Al Forno Pizza | **E 70s**	20
Alloro | **E 70s**	23
Amarone | **W 40s**	20
Amorina | **Prospect Hts**	23
Angelina's | **Tottenville**	23
Angelo's/Mulberry | S | **L Italy**	23
Angelo's Pizza | **multi.**	21
NEW Angolo SoHo | **SoHo**	24
Ann & Tony's | **Fordham**	21
Anthony's | **Park Slope**	21
NEW Antica Pesa | **W'burg**	23
Antonio's Trattoria | **Fordham**	23
Antonucci | **E 80s**	23
Ápizz | **LES**	25
Areo | **Bay Ridge**	24
Armani Rist. | N | **E 50s**	23
Arno | N | **Garment**	20
Aroma Kitchen | **NoHo**	24
Arté Café | **W 70s**	18
Arthur on Smith | **Boerum Hill**	21
Arturo's | **G Vill**	23
Asellina | **Murray Hill**	20
Aurora | **multi.**	23
A Voce | **multi.**	24
Babbo | **G Vill**	27
Bamonte's | **W'burg**	22
Baraonda | **E 70s**	19
Barbetta | N | **W 40s**	22
Barbone | **E Vill**	23
Barbuto | **W Vill**	24
Bar Corvo | N | **Prospect Hts**	26
Bar Italia | **E 60s**	19
Barosa | **Rego Pk**	22

Bar Pitti | **G Vill**	23	**NEW** Corvo Bianco | **W 80s**	–
Basso56 | S | **W 50s**	23	**NEW** Costata | **SoHo**	–
Basta Pasta | **Flatiron**	23	Cotta | **W 80s**	22
Becco | **W 40s**	22	Covo | **Harlem**	23
Beccofino | **Riverdale**	23	Crab Shanty | **City Is**	23
Bella Blu | N | **E 70s**	21	Crispo | N | **W Vill**	23
Bella Via | **LIC**	22	Da Andrea | **G Vill**	23
Best Pizza | **W'burg**	24	Da Ciro | **Murray Hill**	22
Bettola | **W 70s**	19	Da Nico | **L Italy**	21
Bianca | N | **NoHo**	26	Da Noi | N | **multi.**	23
Bice | N | **E 50s**	21	Da Silvano | N | **G Vill**	22
Biricchino | N | **Chelsea**	21	Da Tommaso | N | **W 50s**	20
Birreria | **Flatiron**	20	Da Umberto | N | **Chelsea**	25
Bistango | **Murray Hill**	21	Defonte's | **multi.**	24
Bistro Milano | N | **W 50s**	21	DeGrezia | **E 50s**	24
Bocca | S | **Flatiron**	22	Dell'anima | **W Vill**	25
Bocca/Bacco | **multi.**	21	Del Posto | **Chelsea**	26
Bocca Lupo | **Cobble Hill**	23	Destino | S | **E 50s**	19
Bocelli | **Grasmere**	25	Divino | N | **E 80s**	19
Bond 45 | **W 40s**	19	Dominick's | **Fordham**	23
Bottega | **E 70s**	21	Don Antonio | **W 50s**	24
Bottega Del Vino | **E 50s**	22	Donatella | **Chelsea**	20
Bottino | N | **Chelsea**	21	Don Giovanni | **W 40s**	20
Bricco | **W 50s**	21	Don Peppe | **Ozone Pk**	25
Brick Cafe | N | **Astoria**	21	Due | N | **E 70s**	21
Brio | **multi.**	20	Eataly | **Flatiron**	23
Cacio e Pepe | S | **E Vill**	20	Ecco | **TriBeCa**	23
Cafe Fiorello | **W 60s**	20	Elio's | **E 80s**	24
Caffe e Vino | **Ft Greene**	23	Emilia's | **Fordham**	22
Caffe Grazie | **E 80s**	19	Emporio | **NoLita**	23
Caffe Storico | **W 70s**	20	Enzo's | **multi.**	23
Campagnola | **E 70s**	23	Eolo | S | **Chelsea**	21
Canaletto | N | **E 60s**	21	Erminia | S | **E 80s**	24
Cara Mia | **W 40s**	20	Esca | S | **W 40s**	24
Caravaggio | **E 70s**	25	Etc. Etc. | **W 40s**	22
NEW Carbone | **G Vill**	21	Fabio Piccolo | **E 40s**	23
Carmine's | S | **multi.**	21	F & J Pine | **Morris Park**	23
Casa Lever | **E 50s**	23	Felice | **multi.**	21
Casa Nonna | **Garment**	21	Felidia | **E 50s**	26
Celeste | **W 80s**	23	57 Napoli | **E 50s**	23
Cellini | **E 50s**	22	Fiorentino's | S | **Gravesend**	21
'Cesca | S | **W 70s**	23	Fiorini | S | **E 50s**	21
Cibo | N | **E 40s**	20	Firenze | N | **E 80s**	21
Cipriani Club 55 | **Financial**	23	508 | **Hudson Square**	22
Cipriani Dolci | **E 40s**	22	Forcella | S | **multi.**	22
Cipriani D'twn | **SoHo**	23	Forlini's | N | **Chinatown**	19
Circo | N | **W 50s**	23	Fornino | **multi.**	24
Coppola's | **multi.**	21	Fragole | **Carroll Gdns**	24
Corsino | **W Vill**	21	Frank | **E Vill**	23

CUISINES

Frankies	**multi.**	23	La Piazzetta	**W'burg**	23
Franny's	**Park Slope**	25	**NEW** L'Apicio	**E Vill**	22
Fratelli	**Pelham Gardens**	21	La Pizza Fresca	**Flatiron**	22
Fratelli la Bufala	S	**W 70s**	20	L'Artusi	**W Vill**	27
Fred's at Barneys	N	**E 60s**	20	Lattanzi	S	**W 40s**	22
Fresco	N	**E 50s**	22	Lavagna	**E Vill**	24
Gabriel's	N	**W 60s**	23	La Vigna	**Forest Hills**	23
Gargiulo's	S	**Coney Is**	22	La Villa Pizzeria	**multi.**	23
Gemma	N	**E Vill**	21	Lavo	**E 50s**	21
Gennaro	**W 90s**	24	Leopard/des Artistes	S	**W 60s**	21
Gigino	**multi.**	21	Leo's Latticini/Corona	**multi.**	26
Gino's	**Bay Ridge**	24	Le Zie	**Chelsea**	22
Giorgio's	**Flatiron**	21	Lido	N	**Harlem**	22
Giovanni Rana	**Chelsea**	24	Lil' Frankie	**E Vill**	24
Giovanni	N	**E 80s**	23	Lincoln	**W 60s**	24
Girasole	**E 80s**	21	Locale	**Astoria**	21
Gnocco	**E Vill**	22	Locanda Verde	**TriBeCa**	25
Gottino	**W Vill**	20	Locanda Vini	N	**Clinton Hill**	26
Grace's Tratt.	**E 70s**	19	Lorenzo's	**Bloomfield**	22
Gradisca	**W Vill**	24	Luna Piena	**E 50s**	20
Grifone	N	**E 40s**	25	Lunetta	**Boerum Hill**	21
Harry Cipriani	N	**E 50s**	22	Lupa	**G Vill**	25
Harry's Italian	N	**multi.**	21	Lusardi's	N	**E 70s**	23
Hearth	N	**E Vill**	24	Luzzo's	S	**E Vill**	26
Il Bagatto	**E Vill**	25	Macelleria	N	**Meatpacking**	21
Il Bambino	**Astoria**	27	Madison's	**Riverdale**	20
Il Buco	**NoHo**	25	Maialino	**Gramercy**	26
Il Cantinori	N	**G Vill**	23	Malatesta	N	**W Vill**	24
Il Cortile	**L Italy**	23	Manducatis	S	**LIC**	23
Il Giglio	N	**TriBeCa**	25	Manetta's	**LIC**	23
Il Mulino	S	**multi.**	26	Manzo	**Flatiron**	25
Il Postino	**E 40s**	23	Marcony	**Murray Hill**	25
Il Riccio	S	**E 70s**	20	Marco Polo	**Carroll Gdns**	20
Il Tinello	N	**W 50s**	25	Marea	**W 50s**	28
Il Vagabondo	**E 60s**	20	Maria Pia	**W 50s**	19
'Inoteca	**LES**	21	Mario's	S	**Fordham**	22
I Sodi	**W Vill**	25	**NEW** Marrow	**W Vill**	23
Isola	**SoHo**	–	Maruzzella	**E 70s**	20
Italianissimo	**E 80s**	22	Max	S	**TriBeCa**	18
I Trulli	**Murray Hill**	22	Max SoHa/Caffe	**W 100s**	23
Joe & Pat's	**Castleton Corners**	23	Mercato	**Garment**	21
John's/12th St.	**E Vill**	22	Meson Sevilla	**W 40s**	20
La Bottega	**Chelsea**	21	Mezzaluna/Pizza	**multi.**	21
La Follia	**Gramercy**	22	Mezzogiorno	N	**SoHo**	21
La Gioconda	**E 50s**	22	Miranda	**W'burg**	23
La Lanterna	**G Vill**	20	Montebello	N	**E 50s**	24
La Masseria	**W 40s**	23	Monte's	**Gowanus**	20
La Mela	**L Italy**	21	Morandi	**W Vill**	23
L&B Spumoni	**Bensonhurst**	24	Nanni	**E 40s**	24

Naples 45 | S | **E 40s**	19
Nello | N | **E 60s**	18
Nicola's | N | **E 80s**	21
Nicoletta | **E Vill**	19
Nino's | **multi.**	21
Nizza | **W 40s**	19
Nocello | N | **W 50s**	22
Noodle Pudding | **Bklyn Hts**	25
Nove | S | **Eltingville**	24
Novitá | N | **Gramercy**	25
Numero 28 | **multi.**	24
NEW Old School Brooklyn | **Carroll Gdns**	-
101 | **Bay Ridge**	22
Orso | N | **W 40s**	23
Osso Buco | **E 90s**	20
Osteria al Doge | N | **W 40s**	20
Osteria Laguna | **E 40s**	21
Osteria Morini | N | **SoHo**	24
Otto | **G Vill**	23
Padre Figlio | **E 40s**	22
Palma | S | **W Vill**	24
Paola's | **E 90s**	23
Pappardella | **W 70s**	20
Park Side | **Corona**	25
Parm | S | **NoLita**	23
Parma | N | **E 70s**	21
Pasquale's | **Fordham**	21
Patricia's | **Morris Park**	24
Patsy's | **multi.**	20
Patsy's | S | **W 50s**	22
Paul & Jimmy's | **Gramercy**	20
Peasant | **NoLita**	24
Pellegrino's | **L Italy**	24
Pepe Giallo/Rosso | **multi.**	22
Pepolino | N | **TriBeCa**	26
Perbacco | **E Vill**	23
Perla | **G Vill**	24
Per Lei | **E 70s**	20
Pescatore | **E 50s**	20
Petaluma | **E 70s**	18
Piccola Venezia | **Astoria**	25
Piccolo Angolo | **W Vill**	26
Pietro's | **E 40s**	24
Pinocchio | **E 90s**	24
Pisticci | S | **W 100s**	25
PizzArte | S | **W 50s**	21
Pó | **W Vill**	25
Pomodoro Rosso | **W 70s**	21

Ponticello | N | **Astoria**	24
Porchetta | **E Vill**	24
Porsena | **E Vill**	22
Portofino | N | **City Is**	22
Primola | **E 60s**	23
NEW Quality Italian | **W 50s**	-
Quattro Gatti | **E 80s**	21
Queen | **Bklyn Hts**	24
Rao's | S | **Harlem**	22
NEW Red Gravy | **Bklyn Hts**	20
Regional | **W 90s**	19
Remi | **W 50s**	22
Riposo | N | **multi.**	21
Risotteria | **W Vill**	22
Roberta's | **Bushwick**	26
Roberto | **Fordham**	26
Roc | **TriBeCa**	22
Roman's | **Ft Greene**	24
Rosemary's | **W Vill**	21
Rossini's | **Murray Hill**	23
Rubirosa | **NoLita**	23
Rucola | N | **Boerum Hill**	24
Salumeria/Ristoranti Rosi | **multi.**	25
Sambuca | S | **W 70s**	19
Sandro's | **E 80s**	25
San Matteo | **E 90s**	25
San Pietro | **E 50s**	24
Sant Ambroeus | **multi.**	21
Sauce | S | **LES**	26
Scaletta | N | **W 70s**	21
Scalinatella | **E 60s**	24
Scalini Fedeli | N | **TriBeCa**	27
Scarpetta | **Chelsea**	26
Scottadito | N | **Park Slope**	22
SD26 | **Murray Hill**	25
Serafina | **multi.**	18
Sette Mezzo | **E 70s**	24
Settepani | S | **multi.**	23
Sfoglia | N | **E 90s**	23
NEW Sirio | **E 60s**	22
Sistina | N | **E 80s**	25
Solo | **E 50s**	25
Sorella | **LES**	24
Sosa Borella | **W 50s**	20
SottoVoce | **Park Slope**	21
Spasso | **W Vill**	23
Speedy Romeo | **Clinton Hill**	22
Spiga | **W 80s**	23

Spigolo	**E 80s**	24	Amber*	**Murray Hill**	19
Spina	**E Vill**	25	Arirang Hibachi	**multi.**	21
Supper	N	**E Vill**	25	Blue Fin*	**W 40s**	23
Tarallucci	**multi.**	20	Blue Ribbon*	**Park Slope**	25
Teodora	N	**E 50s**	20	Blue Ribbon Sushi*	**SoHo**	26
Terroir	**multi.**	20	Blue Ribbon Sushi B&G*	**W 50s**	25
Testaccio	S	**LIC**	22	Blue Ribbon/Izakaya	**LES**	21
Tevere	S	**E 80s**	24	Bohemian	**NoHo**	25
Tiella	S	**E 60s**	25	Bond St*	**NoHo**	25
Tommaso	**Dyker Hts**	23	Brushstroke/Ichimura	**TriBeCa**	26
Tony's Di Napoli	S	**multi.**	22	NEW Cherry*	**Chelsea**	-
Torrisi	**NoLita**	27	NEW Chez Sardine*	**W Vill**	20
Tosca Café	**Throgs Neck**	23	Chuko	**Prospect Hts**	23
Tra Di Noi	**Fordham**	24	Donguri	**E 80s**	25
Tratt. L'incontro	**Astoria**	26	EN Japanese	**W Vill**	25
Tratt. Dell'Arte	N	**W 50s**	22	15 East*	**Union Sq**	26
Tratt. Pesce	**multi.**	20	Fushimi*	**multi.**	23
Tratt. Romana	**Dongan Hills**	25	NEW Ganso	**Downtown Bklyn**	22
Trattoria Toscana	N	**W Vill**	25	Gari*	**multi.**	27
Trattoria Trecolori	**W 40s**	21	Gyu-Kaku	**multi.**	21
Tre Dici	**Chelsea**	23	Haru*	**multi.**	21
Tre Otto	**E 90s**	21	Hasaki*	**E Vill**	24
NEW Tre Stelle	**Flatiron**	-	Hatsuhana*	**E 40s**	25
Tuscany Grill	N	**Bay Ridge**	25	Hibino*	**Cobble Hill**	25
Umberto's	**L Italy**	21	Hide-Chan	**E 50s**	22
Uva	**E 70s**	22	Hillstone*	**multi.**	23
Valbella	N	**multi.**	24	Hurricane*	**Flatiron**	21
Vesta	**Astoria**	26	Inakaya	**W 40s**	22
Vesuvio	**Bay Ridge**	20	Ippudo	**multi.**	25
Vezzo	**Murray Hill**	23	Ise*	**multi.**	22
Via Emilia	N	**Flatiron**	23	Japonica*	**G Vill**	23
Via Quadronno	N	**E 70s**	23	Jewel Bako*	**E Vill**	25
ViceVersa	**W 50s**	22	Kajitsu	**Murray Hill**	-
Villa Berulia	N	**Murray Hill**	24	Kanoyama*	**E Vill**	25
Villa Mosconi	**G Vill**	23	Katsu-Hama	**multi.**	22
Vincent's	**L Italy**	22	Ki Sushi*	**Boerum Hill**	25
Vivolo/Cucina	**E 70s**	20	Koi*	**multi.**	24
Ze Café	**E 50s**	21	Ko Sushi*	**multi.**	21
Zero Otto	S	**multi.**	24	Kotobuki*	**E Vill**	25
Zito's	**Park Slope**	21	Kouzan*	**W 90s**	19
		Kurumazushi*	**E 40s**	28

JAMAICAN

Miss Lily's	**G Vill**	21
Negril	**G Vill**	23

JAPANESE

(* sushi specialist)

Aburiya Kinnosuke	**E 40s**	26
Aji Sushi*	**Murray Hill**	20
Aki*	**W Vill**	24

Kyo Ya	**E Vill**	27
NEW Maison O	**L Italy**	-
Masa/Bar Masa*	**W 60s**	27
Megu	**multi.**	24
Menchanko-tei	**multi.**	19
Menkui Tei	**multi.**	20
Minca	**E Vill**	23
NEW Mira Sushi*	**Flatiron**	28

Momo Sushi Shack* | **Bushwick**	27
Momoya* | **multi.**	23
Morimoto | **Chelsea**	26
Naruto Ramen | **E 80s**	22
Natsumi* | **W 50s**	24
Neta* | **G Vill**	27
NEW NY Sushi Ko* | **LES**	–
Ninja* | **TriBeCa**	19
Nippon | **E 50s**	23
Nobu | **multi.**	27
Omen A Zen | **SoHo**	25
one or eight* | **W'burg**	24
Poke* | **E 80s**	24
Rai Rai Ken | **E Vill**	20
Ramen Setagaya | **E Vill**	20
Robataya | **E Vill**	23
Rosanjin | **TriBeCa**	25
Sakagura* | **E 40s**	25
Sasabune* | **E 70s**	28
NEW Sen | **Flatiron**	23
Shabu-Shabu 70* | **E 70s**	21
Soba Nippon* | **W 50s**	22
Soba Totto | **E 40s**	24
Soba-ya | **E Vill**	23
Soto* | **W Vill**	27
Sugiyama | **W 50s**	28
SushiAnn* | **E 50s**	25
Sushi Damo* | **W 50s**	23
Sushiden* | **multi.**	24
NEW Sushi Dojo | **E Vill**	–
SushiSamba | **multi.**	22
Sushi Seki* | **E 60s**	28
Sushi Sen-nin* | **Murray Hill**	25
Sushiya* | **W 50s**	22
Sushi Yasuda* | **E 40s**	28
Sushi Zen* | **W 40s**	26
Takahachi* | **multi.**	25
Takashi | **W Vill**	26
NEW Tanoshi | **E 70s**	–
Tenzan* | **multi.**	21
Tomoe Sushi* | **G Vill**	26
Totto Ramen | **W 50s**	26
Ushiwakamaru* | **G Vill**	28
Yakitori Totto | **W 50s**	25
Yama* | **multi.**	23
Yuba* | **E Vill**	23
Yuka* | **E 80s**	22
Zenkichi | **W'burg**	26
Zuzu Ramen | **Park Slope**	23

JEWISH

Barney Greengrass | **W 80s**	24
Ben's Best | **Rego Pk**	23
Ben's Kosher | **multi.**	19
Carnegie Deli | **W 50s**	22
JoeDoe | **E Vill**	24
Katz's Deli | **LES**	24
Kutsher's | **TriBeCa**	20
Lattanzi | **W 40s**	22
Mile End | **Boerum Hill**	23
Mill Basin Deli | **Mill Basin**	22
Sammy's Roumanian | **LES**	20

KOREAN

(* barbecue specialist)

Arirang Korean | **Garment**	22
Bann | **W 50s**	21
BonChon | **multi.**	21
Cho Dang Gol | **Garment**	23
Danji | **W 50s**	25
Do Hwa* | **W Vill**	22
Gahm Mi Oak | **Garment**	20
NEW Gaonnuri* | **Garment**	21
Hangawi | **Murray Hill**	25
NEW Hanjan | **Flatiron**	22
Jungsik | **TriBeCa**	26
Kang Suh* | **Garment**	22
Kum Gang San* | **multi.**	21
Kunjip* | **Garment**	22
Kyochon | **multi.**	20
Madangsui* | **Garment**	22
Mandoo Bar | **Garment**	20
Miss Korea* | **Garment**	22
Moim | **Park Slope**	23
New WonJo* | **Garment**	22
Sik Gaek | **multi.**	22

KOSHER/
KOSHER-STYLE

Abigael's | **Garment**	20
Azuri Cafe | **W 50s**	25
Ben's Best | **Rego Pk**	23
Ben's Kosher | **multi.**	19
Buddha Bodai | **Chinatown**	23
Caravan/Dreams | **E Vill**	23
Colbeh | **Garment**	23
Hummus Kitchen | **multi.**	20
Hummus Pl. | **multi.**	22
Liebman's Deli | **Riverdale**	23
Mike's Bistro | **W 70s**	24

Mill Basin Deli | **Mill Basin**	22
Pastrami Queen | **E 70s**	21
Peacefood Café | **multi.**	23
Pongal | **Murray Hill**	24
NEW Prime Grill | **W 50s**	-
Prime KO | **W 80s**	23
Sacred Chow | **G Vill**	22
2nd Ave Deli | **multi.**	22
Solo | **E 50s**	25
Tevere | **E 80s**	24
Tiffin Wallah | **Murray Hill**	22

LAOTIAN

NEW Khe-Yo | **TriBeCa**	-

LEBANESE

Al Bustan | **E 50s**	21
Almayass | **Flatiron**	22
Byblos | **Murray Hill**	19
Ilili | **Chelsea**	24
Naya | **multi.**	22

MALAYSIAN

Fatty Crab | **W Vill**	22
Laut | **Union Sq**	22
New Malaysia | **Chinatown**	23
Nyonya | **multi.**	23

MEDITERRANEAN

Akdeniz | **W 40s**	21
Aldea | **Flatiron**	25
Alta | **G Vill**	25
Amali | **E 60s**	21
Amaranth | **E 60s**	21
Antique Garage | **SoHo**	20
Ayza Wine | **multi.**	20
Balaboosta | **NoLita**	23
Barbounia | **Flatiron**	21
Bodrum | **W 80s**	21
Boulud Sud | **W 60s**	25
Cafe Centro | **E 40s**	21
Cafe Du Soleil | **W 100s**	19
Cafe Ronda | **W 70s**	20
Conviv. Osteria | **Park Slope**	25
Courgette | **W 50s**	26
Dee's | **Forest Hills**	22
Dervish | **W 40s**	19
NEW Estela | **NoLita**	-
Extra Virgin | **W Vill**	23
Fig & Olive | **multi.**	21
508 | **Hudson Square**	22

5 Points | **NoHo**	21
Hummus Kitchen | **multi.**	20
Il Buco | **NoHo**	25
Ilili | **Chelsea**	24
Isabella's | **W 70s**	20
Kashkaval | **W 50s**	22
Little Owl | **W Vill**	25
Marseille | **W 40s**	21
Mémé | **W Vill**	22
Miriam | **Park Slope**	21
Nice Matin | **W 70s**	19
Nick & Toni | **W 60s**	19
Olea | **Ft Greene**	23
Olives | **Union Sq**	22
1 Bite Med. | **E 50s**	22
Park | **Chelsea**	17
Pera | **multi.**	20
Picholine | **W 60s**	27
Place | **W Vill**	23
Red Cat | **Chelsea**	23
Sezz Medi' | **W 100s**	22
Smile | **multi.**	21
Taboon | **multi.**	24
Tanoreen | **Bay Ridge**	26

MEXICAN

Alma | **Carroll Gdns**	20
Añejo Tequileria | **W 40s**	22
Barrio Chino | **LES**	24
Café Frida | **multi.**	21
Café Habana/Outpost | **multi.**	23
Calexico | **multi.**	21
Casa Enrique | **LIC**	24
Cascabel Taqueria | **multi.**	21
NEW Cocina Economica | **W 80s**	22
Crema | **Chelsea**	23
Dos Caminos | **multi.**	20
Dos Toros | **multi.**	21
El Centro | **W 50s**	21
El Parador | **Murray Hill**	23
El Paso | **multi.**	24
NEW El Toro Blanco | **W Vill**	22
Empellón | **multi.**	22
Fonda | **multi.**	23
Gran Electrica | **Dumbo**	22
Hecho en Dumbo | **NoHo**	23
Hell's Kitchen | **W 40s**	23
La Esquina | **multi.**	23
La Palapa | **E Vill**	22

NEW La Slowteria | **Carroll Gdns**	-|
La Superior | **W'burg**	25|
Mad Dog | **Financial**	19|
Maya | **E 60s**	23|
Maz Mezcal | **E 80s**	20|
Mercadito | **multi.**	24|
Mesa Coyoacan | **W'burg**	24|
MexiBBQ | **Astoria**	21|
Mexicana Mama | **multi.**	23|
Mexican Radio | **NoLita**	21|
Mexico Lindo | **Gramercy**	22|
Mexicue | **multi.**	19|
Móle | **multi.**	21|
Noche Mex. | **W 100s**	22|
Oaxaca | **multi.**	21|
Ofrenda | **W Vill**	23|
Pachanga Patterson | **Astoria**	23|
Pampano | **E 40s**	24|
Pequena | **multi.**	21|
Pinche Taqueria | **multi.**	21|
Pulqueria | **Chinatown**	20|
Rocking Horse | **Chelsea**	22|
Rosa Mexicano | **multi.**	22|
NEW Salvation Taco | **Murray Hill**	22|
Sinigual | **E 40s**	21|
Sueños | **Chelsea**	23|
Tacombi/Fonda Nolita | **NoLita**	23|
Toloache | **multi.**	24|
Tortilleria Nixtamal | **Corona**	26|
NEW Xixa | **W'burg**	-|

MIDDLE EASTERN

Balaboosta | **NoLita**	23|
Gazala's | **multi.**	21|
Mamoun's | **multi.**	23|
Maoz | **multi.**	21|
Mimi's Hummus | **Ditmas Pk**	24|
Moustache | **multi.**	23|
Taboon | **multi.**	24|
Tanoreen | **Bay Ridge**	26|
12 Chairs | **SoHo**	22|
Zaytoons | **multi.**	20|

MOROCCAN

Barbès | **Murray Hill**	20|
Cafe Gitane | **multi.**	21|
Cafe Mogador | **multi.**	23|
Cafe Noir | **SoHo**	20|
Mémé | **W Vill**	22|

NEW ENGLAND

Extra Fancy | **W'burg**	20|
Littleneck | **Gowanus**	24|
Luke's Lobster | **multi.**	23|
Mermaid | **multi.**	21|
Pearl Oyster | **W Vill**	26|

NEW ZEALAND

NEW Musket Room | **NoLita**	-|

NOODLE SHOPS

Arirang Korean | **Garment**	22|
Biang! | **Flushing**	24|
Bo-Ky | **multi.**	22|
Chuko | **Prospect Hts**	23|
Donguri | **E 80s**	25|
NEW Ganso | **Downtown Bklyn**	22|
Great NY Noodle | **Chinatown**	23|
Hide-Chan | **E 50s**	22|
Ippudo | **multi.**	25|
Ise | **W 50s**	22|
NEW King Noodle | **Bushwick**	-|
Menchanko-tei | **multi.**	19|
Menkui Tei | **multi.**	20|
Minca | **E Vill**	23|
Momofuku Noodle | **E Vill**	24|
Naruto Ramen | **E 80s**	22|
NEW Nightingale 9 | **Carroll Gdns**	-|
Noodle Bar | **W Vill**	21|
Pho Bang | **multi.**	22|
Rai Rai Ken | **E Vill**	20|
Ramen Setagaya | **E Vill**	20|
Republic | **Union Sq**	19|
Sammy's Noodle | **G Vill**	20|
Soba Nippon | **W 50s**	22|
Soba Totto | **E 40s**	24|
Soba-ya | **E Vill**	23|
Tasty Hand-Pulled | **Chinatown**	22|
Totto Ramen | **W 50s**	26|
Xi'an | **multi.**	24|
Zuzu Ramen | **Park Slope**	23|

NUEVO LATINO

A.G. Kitchen | **W 70s**	18|
Cabana | **multi.**	22|
Calle Ocho | **W 80s**	21|
Citrus B&G | **W 70s**	20|
Luz | **Ft Greene**	23|
Mamajuana/Taina | **multi.**	21|

CUISINES

PAN-LATIN

NEW ABC Cocina | **Flatiron**	-
A Casa Fox | **LES**	23
Bogota | **Park Slope**	24
Coppelia | **Chelsea**	23
Hudson River | **Harlem**	20
NEW La Pulperia | **W 40s**	-
Macondo | **LES**	22
Miranda | **W'burg**	23
Rayuela | **LES**	23
Yerba Buena | **multi.**	24
Yuca Bar | **E Vill**	21
Zengo | **E 40s**	22

PERSIAN

Colbeh | **Garment**	23
Persepolis | **E 70s**	22
Ravagh | **multi.**	23
Shalezeh | **E 80s**	22

PERUVIAN

Coco Roco | **multi.**	21
Flor/Mayo | **multi.**	21
Pio Pio | **multi.**	23

PIZZA

Acqua | **W 90s**	20
Adrienne's | **Financial**	23
Al Forno Pizza | **E 70s**	20
Amorina | **Prospect Hts**	23
Angelo's Pizza | **multi.**	21
Anthony's | **Park Slope**	21
Ápizz | **LES**	25
Artichoke Basille | **multi.**	22
Arturo's | **G Vill**	23
Basil Brick Oven | **Astoria**	25
Bella Blu | **E 70s**	21
Bella Via | **LIC**	22
Best Pizza | **W'burg**	24
Bettola | **W 70s**	19
Bricco | **W 50s**	21
Brio | **multi.**	20
Co. | **Chelsea**	24
Covo | **Harlem**	23
Da Ciro | **Murray Hill**	22
Dee's | **Forest Hills**	22
Denino | **Port Richmond**	26
Di Fara | **Midwood**	26
Don Antonio | **W 50s**	24
Donatella | **Chelsea**	20

Don Giovanni | **multi.**	20
57 Napoli | **E 50s**	23
Forcella | **multi.**	22
Fornino | **multi.**	24
Franny's | **Park Slope**	25
Fratelli la Bufala | **W 70s**	20
Gigino | **multi.**	21
Grimaldi's | **multi.**	23
Harry's Italian | **multi.**	21
Joe & Pat's | **Castleton Corners**	23
Joe's Pizza | **multi.**	23
John's/12th St. | **E Vill**	22
John's Pizzeria | **multi.**	22
NEW Juliana's | **Dumbo**	27
Keste Pizza | **W Vill**	25
La Bottega | **Chelsea**	21
La Pizza Fresca | **Flatiron**	22
La Villa Pizzeria | **multi.**	23
Lazzara's | **Garment**	24
Lil' Frankie | **E Vill**	24
Lombardi's | **NoLita**	24
Lucali | **Carroll Gdns**	27
Luzzo's | **E Vill**	26
Mezzaluna/Pizza | **multi.**	21
Monte's | **Gowanus**	20
Motorino | **multi.**	25
Naples 45 | **E 40s**	19
Nick's | **multi.**	23
Nicoletta | **E Vill**	19
Nino's | **E 40s**	21
Numero 28 | **multi.**	24
Otto | **G Vill**	23
Patsy's | **multi.**	20
Paulie Gee's | **Greenpt**	26
Pintaile's Pizza | **E 80s**	20
PizzArte | **W 50s**	21
Posto | **Gramercy**	24
Pulino's | **NoLita**	20
Rizzo's Pizza | **multi.**	23
Roberta's | **Bushwick**	26
Rubirosa | **NoLita**	23
San Matteo | **E 90s**	25
Saraghina | **Bed-Stuy**	26
Sezz Medi' | **W 100s**	22
South Brooklyn Pizza | **multi.**	23
Speedy Romeo | **Clinton Hill**	22
Totonno Pizza | **Coney Is**	25
Two Boots | **multi.**	19
Vesta | **Astoria**	26

Vesuvio | **Bay Ridge**	20
Vezzo | **Murray Hill**	23
Zero Otto | **multi.**	24

POLISH

Little Poland | **E Vill**	20
Lomzynianka | **Greenpt**	22

POLYNESIAN

King Yum | **Fresh Meadows**	20

PORTUGUESE

Ipanema | **W 40s**	23
NEW Louro | **W Vill**	21
Macao Trading | **TriBeCa**	20

PUB FOOD

Donovan's | **multi.**	20
NEW Ellington | **W 100s**	–
Fraunces Tavern | **Financial**	18
Henry Public | **Cobble Hill**	20
J.G. Melon | **E 70s**	21
Landmark Tavern | **W 40s**	18
Molly's | **Gramercy**	22
Neary's | **E 50s**	17
Piper's Kilt | **multi.**	21
P.J. Clarke's | **multi.**	17
Walker's | **TriBeCa**	19

PUERTO RICAN

La Taza de Oro | **Chelsea**	22
Sazon | **TriBeCa**	23
Sofrito | **E 50s**	24

QUÉBÉCOIS

Le Pescadeux | **SoHo**	22
NEW M. Wells Dinette | **LIC**	27

RUSSIAN

FireBird | **W 40s**	20
Mari Vanna | **Flatiron**	21
Russian Samovar | **W 50s**	20
Russian Tea | **W 50s**	20
Tatiana | **Brighton Bch**	20

SANDWICHES

(See also Delis)

NEW Aamanns-Copenhagen | **TriBeCa**	20
An Choi | **LES**	21
Baoguette | **multi.**	22
Beecher's Cellar | **Flatiron**	23
Best Pizza | **W'burg**	24

Bonnie's Grill | **Park Slope**	22
Bread | **NoLita**	21
Brennan | **Sheepshead**	22
Defonte's | **multi.**	24
E.A.T. | **E 80s**	20
Eisenberg's | **Flatiron**	18
Friedman's Lunch | **Chelsea**	22
NEW Fritzl's Lunch | **Bushwick**	–
Hanco's | **multi.**	20
Il Bambino | **Astoria**	27
Leo's Latticini/Corona | **multi.**	26
Shorty's | **multi.**	22
Meatball Shop | **multi.**	24
Mile End | **NoHo**	23
Nicky's | **multi.**	21
No. 7 | **multi.**	22
Num Pang | **multi.**	25
Parm | **NoLita**	23
Peanut Butter Co. | **G Vill**	21
Porchetta | **E Vill**	24
Press 195 | **Bayside**	24
Queens Kickshaw | **Astoria**	23
Roll-n-Roaster | **Sheepshead**	22
Smile | **SoHo**	21
sNice | **multi.**	20
Sweet Melissa | **Park Slope**	20
Taboon | **G Vill**	24
Untitled | **E 70s**	21
Via Quadronno | **E 70s**	23
'Wichcraft | **multi.**	17
Yura on Madison | **E 90s**	20
Zaitzeff | **Financial**	21
Zito's | **Park Slope**	21

SCANDINAVIAN

Aquavit | **E 50s**	25
NEW Aska | **W'burg**	23
Smorgas Chef | **multi.**	20

SEAFOOD

Agora Taverna | **Forest Hills**	21
Ammos | **E 40s**	21
Aquagrill | **SoHo**	26
Artie's | **City Is**	22
Atlantic Grill | **multi.**	22
Avra | **E 40s**	25
Black Duck | **Murray Hill**	22
BLT Fish | **Flatiron**	23
Blue Fin | **W 40s**	23
Blue Water | **Union Sq**	24

CUISINES

Bocelli | **Grasmere**	25
Brooklyn Fish | **Park Slope**	22
Catch | **Meatpacking**	23
City Crab | **Flatiron**	19
City Hall | **TriBeCa**	22
City Is. Lobster | **City Is**	22
City Lobster | **W 40s**	20
Cowgirl | **Seaport**	17
Crab Shanty | **City Is**	23
Crave Fishbar | **E 50s**	25
NEW Cull & Pistol | **Chelsea**	–
David Burke Fishtail | **E 60s**	24
Docks Oyster | **E 40s**	20
Ed's Chowder | **W 60s**	20
Ed's Lobster | **NoLita**	24
Elias Corner | **Astoria**	23
NEW El Toro Blanco | **W Vill**	22
Esca | **W 40s**	24
Extra Fancy | **W'burg**	20
Fish | **W Vill**	23
FishTag | **W 70s**	23
Flex Mussels | **multi.**	23
Francisco's | **Chelsea**	23
Fuleen Seafood | **Chinatown**	22
Fulton | **E 70s**	22
NEW Harlow | **E 50s**	19
Ithaka | **E 80s**	19
John Dory Oyster Bar | **Chelsea**	24
Jordans Lobster | **Sheepshead**	22
Jubilee | **E 50s**	21
Kellari | **W 40s**	22
NEW L & W Oyster | **Chelsea**	20
Le Bernardin | **W 50s**	29
Le Pescadeux | **SoHo**	22
Littleneck | **Gowanus**	24
Lobster Box | **City Is**	20
London Lennie | **Rego Pk**	23
Luke's Lobster | **multi.**	23
Lure Fishbar | **SoHo**	23
Marea | **W 50s**	28
Mary's Fish | **W Vill**	25
McCormick/Schmick | **W 50s**	18
Mermaid | **multi.**	21
Millesime | **Murray Hill**	19
Milos | **W 50s**	27
North End Grill | **Financial**	24
Oceana | **W 40s**	24
Ocean Grill | **W 70s**	24
Okeanos | **Park Slope**	21

Oriental Gdn. | **Chinatown**	22
Oyster Bar | **E 40s**	22
Pampano | **E 40s**	24
Parlor Steak | **E 90s**	21
Pearl Oyster | **W Vill**	26
Pearl Room | **Bay Ridge**	23
Periyali | **Flatiron**	23
Pescatore | **E 50s**	20
Ping's Seafood | **multi.**	21
Portofino | **City Is**	22
Randazzo's | **Sheepshead**	21
Redeye Grill | **W 50s**	21
Red Hook Lobster | **Red Hook**	24
NEW River Styx | **Greenpt**	–
Sagaponack | **Flatiron**	18
Sammy's Fishbox | **City Is**	21
Sammy's Shrimp | **City Is**	23
NEW Sea Fire Grill | **E 40s**	28
Sea Shore | **City Is**	21
Shula's | **W 40s**	21
Sik Gaek | **multi.**	22
St. Andrews | **W 40s**	19
Strip House | **W 40s**	25
Taverna Kyclades | **Astoria**	26
Telly's Taverna | **Astoria**	21
Thalassa | **TriBeCa**	24
Thalia | **W 50s**	20
Tratt. Pesce | **multi.**	20
Umberto's | **L Italy**	21
Water's Edge | **LIC**	22
NEW ZZ's Clam Bar | **G Vill**	–

SMALL PLATES

(See also Spanish tapas specialist)

Almayass | Armenian/Lebanese | **Flatiron**	22
Alta | Med. | **G Vill**	25
Añejo Tequileria | Mex. | **W 40s**	22
Beauty & Essex | Amer. | **LES**	22
Beyoglu | Turkish | **E 80s**	22
Bocca Lupo | Italian | **Cobble Hill**	23
Boukiés | Greek | **E Vill**	23
Buvette | French | **W Vill**	24
Caffe Storico | Italian | **W 70s**	20
NEW Cocotte | French | **SoHo**	–
Corsino | Italian | **W Vill**	21
Danji | Korean | **W 50s**	25
Degustation | French/Spanish | **E Vill**	28
EN Japanese | Japanese | **W Vill**	25

NEW Estela | Med. | **NoLita**	⏠
Forty Four | Amer. | **W 40s**	20
Gottino | Italian | **W Vill**	20
Graffiti | Eclectic | **E Vill**	25
NEW Hanjan | Korean | **Flatiron**	22
Ilili | Lebanese | **Chelsea**	24
'Inoteca | Italian | **LES**	21
Kashkaval | Med. | **W 50s**	22
Lunetta | Italian | **Boerum Hill**	21
Macondo | Pan-Latin | **LES**	22
Maze | French | **W 50s**	24
Mehtaphor | Eclectic | **TriBeCa**	24
Mercadito | Mex. | **multi.**	24
Misdemeanor | Eclectic | **Downtown Bklyn**	⏠
Neta | Japanese | **G Vill**	27
1 Bite Med. | Med. | **E 50s**	22
Rayuela | Pan-Latin | **LES**	23
Recette | Amer. | **W Vill**	24
Robataya | Japanese | **E Vill**	23
Sakagura | Japanese | **E 40s**	25
Salt & Fat | Amer./Asian | **Sunnyside**	26
Salumeria/Ristoranti Rosi | Italian | **multi.**	25
Sorella | Italian | **LES**	24
Terroir | Italian | **multi.**	20
Traif | Eclectic | **W'burg**	26
Uva | Italian | **E 70s**	22
Vanderbilt | Amer. | **Prospect Hts**	21
Wong | Asian | **W Vill**	24
Zenkichi | Japanese | **W'burg**	26

SOUL FOOD

Amy Ruth's | **Harlem**	22
Miss Mamie/Maude | **Harlem**	22
Pies-N-Thighs | **W'burg**	24
Sylvia's | **Harlem**	20

SOUTH AFRICAN

Braai | **W 50s**	20
Madiba | **Ft Greene**	23

SOUTH AMERICAN

Cafe Ronda | **W 70s**	20
Empanada Mama | **LES**	23
NEW MP Taverna | **Astoria**	⏠
Super Linda | **TriBeCa**	17

SOUTHERN

Amy Ruth's | **Harlem**	22
B. Smith's | **W 40s**	19

Char No. 4 | **Cobble Hill**	22
Egg | **W'burg**	24
Hill Country Chicken | **Flatiron**	20
Kitchenette | **multi.**	19
Mama Joy's | **Bushwick**	⏠
Melba's | **Harlem**	24
Miss Mamie/Maude | **Harlem**	22
Peaches | **Bed-Stuy**	23
Redhead | **E Vill**	22
Seersucker | **Carroll Gdns**	23
Sylvia's | **Harlem**	20
Tipsy Parson | **Chelsea**	21

SOUTHWESTERN

Agave | **W Vill**	20
Cilantro | **multi.**	19
Cowgirl | **multi.**	17
Mesa Grill | **Flatiron**	23
Mojave | **Astoria**	22

SPANISH

(* tapas specialist)	
Alcala | **E 40s**	21
Aldea | **Flatiron**	25
NEW Andanada 141* | **W 60s**	21
Bar Jamón* | **Gramercy**	23
NEW Barraca | **W Vill**	15
Beso | **St. George**	23
Boqueria* | **multi.**	23
Cafe Espanol | **multi.**	20
Casa Mono* | **Gramercy**	25
NEW Casa Pomona* | **W 80s**	⏠
NEW Cata | **LES**	⏠
NEW Cocotte | **SoHo**	⏠
Degustation | **E Vill**	28
El Porrón* | **E 60s**	23
El Pote | **Murray Hill**	23
El Quijote | **Chelsea**	21
El Quinto Pino* | **Chelsea**	25
NEW Flor de Sol | **Chelsea**	⏠
Francisco's | **Chelsea**	23
Il Bambino | **Astoria**	27
La Fonda/Sol | **E 40s**	22
Las Ramblas* | **W Vill**	23
La Vara* | **Cobble Hill**	27
NEW Manzanilla | **Murray Hill**	23
Meson Sevilla | **W 40s**	20
Real Madrid | **Mariners Harbor**	21
Salinas* | **Chelsea**	22
Sevilla | **W Vill**	23

CUISINES

Socarrat* | **multi.** 22

Solera* | **E 50s** 24

Tertulia* | **W Vill** 24

Tía Pol* | **Chelsea** 25

Txikito* | **Chelsea** 24

STEAKHOUSES

Arirang Hibachi | **multi.** 21

NEW Arlington Club | **E 70s** 21

Artie's | **City Is** 22

Ben & Jack's | **Murray Hill** 24

Benchmark | **Park Slope** 22

Benjamin Steak | **E 40s** 25

Bill's Food & Drink | **E 50s** 18

Bistro Le Steak | **E 70s** 18

BLT Prime | **Gramercy** 25

BLT Steak | **E 50s** 25

Bobby Van's | **multi.** 23

Bond 45 | **W 40s** 19

Buenos Aires | **E Vill** 24

Bull & Bear | **E 40s** 22

Capital Grille | **multi.** 24

Chimichurri Grill | **W 40s** 23

Christos | **Astoria** 25

Churrascaria | **multi.** 23

Circus | **E 60s** 22

City Hall | **TriBeCa** 22

Club A Steak | **E 50s** 24

NEW Costata | **SoHo** -

Del Frisco's | **multi.** 25

Delmonico's | **multi.** 23

E&E Grill House | **W 40s** 21

Embers | **Bay Ridge** 22

Empire Steakhouse | **E 50s** 24

Frankie & Johnnie's | **multi.** 22

Harry's Cafe | **Financial** 22

Hurricane | **Flatiron** 21

Jake's | **Riverdale** 24

Keens | **Garment** 26

Le Marais | **W 40s** 20

Le Relais/Venise | **E 50s** 20

Les Halles | **multi.** 20

Macelleria | **Meatpacking** 21

Maloney/Porcelli | **E 50s** 23

Manzo | **Flatiron** 25

Marble Lane | **Chelsea** 21

MarkJoseph | **Financial** 24

McCormick/Schmick | **W 50s** 18

Michael Jordan | **E 40s** 21

Morton's | **multi.** 22

Nino's | **W 50s** 21

NYY Steak | **Yankee Stadium** 22

Old Homestead | **Meatpacking** 25

Padre Figlio | **E 40s** 22

Palm | **multi.** 24

Parlor Steak | **E 90s** 21

Peter Luger | **W'burg** 27

Pietro's | **E 40s** 24

Porter House | **W 60s** 26

NEW Prime Grill | **W 50s** -

Prime KO | **W 80s** 23

Prime Meat | **Carroll Gdns** 23

NEW Quality Italian | **W 50s** -

Quality Meats | **W 50s** 26

Ricardo | **Harlem** 25

Rothmann's | **E 50s** 23

Ruth's Chris | **W 50s** 23

Shula's | **W 40s** 21

Smith/Wollensky | **E 40s** 23

Sparks | **E 40s** 25

St. Andrews | **W 40s** 19

Steak Frites | **Union Sq** 20

STK | **multi.** 23

Strip House | **multi.** 25

T-Bar Steak & Lounge | **E 70s** 21

Tre Dici | **Chelsea** 23

Uncle Jack's | **multi.** 23

Via Brasil | **W 40s** 21

Wolfgang's | **multi.** 25

Wollensky's | **E 40s** 23

SWISS

Mont Blanc | **W 40s** 23

Trestle on 10th | **Chelsea** 22

TAIWANESE

BaoHaus | **E Vill** 23

Pig Heaven | **E 80s** 21

TEAHOUSE

Alice's Tea | **multi.** 20

Lady Mendl's | **Gramercy** 22

Radiance Tea | **W 50s** 21

Sweet Melissa | **Park Slope** 20

Tea & Sympathy | **W Vill** 22

THAI

Am Thai | **multi.** 23

Ayada | **Woodside** 26

Bann Thai | **Forest Hills** 20

Breeze | **W 40s** 21

Chai Home | **multi.**	22
Erawan | **Bayside**	23
Jaiya | **multi.**	22
Joya | **Cobble Hill**	23
Kin Shop | **W Vill**	24
Kittichai | **SoHo**	24
Kuma Inn | **LES**	25
Land Thai | **W 80s**	23
Laut | **Union Sq**	22
Lemongrass | **Cobble Hill**	19
Ngam | **E Vill**	22
Pam Real Thai | **W 40s**	22
Pok Pok Ny | **Red Hook**	24
Pok Pok Phat Thai | **LES**	–
Pongsri Thai | **multi.**	21
Pure Thai | **W 50s**	25
Qi | **multi.**	22
Room Service | **multi.**	21
Sea | **multi.**	22
Siam Sq. | **Riverdale**	22
Song | **Park Slope**	24
Sookk | **W 100s**	21
Spice | **multi.**	19
Sripraphai | **Woodside**	27
Thai Market | **W 100s**	23
Topaz | **W 50s**	22
NEW Uncle Boons | **NoLita**	–
Wondee Siam | **multi.**	21
Zabb Elee | **multi.**	22

TURKISH

Akdeniz | **W 40s**	21
A La Turka | **E 70s**	19
Ali Baba | **multi.**	20
Beyoglu | **E 80s**	22
Bodrum | **W 80s**	21
Hanci | **W 50s**	21
Pasha | **W 70s**	20
Pera | **SoHo**	20
Sahara | **Gravesend**	22
Seven's Turkish | **W 70s**	20
Sip Sak | **E 40s**	20
Taci's Beyti | **Midwood**	25
Turkish Cuisine | **W 40s**	20
Turkish Grill | **Sunnyside**	22
Turkish Kitchen | **Murray Hill**	22
Turkuaz | **W 100s**	20
Uskudar | **E 70s**	21

UKRAINIAN

Veselka | **E Vill**	20

VEGETARIAN

(* vegan)

Angelica Kit.* | **E Vill**	22
B & H Dairy | **E Vill**	22
Blossom* | **multi.**	23
Butcher's Daughter* | **NoLita**	–
Candle Cafe* | **multi.**	24
Candle 79* | **E 70s**	25
Dirt Candy | **E Vill**	25
Gobo* | **multi.**	23
Hangawi | **Murray Hill**	25
Kajitsu | **Murray Hill**	–
Maoz | **multi.**	21
Peacefood Café* | **multi.**	23
Pongal | **Murray Hill**	24
Pure Food/Wine* | **Gramercy**	24
Quantum Leap* | **G Vill**	21
Saravanaa Bhavan | **multi.**	23
sNice* | **multi.**	20
Taïm | **multi.**	26
Tiffin Wallah | **Murray Hill**	22
Vatan | **Murray Hill**	23
Wild Ginger* | **multi.**	22
Zen Palate* | **multi.**	19

VENEZUELAN

Arepas | **Astoria**	24
Caracas | **multi.**	24

VIETNAMESE

An Choi | **LES**	21
Baoguette | **multi.**	22
Bo-Ky | **multi.**	22
NEW Bunker Vietnamese | **Ridgewood**	–
Hanco's | **multi.**	20
Indochine | **E Vill**	21
Le Colonial | **E 50s**	21
Nha Trang | **Chinatown**	22
Nicky's | **multi.**	21
NEW Nightingale 9 | **Carroll Gdns**	–
Omai | **Chelsea**	24
Pho Bang | **multi.**	22
Rouge et Blanc | **SoHo**	25
Veatery | **E 80s**	22

CUISINES

Locations

Includes names, street locations and Food ratings. Abbreviations key:
(a=Avenue, s=Street, e.g. 1a/116s=First Ave. at 116th St.;
3a/82-83s=Third Ave. between 82nd & 83rd Sts.)

Manhattan

CHELSEA

(26th to 30th Sts., west of 5th;
14th to 26th Sts., west of 6th)

Americano | *27s/10-11a*	22
Artichoke Basille | *10a/17s*	22
BareBurger | *8a/17-18s*	22
Biricchino | *29s/8a*	21
Bistro La Promenade | *23s/9-10a*	23
Blossom | *9a/21-22s*	23
Blue Ginger | *8a/15-16s*	21
Bocca/Bacco | *9a/20s*	21
Bombay Talkie | *9a/21-22s*	20
Bottino | *10a/24-25s*	21
Breslin | *29s/Bway-5a*	23
Brgr | *7a/26-27s*	19
Buddakan | *9a/15-16s*	25
Cafeteria | *7a/17s*	21
NEW Cherry | *16s/8-9a*	-
Chop-Shop | *10a/24-25s*	22
Co. | *9a/24s*	24
Colicchio/Sons | *10a/15-16s*	25
Cookshop | *10a/20s*	23
Coppelia | *14s/7-8a*	23
Crema | *17s/6-7a*	23
NEW Cull & Pistol | *9a/15-16s*	-
Da Umberto | *17s/6-7a*	25
Del Posto | *10a/15-16s*	26
Donatella | *8a/19-20s*	20
Don Giovanni | *10a/23s*	20
El Quijote | *23s/7-8a*	21
El Quinto Pino | *24s/9-10a*	25
Eolo | *7a/21-22s*	21
NEW Flor de Sol | *10a/16s*	-
Francisco's | *23s/6-7a*	23
Friedman's Lunch | *9a/15-16s*	22
Giovanni Rana | *9a/15-16s*	24
Grand Sichuan | *multi.*	20
NEW Hybird | *9a/15-16s*	-
Ilili | *5a/27-28s*	24
John Dory Oyster Bar | *Bway/29s*	24
La Bergamote | *9a/20s*	24
La Bottega | *9a/17s*	21

La Lunchonette | *10a/18s*	21
NEW L & W Oyster | *5a/28-29s*	20
La Taza de Oro | *8a/14-15s*	22
Legend | *7a/15-16s*	21
Le Grainne Cafe | *9a/21s*	20
Le Zie | *7a/20-21s*	22
Lucky's Famous | *23s/7-8a*	20
Marble Lane | *16s/8-9a*	21
Meatball Shop | *9a/22s*	24
Mexicue | *7a/29-30s*	19
Momoya | *7a/21s*	23
NEW Montmartre | *8a/18s*	19
Mooncake | *30s/7-8a*	20
Morimoto | *10a/15-16s*	26
NoMad | *Bway/28s*	27
No. 7 | *Bway/28-29s*	22
Num Pang | *9a/15-16s*	25
Omai | *9a/19-20s*	24
Park | *10a/17-18s*	17
Patsy's | *23s/8-9a*	20
Pepe Giallo/Rosso | *10a/24-25s*	22
Pinche Taqueria | *14s/6-7a*	21
Pongsri Thai | *23s/6-7a*	21
Rare B&G | *26s/6-7a*	21
Red Cat | *10a/23-24s*	23
Rocking Horse | *8a/19-20s*	22
Room Service | *8a/18-19s*	21
Salinas | *9a/18-19s*	22
Sarabeth's | *9a/15-16s*	20
Scarpetta | *14s/8-9a*	26
Socarrat | *19s/7-8a*	22
Son Cubano | *27s/10-11a*	22
Spice | *multi.*	19
Sueños | *17s/8-9a*	23
Tía Pol | *10a/22-23s*	25
Tipsy Parson | *9a/19-20s*	21
Tre Dici | *26s/6-7a*	23
Trestle on 10th | *10a/24s*	22
Txikito | *9a/24-25s*	24
Uncle Nick's | *8a/29s*	21
Westville | *18s/8a*	23
'Wichcraft | *multi.*	17
NEW Willow Road | *10a/15-16s*	23

CHINATOWN

(Canal to Pearl Sts., east of B'way)

Amazing 66 | *Mott/Bayard-Canal* 22
Big Wong | *Mott/Bayard-Canal* 22
Bo-Ky | *Bayard/Mott-Mulberry* 22
Buddha Bodai | *Mott/Worth* 23
Dim Sum Go Go | 21
  E Bway/Catherine-Chatham
Excellent Dumpling | 22
  Lafayette/Canal-Walker
Forlini's | *Baxter/Bayard-Walker* 19
Fuleen Seafood | *Division/Bowery* 22
Golden Unicorn | *E Bway/Catherine* 21
Great NY Noodle | *Bowery/Bayard* 23
Hop Kee | *Mott/Chatham-Mosco* 21
Jing Fong | *Elizabeth/Bayard-Canal* 20
Joe's Shanghai | 22
  Pell/Bowery-Doyers
Joe's | *Pell/Doyers* 20
New Malaysia | 23
  Bowery/Bayard-Canal
Nha Trang | *multi.* 22
Nice Green Bo | 22
  Bayard/Elizabeth-Mott
Nom Wah Tea | 21
  Doyers/Chatham-Pell
Oriental Gdn. | 22
  Elizabeth/Bayard-Canal
Peking Duck | 22
  Mott/Chatham-Pell
Ping's Seafood | 21
  Mott/Chatham-Mosco
Pongsri Thai | *Bayard/Baxter* 21
Pulqueria | *Dyers/Bowery-Pell* 20
Tasty Hand-Pulled | *Doyers/Bowery* 22
Wo Hop | *Mott/Mosco-Worth* 22
Xi'an | *Bayard/Bowery-Mott* 24

EAST 40s

Aburiya Kinnosuke | *45s/2-3a* 26
Alcala | *44s/2-3a* 21
Ali Baba | *2a/46s* 20
Ammos | *Vanderbilt/44-45s* 21
Aretsky's Patroon | *46s/Lex-3a* 22
Avra | *48s/Lex-3a* 25
Benjamin Steak | *41s/Mad-Park* 25
Bobby Van's | *Park/46s* 23
Bukhara Grill | *49s/2-3a* 21
Bull & Bear | *Lex/49-50s* 22
Cafe Centro | *Park/45s* 21
Capital Grille | *42s/Lex-3a* 24

Chin Chin | *49s/2-3a* 23
Cibo | *2a/41s* 20
Cipriani Dolci | *42s/Vanderbilt* 22
Darbar | *46s/Lex-3a* 21
Docks Oyster | *3a/40s* 20
Fabio Piccolo | *44s/2-3a* 23
Grifone | *46s/2-3a* 25
Gyu-Kaku | *3a/49-50s* 21
Hatsuhana | *multi.* 25
Il Postino | *49s/1-2a* 23
Junior's | *42s/Vanderbilt* 19
Katsu-Hama | *47s/5a-Mad* 22
Kurumazushi | *47s/5a-Mad* 28
La Fonda/Sol | *Park/44s* 22
NEW LCL | *42s/2-3a* -
Lexington Brass | *Lex/48s* 18
Megu | *1a/47-48s* 24
Menchanko-tei | *45s/Lex-3a* 19
Michael Jordan | *Vanderbilt/43s* 21
Morton's | *5a/45s* 22
Nanni | *46s/Lex-3a* 24
Naples 45 | *Park/45s* 19
Naya | *3a/43s* 22
99 Mi. to Philly | *45s/2a* 21
Nino's | *2a/47-48s* 21
Num Pang | *41s/Lex-3a* 25
Osteria Laguna | *42s/2-3a* 21
Oyster Bar | *42s/Park* 22
Padre Figlio | *44s/1-2a* 22
Palm | *multi.* 24
Pampano | *multi.* 24
Patsy's | *2a/42-43s* 20
Pera | *Mad/41-42s* 20
Pietro's | *43s/2-3a* 24
Sakagura | *43s/2-3a* 25
NEW Sea Fire Grill | *48s/Lex-3a* 28
Sinigual | *3a/41s* 21
Sip Sak | *2a/49-50s* 20
Smith/Wollensky | *3a/49s* 23
Soba Totto | *43s/2-3a* 24
Sparks | *46s/2-3a* 25
Sushiden | *49s/5a-Mad* 24
Sushi Yasuda | *43s/2-3a* 28
Tulsi | *46s/2-3a* 24
Two Boots | *42s/Vanderbilt* 19
'Wichcraft | *multi.* 17
Wollensky's | *49s/3a* 23
Yama | *49s/1-2a* 23
Zengo | *3a/40s* 22

LOCATIONS

EAST 50s

Al Bustan	53s/1-2a	21
Amma	51s/2-3a	25
Angelo's Pizza	2a/55s	21
Aquavit	55s/Mad-Park	25
Armani Rist.	5a/56s	23
Bice	54s/5a-Mad	21
Bill's Food & Drink	54s/Mad-Park	18
Bistro Vendôme	58s/1a-Sutton	22
BLT Steak	57s/Lex-Park	25
Bobby Van's	54s/Lex-Park	23
BonChon	2a/51s	21
Bottega Del Vino	59s/5a-Mad	22
Brasserie	53s/Lex-Park	22
Brick Ln. Curry	53s/2-3a	21
BXL	51s/2-3a	19
Casa Lever	Park/53s	23
Caviar Russe	Mad/54-55s	26
Cellini	54s/Mad-Park	22
Chola	58s/2-3a	23
NEW Clarke's Standard	Lex/54s	20
Club A Steak	58s/2-3a	24
Crave Fishbar	2a/50-51s	25
Darbar	55s/Lex-3a	21
David Burke/Bloom.	59s/Lex-3a	19
Dawat	58s/2-3a	23
DeGrezia	50s/2-3a	24
Destino	1a/50s	19
Deux Amis	51s/1-2a	20
Dos Caminos	3a/50-51s	20
Empire Steakhouse	52s/5-6a	24
Ethos	1a/51s	21
Felidia	58s/2-3a	26
57 Napoli	57/Lex-Park	23
Fig & Olive	52s/5a-Mad	21
Fiorini	56s/2-3a	21
Four Seasons	52s/Lex-Park	27
Fresco	52s/Mad-Park	22
Fusia	Lex/56s	22
Grand Sichuan	2a/55-56s	20
NEW Harlow	56s/Lex-Park	19
Harry Cipriani	5a/59-60s	22
Hide-Chan	52s/2-3a	22
Hillstone	3a/54s	23
Jubilee	1a/52-53s	21
Kati Roll Company	53s/2-3a	22
La Gioconda	53s/2-3a	22
La Grenouille	52s/5a-Mad	28
La Mangeoire	2a/53-54s	22

La Mediterranée	2a/50-51s	20
Lavo	58s/Mad-Park	21
Le Cirque	58s/Lex-3a	25
Le Colonial	57s/Lex-3a	21
Le Perigord	52s/FDR-1a	25
Le Relais/Venise	Lex/52s	20
Luna Piena	53s/2-3a	20
Lychee Hse.	55s/Lex-3a	22
Maloney/Porcelli	50s/Mad-Park	23
Monkey Bar	54s/Mad-Park	20
Montebello	56s/Lex-Park	24
Mr. Chow	57s/1-2a	22
Mr. K's	Lex/51s	23
National	Lex/50s	20
Naya	2a/55-56s	22
Neary's	57s/1a	17
NEW Nerai	54s/Mad-Park	-
Nippon	52s/Lex-3a	23
1 Bite Med.	3a/52-3s	22
Peking Duck	53s/2-3a	22
Pescatore	2a/50-1s	20
Peter's 1969	Lex/55-56s	20
P.J. Clarke's	3a/55s	17
Rosa Mexicano	1a/58s	22
Rothmann's	54s/5a-Mad	23
San Pietro	54s/5a-Mad	24
Serafina	58s/Mad-Park	18
Shun Lee Palace	55s/Lex-3a	24
Smith	2a/51s	19
Socarrat	2a/50-51a	22
Sofrito	57s/1a-Sutton	24
Solera	53s/2-3a	24
Solo	Mad/55-56s	25
SushiAnn	51s/Mad-Park	25
Tao	58s/Mad-Park	24
Tenzan	2a/52-53s	21
Teodora	57s/Lex-3a	20
Valbella	53s/5a-Mad	24
Wolfgang's	54s/3a	25
Yuva	58s/2-3a	23
Ze Café	52s/FDR-1a	21

EAST 60s

Alice's Tea	64s/Lex	20
Amali	60s/Park	21
Amaranth	62s/5a-Mad	21
NEW Anassa Taverna	60s/3a	-
Arabelle	64s/Mad-Park	24
Bar Italia	Mad/66s	19
Bistro Chat Noir	66s/5a-Mad	20

LOCATIONS

Sette Mezzo	*Lex/70-71s*	24
Shabu-Shabu 70	*70s/1-2a*	21
Shanghai Pavilion	*3a/78-79s*	21
Sojourn	*79s/2-3a*	23
Spice	*1a/77s*	19
Swifty's	*Lex/72-73s*	17
Szechuan Gourmet	*2a/72-73s*	23
NEW Tanoshi	*York/73-74s*	-
T-Bar Steak & Lounge	*3a/73*	21
Untitled	*Mad/75s*	21
Uskudar	*2a/73-74s*	21
Uva	*2a/77-78s*	22
Via Quadronno	*73s/5a-Mad*	23
Vivolo/Cucina	*74s/Lex-Park*	20
V-Note	*1a/79-80s*	23
Yefsi Estiatorio	*York/78-79s*	25

EAST 80s

Alice's Tea	*81s/2-3a*	20
Amber	*3a/80s*	19
Andre's Café	*2a/84-85s*	19
Antonucci	*81s/Lex-3a*	23
Baluchi's	*2a/89-90s*	19
Beyoglu	*3a/81s*	22
Burger Bistro	*1a/86-87s*	22
Café d'Alsace	*2a/88s*	21
Café Sabarsky/Fledermaus	*5a/86s*	22
Caffe Grazie	*84s/5a-Mad*	19
Cascabel Taqueria	*2a/80s*	21
Chef Ho's	*2a/89-90s*	22
Cilantro	*2a/89s*	19
Crown	*81s/5a-Mad*	21
Divino	*2a/80-81s*	19
Donguri	*83s/1-2a*	25
East End Kitchen	*81s/E End-York*	20
E.A.T.	*Mad/80-81s*	20
Elio's	*2a/84-85s*	24
Erminia	*83s/2-3a*	24
Felice	*1a/83s*	21
Firenze	*2a/82-83s*	21
Flex Mussels	*82s/Lex-3a*	23
Giovanni	*83s/5a-Mad*	23
Girasole	*82s/Lex-3a*	21
Gobo	*3a/81s*	23
Heidelberg	*2a/85-86s*	20
Hummus Kitchen	*2a/83-84s*	20
Italianissimo	*84s/1-2a*	22
Ithaka	*86s/1-2a*	19
Jackson Hole	*2a/83-84s*	19

Jaiya	*2a/80-81s*	22
Kings' Carriage	*82s/2-3a*	21
Ko Sushi	*York/85s*	21
Le Pain Q.	*Mad/84-85s*	18
Luke's Lobster	*81s/2-3a*	23
Maz Mezcal	*86s/1-2a*	20
Móle	*2a/89-90s*	21
Naruto Ramen	*3a/89-90s*	22
Nicola's	*84s/Lex-3a*	21
Papaya King	*86s/3a*	21
Penrose	*2a/82-83s*	20
Pig Heaven	*2a/80-81s*	21
Pintaile's Pizza	*York/83-84s*	20
Poke	*85s/1-2a*	24
Quattro Gatti	*81s/3a*	21
Sandro's	*81s/1-2a*	25
Shake Shack	*86s/Lex-3a*	21
Shalezeh	*3a/80-81s*	22
Sistina	*2a/80-81s*	25
Spigolo	*2a/81s*	24
Taste	*3a/80-1s*	21
Tenzan	*2a/89s*	21
Tevere	*84s/Lex-3a*	24
Toloache	*82s/Lex-3a*	24
Tratt. Pesce	*3a/87-88s*	20
Two Boots	*2a/84s*	19
Veatery	*2a/88s*	22
Wa Jeal	*2a/82-83s*	24
Yuka	*2a/80-81s*	22

EAST 90s & 100s

(90th to 110th Sts.)

ABV	*Lex/97s*	20
Brick Ln. Curry	*3a/93-94s*	21
El Paso	*multi.*	24
Maoz	*Harlem Meer*	21
Moustache	*Lex/102s*	23
Nick's	*2a/94s*	23
Osso Buco	*3a/93s*	20
Paola's	*Mad/92s*	23
Parlor Steak	*3a/90s*	21
Pascalou	*Mad/92-93s*	21
Pinocchio	*1a/90-91s*	24
Pio Pio	*1a/90-91s*	23
Rizzo's Pizza	*Lex/93s*	23
San Matteo	*2a/90s*	25
Sarabeth's	*Mad/92s*	20
Sfoglia	*Lex/92s*	23
Table d'Hôte	*92s/Mad-Park*	19
Tre Otto	*Mad/97-98s*	21

Yura on Madison	*Mad/92s*	20
Zebú Grill	*92s/1-2a*	23

EAST VILLAGE

(14th to Houston Sts., east of B'way, excluding NoHo)

NEW Alder	*2a/9-10s*	20
Angelica Kit.	*12s/2a*	22
Apiary	*3a/10-11s*	23
Artichoke Basille	*14s/1-2a*	22
Awash	*6s/1-2a*	22
Back Forty	*Ave B/12s*	22
B & H Dairy	*2a/7s-St Marks*	22
Banjara	*1a/6s*	23
BaoHaus	*14s/2-3a*	23
Barbone	*Ave B/11-12s*	23
BareBurger	*2a/5s*	22
Black Iron Burger	*5s/Aves A-B*	21
Blue 9 Burger	*3a/12-3s*	19
NEW Blue Ribbon Fried Chicken	*1s/2a*	–
Boukiés	*2s/2a*	23
Brick Ln. Curry	*6s/1-2a*	21
Buenos Aires	*6s/Aves A-B*	24
Butter	*Lafayette/Astor-4s*	23
Cacio e Pepe	*2a/11-12s*	20
Cafe Mogador	*St Marks/Ave A-1a*	23
Cafe Orlin	*St. Marks/2a*	22
Calliope	*4s/2a*	22
Caracas	*multi.*	24
Caravan/Dreams	*6s/1a*	23
ChikaLicious	*10s/1-2a*	25
Crif Dogs	*St Marks/Ave A-1a*	23
DBGB	*Bowery/1s-Houston*	24
Degustation	*5s/2-3a*	28
Dirt Candy	*9s/Ave A-1a*	25
Dos Toros	*4a/13s*	21
Dumpling Man	*St Marks/Ave A-1a*	20
Edi & The Wolf	*Ave C/6-7s*	23
Empellón	*1a/6-7s*	22
NEW Exchange Alley	*9s/Ave A-1a*	–
5 Napkin Burger	*14s/3-4a*	21
Fonda	*Ave B/3s*	23
NEW Fourth	*4a/13s*	–
Frank	*2a/5-6s*	23
Gemma	*Bowery/2-3s*	21
Gnocco	*10s/Aves A-B*	22
Graffiti	*10s/1-2a*	25
Grand Sichuan	*St Marks/2-3a*	20

Gyu-Kaku	*Cooper/Astor-4s*	21
Hasaki	*9s/2-3a*	24
Haveli	*2a/5-6s*	21
Hearth	*12s/1a*	24
Hummus Pl.	*St Marks/Ave A-1a*	22
Il Bagatto	*2s/Aves A-B*	25
Indochine	*Lafayette/Astor-4s*	21
Ippudo	*4a/9-10s*	25
NEW Jeepney	*1a/12-13s*	23
Jewel Bako	*5s/2-3a*	25
JoeDoe	*1s/1-2a*	24
Joe's Pizza	*14s/3a*	23
John's/12th St.	*12s/2a*	22
Kanoyama	*2a/11-12s*	25
Kotobuki	*3a/10-11s*	25
Kyo Ya	*7s/1a*	27
La Palapa	*St Marks/1-2a*	22
NEW L'Apicio	*1s/Bowery-2a*	22
Lavagna	*5s/Aves A-B*	24
NEW Library/Public	*Lafayette/Astor-4s*	18
Lil' Frankie	*1a/1-2s*	24
Little Poland	*2a/12-13s*	20
Lucien	*1a/1s*	23
Luke's Lobster	*7s/Ave A-1a*	23
Luzzo's	*1a/12-13s*	26
Maharlika	*1a/6-7s*	25
Mamoun's	*St Marks/2-3a*	23
Menkui Tei	*Cooper/7s-St Marks*	20
Mercadito	*Ave B/10-11s*	24
Mermaid	*2a/5-6s*	21
NEW Mighty Quinn's	*2a/6s*	24
Minca	*5s/Aves A-B*	23
Momofuku Ko	*1a/10-11s*	27
Momofuku Noodle	*1a/10-11s*	24
Momofuku Ssäm	*2a/13s*	25
Motorino	*12s/1-2a*	25
Moustache	*10s/A-1a*	23
Ngam	*3a/12-13s*	22
Nicoletta	*2a/10s*	19
99 Mi. to Philly	*3a/12-13s*	21
Northern Spy	*12s/Aves A-B*	24
Numero 28	*2a/11-12s*	24
Oaxaca	*Extra/Bowery-2a*	21
Papaya King	*St. Marks/3a*	21
Peels	*Bowery/2s*	20
Perbacco	*4s/Aves A-B*	23
Pommes Frites	*2a/7s*	24
Porchetta	*7s/Ave A-1a*	24

LOCATIONS

Porsena	*7s/2-3a*	22
Prune	*1s/1-2a*	25
Pylos	*7s/Ave A-1a*	27
Rai Rai Ken	*10s/1-2a*	20
Ramen Setagaya	*St Marks/2-3a*	20
Redhead	*13s/1-2a*	22
Robataya	*9s/2-3a*	23
S'MAC	*12s/1-2a*	23
Smith	*3a/10-11s*	19
Soba-ya	*9s/2-3a*	23
South Brooklyn Pizza	*1a/7s-St Marks*	23
Spice	*multi.*	19
Spina	*Ave B/11s*	25
Supper	*2s/Aves A-B*	25
NEW Sushi Dojo	*1a/6-7s*	-
Takahachi	*Ave A/5-6s*	25
Tarallucci	*1a/10s*	20
Terroir	*12s/Ave A-1a*	20
26 Seats	*Ave B/10-11s*	22
Two Boots	*Ave A/3s*	19
Vanessa's Dumpling	*14s/2-3a*	21
Veselka	*2a/9s*	20
Westville	*Ave A/11s*	23
Xi'an	*St Marks/1a*	24
Yerba Buena	*Ave A/1-2s*	24
Yuba	*9s/3-4a*	23
Yuca Bar	*Ave A/7s*	21
Zabb Elee	*2a/4-5s*	22
Zum Schneider	*Ave C/7s*	21

FINANCIAL DISTRICT

(South of Murray St.)

Adrienne's	*Pearl/Hanover*	23
Battery Gdns.	*Battery Pk/State*	20
Bill's Bar	*West/Wash*	19
BLT B&G	*Wash/Albany-Carlisle*	22
Blue Smoke	*Vesey/N End-West*	22
Bobby Van's	*Broad/Exchange*	23
NEW Cantine Paris.	*Kenmare/Elizabeth*	-
Capital Grille	*Bway/Pine*	24
Cipriani Club 55	*Wall/William*	23
NEW Clarke's Standard	*Maiden/Pearl*	20
Delmonico's	*Beaver/William*	23
Felice	*Gold/Maiden-Platt*	21
Fraunces Tavern	*Pearl/Broad*	18
Gigino	*Battery/Little West*	21
Harry's Cafe	*Hanover/Pearl-Stone*	22

Harry's Italian	*multi.*	21
Haru	*Wall/Pearl*	21
Ise	*Pine/Pearl-William*	22
Les Halles	*John/Bway-Nassau*	20
Luke's Lobster	*William/Beaver-Broad*	23
Mad Dog	*Pearl/Broad-Hanover*	19
MarkJoseph	*Water/Dover-Peck*	24
Mooncake	*John/Cliff-Pearl*	20
Morton's	*Wash/Albany-Cedar*	22
Nicky's	*Nassau/Ann-Fulton*	21
North End Grill	*N End/Murray-Vesey*	24
P.J. Clarke's	*World Fin/Vesey*	17
Shake Shack	*Murray/N End-West*	21
Shorty's	*Pearl/Broad-Coenties*	22
Smorgas Chef	*Stone/William*	20
Stage Door	*Vesery/Bway-Church*	19
Toloache	*Maiden/Gold-William*	24
2 West	*West/Battery*	22
Wall/Water	*Wall/Water*	21
Zaitzeff	*Nassau/John*	21

FLATIRON

(14th to 26th Sts., 6th Ave. to Park Ave. S., excluding Union Sq.)

NEW ABC Cocina	*19s/Bway-Park*	-
ABC Kitchen	*18s/Bway-Park*	26
Aldea	*17s/5-6a*	25
Alison Eighteen	*18s/5-6a*	21
Almayass	*21s/Bway-Park*	22
Almond	*22s/Bway-Park*	20
A Voce	*Mad/26s*	24
Barbounia	*Park/20s*	21
Basta Pasta	*17s/5-6a*	23
Beecher's Cellar	*Bway/20s*	23
Birreria	*5a/23-24s*	20
BLT Fish	*17s/5-6a*	23
Bocca	*19s/Bway-Park*	22
Boqueria	*19s/5-6a*	23
Brio	*Bway/21s*	20
BXL	*22s/5-6a*	19
Château Cherbuliez	*20s/5-6a*	-
City Bakery	*18s/5-6a*	22
City Crab	*Park/19s*	19
NEW Clarke's Standard	*Bway/17-18s*	20
Craft	*19s/Bway-Park*	26
Craftbar	*Bway/20s*	23
Dévi	*18s/Bway-5a*	23

Eataly	*5a/23-24s*	18
Eisenberg's	*5a/22*	18
Eleven Madison	*Mad/24s*	28
Giorgio's	*21s/Bway-Park*	21
Gramercy Tavern	*20s/Bway-Park*	28
Grimaldi's	*6a/20-21s*	23
NEW Hanjan	*26s/Bway-6a*	22
NEW Harding's	*21s/Bway-Park*	–
Haru	*Park/18s*	21
Hill Country	*26s/Bway-6a*	23
Hill Country Chicken	*Bway/25s*	20
Hurricane	*Park/26s*	21
Junoon	*24s/5-6a*	24
La Pizza Fresca	*20s/Bway-Park*	22
Le Pain Q.	*Bway/21-22s*	18
Manzo	*5a/23-24s*	25
Mari Vanna	*20s/Bway-Park*	21
Markt	*6a/21s*	20
NEW Maysville	*26s/Bway-6a*	22
Mesa Grill	*5a/15-16s*	23
NEW Mira Sushi	*22s/5-6a*	28
Num Pang	*Bway/25-26s*	25
Periyali	*20s/5-6a*	23
Petite Abeille	*17s/5-6a*	19
Rosa Mexicano	*18s/Bway-5a*	22
Sagaponack	*22s/5-6a*	18
Schnipper´s	*23s/Mad-Park*	19
NEW Sen	*21s/5-6a*	23
Shake Shack	*23s/Bway-Mad*	21
SushiSamba	*Park/19-20s*	22
Tamarind	*22s/Bway-Park*	26
Tarallucci	*18s/Bway-5a*	20
NEW Tre Stelle	*24s/5-6a*	–
Veritas	*20s/Bway-Park*	25
Via Emilia	*21s/Bway-Park*	23
'Wichcraft	*20s/Bway*	17
Wildwood BBQ	*Park/18-19s*	19
Zero Otto	*21s/5-6a*	24

GARMENT DISTRICT

(30th to 40th Sts., west of 5th)

Abigael's	*Bway/38-39s*	20
Ai Fiori	*5a/36-37s*	26
Arirang Korean	*32s/Bway-5a*	22
Arno	*38s/Bway*	20
Ayza Wine	*31s/Bway-5a*	20
Ben's Kosher	*38s/7-8a*	19
BonChon	*38s/7-8a*	21
Brother Jimmy's	*8a/31s*	17

Casa Nonna	*38s/8-9a*	21
Chef Yu	*8a/36-37s*	21
Cho Dang Gol	*35s/5-6a*	23
Colbeh	*39s/5-6a*	23
Delmonico's	*36s/7-8a*	23
Frankie & Johnnie's	*37s/5-6a*	22
Gahm Mi Oak	*32s/Bway-5a*	20
NEW Gaonnuri	*Bway/32s*	21
Go Burger	*38s/8-9a*	18
Kang Suh	*Bway/32s*	22
Kati Roll Company	*39s/5-6a*	22
Keens	*36s/5-6a*	26
Kum Gang San	*32s/Bway-5a*	21
Kunjip	*32s/5a*	22
Lazzara's	*38s/7-8a*	24
Madangsui	*35s/5-6a*	22
Mandoo Bar	*32s/Bway-5a*	20
Mercato	*39s/8-9a*	21
Miss Korea	*32s/Bway-5a*	22
New WonJo	*32s/Bway-5a*	22
Sarabeth's	*5a/38-39s*	20
Stage Door	*Penn Plaza/33-34s*	19
Szechuan Gourmet	*39s/5-6a*	23
Uncle Jack's	*9a/34-35s*	23

GRAMERCY PARK

(14th to 23rd Sts., east of Park Ave. S.)

Bar Jamón	*17s/Irving*	23
BLT Prime	*22s/Lex-Park*	25
Brother Jimmy's	*16s/Irving-Union Sq*	17
Casa Mono	*Irving/17s*	25
Defonte's	*3a/21s*	24
Friend/Farmer	*Irving/18-19s*	18
House	*17s/Irving-Park*	21
Lady Mendl's	*Irving/17-18s*	22
La Follia	*3a/19s*	22
Maialino	*Lex/21s*	26
Mexico Lindo	*2a/26s*	22
Molly's	*3a/22-23s*	22
Novitá	*22s/Lex-Park*	25
Paul & Jimmy's	*18s/Irving-Park*	20
Petite Abeille	*20s/1a*	19
Ponty Bistro	*3a/18-19s*	22
Posto	*2a/18s*	24
Pure Food/Wine	*Irving/17-18s*	24
Rolf's	*3a/22s*	17
Yama	*17s/Irving*	23
Zen Palate	*18s/Irving-Park*	19

LOCATIONS

GREENWICH VILLAGE

(Houston to 14th Sts., west of B'way, east of 6th Ave.)

Alta	10s/5-6a	25
Artichoke Basille	MacDougal/Blkr-3s	22
Arturo's	Houston/Thompson	23
Babbo	Waverly/MacDougal-6a	27
BareBurger	Laguardia/3s-Wash Sq.	22
Bar Pitti	6a/Blkr-Houston	23
BLT Burger	6a/11-12s	22
Blue Hill	Wash pl/MacDougal-6a	27
Burger Joint	8s/MacDougal	24
Cafe Espanol	Blkr/Sullivan	20
Camaje	MacDougal/Blkr-Houston	20
NEW Carbone	Thompson/Blkr-Houston	21
Chez Jacqueline	MacDougal/Blkr-Houston	19
Corkbuzz	13-5a/Uni	22
Creperie	MacDougal/Blkr-3s	22
Cuba	Thompson/Blkr-3s	23
Da Andrea	13s/5-6a	23
Da Silvano	6a/Blkr-Houston	22
Gotham B&G	12s/5a-Uni	27
NEW Grape & Vine	13s/6a	-
Gray's Papaya	6a/8s	20
Il Cantinori	10s/Bway-Uni	23
Il Mulino	3s/Sullivan-Thompson	26
Jackson Diner	Uni/10-11s	21
Jane	Houston/La Guardia-Thompson	21
Japonica	Uni/12s	23
Kati Roll Company	MacDougal/Blkr	22
Knickerbocker	Uni/9s	20
La Lanterna	MacDougal/3-4s	20
Le Pain Q.	multi.	18
Lion	9s/5-6a	21
Lupa	Thompson/Blkr-Houston	25
Mamoun's	MacDougal/Bleecker-3s	23
Maoz	8s/Bway-Uni	21
Mermaid	MacDougal/Blkr-Houston	21
Meskerem	MacDougal/Blkr-3s	23
Mexicana Mama	12s/Bway-Uni	23
Mezzaluna/Pizza	Houston/MacDougal	21

Minetta Tavern	MacDougal/Minetta	24
Miss Lily's	Houston/Sullivan	21
Negril	3s/La Guardia-Thompson	23
Neta	8s/6a	27
North Sq.	Waverly/MacDougal	23
Num Pang	12s/5a-Uni	25
Otto	5a/8s	23
Patsy's	Uni/10-11s	20
Peacefood Café	11s/Uni	23
Peanut Butter Co.	Sullivan/Blkr-3s	21
Perla	Minetta/MacDougal-6a	24
Quantum Leap	Thompson/Blkr-3s	21
Sacred Chow	Sullivan/Blkr-3s	22
Sammy's Noodle	6a/10-11s	20
Spice	13s/Bway-Uni	19
Strip House	12s/5a-Uni	25
Taboon	13s/5a-Uni	24
Tomoe Sushi	Thompson/Blkr-Houston	26
NEW Umami Burger	6a/9-10s	-
Ushiwakamaru	Houston/MacDougal-Sullivan	28
Villa Mosconi	MacDougal/Blkr-Houston	23
'Wichcraft	8s/Mercer	17
NEW ZZ's Clam Bar	Thompson/Blkr-Houston	-

HARLEM/ EAST HARLEM

(110th to 155th Sts., excluding Columbia U. area)

Amor Cubano	3a/111s	23
Amy Ruth's	116s/Lenox-7a	22
Chez Lucienne	Lenox/125-126s	21
Corner Social	Lenox/126s	17
Covo	135s/12a	23
Dinosaur BBQ	125s/12a	23
El Paso	116s/2-3a	24
5 & Diamond	Douglass/112-113s	22
NEW Harlem Shake	124s/Lenox	-
Hudson River	133s/12a	20
Lido	Douglass/117s	22
Melba's	114s/8a	24
Miss Mamie/Maude	multi.	22
Patsy's	1a/117-118s	20
Rao's	114s/Pleasant	22
Red Rooster	Lenox/125-126s	22
Ricardo	2a/110-111s	25

LOCATIONS

MEATPACKING

(Gansevoort to 15th Sts.,
west of 9th Ave.)

Bagatelle	*Little W 12s/9a*	20
Beaumarchais	*13/9a-Wash*	22
Bill's Bar	*9a/13s*	19
Brother Jimmy's	*West/Gansevoort-Horatio*	17
Catch	*9a/Little W 12-13s*	23
Dos Caminos	*Hudson/13-14s*	20
Fig & Olive	*13s/9a-Wash*	21
Macelleria	*Gansevoort/Greenwich s-Wash*	21
NEW Manon	*14s/9-10a*	-
Old Homestead	*9a/14-15s*	25
Paradou	*Little W 12s/Greenwich s-Wash*	22
Pastis	*9a/Little W 12s*	22
Sea	*Wash/Little W 12s*	22
Serafina	*9a/Little W 12s*	18
Spice Market	*13s/9a*	23
Standard Grill	*Wash/Little W 12-13s*	22
STK	*Little W 12s/9a-Wash*	23
Valbella	*13s/9a-Wash*	24

MURRAY HILL

(26th to 40th Sts., east of 5th; 23rd to
26th Sts., east of Park Ave. S.)

Aji Sushi	*3a/34-35s*	20
Ali Baba	*34s/2-3a*	20
Amber	*3a/27-28s*	19
Artisanal	*Park/32-33s*	23
Asellina	*Park/29s*	20
Baluchi's	*3a/25s*	19
Baoguette	*Lex/25-26s*	22
Barbès	*36s/5a-Mad*	20
BareBurger	*3a/34-35s*	22
Ben & Jack's	*5a/28-29s*	24
Bistango	*3a/29s*	21
Black Duck	*28s/Lex*	22
Blue Smoke	*27s/Lex-Park*	22
BonChon	*5a/32-33s*	21
Brother Jimmy's	*Lex/31s*	17
Byblos	*Mad/28-29s*	19
Cafe China	*37s/5a-Mad*	24
Cannibal	*29s/Lex-Park*	24
Coppola's	*3a/27-28s*	21
Da Ciro	*Lex/33-34s*	22
Dhaba	*Lex/27-28s*	23
Dos Caminos	*Park/26-27s*	20

East Pacific	*34s/Lex-Park*	22
El Parador	*34s/1-2a*	23
El Pote	*2a/38-39s*	23
Ethos	*3a/33-34s*	21
Forcella	*Park/26-27s*	22
Grand Sichuan	*Lex/33-34s*	20
Grimaldi's	*2a/26s*	23
Hangawi	*32s/5a-Mad*	25
Hillstone	*Park/27s*	23
Hummus Kitchen	*3a/30-31s*	20
I Trulli	*27s/Lex-Park*	22
Jackson Hole	*3a/35s*	19
Jaiya	*3a/28s*	22
Kajitsu	*39s/Lex-Park*	-
Kyochon	*5a/32-33s*	20
Le Parisien	*33s/Lex-3a*	22
Les Halles	*Park/28-29s*	20
Shorty's	*Mad/27-28s*	22
Madison Bistro	*Mad/37-38s*	20
NEW Manzanilla	*Park/25-26s*	23
Marcony	*Lex/31-32s*	25
NEW Meli	*35s/5a*	-
Millesime	*Mad/29s*	19
Morgan	*Mad/36-37s*	19
Nirvana	*Lex/39-40s*	22
Penelope	*Lex/30s*	22
Phoenix Gdn.	*40s/2-3a*	23
Pio Pio	*34s/2-3a*	23
Pongal	*Lex/27-28s*	24
Pranna	*Mad/28-29s*	18
Rare B&G	*Lex/37s*	21
Ravagh	*30s/5a-Mad*	23
Resto	*29s/Lex-Park*	21
Riverpark	*29s/FDR-1a*	24
Rossini's	*38s/Lex-Park*	23
NEW Salvation Taco	*39s/Lex-3a*	22
Sarabeth's	*Park/27-28s*	20
Saravanaa Bhavan	*Lex/26s*	23
SD26	*26s/5a-Mad*	25
2nd Ave Deli	*33s/Lex-3a*	22
S'MAC	*33s/Lex-3a*	23
Smorgas Chef	*Park/37-38s*	20
Sushi Sen-nin	*33s/Mad-Park*	25
Terroir	*3a/30-31s*	20
Tiffin Wallah	*28s/Lex-Park*	22
Turkish Kitchen	*3a/27-28s*	22
Vatan	*3a/29s*	23
Vezzo	*Lex/31s*	23
Villa Berulia	*34s/Lex-Park*	24

Water Club	*E River/23s*	22
Wolfgang's	*Park/33s*	25
Zen Palate	*3a/34*	19

NOHO

(Houston to 4th Sts., Bowery to B'way)

Acme	*Gr. Jones/Lafayette*	22
Aroma Kitchen	*4s/Bowery-Lafayette*	24
Bianca	*Blkr/Bowery*	26
Bohemian	*Gr Jones/Bowery-Lafayette*	25
Bond St	*Bond/Bway-Lafayette*	25
5 Points	*Gr Jones/Bowery-Lafayette*	21
Forcella	*Bowery/Bond-Gr Jones*	22
Great Jones Cafe	*Gr Jones/Bowery-Lafayette*	21
Hecho en Dumbo	*Bowery/4s-Gr Jones*	23
Il Buco	*multi.*	25
NEW Lafayette	*Lafayette/Gr Jones*	19
NEW Le Philosophe	*Bond/Bowery-Lafayette*	24
Mile End	*Bond/Bowery-Lafayette*	23
NoHo Star	*Lafayette/Blkr*	19
Pinche Taqueria	*Lafayette/Blkr*	21
Saxon & Parole	*Bowery/Blkr*	22
Smile	*Bond/Bowery-Lafayette*	21
Two Boots	*Blkr/Bway*	19

NOLITA

(Houston to Kenmare Sts., Bowery to Lafayette St.)

Balaboosta	*Mulberry/Spring*	23
Bread	*Spring/Elizabeth-Mott*	21
Butcher's Daughter	*Kenmare/Elizabeth*	-
Cafe Gitane	*Mott/Prince*	21
Café Habana/Outpost	*Prince/Elizabeth*	23
NEW Cleveland	*Cleveland/Kenmare-Spring*	-
Delicatessen	*Prince/Lafayette*	19
Ed's Lobster	*Lafayette/Broome-Spring*	24
Emporio	*Mott/Prince-Spring*	23
NEW Estela	*Houston/Mott-Mulberry*	-
Lombardi's	*Spring/Mott-Mulberry*	24

Mexican Radio	*Cleveland/Kenmare-Spring*	21
NEW Musket Room	*Elizabeth/Houston-Prince*	-
Parm	*Mulberry/Prince-Spring*	23
NEW Pearl & Ash	*Bowery/Prince-Spring*	-
Peasant	*Elizabeth/Prince-Spring*	24
Pinche Taqueria	*Mott/Prince-Spring*	21
Public	*Elizabeth/Prince-Spring*	23
Pulino's	*Bowery/Houston*	20
Rubirosa	*Mulberry/Prince-Spring*	23
Socarrat	*Mulberry/Houston-Prince*	22
Spring/Natural	*Spring/Lafayette*	20
Tacombi/Fonda Nolita	*Elizabeth/Houston-Prince*	23
Taïm	*Spring/Mulberry*	26
Torrisi	*Mulberry/Prince-Spring*	27
NEW Uncle Boons	*Spring/Bowery-Elizabeth*	-

SOHO

(Canal to Houston Sts., west of Lafayette St.)

NEW Angolo SoHo	*W Bway/Grand*	24
Antique Garage	*Mercer/Broome-Grand*	20
Aquagrill	*Spring/6a*	26
Aurora	*Broome/Thompson-W Bway*	23
Back Forty	*Prince/Crosby*	22
Balthazar	*Spring/Crosby*	24
B&B Winepub	*Houston/Greene-Mercer*	22
Bistro Les Amis	*Spring/Thompson*	22
Blue Ribbon	*Sullivan/Prince-Spring*	25
Blue Ribbon Sushi	*Sullivan/Prince-Spring*	26
Boqueria	*Spring/Thompson-W Bway*	23
Cafe Noir	*Grand/Thompson*	20
NEW Charlie Bird	*King/6a*	-
Cipriani D'twn	*W Bway/Broome-Spring*	23
NEW Cocotte	*Thompson/Prince-Spring*	-

NEW Costata | _Spring/6a-Sullivan_ — |

David Burke Kitchen | _Grand/6a_ 24

Dos Caminos | _W Bway/Houston-Prince_ 20

Dutch | _Sullivan/Prince_ 23

Hampton Chutney | _Prince/Crosby-Lafayette_ 21

Hundred Acres | _MacDougal/Prince_ 20

Isola | _Crosby/Grand-Howard_ —

Jack's Wife Freda | _Lafayette/Broome-Spring_ 19

Kittichai | _Thompson/Broome-Spring_ 24

Koi | _Spring/6a-Varick_ 24

L'Ecole | _Bway/Grand_ 24

Le Pain Q. | _Grand/Greene-Mercer_ 18

Le Pescadeux | _Thompson/Prince-Spring_ 22

Lure Fishbar | _Mercer/Prince_ 23

Mercer Kitchen | _Prince/Mercer_ 22

Mezzogiorno | _Spring/Sullivan_ 21

Mooncake | _Watts/6a-Thompson_ 20

Omen A Zen | _Thompson/Prince-Spring_ 25

Osteria Morini | _Lafayette/Broome-Spring_ 24

Pepe Giallo/Rosso | _Sullivan/Houston-Prince_ 22

Pera | _Thompson/Broome-Spring_ 20

Raoul's | _Prince/Sullivan-Thompson_ 25

Rouge et Blanc | _MacDougal/Houston-Prince_ 25

Smile | _Howard/Crosby-Lafayette_ 21

Snack | _Thompson/Prince-Spring_ 23

sNice | _Sullivan/Houston-Prince_ 20

12 Chairs | _MacDougal/Houston-Prince_ 22

SOUTH STREET SEAPORT

Cabana | _South/Beekman-John_ 22

Cowgirl | _Front/Dover_ 17

TRIBECA

(Canal to Murray Sts., west of B'way)

NEW Aamanns-Copenhagen | _Laight/6a-Varick_ 20

Acappella | _Hudson/Chambers_ 24

Atera | _Worth/Church-W Bway_ 25

Baluchi's | _Greenwich s/Murray-Warren_ 19

Blaue Gans | _Duane/W Bway_ 22

Bouley | _Duane/Hudson-W Bway_ 29

Brushstroke/Ichimura | _Hudson/Duane_ 26

Bubby's | _Hudson/N Moore_ 20

NEW Butterfly | _W Bway/Franklin-White_ —

Cercle Rouge | _W Bway/N Moore_ 19

Churrascaria | _W Bway/Franklin-White_ 23

City Hall | _Duane/Church-W Bway_ 22

NEW Distilled | _W Bway/Franklin-White_ —

Ecco | _Chambers/Church-W Bway_ 23

Gari | _W Bway/Duane_ 27

Gigino | _Greenwich s/Duane-Reade_ 21

Harrison | _Greenwich s/Harrison_ 22

Il Giglio | _Warren/Greenwich s-W Bway_ 25

Jungsik | _Harrison/Hudson_ 26

NEW Khe-Yo | _Duane/Hudson-W Bway_ —

Kitchenette | _Chambers/Greenwich s-W Bway_ 19

Kutsher's | _Franklin/Greenwich s-Hudson_ 20

Landmarc | _W Bway/Leonard-Worth_ 21

Locanda Verde | _Greenwich s/N Moore_ 25

Macao Trading | _Church/Lispenard-Walker_ 20

Marc Forgione | _Reade/Greenwich s-Hudson_ 26

Max | _Duane/Greenwich s-Hudson_ 18

Megu | _Thomas/Church-W Bway_ 24

Mehtaphor | _Duane/Church_ 24

Mr. Chow | _Hudson/N Moore_ 22

Ninja | _Hudson/Duane-Reade_ 19

Nobu | _Hudson/Franklin_ 27

Odeon | _W Bway/Thomas_ 19

Palm | _West/Chambers-Warren_ 24

Pepolino | _W Bway/Canal-Lispenard_ 26

Petite Abeille | _W Bway/Duane-Thomas_ 19

Roc | _Duane/Greenwich s_ 22

Rosanjin | _Duane/Church-W Bway_ 25

Sarabeth's | Greenwich s/Harrison-Jay | 20

Sazon | Reade/Church-W Bway | 23

Scalini Fedeli | Duane/Greenwich s-Hudson | 27

Super Linda | W Bwy/Reade | 17

Takahachi | Duane/Church-W Bway | 25

Tamarind | Hudson/Franklin-Harrison | 26

Terroir | Harrison/Greenwich s-Hudson | 20

Thalassa | Franklin/Greenwich s-Hudson | 24

Tiny's | W Bway/Duane-Thomas | 21

Tribeca Grill | Greenwich s/Franklin | 22

Walker's | N Moore/Varick | 19

'Wichcraft | Greenwich s/Beach | 17

Wolfgang's | Greenwich s/Beach-Hubert | 25

UNION SQUARE

(14th to 17th Sts., 5th Ave. to Union Sq. E.)

Blue Water | Union sq W/16s | 24

Coffee Shop | Union sq W/16s | 17

15 East | 15s/5a | 26

Laut | 17s/Bway-5a | 22

Maoz | Union sq E/16-17s | 21

Olives | Park/17s | 22

Qi | 14s/5-6a | 22

Republic | Union sq W/16-17s | 19

Steak Frites | 16s/5a-Union Sq. W. | 20

Tocqueville | 15s/5a-Union sq W | 27

Union Sq. Cafe | 16s/5a-Union sq W | 27

WASHINGTON HTS./ INWOOD

(North of W. 155th St.)

Garden Café | Bway/Isham-207s | 20

Malecon | Bway/175 | 21

Mamajuana/Taina | Dyckman/Seaman | 21

New Leaf | Corbin/190s | 21

Piper's Kilt | Bway/Isham-207s | 21

WEST 40s

Akdeniz | 46s/5-6a | 21

Amarone | 9a/47-48s | 20

Añejo Tequileria | 10a/47s | 22

Aureole | 42s/Bway-6a | 26

Barbetta | 46s/8-9a | 22

Becco | 46s/8-9a | 22

Blossom | 9a/43-44s | 23

Blue Fin | Bway/47s | 23

Bobby Van's | 45s/6-7a | 23

Bocca/Bacco | 9a/44-45s | 21

Bond 45 | 45s/6-7a | 19

Bouchon Bakery | 48s/5-6a | 24

Breeze | 9a/45-46s | 21

Bryant Park Grill/Cafe | 40s/5-6a | 19

B. Smith's | 46s/8-9a | 19

BXL | 43s/6-7a | 19

Cara Mia | 9a/45-46s | 20

Carmine's | 44s/7-8a | 21

Ça Va | 44s/8-9a | 21

Chez Josephine | 42s/9-10a | 20

Chimichurri Grill | 9a/43-44s | 23

Churrascaria | 49s/8-9a | 23

City Lobster | 49s/6a | 20

Counter | Bway/41s | 20

Dafni Greek | 42s/8-9a | 19

Daisy May's | 11a/46s | 21

db Bistro Moderne | 44s/6a | 25

Del Frisco's | 6a/48-49s | 25

Delta Grill | 9a/48s | 20

Dervish | 47s/6-7a | 19

Don Giovanni | 44s/8-9a | 20

E&E Grill House | 49s/Bway-8a | 21

Ember Room | 9a/45-46s | 21

Esca | 43s/9-10a | 24

Etc. Etc. | 44s/8-9a | 22

FireBird | 46s/8-9a | 20

5 Napkin Burger | 9a/45s | 21

Forty Four | 44s/5-6A | 20

44 & X/44½ | 10a/44-45s | 22

Frankie & Johnnie's | 45s/8a | 22

Gari | 46s/8-9a | 27

Gazala's | 9a/48-49s | 21

Glass House | 47s/Bway-8a | 19

Grand Sichuan | 46s/8-9a | 20

NEW Guy's American | 44s/7-8a | 17

Gyu-Kaku | 44s/8-9a | 21

Hakkasan | 43s/8-9a | 23

Harry's Italian | 6a/49-50s | 21

Haru | 43s/7-8a | 21

Havana Central | 46s/6-7a | 19

Hell's Kitchen | 9a/46-47s | 23

Inakaya | 40s/7-8a | 22

Ipanema | 46s/5-6a | 23

Joe Allen | 46s/8-9a | 19

John's Pizzeria | 44s/7-8a	22
Junior's | Bway/7a	19
Kellari | 44s/5-6a	22
Koi | 40s/5-6a	24
La Masseria | 48s/Bway-8a	23
Lambs Club | 44s/6-7a	22
Landmark Tavern | 11a/46s	18
NEW La Pulperia | 46s/8-9a	-
Lattanzi | 46s/8-9a	22
Le Marais | 46s/6-7a	20
Le Rivage | 46s/8-9a	21
Shorty's | 9a/41-42s	22
Maoz | multi.	21
Marseille | 9a/44-45s	21
Meson Sevilla | 46s/8-9a	20
Mont Blanc | 48s/8-9a	23
Nizza | 9a/44-45s	19
Oceana | 49s/6-7a	24
Orso | 46s/8-9a	23
Osteria al Doge | 44s/Bway-6a	20
Pam Real Thai | 49s/9-10a	22
Pio Pio | 10a/43-44s	23
Pongsri Thai | 48s/Bway-8a	21
Print | 11a/47-48s	22
Qi | 8a/43s	22
Queen of Sheba | 10a/45-46s	22
Riposo | 9a/46-47s	21
Room Service | 9a/47-48s	21
Ruby Foo's | Bway/49s	18
Saju Bistro | 44s/Bway-6a	20
Sardi's | 44s/7-8a	18
Schnipper´s | 8a/41s	19
Sea Grill | 49s/5-6a	23
Serafina | 49s/Bway-8a	18
Shake Shack | 8a/44s	21
Shula's | 43s/Bway-8a	21
St. Andrews | 44s/Bway-6A	19
STK | 6a/42-43s	23
Strip House | 44s/5-6a	25
Sushiden | 49s/6-7a	24
Sushi Zen | 44s/Bway-6a	26
Tony's Di Napoli | 43s/6-7a	22
Trattoria Trecolori | 47s/Bway-8A	21
Triomphe | 44s/5-6a	23
Turkish Cuisine | 9a/44-45s	20
Two Boots | 9a/44-45s	19
Utsav | 46s/6-7A	21
Via Brasil | 46s/5-6a	21
View | Bway/45-46s	16

Virgil's BBQ | 44s/Bway-6a	20
West Bank | 42s/9-10a	19
'Wichcraft | multi.	17
Wolfgang's | 41s/7-8a	25
Wu Liang Ye | 48s/5-6a	23
Zen Palate | 9a/46s	19

WEST 50s

Abboccato | 55s/6-7a	21
Afghan Kebab | 9a/51-52s	20
Angelo's Pizza | multi.	21
Azuri Cafe | 51s/9-10a	25
Bann | 50s/8-9a	21
Bar Americain | 52s/6-7a	23
Basso56 | 56s/Bway-8a	23
Benoit | 55s/5-6a	21
NEW Betony | 57s/5-6a	-
Bill's Bar | 51s/5-6a	19
Bistro Milano | 6a/54-55s	21
Blue Ribbon Sushi B&G | 58s/8-9a	25
Bobby Van's | 50s/6-7a	23
Bocca/Bacco | 9a/54-55s	21
Bombay Palace | 52s/5-6a	20
Braai | 51s/8-9a	20
Brasserie Cognac | Bway/55s	19
Brasserie 8½ | 57s/5-6a	22
Brass. Ruhlmann | Rock plz/50-51s	19
Bricco | 56s/8-9a	21
Burger Joint | 56s/6-7a	24
Capital Grille | 51s/6-7a	24
Carnegie Deli | 7a/55s	22
Chai Home | 8a/55s	22
Chez Napoléon | 50s/8-9a	22
China Grill | 53s/5-6a	23
Circo | 55s/6-7a	23
NEW Clarke's Standard | 8a/57-58s	20
Courgette | 55s/Bway-7a	26
Danji | 52s/8-9a	25
Da Tommaso | 8a/53-54s	20
Del Frisco's | Rock plz/51s	25
Don Antonio | 50s/8-9a	24
Eatery | 9a/53s	21
El Centro | 9a/54s	21
Empanada Mama | 9a/51-52s	23
Gari | 59s/5a	27
Gordon Ramsay | 54s/6-7a	23
Greek Kitchen | 10a/58s	20
Guantanamera | 8a/55-56s	20
Hanci | 10a/56	21

Hummus Kitchen	*9a/51-52s*	20
Il Tinello	*56s/5-6a*	25
Ippudo	*51s/8-9a*	25
Ise	*56s/5-6a*	22
Island Burgers	*9a/51-52s*	21
Joe's Shanghai	*56s/5-6a*	22
Kashkaval	*multi.*	22
Katsu-Hama	*55s/5-6a*	22
La Bergamote	*52s/10-11a*	24
La Bonne Soupe	*55s/5-6a*	19
La Silhouette	*53s/8-9a*	24
Le Bernardin	*51s/6-7a*	29
Le Pain Q.	*7a/58s*	18
Lucky's Famous	*52s/8-9a*	20
Luke's Lobster	*59s/5a*	23
Má Pêche	*56s/5-6a*	23
Marea	*CPS/Bway-7a*	28
Maria Pia	*51s/8-9a*	19
Maze	*54s/6-7a*	24
McCormick/Schmick	*6a/51-52s*	18
Menchanko-tei	*55s/5-6a*	19
Menkui Tei	*56s/5-6a*	20
Michael's	*55s/5-6a*	22
Milos	*55s/6-7a*	27
Modern	*53s/5-6a*	26
Molyvos	*7a/55-56s*	23
Mooncake	*54s/8-9a*	20
Natsumi	*50s/Bway-8a*	24
Nino's	*58s/6-7a*	21
Nobu	*57s/5-6a*	27
Nocello	*55s/Bway-8a*	22
Nook	*9a/50-51s*	23
Norma's	*56s/6-7a*	25
No. 7	*59s/5a*	22
Palm	*50s/Bway-8a*	24
Palm Court	*5a/59s*	21
Patsy's	*56s/Bway-8a*	22
Petrossian	*58s/7a*	24
PizzArte	*55s/5-6a*	21
Plaza Food Hall	*59s/5a*	22
NEW Prime Grill	*56s/5-6a*	-
Pure Thai	*9a/51-52s*	25
NEW Quality Italian	*57s/6a*	-
Quality Meats	*58s/5-6a*	26
Radiance Tea	*55s/6-7a*	21
Redeye Grill	*7a/56s*	21
Remi	*53s/6-7a*	22
Rice 'n' Beans	*9a/50-51s*	21
Robert	*Bway/8a*	20

Rock Ctr.	*50s/5-6a*	19
Rue 57	*57s/6a*	19
Russian Samovar	*52s/Bway-8a*	20
Russian Tea	*57s/6-7a*	20
Ruth's Chris	*51s/6-7a*	23
Sarabeth's	*CPS/5-6a*	20
Seäsonal	*58s/6-7a*	25
Serafina	*55s/Bway-7a*	18
Soba Nippon	*52s/5-6a*	22
Sosa Borella	*8a/50s*	20
South Gate	*CPS/6-7a*	21
Steak 'n Shake	*Bway/53-54s*	20
Sugiyama	*55s/Bway-8a*	28
Sushi Damo	*58s/8-9a*	23
Sushiya	*56s/5-6a*	22
Szechuan Gourmet	*56s/Bway-8a*	23
Taboon	*10a/52s*	24
Tang Pavilion	*55s/5-6a*	23
Thalia	*8a/50s*	20
Toloache	*50s/Bway-8a*	24
Topaz	*56s/6-7a*	22
Totto Ramen	*52s/8-9a*	26
Tratt. Dell'Arte	*7a/56-57s*	22
21 Club	*52s/5-6a*	23
Uncle Jack's	*56s/5-6a*	23
Uncle Nick's	*9a/50-51s*	21
ViceVersa	*51s/8-9a*	22
Victor's Cafe	*52s/Bway-8a*	22
Whym	*9a/57-58s*	19
Wondee Siam	*multi.*	21
Yakitori Totto	*55s/Bway-8a*	25

WEST 60s

NEW Andanada 141	*69s/Bway-Colum*	21
Asiate	*60s/Bway*	25
Atlantic Grill	*64s/Bway-CPW*	22
A Voce	*60s/Bway*	24
Bar Boulud	*Bway/63-64s*	24
Blossom	*Amst/67-68s*	23
Bouchon Bakery	*60s/Bway*	24
Boulud Sud	*64s/Bway-CPW*	25
Cafe Fiorello	*Bway/63s*	20
Ed's Chowder	*63s/Bway-Colum*	20
Gabriel's	*60s/Bway-Colum*	23
Grand Tier	*Lincoln Ctr/63-65s*	20
Jean Georges	*CPW/61s*	28
Jean-Georges' Noug.	*CPW/61s*	27
La Boîte en Bois	*68s/Colum-CPW*	21
Landmarc	*60s/Bway*	21

Leopard/des Artistes | 67s/Colum-CPW — 21

Le Pain Q. | 65s/Bway-CPW — 18

Lincoln | 65s/Amst-Bway — 24

Masa/Bar Masa | 60s/Bway — 27

Nick & Toni | 67s/Bway-Colum — 19

Per Se | 60s/Bway — 28

Picholine | 64s/Bway-CPW — 27

P.J. Clarke's | 63s/Colum — 17

Porter House | 60s/Bway — 26

Rosa Mexicano | Colum/62s — 22

Sapphire Indian | Bway/60-61s — 21

Shun Lee Cafe | 65s/Colum-CPW — 21

Shun Lee West | 65s/Colum-CPW — 22

Smith | Bway/63s — 19

Telepan | 69s/Colum — 26

'Wichcraft | 62s/Colum — 17

WEST 70s

A.G. Kitchen | Colum/73s — 18

Alice's Tea | 73s/Amst-Colum — 20

Amber | Colum/70s — 19

Arté Café | 73s/Amst-Colum — 18

Bettola | Amst/79-80s — 19

Bistro Cassis | Colum/70-71s — 20

Café Frida | Colum/77-78s — 21

Cafe Luxembourg | 70s/Amst-W End — 21

Cafe Ronda | Colum/71-72s — 20

Caffe Storico | CPW/77s — 20

'Cesca | 75s/Amst — 23

Citrus B&G | Amst/75s — 20

Coppola's | 79s/Amst-Bway — 21

Dovetail | 77s/Colum — 25

FishTag | 79s/Amst-Bway — 23

Fratelli la Bufala | Bway/76s — 20

Gari | Colum/77-78s — 27

Gazala's | Colum/78s — 21

Grand Sichuan | Amst/74-75s — 20

Gray's Papaya | Bway/72s — 20

Hummus Pl. | Amst/74-75s — 22

Isabella's | Colum/77s — 20

Josie's | Amst/74s — 20

Legend | 72s/Amst-Colum — 21

Le Pain Q. | 72s/Colum-CPW — 18

Loi | 70s/Amst-W End — 22

Maoz | Amst/70-71s — 21

Mike's Bistro | 72s/Bway-W End — 24

Mughlai | Colum/75s — 20

Nice Matin | 79s/Amst — 19

Ocean Grill | Colum/78-79s — 24

Pappardella | Colum/75s — 20

Pasha | 71s/Colum-CPW — 20

Patsy's | 74s/Colum-CPW — 20

Pomodoro Rosso | Colum/70-71s — 21

Riposo | 72s/Colum-CPW — 21

Salumeria/Ristoranti Rosi | Amst/73-74s — 25

Sambuca | 72s/Colum-CPW — 19

Saravanaa Bhavan | Amst/79-80s — 23

Scaletta | 77s/Colum-CPW — 21

Serafina | Bway/77s — 18

Seven's Turkish | 72s/Amst-Colum — 20

Shake Shack | Colum/77s — 21

Tenzan | Colum/73s — 21

Tolani | Amst/79-80s — 20

WEST 80s

Barney Greengrass | Amst/86-87s — 24

B. Café | Amst/87-88s — 21

Bistro Citron | Colum/82-83s — 20

Bodrum | Amst/88-89s — 21

Brother Jimmy's | Amst/80-81s — 17

Blossom | Colum/82-83s — 23

Cafe Lalo | 83s/Amst — 20

Calle Ocho | 81s/Colum-CPW — 21

Candle Cafe | Bway/98-90s — 24

NEW Casa Pomona | Colum/84-85s — -

Celeste | Amst/84-85s — 23

Cilantro | Colum/83-84s — 19

NEW Cocina Economica | Amst/82s — 22

NEW Corvo Bianco | Colum/81s — -

Cotta | Colum/84-85s — 22

5 Napkin Burger | Bway/84s — 21

Flor/Mayo | Amst/83-84s — 21

Good Enough/Eat | Colum/85s — 21

Hampton Chutney | Amst/82-83s — 21

Haru | Amst/80-81s — 21

Hummus Kitchen | Amst/80s — 20

Island Burgers | Amst/80s — 21

Jackson Hole | Colum/85s — 19

Jacob's Pickles | Amst/84-85s — 20

Land Thai | Amst/81-82s — 23

Luke's Lobster | Amst/80-81s — 23

Mamajuana/Taina | Amst/87-88s — 21

Mermaid | Amst/87-88s — 21

Momoya | Amst/80-81s — 23

Oaxaca | Amst/80-81s — 21

Ouest	*Bway/84s*	24
Peacefood Café	*Amst/82a*	23
Prime KO	*85s/Amst-Bway*	23
Sarabeth's	*Amst/80-81s*	20
Spice	*Amst/81s*	19
Spiga	*84s/Amst-Bway*	23
Spring/Natural	*Colum/83s*	20
Tarallucci	*Colum/83s*	20

WEST 90s

Acqua	*Amst/95s*	20
NEW Amsterdam Burger	*Amst/92s*	25
Café Frida	*Amst/97-98s*	21
Carmine's	*Bway/90-91s*	21
Gennaro	*Amst/92-93s*	24
Kouzan	*Amst/93s*	19
Malecon	*Amst/97-98s*	21
Numero 28	*Amst/92s*	24
Pio Pio	*Amst/94s*	23
Regional	*Bway/98-9s*	19
Tratt. Pesce	*Colum/90-91s*	20
Two Boots	*Bway/95-96s*	19

WEST 100s

(See also Harlem/East Harlem)

Awash	*Amst/106-107s*	22
Bistro Ten 18	*Amst/110s*	19
Cafe Du Soleil	*Bway/104s*	19
Cascabel Taqueria	*Bway/108s*	21
Community Food	*Bway/112-113s*	23
NEW Ellington	*Amst/106s*	-
Flor/Mayo	*Bway/100-101s*	21
Havana Central	*Bway/113-114s*	19
Henry's	*Bway/105s*	20
Indus Valley	*Bway/100s*	22
Kitchenette	*Amst/122-123s*	19
Legend	*109s/Amst-Bway*	21
Maoz	*Bway/110-111s*	21
Max SoHa/Caffe	*multi.*	23
Noche Mex.	*Amst/101-102s*	22
107 West	*Bway/107-108s*	20
Pisticci	*La Salle/Bway*	25
Sezz Medi'	*Amst/122s*	22
Sookk	*Bway/102-103s*	21
Symposium	*113s/Amst-Bway*	20
Thai Market	*Amst/107-108s*	23
Turkuaz	*Bway/100s*	20
Vareli	*Bway/111-112s*	23
Wondee Siam	*Amst/107-108s*	21

WEST VILLAGE

(Houston to 14th Sts., west of 6th Ave., excluding Meatpacking)

Agave	*7a/Charles*	20
Aki	*4s/Barrow*	24
Amber	*Christopher/Hudson*	19
Annisa	*Barrow/7a-4s*	27
A.O.C.	*Blkr/Grove*	20
A Salt & Battery	*Greenwich a/12-3s*	22
August	*Blkr/Charles-10s*	22
Ayza Wine	*7a/Carmine*	20
Baoguette	*Christopher/Bedford*	22
Barbuto	*Wash/Jane-12s*	24
NEW Barraca	*Greenwich a/Bank*	15
NEW Beatrice Inn	*12s/4s-Hudson*	17
Bell Book/Candle	*10s/Greenwich a-Waverly*	20
Betel	*Grove/Blkr-7a S*	21
Blue Ribbon Bakery	*Downing/Bedford*	24
Bobo	*10s/7a*	23
Buvette	*Grove/Bedford-Blkr*	24
Cafe Asean	*10s/Greenwich-6a*	22
Blossom	*Carmine/Bedford-Blkr*	23
Cafe Cluny	*12s/4s*	22
Cafe Espanol	*Carmine/7a*	20
Cafe Gitane	*Jane/Wash-West*	21
Café Henri	*Bedford/Downing-Houston*	20
Cafe Loup	*13s/6a*	19
NEW Chez Sardine	*10s/4s*	20
NEW Clarkson	*Varick/Houston*	20
NEW Cole's	*Greenwich a/13s*	21
Commerce	*Commerce/Barrow*	23
Cornelia St. Cafe	*Cornelia/Blkr-4s*	19
Corner Bistro	*4s/Jane*	22
Corsino	*Hudson/Horatio*	21
Cowgirl	*Hudson/10s*	17
Crispo	*14s/7-8a*	23
Dell'anima	*8a/Jane*	25
Do Hwa	*Carmine/Bedford-7a*	22
Dos Toros	*Carmine/Blkr-6a*	21
NEW El Toro Blanco	*6a/Bedford-Downing*	22
Empellón	*4s/10s*	22
EN Japanese	*Hudson/Leroy*	25
Extra Virgin	*4s/Perry*	23

LOCATIONS

Fatty Crab | *Hudson/Gansevoort-Horatio* 22

Fatty 'Cue | *Carmine/Bedford-Blkr* 22

Fedora | *4s/Charles-10s* 23

Fish | *Blkr/Jones* 23

Flex Mussels | *13s/6-7s* 23

Frankies | *Hudson/11s* 23

Gobo | *6a/8s-Waverly* 23

Good | *Greenwich a/Bank-12s* 21

Gottino | *Greenwich a/Charles-Perry* 20

Gradisca | *13s/6-7a* 24

Grand Sichuan | *7a/Carmine-Leroy* 20

Havana Alma | *Christopher/Bedford-Blkr* 21

Home | *Cornelia/Blkr-4s* 22

Hudson Clearwater | *Hudson/Morton* 23

Hummus Pl. | *7a/Barrow-Blkr* 22

I Sodi | *Christopher/Blkr-Hudson* 25

Jeffrey's Grocery | *Waverly/Christopher* 22

Joe's Pizza | *Carmine/Blkr-6a* 23

John's Pizzeria | *Blkr/Jones* 22

Joseph Leonard | *Waverly/Grove* 24

Keste Pizza | *Blkr/Morton* 25

Kin Shop | *6a/11-12s* 24

Landbrot | *7a/Charles* 20

L'Artusi | *10s/Blkr-Hudson* 27

Las Ramblas | *4s/Cornelia-Jones* 23

Left Bank | *Perry/Greenwich s* 20

Le Gigot | *Cornelia/Blkr-W 4s* 24

Little Owl | *Bedford/Grove* 25

NEW Louro | *10s/Greenwich a-Waverly* 21

Malatesta | *Wash/Christopher* 24

Market Table | *Carmine/Bedford* 23

NEW Marrow | *Bank/Greenwich s* 23

Mary's Fish | *Charles/4s* 25

Mas | *Downing/Bedford-Varick* 27

Mas (La Grillade) | *7a/Leroy-Morton* 23

Meatball Shop | *Greenwich a/Perry* 24

Mémé | *Hudson/Bank* 22

Mercadito | *7a/Grove* 24

Mexicana Mama | *Hudson/Charles-10s* 23

Móle | *Jane/Hudson* 21

Morandi | *Waverly/Charles* 23

Moustache | *Bedford/Barrow-Grove* 23

NEW Murray's Cheese | *Blkr/Leroy-Morton* 24

Noodle Bar | *Carmine/Bedford-Blkr* 21

Numero 28 | *Carmine/Bedford-Blkr* 24

Oaxaca | *Greenwich a/Charles-Perry* 21

Ofrenda | *7a/Christopher-10s* 23

One if by Land | *Barrow/7a-4s* 24

Palma | *Cornelia/Blkr-W 4s* 24

Pearl Oyster | *Cornelia/Blkr-4s* 26

Perilla | *Jones/Blkr-4s* 26

Perry St. | *Perry/West* 26

Petite Abeille | *Hudson/Barrow* 19

Philip Marie | *Hudson/11s* 19

Piccolo Angolo | *Hudson/Jane* 26

Place | *4s/Bank-12s* 23

Pó | *Cornelia/Blkr-4s* 25

Recette | *12s/Greenwich s* 24

RedFarm | *Hudson/Charles-10s* 25

Risotteria | *Blkr/Morton* 22

Rosemary's | *Greenwich a/10s* 21

Sant Ambroeus | *4s/Perry* 21

Sevilla | *Charles/4s* 23

Smorgas Chef | *12s/4s* 20

Snack | *Bedford/Morton* 23

sNice | *8a/Horatio-Jane* 20

Soto | *6a/Wash-4s* 27

Spasso | *Hudson/Perry* 23

Spotted Pig | *11s/Greenwich s* 24

SushiSamba | *7a/Barrow* 22

Taïm | *Waverly/11s-Perry* 26

Takashi | *Hudson/Barrow-Morton* 26

Tartine | *11s/4s* 22

Tea & Sympathy | *Greenwich a/Jane s* 22

Tertulia | *6a/Wash* 24

Tratt. Pesce | *Blkr/Leroy* 20

Trattoria Toscana | *Carmine/Bedford-7A* 25

Two Boots | *11s/7a* 19

Wallsé | *11s/Wash* 26

Waverly Inn | *Bank/Waverly* 21

Westville | *10s/Blkr* 23

Wong | *Cornelia/Blkr-4s* 24

Yama | *Carmine/Bedford-Blkr* 23

Yerba Buena | *Perry/Greenwich a* 24

Bronx

CITY ISLAND

Artie's | *City Is/Ditmars* — 22
Bistro S K | *City Is/Carroll-Hawkins* — 26
Black Whale | *City Is/Hawkins* — 22
City Is. Lobster | *Bridge/City Is* — 22
Crab Shanty | *City Is/Tier* — 23
Lobster Box | — 20
  City Is/Belden-Rochelle
Portofino | *City Is/Cross* — 22
Sammy's Fishbox | *City Is/Rochelle* — 21
Sammy's Shrimp | *City Is/Horton* — 23
Sea Shore | *City Is/Cross* — 21

FORDHAM

Ann & Tony's | *Arthur/187-188s* — 21
Antonio's Trattoria | — 23
  Belmont/Crescent
Dominick's | *Arthur/184-187s* — 23
Emilia's | *Arthur/Crescent* — 22
Enzo's | *Arthur/184-187s* — 23
Mario's | *Arthur/Crescent-184s* — 22
Pasquale's | *Arthur/Crescent* — 21
Roberto | *Crescent/Hughes* — 26
Tra Di Noi | — 24
  187s/Belmont-Hughes
Zero Otto | *Arthur/186s* — 24

KINGSBRIDGE

Malecon | *Bway/231* — 21
Piper's Kilt | *231s/Albany Crescent* — 21

MORRIS PARK

Enzo's | *Williamsbridge/Neill* — 23
F & J Pine | — 23
  Bronxdale/Matthews-Muliner
Patricia's | — 24
  Morris Pk/Haight-Lurting

MOTT HAVEN

Pio Pio | *Cypress/138-139s* — 23

PELHAM GARDENS

Fratelli | *Eastchester/Mace* — 21

RIVERDALE

Beccofino | — 23
  Mosholu/Fieldston-Spencer
Jake's | *Bway/242s* — 24
Liebman's Deli | *235s/Johnson* — 23
Madison's | *Riverdale/258-259s* — 20
Siam Sq. | *Kappock/Knolls* — 22

THROGS NECK

Tosca Café | — 23
  Tremont/Miles-Sampson

YANKEE STADIUM

NYY Steak | *161s/River* — 22

Brooklyn

BAY RIDGE

Areo | *3a/84-85s* — 24
Arirang Hibachi | *4a/88-89s* — 21
Burger Bistro | *3a/72-73s* — 22
Cebu | *3a/88s* — 20
Chadwick's | *3a/89s* — 24
Eliá | *3a/86-87s* — 25
Embers | *3a/95-96s* — 22
Fushimi | *4a/93-94s* — 23
Gino's | *5a/Bay Ridge-74s* — 24
Greenhouse | *3a/77-78s* — 20
Omonia | *3a/76-77s* — 20
101 | *4a/100s* — 22
Pearl Room | *3a/82s* — 23
Schnitzel Haus | *5a/74s* — 23
Tanoreen | *3a/76s* — 26
Tuscany Grill | *3a/86-87s* — 25
Vesuvio | *3a/73-74s* — 20

BEDFORD-STUYVESANT

Ali's Roti | *Fulton/Arlington* — 25
Do or Dine | *Bedford/Lex-Quincy* — 25
Peaches | *multi.* — 23
Saraghina | *Halsey/Lewis* — 26

BENSONHURST

L&B Spumoni | *86s/10-11s* — 24
Nyonya | *86s/Bay 34s* — 23
Tenzan | *18a/71s* — 21

BOERUM HILL

Arthur on Smith | — 21
  Smith/Degraw-Sackett
Bacchus | *Atlantic/Bond-Nevins* — 20
Hanco's | *Bergen/Smith* — 20
Ki Sushi | *Smith/Dean-Pacific* — 25
Lunetta | *Smith/Dean-Pacific* — 21
Mile End | *Hoyt/Atlantic-Pacific* — 23
Nicky's | *Atlantic/Hoyt-Smith* — 21
Rucola | *Dean/Bond* — 24
South Brooklyn Pizza | — 23
  4a/Bergen-St Marks

BOROUGH PARK

Nyonya | 8a/54s — 23

BRIGHTON BEACH

Tatiana | Brighton 6s/Brightwater — 20

BROOKLYN HEIGHTS

ChipShop | — 20
  Atlantic/Clinton-Henry
Colonie | Atlantic/Clinton-Henry — 25
Hanco's | — 20
  Montague/Clinton-Henry
Henry's End | — 25
  Henry/Cranberry-Middagh
Jack Horse | Hicks/Cranberry — 23
Noodle Pudding | — 25
  Henry/Cranberry-Middagh
Queen | — 24
  Court/Livingston-Schermerhorn
NEW Red Gravy | — 20
  Atlantic/Clinton-Henry
Teresa's | Montague/Hicks — 20

BUSHWICK

Blanca | Moore/Bogart — 29
NEW Fritzl's Lunch | — ‒
  Irving/Stanhope-Stockholm
NEW King Noodle | — ‒
  Flushing/Morgan
Mama Joy's | Flushing/Porter — ‒
Momo Sushi Shack | — 27
  Bogart/Moore
Roberta's | Moore/Bogart — 26

CARROLL GARDENS

Alma | Columbia/Degraw — 20
Battersby | Smith/Degraw-Sackett — 27
Brooklyn Farmacy | Henry/Sackett — 23
Buttermilk | Court/Huntington — 25
Calexico | Union/Columbia-Hicks — 21
Fragole | Court/Carroll-1pl — 24
Frankies | Court/4pl-Luquer — 23
Grocery | Smith/Sackett-Union — 27
NEW La Slowteria | Court/9s — ‒
Lucali | Henry/Carroll-1pl — 27
Marco Polo | Court/Union — 20
NEW Nightingale 9 | Smith/Carroll — ‒
NEW Old School Brooklyn | — ‒
  Court/Huntington-Nelson
Prime Meat | Court/Luquer — 23
Seersucker | — 23
  Smith/Carroll-President

South Brooklyn Pizza | — 23
  Court/4pl-Lucquer
Zaytoons | Smith/Sackett — 20

CLINTON HILL

Locanda Vini | — 26
  Gates/Cambridge-Grand
Maggie Brown | — 23
  Myrtle/Wash-Waverly
Speedy Romeo | Classon/Greene — 22

COBBLE HILL

Awash | Court/Baltic-Kane — 22
Bocca Lupo | Henry/Warren — 23
Cafe Luluc | Smith/Baltic-Butler — 21
Char No. 4 | Smith/Baltic-Warren — 22
Chocolate Room | — 25
  Court/Butler-Douglass
Coco Roco | Smith/Bergen-Dean — 21
Henry Public | — 20
  Henry/Atlantic-Pacific
Hibino | Henry/Pacific — 25
Joya | Court/Warren-Wyckoff — 23
La Vara | — 27
  Clinton/Verandah-Warren
Lemongrass | — 19
  Court/Amity-Pacific
Wild Ginger | — 22
  Smith/Dean-Pacific

CONEY ISLAND

Gargiulo's | 15s/Mermaid-Surf — 22
Grimaldi's | Surf/Stillwell-12a — 23
Tom's | Boardwalk/Stillwell — 21
Totonno Pizza | Neptune/15-16s — 25

CROWN HEIGHTS

Ali's Roti | Utica/Carroll — 25

DITMAS PARK

Am Thai | Church/10-11s — 23
Farm/Adderley | — 24
  Cortelyou/Stratford-Westmin
Mimi's Hummus | — 24
  Cortelyou/Argyle-Westmin
Purple Yam | — 22
  Cortelyou/Argyle-Rugby

DOWNTOWN BROOKLYN

Chef's/Brooklyn Fare | — 27
  Schermerhorn/Bond-Hoyt
NEW Ganso | Bond/Livingston — 22
Junior's | Flatbush/DeKalb — 19

Misdemeanor | Smith/Atlantic-State ⏤

Shake Shack | Fulton/Adams 21

DUMBO

NEW Atrium Dumbo | Main/Plymouth-Water ⏤

Gran Electrica | Front/Old Fulton 22

Grimaldi's | Front/Dock-Old Fulton 23

NEW Juliana's | Old Fulton/Front-Water 27

Luke's Lobster | Water/New Dock 23

No. 7 | Water/New Dock 22

River Café | Water/Furman-Old Fulton 26

Smorgasburg | Water/Dock 27

DYKER HEIGHTS

Tommaso | 86s/Bay 8s-15a 23

FORT GREENE

Café Habana/Outpost | Fulton/Portland 23

Caffe e Vino | Dekalb/Ashland-St Felix 23

Chez Oskar | DeKalb/Adelphi 20

General Greene | DeKalb/Clermont 20

Luz | Vanderbilt/Myrtle-Willoughby 23

Madiba | DeKalb/Adelphi-Carlton 23

No. 7 | Greene/Cumberland-Fulton 22

Olea | Lafayette/Adelphi 23

Pequena | Portland/Fulton-Lafayette 21

Roman's | DeKalb/Clermont-Vanderbilt 24

67 Burger | Lafayette/Elliott-Fulton 21

Smoke Joint | Elliott/Fulton-Lafayette 22

Stonehome | Lafayette/Portaland 21

Walter | Dekalb/Cumberland 23

Zaytoons | Myrtle/Hall-Wash 20

GOWANUS

Dinosaur BBQ | Union/4a 23

NEW Fletcher's | 3a/7-8s 22

Littleneck | 3a/Carroll-President 24

Monte's | Carroll/Nevins-3a 20

NEW Pines | 3a/Carroll-President 23

NEW Runner & Stone | 3a/Carroll-President 23

GRAVESEND

Fiorentino's | Ave U/McDonald-West 21

Sahara | Coney Is/Aves T-U 22

GREENPOINT

NEW Alameda | Franklin/Green ⏤

Calexico | Manhattan/Bedford 21

Five Leaves | Bedford/Lorimer 26

Fornino | Manhattan/Milton-Noble 24

Lomzynianka | Manhattan/Nassau-Norman 22

NEW Luksus | Manhattan/Nassau ⏤

No. 7 | Manhattan/Java-Kent 22

Paulie Gee's | Greenpoint/Franklin-West 26

NEW River Styx | Greenpoint/East River-West ⏤

Xi'an | Beadel/Morgan-Vandervoort 24

KENSINGTON

Am Thai | McDonald/Albermale 23

MIDWOOD

Di Fara | Ave J/15s 26

Taci's Beyti | Coney Is/Ave P-Kings 25

MILL BASIN

La Villa Pizzeria | Ave U/66 23

Mill Basin Deli | Ave T/58-59s 22

PARK SLOPE

Al Di La | 5a/Carroll 27

Anthony's | 7a/14-15s 21

A.O.C. | 5a/Garfield 20

Applewood | 11s/7-8a 25

Baluchi's | 5a/2s 19

BareBurger | 7a/1s-Garfield 22

Bark | Bergen/5a-Flatbush 22

Benchmark | 2s/4-5a 22

Blue Ribbon | 5a/1s-Garfield 25

Bogota | 5a/St Johns 24

Bonnie's Grill | 5A/1s-Garfield 22

Brooklyn Fish | 5a/Degraw 22

Burger Bistro | 5a/Berkeley-Lincoln 22

Cafe Dada	*7a/Lincoln*	22
Cafe Steinhof	*7a/14s*	18
ChipShop	*5a/6s*	20
Chocolate Room	*5a/St Marks-Warren*	25
Coco Roco	*5a/6-7s*	21
Conviv. Osteria	*5a/Bergen-St Marks*	25
Cubana Café	*6a/St Marks*	21
Flatbush Farm	*St Marks/Flatbush*	21
Fonda	*7a/14-15s*	23
Franny's	*Flatbush/8a-Sterling*	25
Hanco's	*7a/10s*	20
Juventino	*5a/5-6s*	25
La Villa Pizzeria	*5a/1s-Garfield*	23
Miriam	*5a/Prospect*	21
Moim	*Garfield/7a*	23
Oaxaca	*4a/Carroll-President*	21
Okeanos	*7a/8s*	21
Rose Water	*Union/5-6a*	25
Scottadito	*Union/6-7a*	22
Sidecar	*5a/15-16s*	23
67 Burger	*Flatbush/Bergen-6a*	21
sNice	*5a/3s*	20
Song	*5a/1-2s*	24
SottoVoce	*7a/4s*	21
South Brooklyn Pizza	*1a/6-7a*	23
Spice	*7a/Lincoln*	19
Stone Park	*5a/3s*	24
Sweet Melissa	*7a/1-2s*	20
Talde	*7a/11s*	25
Terroir	*5a/1s*	20
Thistle Hill	*7a/15s*	20
12th St. B&G	*8a/12s*	22
Two Boots	*2s/7-8a*	19
Zito's	*multi.*	21
Zuzu Ramen	*4a/Degraw*	23

PROSPECT HEIGHTS

Ali's Roti	*Flatbush/Midwood-Rutland*	25
Amorina	*Vanderbilt/Prospect*	23
Bar Corvo	*Wash/Lincoln-St John*	26
Chuko	*Vanderbilt/Dean*	23
James	*Carlton/St Marks*	24
Pequena	*Vanderbilt/Bergen*	21
606 R&D	*Vanderbilt/Prospect-St Marks*	23
Tom's	*Wash/Sterling*	21

Vanderbilt	*Vanderbilt/Bergen*	21
Zaytoons	*Vanderbilt/St Marks*	20

RED HOOK

Defonte's	*Columbia/Luquer*	24
Good Fork	*Van Brunt/Coffey-Van Dyke*	25
Pok Pok Ny	*Columbia/Degraw-Kane*	24
Red Hook Lobster	*Van Brunt/Pioneer-Visitation*	24

SHEEPSHEAD BAY

Brennan	*Nostrand/Ave U*	22
Jordans Lobster	*Harkness/Plumb 2s*	22
Randazzo's	*Emmons/21s*	21
Roll-n-Roaster	*Emmons/Nostrand-29s*	22

SUNSET PARK

Pacificana	*55s/8a*	23

VINEGAR HILL

Vinegar Hill Hse.	*Hudson/Front-Water*	24

WILLIAMSBURG

Allswell	*Bedford/N 10s*	23
NEW Antica Pesa	*Berry/N 7-8s*	23
NEW Aska	*Wythe/N 11s*	23
Aurora	*Grand/Wythe*	23
Bamonte's	*Withers/Lorimer-Union*	22
Beco	*Richardson/Lorimer*	23
Best Pizza	*Havemeyer/N 7-8s*	24
NEW BrisketTown	*Bedford/S 4-5s*	25
Cafe Mogador	*Wythe/N 7-8s*	23
Caracas	*Grand/Havemeyer-Roebling*	24
Chai Home	*N 6s/Berry*	22
Crif Dogs	*Driggs/N 7s*	23
Diner	*Bway/Berry*	24
Dos Toros	*Bedford/N6-7s*	21
DuMont	*multi.*	23
Egg	*N 5s/Bedford-Berry*	24
NEW Elm	*N 12s/Bedford-Berry*	-
Extra Fancy	*Metro/Roebling*	20
Fatty 'Cue	*S 6s/Berry*	22
Fette Sau	*Metro/Havemeyer-Roebling*	26

Forcella | Lorimer/Grand-Powers | 22

Fornino | Bedford/N 7s | 24

Fushimi | Driggs/N 10-11s | 23

Gwynnett St. | Graham/Ainslie-Devoe | 27

La Esquina | Wythe/N 3s | 23

La Piazzetta | Graham/Frost-Richardson | 23

La Superior | Berry/S 2-3s | 25

Mable's Smokehouse | Berry/N 11s | 23

Marlow/Sons | Bway/Berry-Whythe | 24

Meatball Shop | Bedford/N 7-8s | 24

Mesa Coyoacan | Graham/Conselyea-Skillman | 24

Miranda | Berry/N 9s | 23

Móle | Kent/N 4s | 21

Motorino | Bway/Bedford-Driggs | 25

one or eight | S 2s/Wythe | 24

Peter Luger | Bway/Driggs | 27

Peter's 1969 | Bedford/N 7-8s | 20

Pies-N-Thighs | S 4s/Driggs | 24

Qi | N 9s/Bedford-Driggs | 22

Reynard | Wythe/N 11s | 23

Rye | S 1s/Havemeyer-Roebling | 25

Sea | N 6s/Berry | 22

Settepani | Lorimer/Conselyea-Skillman | 23

Smorgasburg | Kent/N 7s | 27

St. Anselm | Metro/Havemeyer | 27

Traif | S 4s/Havemeyer-Roebling | 26

Vanessa's Dumpling | Bedford/S 1-2s | 21

Walter | Grand/Roebling | 23

Wild Ginger | Bedford/N 5-6s | 22

NEW Xixa | 4s/Havemeyer | -

Zenkichi | N 6s/Wythe | 26

Queens

ASTORIA

Agnanti | Ditmars/19s | 24

Arepas | multi. | 24

Astor Room | 36s/35-36a | 20

Bahari Estiatorio | Bway/31 | 24

BareBurger | multi. | 22

Basil Brick Oven | Astoria/27-29s | 25

Brick Cafe | 33s/31a | 21

Butcher Bar | 30a/37-38s | 24

Cávo | 31a/42-43s | 21

Christos | 23a/41s | 25

Elias Corner | 31s/24a | 23

5 Napkin Burger | 36s/35a | 21

Il Bambino | 31a/34-35s | 27

Locale | 34a/33s | 21

Loukoumi | Ditmars/45-46s | 24

Malagueta | 36a/28s | 24

MexiBBQ | 30a/37-38s | 21

Mojave | 31s/Ditmars-23a | 22

NEW MP Taverna | Ditmars/33s | -

Omonia | Bway/33s | 20

Ovelia | 30a/34s | 23

Pachanga Patterson | 31a/33-34s | 23

Piccola Venezia | 28a/42s | 25

Ponticello | Bway/46-47s | 24

Queens Kickshaw | Bway/41-Steinway | 23

Rizzo's Pizza | Steinway/30-31a | 23

Sanford's | Bway/30-31s | 22

Seva Indian | 34s/30a | 24

Stamatis | 23a/29-31s | 23

NEW Strand | Bway/Crescent-29s | 21

Sugar Freak | 30a/36-37s | 22

Taverna Kyclades | Ditmars/33 | 26

Telly's Taverna | 23a/28-29s | 21

Tratt. L'incontro | 31s/Ditmars | 26

Vesta | 30a/21s | 26

BAYSIDE

BareBurger | Bell/42-43s | 22

Ben's Kosher | 26a/Bell | 19

BonChon | Bell/45dr-45r | 21

Donovan's | 41a/Bell | 20

Erawan | Bell/42-43a | 23

Jackson Hole | Bell/35a | 19

Press 195 | Bell/40-41a | 24

Uncle Jack's | Bell/40a | 23

CORONA

Leo's Latticini/Corona | 104s/46a | 26

Park Side | Corona/51a-108s | 25

Tortilleria Nixtamal | 47a/104-108s | 26

DOUGLASTON

Grimaldi's | 61a/Douglaston | 23

ELMHURST

Pho Bang | *Bway/45s-Whitney* 22
Ping's Seafood | *Queens/Goldsmith* 21

FLUSHING

Biang! | *Main/41a-41r* 24
Blue Smoke | *126s/Roosevelt* 22
Joe's Shanghai | *37a/Main-Union* 22
Kum Gang San | 21
  Northern/Bowne-Union
Kyochon | *Northern/156-157s* 20
Leo's Latticini/Corona | 26
  126s/Roosevelt
Pho Bang | *Kissena/Barclay-41a* 22
Shake Shack | *126s/Roosevelt* 21
Sik Gaek | *Crocheron/162s* 22
Spicy & Tasty | *Prince/Roosevelt* 24
Szechuan Gourmet | 23
  37a/Main-Prince
Xi'an | *Main/41r* 24

FOREST HILLS

Agora Taverna | *Austin/71a* 21
Alberto | *Metro/69-70a* 23
Baluchi's | *Queens/76a* 19
Bann Thai | 20
  Austin/69r-Yellowstone
BareBurger | *Austin/71r-72a* 22
Cabana | *70r/Austin-Queens* 22
Danny Brown | *Metro/71dr* 26
Dee's | *Metro/74a* 22
La Vigna | *Metro/70a* 23
Nick's | *Ascan/Austin-Burns* 23

FRESH MEADOWS

King Yum | *Union/Kent-Surrey* 20

GLENDALE

Zum Stammtisch | 24
  Myrtle/69pl-70s

HOWARD BEACH

La Villa Pizzeria | *153a/82s* 23

JACKSON HEIGHTS

Afghan Kebab | *37a/74-75s* 20
NEW Alchemy, TX | -
  35a/Leverich-72s
Jackson Diner | *74s/37a-37r* 21
Jackson Hole | *Astoria/70s* 19
Pio Pio | *multi.* 23
Zabb Elee | *Roosevelt/72s* 22

JAMAICA

Bobby Van's | *JFK/Amer. Air* 23

LITTLE NECK

La Baraka | 23
  Northern/Little Neck

LONG ISLAND CITY

Bella Via | *Vernon/48a* 22
Café Henri | *50a/Vernon* 20
Casa Enrique | *49a/5s-Vernon* 24
Corner Bistro | *Vernon/47r* 22
Manducatis | *multi.* 23
Manetta's | *Jackson/11s* 23
NEW M. Wells Dinette | 27
  Jackson/46a
Riverview | *50s/Ctr.-49s* 21
Shi | *Ctr./Vernon* 24
Spice | *Vernon/48s* 19
Testaccio | *Vernon/47r* 22
Tournesol | *Vernon/50-51a* 24
Water's Edge | *44d/E River* 22

OZONE PARK

Don Peppe | *Lefferts/149a* 25

REGO PARK

Barosa | *Woodhaven/62r* 22
Ben's Best | *Queens/63r-64a* 23
Grand Sichuan | *Queens/66r-67a* 20
London Lennie | 23
  Woodhaven/Fleet-Penelope
Pio Pio | 23
  Woodhaven/Dry Harbor-62r

RIDGEWOOD

NEW Bunker Vietnamese | -
  Metro/Woodward

ROCKAWAY BEACH

Caracas | *Shore Front/Beach 106s* 24

SUNNYSIDE

Salt & Fat | *Queens/41-42s* 26
Turkish Grill | *Queens/42-43s* 22

WOODSIDE

Ayada | *Woodside/77-78s* 26
Donovan's | *Roosevelt/58s* 20
Mamajuana/Taina | *56s/Bway* 21
Sik Gaek | *Roosevelt/50s* 22
Sripraphai | *39a/64-65s* 27

Staten Island

BLOOMFIELD

Lorenzo's | *South/Lois*   22

CASTLETON CORNERS

Joe & Pat's | 23
  Victory/Manor-Winthrop

DONGAN HILLS

Carol's | 25
  Richmond/Four Crnrs-Garretson
Tratt. Romana | *Hylan/Benton*   25

ELTINGVILLE

Nove | *Richmond/Amboy*   24

GRANT CITY

Fushimi | 23
  Richmond/Colfax-Lincoln

GRASMERE

Bocelli | *Hylan/Parkinson*   25

GREAT KILLS

Arirang Hibachi | *Nelson/Locust*   21

MARINERS HARBOR

Real Madrid | 21
  Forest/Bruckner-Union

NEW BRIGHTON

Nurnberger | 23
  Castleton/Davis-Pelton

NEW SPRINGVILLE

East Pacific | 22
  Richmond a/Richmond Hill

PORT RICHMOND

Denino | 26
  Port Richmond/Hooker-Walker

ROSEBANK

Bayou | *Bay/Chestnut-St Mary*   23

SHORE ACRES

Da Noi | *Fingerboard/Tompkins*   23

ST. GEORGE

Beso | *Schuyley/Richmond*   23

TOTTENVILLE

Angelina's | *Ellis/Arthur Kill*   23

TRAVIS

Da Noi | *Victory/Crabbs*   23

LOCATIONS

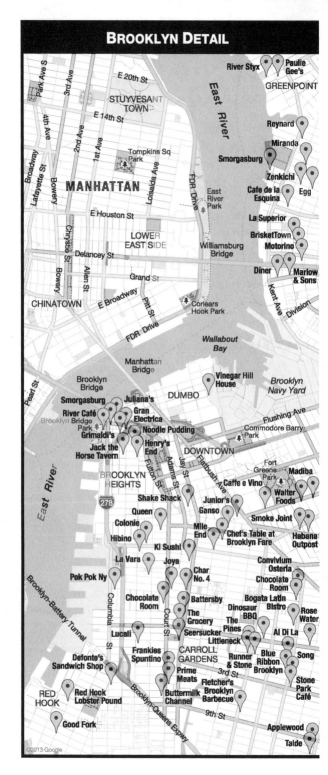

BROOKLYN DETAIL

River Styx
Paulie Gee's
GREENPOINT

Reynard
Miranda
Smorgasburg
Zenkichi
Cafe de la Esquina
Egg
La Superior
BrisketTown
Motorino
Diner
Marlow & Sons

E 20th St
STUYVESANT TOWN
E 14th St
Tompkins Sq Park
MANHATTAN
E Houston St
LOWER EAST SIDE
Delancey St
Grand St
CHINATOWN
E Broadway
Pitt St
FDR Drive

East River
East River Park
Williamsburg Bridge
Corlears Hook Park
Wallabout Bay
Kent Ave
Division

Vinegar Hill House
Brooklyn Navy Yard

Manhattan Bridge
DUMBO

Brooklyn Bridge
Smorgasburg
Juliana's
Gran Electrica
River Café
Brooklyn Bridge Park
Grimaldi's
Noodle Pudding
Jack the Horse Tavern
Henry's End
DOWNTOWN
Flushing Ave
Commodore Barry Park

East River

BROOKLYN HEIGHTS
278

Shake Shack
Queen
Colonie
Hibino
La Vara
Pok Pok Ny

Caffe e Vino
Madiba
Junior's
Ganso
Walter Foods
Mlle End
Smoke Joint
Chef's Table at Brooklyn Fare
Habana Outpost
Kl Sushi
Joya
Char No. 4
Battersby
The Grocery
Seersucker
Littleneck
Convivium Osteria
Chocolate Room
Bogata Latin Bistro
Dinosaur BBQ
The Pines
Rose Water
Al Di La
Chocolate Room

Lucali
Frankies Spuntino
CARROLL GARDENS
Prime Meats
Runner & Stone
Blue Ribbon Brooklyn
Song
3rd St
Stone Park Café
Fletcher's Brooklyn Barbecue

Defonte's Sandwich Shop
Red Hook Lobster Pound
RED HOOK
Buttermilk Channel
9th St
Good Fork
Applewood
Talde

©2013 Google

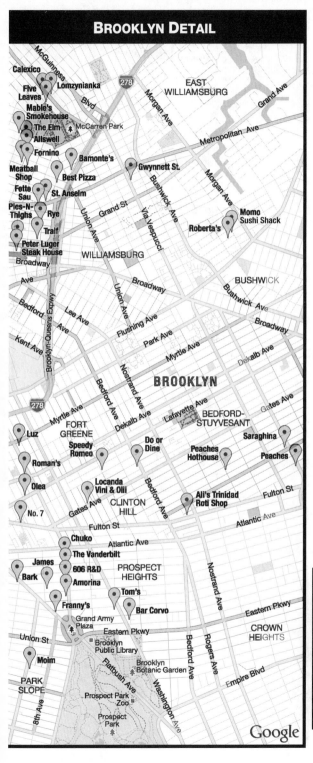

BROOKLYN DETAIL

Calexico
Five Leaves
Lomzynianka
Mable's Smokehouse
The Elm
Allswell
Fornino
Bamonte's
Meatball Shop
Best Pizza
Fette Sau
St. Anselm
Ples-N-Thighs
Rye
Tralf
Peter Luger Steak House
Gwynnett St.
Roberta's
Momo Sushi Shack

EAST WILLIAMSBURG
WILLIAMSBURG
BUSHWICK
BROOKLYN

McGuinness Blvd
Morgan Ave
Grand Ave
Metropolitan Ave
Bushwick Ave
Grand St
Via Vespucci
Union Ave
Broadway
Ave
Bedford Ave
Kent Ave
Brooklyn-Queens Expwy
Lee Ave
Union Ave
Flushing Ave
Park Ave
Myrtle Ave
Dekalb Ave
Broadway

McCarren Park

Luz
FORT GREENE
Speedy Romeo
Do or Dine
Saraghina
Roman's
Peaches Hothouse
Peaches
Olea
Locanda Vini & Olii
Ali's Trinidad Roti Shop
No. 7
CLINTON HILL
Chuko
The Vanderbilt
James
606 R&D
Bark
Amorina
PROSPECT HEIGHTS
Franny's
Tom's
Bar Corvo
Moim
PARK SLOPE

BEDFORD-STUYVESANT
CROWN HEIGHTS

Myrtle Ave
Bedford Ave
Dekalb Ave
Lafayette Ave
Gates Ave
Bedford Ave
Fulton St
Atlantic Ave
Gates Ave
Fulton St
Atlantic Ave
Nostrand Ave
Eastern Pkwy
Rogers Ave
Bedford Ave
Empire Blvd
Washington Ave
Union St
8th Ave

Grand Army Plaza
Eastern Pkwy
Brooklyn Public Library
Brooklyn Botanic Garden
Flatbush Ave
Prospect Park Zoo
Prospect Park

Google

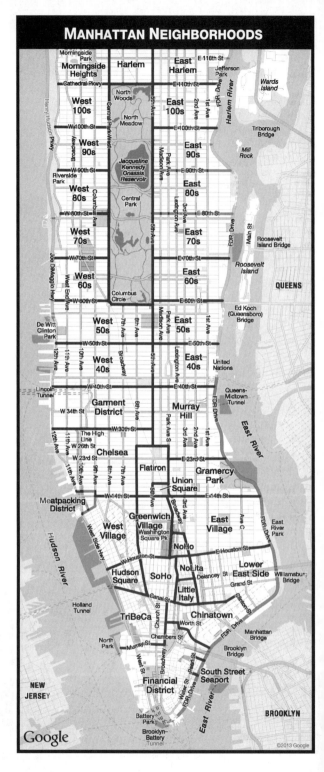

MANHATTAN NEIGHBORHOODS

Best in Glass

SAVE $100

Enjoy
12 Great Wines
for Just $69.99*
Plus Free Gift